One
Thousand
Roads to Mecca

Books by Michael Wolfe

FICTION
Invisible Weapons

TRAVEL
In Morocco
The Hadj: An American's Pilgrimage to Mecca

VERSE
How Love Gets Around
World Your Own
No, You Wore Red

One Thousand Roads to Mecca

*Ten Centuries of Travelers Writing about
the Muslim Pilgrimage*

Edited and Introduced by

Michael Wolfe

Grove Press
New York

Published simultaneously in Canada
Printed in the United States of America
FIRST EDITION

Library of Congress Cataloging-in-Publication Data
Wolfe, Michael, 1945–
One thousand roads to Mecca : ten centuries of travelers writing
about the Muslim pilgrimage / Michael Wolfe. — 1st ed.
p.   cm.
includes bibliographical references and index.
ISBN 0-8021-1611-6
1. Muslim pilgrims and pilgrimages—Saudi Arabia—Mecca.
I. Title.
BP187.3.W66   1997
297.3'52—DC21   97-1329

DESIGN BY LAURA HAMMOND HOUGH

Grove Press
841 Broadway
New York, NY 10003

10 9 8 7 6 5 4 3 2 1

Contents

꾼꿈

Contents

Five: The Jet Age Hajj, 1947–90

preface

In the years when I performed the Hajj, then wrote a book about it, between 1990 and 1993, I became aware of a string of accounts by Muslims and non-Muslims who over the last one thousand years had gone to Mecca on the pilgrimage. A little later, I began to read these works in order. I had no trouble locating the first three authors excerpted in this collection. Naser-e Khosraw (in Mecca in 1050), Ibn Jubayr (1185), and Ibn Battuta (1326) are all classics. Other books, deservedly well-known, by Western authors like Sir Richard Burton (1853) and Malcolm X (1964), are readily available in bookstores. Bibliographical searches and the polling of scholars uncovered many more works I did not know. Some were rare volumes, ordered and shipped from libraries across the country. Tracking them down, even handling them—at times in first editions that threatened to crumble in one's hands—was an adventure. But that was not the end of my reading. The job of placing each book in its context led to other books, of history, of Muslim theology, of Western literary criticism.

I began this work for the pleasure of it. I continued in the growing belief that it brings together a literature worth collecting. Certainly practicing Muslims will find plenty here to interest them. Others may find these stories entertaining as adventures. As cultural artifacts, they may have importance, too, especially for Westerners in this period of deep misunderstandings about Islam. Islam is a majority faith in fifty-four countries around the globe, most of them in the Middle East, the East, and Africa. In addition, millions of Muslims now live in Western countries, Western cities, Western neighborhoods. It is no secret that in these latter settings, Muslim–non-Muslim relationships suffer from misconceptions on all sides. If Westerners have more pressing reasons now to learn about Islam, perhaps the Hajj can provide a way to that knowledge. After all, the annual pilgrimage to Mecca is a supreme expression of the Muslim religion. All the principle practices of the faith are contained and made more apparent in its rites. Furthermore, the records of this journey that pilgrims have been making now for thirteen centuries reveal Islamic civilization as a vital global society with many centers and with a stronger religious aspect than many Westerners imagine. Performing the Hajj is not a case of the hollow fulfillment of an empty rite. These accounts are proof, if that were needed, of its persistent and attractive force for every kind of Muslim. The Hajj has drawn people across thousands of miles, in huge numbers, through every sort of calamity. It continues to do so. It has not died out with modernity. It has flourished.

The Hajj and the writing that surrounds it, then, may offer non-Muslim readers a fresh way of envisioning Islam, particularly when so many of its best written records are by Western authors. Two thirds of the accounts collected here are by Europeans and Americans. Together, they help make palpable the breadth and cultural richness of Islamic civilization, framed in Western languages and thought. Some of these books were popular in their day; some have remained so. Burton's work on Mecca and Medina is one of the finest travel books in nineteenth-century English; Malcolm X's Hajj account appears in a twentieth-century best-seller. How is it, one wonders, that non-Muslims know these books yet have no clear conception of Islam or the pilgrimage to Mecca? I began to hope this collection might even prove instructive, both for non-Muslim area experts who may be familiar with Islam but not with the Hajj and for that majority of the Western reading public who admit they know almost nothing about either.

This book is a literary anthology containing works by travelers who performed the Hajj and wrote at least passingly well about it. It proceeds chronologically from the mid-eleventh century to the end of the twentieth. I have chosen the accounts for their variety, in order to give readers a sense of the changing aspects of the Hajj over the centuries as well as a feel for how perennial the rites themselves have proved. Secondhand accounts and the flood of ephemeral works by returning hajjis who wrote to memorialize a journey for friends or family have been omitted. I wanted primary documents that were more carefully observed than sentimental. Unfortunately, no accounts by Turkish authors appear here, although the Ottoman court in Istanbul oversaw Hajj travel for five centuries. My only excuse is a lack of suitable translations. A similar problem occurred with the narratives of Southeast Asia, for although the region supplies a huge number of pilgrims to this day, the only full-length account in English of such a journey is a third-person retelling by the journalist Owen Rutter of David Chale's 1937 journey. The 1848 *Pilgrimage of Ahmad* and Léon Roches's *Dix ans à travers d'Islam, 1834–1844* are both wonderful books, but I have had to omit them. The collection is selective, not exhaustive.

The three accounts translated from Persian retain spellings found in English editions of these works. With Arabic, approximations in English have varied widely over the centuries. For example, I have counted half a dozen different spellings of the central term Tawaf in the originals of these accounts. Spellings of names and places can be equally confusing. Is the goal of the pilgrim Mecca, Makkah, Macca, or Mek? Was the famous twelfth-century ruler of Egypt Saladin (a Western preference) or Salah al-Din (his real name)? With exceptions that would cloud their recognition were spellings altered, I have standardized the orthography throughout this collection. Most diacritical marks have been omitted. Footnotes to the editions, whether by an author or later editors, have been omitted, too, except where they assist the nonacademic reader. Footnotes by the present editor are marked with the abbreviation "Ed."

These twenty-four accounts are arranged into five historical periods and supplied with brief introductory essays. The dates below the essay titles indicate the year when the authors performed the pilgrimage. A longer General Introduction follows this Preface and sets the pilgrimage in a broader context. Occasionally, the excerpted selections have been edited or cut here to make the text more readable. Readers seeking fuller historical treatment of the Hajj and Mecca, based on primary sources, may turn to F. E. Peters's 1994 volumes. This book, on the other hand, is the story of a journey— from home, wherever home might be, to Mecca, as recorded by travelers over a thousand years.

The tale of the Hajj is not always a simple one. Its administration through the years has been in the hands and sometimes at the mercy of many a facile potentate, and the cynicism with which it has been manipulated as a symbol can be shocking. In another vein, the Hajj has drawn every kind of traveler to it, making a collection such as this a complex medley of cultures and personalities. Poets, bureaucrats, spies, ne'er-do-wells, queens, slaves, the fabulously wealthy, old and young, lawyers, judges, confidence men, scholars, novelists, existentialists, and devout believers all are represented in these pages. So, too, are Persians, Moroccans, Afghans, Meccans, Spaniards, Australians, Hindi Indians, Austrians, Italians, Swiss, Americans, and Britons, just to mention the authors represented in this volume. Each excerpt adds its part to a larger story. In order to appreciate these travelers more, we have to comprehend something of their times. I say *something* by way of reservation because the necessary brevity of my introductions limits their scope severely. The books listed in the Bibliography are intended as a first layer of recommended reading.

—M. W., SPRING 1997

General Introduction

A ceremony is like a book in which a great deal is written. One ceremony often contains more than a hundred books.
—George Gurdjieff, *Meetings with Remarkable Men*

The Hajj, or annual pilgrimage to Mecca, is one of mankind's most enduring rites. For almost fourteen hundred years, it has provided a spiritual destination to millions of men and women around the globe. Its attractive power has outlasted great empires, shaped trade routes through half the world, and persisted despite war, famine, and plague. Today, Islam is the world's second largest and fastest growing religion; the Hajj is its greatest public rite. Over two million Muslims from 125 countries perform the Hajj every year, forming the largest single gathering in one place at one time for one purpose on Earth. The point of this journey has always been the same: to detach a representative number of people from their homes and, by bringing them to Islam's birthplace, to emphasize the unity of all human beings before their Creator. The Hajj's first requirement is to arrive on time, to keep an appointment with God and the Muslim community. Once in Mecca, pilgrims perform a week-long set of rites.

The Hajj is both a collective celebration and an intensely personal experience, the religious apex of a Muslim's life. From early times, it has also been a central theme in Islamic travel writing. Called *rihla* in Arabic, *safarnameh* in Persian, these accounts have informed and entertained readers since the early Middle Ages with firsthand descriptions of cities, exotic regions, and local mores encountered on journeys to and from Mecca. In addition, beginning with the European Renaissance, Mecca became for about four centuries the occasional destination for a handful of writers from the Christian West who, through pretense and connivance, managed to enter a city forbidden to non-Muslims. Read in counterpoint, these two quite different traditions supply opposing voices in a spirited conversation for which Mecca and Islam are common ground. Filled with feats of daring and endurance, with moments of heightened religious perception and great risk, the travelers (whether Muslims or pretenders) were close observers of their journey. Accounts drawn from both these traditions form the body of the book before us. In order to appreciate them, readers should first know something more about Islam, Mecca, and the rites of pilgrimage.

The Tradition of Islam

Viewed outside its divergent history, Islam is as much a "Western" religion as Judaism or Christianity. Semitic at heart, these three related faiths touch so profoundly at so many points that they clearly form contiguous layers in a single cultural substratum, the ancient West Asian tradition of prophetic monotheism. This relationship is more than geographic. Like its elder cousins, Islam is an Abrahamic faith and has frequent recourse to the contents of the Torah. On this score alone, it may be likened to the third panel in a spiritual triptych. Its own sacred book, the Holy Quran, defines Islam as a continuer of a perennial religion that existed long before Judaism, one that Jews revived, as Jesus would do later. As the Quran says,

> *We believe in God*
> *and in what has been sent down to us,*
> *what has been revealed to Abraham and Ishmael*
> *and Isaac and Jacob and their offspring,*
> *and what was given to Moses and to Jesus*
> *and all the other prophets by the Lord.*
> *We make no distinction among them.*

In one of the book's many comments on itself, we also read that "the Quran is not a story that was forged. It is the confirmation of what preceded it." Two thirds of its chapters contain allusions to the Bible and its prophets. Adam, Eve, Abraham, Noah, Lot, Jonah, Moses, Aaron, David, Enoch, as well as John the Baptist, Jesus, and Mary, are singled out as spiritual heroes inspired by the same "Lord of all the worlds." This is not a literary trope; it is the prophetic lineage in which Muslims believe. In daily prayers, they speak of Muhammad and Abraham as prophets in one tradition. Allah* and the God of the Flood are identical.

Unlike the Torah and the Gospels, however, the Quran does not aspire to set an historical record in a context. In the Quran, the time is always

---

*Allah is simply the Arabic word for God, used alike by all Arabic speakers regardless of religion, and not a separate sacred figure peculiar to Islam.

now, and the words on every page are the voice of God. In this sense, its relation to Islam is akin to that of Jesus for Christianity. In place of the Word incarnate, we have what might be called the Voice *inlibrate*. The Book, not the man who delivered it, is the truth and the way. Muslims venerate Muhammad as an exemplary human being and a great prophet. He worked for a living, married, had children, transformed his society, and died at sixty-two. He mourned the death of several children; he could be angry, even peevish; he had a sense of humor. Every step of his life is well recorded, and his words and deeds are considered useful guides, but he was mortal. He is not worshiped or even prayed to. He considered himself a servant and advised his followers to do the same.

Today, of course, we have more than books and a common tradition to help locate Islam as a Western religion. We have population statistics. With 1.2 billion Muslims in the world, Islam is the only world faith that is gaining numbers. In Europe, it is the second largest religion. In the United States, there are now more Muslims than Episcopalians or Jews, and half of them were born here. This new popularity in the West is due to the fact that Islam speaks to people in universal ways. Its roots, however, reach back to a distant period and to a distant city, Mecca. To understand Islam today and the meaning of the Hajj for modern Muslims, readers of the accounts to come need some acquaintance with the city's background.

Mecca, the Birthplace of Islam

Mecca lies midway along the west coast of Arabia in a mountainous barrier region named the Hijaz. (See Figs. 1 and 2.) This is a narrow tract of barren land about nine hundred miles long with the Tropic of Cancer passing through its center. The second-century Greco-Egyptian geographer Ptolemy called the city Makoraba, the Temple. It occupies a north-south basin two miles long by half a mile wide fifty miles east of the Red Sea. Mecca owes its existence to the Zamzam Well, the sole water source in a barren valley surrounded by rugged, treeless peaks. (See Figs. 3 and 4.) Its usual climate has been described as a combination of "suffocating heat, deadly winds, and clouds of flies."* No crops seem ever to have grown there. In its prehistoric period, this place "without sown land" was considered too sacred for regular habitation. Perhaps a special status was connected to its well or to the falling of a meteor in the area. In any

---

*From the Arab geographer Maqdisi's description, ca. 966 C.E.

case, its plants could not be cut nor its wildlife hunted. In spite of these pro-
hibitions, a town gradually grew up there and derived a modest income from
visiting pilgrims. By the late sixth century, when Muhammad was a boy, his
own tribe, the Quraysh, controlled Mecca, occupied its central hollow, and
were providing visitors security and water.

In the town's principal crossroads stood the Ka'ba, a cube-shaped
building of ancient origins located a few yards from the Zamzam Well. It
seems to have been there from time immemorial. Buildings like it are known
to have existed, marking similar asylums, in other parts of the Arabian Peninsula from Jordan to Yemen. As with most Semitic shrines, the Meccan
Ka'ba's surrounding area formed a sacred territory with special laws of sanctuary and dress. Here many Middle Eastern cults set up idols, creating a pre-
Islamic pantheon that included Hubal (a Nabatean god imported from
Jordan), Venus, the moon, and the Virgin Mary, among many others. The
principal deity of the Meccans, Al-Llah, the High God of the Arabs, was
probably linked in forgotten ways with the God of Abraham. In any case,
the city welcomed the gods of many tribes. Thus people throughout the
region were drawn to Mecca as pilgrims to pay their respects and execute
old rites, traveling by seasonal caravan from Yemen, Syria, and the Persian
Gulf. Once arrived, they circuited the Ka'ba seven times and (probably depending on their cult) ran between two hills, lit fires to rain gods, cast stones
at solar obelisks, and held poetry contests, fixing verses inscribed on animal
skins to the Ka'ba's walls. The pre-Islamic rites at Mecca embodied an inexplicable element, something ancient and almost precerebral, that matched
the volcanic landscape all around it. Then gradually the place began to change.

Even before Muhammad's birth, earthen buildings were replacing tents
in the central district and an urban establishment was growing up, supplant-
ing older, more nomadic tribal codes. Increased income among the ruling
clans finally promised to free a portion of Meccans from the perennial grip
of desert poverty. At the same time, old forms of loyalty were dying. The
Quraysh's quick transition to urban independence seems to have eroded their
social fabric, concentrating wealth in a few successful families while slight-
ing the needs of the weak and less well born. Judging from reforms a few
decades later, the society into which Muhammad was born in 570 c.e. was
polytheistic, plutocratic, and deeply divided along economic lines. Female
infanticide was rife, interest rates were uncontrolled, and most women and
orphans had no rights or real property. When Muhammad was forty, in 610,
he retreated to the mountains outside town for a period of fasting and reflection. After a numinous experience with the archangel Gabriel, he returned
to town shaken, with the first revelation of the Quran. From this experi-

ence, there gradually developed the core of a monotheistic religion called Islam, or Self-Surrender. It met with immediate resistance from the Meccans and only slowly attracted followers. Muhammad's insistence on worshiping one God threatened his people, who housed the principal gods of the Middle East and earned their revenues from many cults. To the landlords of the Ka'ba, a claim that God is everywhere appeared subversive. In September 622, Muhammad and his few hundred followers were forced into exile.

The Muslims moved north to the oasis of Medina, where they prospered, absorbing most of that city's population, forming a new community, and rebuffing occasional attacks from Mecca. Battles raged, trade routes were interrupted. Finally, in 628, treaties were signed between Muhammad and the Meccans permitting a Muslim contingent to visit Mecca for a pilgrimage. When the Quraysh broke the truce a year later, Muhammad marched on the city with an army, and the Meccans gave up without a fight. Much to their surprise, the city prospered under Islam, although Muhammad continued living in Medina. Between the two cities a few hundred miles apart, Islam spread quickly.

About three months before he died, Muhammad led ninety thousand followers on a march to Mecca called the Farewell Hajj. At this time, he swept the Ka'ba of its idols, pronouncing it the Muslim House of God, then designated a pilgrim route that looped between the city and the desert, requiring several days to move around it. Along this route, he led a great procession, integrating as he went diverse pagan rites into a coherent ritual performance that pilgrims still execute today. In the process of performing it, Muhammad redefined the ancient Hajj as a concentrated expression of Islam. By retaining certain of its timeless rites, he preserved in ritual form a profound evocation of the ancient impulse that first gave birth to religion. He also broadened the context of the Hajj ceremonies, linking them and their Meccan sites to the legends of five prophets—Abraham, Hagar, Ishmael, Adam, and Eve. The Farewell Hajj completed Muhammad's role as a spiritual messenger. At its climax, in the desert on the Plain of Arafat, he delivered the last verses of the Quran, completing the foundation of the Muslim religion, making the Hajj and the sacred book its capstones. This creation of a distinctly Muslim Hajj was his final public act. It is sometimes called Islam's last pillar.

Mecca was probably never a great commercial center.* Even in pre-Islamic times, it was neither easy to reach nor rich in any commodities we know of.

*See Patricia Crone, *Meccan Trade and the Rise of Islam.*

xvii

From the beginning, people seem to have flocked there because the place was sacred. In a stark desert made more inhospitable by raiding and inter-tribal wars, the attractions of such an asylum, where safety is guaranteed and water free, must have been great. After Muhammad, from about 750 on, the tour was supported by powerful rulers in distant capitals like Damascus, Baghdad, and Cairo who subsidized regional caravan routes with way stations and wells. These prestigious public works were meant to benefit their Muslim subjects and connect their reign to the service of religion. They were not undertaken to better trade but, rather, to accommodate an enormous increase in pilgrims as Islam spread through the world.

Little has stayed the same in Mecca from one age to the next. Fire, flood, adobe, and dynastic building projects have wrought consistent rapid change in the city's appearance through the centuries. Wells, dams, walls, gates, houses, markets, neighborhoods, and thoroughfares have come and gone with dramatic speed. One might almost say that the literary record is all that re-mained of Mecca from era to era. There have only been two constants in this flux. The rites and sites of the Hajj itself have undergone surprisingly little variation over time; and for more than seven hundred years, the city was governed continuously by a single family. Claiming descent from the Prophet Muhammad, they called themselves the nobles, or sharifs.

This line emerged around the time our book begins, in the late 1100s, when a handful of regional rulers were vying for control of the Hijaz. One, named Sharif Qitada, governor of the Red Sea port of Yanbu, sent cavalry troops against Mecca in 1201 and captured it. Making the city their capital, branches of his family continued to rule the Hijaz until 1925. Successions were frequently bloody, involving war and fratricide, and corruption was endemic. But by cleaving to their role as caretakers of the Hajj and its sacred sites, they maintained their throne and prospered. The sharifs in turn were patronized by more distant and powerful rulers who, with annual gifts to the sharifal treasury, purchased the prestige of supporting Mecca. The fam-ily earned added revenues from taxes on goods and pilgrims; in return, they guaranteed secure roads. The results of these complex arrangements are dis-cussed by almost every pilgrim author throughout the sharifs' protracted reign.

The twentieth century brought enormous changes to the balance of power in the Hijaz. Reduced to a pawn in a game during World War I, the last sharif fled Mecca, and a new regime, led by Abd al-Aziz ibn Sa'ud, took over the city. By 1933, Ibn Sa'ud had unified most of the Arabian Peninsula for the first time in recorded history. He also reorganized the Hajj adminis-tration and put an end to raiding on the roads. A few decades later, rapid transportation and the introduction of modern technology in the Hijaz led to a physical transformation of Mecca. Yet the city's principal role remains unchanged. With a resident population of 1.2 million Mecca continues to host the pilgrimage and care for the well and shrine that gave it birth.

The Rites of the Hajj

In the twenty-four selections in this book, the serial rites of the pilgrimage are described from many angles. Before they are outlined here, it is worth remarking that pilgrims who perform them are taking part in a drama that reaches back to the first prophets and to the testing of the human family's faith in God. In this sense, the Hajj is a journey through time as well as space for the purpose of bonding people to a primordial religion, the ethical monotheism of Abraham. This is the secret dimension of the Hajj that penetrates its entire ritual process, connecting the present moment to the past so that even today's very modern pilgrims, with their ritual choreography and ancient-looking robes, seem to have stepped out of the pages of Scripture. Most of the rites described here are like bookmarks in a very ancient story. As pilgrims perform them, the old drama unfolds.

THE HARAM, OR SACRED TERRITORY   The word *haram,* meaning "sanctuary," runs through all the Hajj accounts. The term may be applied in different ways. For pilgrims arriving in the Hijaz, it refers to the whole of Mecca and its surrounding lands as marked by pillars at five principal stations beyond the town. "All of Mecca is a sanctuary," the Meccans say. Only Muslims may pass into this precinct, where special laws of the sanctuary take over. In addition to this wider area, the word *haram* is also applied to the Great Mosque at Mecca. Pilgrims routinely refer to it as the Haram Mosque or Haram al-Sharif, the Noble Sanctuary. They may also call it Bayt Allah, God's House, or simply the House.

HARAM LAW AND IHRAM DRESS   Most religions protect their rites with special codes and dress. Pilgrims entering the Haram territory assume a sanctified condition, called *ihram.* The term indicates an adopted state of consecration or dedicated abstinence, symbolized by special *ihram* clothes. Arriving at one of the five stations, called *miqat*s, all haijis bathe and state their intention to make the Hajj. Women may wear national dress, although many change into robes of a light color, leaving their hands and faces bare. For men, the demands are more specific. They must go bareheaded and unshod (sandals are acceptable) and replace their daily clothes with two plain lengths of unstitched cloth, one worn around the waist (it may be belted), the other draped over the left shoulder, leaving the right shoulder bare. The custom is pastoral, prehistoric, and symbolic: *ihram* clothes are an outward sign that while inside the territory, pilgrims agree to obey the *haram* laws and to behave in ways conducive to peace and spiritual dedication. Sexual activity is suspended for the time being. Violence is forbidden in all its forms, right down to disturbing local wildlife and expressing anger or impatience. Likewise, unseemly attention to one's appearance is proscribed, from cutting the hair and nails to wearing cosmetics. *Haram* law also requires pilgrims approaching Mecca to repeat in unison a round of verses, the Talbiyya, indicating spiritual readiness: "Here I am, Lord, at your service. Here I am." *Ihram* is the recommended condition for anyone entering the Haram Territory and is required for a pilgrimage. Its simplified, uniform appearance blunts the usual distinctions of wealth and station and helps to render everybody equal, in keeping with the Hajj's purpose.

THE REQUIREMENTS OF THE HAJJ Islam is a world religion with a journey at the center of its practice. All Muslims are required to go on the Hajj once in a lifetime, provided they are healthy, sane, mature, and unindebted, endangered by neither war nor epidemic, and have the means both to make the journey and to support any dependents left behind. The annual pilgrimage is a strict appointment, too. It begins on the eighth day of the last month of the Muslim lunar year, and those who miss its central rites commencing on the ninth day miss the Hajj altogether, although they may return another year. By contrast, the Lesser or Minor Pilgrimage, the Umra, contains some but not all the rites of the Hajj and may be performed at any time. Every Muslim who enters Mecca is obliged to perform one or the other. Exceptions are made for those whose work requires frequent visits, but the obligation is generally viewed as an opportunity. People are not simply required to make the Hajj. Most long to go, save up for years to do so, and consider the trip a blessing in their lives.

THE HARAM MOSQUE All the initial rites of the Hajj take place inside the Haram Mosque in Mecca. The core of this building is an immense open courtyard with the stately granite cube of the Ka'ba at its center. The Zamzam Well stands nearby, and at some distance runs a straight course, called the Masa'a, a quarter-mile stretch of covered mall running on a tangent between Safa and Marwa, two hills adjacent to the Shrine. A glance at this eccentric floor plan (see Fig. 5) makes it clear that the "surrounding" mosque has been arranged to preserve these ancient ritual locations.

The Meccan Haram is the only mosque in the world built in the round. Its surrounding prayer halls all face the Ka'ba, and the whole building is organized around it. The Ka'ba, the lodestone of Islam, stands fifty feet high and is draped in an embroidered black silk cover called the *kiswa*. Pilgrims often refer to this sanctum sanctorum as the Shrine. It contains no relics and is not itself an object of prayer.* Rather, it provides spiritual focus, marking the direction in which all Muslims pray throughout their lives. Set squarely on the compass points, its monolithic lines symbolize God's location at the center of creation. Simply to have the Ka'ba physically before them brings tears to many pilgrims' eyes, and day or night it serves as an object of prayer and meditation.

Many legends surround the Haram Mosque, but the chief ones form a cycle of myth reflected in the building's architecture. These stories and the Hajj rites that express them illustrate in different stages the birth of ethical monotheism in the Middle East. To commemorate the founder of this project, there stands to one side of the Shrine a smaller, booth-shaped station, the Maqam Ibrahim, named for the Ka'ba's original architect, Abraham. On the Ka'ba's northwest side, enclosed by a marble railing, lie the legendary graves of Hagar and Ishmael, Abraham's wife and son. The lives of these three prophets are familiar to every Muslim child. They form a mental geography of which pilgrims are inescapably reminded as they move about the sites of the Hajj and execute its rites. Particular parts of the saga are emphasized in Mecca: how Abraham, in deference to Sarah, first consigned Hagar and her son to exile in a desert sanctuary; how in repentance he constructed the Ka'ba there; how the family's faith was tested by God's command to sacrifice the son; and how his life was spared at the last moment by the substitution of a ram.† This timeless test of faith and mercy forms the ethical backbone of the Hajj. It runs through all the forthcoming accounts.

*The Black Stone, the only surviving part of the original building, is lodged in a silver band in the Shrine's east corner, at shoulder height. Pilgrims ritually circling the Ka'ba start their circuits here and salute or try to touch or even kiss the stone in passing. A few other sanctified spots around the building command special reverence; however, the Ka'ba is not sacred due to them but, rather, because of its symbolic value as a marker of the *qibla*, the direction of prayer.
†Non-Muslim readers may want to consider the biblical story of Abraham and Isaac and this later, somewhat different Muslim legend as two versions of a common narrative concerned with the themes of covenant and origins.

THE SEQUENCE OF THE HAJJ The Hajj may be divided into two groups of ritual performances: a three-fold set of urban rites performed in a matter of hours at the Haram Mosque in downtown Mecca and a four-part procession that carries the whole pilgrim population on a fifteen-mile march to and from the desert over a period of several days. The initial, city-centered ceremonies include completing seven circuits around the Ka'ba, visiting the Zamzam Well, and walking seven times between the Safa and Marwa hills.

TAWAF The seven circuits around the Ka'ba are called the turning, or *tawaf.* Their number and counterclockwise direction suggest the ancient world's seven planets circling the sun. They have more recently been likened to the nuclear paths of atomic particles. The *tawaf* is a form of prayer at the Meccan mosque, and visitors may perform it often. In season, the turns are inevitably made in a wheeling band of many thousand people. During the Hajj, the rite is required on three occasions. A pilgrim's first Turning of Arrival should take place sometime before the desert procession from Mecca on the eighth day of the month.

ZAMZAM AND SA'Y Immediately after their last circuit, pilgrims repair to the Zamzam Well in a symbolic act of spiritual refreshment. The story of the well is linked to the rite of running (*sa'y*), which follows next. To perform it, pilgrims cross the mosque to the east side of the building, where a course about a third of a mile long, the Masa'a, stretches between the Safa and Marwa hills. Here Ishmael's mother, Hagar, is said to have run back and forth seven times in a frantic search for water in the desert. During her final lap, the child cried out. Returning, she found an unearthed desert spring. Today, this rite gives pilgrims a participatory taste of a timeless drama in which parental love and religious faith are weighed in the balance. At an ethnic level, the story explains the survival of all Arabs, Ishmael being their progenitor.

THE DESERT PROCESSIONAL On the eighth day of the Hajj month, pilgrims, wearing their *ihram,* all leave the city and move five miles east, into Mina Valley, where they spend the night in tents. This exchange of urban comfort for a more timeless desert life further dissolves class distinctions and binds the Hajj community more closely. The next morning the exodus pushes another five miles east, to Arafat. Here the zenith of the Hajj takes place in the form of a group vigil, called the Day of Standing Together before God (Yawm al-Wukuf). Arafat, with its signature hill, Mount Mercy (Jabal al-Rahma), forms a broad plain lying a short distance outside the Haram Territory. Appropriately, the legends informing this supreme Hajj rite transcend remembered time, stretching back past Abraham to the days of Genesis. Here, in a volcanic negative of the Garden, mankind's parents, Adam and Eve, are said to have rendezvoused after the Fall and been taught by Gabriel to pray—in a stone niche on the west face of Mount Mercy. Muslims, then, see Arafat as a place set aside for spiritual reunion, where pilgrims travel to re-form family ties, seek pardon, reclaim faith, and re-collect their spirits. In addition to a limitless past, Arafat has an impressive future too, being a yearly rehearsal place for the Day of Judgment.* In every sense, the Hajj reaches its outer limits here.

THE MUZDALIFA VIGIL From the moment the Hajj leaves Arafat, at sunset, the procession becomes a recessional, turning back on a westward path to Mina Valley. The first night, the crowds accomplish half the journey, stopping at Muzdalifa, a group of hills three miles down the plain. Here they camp beneath the stars and undertake a second vigil, this time within the Haram Territory. During the night they meditate and gather pebbles for the next day's rite.

THE DAYS OF STONING AND FEASTING At dawn, the hajjis begin their return to Mina Valley, a few miles farther west, where they celebrate the Feast of Sacrifice (Id al-Adha), a major holiday throughout the Muslim world. Before the feast, however, pilgrims first proceed to a part of Mina specially reserved for three tall pillars (*jamarat*). These mark three legendary spots in another chapter of the Abrahamic story. Here it is said that the angel of darkness appeared to tempt Ishmael, arguing that God's command to Abraham to sacrifice his son was a product of Satan's work and Abraham's madness. Ishmael, who knew the difference between Satan's voice and God's, responded by stoning the devil seven times. Pilgrims today follow his example, stoning one pillar on the first day and all three pillars on the next two days. In the vicinity of the third pillar, it is said, there grew a bush in which the sacrificial ram was caught and slain.

THE RETURN TO MECCA Pilgrims are freed from most of the *ihram* restrictions after their first throws. They are, however, required to return to Mecca sometime in the next three days to perform a return *tawaf.* In coming days, most pilgrims who have not already visited the Prophet's Mosque (Masjid

---

*"Only our concept of time makes it possible for us to speak of the Day of Judgment by that name; in reality it is a summary court in perpetual session."—Franz Kafka.

al-Nabi) in Medina will travel north to pay their respects at Muhammad's grave site. Before departing, however, pilgrims should perform a final *tawaf*, after which they leave the mosque by the Farewell Gate.

SIGNIFICANCE OF THE HAJJ Even today, when travel is comparatively easy, only two in a thousand adult Muslims perform the Hajj each year. The largest part of this population is composed of middle-aged people. They have earned and been able to set aside the money for the journey. Their children have been raised, their obligations met. Now they turn to fulfilling religious duties or younger family members may pool resources to send their parents. Newlyweds often go to Mecca, too, to cement a marriage. People who have suffered a powerful crisis in their lives—the loss of a relation or mate, a period of personal depression—may go on the Hajj to regenerate their spirits. Its successful completion confers new social status too, marked by a voluntary name change: the addition of a title (*hajji* for men or *hajja* for women) before their name. As we shall see, this chance to join a social elite has remained a powerful inducement to pilgrims as different as the fourteenth-century Moroccan Ibn Battuta and the twentieth-century American Malcolm X. The real goal of the Hajj, however, is to perform it well. In the final analysis, its admissibility is up to God. It is something one *offers*.

Muslims are drawn to Mecca like filings to a magnet, attracted by the integrative power of a journey to the heartland. More than a city, Mecca is a principal part of speech in a sacred language and the direction Muslims pray in throughout their lives. Simply to set foot there may answer years of longing. Muhammad's story takes on new meaning in Mecca too, as that of an exemplary human being who, when he went to make the Hajj, made it over in the spirit of Islam. Over the centuries, in times of peace and war, Mecca has offered its visitors a dependable retreat, a sort of ritual greenhouse reserved for forcing the spirit into blossom no matter what may be going on beyond the Haram borders. As a reminder of how life ought to be lived, the journey has inspired peasants, princes, mystics, and revolutionaries. For all these reasons, it represents a literal trip of a lifetime.

Hajj Travel

Those who find the sinuous rites of the Hajj confusing should know in advance that pilgrims themselves usually require the help of a guide, or *mutawwif*, to execute them. Neither simple nor self-evident, they are, however, so frequently described, referred to, and repeated in these pages that even non-Muslims will come to know them better as they read. At this stage, it is more important to understand that the pilgrimage is not just a matter of traveling to Mecca. Arrival is only a beginning. The Hajj itself is a protean event composed of many stages, each one marked by a collective rite. Changing its shape and purpose day by day, the ceremony does not *take place* so much as it unfolds, first in a city, then on a desert, becoming by turns a circle dance, a spiritual racecourse, a procession, a camping trip in the dunes, an athletic event, a trade fair, and a walking meditation. It is a kind of Muslim United Nations, too, in which people from around the world collaborate and even live together. And yet of course the Hajj means travel, too.

As these accounts make clear, the journey to Mecca has always been more than a means to a destination. Until the advent of modern transportation, the trip required months or even years. Not surprisingly, most of the writing in most of this collection concerns going and coming, crossing mountains, seas, and sandy wastes, encountering sacred shrines, enormous cities, exotic ways, strange customs, and stranger people. Hajj literature is fraught with trouble too: earthly trouble, social trouble, physical injury, fateful loss, and unexpected pathos. Pilgrims have never been immune to risk and danger—thieves and tricksters, greedy border agents, war, enslavement, financial ruin, political upheaval, prejudice, disease, bad faith, foul play, and false protectors. It is a principal truth of travel writing that trouble goes with the territory, even (perhaps especially) for pilgrims. Of three Hajj authors picked almost at random, Ibn Battuta returned home in 1350 with a plague licking at his heels, Joseph Pitts (in Mecca ca. 1685) spent fifteen years in slavery, while John Lewis Burckhardt (in Mecca, 1814) died in Cairo of an illness contracted on the Hajj.

Getting to Mecca has never been a picnic. Perhaps the most brutal irony of all, repeated in account after account, is that until about 1930 the nearer pilgrims came to their hallowed goal, the more dangerous life became for them. Raiding clans like the Banu Harb and the Banu Utayba, who made travel through the Hijaz a living hell, appear often in these pages. These and other Bedouin tribes derived their wealth by extorting payment from traders and pilgrims passing through their territories and by raiding their caravans mercilessly when they could not pay. This was no quaint medieval tactic. As recently as World War I, the lion's share of subsidies from Istanbul and London went to buying off these predatory tribes in order to keep the land routes open, especially during the months of pilgrimage.

The Hijazi tribes were not unique in these predations, nor were pilgrims the only victims of attack. Identical nightmares attended any caravan traveling through Syria, Arabia, Iraq, Libya, or Egypt. They did not abate until new forms of transportation began to outpace the camel in the nineteenth and twentieth centuries. In 1922, for instance, the American novelist John Dos Passos, traveling with a caravan of five hundred camels from Baghdad to Damascus, encountered precisely the same protection racket that our first Hajj author, Naser-e Khosraw, endured east of Mecca in the eleventh century. Both men were forced to ransom their baggage over and over as they proceeded, paying one tribe to defend them from all comers, only to watch attackers and defenders change their roles the moment the caravan entered a new fiefdom. In Dos Passos's case, this happened every fifty miles.

The journey, however, was not all hardship. Along the way, pilgrims stopped at well-established stations, famous mosques, saints' shrines, and Sufi centers. According to their status, they worked in cities, earning the means to travel on, or were hosted in the courts of lavish rulers. The caravans they joined ranged from a single string of camels to giant tented cities on the move. Readers who enter the medieval version of this trip, in Part One of this volume, will be rewarded with portraits of Cairo and Damascus at the height of their glory. By the fourteenth century, the Muslim world had greatly exceeded its birthplace in the Arab Middle East. Stretching from Morocco across India to China, it formed a vast, interconnected global society through which pilgrims could travel toward Mecca from any corner and not lose touch with Muslim culture. Once these more distant Hajj routes opened, they did not close. Burckhardt, in the early 1800s, joins a largely Malay caravan to Medina. In the 1930s, large numbers of pilgrims from Indonesia cross thousands of miles of ocean to make the Hajj. With its anecdotes and personal observations over time, the Hajj literature records this international and cosmopolitan character of pilgrim travel, which modern transportation has expanded.

The dangers and risks of the Hajj were steeply reduced in the twentieth century by technology, advances in hygiene, and new administrative methods. As with all modern travel, the structure of the journey was radically altered. In a period of seventy-five years, the old pilgrim routes to Mecca were rendered largely obsolete by steamships, trains, and other means of automated transport. The airplane, a few decades later, made the roads all but superfluous. By the 1980s, 90 percent of foreign pilgrims were arriving for the Hajj on chartered flights while overland pilgrims from around the Middle East used high-speed freeways, reducing the desert to a blur. Pressed by economics, a very few hajjis still were walking across Africa to Mecca when I performed the Hajj in 1990, but this practice will probably vanish soon. Airplanes have made the Hajj less costly, in terms of both the price of travel and the greatly reduced absence from business and family. Air travel is the main cause of the geometric rise in pilgrim numbers during the last half of the twentieth century.

The Contents and Organization of This Book

THE TEXTS The excerpts included here are drawn from the accounts of twenty-three travelers from around the world. They appear in chronological order, grouped in five sections according to their era, from medieval to contemporary times.

Part One contains three classics from the Islamic Middle Ages, a period of global ascendancy for Islam. The section opens with an eleventh-century account of a trek to Mecca by the classical Persian poet and mystic Naser-e Khosraw. It continues with a late-twelfth-century book by Ibn Jubayr, who sailed east from Muslim Spain, and ends with excerpts from Islam's most famous traveler, the fourteenth-century Moroccan, Ibn Battuta. Damascus and Cairo loom large as the overall sponsors of the Hajj in this period. Here we also witness the emergence of the sharifs as local governors in Mecca and the Hijaz, rub shoulders with Crusaders as they invade the Arab world, and view the capitals of great rulers like Saladin. These opening selections, all from works important in their time, should help ground even uninitiated readers in the complexities of the Hajj and pilgrim travel. The introductory essays are slightly longer here, to establish points important throughout the literature.

Part Two introduces the Western side of the travel ledger. It consists of five accounts bridging the Renaissance, the Enlightenment period, and the early Romantic Age, written by Europeans from Italy, Britain, Spain, and Switzerland. They begin with the unlikely Ludovico di Varthema of Bologna, who slipped into Mecca in 1503, attached as a guard to a pilgrim caravan, and who wrote his account in Latin. Varthema's work is followed by an anonymous report in the 1580s of the Damascus-to-Mecca caravan and leads, a century later, to a most unusual book by an English sailor, Joseph Pitts, containing some of the first accurate writing about Islam in Western sources. The section concludes with works by two highly educated observers, the Spanish Muslim noble Domingo Badia y Leblich (1807), traveling under the name Ali Bey al-Abbasi, and the Swiss explorer John Lewis

Burckhardt (1814). During all but the first few years of this long period, the Ottoman government in Istanbul financed, protected, and oversaw the Hajj.

Part Three continues in a European vein with Sir Richard Burton's famous 1856 *Personal Narrative,* then alternates between accounts by an Indian princess, the Begum of Bhopal (1864), and a Persian diplomat, Mohammad Farahani (1885), on the one hand, and works by the later European pretenders John Keane (1877) and Arthur Wavell (1908), on the other. With Burton's romantic treatment of Hajj travel, the participating eye of the expert traveler replaces the cooler observers of the Enlightenment. The tone of the traditional Muslim *rihla* changes too in this period. With Mohammad Farahani's encyclopedic treatment, a scientific approach enters the record. Modernity no longer belongs to Europeans only. A modern tone and a modern world are being shaped to serve the needs of Muslim travelers.

The end of Part Three forms a watershed in this literature: To our day, Arthur Wavell's 1908 account remains the last representation of the Hajj by a non-Muslim. In retrospect, it is possible to view these works by pseudo-pilgrims as products of a long historical project that joined European and Middle Eastern territorial and trade interests. Like their Muslim counterparts, the Hajj masqueraders traveled in response to forces built into their culture. But whereas for Muslims this meant fulfilling religious commitments and social expectations, the forces that summoned Westerners to Mecca were a call to adventure as old as Ulysses, a wish to add to the sum of human knowledge, and personal desires for fame or fortune. It is easy to slight them on moral grounds as mere intruders, yet the fact remains that they contributed substantially to the Hajj genre and in some instances helped to correct Europe's flawed vision of Islam. At the same time, the shortcomings inherent in their efforts should not be lost on modern readers. The Hajj they undertook to describe remained an experience only Muslims may have.

Part Four moves on to the interwar period of the twentieth century, with five works by European converts to Islam. It begins in 1925 with the English Muslim Eldon Rutter's two-volume account written in the last decade of the camel. It continues with works by two English-speaking women converts: a spunky, offhand memoir by Winifred Stegar detailing her family's third-class pilgrimage from Australia in 1927 and Lady Evelyn Cobbold's more mandarin volume written in 1933. Due to chronology, these two accounts are separated by excerpts from the philosophical memoir of scholar-adventurer Muhammad Asad, a Galician journalist who embraced Islam and lived for some years at the court of Ibn Saʿud, and by a Hajj memoir by Harry St. John Philby, the British Middle East diplomat and explorer, who, like

Asad, lived at the Saudi court for years. Although Part Four spans only a decade, the period is crucial for the Hajj. During this time, the House of Saʿud put an end to sharifal rule in Mecca, and in the wake of World War I the Ottoman Empire dissolved. The foundations of the modern Hajj all date from this period. For the first time in many centuries, it came under direct local control.

Part Five concludes the collection with five records of the postcolonial, Jet Age pilgrimage. These accounts by Muslims from Mecca, Afghanistan, Iran, Britain, and the United States were composed after World War II, when a war-torn Europe at last began to relinquish its global empire, granting independence to Muslim colonies and mandates and ceding strategic authority to the United States. They bear witness to Islam's spread into the West, to the arrival of global modernity in Saudi Arabia, and to the physical transformation of the Hajj, including the replacement of camels by cars and airplanes and a massive expansion of the pilgrim sites. Opening this section Hamza Bogary's childhood memoir of 1940s Mecca provides a baseline for the rapid changes that follow. Readers may track the stages of this process through subsequent accounts by a pair of notable pilgrims of the 1960s. The Iranian novelist Jalal Al-e Ahmad, and the African American leader Malcolm X. Al-e Ahmad (1964) used the Hajj to point up Islam's continued importance in the radically secularizing Iran of Shah Muhammad Reza Pahlavi; Malcolm X enlisted Islam in the last year of his life as a liberation theology in his struggle against American racism. Both were countercultural figures. Part Five concludes with selections from two less politicized accounts: Saida Miller Khalifa's *The Fifth Pillar of Islam,* detailing her 1970 pilgrimage from Cairo, and my own book on the 1990 Hajj.

The twentieth century will probably be remembered as the century par excellence of the diaspora. As for Islam, about half the world's Muslim population now lives in countries where Islam is a minority religion. In keeping with this trend, most of the Hajj accounts in Parts Four and Five were written by converts from countries outside Islam's more traditional borders. Among born Muslims, only Jalal Al-e Ahmad (1964) returned to his traditional homeland after the Hajj. Just as technology reshaped the look and timetable of the Hajj, so has modernity infused its literature and intellectual traditions. There is nothing antique in the points of view expressed by these modern Muslim hajjis. Muhammad Asad and Bogary both know their Freud, Al-e Ahmad and Malcolm X their Marx. Whether world travelers or local figures, they inhabit a global culture and have shaped it to their needs. All are at home on trains (and, later, airplanes), just as their predecessors were on camels. Westerners who treat modernity as exclusive territory may be surprised to meet it here, not as a form of ineffectual imitation but as an adaptable methodology put to local uses around the world.

THE ESSAYS A general essay precedes each of these five sections, touching on some of the main forces of the period, particularly as they affected Mecca and the pilgrimage. Each traveler's account is prefaced, too, by shorter essays placing the authors in their time and context and addressing specific aspects of the Hajj. All these introductions are historical in nature, their purpose being to present and frame the excerpts. They focus on the pilgrimage itself and on the travelers who wrote about it. I have not paid much more attention to Meccan politics than they did. Where an author demonstrates interest in a ruler or regime, I have tried to shed light on that for readers. Otherwise, the attention remains on the Hajj, not on the palace. Each excerpt adds a small part to a larger story. Presenting the excerpts in chronological order may help illuminate the subject as a whole; they do not, however, add up to an overview of Islamic or Middle Eastern history. In some cases, hundreds of years separate one traveler from the next, and inevitably a lot has been omitted. Readers seeking more historical background are directed to the Bibliography.

Setting aside chronology for a moment, it is easy to distinguish three categories among these travelers.

In the Islamic group, we have seven insider accounts composed by Muslims born and bred that run through four of the five periods. On the Western side, we find eight outsider works by travelers from Europe, grouped together in Parts Two and Three. Finally, we have a third cluster of eight twentieth-century converts from the West, whose works bulk large in the last two sections. The yawning differences between these groups, in motive, temperament, and point of view, will be touched on again and again throughout this volume. By and large, we will find that the Muslim traveler treats Mecca as a well-known capital in an enormous and unified social system, a place where in addition to spiritual fulfillment one may properly pursue one's education and, even, professional career. Non-Muslim travel writers, on the other hand, treat the East as closed, mysterious, inimical. For them, the Holy Land (whether Muslim or Christian) lies elsewhere, while for Muslims the sacred territories (Mecca and Jerusalem) are centers of a more familiar world. Finally, Muslim travelers are more intimately aware of where they are going, while the outsiders explore a strange unknown. Paradoxically, the latter group tells us much about Mecca and the Hajj because their appointed role is usually to report new facts to unaccustomed readers. From the ill-informed Varthema (1503) to the studious Burckhardt and Burton, readers may watch this Western advance guard improving and transmitting its new knowledge.

For some readers, the continued appearance of non-Muslim interlopers on the Hajj may be contradictory, even repugnant. Barred from the city by religious law, they seemed to think nothing of making the Hajj their masquerade. And then there are the uses to which their books were put. Whether by dedicated, sympathetic scholars, author-adventurers, or professional spies, these reports almost invariably flowed back to rulers with conquest in mind. Especially during the colonial nineteenth century, one generation's works of exploration often provided the maps for political domination a few years later. In that light, even these Hajj accounts may be read as products of a global exploitation, of what is referred to in academic circles as the Western hegemonic thrust—that lawless free-for-all for the rest of the planet's resources that began with the Renaissance and is now entering a computerized phase in the transnational trade zones of the twenty-first century. On the other hand, however broadly true the interpretation, it does not very well apply to Mecca, which after all was never colonized. Such blanket theories also have the dismal effect of causing Mecca and the Hajj to vanish into their framework. Nor are they very sensitive to good writing.

This is a sample collection of works that span a millennium. They were composed by a band of travelers who, following various routes for different motives, moved toward the same destination, Mecca. Their pages constitute a literal journey with a thousand roads.

part one

The Medieval Period:
Three Classic
Muslim Travelers
1050—1326

The Persian Naser-e Khosraw (1003–1077), the Iberian Ibn Jubayr (1145–1217), and the Moroccan Ibn Battuta (1303 or 1304–1368 or 1369) were all civil servants, educated men, and devout Muslims. Although separated by centuries, they are often grouped as near contemporaries inhabiting phases of a single age, Islam's expansive Middle Period. This epoch has been called the Golden Age of Muslim travel, partly through the efforts of these authors. To enjoy them, a reader may want to understand the lines along which the Islamic world developed after Muhammad's death.

As Western readers are generally aware, early Islam (620–800) spread quickly in two directions, from Mecca northeast to Afghanistan on the one hand and west to Morocco and Spain on the other. It remains less well known that during the next six centuries, Islam did not endure a long Dark Age like Europe's. As a religion and as a social order, it went on steadily expanding into Africa, India, and Asia, bearing with it a legal system, a trading network, and a coherent way of life. By all accounts, this gradual, often chaotic elaboration resulted in Earth's first global culture. It created a composite civilization, a vast Eurasian common ground across which pilgrims, traders, merchants, and bureaucrats traveled with surprising ease.

It was a thoroughly Muslim world they moved through, a loosely cohesive network with many capitals. In Arabia, the remote, sacred city of Mecca retained its status as a pilgrim center, and hajjis continued to flock there every year, but by the eighth century real political power had drained away to more accessible cities, like Damascus and Baghdad. About two centuries later, when our first author, Naser-e Khosraw, was on the road, power shifted once again, to Cairo. By then, however, the classical notion of an empire ruled from a single capital was already giving way to what the American historian Marshall Hodgson has described as a constantly expanding international society governed by numerous independent Muslim powers.

Centers like Baghdad and Cairo continued to hold sway in the Near East, but beyond them in every direction for many thousands of miles lay other regions of political and mercantile influence, including full-fledged Muslim empires in Spain, North Africa, and India. As our travelers keep reminding us, these regions boasted great capitals too—Córdoba, Tunis, Delhi; yet 90 percent of humanity lived outside them, in towns and villages along the roads. Scholars today reject the ingrained Western view that this expansion was accomplished by military force. In most regions and in most cases, the local populations seem to have willingly adopted a system that taxed them less and offered new options. Generally speaking, Islam proved adaptable and attractive in both urban and pastoral settings across three continents.

The forces nourishing this far-flung network were not political, commercial, or even urban. The real unifying factors were a common social pattern, expressed in the daily traditions of Islam (prayer, ablution, diet, and manners); a common book, the Quran; and a common set of laws, the Sharia, which stresses fair trade. Commerce between, say, Tangier, Cairo, Damascus, and Delhi was further supported by a complex system of caravan and sea routes for transferring goods over many thousands of miles. Throughout the Near East, the Hajj roads were the arteries of this system. During a three-month season every year, they were swollen with pilgrims from all points on the compass carrying goods to pay their way to Mecca, bearing news between the provinces. Because everyone knew someone who had been there and because it was the birthplace of their faith, Mecca, forbidden, mysterious to the West, was always the best-known Muslim city. Any urban ten-year-old, whether in Persia or Morocco, would have been familiar with the pilgrim rites, would in all likelihood have heard some returning uncle or aunt describe the Hajj. In the villages, too, Mecca captured the imagination of the people whether or not they had been there, whether or not they were especially devout.

In Ibn Battuta's fourteenth century, the Hajj was already an organized adventure. At appointed times and for a modest price pilgrims arriving at Cairo, Damascus, or Baghdad would set out together on specific roads, traveling in official caravans scheduled to deliver them to Mecca in time to undertake the appointed rites. The hajjis came from all parts of the Eastern Hemisphere, spoke dozens of different languages, and dressed distinctively. They set out as small families. A few would have some village or city in common, but for the most part they traveled as strangers. In this sense, one's announced intention to perform the Hajj was like keeping a rendezvous at an appointed place with a few hundred thousand people you did not know yet. In a world where clan and blood were emphasized, this aspect of Hajj travel overruled the more usual loyalties, proving Muhammad's point again each year, that Muslim people are bound together by something greater than tribe or race. In addition to strangeness, the Hajj exposed pilgrims to real danger, too. In times of political upheaval, travelers literally risked their lives to get to Mecca. Given the heat, the desert roads, the threat of Bedouin highwaymen and violent Crusaders, to plan to arrive at all was an act of faith—as we shall see.

These huge caravans from the capitals were like cities on the move. Supported and defended by regional rulers, they traveled in stages through treeless regions, over sandy wastes dotted with oases and encampments. To the social historian, their logistical feats indicate high organizational sophistication. The routes themselves were achievements. The nine-hundred-mile Baghdad Road from Kufa to Medina, for example, dates back to pre-Islamic times. By the mid-ninth century, however, the route was marked with milestones and offered fifty-four major way stations, with cisterns, reservoirs or wells, fire-signal towers, hostels, and fortresses paid for from the Abassid caliphal treasury. Like other main routes from Suez and Damascus, the Baghdad Road developed revictualing stations too, to which local traders rode out to sell their produce. As Ibn Battuta tells us, each caravan had its own administration. An annually appointed leader, or amir, oversaw a collection of high officials who in turn governed a complex pilgrim-service industry of cameleers, medics, water carriers, torch bearers, cooks, fireworks experts, scouts, guides, battalions of soldiers, and of course musicians. Besides the main arterial routes from Cairo, Damascus, and Baghdad, other trails were well traveled too—south up the Nile through Egypt, then across the Red Sea from Aydhab, or north through mountainous Yemen, for example. (See Fig. 6.)

Most of these routes are depicted (and redepicted) in these pages. Some of the best descriptive writing of the age is trained on the Meccan caravans. Their annual treks were spectacles, steeped in the symbols of nomadic culture: sweeping trains of silent camels pacing down the sands at night, lit by swaying lanterns, to the faint accompaniment of tambourines. Beguiling today, such scenes must have been even more attractive to urban Muslim readers of the period. The Hajj authors wrote to entertain, but also to forewarn prospective pilgrims, for the caravans were mortal affairs rife with risk and ever-present danger: scarce water, desiccating winds, marauding thieves, and the bleached bones of last year's unfortunates dotting the wayside. The routes demanded description because they held so many pitfalls. Armed escorts as protection from raiders were a must. In 1051, Naser-e Khosraw, returning home from Mecca, diverged from the security of the Baghdad caravan and barely lived to write about it. A century later, in southern Egypt, Ibn Jubayr, our second traveler, remarked on the "many hells that strew the road" to Mecca. Still later, Ibn Battuta mentions an escort of "a hundred or more cavalry and a troop of archers" attached to his Libyan caravan. It should not cause surprise that half the accounts in this book were written in part to warn and protect later pilgrims.

In our opening section, the eleventh and twelfth centuries of the Earlier Middle Period form the stage for a power struggle between two distinct branches of Islam, the Sunni and the Shi'ite. Both groups emerged from a rift in the Muslim community thirty years after Muhammad's death. They are distinguished by opposing views of succession. The larger, Sunni branch preferred an elective process for each new caliph; Shi'ites, on the other hand, believed the leadership belongs to the Prophet's nephew and son-in-law, Ali, and to his heirs. By 945, however, the post of *khalifah* (caliph, or successor to the Prophet), once the spiritual and temporal ruler of Islam, was being reduced to a figurehead in a greatly expanding Muslim world that could no longer be controlled from one Arab center. The caliph came to preside over an idea, the overall unity of the Muslim world, while sultans (the overlords of sometimes quite extensive regions) and amirs (who governed more local territories) assumed the reins of practical government completely. Supported by a fourth force, the military, these broad divisions of power became the norm almost everywhere until 1500. Through most of the Earlier Middle Period (945–1250), the central Arab region was split between two powers: a Sunni Abassid Empire, centered in Baghdad, and an emerging Shi'ite power, the Fatimid Caliphate (961–1171), with the new city of Cairo as its capital. Their long, uneven contest to establish a single, stable dominion from Morocco to the Iranian plateau shaped the whole period.

Mecca influenced and was affected by this struggle. First as the Fatimid rule gained ascendancy in the eleventh century and again as the Abbasids recovered it after 1170, each of these titanic urban powers pressed to have its sovereignty confirmed in *Mecca*—a poor, provincial, inclement desert city with nothing but the Hajj to recommend it. The Meccan trade could not have interested such rich mercantile centers; apart from the Hajj, it was probably negligible, anyway. Rather, they sought the wholly symbolic power conferred by Meccan recognition and the charisma derived from serving as protectors of Islam's most sacred shrine. Without acknowledgment from the heartland, the caliph's title "Commander of the Faithful" lacked moral force among his subjects. Mecca's seal of approval was also crucial because at one time or another almost everybody went there from every part of the vaunted caliph's realm. In exchange for recognition in the mosque there (expressed

6

by blessing the ruler's name at Friday prayers), the imperial treasuries gave liberally to the local rulers (the sharifs) and to the mosques in Mecca and Medina. They also pursued the important task of protecting the pilgrim roads.

Our first two accounts depict the ins and outs of this arrangement. In the opening selection, Naser-e Khosraw, a Shi'ite, attends a Hajj in 1047. It is largely supported by the Shi'ite ruler in Egypt, al-Mustansir. A century later, as power swings back in the Abassid direction, Ibn Jubayr arrives in Cairo, too, to find a *Sunni* controlled city and a *Sunni* supported Hajj in the Hijaz. A revolution in government has taken place; the Hijaz and many other lands have shifted hands. Yet during both periods, *the same strategic alliance remains in place* between Mecca and the region's prevailing power. Each regime has had its sovereignty proclaimed in the Sacred City in return for support and security. From about 1180 on, the Meccan sharifs were supposed to use part of these funds to mollify the Hijazi raiding clans and so reduce their plundering of pilgrims. The basic outlines of this arrangement continued for centuries. Under the Mamluks (1250–1517), the armed guards of the caravans were greatly augmented. Under Ottoman rule (1517–1924), the protection of the Hajj caravans became a major budgetary item, equal to waging a large, annual war.

Who were the sharifs? Ibn Battuta tells us that when he first arrived in Mecca, the town's co-governors were brothers, sons of a previous ruler, Abu Numayy Qitada. The Qitada line went back more than a century, to the days of Abu Aziz "al-Nabigha" Qitada, ruler of Yanbu and a Hashimite, a member of the Prophet's clan. Al-Nabigha means "the Genius," a nickname he probably earned after sending his son at the head of an army to seize Mecca on May 3, 1201. Certainly this stroke of political wisdom served his descendants. From that date, the Qitada line flowed forward for seven more centuries. The last sharif (Husayn ibn Ali, reigned 1908–24) was both a Qitada and a Hashimite. In all that time, the line remained unbroken. The dynasties of Abu Numayy I (1255–1425), the Barakats (1425–1524), Abu Numayy II with his several clans (1524–1636), and Sharif Ghalib and his relations (1771–1881) each lasted a century or more. Their reigns, however, were anything but stable. For one thing, each sharif bore many sons, who often became mortal enemies, sometimes of Shakespearean proportions. Externally, too, the pressures toward disintegration were enormous, with Egyptian, then Turkish, forces occasionally garrisoning the city, sometimes for decades, over the centuries.

Like petty rulers anywhere, the Qitadas held on by adroitness and guile, but also by passing down from father to son their founder's deathbed advice on how to govern. There were, they believed, five principles by which the ruler of such a poor province might prevail: First, he must take advantage of the unassailable remoteness of the Hijaz, barricading himself inside it as if in a fortress, and not risk his limited strength in foreign struggles. Second, he ought always to maintain a shrewd balance between the centers of power to the north (Cairo and Baghdad) while looking south to Yemen for true allies. Third, he should permit the name of the foreign sultan strong enough to impose it to be mentioned in prayers at the Holy Mosque, as a symbol of sovereignty. Fourth, he should obtain grants and presents from richer Muslim rulers in order to maintain the Holy Places and the roads. Last, he must be careful to hold down pilgrim taxes to tolerable limits. This last rule, placing a check on noble greed, was largely dishonored; yet by sticking to the rest of the prescription, the Qitadas managed to reign over Mecca into the twentieth century. Although the deathbed scene is probably apocryphal, their ancient code pretty well sums up the best course open to a family hoping to maintain a throne in Mecca.

These early accounts are not reports of visits to an exotic city. Nor are they works of pure geography, like *The Book of Routes and Provinces* by Ibn Khurdadhbih (died 893 or 894) or *The Book of Earth's Roads* (ca. 977) by Ibn Hawkal. Whereas those books state correctly that the Sinai Road to Mecca was composed of thirty-four stages, each twenty-eight to thirty miles long, they do not report how the caravan appeared or give the pomp and feel of the procession. Readers must turn to the travelers for that. Yet this is not adventure literature either, or exploration. These authors are aware of their destination; they possess knowledge about the place before they set out. Nor is it commerce or curiosity that draws them. The underlying goal of these first travelers is spiritual and penitent in nature. They are not just out to see the world (though they see quite a lot of it). Principally, they are going to Mecca to fulfill a vow and to experience God more deeply. That is one salient difference between, say, Ibn Battuta and Marco Polo.

Matters of interwoven texts, not to say plagiarism, abound in this literature from the start. Ibn Jubayr, for example, a twelfth-century Arab from Spain, knew Naser-e Khosraw's Hajj book very well, although it was written in Persian a century earlier. He quotes from it, as he quotes from Azraqi and other early historians of Mecca. A century and a half later Ibn Battuta quotes all three, even incorporating swatches of Ibn Jubayr's account in his own descriptions. The cribbing and quoting starts early. It continues through the nineteenth century (see especially Burckhardt [1814] and Burton [1853]), as both Muslim and non-Muslim travelers redeploy the very small shelf of their predecessors.

These ancient accounts continue to be published, drawn upon, and read because they shed valuable light on the human workings of pilgrim travel and because people still enjoy reading them. Ibn Jubayr's, the most compact in space and time, describes a round-trip of about two years—the average span of the journey before trains and airplanes. A century earlier, Naser-e Khosraw recorded a round-trip, too, but his journey lasted seven years and was mystically motivated. The last and longest account in this section, by Ibn Battuta, starts as a conventional Hajj report, then opens out into a description of the world. The editorial comments introducing these first three authors are somewhat longer than in later sections of the book because they present concepts that are foundational. Topics essential to the later record—the caliphate, Sunni and Shi'ite Islam, and the expansion of the Muslim world—are first presented here.

These initial selections are by medieval authors writing for a Muslim audience. Their notion of life's necessities, their definitions of comfort and roadside attractions, are their own. Their cities seem less dangerous than ours, their roads more precarious. Their narrative voice may strike us oddly, too. Even Ibn Battuta, perhaps the most personal, can seem withdrawn when compared to more contemporary writers, for whom the private psyche is more naturally a matter of public record. The pace of travel differs too. The first private carriage on the Hajj does not appear in writing until the early 1800s. Meanwhile, the nearest thing to a conveyance, the camel-borne *shugduf,* is a saddled-mounted tent to deflect the sun. Ibn Jubayr described such conveyances in 1184. Sir Richard Burton could still recommend them almost seven centuries later. Inside Arabia until the 1930s, the speed of pilgrim travel was determined not by wheels but by padding feet.

Naser-e Khosraw
Persia
1050

Naser-e Khosraw's Book of Travels *is a classic text that has set the tone for a thousand years of Persian travel writing. In this offhand roadside diary, a seasoned traveler records great sights and endures hardship gamely. He may not strike us as a self-revealing narrator, and yet his book begins with a confession: that his travels are the result of a midlife crisis.*

Naser-e Khosraw was born in 1003 in the province of Khurasan in eastern Persia. Until he left for Mecca at forty-two, he occupied administrative posts at Marv (present-day Mary) and Balkh and occasionally attended upon princes. His satiric poem "The Aging Rake" appears to be based on firsthand knowledge of a dissolute court life. By his own account, he overindulged in the most un-Islamic vice of alcohol until in the fall of 1045 he had a dream. He had been traveling for about a month, he says, and drinking steadily, when a figure appeared in his sleep one night and advised him to seek wisdom. When Khosraw asked where wisdom lay, his visitor pointed toward Mecca and disappeared.

In eleventh-century Persia, a dream like this marked a turning point on the spiritual path of an esoteric Shi'ite sect, the Isma'ilis. Intellectually, they were sophisticated scholars with a passion for science and hidden meanings. Politically, they were tainted in Sunni-governed Khurasan for their allegiance to the Fatimid ruler in Cairo and for their faith in an imminent millennium, with its promise of revolution and social justice. Whether Khosraw was already an Isma'ili or whether he became one on the road remains unclear. We do know, however, that at about this time Isma'ilis were being increasingly persecuted by the newly arrived and aggressively Sunni Seljuks. For these mercenary soldiers, the sect (and Shi'ism in general) posed a threat by insisting on allegiance to a special leadership apart from the Caliph and by honoring a secret body of traditions. Holding a government post under the Seljuks may have been one of the "torments of the world" Khosraw complained of.

For whatever reasons, he dropped everything to be under way. He resigned his post at the treasury in Marv, announced he was going to Mecca, and apparently destroyed his early poems. Departing ahead of the annual caravan, joined by one brother and a servant, Khosraw was packed and on the road without delay. He did not make straight for Baghdad, however, then drop south by the usual route to Mecca. (See Fig. 7.) Instead, he took a roundabout way across northern Persia, moving by twists and turns through towns and regions friendly to Isma'ilis. (In this part of his book, notes on food, architecture, and culture are mixed with accounts of visits to scholars and pre-Crusader shrines in Persia, Syria, Jordan, Palestine, and Egypt.) Avoiding the Hajj caravan is telling, for after all it provided security. In his present situation, however, Khosraw valued anonymity over safety, especially on roadways secured by Sunni guards.

If the Isma'ilis were suspect in much of Persia and Mesopotamia, in Fatimid Egypt they were on the throne. Not surprisingly, after a first pilgrimage to Mecca, Khosraw headed for Egypt. Cairo was in its heyday then, under the great Fatimid Sultan al-Mustansir (reigned 1036–94), whose ancestors had laid out the city on the Nile. Under his enlightened policies, Cairo became the center of a rich market ranging over a vast trade zone from Tunisia to Gujarat (India). The first Muslim university, al-Azhar, was founded here, adding prestige and scholarship to a well-governed capital famed for its support of arts and letters. Khosraw's fluent descriptions of the prosperity he found, the rooftop gardens and several thousand mosques, free hospitals, safe roads, worthy scholars, and charitable laws all bespeak a cultural golden age. The extent of the Sultan's sway and the fanfare surrounding him may seem flamboyant to modern readers, but they are not exaggerations. Al-Mustansir's reign of nearly six decades marks one of the high points of Muslim culture.

Khosraw seems to have taken up permanent quarters at the royal court, becoming a pupil of Daud Shirazi, a great Isma'ili sage, and being prepared as a da'i, or chief missionary. During his extended stay, he also visited Mecca three more times. The last journey forms the center of his book. The excerpts from it presented here condense the stages of his itinerary. They begin with early travels through Persia and Syria. They continue with a longer view of the wonders of Fatimid Cairo, include extracts from his period in Mecca, and end with enough of his hard trek home to indicate the risks in traveling through Arabia alone at the time of the Battle of Hastings.

Khosraw's description of Mecca is spare—a matter of a few pages. In this, it resembles the accounts of other early Muslim pilgrims. The reason for their brevity is simple: they wrote for an audience of fellow Muslims, readers to whom Mecca was the most familiar, not the most secret, city on Earth. Although unadorned, Khosraw's view of the ritual grounds within the Meccan mosque is not *only accurate; it presents the core arena as it stands today: the two-story Kaʿba at its center, where pilgrims circulate; the Zamzam Well, where they quench their thirst; and Safa and Marwa, the hills they pace between. Here we have our first course in the arrival rites of the Hajj, the sacred geography of Mecca, and the procession from the city to the Plain of Arafat. These and other themes (the economy of Mecca, the "sojourner" pilgrims who extend their stay, the city's water system) appear here in miniature. Later travelers will treat these topics extensively. Khosraw's book articulates them first.*

After his fourth pilgrimage, Khosraw did not return to Cairo. He struck out for home instead, on a roundabout route through eastern Arabia. His choice of itineraries led to disaster. Preyed upon by raiders, without the protection of a caravan, here Khosraw gives us our first grim look at the merciless deserts of Arabia and at the predatory ways of the Arab Bedouin, whose control of the roads traversing their lands provides a gruesome set piece in pilgrim books for centuries to come. In Khosraw's case, the desert quickly devolved into a toll road manned by camel-riding pirates. The price of safe passage cost his party their money, then their clothes.

This choice of routes yields one great consolation—a purported nine-month stay in the city of Lahsa. A legendary land of plenty in the eastern Hasa Desert, Lahsa lay a day's ride from Bahrain. Khosraw seems to have felt it worth the detour to experience firsthand this (not coincidentally) Shiʿite capital, with its six monarchs sharing power and an equitable society protected from attack behind high walls. Here, in a place surrounded by social chaos, Khosraw treats us to a brief, meticulous portrait of a city where the arts of civilization plainly flourished. Forsaking its comforts to travel north could not have been easy. The long trip through savage deserts was unbearably exhausting. Limping into Basra eight months later, Khosraw and his two companions appeared so destitute that the head of the public baths refused to admit them.

from Naser-e Khosraw's
Book of Travels

INTRODUCTION I was a clerk by profession and one of those in charge of the sultan's revenue service. In my administrative position I had applied myself for a period of time and acquired no small reputation among my peers.

13

In the month of Rabi‘ II in the year 437 [October 1045], when the prince of Khurasan was Abu Solayman Chaghri Beg Daud son of Mika'il son of Seljuk, I set out from Marv on official business to the district of Panjdeh in Marv Rud, where I stopped off . . .

From there I went to Juzjanan, where I stayed nearly a month and was constantly drunk on wine. (The Prophet says, "Tell the truth, even if on your own selves.") One night in a dream I saw someone saying to me, "How long will you continue to drink of this wine, which destroys man's intellect? If you were to stay sober, it would be better for you."

In reply I said, "The wise have not been able to come up with anything other than this to lessen the sorrow of this world."

"To be without one's senses is no repose," he answered me. "He cannot be called wise who leads men to senselessness. Rather, one should seek out that which increases reason and wisdom."

"Where can I find such a thing?" I asked.

"Seek and ye shall find," he said, and then he pointed toward the *qibla** and said nothing more. When I awoke, I remembered everything, which had truly made a great impression on me. "You have waked from last night's sleep," I said to myself. "When are you going to wake from that of forty years?" And I reflected that until I changed all my ways I would never find happiness.

On Thursday . . . [19 December 1045] . . . , I cleansed myself from head to foot, went to the mosque, and prayed to God for help both in accomplishing what I had to do and in abstaining from what he had forbidden.

Afterwards I went to Shoburghan and spent the night in a village in Faryab. From there I went via Samangan and Talaqan to Marv Rud and thence to Marv. Taking leave from my job, I announced that I was setting out for the Pilgrimage to Mecca, I settled what debts I owed and renounced everything worldly, except for a few necessities.

CROSSING PERSIA On . . . [5 March 1046] I set out for Nishapur, traveling from Marv to Sarakhs, which is a distance of thirty parasangs.† From there to Nishapur is forty parasangs. . . .

---

qibla: the direction of the Ka‘ba in Mecca, toward which Muslims orient themselves when they pray. [Ed.]

†parasang: three and a half miles. [Ed.]

On the second of Dhu al-Qada I left Nishapur and, in the company of Khwaja Mowaffaq, the sultan's agent, came to Qumes via Gavan. There I paid a visit to the tomb of Shaykh Bayazid of Bestam.

On Friday the eighth of Dhu al-Qada [17 May] I went out to Damghan. The first of Dhu al-Hijja 437 [9 June 1046] I came to Semnan by way of Abkhwari and Chashtkhwaran, and there I stayed for a period of time, seeking out the learned. I was told of a man called Master Ali Nasa'i, whom I went to see. He was a young man who spoke Persian with a Daylamite accent and wore his hair uncovered. He had a group of people about him reading Euclid, while another group read medicine and yet another mathematics. During our conversation he kept saying, "I read this with Avicenna," and "I heard this from Avicenna." His object of this was, of course, for me to know that he had been a student of Avicenna.* When I became engaged in discourse with some of these people, he said, "I know nothing of arithmetic [*siyaq*] and would like to learn something of the arithmetic art." I came away wondering how, if he himself knew nothing, he could teach others. . . .

SYRIA   On the eleventh of Rajab [11 January] we left the city of Aleppo. Three parasangs distant was a village called Jond Qennasrin. The next day, after traveling six parasangs, we arrived in the town of Sarmin, which has no fortification walls.

Six parasangs farther on was Ma'arrat al-No'man, which is quite populous. It has a stone wall. Beside the city gate I saw a cylindrical column of stone, which had something written on it in a script that was not Arabic. I asked someone what it was, and he said that it was a talisman against scorpions. If ever a scorpion were brought in from outside and turned loose, it would run away and not stay in the town. I estimated that column to be about ten ells† high. I found the bazaars to be flourishing, and the Friday mosque built on a rise in the middle of town so that from whatever place one wants to go up to the mosque, one has to ascend thirteen steps. Their whole agriculture consists of wheat, which is plentiful. Figs, olives, pistachios, almonds, and grapes also abound. The city water comes from both rain and wells.

*Avicenna: Western name of Ibn Sina (980–1037), renowned Persian philosopher and physician. [Ed.]

†ell: roughly one and a half feet. [Ed.]

In the city was a man named Abu al-Ala of Ma'arra. Although blind, he was the head of the city and very wealthy, with many slaves and servants. Everyone in the city, in fact, was like a slave to him, but he himself had chosen the ascetic life. He wore coarse garments and stayed at home. Half a *maund*** of barley bread he would divide into nine pieces and content himself with only one piece throughout the entire day and night. Besides that, he ate nothing. I heard it said that the door to his house was always open and that his agents and deputies did all the work of the city, except for the overall supervision, which he saw to himself. He denied his wealth to no one, although he himself was constantly fasting and vigilant at night, taking no part in the affairs of the world. This man has attained such a rank in poetry and literature that all the learned of Syria, the Maghrib, and Iraq confess that in this age there is no one of comparable stature. He has composed a book . . . in which he speaks in enigmatic parables. Although eloquent and amazing, the book can be understood only by a very few and by those who have read it with him. He has even been accused of trying to rival the Quran. There are always more than two hundred persons from all over gathered about him reading literature and poetry. I have heard that he himself has composed more than a hundred thousand lines of poetry. Someone once asked him why, since God had given him all this wealth and property, he gave it away to the people and hardly ate anything himself. His answer was, "I own nothing more than what I eat." When I passed through that place he was still alive. . . .

JOURNEY TO EGYPT After Jerusalem I decided to voyage to Egypt by sea and thence again to Mecca. . . . Shortly, I arrived at a port called Tina, from which you proceed to Tennis. I boarded a boat and sailed over to Tennis, which is on an island. It is a pleasant city and so far from the mainland that you cannot even see the shore from rooftops. The city is populous and has good bazaars and two cathedral mosques. I estimated there were ten thousand shops, a hundred of which were pharmacies. . . .

They weave multicolored linen for turbans, bandages, and women's clothing. The colored linen of Tennis is unequaled anywhere except by the white linen woven in Damietta. That which is woven in the royal workshop is not sold to anyone. I heard that the king of Fars once sent twenty thousand dinars to Tennis to buy one suit of clothing of their spe-

---

maund: roughly three and a half pounds. [Ed.]

cial material. [His agents] stayed there for several years but were unsuccessful in obtaining any. What the weavers are most famous for is their "special" material. I heard that someone there had woven a turban for the sultan of Egypt that cost five hundred gold dinars. I saw the turban myself and was told it was worth four thousand dinars. In this city of Tennis they weave [a type of cloth called] *buqalamun,* which is found nowhere else in the world. It is an iridescent cloth that appears of different hues at different times of the day. It is exported east and west from Tennis. I heard that the ruler of Byzantium once sent a message to the Sultan of Egypt that he would exchange a hundred cities of his realm for Tennis alone. The sultan did not accept, of course, knowing that what he wanted with this city was its linen and *buqalamun.*

When the water of the Nile rises, it pushes the salt water of the sea away from Tennis so that the water is fresh for ten parasangs. For that time of the year large, reinforced, underground cisterns called *masna'as* have been constructed on the island. When the Nile water forces the salty seawater back, they fill these cisterns by opening a watercourse from the sea into them, and the city exists for a whole year on this supply. When anyone has an excess of water, he will sell to others, and there are also endowed *masna'as* from which water is given out to foreigners.

The population of this city is fifty thousand, and there are at any given time at least a thousand ships at anchor belonging both to private merchants and to the sultan; since nothing is there, everything that is consumed must be brought in from the outside. All external transactions with the island are made therefore by ship, and there is a fully armed garrison stationed there as a precaution against attack by Franks and Byzantines. I heard from reliable sources that one thousand dinars a day go from there into the sultan's treasury. Every day the people of the city turn that amount over to the tax collector, and he in turn remits it to the treasury before it shows a deficit. Nothing is taken from anyone by force. The full price is paid for all the linen and *buqalamun* woven for the Sultan, so that the people work willingly— not as in some other countries, where the artisans are forced to labor for the Vizier and Sultan! They weave covers for camel litters and striped saddlecloths for the aristocrats; in return, they import fruits and foodstuffs from the Egyptian countryside.

They also make superior iron tools such as shears, knives, and so on. I saw a pair of shears imported from there to Egypt and selling for five dinars. They were made so that when the pin was taken out, the shears came apart, and when the pin was replaced they worked again . . .

We set out for Egypt. When we reached the seashore, we found a boat going up the Nile. As the Nile nears the coast, it splits into many branches and flows fragmented into the sea. The branch we were on is called Rumesh. The boat sailed along until we came to a town called Salehiyya, which is very fertile. Many ships capable of carrying up to two hundred *kharvar*s* of commodities for sale in the groceries of Cairo are made there. Were it not done in that manner, it would be impossible to bring provisions into the city by animal with such efficiency. We disembarked at Salehiyya and proceeded that very night to the city.

On Sunday . . . [3 August 1047], . . . we were in Cairo.

THE PROVINCES OF THE NILE The city of Cairo lies between the Nile and the sea, the Nile flowing from south to north into the sea. From Cairo to Alexandria is thirty parasangs, and Alexandria is on the shore of the Mediterranean and the banks of the Nile. From there much fruit is brought to Cairo by boat. There is a lighthouse that I saw in Alexandria, on top of which used to be an incendiary mirror.† Whenever a ship came from Istanbul and approached opposite the mirror, fire would fall from the mirror and burn the ship up. The Byzantines exerted great effort and employed all manner of subterfuge, until they finally sent someone who broke the mirror. In the days of al-Hakim, the Sultan of Egypt, a man appeared who was willing to fix the mirror as it had once been, but al-Hakim said it was not necessary, that the situation was well under control, since at that time the Greeks sent gold and goods in tribute and were content for the armies of Egypt not to go near them. . . .

Whoever wants to go to Mecca from Egypt must go east. From Qolzom there are two ways, one by land and one by sea. The land route can be traversed in fifteen days, but it is all desert and three hundred parasangs long. Most of the caravans from Egypt take that way. By sea it takes twenty days to reach Jar, a small town in the Hijaz on the sea. From Jar to Medina it takes three days. From Medina to Mecca is one hundred parasangs. Following the coastline from Jar, you will come to the Yemen and the coast

---

kharvar: 100 *maunds*, or roughly 350 pounds. [Ed.]

†the Pharos lighthouse of antiquity, one of the Seven Wonders of the World. See page 57 for Ibn Battuta's description three centuries later. [Ed.]

of Aden; continuing in that direction, you will eventually wind up in India and China. Continuing southward from Aden and slightly westward, you will come to Zanzibar and Ethiopia, which will be described presently. Going south from Egypt through Nubia, you come to the province of the Masmudis, which is a land of broad pasturelands, many animals, and heavyset, strong-limbed, squat, black-skinned men; there are many soldiers of this sort in Egypt . . .

A DESCRIPTION OF THE CITY OF CAIRO Coming south from Syria, the first city one encounters is (New) Cairo, Old Cairo being situated farther south. Cairo is called al-Qahera al-Mo'ezziyya, and the garrison town is called al-Fustat. . . . I estimated that there were no less than twenty thousand shops in Cairo, all of which belong to the Sultan. Many shops are rented for as much as ten dinars a month, and none for less than two. There is no end of caravansaries, bathhouses, and other public buildings—all property of the Sultan, for no one owns any property except houses and what he himself builds. I heard that in Cairo and Old Cairo there are eight thousand buildings belonging to the Sultan that are leased out, with the rent collected monthly. These are leased and rented to people on tenancy-at-will, and no sort of coercion is employed.

The Sultan's palace is in the middle of Cairo and is encompassed by an open space so that no building abuts it. . . . As the ground is open all around it, every night there are a thousand watchmen, five hundred mounted and five hundred on foot, who blow trumpets and beat drums at the time of evening prayer and then patrol until daybreak. Viewed from outside the city, the Sultan's palace looks like a mountain because of all the different buildings and the great height. From inside the city, however, one can see nothing at all because the walls are so high. They say that twelve thousand hired servants work in this palace, in addition to the women and slave girls, whose number no one knows. It is said, nonetheless, that there are thirty thousand individuals in the palace, which consists of twelve buildings. The harem has ten gates on the ground level, each with a name. . . .

A DESCRIPTION OF THE OPENING OF THE CANAL When the Nile is increasing, . . . with its level rising eighteen ells above the winter level, the heads of the canals and channels are closed throughout the land. Then the canal called al-Khalij, which begins in Old Cairo and passes through New Cairo, and which is the Sultan's personal property, is opened with the Sultan* in attendance. Afterward, all the other canals and channels are opened throughout the countryside. This day is one of the biggest festivals of the year and is called Rokub Fath al-Khalij ("Riding Forth to Open the Canal").

When the season approaches, a large pavilion of Byzantine brocade spun with gold and set with gems, large enough for a hundred horsemen to stand in its shade, is elaborately assembled at the head of the canal for the sultan. In front of this canopy are set up a striped tent and another large pavilion. Three days before the Rokub, drums are beaten and trumpets sounded in the royal stables so that the horses will get accustomed to the sound. When the Sultan mounts, ten thousand horses with gold saddles and bridles and jewel-studded reins stand at rest, all of them with saddlecloths of Byzantine brocade and *buqalamun* woven seamless to order. In the borders of the cloth are woven inscriptions bearing the name of the Sultan of Egypt. On each horse is a spear or coat of armor and a helmet on the pommel, along with every other type of weapon. There are also many camels and mules with handsome panniers and howdahs, all studded with gold and jewels. Their coverings are sewn with pearls.

Were I to describe everything about this day of [the opening of] the canal, it would take too long. . . . On the morning when the Sultan is going out for the ceremony, ten thousand men are hired to hold the steeds we have already described. These parade by the hundred, preceded by bugles, drums, and clarions and followed by army battalions, from the Harem Gate up to the head of the canal. Each of these hirelings who holds a horse is given three dirhems. Next come horses and camels fitted with litters and caparisons, and following these come camels bearing howdahs. At some distance behind all of these comes the Sultan, a well-built, clean-shaven youth with cropped hair, a descendant of Husayn son of Ali. He is mounted on a camel with plain saddle and bridle with no gold or silver and wears a white shirt, as is the custom in Arab countries, with a wide cummerbund. . . . The value of this alone is said to be ten thousand dinars. On his head he has a turban of the same color, and in his hand he holds a large, very costly whip. Before him walk three hundred Daylamites wearing Byzantine gold-spun cloth with cummerbunds and wide sleeves, as is the fashion in Egypt. They all carry spears and arrows and wear leggings. At the Sultan's side rides a parasol bearer with a bejeweled, gold turban and a suit of clothing worth ten thousand dinars. The parasol he holds is extremely

---

*al-Mustansir (reigned 1036–94). [Ed.]

ornate and studded with jewels and pearls. No other rider accompanies the Sultan, but he is preceded by Daylamites. To his left and right are thurifers burning ambergris and aloe. The custom here is for the people to prostrate themselves and say a prayer as the Sultan passes. After the Sultan comes the Grand Vizier with the Chief Justice and a large contingent of religious and governmental officials.

The Sultan proceeds to the head of the canal, where court has been set up, and remains mounted beneath the pavilion for a time. He is then handed a spear, which he throws at the dam. Men quickly set to work with picks and shovels to demolish the dam, and the water, which has built up on the other side, breaks through and floods the canal.

On this day the whole population of Old and New Cairo comes to witness the spectacle of the opening of the canal and to see all sorts of wonderful sporting events. The first ship that sails into the canal is filled with deaf-mutes, whom they must consider auspicious. On that day the Sultan distributes alms to these people.

There are twenty-one boats belonging to the Sultan, which are usually kept tied up like animals in a stable, in an artificial lake the size of two or three playing fields next to the Sultan's palace; each boat is fifty yards long and twenty wide and is so ornate with gold, silver, jewels, and brocade that were I to describe them I could fill many pages.

A DESCRIPTION OF THE CITY OF MECCA The city of Mecca is situated low in the midst of mountains such that from whatever direction you approach, the city cannot be seen until you are there. The tallest mountain near Mecca is Abu Qubays, which is round like a dome, so that if you shoot an arrow from the foot of the mountain it reaches its top. Abu Qubays is to the east of the city, so that if you should be in the Haram Mosque in the month of Capricorn you see the sun rise from behind the top of the mountain. On top of the mountain is a stone stele said to have been erected by Abraham. The city lies on a plain between the mountains and measures only two arrow shots square. The Haram Mosque is in the middle of the plain, and the city lanes and bazaars are built all around it. Wherever there is an opening in the mountain a rampart wall has been made with a gate. The only trees in the city are at the western gate to the Haram Mosque, called Abraham's Gate, where there are several tall trees around a well. On the eastern side of the Haram Mosque a large bazaar extends from south to north. At the south end is Abu Qubays. At the foot of Abu Qubays is Mount Safa, which is like a staircase, as rocks have been set in such a fashion that people can go up to pray, which is what is meant by [the expression] "to do Safa and Marwa." At the other, the north end of the bazaar, is Mount Marwa, which is less tall and has many edifices built on it, as it lies in the midst of the city. In running between Safa and Marwa the people run inside this bazaar.

For people who have come from faraway places to perform the Minor Pilgrimage, there are milestones and mosques set up half a parasang away from Mecca, where they bind their *ihram*. To bind the *ihram* means to take off all sewn garments and to wrap a seamless garment about the waist and another about the body. Then, in loud voice, you say, *"Labayk Allahumma, labayk,"** and approach Mecca. When anyone already inside Mecca wants to perform the Minor Pilgrimage, he goes out to one of the markets, binds his *ihram,* says the Labayk, and comes back into Mecca with an intention to perform the Minor Pilgrimage. Having come into the city, you enter the Haram Mosque, approach the Ka'ba, and circumambulate . . . always keeping the Ka'ba to your left [shoulder]. Then you go to the corner containing the Black Stone, kiss it, and pass on. When the Stone is kissed once again in the same manner, one *tawaf,* or circumambulation, has been completed. This continues for seven *tawaf*s, three times quickly and four slowly. When the circumambulation is finished, you go to the Station of Abraham opposite the Ka'ba and stand behind the Station. There you perform two *rakat*s called the Circumambulation Prayer. Afterwards you go the Well of Zamzam, drink some water or rub some on the face, and leave the Haram Mosque by the Safa Gate. Just outside this gate are the steps up Mount Safa, and here you face the Ka'ba and say the prescribed prayer, which is well-known. When the prayer has been said, you come down from Safa and go from south to north through the bazaar to Marwa. Passing through the bazaar, you go past the gates to the Haram Mosque, where the Prophet ran and commanded others to run also. The length is about fifty paces, and on either side are two minarets. When the people coming from Safa reach the first two minarets, they break into a run until they pass the other two at the other end of the bazaar. Then they proceed slowly to Marwa. Upon reaching the end they go up Marwa and recite the prescribed prayer. Then they return through the bazaar and repeat the run until they have gone four times from Safa to Marwa and three times from

*The words of the *labayk* mean approximately "[Thy servant] has answered thy call, O God."

Marwa to Safa, making seven runs the length of the bazaar. Coming down from Marwa the last time, you find a bazaar with about twenty barber-shops facing each other. You have your head shaved and, with the Minor Pilgrimage completed, come out of the Sanctuary. The large bazaar on the east side is called Souk al-Attarin [Druggists' Market]. It has nice build-ings, and all the shopkeepers are druggists. In Mecca there are two [public] baths each paved with a green stone from which flints are made.

I reckoned that there were not more than two thousand citizens of Mecca, the rest, about five hundred, being foreigners and *mojawirs*.* Just at this time there was a famine, with sixteen maunds of wheat costing one dinar, for which reason a number of people had left.

Inside the city of Mecca are hospices for the natives of every region—Khurasan, Transoxiana, the Iraq, and so on. Most of them, however, had fallen into ruination. The Baghdad caliphs had built many beautiful struc-tures, but when we arrived some had fallen to ruin and others had been ex-propriated. All the well water in Mecca is too brackish and bitter to drink, but there are many large pools and reservoirs, costing up to ten thousand dinars each, that catch the rainwater from the hills. When we were there, however, they were empty. A certain prince of Aden, known as Pesar-e Shaddel, had brought water underground to Mecca at great personal expense. This water was used to irrigate crops at Arafat and was limited to there, al-though conduits had been constructed and a little water reached Mecca, but not inside the city; therefore, a pool had been made to collect the water, and water carriers drew the water and brought it to the city to sell. Half a parasang out on the Borqa Road is a well called Bir al-Zahed [the Ascetic's Well]. A nice mosque is located there, and the water is good. The water carriers also bring water from that place for sale.

The climate of Mecca is extremely hot. I saw fresh cucumbers and eggplants at the end of the month of Aquarius. This was the fourth time I had been to Mecca.

From . . . [19 November 1050] until . . . [5 May 1051] I was a *mojawer* in Mecca. On the fifteenth of Aries the grapes were ripe and were brought to town from the villages to be sold in the market. On the first of Taurus melons were plentiful. All kinds of fruit are available in winter, and [the mar-kets] are never empty.

**mojawir:* a sojourner, one who resides for an unusually long period near a holy place or sacred shrine to receive the blessings attendant upon it. [Ed.]

THE HAJJ On the ninth of Dhu al-Hijja 442 [24 April 1051], with God's help, I completed my fourth pilgrimage. After the sun had set and the pilgrims and preacher had left Arafat, everyone traveled one parasang to Mash'ar al-Haram [Sacred Shrine], which is called Muzdalifa. Here a nice structure like a *maqsura** has been built for people to pray in. The stones that are cast in Mina are gathered up here. It is customary to spend the holiday eve in this spot and then to proceed to Mina early the next morning after the dawn prayer for making the sacrifice. A large mosque called Khayif is there, although it is not customary to deliver the sermon or to perform the holiday prayer at Mina, as the Prophet did not establish a precedent.

The tenth day is spent at Mina, and stones are cast, which practice is explained as a supererogatory act connected with the Pilgrimage.

On the twelfth, everyone who intends to leave departs directly from Mina, and those who intend to remain awhile in Mecca go there. Hiring a camel from an Arab for the thirteen-day journey to Lahsa, I bade farewell to God's House.

MECCA TO TA'IF On Friday . . . [4 May 1051], the first of the old month of Gemini, I traveled seven parasangs from Mecca. There was an open plain with a mountain visible in the distance. Heading toward that mountain, we passed by fields and villages. There was a well called Bir al-Husayn ibn Salama [Well of Husayn son of Salama]. The weather was cold. We continued eastward and on Monday arrived in Ta'if, which is twelve parasangs from Mecca. . . .

JAZ' We continued on past that place and saw a fortress called Jaz'. Within half a parasang we passed four fortresses, the largest of which, where we stopped, was called the Banu Nosayr Fortress, and it had a few date palms.

As the man from whom I had hired my camel was from Jaz', I stayed there for fifteen days, there being no *khafir* [safe-conduct] to take us on farther. The Arab tribes of that region each have a particular territory in which they graze their flocks, and no stranger can enter one of these territories, since anyone who does not have a *khafir* will be captured and plundered. Therefore, from each tribe there is a *khafir*, who can pass through a given territory. The *khafir* is also called *qalavoz*.

---

maqsura: an enclosed or screened-off portion of a mosque originally reserved to protect a ruler while praying. [Ed.]

By chance, the leader of the Arabs with whom we had traveled, the Banu Sawad, came to Jaz', and we took him as our *khafir*. His name was Abu Ghanem Abs son of al-Ba'ir, and we set out under his protection. A group of Arabs, thinking they had found "prey" (as they call all strangers), came headed toward us; but since their leader was with us, they passed without saying anything. Had he not been with us, they most certainly would have destroyed us.

We had to remain among these people for a while because there was no *khafir* to take us farther. Finally, we found two men to act as *khafir*s and paid them ten dinars each to take us to the next tribe.

Among one tribe, some seventy-year-old men told me that in their whole lives they had drunk nothing but camels' milk, since in the desert there is nothing but bitter scrub eaten by the camels. They actually imagined that the whole world was like this!

Thus I was taken and handed over from tribe to tribe, the entire time in constant mortal danger. God, however, willed that we [should] come out of there alive.

In the midst of an expanse of rubble, we reached a place called Sarba, where there were mountains shaped like domes. I have never seen anything like them anywhere. They were not so high that an arrow could not have been shot to the top, and they were as bald and smooth as an egg, not the slightest crack or flaw showing.

Along the way, whenever my companions saw a lizard they killed and ate it. The Arabs, wherever they are, milk their camels for drink. I could neither eat the lizard nor drink camels' milk; therefore, wherever I saw a kind of bush that yielded small berries the size of a pea, I picked a few and subsisted on that.

FALAJ After enduring much hardship and suffering great discomfort, on . . . [6 July] we came to Falaj, a distance of 180 parasangs from Mecca. Falaj lies in the middle of the desert and had once been an important region, but internal strife had destroyed it. The only part left inhabited when we arrived was a strip half a parasang long and a mile wide. Inside this area there were fourteen fortresses inhabited by a bunch of filthy, ignorant bandits. These fourteen fortresses had been divided up between two rival factions who were constantly engaged in hostilities. They claimed to be the Lords of al-Raqim mentioned in the Quran.* They had four irrigation canals for their palm

*Quran XVIII: 9. [Ed.]

grove, and their fields were on higher ground and watered from wells. They plow with camels, not cows. As a matter of fact, I never saw a cow there. They produce very little in the way of agriculture, and each man has to ration himself with two seers of grain a day.* This is baked as bread and suffices from the evening prayer until the next evening, as in the month of Ramadan, although they do eat dates during the day. I saw excellent dates there, much better than in Basra and other places. These people are extremely poverty stricken and destitute; nonetheless, they spend the whole day fighting and killing each other. They have a kind of date called *maydun* that weighs ten dirhems,† the pit weighing not more than one-half *danaks*.‡ They claimed that this particular date could be kept for twenty years without spoilage. Their currency is Nishapuri gold.

I stayed four months in this Falaj under the worst possible conditions: nothing of this world remained in my possession except two satchels of books, and they were a hungry, naked, and ignorant people. Everyone who came to pray brought his sword and shield with him as a matter of course. They had no reason to buy books.

There was a mosque in which we stayed. I had a little red and blue paint with me, so I wrote a line of poetry on the wall and drew a branch with leaves up through the writing. When they saw it, they were amazed, and everybody in the compound gathered around to look at what I had done. They told me that if I would paint the *mihrab* they would give me one hundred *maunds* of dates. Now a hundred *maunds* of dates was a fortune for them. Once while I was there, a company of Arab soldiers came and demanded five hundred *maunds* of dates. They refused to give it and fought, which resulted in the death of ten people from the compound. A thousand palms were cut down, but they did not give up even ten *maunds* of dates. Therefore, when they offered me that much, I painted the *mihrab,* and that hundred *maunds* of dates was an answer to our prayers, since we had not been able to obtain any food.

We had almost given up hope of ever being able to get out of that desert, the nearest trace of civilization in any direction being two hundred parasangs away through fearful, devastating desert. In all those four months, I never saw five *maunds* of wheat in one place. Finally, however, a caravan came from

---

*seer: about one and a half ounces. [Ed.]

†*dirhem:* the equivalent of four *danaks*. [Ed.]

‡*danak:* the equivalent of eight grains. [Ed.]

Yamama to take goat's leather to Lahsa. Goat's leather is brought from the Yemen via Falaj and sold to merchants. An Arab offered to take me to Basra, but I had no money to pay the fare. It is only two hundred parasangs to Basra from there, and the hire for a camel was one dinar, whereas a good camel can be bought outright for two or three dinars. Since I had no cash with me, they took me on credit on condition that I pay thirty dinars in Basra. I was forced to agree to these terms, although I had never in my life so much as set foot in Basra!

The Arabs packed my books and seated my brother on a camel, and thus, with me on foot, we set out, headed toward the ascent of the Pleiades. The ground was flat, without so much as a mountain or hill, and wherever the earth was a bit harder, there was rainwater standing in pools. As these people travel night and day, without the slightest trace of a road visible, they must go by instinct. What is amazing is that, with no indication or warning, suddenly they come upon a well.

To make a long story short, in four days and nights we came to Yamama, which has inside a large, old fortress and outside a town with a bazaar containing all sorts of artisans and a fine mosque. The amirs there are Alids of old, and no one has ever been able to wrest the region from their control, since, in the first place, there is not, nor has there been, a conquering sultan or king anywhere near and, in the second, those Alids possess such might that they can mount three to four hundred horsemen. They are of the Zaydi sect, and when they stand in prayer they say, "Mohammad and Ali are the best of mankind," and "Come to the best deed!"* The inhabitants of this town are sharifs, and they have running water, irrigation canals, and many palm groves in the district. They told me that when dates are plentiful, a thousand *maund*s are only one dinar.

It is forty parasangs from Yamama to Lahsa. During the winter it is possible to travel because potable rainwater collects in pools, but not in summer.

A DESCRIPTION OF LAHSA To reach the town of Lahsa from any direction, you have to cross vast expanses of desert. The nearest Muslim city to Lahsa that has a ruler is Basra, and that is one hundred and fifty parasangs away. There has never been a ruler of Basra, however, who has attempted an attack on Lahsa.

---

*These words characterize the Shi'ite (including the Zaydi) call to prayer. The Sunni call to prayer includes neither phrase. In Khosraw's terminology, "Alid" refers to any of the Shi'a.

All of the town's outlying villages and dependencies are enclosed by four strong, concentric walls made of reinforced mud brick. The distance between these walls is about a parasang, and there are enormous wells inside the town, each the size of five millstones around. All the water of the district is put to use so that none goes outside the walls. A really splendid town is situated inside these fortifications, with all the appurtenances of a large city, and there are more than twenty thousand soldiers.

They said that the ruler had been a sharif who prevented the people from practicing Islam and relieved them of the obligations of prayer and the fast by claiming that he was the ultimate authority on such matters. His name was Abu Sa'id and when you ask the townspeople what sect they belong to, they say they are Busa'idis. They neither pray nor fast, but they do believe in Muhammad and his mission. Abu Sa'id told them that he would come among them again after his death, and his tomb, a fine shrine, is located inside the city. He directed that six of his [spiritual] sons should maintain his rule with justice and equity and without dispute among themselves until he should come again. Now they have a palace that is the seat of state and a throne that accommodates all six kings in one place, and they rule in complete accord and harmony. They have also six viziers, and when the kings are all seated on their throne, the six viziers are seated opposite on another bench. Thus all affairs are handled in mutual consultation. At the time I was there they had thirty thousand Zanzibari and Abyssinian slaves working in the fields and gardens.

They take no tax from the peasantry, and whenever anyone is stricken by poverty or contracts a debt, they take care of his needs until the debtor's affairs should be cleared up. And if anyone is in debt to another, the creditor cannot claim more than the amount of the debt. Any stranger to the city who possesses a craft by which to earn his livelihood is given enough money to buy the tools of his trade and establish himself, when he repays however much he has given. If anyone's property or implements suffer loss and the owner is unable to undertake necessary repairs, they appoint their own slaves to make the repairs and charge the owner nothing. The rulers have several gristmills in Lahsa, where the citizenry can have their meal ground into flour for free, and the maintenance of the buildings and the wages of the miller are paid by the rulers. The rulers are called simply "lord" and the viziers, "counsel."

There was once no Friday mosque in Lahsa, and the sermon and congregational prayer were not held. A Persian man, however, named Ali son of Ahmad, who was a Muslim, a pilgrim and very wealthy, did build a mosque in order to provide for pilgrims who arrived in the city . . .

They do not prevent anyone from performing prayers, although they themselves do not pray. The ruler answers most politely and humbly anyone who speaks to him, and wine is not indulged in.

A horse outfitted with collar and crown is kept always tied close by the tomb of Abu Saʿid, and a watch is continually maintained day and night for such time as he should rise again and mount the horse. Abu Saʿid said to his sons, "When I come again among you, you will not recognize me. The sign will be that you strike my neck with my sword. If it be me, I will immediately come back to life." He made this stipulation so that no one else could claim to be him.

In the time of the Baghdad caliphs one of the rulers attacked Mecca and killed a number of people who were circumambulating the Kaʿba at the time. They removed the Black Stone from its corner and took it to Lahsa. They said that the Stone was a "human magnet" that attracted people, not knowing that it was the nobility and magnificence of Muhammad that drew people there, for the Stone had lain there for long ages without anyone paying any particular attention to it. In the end, the Black Stone was bought back and returned to its place.

Seven parasangs east of Lahsa is the sea. In this sea is the island of Bahrain, which is fifteen parasangs long. There is a large city there and many palm groves. Pearls are found in the sea thereabouts, and half of the divers' take belongs to the Sultan of Lahsa. South of Lahsa is Oman, which is on the Arabian Peninsula, but three sides face desert that is impossible to cross. The region of Oman is eighty parasangs square and tropical; there they grow coconuts, which they call *nargil*. Directly east of Oman across the sea are Kish and Mokran. South of Oman is Aden, while in the other direction is the province of Fars.

There are so many dates in Lahsa that animals are fattened on them and at times more than one thousand *maunds* are sold for one dinar. Seven parasangs north of Lahsa is a region called Qatif, where there is also a large town and many date palms. An Arab amir from there once attacked Lahsa, where he maintained seige for a year. One of those fortification walls he captured and wrought much havoc, although he did not obtain much of anything. When he saw me, he asked whether or not it was in the stars for him to take Lahsa, as they were irreligious. I told him what was expedient [for me to say], since, in my opinion also, the Bedouins and people of Lahsa were as close as anyone could be to irreligiosity, there being people there who, from one year to the next, never perform ritual ablutions. This that I record is told from my own experience and not from false rumors, since I was there among them for nine consecutive months, and not at intervals. . . .

A DESCRIPTION OF BASRA The city has a large wall, except for the portion that faces the water, where there is no wall. The water here is all marsh, the Tigris and Euphrates coming together at the beginning of the Basra district, and when the water of the Hawiza joins the confluence, it is called Shatt-al-Arab. From this Shatt-al-Arab, two large channels have been cut, between the mouths of which is a distance of one parasang, running in the direction of the *qibla* for four parasangs, after which they converge and run another one parasang to the south. From these channels numerous canals have been dug in all directions among palm groves and orchards. Of these two channels, the higher one, which is northeast, is called Nahr Ma'qel, whereas the southwestern one is called Nahr Obolla. These two channels form an enormous rectangular "island," on the shortest side of which Basra is situated. To the southwest of Basra is open plain that supports neither settlement nor agriculture.

When I arrived, most of the city lay in ruins, the inhabited parts being greatly dispersed, with up to half a parasang from one quarter to another. Nonetheless, the walls were strong and well kept, the populace numerous, and the ruler with plenty of income. At that time, the Amir of Basra was the son of Aba Kalijar the Daylamite, King of Fars. His Vizier was a Persian, Abu Mansur Shahmardan by name.

Every day there are three bazaars in Basra: in the morning transactions are held at a place called Souk al-Khoza'a [Market of the Khoza'a tribe]; in the middle of the day at Souk 'Othman ['Othman's Market]; and at the end of the day at Souk al-Qaddahin [Flintmakers' Market]. The procedure at the bazaar is as follows: you turn over whatever you have to a money changer and get in return a draft; then you buy whatever you need, deducting the price from the money changer's draft. No matter how long one might stay in the city, one would never need anything more than a money changer's draft.

When we arrived we were as naked and destitute as madmen, for it had been three months since we had unloosed our hair. I wanted to enter a bath in order to get warm, the weather being chilly and our clothing scant. My brother and I were clad only in old *lungi*s with a piece of coarse fabric on our backs to keep out the cold. "In this state who would let us into a bath?" I asked. Therefore, I sold a small satchel in which I kept my books and wrapped the few rusty dirhems I had received in a piece of paper to give the bath attendant, thinking that he might give us a little while longer in the bath in order for us to remove the grime from our bodies. When I handed him the change, he looked at us as though we were madmen and said, "Get away from here! People are coming out of the bath." As he would not allow us in, we came away humiliated and in haste. Even the children who were playing at the bathhouse door thought we were madmen and, throwing stones and yelling, chased after us. We retired into a corner and reflected in amazement on the state of the world.

Now, as we were in debt to the camel driver for thirty dinars, we had no recourse save the Vizier of the King of Ahwaz, Abu al-Fath Ali son of Ahmad, a worthy man, learned in poetry and belles lettres, and very generous, who had come to Basra with his sons and retinue and taken up residence but who, at present, had no administrative position. Therefore, I got in touch with a Persian, also a man of learning, with whom I had some acquaintance and who had entrée to the Vizier but who was also in straightened circumstances and totally without means to be of assistance to me. He mentioned my situation to the Vizier, who, as soon as he heard, sent a man with a horse for me to come to him just as I was. Too ashamed of my destitution and nakedness, I hardly thought it fitting to appear before him, so I wrote a note of regret, saying that I would come to him later. I had two reasons for doing this: one was my poverty, and the other was, as I said to myself, that he now imagines that I have some claim to being learned, but when he sees my note he will figure out just what my worth is, so that when I go before him I need not be ashamed.

Immediately he sent me thirty dinars to have a suit of clothing made. With that amount I bought two fine suits and on the third day appeared at the Vizier's assembly. I found him to be a worthy, polite, and scholarly man of pleasant appearance, humble, religious, and well-spoken. He had four sons, the eldest of whom was an eloquent, polite, and reasonable youth called Ra'is Abu Abd Allah Ahmad son of Ali son of Ahmad. Not only a poet and administrator, he was wise and devout beyond his youthful age. We were taken in and stayed there from the first of Shaban until the middle of Ramadan. The thirty dinars due the Arab for our camel were paid by the Vizier, and I was relieved of that burden. (May God thus deliver all his servants from the torment of debt!)

When I desired to depart he sent me off by sea with gifts and bounteous good things so that I reached Fars in ease and comfort, thanks to the generosity of that noble man. (May God delight in such noble men!) . . .

After our worldly condition had taken a turn for the better and we each had on decent clothing, we went back one day to the bathhouse we had not been allowed to enter. As soon as we came through the door the attendant and everyone there stood up respectfully. We went inside, and the scrubber and servant came to attend to us. When we emerged from the bath all who were in the dressing room rose and remained standing until we had put on our clothes and departed. During that time the attendant had said to a friend of his, "These are those very young men whom we refused admission one day." They imagined that we did not know their language, but I said in Arabic, "You are perfectly correct. We are the very ones who had old sacks tied to our backs." The man was ashamed and most apologetic. Now these two events transpired within twenty days, and I have included the story so that men may know not to lament adversity brought on by fate and not to despair of the Creator's mercy, for he is merciful indeed.

2

Ibn Jubayr
Spain
1183—84

꧁꧂

The months of travel, thousands of miles, dozens of languages and regional cultures, that separate Khosraw's Khurasan from Ibn Jubayr's Granada should give any reader pause. By the time the following account was made, the contiguous sweep of Islamic lands encompassed capitals and trade routes from India to Morocco, including Iberia up to the Pyrennes.

Abu al-Husayn ibn Jubayr was born in Grenada, Spain, in 1145 and served as first secretary to its Muslim governor in the second half of the twelfth century. Like Naser-e Khosraw, Ibn Jubayr was a courtier, a scholar, and a poet, but when read in succession Khosraw's work appears sketchy. Besides a vivid record of a pilgrimage performed during the Crusades, Ibn Jubayr supplies the prototype for the rihla, *or traveler's account, a popular literary form in the Arab Middle Ages. It has rightly been called the most elegant of the medieval Muslim travel books. In 1189, when it first appeared, Ibn Jubayr's Grenada was emerging as a capital of Europe's first Islamic region, Muslim Spain.*

The origins of Muslim Spain reach back to the last years of the seventh century and to that part of the western Mediterranean where Europe and Africa almost meet. (See Fig. 8.) The Muslim invaders who drew up here from Syria, Arabia, and Egypt were diligent soldiers inspired by a powerful sense of manifest destiny. Running out of continent, they looked north. In 711, an Arab general named Tariq crossed over to Gibraltar at the head of a largely Moroccan Berber army. A decisive battle ensued, and the Arabs marched north to the Visigoths' capital, Toledo. Two years later most of the Iberian Peninsula lay in their hands.

Ibn Jubayr's family arrived from Mecca as part of an army dispatched by the Caliph of Damascus in 740. In southern Spain, known to them as Andalus, they came upon a Christian world with Roman roots—the birthplace of the emperors Hadrian and Trajan, the Stoic philosopher Seneca, and the poet Lucan. They found theaters, aqueducts, bridges, and a society governed by the Visigothic code. Upon these rich foundations, they installed the cultural hallmarks of the

East: the "Moorish" arch from Sassanid Persia, the stylized and luminous art of Byzantium, the new science of Ptolemy's school at Alexandria, and of course Islam. A day's sail north of Morocco's rocky coast, in the lush Mediterranean valleys of Andalusia, these settlers set off a fusion of civilizations that illuminated Europe for eight centuries.

At Córdoba, for example, beginning in 756, the first Amir, Abd al-Rahman I, extended along the river Guadalquivir a city whose plan, fortifications, palaces, and suburbs mirrored those of Damascus. The first palm tree in Spain grew in his courtyard. Abd al-Rahman did not come to Spain for the sunlight. He was driven out of Syria during the Abbasid revolution, fleeing the extermination of his family and the whole Umayyad court. A survivor of cross-tribal violence, Abd al-Rahman made a point of avoiding the same catastrophe in Spain. In this, he had the support of a school of Islam that encouraged religious and racial tolerance. Like the light of a dying star, the Umayyad tradition, extinguished in Damascus, continued to shed its rays on far-off Spain. Its open, pluralistic nature prompted Abd al-Rahman and his heirs to develop a highly civilized Muslim state. Assuming command of the region, he announced a plan to treat all its faiths and races impartially, each one according to its laws. In the next thirty years, he established justice in the markets and the courts, laying the groundwork for a centuries-long experiment in social toleration such as neither Europe nor the Middle East had ever seen. Convivencia, Spain's golden age of tolerance, dates from Abd al-Rahman. Under its banner, Arab, Christian, and Jewish cultures flourished side by side for centuries. Before he died, in 788, Abd al-Rahman had subdued and organized a region stretching from Portugal to southern France. By helping the Basques chase Charlemagne over the Pyrenees, he also unwittingly supplied a plot line for France's national epic, The Song of Roland.

During the next three centuries, a succession of talented rulers and their court philosophers, scholars, poets, architects, inventors, and musicians set the cultural standards for their age. By Ibn Jubayr's day, Seville boasted five hundred public baths and a thousand mosques, and Córdoba was western Europe's largest city, with a population of seven hundred thousand, where Muslim and Jewish scholars taught side by side in tax-supported universities. It is rare when we can pinpoint where one civilization went on to learn from another, but Muslim Spain provides a clear-cut case. It became the site for the most prolonged and intimate encounter in Europe among Judaism, Christianity, and Islam. In the explosion of philosophical thought triggered during this period, most of the "lost" works of Aristotle, Plato, Hippocrates, Galen, Ptolemy, and Euclid were reintroduced into Europe through Arabic translations and the commentaries of Muslim philosophers and scholars. The full extent of this wealth of translations may never be uncovered, but on two points modern scholarship agrees: the works revived in Muslim Spain fueled Europe's renaissance, and the flow of information was all one way, from the libraries of Cairo and Baghdad to the libraries of Spain and thence toward the rest of Europe. Christian scholars traveled south in numbers. In the decade of Ibn Jubayr's birth, at Toledo alone, the Englishman Robert of Ketton, the Italian Gerard of Cremona, and the Austrian Hermann of Carinthia could all be found actively translating hundreds of Greek classics from Arabic to Latin for European scholars. Meanwhile, Spain's Muslim rulers scoured the Levant for more. Hakim II (reigned 961–976), to cite one example, employed spies in Egypt and Syria to alert him to the presence not of gold or of concubines but of rare books and new translations. His alabaster library in Córdoba held thousands of volumes.

This surge of cultural attention reached an apex around the time of Ibn Jubayr's birth. His Iberian contemporaries include the iconoclastic Muslim mystic Ibn 'Arabi of Ronda (1165–1240), the polymath Ibn Rushd of Seville (1126–1198, called Averroës in Europe), and Moses Maimonides of Córdoba (Musa ibn Maymun, 1135–1204). Maimonides' early career as Judaism's greatest medieval thinker demonstrates the extent to which a multicultural context flourished for centuries in Muslim Spain, benefiting not only Islam but other religions then under Muslim rule. Ibn Jubayr's Granada was more civilized than most urban centers farther east. As his book makes plain, he was often shocked by the greed and inequity of Christian Europe and *the Arabian Hijaz.*

The following selections include Ibn Jubayr's arrival in Egypt, his departure by a Red Sea ship for Arabia, and his stay in Jidda. They continue with excerpts from his eight-month stay at Mecca. He set out from Grenada in early February 1183. Traveling with one companion, a physician, he embarked on a Genoese ship at Ceuta and sailed with a Christian crew to Egypt. The passage, frequently stormy, took thirty days. Along the way, he appears to have been unnerved by more than weather. With a third crusade brewing in Palestine, prisoners were being sold into slavery on all sides. Within a few pages, while docked at Cape St. Mark in Sardinia, Ibn Jubayr records that he observed eighty Muslim captives standing for auction in the market. "The enemy," he writes, "had just returned with them from the Muslim coast." In Egypt, where our first excerpt begins, the fate of the contestants is reversed. Disembarking at Alexandria, Ibn Jubayr meets a camel train of Christian soldiers being led away to prison. Not just any soldiers, these were the troops of Reynald de Chatillon, a legendary figure in the Crusader annals who made a special practice of raiding Hajj caravans. This time, his men had been stopped a day's march short of Medina by an army sent from Cairo. The prisoners met by Ibn Jubayr were captives from this failed expedition.

    The European invasion of the Levant runs like a dark current through Ibn Jubaye's pages. Performing the Hajj under such conditions would not be easy. For one thing, the principal trans-Sinai route from Egypt to Mecca ran right through Reynald's raiding grounds. Sobered, Ibn Jubayr made for Cairo, now a Sumi capital where he found the famous Saladin in power. The consolidating genius of this new Kurdish sultan had already improved the pilgrims' lot. Calling them sons and daughters of the road, he provided them food and abolished the city's Hajj tax. The farther one moved from the capital, however, the more dangerous things became. If the Sinai route was impassable, the alternative—a nine-day southern march up the Nile to Qus in Upper Egypt, then overland across scorching sand to the Red Sea port of Aydhab—was not much safer. A year before, Crusaders had attacked a train of pilgrims outside Qus and slaughtered the lot of them. Ibn Jubayr saw no choice. He traveled south from Cairo in a camel caravan. Although he reached the coast alive, the port of Aydhab turned out to be a hellhole, and the Red Sea crossing to the Hijaz was horrendous.

    Matters grew worse in Arabia. Indeed, the riskiest parts of Ibn Jubayr's journey occurred in the Hijaz along the routes that linked the coast to Mecca and Medina. Since long before Islam was born, these ancient trails had bristled with fractious local tribes whose only wealth derived from raiding passing travelers. In the late twelfth century, the annual Syrian caravan ran a gauntlet of these rapacious clans, starting at the gates of Damascus and continuing almost unbroken right to Mecca—a distance of a thousand miles. The sanctity of pilgrimage was the last thing on the minds of these marauders. They viewed the untaxed Hajj caravans winding through their lands as an invitation to plunder, nothing more. As for pilgrims foolish enough to brave the Hijaz without protection, the usual method was to strip them bare and take their camels. We have already seen where this could lead, with Naser-e Khosraw.

    Muslims have always viewed the Hajj as an opportunity for overcoming obstacles. Acceptance, forbearance, and vigilant efforts in behalf of fellow pilgrims bear a promise of spiritual rewards throughout the Hajj record. Yet even a man as devout as Ibn Jubayr could not mistake for God's will the violence of these venal Hijazi raiders. Outraged by their methods, he recommends at one point that the whole region be "purified by the sword," then concludes that the Hajj simply isn't worth it, that those jurists were wise who released prospective pilgrims from the fulfillment of their duties in bad times. It is not surprising to read later that no caliph had risked his neck on the Hajj in four hundred years.

    Once safely inside Mecca's gates, however, Ibn Jubayr strikes a very different tone. A precinct exclusively governed by sacred law, the city appears like a corner of heaven on Earth, a peaceable kingdom steeped in spirituality and order, where every visitor takes to heart the proscriptions against partisan argument and any form of violence. The crowds do not push or shove; pilgrims at their rites respect one another. Canonical hours divide the day with calls to prayer, and the whole population takes up lives of customary action. This profound security of the Haram district is all the more arresting in contrast to the rest of the Hijaz. Even the markets flow with milk and honey, thanks to the charity of Yemeni Muslims, who sustain the town all year with free produce.

When Hajj-time finally comes around, Ibn Jubayr records it meticulously, not as an outside observer but as a participant with a sharp eye for details. He provides a vivid depiction of the Arafat encampments and proves a first-class pilgrim guide, giving his readers at home in Spain a real taste of the distant sacred rites. He is also the first Hajj author to note big improvements to the pilgrimage infrastructure, from its water system to the steps carved at great expense into Mount Mercy. Along the way, he conveys the feel of pedestrian travel as well as of the deluxe camel litters of the wealthy, in which passengers rode beneath protective canopies undisturbed by wind and sun, napping on mattresses, playing chess and reading.

Ibn Jubayr turned back toward Spain when the Hajj was over, traveling through Mesopotamia, Syria, and Sicily. He reached Grenada in April 1185, and his book appeared four years later. Organized in diary form yet carefully constructed, it divides into twenty-seven chapters, one for each month the author was away. Addressed to a community of believers, it is the work of a devout Muslim, complete with praise for God's providence and theological shrugs when times grow tough. It is also shrewdly observant and candid in its views. Whereas Khosraw was laconic, Ibn Jubayr speaks his mind on every page. He is not always pleased, and he knows a good town when he sees one—qualities of first importance in all good travel writing. Nowhere in the Hajj literature are the security and spirit of the sacred Territory move vividly expressed.

from *The Travels of Ibn Jubayr*

EGYPT TO MECCA. APRIL–AUGUST 1183 The first thing we saw upon landing at Alexandria was a large crowd gathered along the road to watch a train of European prisoners being led through town on camelback. The captives rode backward, facing the camels' tails, and a band of horns and cymbals played around them. We asked what had happened and were told a painful story. Earlier that year, a number of Syrian Crusaders had constructed sailing ships in a part of that country close to the Red Sea. From there they loaded the parts of the ships on camels hired out from local Arabs and had the ships transported to the water. There they nailed them together and launched them into the sea, to harass the pilgrims coming and going to Mecca. In the Yemen Sea they burned sixteen Muslim ships. Then they sailed on to Aydhab and attacked a boatload of pilgrims coming from Jidda. On the Egyptian side, they seized a large Hajj caravan traveling from Qus to Aydhab and killed everyone in it. Next they captured two vessels bringing merchandise from Yemen. Back on the Arabian side, all along the beaches, they burned down many revictualing stations providing food to God's exalted cities, Mecca and Medina. These are unparalleled atrocities. No European had ever come so near the sacred sites. The most shocking outrage, however, was their aim to enter Medina, the City of the Prophet, and rob his tomb.

They made no secret of this plan, spreading word of it far and wide to frighten people, but Allah foiled their attempt. Less than a day's ride from Medina, they were repelled by ships sent all the way from Cairo and Alexandria. The Chamberlain Husam al-Din Lu'lu' and many brave sailors pursued the enemy into the hills and captured everyone. We saw in this a sign from God, for the ships from Egypt were a month and a half away when they set out, and they arrived at the last possible moment. All the invaders were either killed on the spot or captured and subsequently executed in many different countries as a warning. Some were sent to Mecca and Medina. Allah watches over Islam. Praise to the Lord of the Universe. . . .

THE RED SEA CROSSING   The ships that ply the Red Sea from Aydhab to Jidda are sewn together without a single nail. They are bound by cord made from coconut fiber, which the builders pound until it takes the form of thread. . . . The ships are caulked with palm-tree shavings, and when the construction is finished, they smear it with grease, castor oil, or shark oil, the last of which is best. . . . They grease the boats to soften the shell and make it supple, protecting it against the inevitable contact with the reefs, which prevent nailed ships from making passage in these waters. The wood and the coconut fiber both come from India. The sails, amazingly, are woven from the leaves of a gum tree, but their sheets are weakly joined and poorly made. . . .

Our sea passage [from Aydhab to Jidda] on Tuesday and Wednesday took longer than usual, the winds being light. Then, after Thursday's evening prayer, just as we saw the first birds from Arabia start to circle in the air, lightning bolts flashed off the mountains in the east and a rising storm darkened the skies, covering everything. The tempest raged, driving the ship off course and, finally, backward. The wind's fury continued. The darkness grew thick and filled the air so that we couldn't stay our course. Finally, a few stars reappeared to guide us. The sail was lowered to the bottom of the mast, and we passed the night in a storm that made us desperate. The Pharaoh's Sea is famous for these rages, but in the morning God brought us relief. The wind fell, the clouds broke up, the sky grew clear. In the distance the lands of the Hijaz appeared before us. We could only make out the mountains east of Jidda. Our captain said they lay two days away. . . .

We sailed all day under a favorable light breeze, meeting many reefs along the way which broke the water and made it laugh around us. We entered these watery alleys with great care. The captain was skilled and artful, and God kept us off the reefs until we finally anchored at a small island near the coast, named the Obstacle of Ships. God saved us from its unpleasant name. We disembarked here and passed Friday night. The morning was calm, but the wind blew from an unsuitable direction, so there we remained through the day. On Saturday a slight breeze rose, and we sailed out quietly into a calm sea that resembled a dish of blue crystal. . . .

On Monday evening we anchored near Jidda. The city lay in plain view. The wind raged the following morning and prevented us from making port. The entry was made difficult by the presence of many reefs and winding shallows. We admired the dexterity with which these pilgrim captains and their sailors handled their ships among the reefs. It was truly marvelous. They would enter the narrow channels and make their way through them the way a horseman manages a mount that is light on the bit and docile.

At Jidda we lodged in the house of the Governor, Ali, who rules this port in the name of Saladin. Most of the houses here are made of reed. There are also inns of stone and mud with palm-frond lean-tos serving as upper chambers, beneath which people sleep at night to escape the heat. We stayed in one of these apartments on the rooftop. The many ancient remains in town attest to its great age. Traces of prehistoric walls still rise around it, and there is one place with an old and lofty dome which is said to mark the house of the prophet Eve, humanity's mother, in the days when she was on her way to Mecca. Allah knows best in these matters.

Most of the people living in this town and in the desert and mountains around it are descendants of the Prophet, Ali [his cousin and son-in-law], Hasan, and Husayn [Ali's sons] or they are descendants of Jafar—God keep their noble ancestors in his favor. The life of the Jiddans is heartbreaking. They support themselves in many ways, hiring out camels if they have them, selling milk or water, dates when they can find them, or driftwood, which they gather off the beaches. Sometimes their women, daughters of the Prophet, do these jobs, too. Beyond a doubt theirs is a family to which God has granted a future, not a present. . . .

The majority of these people are sectarians and schismatics divided into various doctrines. They have no real religion. They treat foreign pilgrims worse than they treat the Christians and Jews under their tribute, seizing most of the hajjis' collective provisions, robbing them blind, and finding new ways to divest them of their goods. Pilgrims passing through their territories pay endless tolls and part constantly with food until they reach their homelands. Without Saladin's efforts to improve conditions, the oppression of pilgrims in this region would be universal and unending. For Saladin lifted the pilgrim tax, sending money and goods to Mukthir, the Amir of Mecca. But when these payoffs are delayed even a little, the Amir goes back to intimidating pilgrims and jailing those who cannot pay the tax.

So it was when we arrived at Jidda and were arrested by Amir Mukthir. That year he had ordered the pilgrims to guarantee each other's payment against the arrival of Saladin's allocation; only then might we enter the Sacred Mosque at Mecca. Should the bribes arrive in time, all would go smoothly; otherwise, he would demand his tax from the pilgrims. So ran his speech, as if God's Sacred City were an heirloom in his hand which he had a lawful right to lease to the hajjis. Glory to God, who has the power to alter laws.

Saladin had paid two thousand dinars and 2,002 *irdabb** of wheat, exclusive of the land rents in Upper Egypt and Yemen assigned to the Amir as a substitute for the tax. It should be said that had Saladin not been absent, fighting Crusaders in Syria, the Amir would not have dared act in this way.

The part of Islam that most deserves a cleansing by the sword is the Hijaz, both for flying in the face of faith and for robbing the pilgrims' goods and shedding their blood. The Spanish judges who say that Muslims should be absolved of the pilgrim's obligation speak rightly for this very reason. Anyone coming this way faces danger and oppression, though God intends something quite different for those who come to share this place. How can the House of God have fallen into the hands of people who use it illegally, as a source of income, making it a means of seizing property and of detaining pilgrims whom they humiliate and reduce to poverty? . . .

JIDDA TO MECCA   On Tuesday evening, the second day of August, we left Jidda—only after the pilgrims had guaranteed each other's tax and their

---

**irdabb:* the equivalent of forty-three and a half gallons. [Ed.]

names had been recorded in a book by the governor of Jidda. . . . We traveled all night and arrived at al-Qurayn as the sun was rising. This is a staging post and camp for pilgrims. Here they put on the *ihram*. If they rest through the day, as is the custom, leave at dusk, and travel throughout the night, in the morning they will reach the Sacred Mosque, God increase its honor. Returning hajjis rest at Qurayn, too. The place has a well of sweet spring water, so the pilgrims do not have to overburden themselves with water coming up through the mountains the night before. We rested there all Wednesday. When darkness fell, we left in our pilgrim clothes to perform the Umra [Lesser Pilgrimmage] and marched all night. A full moon threw its light over the earth, and the night raised its veil. Voices chanted "Here am I, Lord. Here am I" on every side, and the pilgrims prayed to Allah to grant their requests. Bride of all life's nights, Time's virgin maiden.

We reached the mosque at dawn, coming down the hill into town as the light spread, and saw before us the venerable Haram where Abraham stayed, the friend of God, and where he found the Ka'ba, the sacred House that is led like an unveiled bride to Paradise, surrounded by pilgrims, the envoys of God. We circled the Ka'ba to celebrate our arrival and then prayed at the Station of Abraham. We clung to the covering of the Ka'ba, on the wall between the Black Stone and the door, where prayers are answered. We went into the Zamzam pavilion and drank the water that in the Prophet's words is good for every purpose.* Then we performed the rite of *sa'y*, running between the hills of Safa and Marwa. After this we shaved our heads and, so, entered a state of purity. . . .

In Mecca we lodged at a house called Purity, near the Mosque's al-Suddah Gate, in a room with many amenities, overlooking the Haram and the Ka'ba.

MECCA. THE MONTH OF JUMADA 'L-ULA, AUGUST–SEPTEMBER 1183 This town and its people from very ancient times have profited from the prayers of Abraham, the friend of God, as it is written. . . . "Have we not established a safe sanctuary for [the believers] to which all kinds of products shall be carried."† The proof of this verse is obvious in Mecca, and will remain so until the Day of Judgment, for people's hearts yearn toward it from distant places.

---

*"Zamzam water is for the end for which one drinks it. If you drink it for a cure, it will cure you; if to fill your stomach, it will satisfy you; and if to ease a burning thirst, it will quench it. This well is the hollow Gabriel made with his feet. With its waters God quenched Ishmael's thirst." (*Kitab al-Kawkab al-Durri*, manuscript, Leiden, 607)

†Quran XXVIII: 57. [Ed.]

The roads to it are a meeting place for those to whom Islam's teachings have spread. Produce is brought here from everywhere, and in its fruits, goods, and commerce it is the most prosperous of regions. And although there is no substantial trade outside the pilgrim season, nevertheless, since people flock this way from the East and West, you can find sold here in a single day pearls, sapphires, and other precious stones, a great variety of perfumes, including musk, camphor, amber, and aloes, Indian medicines, and other goods from India and Ethiopia, products from the factories of Iraq and Yemen, merchandise from Khurasan, the goods of northwestern Africa, and many more goods too extensive to assess. . . .

As for . . . fruits, we had imagined that Spain was the most favored region in the world, and so it seemed until we came here and found it overflowing with good things, figs, grapes, pomegranates, quince, peaches, lemons, walnuts, palm fruit, watermelons, cucumbers, and other vegetables, like eggplant, pumpkin, carrot, cauliflower, and aromatic herbs. . . . The best of the fruits we tried were the watermelon and the quince. All the fruit here is good, but the watermelon is particularly fragrant. When someone approaches you with one of these, you smell the fruit before it reaches you, and the sweetness is such that you almost don't need to eat it. When you do taste it, the sweetness is like candy or pure honey. The reader may think I exaggerate. Actually, it is better than I describe. As for honey, Mecca has a honey so fine it has passed into proverbs; they call it *al-mas'udi*. The various kinds of milk are of the first quality too, so that butter made from it can scarcely be distinguished from the honey. . . .

MECCA. THE MONTH OF RAJAB, OCTOBER 20, 1183 . . . The people of Mecca regard this month as a solemn occasion for pilgrims to meet each other. It is the occasion of a great local festival, one they have observed without a break since long before the days of the Prophet Muhammad. People perform the Umra during this month in numbers nearly equivalent to the Arafat vigil during the month of Hajj. Pilgrims from neighboring countries flock to Mecca for it. . . .

The events on the night of the new moon and the day after are almost impossible to describe. That afternoon the streets and alleys of Mecca were thronged with camels bearing small dome-shaped enclosures, or howdahs, roped onto their backs and covered with silk drapes and trappings of fine linen. The quality of the decorations varied according to the affluence of each owner, but everyone gave them all the care and attention in their power. They set out in great numbers for Tan'im, the ritual starting point for those making the Umra, so that the howdahs appeared to flow through the valleys and mountain tracks, the camels beneath them adorned with ornaments and moving toward the sacred places without drivers, in collars of silk and with beautiful trappings that sometimes dragged along the ground. There was no one in the city who did not perform the Umra that evening. Fires lined the roads on either side and lit torches preceded the howdahs of the Meccan women. When we had completed the rites, circled the Ka'ba seven times, and arrived at the concourse between the Safa and Marwa hills, we found the road completely lit with fires and lanterns, and thronged with men and women performing the rite on their camels. . . . This remarkable sight, the crowds of people dressed in pilgrim robes, crying out "Here I am, Lord, at your service. Here am I" and the mountains answering with echoes, made one imagine the gathering on the Day of Resurrection. People cried, tears flowed, hearts melted at this sight. . . .

On Friday the road was almost as jammed as the day before with horsemen and pedestrians, men and women walking along the blessed way in hope of a heavenly reward. Throughout all this, whenever men met, they shook hands, offering prayers and seeking God's forgiveness on each other's behalf, and the women did the same. Everyone wore their finest clothes, according to the fashion of their homeland and their tribe. The people of Mecca make elaborate preparations for this festival. They amass in great numbers, compete in the fineness of their appearance, and indulge in great ceremony. The markets are also very active at this time, and sales are brisk, so that the vendors often prepare for these few days months in advance. . . .

A tribe from Yemen, the Saru, make a tradition of arriving ten days before this festival begins, with a double purpose of performing the Umra, on the one hand, and of providing Mecca, on the other, with wheat, grains, kidney beans, and other coarser products, bringing butter, honey, raisins, almonds, condiments, and fruit. This year they arrived by the thousands, men and camels laden with goods, and bringing an abundance of supplies to the Blessed City and to the pilgrims who have settled here, to nourish and sustain them. Prices are lowered at this time and produce is easy to come by. Indeed, many people acquire from the Saru everything they will need for the next year. Without these provisions, the people of Mecca would lead a miserable existence.

Strangely enough, the Saru do not sell any of this produce for dirhems or dinars. Instead they exchange them for clothes, principally for two kinds of cloaks, the 'abat and the shimal. The Meccans produce these garments for them, along with women's veils, heavy quilts, and other things popular with the Bedouin. They say that when the Saru remain at home and fail to bring provisions to the Blessed City, they are afflicted there by drought and their flocks and herds die, but when they come, their lands produce a full harvest and they are blessed. So when the time for departure arrives, if preparations are careless and the men malinger, the women collect the provisions and drive their husbands from the houses. Their lands are fertile and extensive, abounding in figs and vines, with wide fields and rich crops, and the Saru firmly believe that this prosperity is due to the provisions they bring and that they are doing business not just with the Meccans but with God. All this is Allah's way of looking after Mecca, the Safe City.

MECCA. THE MONTH OF SHABAN, NOVEMBER–DECEMBER 1183 The blessed night of the middle of Shaban is esteemed by Meccans because of the noble tradition that has come down to us about it.* They compete with each other in performing sacred rites like the Umra, the *tawaf,* and prayers both individual and congregational. . . . In the middle of the month, which fell on Saturday this year, immediately after the evening prayers we saw a great throng in the Haram. Men began to say special prayers in groups, reciting the first chapter of the Quran and repeating "God is One" ten times for each prayer sequence until they had done one hundred sequences. Each group had chosen an imam, mats were spread out, candles lit, torches kindled. In addition, the lamp of the moonlit sky shed its brightness on the earth, the rays converging in the Haram, which is itself a light. An unimaginable scene, sublime beyond your dreams! . . .

That night Ahmad ibn Hassan, my traveling companion, witnessed something amazing, one of those remarkable events that prove unforgettable. As it happened, he felt weary in the last third of night and retired to rest on the bench that surrounds the dome of the Zamzam Well. Here he lay down to take a nap, facing the Black Stone and the door of the Kaʿba. Suddenly a foreign man appeared and seated himself on a corner of the bench near Hassan's head. There he began to recite the Quran in a moving and tender voice, interspersed with sighs and sobbing. He recited the verses beautifully, instilling their feeling and meaning into the soul. My comrade Hassan gave up his nap to enjoy the beauty of what he heard, with all its yearning and emotion. When the man finally finished, he said,

---

*"According to popular belief, in the night preceding the fifteenth [of Shaban] the tree of life on whose leaves are written the names of the living is shaken. The names written on the leaves which fall down indicate those who are to die in the coming year. In *hadith* [the Muslim tradition] it is said that in this night Allah descends to the lowest heaven; from there he calls mortals in order to grant them forgiveness of sins (Tirmidhi, *Sunan,* b. 39)." (*The Shorter Encyclopedia of Islam*)

If evil deeds have taken me far from You,
My honest thoughts have brought me near again,

repeating the words like a melody designed to break the heart. Again and again he repeated these lines while his tears flowed and his voice shook and grew weak, until Hassan feared that the man was about to faint. No sooner had this crossed his mind than the man fell to the ground, lying there like something tossed aside, without a movement. Ibn Hassan sat up at once, alarmed by the frightening thing he had seen, unsure whether the man was alive or dead, for he had fallen quite a distance—the bench was considerably higher than the ground. A man who had been asleep nearby wakened then, too, and they both were bewildered, afraid to awake the man or even approach him. Finally a foreign woman passed and shouted at them, "Is this the way you leave a man in such a condition?" and she quickly fetched a little water from the well and wet his face. The other two came nearer then and raised the man to a sitting position. When he saw them, however, he hid his face, afraid they might identify him later, and quickly fled toward the Gate of the Guardians. The two men sat wondering what they had seen. Ibn Hassan soon regretted missing his chance to gain the man's blessings, for things had happened quickly and prevented him from asking, nor could he remember the man's face. These foreign hajjis are really remarkable for their sensibility, emotionalism, their capacity for ecstasy, and the ardor of their worship. Such grace, of course, is in God's hands. He bestows it on whom he wishes.

MECCA. THE MONTH OF THE PILGRIMAGE, MARCH–APRIL 1184 The new moon of this month rose on Thursday night, corresponding with the fifteenth of March of the Christians. . . . This is the third of the sacred months. During its first ten days the people assemble [and perform the Hajj]. It is the great period of the pilgrimage, the month of chanting "Here am I, Lord," the time of sacrifice, when God's envoys from every country come together. It is the target of Allah's mercy and blessing, the month of the solemn vigil on the Plain of Arafat. . . .

During this period large crowds of pilgrims from the Yemen and many other lands were converging on the city in such numbers that only God could count them. Mecca lies in a valley about a bow shot wide. Its ability to expand and to accommodate such crowds is one of God's miracles. The learned doctors are right to compare it to the mother's uterus that miraculously makes room for its child. Were such a crowd brought into the largest city on the earth, it could not contain it.

From the start of the month the drums of the Amir were beaten morning and evening and at the hours of prayer, to mark the solemnity of the period. The drums continued until the day when we went up to Arafat. . . .

The people flowed out of Mecca all that day, all night, and all Friday, stopping about five miles outside town, at Mina, then going on another five to Muzdalifa, then another five to Arafat, so that an uncountable number were finally assembled on the plain there. About a mile away from Muzdalifa . . . lies the Valley of Muhassir, a boundary between Mina and Muzdalifa, through which custom requires the pilgrims to pass at a quickened pace. Muzdalifa itself is a wide expanse of land between two mountains. Around it lie the reservoirs and cisterns built in the time of Queen Zubayda,* God rest her soul. In the middle of this plain is an enclosure, called Mash'ar al-Haram [Sacred Shrine]. At the center of the enclosure is a round knoll with a mosque on top and steps leading up two sides. Pilgrims amass in crowds as they climb up to pray inside it. They pass the night at Muzdalifa.

Arafat is a wide plain too, broad enough to contain the whole congregation of mankind on Resurrection Day. The plain is surrounded by many mountains. At its most eastern extreme stands the Mount of Mercy (Jabal al-Rama). The standing ground for the Hajj vigil lies all around it. . . . It rises in the middle of the plain, separated from the other mountains. It is composed of discrete sections of granite and hard to climb. Jamal al-Din,† whose works have already been cited in this journal, built low steps on all four sides so wide that laden animals climb it. Great sums were spent on their construction. At the summit stands a cupola named after Umm Salima.‡ A mosque stands beneath the cupola. Into this the pilgrims crowd to pray. Around it runs a terrace, broad and lovely to the eye, overlooking the Plain of Arafat. A southern wall holds many prayer niches for the pilgrims. At the mountain's foot is an ancient house with a vaulted upper room, attributed to Adam, may God preserve him. To its left, facing Mecca, is the rock beside which the Prophet traditionally stood, on a small hill. Around the mountain and the house are many wells and cisterns. To the left of the house is a small mosque. Near the mileposts marking the sacred territory stand the ruins of a much larger mosque, of which the south wall, named for Abraham,

---

*Queen Zubayda (reigned 786–809). [Ed.]

†Jamal al-Din al-Jawad al-Isphahani (died 1164): Vizier of Mosul who built many public works in Mecca and Medina. [Ed.]

‡Umm Salima: one of Muhammad's later wives; the domed shrine was destroyed in the early nineteenth century by the Wahhabis. [Ed.]

remains. The imam delivers a sermon here on the day of the vigil, then he leads the combined midday and afternoon prayers. To the left of the markers facing Mecca lies the Valley of the Thorn Tree, whose green spines stretch in the distance across the plain. . . .

The next morning a multitude filled the plain, greater than anyone living could remember. . . . Some very judicious pilgrims who have settled here in Mecca swore they had never seen such crowds. Personally, I don't believe that since the time of Harun al-Rashid,* the last caliph to perform the pilgrimage, there has been such a gathering of Muslims. May God grant them immunity and mercy.

The people stood in tears during the prayers, begging God for mercy. The cries of *"Allahu akbar!* God is great!" rose in the air. It was a day unequaled in weeping and penitence, of necks bent down in reverent submission and humility before God. The hajjis went on this way, while the sun burned their faces, until the time arrived for the sunset prayers.

The Amir of the Hajj had appeared by now with numerous soldiers dressed in mail. They took up a position near the small mosque on the rocks. The Saru tribes from Yemen took up their appointed posts on the Mount of Mercy, places they have occupied by inheritance since the days of the Prophet. No tribe encroached on the positions of another. The Amir of Iraq arrived too, with a record crowd around him, accompanied by dignitaries from Khurasan and by royal princesses and many women, the daughters of amirs among them. . . . This encampment was beautiful to see and superbly equipped with large handsome tents and wonderful pavilions and awnings, an incomparable scene. The grandest camp, the Amir's, is surrounded by a linen screen, forming a kind of closed-in garden. The tents are pitched within, all black on a white background, dappled and variegated like flowers in a garden. The screen is decorated on all sides with startling black shields painted on the linen with such realism that passersby might take them for the shields of mounted knights. The screens are pierced by tall doors as in a castle, through which one enters a confusing maze of halls, beyond which the tents and pavilions stand on open ground. It is as though the Amir inhabits a walled city that moves when he moves and settles where he settles. This piece of royal splendor is like nothing seen among the Western kings. Beyond the doors are the Amir's chamberlains, servants, and other followers. The doors are so high that a horseman with a banner can pass through without bowing his head. All these constructions are remarkably arranged and secured to the

*Harun al-Rashid (died 809): husband of Zubayda. [Ed.]

ground with linen cords and wooden stakes. The other amirs that year had lesser camps, but all of them were similar in style, with splendid pavilions that closely resembled giant crowns. By the size and equipment of their encampments, the profusion of their wealth was beyond question.

When the inhabitants of these camps travel by camel they ride beneath the shade of canopies raised over wooden litters. These are like cradles, and the travelers ride like infants in a bed, for the litters are filled with soft mattresses on which the traveler sits in comfort, as on a bed. Facing him, in the other half of the litter, sits his companion, man or woman, and above their heads the canopy protects them. They move along undisturbed, napping or reading the Quran or playing chess. When they reach their destination, once the screens are set in place, they enter the enclosure without descending. Ladders are then brought up and they get down, passing from the shade of the canopy into their bedroom tents without being touched by the wind or a ray of sun. . . .

The pilgrims departed Arafat after sunset, as I have said. Late that night they came to Muzdalifa, where they combined their sundown and early-evening prayers, as the Prophet did before them. Throughout the night the Mash'ar al-Haram was illuminated by candle lamps. The mosque was lighted too, so that looking out over the plain it was as if all the stars of the sky twinkled upon it. It looked the same on the Mount of Mercy and its mosque, for the foreigners from Khurasan and some of the Iraqis make it a point to bring great numbers of candles to these shrines. The Haram Mosque at Mecca looked the same during their stay, because every time they entered it, they went in carrying a candle. We saw one enormous example, the size of a cypress tree, which they set before the Hanafi imam, for most of the Iraqis follow that practice.*

That night the pilgrims stayed at Muzdalifa. Here during the night a majority of them collected the little pebbles they would throw at the *jamarat* pillars in the next three days. (Gathering them here is the more popular tradition, although others collect them around the Khayif mosque in Mina.) After the predawn prayer they left for Mina. When they reached it, they hurried to throw their first seven stones at the largest pillar, then they sacrificed an animal. After this, in keeping with the laws of pilgrimage, they were free to return to the normal activities of life, except for sexual relations and use of perfume. From these two pleasures they must abstain until they have circled the Ka'ba again in Mecca. Most people stoned the largest pillar around sunrise on the day of the sacrifice, then they left for Mecca to perform their

*See footnote on the four schools of Sunni Islam, p. 60. [Ed.]

circumambulations. Some stayed on until the second day, and some remained until the third, the official day for returning to city. On the day after the sacrifice, as the sun falls off the meridian, the hajjis cast seven stones at each of the three pillars, saying prayers at the first two places, all of which follows the example of the Prophet, God bless and preserve him. The great pillar is stoned last on these two days, but on the day of sacrifice it is the first and only pillar stoned.

On Saturday, the day of the sacrifice, the *kiswa*, or covering of the holy Ka'ba, was borne on four camels into Mecca from the camp of the Iraqi Amir. The newly appointed judge of the city walked before it, wearing black robes provided by the Caliph, led by banners and followed by rolling drums. . . . The *kiswa* was placed on the roof of the Ka'ba, and on Tuesday the thirteenth the guardians were busy draping it over the building. Its beautiful ripe-green color dazzled the eye. A broad red band ran around its upper section. On the side facing the Station of Abraham, the side with the door in it, there was written on this band the words *Bismillah:** "Surely the first Sanctuary appointed for humanity was that at Bekkah [Mecca]."† The Caliph's name was written on the other sides, along with some invocations in his favor. Running around the band were two reddish zones with small white lozenges holding finely written verses from the Quran and other references to the Caliph. When the Ka'ba was completely covered, the hem of the *kiswa* was tucked up to protect it from the hands of visiting pilgrims, who pull the cloth violently and throw themselves upon it with emotion. At this moment the House of God presented the most beautiful sight imaginable, like an unveiled bride in the best green silk brocade. May God let it be viewed by everyone who wants to see it. . . .

On Thursday night the fifteenth, after the prayers at nightfall, a pulpit and stairs were set before Abraham's Station, and a preacher from Khurasan went up the steps, a man with a handsome face and graceful gestures. He spoke fluent Arabic and Persian, employing them both according to the best rules of oratory, with eloquence and clarity. When he spoke to the Persians, he made them shake with emotion and melt with sighs. The next evening a pulpit was set before the Hanafi pavilion, and after the evening prayer a dignified shaykh with white mustaches mounted the steps and de-

Bismillah: "in the name of God." [Ed.]

†Quran III:95. [Ed.]

livered a graceful sermon, through which he strung, word by word, the Throne Verse,* employing every sort of exhortation, utilizing every branch of knowledge. He, too, used both languages, moving listeners to a state of rapture, then setting fire to their emotions. Questions flew from the audience like arrows and were met by long replies that ravished the mind and left us transfixed with wonder and admiration. It was as if his words were inspired by God. . . . At times men tried to confuse and distract these preachers with questions, but they invariably replied as fast as lightning, in the twinkling of an eye. Superiority is in Allah's hands.

Reciters stood in front of the preachers, intoning the Quran in harmonies that could seduce hard rock, like David's psalms. The congregation seemed at a loss what to admire most. In order to give credence to a story about the Prophet, the shaykh mentioned above quoted five of his own ancestors in succession, one after another from his father back. Each one had a special name indicating his fame in the world of scholars and his standing as a conservator of knowledge. The man was steeped in his calling, where the glory is hereditary. . . .

Our stay in the Sanctified City—from August 4, 1183, when we arrived, until April 5, 1184, when we departed—amounted to eight and a third [lunar] months in all, or 245 blessed days. Throughout this period we were out of sight of the Ka'ba for just three days. May God grant that it will not be my last visit to his Sacred Territory.

*Quran II:256. [Ed.]

3

Ibn Battuta
Morocco
1326

✴︎✴︎✴︎

Ibn Battuta, who traveled farther than any writer before him, is rightly consid-
ered one of the great medieval voyagers. He set out from Morocco on the pilgrim-
age to Mecca, then continued moving east for twenty years, covering most of the
known world from North Africa to China before returning home to dictate his
book to a young scribe. Neither a miniaturist like Khosraw nor a sophisticate
like Ibn Jubayr, Ibn Battuta was more a force of nature, contradictory, opinion-
ated, anecdotal, sweeping, and a shrewd observer of humanity. He traveled longer
and farther, and wrote more, than Marco Polo. Jammed with vivid description
and adventure, his book, exceeding a thousand pages, is the longest and most
complex travel work in Arabic to survive the Middle Ages.

Ibn Battuta was born in 1303 or 1304 into a family of lawyers in Tangier,
Morocco, just across the strait from Muslim Spain. He studied law as a young
man, then set out alone for Mecca in 1325. He crossed North Africa slowly by
horse, burro, and camel, taking the coastal land routes, always in the company
of strangers. In Libya, he joined the annual pilgrim caravan. After an eight-month
tour through Egypt, Palestine, and Syria, he finally performed his initial Hajj
in 1326. (See Figs. 9 and 10.) He was twenty-three years old.

Probably, on leaving home, he had intended to return, after his Hajj, to
take up a job at the Sultan's court in Fez, but the journey changed him. Smitten
by travel, sensing the very real opportunities before him, he traveled on. From
Medina, he continued to Mesopotamia and Persia, then doubled back to Mecca
and stayed a year. Next he visited Africa, then the Persian Gulf, performed the
Hajj again, and set out for India, probably in 1332. He took the long way,
through Syria and Asia Minor to Constantinople and the Asian steppes. In
India for at least eight years, he rose to the post of grand judge in Delhi, then was
appointed ambassador to the court of the Mongol emperor of China. After a ship-
wreck and several years in Ceylon and the Maldive Islands, he continued east-
ward, visiting Nepal, Burma, Sumatra, and perhaps China.

Returning west in 1347, Ibn Battuta stopped off in Mecca one last time. He reached Tangier early in 1350. Three years later the Sultan at Fez commissioned him to set down his adventures. By then, he had been on the road for two and a half decades, had visited the equivalent of fifty modern countries, and had covered more than seventy-five thousand miles. "I have realized my deepest desire in this world," he wrote, "which was to travel through it. In this respect, I have accomplished something no one else to my knowledge has done."

Ibn Battuta's experiences abroad confirm the existence of a single, intercommunicating culture extending from the Atlantic Ocean to the South China Sea; not a narrow corridor spanned by a handful of trade routes east and west over which privileged figures traveled on official business but a global arena, an Afro-Eurasian zone actively crisscrossed by large populations of itinerant professionals who settled where they chose, furthered a career, and felt at home. Ibn Battuta was not unique in this milieu—he was representative. The roads of his time were filled with provincial scholars, judges, lawyers, teachers, businessmen, and traders from every corner of the earth who shuttled almost routinely among North Africa, Egypt, Persia, India, and Indonesia. Not only Muslims but Christians and Jews, too, took advantage of this trading network. They moved along lines that appear to have provided real support to a large class of mobile professionals. Ibn Battuta moved with them, working and traveling, recording a way of life that in certain ways prefigures the social flux of modern, free market capitalism. Bangladeshis at work in Silicon Valley, Iranian families thriving in Japan, would not have surprised Ibn Battuta. In fourteenth-century Damascus, he assures us, any Moroccan running out of money would be sure to find the means to earn his way. When he himself fell sick there, then went broke, benefactors appeared out of the woodwork. Later, in India, he met lawyers from around the world working at the sultan's court in Delhi, earning handsome salaries and socializing with the upper classes. Still later, in China, as a guest of prosperous Egyptians in the huge city of Hang-chou, with whom should he cross paths in its large Muslim quarter but a neighbor from his own street in Tangier.

Ibn Battuta's account is greatly enriched by this sense of belonging and by the social opportunities it allowed. A non-Muslim author would have been stopped short at most of the doors that Ibn Battuta passed through; many a Muslim merchant, too, must have lacked his access to first families and potential patrons. In addition to a magnetic manner, Ibn Battuta made astute use of his knowledge in the law and in Sufi doctrine. These assertions of specialized knowledge earned him deference and respect in the wider world of Islamic values. They smoothed his way over thousands of miles and, very often, paid it, too, with lucrative appointments at court and hospitality along the roads.

Ibn Battuta's pages offer what in many cases seem to be the only surviving views of daily life at court and in the streets of fourteenth-century Muslim Asia. As an author, he made productive use of even the most trivial-seeming scenes. Seeing a servant drop a plate in the streets of Damascus, for example, he puts to use this fleeting accident to shed light on the city's social institutions. Like Herodotus, he is a productive gossip, too, providing the reader with mosque and court intrigues and depicting his own negotiations with local dignitaries, all in order to enrich his record. For this purpose, he willingly discoursed on any topic, from the court system in Delhi to the sexual customs of Maldive Islanders.

Shaped by the world he traveled, Ibn Battuta was socially inclusive to a radical degree. Religiously, he was a walking resolution to the sometime antagonism between Sufi mysticism and Sunni orthodoxy. He was both a paid practitioner of Muslim law and a devotee of several Sufi orders, without apology to either side. Again and again in North Africa, approaching a Sufi hermitage or lodge, he would leave the road at a moment's notice, sometimes riding all day to visit some legendary sage or teacher. Such detours increase spiritual capital, he tells us. Indeed, the Hajj roads of the Maghrib are circuitous to a degree surprising to any modern traveler. Rarely laid out on the shortest distance between points, they describe an altogether different purpose: to allow pilgrims to touch base with all the important mosques and shrines along the way. In Ibn Battuta's case, these "detours" also helped an uncertain youth define his long-range goals. This binding force of spiritual societies throughout the Muslim world is often ignored by Western scholars. Ibn Battuta shows it working everywhere.

Lawyer, lay mystic, itinerant judge, scholar, courtier, and sometime spy— Ibn Battuta's professional life touched every social stratum of the period. He was not a successful public servant like Naser-e Khosraw and Ibn Jubayr, who in middle age threw off their courtly clothes to go to Mecca. He was not a man of independent means. He went broke once at least before he reached Mecca. There and in Damascus, he acquired diplomas at a frantic pace, knowing that later he must keep on working. Fourteenth-century Mecca appears to have been a popular finishing school for fledgling lawyers like himself, a place to make contacts and qualify oneself to earn a living. All the major paths of Islamic thought maintained schools there, with influential scholars who tutored students from around the world. In the lives of these young aspiring elites, Mecca functioned as an influential hub, not as a terminus.

For Naser-e Khosraw, the pilgrimage was a watershed experience; for Ibn Jubayr, a journey of devotion. In each case, the route was circular. After the Hajj, both men turned home. For Ibn Battuta, Mecca marked the first leg of a much longer journey. His Hajj was a precipitating event, a catalyst that transformed him into a world traveler. His meetings and friendships during this period opened his eyes to a region full of promise farther east. "Seek out knowledge even as far as China" is one of the Prophet Muhammad's best-known sayings. Ibn Battuta took it literally. He did not look back after Mecca. In 1328, after passing a year there, he made a vow: never to travel the same route twice so far as he was able. He set out for India, taking the long way, through Turkey, through Russia.

Ibn Battuta began his travels the year after Marco Polo died. Although he visited more places and traveled somewhat longer, the deeper distinction between their works is not a question of distance or years on the road but a matter of viewpoint. Whereas Marco Polo was always an outsider, Ibn Battuta, through most of his wanderings, remained within the borders of Islam. Music and dress changed a dozen times between Tangier and Delhi, yet the calendar and etiquette remained almost identical. Even in Canton, Muslims prayed five times a day, fasted together for a month, practiced Muslim hospitality, and lived by the same religious law. Ibn Battuta could always find work because the network of a global Islam provided it. He settled down, sometimes for years (in Mecca, Damascus, Baghdad, Delhi), married six times, had children, earned and spent small fortunes, and held official positions many times. The law he had studied as a young man in Morocco supported him in India and Sumatra. Over most of the lands he crossed, he remained immersed in a single community, a guest among fellow Muslims and an equal, speaking Arabic, sharing in a culture that ate, bathed, judged, and thought in common ways. Marco Polo was always an alien. Ibn Battuta, for all his mileage, remained at home.

When Ibn Battuta settled in Fez in 1353, the Sultan, Abu Inan, requested him to set down his travels; a young secretary named Ibn Juzayy, a poet and traveling scholar, was appointed to assist him. Ibn Juzayy describes the book they composed together as his own "abridgment" of the traveler's "notations" and "dictation." To these materials, in the spirit of his day, he occasionally inserted passages from the works of earlier travelers. For the physical descriptions of Damascus, Mecca, and Medina, the book relies heavily on Ibn Jubayr. These, and the swatches of purple prose Ibn Juzayy composed to introduce them, stand out clearly from the more direct voice of Ibn Battuta. The secretary's shaping hand may also be seen pressing into more logical shape his author's confusing itinerary. They worked together for two years. Of that process, Ibn Juzayy wrote, "I have rendered the sense of the narrative in language that adequately expresses the purposes he had in mind, and I have set forth clearly the ends he had in view. Frequently I have reported his words in his own phrasing, without omitting either root or branch." Still, he clearly had his orders: to smooth, and impose a more graceful shape on, the rough reminiscences of a traveled man who was not a writer.

Over the centuries, this work was considered lost. Then, in the early 1800s, the Swiss explorer J. L. Burckhardt (whose Hajj account appears here later) discovered and sent back from Cairo an Arabic excerpt of Ibn Battuta's travels, which was translated into English in 1829. Thirty years later, five manuscripts were unearthed in Algeria during the French occupation. From these, a complete French edition was prepared in 1858. Although it remains the accepted text, no one can say if we are reading a draft or a finished work. Nor can we know if Ibn Battuta gave it his blessing, nor how much Ibn Juzayy may have added later, nor how much is the work of copyists.

The selections that follow contain none of Ibn Juzayy's additions. Although this is merely a sliver of the total work, we are shown a surprising amount in a few pages: the disrupted state of North Africa in the fourteenth century, civil and religious life along the Nile, the aftermath of the Crusades, the social infrastructure of Damascus, the Syrian caravan to Medina, and the mystical devotees of Mecca.

from *The Travels of*
Ibn Battuta

TANGIER TO TUNIS. JUNE–JULY 1325 I left Tangier, my birthplace, on Thursday the second of Rajab, . . . intending to make the pilgrimage to the Sacred House at Mecca and to visit the tomb of the Prophet at Medina. I set out by myself, with no companion to cheer me along or any caravan to join with, compelled by an overwhelming urge and a long-held desire in my heart to visit these famous sanctuaries. So I confirmed my decision to leave everyone dear to me, men and women, and flew from my home as birds desert their nests. My parents were still alive at the time, and it weighed me down terribly to leave them. Both they and I were saddened when we parted. I was twenty-two then.

I came to Tlemcen when Ibn Zayyan was its Sultan. My arrival there happened to coincide with a visit by two envoys from the King of Ifriqiya. These men were justices of the peace at Tunis. Their names were Muhammad al-Nafzawi, a judge, and Muhammad al-Zubaidi, a Berber shaykh from a coastal town near Mahdiya. Shaykh al-Zubaidi was one of the foremost scholars of his time. He died in 1340.

The day I arrived, these two were leaving town, and an intermediary advised me to go with them. I consulted the Quran for a sign in the matter, and after three nights in Tlemcen spent procuring my provisions, I left town, riding after them at a gallop, and caught up with them in the town of Miliana. This was in the hottest part of the summer. Both envoys fell ill, and so we halted there ten nights. We had no sooner started out again than al-Nafzawi's condition became much worse. We stopped near a stream a few miles outside town, but the man died on our fourth morning there, and his son and al-Zubaidi went back to Miliana and buried him. At this point we parted company, and I continued my travels with a group of merchants from Tunis. When we reached Algiers, we camped outside town for several days, until al-Zubaidi and the dead man's son overtook us. Then we went on together through the dry flats of Mitija into the eastern Kabyle Mountains.

In Bejaïa, I was stricken by fever. Al-Zubaidi advised me to stay behind until I had fully recovered, but I refused, saying, "If God says I must die then let it happen on the road, while I'm facing Mecca." "Well," he answered, "if you really mean it, then sell your mount and your heavy baggage. I'll lend you a mule and a tent. That way you can keep up with us. We have to move quickly. There are thieves along these roads." I took his suggestion.

We continued on to Constantine and stopped outside it. During the night, heavy rains drove us from our tents and we ran for cover to some nearby buildings. In the morning the Governor of the town, a man named Abu al Hasan, a descendant of the Prophet, came to greet us. Seeing my clothes, which were soaked and muddy from the rain, he sent them to be laundered at his home. My mantle was in such ragged shape that he sent me a new one of fine cloth from Baalbek. Tied into one of its corners were two gold dinars, the first alms of my journey.

From Constantine we rode on to Annaba and lodged inside the city walls. A few days later, due to the dangers of the road, we parted from the merchants and traveled light with greater speed, pushing on day and night without a stop. I fell ill again with a fever and actually tied myself to the saddle with a turban to keep from falling off in my weakened state. It wasn't possible to dismount because of the danger. When we finally reached the town of Tunis, people came out to welcome Shaykh Zubaidi and the others home. They surrounded these men on every side with greetings and questions, but no one spoke to me because nobody knew me. I felt such loneliness I could not keep back my tears. One of the people noticed this and made a point of greeting me warmly. He continued to comfort and talk to me until I came into the city, where I found lodgings in the college of the booksellers.

ALEXANDRIA TO AYDHAB, EGYPT. APRIL—JULY 1326 I went to visit the Pharos lighthouse and found one side of it in total ruin. It is a square building soaring into the sky, with a single door far above ground level. The only way to enter it was over wooden planks laid between the door and an adjacent building. There was a place for a guardian just inside the door, and within the lighthouse itself lay many chambers. The inner passage is about 7 feet wide. The wall is 7½ feet thick; each of the lighthouse's four faces is 105 feet broad. It stands on a high mound three miles from the city on a long finger of land extending into the water on three sides. The town cemetery is on the same peninsula. I visited the lighthouse again on my return to Morocco in 1349, but it had fallen into such ruin by then that I couldn't enter it or even climb up to the doorway. . . .

During my time in Alexandria, I heard about a pious sage named al-Murshidi, who lived a life of pure devotion cut off from the world and who supplied all his needs from divine sources. He was certainly a true sage with real insight into the unseen. I learned that he was living in isolation in a village called Munyat Bani Murshid. He lived alone in a hermitage there, without servants or companions, and he was constantly sought out by ministers of state. Men from every walk of life came to him daily, and he would serve them. Because food prepared by such a man is blessed, everyone who came to see him would ask to eat some meat or fruit or candy in his dwelling, and he would bring whatever they asked for, even when it was out of season. Doctors of theology came to seek appointments from him too, and he would give them or retract them, depending on each man's merit.

Shaykh al-Murshidi's retreat lies close to Fawa, separated from the town by a canal. I passed through the town and reached the shaykh's cell before the afternoon prayer hour. I found him with a visitor, an officer of the Sultan's bodyguard, who had camped with his troops outside the cell. When I came to the Shaykh, he rose to meet me, embraced me, and invited me to eat. He wore a black wool tunic. When the time arrived, he asked me to lead the prayer, and I continued this throughout my stay there. When I was ready to go to sleep that night, he said: "Go up on the roof of the cell and sleep there." This was during the worst of the summer heat and he wanted me to be comfortable. I deferred to the Sultan's officer, but he replied by quoting the Quran: "Everyone has his appointed place." I went up to the roof and found a bed of straw, a leather mat, and water jugs for washing and drinking. I lay down to sleep there.

That night I dreamed I was perched on the wing of an enormous bird which flew with me in the direction of Mecca. There it turned south to Yemen, then east, then south again, and finally made a long flight toward the east, alighting in a dark and greenish country, where it left me. I woke astonished. I said to myself: "If the shaykh shows me that he knows about this dream, he is all that people say he is." In the morning I led the prayer again, then the Sultan's officer went on his way. Shaykh al-Murshidi gave small cakes to his other visitors and they departed. After the mid-morning prayer, he called me in and asked what I had dreamed. I told him. He replied: "You are going to make the pilgrimage to Mecca and visit the Prophet's tomb (at Medina), then you will travel to Yemen, Iraq, Turkey, and India. You will remain in India a long time and meet my brother Dilshad there. He will save you from a dangerous situation." Then he provided me with cakes and silver coins and I departed. . . .

I passed through a region of sand to Damietta, a city of spacious neighborhoods laden with fruit. It lies on a bank of the Nile, and the people in the houses near the river go down to it easily with buckets, for many homes have stairs right to the shore. Damietta is richly endowed and well laid out. Bananas thrive there; the fruit is carried down to Cairo on boats. Because its sheep and goats graze freely day and night, there is a saying about the city: "Its walls are made of sweet fruit and its dogs are sheep." Once you have entered the city, you may leave it only by showing a "pass" from the Governor. People of standing carry a seal stamped on a piece of paper, which they show at the gate. Others have the seal stamped on their forearms and must show that.

Seabirds* are in abundance in the market, as are various forms of a buffalo milk unsurpassed in their sweetness and a type of mullet exported not only to Cairo but to Syria and Anatolia. Outside town an island lies between the sea and the river, called the isthmus. Here there are a mosque and a hermitage whose shaykh I met, a man named Ibn Qufil, who has around him numerous dervishes all devoted to a life of faith. I spent a Thursday night with him, listening to their prayers and incantations.

The present city of Damietta is new; the old town was destroyed after being freed a second time from the Crusaders in the days of al-Malik al-Salih (1249–50). Here lies the hermitage of Shaykh Jamal al-Din al-Sawi, now deceased, who set the style for a group of wandering dervishes called the Qalandariya. These Qalandariya shave off their beards and eyebrows. The story goes that as a young man Shaykh al-Sawi was well built and handsome, and a Persian woman living here conceived a passion for him, sending him letters and stopping him on the street with invitations to come and see her.

*Seabirds: geese, ducks, teal, and ibis. [Ed.]

One day, baffled by his refusals, she posted a woman along his usual route to the mosque. As he passed, she stepped from the doorway with a letter. "Sidi, can you read?" she asked. "It's a letter from my son. Can you tell me what's in it?" Then, before he had broken the seal, she added: "My son's wife is in the hallway of this house. Would you read it to her through the door, so she may hear it?" He agreed, but when he was between the inner door and the outer one, the old woman locked the first door and the Persian lady came through the second with her servants. They seized him and dragged him into the house, where the woman attempted to seduce him. Seeing no way out, the Shaykh played along. "Where is your toilet?" he asked, and the woman showed him. He took a jar of water in with him and shaved off his beard and eyebrows with a razor, then returned to her side. She was so horrified and angered by what he had done that she forgot herself and threw him out. He kept up the practice afterwards, and so have his followers. . . .

There was a governor in Damietta named al-Muhsini, a good man and charitable too, who had built a college on the riverbank. I lodged in this college during my stay there, and a strong friendship grew up between us. When I finally left town and was on my way to Fariskur, a rider sent out by al-Muhsini overtook me. He said, "The Amir asked after you today. Hearing you had left, he sent you this—" and he handed me a little sack of coins. May Allah reward him. . . .

I continued on my journey from Ikhmim to Hu, another large town on the riverbank. I stayed here at the college of Ibn al-Sarraj and watched his followers recite a section of the Quran every day after the dawn prayer, followed by the devotions of al-Shadhili.* The noble Abdullah al-Hasani, a descendant of the Prophet and one of the saintliest of men, lives in Hu. I went to visit him, to receive his blessing. When he asked me my plans, I told him that I intended to make the pilgrimage to Mecca by way of Jidda, over the Red Sea. He said: "You won't succeed in doing that this time. Go back. Your first Hajj will be performed by the road from Damascus." I left him. Instead of taking his advice, I continued on my way . . . and finally, after fifteen days through the desert, I reached Aydhab. . . . There the current King was locked in a battle with the troops of the Sultan of Egypt. As a result he had sunk all the ships [that would have taken us to Jidda]. It was impossible for us to cross the sea, so we sold the provisions we had brought with us for the trip and returned to Upper Egypt with the Arabs who had rented us our

*al-Shadhili (1196–1258): a Moroccan Sufi theologian who, while in Egypt, founded the Shadhiliyah order, which later became one of the most popular mystical schools of the Middle East and North Africa, giving rise to fifteen other orders. [Ed.]

camels. From Qus we sailed back down the Nile (which was in flood) and after a passage of eight nights arrived back in Cairo. I stayed one night there before setting out for Syria.

DAMASCUS. AUGUST 1326 On Thursday, the ninth day of the fast of Ramadan, I reached Damascus. I lodged there at the Maliki college.* For sheer beauty Damascus surpasses any other city I have seen. . . . It is surrounded on three sides by extensive suburbs, whose districts are more pleasant than the city center, where the streets are very narrow. To the north lies the suburb of Salihiya, a city in itself, with beautiful markets, a congregational [Friday] mosque, and a public hospital. There is a college there, named for Ibn Omar, exclusively endowed for older people who want to turn to the study of the Quran. Here food and clothing are provided for both students and professors. Damascus has such a college, too. . . .

I was walking one day in a narrow lane in Damascus when I saw a young servant let slip from his hands an expensive-looking dish of Chinese porcelain. It broke into bits and a crowd gathered around him. Then one of these onlookers advised the boy: "Pick up the pieces and take them to the office of the Utensils Fund." The boy picked them up and the man went along with him to the office, where they showed the broken platter to a custodian. The boy was then given enough money to buy a suitable replacement. This fund is one of the best things about Damascus, for the boy's master would undoubtedly have beaten him for dropping such a dish. The fund is a service to mend the human heart. May God reward its benefactors.

People of means here compete with each other in the endowment of mosques, colleges, and sanctuaries. Because they have a high opinion of Moroccans, any of my countrymen who runs out of money in Damascus will find some way of earning a living open to him. He might be given an appointment as an imam in a mosque, as a teacher in a college with free room and board, as a reciter of the Quran, or as the keeper of a sanctuary; or he might go and live at a Sufi hermitage and there receive both food and clothes.

---

*The four orthodox "schools" of jurisprudence in Sunni Islam are Maliki, Hanbali, Hanafi, and Shafi'i. They take their names from their founders. With slight variations, all four interpretations follow the path, or *sunna,* of the Prophet Muhammad.

At Mecca until this century, each school was represented by a pulpit facing one of the four sides of the Ka'ba. From here, their imams took turns leading the prayers.

To some degree, the sway of each rite is regional. Morocco, for example, follows the Maliki rite almost exclusively. Being far from home, it makes sense that Ibn Battuta would find hospitality among their representatives. He frequently did so. [Ed.]

Furthermore, anyone living on charity here is protected from having to earn his keep at the cost of his self-respect and dignity. In this way manual workers and domestics may wind up guarding an orchard, attending to a mill, or caring for children, walking them to their morning classes and returning with them in the evening. If they want to pursue a course of studies or enter the religious life, they receive every assistance in the matter. . . .

When I first arrived here, I became good friends with the Malikite professor Nur al-Din al-Sakhawi, and he encouraged me to breakfast at his house each night during Ramadan.* I visited him four nights in a row, then had a stroke of fever and stayed away. He sent someone to search for me, and although my weakened state gave me good reason, he would not accept any excuse, and I wound up going to his house and spending the night there. When I tried to leave in the morning, he objected. "Think of my house as yours or your father's or brother's," he told me. He sent for a doctor, arranged for medical prescriptions, and ordered special foods to be prepared which the doctor prescribed for me. I remained with him in the same condition until the end of Ramadan. On the day of the festival prayers ending the fast, which I attended, God healed me, but by then the funds reserved for my Hajj had run out. Nur al-Din, hearing this, hired camels for me and provided me provisions and money, too. He said: "The money will be useful for anything of importance you may need." May God reward him.

THE DAMASCUS CARAVAN TO MECCA. SEPTEMBER–OCTOBER 1326 When the new moon of Shawal appeared, the Hijaz caravan trooped out to the south side of the city and camped at a village called Kiswé. I set out with them, traveling with a tribe of Bedouin called the Ajarima, whose Amir was Muhammad al-Rafi'. We marched from Kiswé to a sizable village, Sanamayn, and went on from there to the small town of Zur'a in the district of Hauran. After a stop near Zur'a we continued on to the small town of Busra. The caravan usually stops there for four nights, to await any stragglers from Damascus. When Muhammad was a young man and a trader in the employ of his wife, Khadija, he met a Christian monk [Bahira] here who foretold his future mission as a prophet. Today a large mosque stands on the place where his camel rested. People from all over the district of Hauran flock to this town, bringing produce to sell the pilgrims for their journey. From Busra the caravan traveled on to the Pool of Ziza, stopped there for a day, then

*The annual, month-long fast of Ramadan lasts each day from dawn until sunset. Thus, the Ramadan "breakfast" takes place at dusk. [Ed.]

continued on to Lajjun, where there is running water. From Lajjun we marched to the castle of Karak.*

Karak is one of the most remarkable, inaccessible, and famous of the Sinai fortresses. It is sometimes called the Raven's Castle. The river wraps around it on all sides, and it has only one gate, the entrance to which is hewn out of the rock. Today this castle is a stronghold for neighboring kings in times of trouble. . . . We stopped outside Karak for four days, at a place named Thaniyya. Here we prepared to enter the real desert. From Thaniyya we traveled on to Ma'an, the last town in Syria, then descended through the Pass of Flints into the wilderness. People say of this region that anyone entering it is lost and anyone leaving it is reborn. After a two-day march we stopped at Dhat Hajj, where water lies in beds deep in the ground and there are no houses. We continued on from there to Wadi Balda, a dry river, and then to Tabuk. This is the same place the Prophet raided [in 631]. . . .

The enormous caravan camps near the spring, and everybody satisfies his thirst. The pilgrims stay here for four days to refresh themselves, water their camels, and stock up on water for the even more fearsome emptiness between Tabuk and Ula. The water bearers set up buffalo-hide tanks beside the spring, filling them up like reservoirs. They water the camels and also fill water bags for the caravan and smaller skins for individuals. Each amir and person of rank has a private tank; the rest of the pilgrims make arrangements with the bearers for a fixed amount of money. Then the whole caravan leaves Tabuk and pushes on with haste, traveling night and day without stopping, for the wilderness is at its worst here. Halfway through lies the valley of Ukhaidir [Little Green Place], which might be more aptly named Valley of Hell. One year the hajjis suffered terribly in this place, for the *samoom* [poison wind] began blowing, their waterskins dried up, and the price of a drink rose to a thousand dinars. Both seller and buyer perished. The story is inscribed on one of the rocks as you pass through the valley. . . .

Five days beyond Tabuk the pilgrims reach the well of Thamud, which is full of water. In spite of their violent thirst, however, nobody draws a single bucket from this well, for the Prophet, when he passed here, told his people not to drink from it. (A few had already used the water to make dough; they subsequently fed it to their camels.) Here the dwellings of ancient Thamud stand carved into the hills, hewn out of reddish rock with elaborately deco-

---

*In the days of Ibn Jubayr, Karak was held by "the demon of the West," Reynald de Chatillon, among the most violent and fanatical of the Crusaders. From here, he raided the pilgrim caravans. In 1188, Saladin's general al-Adil captured the castle. Saladin executed Reynald with his own hand, and the balance of power shifted for good away from the Crusaders. [Ed.]

rated thresholds that look quite modern.* Their builders' bones lie turning to dust inside them, "a real sign for those with eyes to see."†

From Thamud to Ula is about a half-day journey. It is a large, pleasant village with palm groves and springs. Here the pilgrims stop for four nights to reprovision and to wash their clothes. The local people are honest and many pilgrims leave surplus provisions on deposit with them for the return journey, taking along only what they may need to reach Medina. Ula marks a boundary line, south of which the Syrian Christian merchants may not go. These people trade in provisions and goods with the pilgrims.

The day after the caravan leaves this town, the pilgrims camp in the valley of Itas. The heat here is killing and the fatal *samoom* is common. The last time it blew in this season, only a few pilgrims escaped with their lives. Past Itas they camp at Hadiyya, a place with underground water in a valley, where they dig shallow pits and water magically appears, but it is brackish. On the third day out we caught sight of the sanctified city of Medina, the City of the Prophet. . . .

When it came time to leave Medina and head for Mecca, we halted near the Dhu al-Hulayfa mosque, where the Prophet himself put on his pilgrim clothes for the Farewell Hajj. The mosque is five miles from Medina, near the stream of Aqiq. It marks the limit of Medina's sacred territory. Here I put away my tailored clothes, bathed, put on my consecrated lengths of unstitched cotton, and performed the customary prayers. I entered the life of a pilgrim at this stage, stating my intention to perform the Hajj as a rite separate from the Umra. I felt such enthusiasm then that I took up the chant of the caravan‡ and went on with it through every hill and valley until we reached the Pass of Ali, where we stopped for the night.

MECCA. OCTOBER–NOVEMBER 1326 At the time of my arrival there, the title of Amir of Mecca was held by two brothers, Rumaytha and Atayfa, sons of Abu Numayy Quitada, all descendants of the Prophet through Hasan. Rumaytha, although older, insisted that Atayfa be named before him in the Friday sermon at the mosque, because of the latter's widespread reputation

---

*The modern name of the site is Mada'in Salih. Along the caravan route rise many freestanding buttes carved away by the wind into grotesque shapes that, by some feat of unexplained genius, contain near their tops rock-hewn dwellings with plinths, peristyles, columns, and classic arches around the entries. At first glance, these dwellings resemble works of ancient Rome. In fact, they are architectural cousins of the rock-hewn houses at Petra, Jordan. [Ed.]

†Quran III:13. [Ed.]

‡"Here I am, Lord. What is your command?" [Ed.]

for justice. Atayfa's home stands to the right of the Marwa Hill; Rumaytha lives in the hermitage of al-Sharabi, near the Shayba Gate. Drums are beaten outside their doors every morning.

The generosity and good manners of the Meccans are outstanding. Not only do they give food to the poor before they start a feast; they invite them in and serve the food themselves. Meccans routinely give a third to a half of all their bread away. They are particular about their dress and usually wear white. The men wear perfume, darken their eyes with kohl, and frequently carry toothpicks made from the branches of a local tree. The women are beautiful. They also use scents and unguents liberally, and some go without food in order to buy them. When they perform the *tawaf* on Thursday nights, their perfumes fill the mosque and remain behind them long after they leave. . . .

During the week, the first of the four imams to recite the daily prayers is the Shafi'i imam. The majority of the Meccans belong to this rite and he is appointed by those in authority. He performs his prayer behind the Station of Abraham, in an admirable enclosure made especially for him. It is formed by beams joined in the shape of two ladders affixed to a plaster pedestal. A top beam supports many rows of glass lamps hanging on hooks. When the Shafi'i imam has finished his prayer, the imam of the Malikites prays in a separate oratory facing the Ka'ba's southern angle; the imam of the Hanbalites prays along with him, facing the eastern wall of the shrine. Lastly, the Hanafi imam prays, facing the roof spout of the shrine. He stands in an enclosure quite similar to the leader of the Shafi'ite's. This order of prayer remains the same for four of the five daily prayers. At the sunset prayer they pray in unison, each imam leading his own congregation. One notices some distraction among the people at these times, Malikites bowing in time with the Shafi'ites, Hanafites prostrating with the Hanbalites. You can see the people listening with great attention to the voice of their particular muezzin, in order to avoid confusion.

At the Friday sermon the imam enters dressed entirely in black, with a turban and a muslin veil hanging down his back, furnished by the King of Egypt. He walks at a dignified pace between two black flags borne along by two of the muezzins who will call the prayer. A chamberlain precedes him carrying a tall stick, the *farqa'a*, with a thin twist of cord tied at one end, which is cracked like a whip as a signal to everyone that the imam is coming. First he goes to kiss the Black Stone. Beside him comes the senior muezzin of Zamzam, dressed in black, bearing a sword on one shoulder. Then the two flags are placed on either side of the pulpit, which stands very near the Ka'ba, close to the wall between the Black Stone and the northern (Iraqi) angle of the shrine. As the imam prepares to mount the steps, the muezzin gives him the sword, and the imam strikes the first step with it. This draws the attention of the crowds. He does the same with the other steps and strikes a fourth time at the top. Next, he prays in a low voice, facing the Ka'ba, then turns to the public, bowing to his right and to his left. The congregation returns the gesture. At the very moment that he sits down, the muezzins begin the call to prayer, standing on the dome of the Zamzam Well.

The imam prays for Allah's Prophet many times, then for the Prophet's family: his uncles, Hamza and Abbas; his grandsons, Hasan and Husayn; Fatima, their mother, and Khadija, his first wife, too; then for Malik al-Nasir of Egypt; for the Sultan, Nur al-Din Ali; for the two amirs of Mecca; and for the Sultan of Iraq (though not recently for this last one). After his sermon he prays again, then returns the way he came, and the order of his departure is the reverse of his arrival.

SOME SOJOURNERS AT MECCA Among those who had come to perform the Hajj, then remained long after, there were the following:

—A wise and pious imam known as al-Yafi'i, who was also a Sufi adept and devotee. This man was almost constantly circling the Ka'ba "by night and at the odd hours of the day."* Often, after performing his evening circuits, he would climb to the roof of the Muzaffariya college and sit there watching the Ka'ba until he fell asleep. He would place a flat stone beneath his head and rest a little, then renew his ablutions [wudu']† and take up his circling again until the time came for the morning prayer. He was married to the daughter of Shihab ibn Burhan, a lawyer and fellow Sufi. A young woman, she constantly complained to her father of neglect; he advised her to be patient, and she stayed with al-Yafi'i for some years, but things did not improve and she divorced him.

—Shaykh Abu al-Abbas ibn Marzuq, who often resided in Mecca. I saw him there in 1328 and he was by far the most determined in circling the Ka'ba. His persistence in spite of the heat always amazed me, for the pavement around the shrine is flagged with black stones and the midday sun heats them up like red-hot plates. I have seen the water bearers attempt to wet them down, but no sooner does the water hit the stone than the spot changes color

*Quran XX:130. [Ed.]

†*wudu'*: a light washing of the face and limbs, establishing a state of purity required before Muslim prayer. [Ed.]

and starts steaming. Most people performing the *tawaf* at that hour wear sandals, but this man did it with bare feet. One afternoon I saw him circling and thought I would like to join him. But when I crossed the pavement to kiss the Black Stone, the heat of its surface overpowered me. I steeled myself enough to reach the Stone but hurried away without making the first circuit, laying my head scarf on the ground and treading on it again and again until I reached the colonnades.

—Najm al-Din al-Usfuni had been a judge in Upper Egypt, then quit the post, became a devotee, and then a sojourner at the Sanctuary. He used to perform the Umra every day and, during the fast at Ramadan, twice a day, relying upon a statement attributed to the Prophet that performing this rite during Ramadan is equivalent to the performance of the Hajj.*

—Abu Bakr al-Shirazi, known as the Silent. He was almost constantly engaged in circling the shrine and stayed at Mecca for many years, during which he never spoke a word.

—Izz al-Din al-Wasiti, a man of tremendous wealth who received a large remittance from his native town each year. He used to buy grain and dried dates with the money and distribute them to the poor and those in need, transporting the goods to their homes himself. He occupied himself this way until he died.

—Abu al-Hasan al-Anjari, a lawyer from the district of Tangier. He sojourned at Mecca for some years and died there. My father and he had a long-standing friendship, and whenever he came to Tangier, he stayed in our home. At Mecca he had a room at the Muzaffariya college, where he taught theology during the day. At night he retired to a dwelling in the hermitage of Rabi'. (The people of the Hijaz hold this hermitage in high esteem and bring offerings to it. The people of Ta'if supply it with fruit. Anyone in Ta'if with a garden of date palms, grapes, peaches, or figs has long ago agreed to give a share of the produce to this place and to convey it there on their own camels. Ta'if is a two-day ride from Mecca.)

THE STORY OF HASAN, THE MAD In the later days of my own sojourn in Mecca, in 1328, there lived a man named Hasan of the West. He was possessed and had a strange life and a remarkable character. He had not always been insane. Formerly he had served the sage Najm al-Din al-Isbahani.

*In orthodox Islamic law, there is no substitute for or "equivalent" to the Hajj. [Ed.]

During the years when Najm al-Din was at Mecca, Hasan used to circle the Shrine many times at night, and he often saw a Sufi student making the turns, too, but the man never appeared to him in the daytime. One night the man approached him and said, "Hasan, your mother is weeping for you. She wants to see you. Would you like to meet with her?" Hasan replied, "Yes, but it's impossible. She is no longer with us." The student said, "Meet me here tomorrow night. We will see what Allah brings." The following night, a Thursday, Hasan met the man and they circled the Shrine together many times. Then the student left the mosque and Hasan followed. Outside the Ma'la Gate, the man told him to close his eyes and hold on to his sleeve. Hasan took the man's sleeve. In a little while the student said, "Would you know your hometown if you saw it?" Hasan opened his eyes and found himself at the gate of his mother's home. (I think his town was the city of Asafi.) He went inside and stayed with her about three weeks, not saying a thing about how he had come there. Finally one day he went out to the cemetery and crossed paths with the student. "How are you?" he asked. Hasan replied, "I've been trying to find Shaykh Najm al-Din. I left his home in the normal way, but now I've been away too many days, and I'd like you to take me back to him." The student said, "Certainly," and they made an appointment to meet that night. When Hasan returned to the graveyard, the student had him close his eyes and take his sleeve. In a little while they were back in Mecca. The student made Hasan swear not to tell Shaykh Najm or anyone else what had happened. When the Shaykh asked Hasan where he had been, he would not tell him. When he was pressed, he told Najm the story. The Shaykh said, "Show me the man," and went to the Shrine with him that night. The student was there, and Hasan pointed him out. The student heard him and struck him on the mouth, saying "Be silent." Hasan's tongue became tied at that moment and his reason left him forever. He remained in the mosque, a demented figure, performing the circuits night and day without washing or saying prayers. The people saw him as a means to acquire blessings and clothed and fed him. When he felt hungry, he would step out to the market, pick out any booth, and eat what he liked from it. No one drove him away or tried to stop him. On the contrary, people were pleased if he ate their food, for it brought them blessings and seemed to improve their sales. He did the same with the water bearers when he wanted to drink. He went on this way until 1329, when the same soldier of the Sultan's guard whom I had crossed paths with at al-Murshidi's hermitage in Egypt came for the Hajj and took Hasan back to Egypt. Since that time I have not heard of him.

part two

Enter the Europeans:
renegades, impostors, slaves,
and scholars. The awakening
of european interest
1503 — 1814

The Orient is not only adjacent to Europe; it is also the place of Europe's greatest and richest and oldest colonies, the source of its civilizations and languages, its cultural contestant, and one of its deepest and most recurring images of the Other.
                                        —*Edward Said,* Orientalism

Starting in the early 1500s, a new breed of traveler began to arrive in the Red Sea area. Attaching themselves to trading caravans, learning enough Arabic to pass, a few of these adventurers made it all the way to Mecca, and a handful even wrote about it. They were not citizens of Islamdom's international community. In most cases, they were not Muslims at all but, rather, European Christians in disguise. As authors, they addressed a Western audience. As travelers, they were propelled by forces very different from those that drew Naser-e Khosraw or Ibn Jubayr. Before we can comprehend their books or motives, however, we need to understand how the times that produced them reshaped Europe and its vision of Islam. To do this, we have to reverse our previous perspective and examine Islam and the Hajj itself from the point of view of Western thought at the end of the Middle Ages.

About the time that Ibn Battuta returned to Fez to write his book, a Benedictine monk named Uthred of Bolden at Oxford University submitted an innovative proposition. He suggested that "at the moment of death all human beings, whether Christian or Muslim, or whatever faith, enjoy the direct vision of God and receive everlasting judgment in the light of their response to this experience."* Uthred was in every other way a laborious conservative, yet his proposal, to grant unbelievers a privilege previously reserved for Christians, was apparently original with him. Although later condemned and withdrawn, the conception and publication of such a notion illustrates the relative openness of his cultural milieu. How Christian Europe declined in the next 150 years, from a world where new ideas were still possible to the often violently exclusive atmosphere of the premodern inquisition, is a complex story.

*R. W. Southern, *Western Views of Islam in the Middle Ages,* p. 76.

The years between Roger Bacon's birth, in 1220, and Uthred's death, in 1370, are considered the final flowering of the Middle Ages. They were followed by a longer, grimmer period in Europe, during which the machinery for rooting out heresy defeated enlightened discourse almost completely. The early condemnation of works by William Ockham, Johannes Eckehart, the spiritual Franciscans, and Dante signaled the start of a breakdown in the integrity of Western thought. During this Great Interruption, xenophobia replaced curiosity, interest in Islam and the classics withered, and Muslim thought was anathematized or ignored. Fifty years later, it was no longer wise to learn Arabic, Hebrew, or even Greek. In 1453, when John of Segovia proposed a new translation of the Quran, he could not find a single Christian scholar of Arabic in Europe. Already, native Iberian Muslims and Jews in vast numbers were being deported or were fleeing persecution from long-pluralistic Muslim Spain into North Africa, Bosnia, and Turkey. The complete extinction of this eight-hundred-year-old culture is one of the great tragedies of Europe. The great age of translation had given way to repression, narrowness, and fear.

Historians usually cite three causes for this retrenchment. First, the thirteenth- and fourteenth-century Mongol invasions from Asia enlarged many times the known population of the world, so that Roman Catholics felt suddenly outnumbered by fifty times. Second, the hope that Islam would fade away was constantly disappointed. Rather than wither, as an inferior force should do, Islam was expanding. By the end of the fourteenth century, most of the Balkans were Turkish tributaries, and the resulting loss of access to the wealth of the India trade was strapping the economy of Europe. Third came the plague, which followed Ibn Battuta home through Syria and Egypt, wasting Damascus and Cairo as it went and depleting Europe, by 1350, of a third of its people. Ignorant of the plague's pathology and with a theology geared to interpreting catastrophe as punishment for sin, Catholic Europe was plunged into a long, apocalyptic twilight. These three factors—the Mongols, the westward expansion of Islam, the Black Death—joined to close down and weirdly addle Western Europe.

In place of the remote, failed Crusades, a new, isolationist strategy took hold: to set one's own house in order, to weed out heresy, to cleanse the ranks. On a continent ravaged by buboes and pneumonia, the Roman Catholic Church discovered enemies within. Salvation came to lie in a purifying justice. Libraries were cleansed by fire, as were thousands of Gypsies, "heretical" Catholics, Muslims, and Jews. Anathema was punished, rooted out. Interestingly, this new war on blasphemy was shaped in crucial ways by the Muslim question. In purely theological terms, Islam had always deeply riled the

Church. Here was a faith that acknowledged one God as the all-knowing Creator, concurred on the immortality of the soul, treated both Testaments as sacred, accepted Jesus' virgin birth, and deeply respected his status as a prophet—yet denied his divinity, possessed no priesthood, followed its own Book, and seemed to imply that sexuality and wealth were a part of God's blessings. Worse yet, Islam was enormously successful.

From its early days, Islam remained a European measure of what real heresy was all about. In the fifteen and sixteenth centuries, however, after most Muslims had been expelled from Spain and as real knowledge of them dwindled, the European image of Islam grew more distorted, becoming a colossal parody of Catholicism. From a well-defined other, its face was re-cast as a monstrous double, a reverse image of Christianity in all its virtue: the face of the scapegoat. This was not due to new thinking on the subject. Rather, cultural propaganda from the Crusades was simply dusted off and reapplied to the Inquisition. In the intellectual history of the West, Islam was delivered full circle, back to the demonizing portraits enshrined in the Old French epic of *Roland*. A Muslim became everything a good Christian was not. Islam was reduced to a set of self-referential signs and symbols. As we shall see, this cultural hallucination found a supporting fiction in medi-eval Western travel writing.

The Evolution of Western Travel Writing

European accounts of Mecca begin with the Renaissance, but they share an older literary background. Until Marco Polo (flourished 1295), Western travel writing about the Near East was mostly a product of the imagination. Throughout the Dark Ages, when Europeans produced books about the East, they approached the project crabwise, from one of two angles. Either they recorded a timeless Holy Land shaped by the Bible, or they depicted an ex-otic nightmare world of infernal monsters that stretched from the gates of Jerusalem to China. The first, ahistorical approach, the Latin *itinerario*, employed a rhetoric of piety. The other, more secular view affected a scien-tific tone and emphasized grotesquerie. Pious tomes and fantastical collec-tions—both were devoid of real-life encounters.

The religious works, by pilgrim monks and nuns, did not record an actual place at all. When these authors looked at Jerusalem, they saw neither Muslims, Jews, and Eastern Christians nor their markets, donkeys, villages, and forts but an eternal topography "quoted" from the Bible. They offered up false geography in a timeless literary landscape. Their pages flow along without the least reference to travel or even physical perception. Examples abound throughout the literature. In an early depiction from Saint Jerome (ca. 347–419/20) for instance, the Jordan River is anything but wet:

> Scarcely was the night past before she, with fervent zeal, came to the Jordan, stood on the bank of the river, and, as the sun rose, remembered the Sun of Righteousness, how the priests stood on dry ground in the middle of the bed of Jordan; . . . and how, by His Baptism, the Lord cleansed the waters which had been defiled by the Flood and stained by His death.

There are developments and exceptions through the centuries, but overall the pious travel record shrank the actual East to a spiritual theme park. In these upright, selective, and fleshless exercises, even the leaves on the trees at Gethsemane were reduced to black ink and Latin letters.

The more secular sort of travel record was still less informative. It took the form of an illustrated wonder book, a cross between atlas, bestiary, and Ripley's *Believe It or Not!* To appreciate its popularity, we have to remember that except for commerce and pilgrimage, Europeans before 1250 rarely ventured past the Holy Land to write about it. Instead, they invented "Eastern" places out of whole cloth and peopled them with fabulous inhabitants. The typical wonder book contained short descriptive items of a great beyond, its exotic places and nonexistent creatures. These texts were usually accompanied by woodcuts of surreal maps and nightmare creatures: headless men with eyes in their breasts, humans eight feet tall and eight feet wide, naked goat-footed women with hoof-length hair, sciopods, cyclopes, dog-headed humans, two-headed babies, and cauldrons pinpointing the exact locale of Hell. These so-called *monstra,* inventions devised to entertain and warn, provided the reader an armchair thrill as they enforced the self-congratulatory image of a world with a normal Europe at its center and a monstrous East at the margins. A medieval equivalent of Joel-Peter Witkin's photography, the wonder books were read as allegories. They reminded Christian Europe that everything *contra naturam* lay in the East.

The end of the Crusades and the opening of Asian roads in the thirteenth and early fourteenth centuries abetted travel on a global scale. During this all too brief period, a handful of works by actual travelers shifted the emphasis away from pious content and grotesquerie to an actual East experienced by a narrator with a purpose. The best of these authors, Marco Polo (1254–1324) and William of Rubruck (ca. 1215–ca. 1295), displaced the pious and fantastic with a credible, human narration that interprets exotic settings in a more objective tone. Marco Polo in particular provided Europe with a description of the East that simply made more sense than the Church's version. Even after the Mongol invasions and after plague and the Inquisition conspired to wall off the East again, curious merchants, lawyers, gentleman scholars, and general readers across Europe continued to make popular the many editions and translations of this work.

As his book got around, Marco Polo's "realism" inspired subsequent authors to new amalgams of fact and fiction. With one foot in the age of the wonder book and the other foot in the Renaissance, these authors adopted his "truthful" tone, applying it uniformly to hearsay as well as observation. Today, they are sometimes referred to as travel liars, for their habit of "factually" reporting on places they had not seen. At one end of the period stands the work of Sir John Mandeville (flourished 1356), an encyclopedist whose mostly invented stories still ring true, thanks to his gift for writing the first realistic Western fiction since Petronius. We do not know who this man was or even what language he wrote in, but modern textual analysis suggests that he rarely left his study. Rather than travel, he scavenged and plagiarized the works of others, improving their prose as he claimed their discoveries. In a period of continental isolation, Mandeville satisfied Europe's appetite for news by making up an East that sounded real. In expanding editions and translations, his *Voyage and Travels* became the most popular prose book of the Middle Ages. A fictional work, it nonetheless demystified the East for Western readers, simply because the writing imitated a believable product: the voice of the secular traveler encountering a forbidden, real world.

At the latter end of the period, there came a specific brand of liar: men who in fact had traveled far and who claimed to have been to Mecca but never reached it. The Dominican friar Felix Fabri's 1484 account is of this type. Here, in the midst of a true report of a trip to Jerusalem, one suddenly finds a garbled batch of mediated lore concerning Mecca: the Black Stone protruding from the northeast corner of the Ka'ba is wrongly identified as the back of a statue of Saturn cemented into the Shrine by the Prophet Muhammad. The pilgrims (Fabri continues) worship Venus and perform the *jamarat* rites by casting stones "backward between their thighs to pelt the devil." Moreover, many pilgrims come to Mecca to "see Muhammad's coffin hung in the air without rope or chain"—although his tomb lies in Medina, two hundred miles to the north. Only at the end of his five-page entry does the friar confess that he made his pilgrimage "in imagination, that I might see [show] the difference between our pilgrimage and their pilgrimage."

Two years later Arnold von Harff, a wealthy German youth, set out from Cologne on a pilgrimage to Rome, then continued to Egypt. The account of his caravan journey to Mecca, taking up about a page, begins a section of Arabian travel so confusing it makes no sense. Harff claims to have been sneaked into Mecca by a Christian Mamluk soldier, a *"renegado."* He finds "a very pleasant town surrounded by beautiful gardens with rare fruit. Beside the town a fine and large river runs southward to the Red Sea." (Had there been such a river, would it be running in the desert in mid-August?) Harff, too, claims to have visited Muhammad's tomb at Mecca. Medina he wrongly locates to the south, calling it Trippa, an ancient, pre-Islamic name out of use for more than a thousand years. Arriving in Aden, he calls it Madach, another anachronism, taken from the second-century Greco-Egyptian geographer Ptolemy.

These fictional visits to Mecca go hand in hand with the rise of a mercantile interest in the East, which sprang up in Europe in the 1490s. While Columbus sailed west for Spain, the Portuguese, that other arm of old Andalus, sailed east in search of navigable alternatives. It is no accident that the two Western monarchies most intimate with Arab ship design and sailing techniques should also have been the first to blaze these sea routes. As the historian Daniel J. Boorstin rightly observes, "The lateen sail, which the Arabs brought into the Mediterranean, by its adeptness at sailing into the wind, had made the Portuguese ventures possible. The Arabs also pioneered in developing the stern rudder, which made any ship more maneuverable."* It is also worth noting in this context that Vasco da Gama, on his first great eastward voyage, was guided across the Indian Ocean from East Africa by an Arab pilot named Ibn Majid, who also happened to be the author of the *Nautical Directory* (1490), a popular Arabic compendium of contemporary nautical science, including all the information then available for sailing the Red Sea and the Indian Ocean.

With the opening of a lane to Calicut in 1498, a new kind of traveler began drifting into the Red Sea area. Harff is the first to mention *renegados* (the word was originally Portuguese), and he rightly links them to the Mamluk armies of Cairo and Damascus. From the sixteenth century on, these new adventurers arrived in growing numbers—runaway adolescents, deserters of merchant navy ships, riffraff, freebooters, here and there a disillusioned priest—all entering the Muslim world in search of something different, wealth or adventure, fleeing hometown trouble, washed up in shipwrecks, or (as we shall see) impressed into slavery. The *renegado* gives credence to

*Daniel J. Boorstin, *The Discoverers,* p. 184.

76

Freud's remark that "if one motive for traveling is curiosity, a stronger motive is that which impels adolescent runaways." For reasons particular to each, Italian, Greek, Spanish, Portuguese, French, German, English, Irish, Scots, and Dutch examples of the type all began turning up in unexpected places, frequently as mercenaries with expertise in firearms and warships. Many became Muslims. (Even to join the Mamluk army required a nominal conversion. The English term "to turn Turk" derives from a similar practice in Ottoman times.) Some rose to high positions. Many more died obscurely in nameless battles, often against European troops.

It was just a matter of time until one of these characters reached Mecca. Probably a few had come and gone as slaves or impostors before Ludovico di Varthema, an Italian *renegado* from Bologna, produced the first Western narrative of the Hajj in 1503. His account occurs in the first fifty pages of a much longer book of travels. His motive for going is anything but religious:

> On the eighth day of April, the [Damascus] caravan being set in order to go to Mecca, and I being desirous of beholding various scenes and not knowing how to set about it, formed a great friendship with the captain of the Mamluk guard of the caravan, who was a Christian renegade, so that he clothed me like a Mamluk and gave me a good horse, and placed me in company with other Mamluks, and this was accomplished by means of the money and other things which I gave him; and in this manner we set ourselves on the way.

We are a long way from the devout pilgrim's account with Varthema. On the other hand, we are definitely in the Hijaz with a clear-eyed if unscrupulous observer.

The five accounts that make up Part Two of this collection are all by Europeans. Only one of them died a Muslim. Whereas Khosraw, Ibn Jubayr, and Ibn Battuta each journeyed toward a known center, the authors of the next accounts all set out through an exotic elsewhere on their way to a forbidden goal. Whereas spiritual credit accrues to a believer's efforts, these men are taking their chances for the sake of compulsions unrelated to belief. The section opens with Varthema. It continues on a more objective note with a richly detailed Hajj report that is accurate and, unfortunately, anonymous. With this brief account of 1575, the wonder books and their infernal Eastern landscapes give way to more perspicuous reporting. The period starts with a penniless, semiliterate soldier (Varthema) and ends, in 1814, with John Lewis Burckhardt, a Cambridge-educated classicist. The two most comprehensive reporters, Ali Bey al-Abbasi (1807) and Burckhardt, provide accurate, eyewitness testimony to the rise of independence movements throughout the nineteenth-century Arab world, with a particular focus on the Saudi rebellion in the Hijaz.

Varthema, Ali Bey, and Burckhardt all traveled willingly as Muslims. Joseph Pitts visited Mecca under duress, as a pilgrim's slave. Muslim readers may be shocked by the secular motives of some of these trespassers while non-Muslims may find them spiritually vacant or latently racist. Like it or not, this odd handful of figures constitutes the ragtag band that will form a basis for all later Western treatments of the subject.

4

Ludovico di Varthema
Bologna
1503

꧁꧂

He shall pass into strange countries, he shall try good and evil in all things.

—*Ecclesiastes*

When Ludovico di Varthema reached Damascus in 1502, he found a well-established European presence. Venetians had been active in the region since the thirteenth century, monopolizing the western end of the India trade. There were Greek merchants as well, and many European soldiers: Mamluk military slaves from Georgia and Circassia in the pay of the Sultan, the occasional Austrian or Russian prisoner captured in battle, and quite a number of Western renegados. Varthema soon met a lot of these, including a European captain in charge of a cavalry unit assigned to guard the Meccan caravan. By befriending this man, by paying him money and becoming a nominal Muslim, Varthema managed to join the Mamluk army, draw a wage, and under its protection further his fascination with new scenes. He seems to have had no trouble picking up Arabic. He went off to Mecca as a mercenary soldier.

This start as a Mamluk is not surprising. A slave soldiery introduced into Egypt in 1169, the Mamluks solved the need for a reliable military class in a state riven by factions. Like the Seljuks of Naser-e Khosraw's day, they began as a private guard attached to the ruler, then grew into an urban-based elite. When the Mongols sacked Baghdad in 1258, then pillaged westward, it was the Mamluks who stopped them. After their victory, they settled down to rule a sizable sultanate in Egypt and Syria. From their capital, Cairo, they installed a political agent in the Hijaz and a cavalry in Mecca. They took charge of the Jidda customs, too, sharing its revenues with the Sharif. Mamluks were numerous enough in the Hijaz by Varthema's time to provide a Christian adventurer like Varthema with a credible disguise.

Varthema's experience in Arabia is certainly firsthand. Three hundred fifty years later, Richard Burton could write that "for correctness of observation . . . [he] stands in the foremost rank of the old Oriental travelers." On the other hand, he is hardly representative of Hajj authors. The change of tone we encounter in his pages reflects a radical alteration in point of view. With Khosraw, Ibn Jubayr, and Ibn Battuta, we were guided into Mecca by believers. With Varthema, we are suddenly in forbidden territory, confronting the Haram through the eyes of a trespasser. This man is not fulfilling a religious duty with his visit. He is performing the unimaginable. Why?

Varthema traveled in the East for about five years. At the start, in Damascus, he was already "desirous of beholding various scenes" but had no way to set about it until he hit upon the plan to go to Mecca. If his own book is anything to go by, the "various scenes" he longed to behold were all located in the Indian Ocean area, in the vicinity of an enormously lucrative spice trade, which the Portuguese navy was busy capturing in Muslim harbors and sea-lanes across the region. Varthema passed through Arabia in a few months; he traveled in India and the Spice Islands for four years. These adventures took place during the second wave of Portuguese expansion. Vasco da Gama had given Europe a navigable sea route from Lisbon to India in 1498. Now, a consolidation of the Spice Islands was under way. Varthema, by masquerading as a Muslim, was able to travel to the farthest reach of this new empire at a time when life was dangerous there for Westerners.

Varthema seems perfectly disposed to the spy's profession. He was a young man drunk on travel, insatiably curious, and his natural duplicity was boundless. He hoodwinked so many strangers on the way that a suggestion of Iago runs through the narrative. The whole book is laced with narrow escapes and the double-crossing of innocent figures whom Varthema bests (and sometimes cuckolds). How much of this audacity is window dressing devised to attract Renaissance readers? No one can say. He appears to have been a cat with nine lives, a self-serving rascal who entertained a passion for travel and dreamed of great rewards awaiting him at home. Yet despite his tricks, something about Varthema made Muslims like him. In Mecca, a local trader helped him desert the Mamluk army. In Aden, the Sultan's wife arranged his release from jail. Varthema was definitely a rogue, but he must have been likable.

As an author, Varthema straddles the divide between ancient and modern travel writing in the West. On the one hand, where crowds and battles are concerned, he consistently exaggerates their numbers. With a nod to the wonderbook market, he even includes an "eyewitness" report of unicorns in the Haram Mosque. At moments like these, he appears to be mired in a superstitious age. Yet he could be "scientific," too, concerned with accuracy to a degree that sets him apart from the travel liars. He rightly locates the Prophet's tomb in Medina, not Mecca, and deflates other myths. His book as a whole is freighted with cultural distortions, yet he kept his prejudices well enough in check to present the rites of the Hajj without invention.

Varthema's account is a curious prelude to Western writing about the Hajj. After centuries of sharp-eyed reporting by Muslims, we have these first few pages by an impostor. For better or worse, however, the man was in the Sacred Territory. He wrote with interest and relative restraint, and he went some way to dispelling old confusions about the East. In this sense, Varthema's work marks the beginning of an arduous development in Western travel writing, away from fantasy, toward more accurate reporting. His account was one of the first printed books to gain wide popularity in Europe. The first edition (Rome, 1510) attracted immediate attention. A Latin translation appeared six months later, followed by editions in German, Spanish, French, Dutch, and English. Keeping in mind, as he says himself, "that one eyewitness is worth more than ten rumors," I have started this section with some excerpts from his Travels.

from *The Travels of*
Ludovico di Varthema

HOW MECCA IS CONSTRUCTED, AND WHY THE MOORS GO THERE   We will now speak of the very noble city of Mecca, what it is, its state, and who governs it. The city is most beautiful, and is very well inhabited, and contains about six thousand families. The houses are extremely good, like our own, and there are houses worth three or four thousand ducats each. This city is not surrounded by walls. A quarter of a mile distant from the city we found a mountain where there was a road cut by human labor. And then we descended into the plain. The walls of the city are the mountains, and it has four entrances. The governor of this city is a sultan, that is, one of four brothers, and is of the family of Muhammad, and is subject to the Grand Sultan of Cairo. His three brothers are always at war with him. On the eighteenth of May we entered into the city of Mecca; we entered from the north, and afterward we descended into the plain. On the side toward the south there are two mountains which almost touch each other, where lies the pass to the gate of Mecca. On the other side, where the sun rises, there is another mountain pass, like a valley,* through which is the road to the mountain where they celebrate the [near] sacrifice of Isaac by Abraham,† distant from the city about eight or ten miles.‡ The height of this mountain is two or three casts of a stone by hand, and it is of some kind of stone, not marble, but of another color. On the top of this mountain there is a mosque according to their custom, which has three doors. At the foot of the mountain there are two very beautiful reservoirs of water. One is for the caravan from Cairo, and the other for the caravan from Damascus; which water is collected there from the rain and comes from a great distance.

Now, let us return to the city. (At the proper time we will speak of the sacrifice which they make at the foot of the said mountain.) When we entered into the city, we found the caravan from Cairo, which had arrived eight days before us because they had not traveled by the same route as ourselves. In the caravan there were sixty-four thousand camels and one hundred Mamluks. You must know that, in my opinion, the curse of God has been laid upon the city, for the country produces neither grass nor trees, nor any one thing. And they suffer from so great a dearth of water that if everyone were to drink as much as he might wish, four *quattrini*§ worth of water daily would not suffice them.

I will tell you in what manner they live. A great part of their provisions comes from Cairo, that is, from the Red Sea. There is a port called Jidda, which is distant from the city forty miles. A great quantity of food also comes there from Arabia Felix [Yemen], and also a great part comes from Ethiopia. We found a great number of pilgrims, of whom some came from Ethiopia, some from India Major, some from India Minor, some from Persia, and some from Syria. Truly I never saw so many people collected in one spot as during the twenty days I remained there. Of these people some had come for the purposes of trade, and some on pilgrimage for their pardon, in which pardon you shall [soon] understand what they do.

*"This is the open ground leading to the Mina Pass." (Sir Richard Francis Burton, *Personal Narrative of a Pilgrimage to al-Madinah and Meccah*, II:362*n*)

†Varthema mistakenly transposes the biblical version of Abraham's trial to the Meccan rite. In the Islamic story, the son God asks him to sacrifice is Ishmael, not Isaac. [Ed.]

‡"An error. The sacrifice is performed at Mina not at Arafat, the mountain here alluded to." (Burton, *Personal Narrative*, II:362*n*)

§*quattrini:* a Venetian liquid measure. [Ed.]

THE MERCHANDISE IN MECCA First we will speak of the merchandise, which comes from many parts. From India Major there come a great many jewels and all sorts of spices, and part comes from Ethiopia; and there also comes from India Major, from a city called Bangehella [Bengal], a very large quantity of stuffs of cotton and of silk, so that in Mecca there is carried on a very extensive traffic of merchandise, that is, of jewels, spices of every kind in abundance, cotton in large quantities, wax and odoriferous substances in the greatest abundance.

CONCERNING THE PARDONING IN MECCA Now let us turn to the pardoning of the pilgrims. In the midst of the city there is a very beautiful temple, similar to the Colosseum of Rome, but not made of such large stones, but of burned bricks, and it is round in the same manner; it has ninety or one hundred doors around it and is arched.* On entering the temple, you descend ten or twelve steps of marble, and here and there about the entrance there stand men who sell jewels, and nothing else. And when you have descended the steps, you find the temple all around, and everything, that is, the walls, covered with gold. And under the arches there stand about four thousand or five thousand persons, men and women, which persons sell all kinds of odoriferous things; the greater part are powders for preserving human bodies,† because pagans come there from all parts of the world. Truly, it would not be possible to describe the sweetness and the odors which are smelled within this temple. It appears like a spicery full of musk, and of other most delicious odors.

On the twenty-third of May the pardon commenced in the temple. The pardon is this: Within the temple, and uncovered, and in the center, there is a tower, the size of which is about five or six paces on every side,‡ around which there is a cloth of black silk.§ And there is a door all of silver, of the height of a man, by which you enter into the tower. On each side of the door there is a jar, which they say is full of balsam, and which is shown

---

*Burton says: "The principal gates are seventeen in number. In the old building they were more numerous." The latter fact, coupled with Burckhardt's description of the double and triple division in each gate, may account for Varthema's approximate estimate and might have spared him Burton's remark thereon, who calls it "a prodigious exaggeration."

†"I saw nothing of the kind, though constantly in the Haram at Mecca." (Burton, *Personal Narrative*)

‡The Ka'ba is described here.

§The *kiswa,* or curtain covering the Ka'ba. Burton says that the material now is a mixture of silk and cotton. It is renewed annually at the time of the Hajj.

on the day of Pentecost.* And they say that that balsam is part of the treasures of the Sultan. On each side of the said tower there is a large ring at the corner.† On the twenty-fourth of May all the people begin, before day, to go seven times around the tower, always touching and kissing each corner. And at about ten or twelve paces distant from the tower there is another tower, like one of your chapels, with three or four doors. In the center of this tower there is a very beautiful well, which is seventy fathoms deep, and the water is brackish.‡ At this well there stand six or eight men appointed to draw water for the people. And when the people have gone seven times around the first tower, they go to this well and place themselves with their backs toward the brink of the well, saying: *"Bismillah al-Rahman, al-Rahman. Istaghfir lana,"* which means, In the name of God, the Pitiful, the Compassionate. Pardon us. And those who draw the water throw three bucketsful over each person, from the crown of their heads to their feet, and all bathe, even though their dress be made of silk. And they say in this wise that all their sins remain there after this washing. And they say that the first tower which they walked round was the first house that Abraham built.§ And all having thus bathed, they go by way of the valley to the mountain of which we have before spoken and remain there two days and one night. And when they are all at the foot of the mountain, they make the sacrifice there.**

THE MANNER OF THE SACRIFICES IN MECCA   Every generous mind is the most readily delighted and incited to great deeds by novel events. Wherefore, in

---

*Varthema was probably thinking of Good Friday and the Easter which follows, and connecting in his mind the Muslim sacrifices at Mina with the solemnities of those Christian seasons, when he spoke of "the day of Pentecost."

†"These are the brazen rings which serve to fasten the lower edge of the *kiswa*, or covering." (Burton, *Personal Narrative*)

‡The building which encloses the well (Varthema's "chapel") was erected, according to Burckhardt, A.D. 1072.

§"Muslim mythology affirms that the Ka'ba was constructed in heaven two thousand years before the creation of this world and that it was then adored by the angels, whom the Almighty ordered to perform the *tawaf*, or walk round it. Adam, who was the first true believer, erected the Ka'ba on earth on its present site, which is directly below the spot it occupied in heaven. . . . The sons of Adam repaired the Ka'ba, and after the deluge Ibrahim [Abraham], when he abandoned the idolatry of his forefathers, was ordered by the Almighty to reconstruct it. His son Ishmael, who from his infancy resided with his mother, Hagar, near the site of Mecca, assisted his father, who had come from Syria to obey the commands of Allah." (John Lewis Burckhardt, *Travels in Arabia,* 297)

**Burton justly observes that there is great confusion in this part of Varthema's narrative.

order to satisfy many of this disposition, I will add concisely the custom which is observed in their sacrifices. Every man and woman kills at least two or three, and some four and some six sheep;* so that I really believe that on the first day more than thirty thousand sheep are killed by cutting their throats, facing the east. Each person gives them to the poor for the love of God, for there were about thirty thousand poor people there, who made a very large hole in the earth, and then put in it camels' dung, and thus they made a little fire, and warmed the flesh a little, and then ate it. And truly, it is my opinion, that these poor men came more on account of their hunger than for the sake of the pardon; and as a proof that it was so, we had a great number of cucumbers, which came from Arabia Felix, and we ate them all but the rind, which we afterward threw away outside our tent. And about forty or fifty poor people stood before our tent and made a great scrambling among themselves in order to pick up the rinds, which were full of sand. By this it appeared to us that they came rather to satisfy their hunger than to wash away their sins.† On the second day a *qadi* of their faith, like one of our preachers, ascended to the top of the mountain and made a discourse to all the people, which discourse lasted for about an hour;‡ and he made in their language a sort of lamentation and besought the people that they should weep for their sins. And he said to them in a loud voice: "Oh, Abraham, well-wished for and well-loved of God!" And then he said: "Oh, Isaac [Ishmael], chosen of God, friend of God, beseech God for the people of the Prophet!" and then were heard very great lamentations.

And when he had finished his sermon, the whole caravan rushed back into Mecca with the greatest haste, for at the distance of six miles there were more than twenty thousand Arabs§ who wanted to rob the caravan, and we [the Mamluk guard] arrived for the defense of Mecca.**

But when we had gone halfway, that is, between Mecca and the mountain where the sacrifice is made, we found a certain little wall four fathoms

---

*The numbers cited so far exceed the ritual requirement (one victim per adult pilgrim) that they are suspect. [Ed.]

†Burton remarks that "this well describes the wretched state of the poor Takruri and other Africans, but it attributes to them an unworthy motive." (Burton, *Personal Narrative*, III:7, 8)

‡The Qutba al-Wukuf, or Sermon of the Standing, usually preached by the Qadi of Mecca from Arafat, the orator taking his stand on the stone platform near the top.

§Varthema invariably exaggerates the strength of the attacker. [Ed.]

**On this particular occasion the return of the pilgrims may have been hastened by fear of an apprehended attack from the Bedouin; but the same rush, often attended with fatal re-

high, and at the foot of the said wall a very great quantity of small stones, which stones are thrown there by all the people when they pass that way, for the objects which you shall hear.

They say that when God commanded Abraham that he should go and sacrifice his son, he went before him, and he said to his son that he must follow after him, because it was necessary to fulfill the commandments of God. The son answered him: "I am well pleased to fulfill the commandment of God." And when Isaac* arrived at the above-mentioned little wall, they say that the devil appeared to him in the form of one of his friends and said to him: "My friend Isaac, where art thou going?" He answered him: "I am going to my father, who is waiting for me in such a place." The devil answered him: "Do not go, my son, for thy father will sacrifice thee to God and will put thee to death." And Isaac replied: "Let it be so; if such be the will of God, so let it be." The devil then disappeared, and a little farther on he appeared in the form of another dear friend of Isaac, and said to him the above-mentioned words. They relate that Isaac answered with anger: "Let it be so"; and took a stone and threw it in the devil's face: and for this reason, when the people arrive at the said place, each one throws a stone at the said wall, and then they go to the city.†

THE DOVES OF MECCA We found in the street of the said city fifteen thousand or twenty thousand doves, which they say are of the stock of that dove which spoke to Muhammad in the form of the Holy Spirit,‡ which doves fly about the whole district at their pleasure, that is, in the shops where they sell grain, millet, rice, and other vegetable productions. And the owners of

---

sults, occurs at every Hajj and has given to that part of the ceremonies the name of the Rush from Arafat. The cause is that, in accordance with the example of Muhammad, the prayer shortly after sunset should be said at the mosque of Muzdalifa, about three hours distant.

*Here Varthema is [again] in error. According to Muslim theology it was Ishmael and not Isaac who was ordered to be sacrificed.

†"[V]arthema alludes to the Shaytan al-Kabir, the Great Devil, as the buttress at Mina is called. His account of Satan's appearance is not strictly correct. Most Muslims believe that Abraham threw the stone at the Rajim—the lapidated one; but there are various traditions on the subject." (Burton, *Personal Narrative*)

This custom of maledictory lapidation prevails elsewhere in the East. See also Joshua 8:29; 2 Samuel 18:17.

‡"A Christian version of an obscure Muslim legend about a white dove alighting on the Prophet's shoulder, and appearing to whisper in his ear whilst he was addressing a congregation." (Burton, *Personal Narrative*)

the said articles are not at liberty to kill them or catch them. And if anyone were to strike any of those doves, they would fear that the country would be ruined. And you must know that they cause very great expense within the temple.

CONCERNING THE UNICORNS IN THE TEMPLE OF MECCA In another part of the said temple is an enclosed place in which there are two live unicorns,* and these are shown as very remarkable objects, which they certainly are. I will tell you how they are made. The elder is formed like a colt of thirty months old, and he has a horn in the forehead, which horn is about three *braccia* in length. The other unicorn is like a colt of one year old, and he has a horn of about four *palmi* long.† The color of the animal resembles that of a dark bay horse, and his head resembles that of a stag; his neck is not very long, and he has some thin and short hair which hangs on one side; his legs are slender and lean like those of a goat; the foot is a little cloven in the fore part, and long and goatlike, and there are some hairs on the hind part of the legs. Truly this monster must be a very fierce and solitary animal. These two animals were presented to the Sultan of Mecca as the finest things that could be found in the world at the present day, and as the richest treasure ever sent by a king of Ethiopia, that is, by a Moorish king. He made this present in order to secure an alliance with the Sultan of Mecca.

SOME OCCURRENCES BETWEEN MECCA AND JIDDA I must here show how the human intellect manifests itself under certain circumstances, insofar as it became necessary for me to exercise it in order to escape from the caravan of Mecca. Having gone to make some purchases for my captain, I was recognized by a Moor who looked me in the face and said to me: "*Anta min ain?*" that is, "Where are you from?" I answered: "I am a Moor." He replied: "*Anta kadh-dhab,*" that is, "You are not telling the truth." I said to him: "*Wa-ras en-Nabi ana Muslim,*" that is, "By the head of Muhammad, I am a Muslim." He answered: "*Taal ila beitana,*" that is, "Come to my house"; and I went with him. When I had arrived at his house, he spoke to me in Italian and told me where I had come from and that he knew that I was not a Moor,

---

*Burton remarks that these animals "might possibly have been African antelopes, which a *lusus naturae* had deprived of their second horn," adding, "but the suspicion of fable remains."

†Varthema's scale of measurements was probably Venetian. The modern *braccia* at Venice varies from 25.08 to 26.87 inches. The *palmo* is 3.937 inches.

and he told me that he had been in Genoa and in Venice and gave me proofs of it. When I heard this, I told him that I was a Roman and that I had become a Mamluk at Cairo. When he heard this, he was much pleased and treated me with very great honor. As it was my intention to proceed further, I began to say to him if this was the city of Mecca which was so renowned through all the world, where were the jewels and spices, and where were all the various kinds of merchandise which it was reported were brought there. I asked him this only that he might tell me why they had not arrived as usual, and in order not to ask him if the king of Portugal was the cause, he being Lord of the Atlantic and of the Persian and Arabian Gulfs. Then he began to tell me by degrees why the said articles had not come as they were accustomed to do. And when he told me that the king of Portugal was the cause, I pretended to be much grieved, and spoke great ill of the said king, merely that he might not think that I was pleased that the Christians should make such a journey.* When he saw that I displayed hostility to the Christians, he showed me yet greater honour, and told me everything point by point.

And when I was well informed, I said to him: "O, my friend, I beg you to tell me some mode or way by which I may escape from the caravan, because my intention is to go to find those beings who are hostile to the Christians; for I assure you that, if they knew what I am capable of, they would send to find me even to Mecca." He answered me: "By the faith of our prophet what can you do?" I answered him that I was the most skilful maker of large mortars in the world. Hearing this he said: "Muhammad be ever praised, who has sent us such a man to serve the Moors and God." So he concealed me in his house with his wife. And he begged me that I would induce our captain to drive out from Mecca fifteen camels laden with spices, and this he did in order not to pay thirty *seraphim*† to the Sultan for the toll. I replied that if he would save me in this house, I would enable him to carry off a hundred camels if he had so many, for the Mamluks have this privilege. And when he heard this, he was much pleased. Afterward, he instructed me in the manner in which I should conduct myself and directed me to a king who is in the parts of India Major and who is called the King of Deccan. When the time comes, we will speak of that king.

The day before the caravan set out, he concealed me in his house in a secret place. In the morning, two hours before day, there went through the

---

*The Portuguese had seized seven Muslim ships between India and the Persian Gulf, and massacred their crews, prior to Varthema's visit to Mecca.

†*seraphim:* a coin of some value in sixteenth-century Mecca.

city a great quantity of instruments and trumpets, sounding according to their custom, and making proclamation that all the Mamluks, under pain of death, should mount their horses and commence their journey toward Syria. Whereupon, my heart was seized with a great perturbation when I heard this proclamation, and I earnestly recommended myself with tears to the wife of the said merchant, and besought God that he would save me from such violence.

On Tuesday morning the said caravan departed, and the merchant left me in his house with his wife; and he went with the caravan and told his wife that on the following Friday she must send me away in company with the caravan of India, which was going to Jidda, which is a port of Mecca, forty miles distant. I cannot express the kindness I received from this lady, and especially from her niece of fifteen years old, they promising me that if I would remain there, they would make me rich. But I declined all their offers on account of the present danger. When Friday came, I set out with the caravan at noon, to the no small regret of the said ladies, who made great lamentations, and at midnight we arrived at a certain city of Arabia, and remained there all night and until noon of the following day. On Saturday we departed and traveled until midnight, when we entered into the said port of the city of Jidda.

5

A Pilgrim with No Name
Italy
c. 1575

※※※

Some moved by devotion, and some for traffic's sake, and some to pass away the time.

—Anonymous

Sometime around 1575, a highly observant European attached himself to the Cairo-Sinai-Mecca caravan. His report of the journey runs to thirty-five pages in Elizabethan English. Composed in the third person, it is usually classed as a geographic essay. It does not read like geography. The author shows no interest in measuring distances between oases, and his treatment of social detail and human behavior is too vivid. The account appears in Richard Hakluyt's The Principal Navigations, Voyages, Traffiques, and Discoveries of the English Nation *(1599), an extensive collection of reports by Tudor explorers. It appears to be a translation from Italian.*

Varthema en route to Mecca seems half-informed compared with this traveler. Before the caravan gets under way, we have a clear portrait of international Alexandria, where Venetians, Frenchmen, Portuguese, and Genoese outnumber Arabs and live at peace in their own gated quarter. In Cairo, the pyramids lead to talk of grave robbers, medicines made of mummy dust, and a view of the long-neglected Sphinx, with just its head and neck above the sand. Farther upriver, we come to mammoth statues on a site that sounds very much like Abu Simbel, although Abu Simbel will not be "discovered" for two more centuries.*

As the caravan sets out, the narration becomes participatory, placing us front and center on the Hajj. By now, the Ottoman Sultan enthroned in Istanbul had wrested control of the Mamluk caravan and was busy expanding it into the foremost engine of travel and trade in the region. Its dimensions in 1575 were

---

*By John Lewis Burckhart, excerpts of whose 1814 Hajj account form the last selection in this section.

those of a large metropolis on the move. The narration surveys this machine from every angle. The order of march and pace of travel are clearly established. Levels of leadership are described, the makeup of the transient population, the tax-free status of its goods. As the train departs Cairo for Suez, it is thronged by thousands of well-wishers throwing flowers. At its head rides the camel-mounted ark, or mahmal, *a Hajj symbol of sovereignty since the thirteenth century. Behind rides the* kiswa, *the Ka'ba's woven cover that must be annually renewed. Steeped in tradition, depicted at length, the caravan has all the complexity of a trade fair crossed with a military campaign. Great stores of goods are packed off to sell in Mecca during this season, and a substantial mounted guard rides along to repel attacks by Bedouin raiders. A few pages later, we find the caravan's Amir bribing clan leaders for safe passage. We also watch the governor of Mecca in his tent, acknowledging the authority of Cairo. We see uniforms, equipment, the colors of the guard.*

The Hajj rites receive close treatment, too. Readers who have had difficulty grasping their shape and sequence until now will see them more clearly after reading this account. It contains a good description of the mosque, with its outermost walls half a mile long on all sides, and each of the ritual sites is well presented. The procession from Mecca to Arafat receives special care. We see each stage of its complicated passage through Mina Valley. The depiction of the Arafat vigil, the precise arrangement of the caravans, the message of the sermon, even the mood and movement of the crowd, are documented. We hear legends, too, of a more completely Muslim content than Varthema's. The stories related here, of the Black Stone and Mount Mercy, are the same ones pilgrims hear today. The flavor and feel of pilgrimage run through this record. It is the focused work of an observer who missed nothing, who saw the Hajj whole and makes his readers see it, too.

from A Description of the Yearly Voyage or Pilgrimage of the Muslims, Turks, and Moors unto Arabia

OF THE PREPARATION OF THE CARAVAN TO GO TO MECCA The Muslims observe a kind of Lent continuing one whole moon and being a movable ceremony which sometimes falls high, sometimes low in the year. It is called

Ramadan, and their feast is called Seker Bayrami.* During this time of Lent all those who intend to go to Mecca resort to Cairo; twenty days after the feast the caravan is ready to depart on the voyage. Then thither come a great multitude of people from Asia, Greece, and Barbary to go on this voyage, some moved by devotion, and some for traffic's sake, and some to pass away the time.

Now [a] few days after the feast they who go on the voyage depart out of the city two leagues to a place called Birca, where they expect the Captain of the caravan. This place has a great pond caused by the inundation of [the] Nile, and so made that the camels and other beasts may drink therein. . . . Of mules, camels, and dromedaries there are at least forty thousand, and the people who follow the caravan every year are about fifty thousand, [a] few more or less, according to the times. Moreover, every three years they appoint a new Captain, called the Amir al-Hajj, to whom the Pasha gives every voyage eighteen purses containing each of them 625 ducats of gold . . . for the [benefit] of the caravan and also to distribute as alms to the needful pilgrims.

This Captain, besides other serving men who follow him, has four *chausi* [officers] to serve him. Likewise he has with him for the security of the caravan four hundred soldiers: two hundred *spachi* or cavalry mounted on dromedaries and two hundred janissaries riding camels. The *chausi* and the *spachi* are at the charge of the Captain, but the janissaries not so, for their provision is made them from Cairo. The *spachi* wear caps or bonnets like the caps of sergeants, but the janissaries [dress] after another sort, with a lap falling down behind like a French hood, and having before a great piece of wrought silver on their heads. The charge of these is to cause the caravan to march in good array when need requires; they are not at the commandment of any but the Captain of the caravan. Moreover, the Captain has for his guide eight pilots, whose office is always stable and firm from year to year, and these go before, guiding the caravan and showing the way, being well experienced in the place. In the night they govern them as the mariners [do], by the stars. These also . . . send before [the caravan] four or five men carrying pieces of dry wood which give light, so that they do not stray. And if at any time through their ill hap [the caravan should] wander astray out of the way, they are cast down and beaten with many bastinadoes on the soles of their feet, to serve them as a perpetual remembrance.

The Captain of the caravan has his lieutenant accompanied continually by fifteen *spachi*. He has the charge to set the caravan in order and to

* Seker Bayrami: Turkish term for the feast that ends the month of Ramadan; in Arabic, Id al-Fitr. [Ed.]

cause them to depart on their journey when need requires. The caravan carries with it six pieces of ordnance drawn by twelve camels, which serve to terrify the Arabians and also to make triumph at Mecca and other places. The merchants which follow the caravan . . . carry cloth of silk, some coral, some tin, others wheat, rice, and all sorts of grain. Some sell by the way, some at Mecca, so that everyone brings something to gain by, because merchandize that goes by land pays no custom, but that which goes by sea is bound to pay 10 percent.

THE BEGINNING OF THE VOYAGE The Captain and all his retinue and officers resort to the castle of Cairo [to stand] before the Pasha, who gives to every man a garment. That of the Captain is wrought with gold and the others are served according to their degree. Moreover, he delivers to them the Kiswa al-Nabi, which signifies in the Arabian tongue the Garment of the Prophet. This vestment is of silk, wrought in the midst with letters of gold which read, *La ilaha il-Allah, Muhammad al-Rasu'allah,* that is to say, "There are no gods but God, and his ambassador is Muhammad." This garment is made to cover from top to bottom a little house in Mecca standing in the midst of the mosque, which they say was built by Abraham or by his son Ishmael. After this, he delivers to him a gate made for the House of Abraham wrought all with fine gold, of excellent workmanship, a thing of great value. Besides, he delivers to him a covering of green velvet made in [the] manner of a pyramid, about nine palms high and artificially wrought with most fine gold. This is to cover the tomb of their Prophet within Medina, which is built [somewhat] in the shape of a pyramid. Besides that covering there are brought many others of gold and silk, to ornament the tomb.

Which things consigned, the Pasha does not depart his place, but the Captain of the caravan takes his leave with his officers and soldiers and departs accompanied with all the people of Cairo in an orderly procession, with singing, shouting, and a thousand other ceremonies too long to recite.

From the [Pasha's] castle they go to a gate of Cairo called Bab al-Nasir, beyond which stands a mosque, and there they lay up the vestments very well kept and guarded. . . . The camels which bring the vestments are all adorned with cloth of gold, with many little bells, and passing along the street, you may see the multitude casting upon the vestments thousands of beautiful flowers of diverse colours and sweet water. Others bring towels and fine cloth and touch the vestments, which ever after they keep as relics with great reverence.

After having left the vestments in the mosque, they return again into the city, where they remain for twenty days. Then the Captain departs again with his company and, taking the vestments out of the mosque, carries them to Birca. Here, having pitched his tent with the standard of the Pasha over the gate, and the other principal tents standing about his, he stays some ten days, but no more. In this time all those resort there that mean to follow the caravan in this voyage to Mecca. Here you see certain women who intend to go, accompanied with their parents and friends, mounted upon camels, adorned with many trifles, tassels, and knots, that in beholding them a man cannot refrain from smiling. The last night before their departure they make great feasting and triumph within the caravan, with [fireworks displays called] castles and other infinite devises of fireworks. The janissaries all this time stand round about the tent of the Captain with such shouting and joy that on every side the earth resounds. On this night they discharge all their ordnance from four to six times. At daybreak, upon the sound of a trumpet, they march forward on their way.

WHAT TIME THE CARAVAN TRAVELS AND WHEN IT RESTS   From Cairo to Mecca they make forty days' journey or thereabouts, and the days are long ones. For the custom of the caravan is to travel much and rest little. Ordinarily they journey in this manner: They travel from two o'clock in the morning until the sun rises. Then having rested until noon, they set forward and so continue until night. Then they rest again until two o'clock. They observe this order until the end of the voyage, never changing it, except in some places where for respect of water they rest sometimes a day and a half to refresh themselves. Otherwise both man and beast would die.

IN WHAT ORDER THE CARAVAN TRAVELS   The manner and order which the caravan observes in marching is this. It goes divided into three parts—the forward, the main battle, and the rearward.

In the forward go the eight pilots before with a *chaus,* who has four knaves. Each knave carries the sinew of a bull, [so that] if occasion requires, the bastinado may be given to [those who deserve it]. . . . This *chaus* is the captain of the forward. He commands the lights carried before when they travel in the night. Also there go in the forward six *santones* [clergymen] with red turbans upon their heads, who eat and ride at the cost of the caravan Captain. When the caravan arrives at a good lodging, [the moment] they have sighted the place, they cry with a loud voice, saying "Good news, good news! We are near our destination!" For this news the chiefs of the company bestow benevolence upon them. In this forward goes very near the third part of the people of the caravan, behind whom [come] twenty five *spachi* armed with swords, bows, and arrows to defend them from thieves.

Next to the forward, within a quarter of a mile, follows the main battle. Before it are drawn the six pieces of ordnance with their gunners and fifteen *spachi* archers. Next comes the chief physician, who is an old man of authority with many medicines, ointments, salves, and other refreshments for the sick. He also has camels with him for the sick to ride on, when they have no horse or beast. Beside him goes one camel alone, the fairest that can be found: for with great industry is sought the greatest and fairest which may be found within the dominions of the Pasha. This camel also is decked with cloth of gold and silk and carries a chest [*mahmal*] . . . made in likeness of the ark of the Old Testament, but without gold or any other thing of cost. Within this chest is the Quran all written with great letters of gold, bound between two tablets of massy gold. The chest during their voyage is covered with silk, but at their entering into Mecca it is all covered with cloth of gold and adorned with jewels and the like, as at the entrance into Medina. The camel which carries the chest is compassed about with many Arabian singers and musicians, always singing and playing upon instruments. After this follow fifteen other very fair camels, every one carrying one of the vestments and covered from top to toe in silk. Behind go twenty more camels, which carry the money, apparel, and provision of the Captain. After these follows the royal standard of the Pasha, accompanied continually with the musicians of the Captain, twenty-five *spachi* archers, and a *chaus*. About these marvellous things go all the people and camels which follow the caravan.

Behind these less than a mile follow the rearward, whereof the greater part are pilgrims. This is because, while the merchants seek always to be in the forward for the security of their goods, the pilgrims, who have little to lose, care not though they come behind. Behind them always go twenty-five well-armed *spachi* with a *chaus* as captain, and forty Arabian archers to guard the rear.

Because the caravan always goes along the Red Sea bank, which in going forth they have on their right hand, the two hundred janissaries divided into three companies go upon their left hand well armed and mounted upon camels bound one to another. For upon that side is all the danger of thieves, and on the other no danger at all. Meanwhile the Captain of the caravan is always going among his people, sometimes on the one side and sometimes on the other, never keeping any firm place. He is continually accompanied with a *chaus* and twenty-five *spachi,* armed and mounted upon dromedaries, and eight musicians with viols in their hands, which cease not sounding till the Captain take his rest. They attend upon him until such time as he enters his pavilion, and then ordering all his attendants and followers to depart, they go each man to their lodging.

OF NOTABLE THINGS SEEN ON THIS VOYAGE . . . It is needful and a usual thing that the Captain put his hand to his purse in these places and bestow presents, garments, and turbans upon certain of the chiefs of the Arabians, to the end they may give him and his caravan free passage and promise that their followers likewise shall do no damage to the caravan . . . and [that] by word of mouth, if the caravan be robbed, they will make restitution of such things as are stolen. Notwithstanding the caravan is oftentimes damnified by them, and those who are robbed receive no other restitution at the Arabians' hands than the sight of their heels as they fly into places where it is impossible to find them.

At length the caravan comes to a place called Jehbir, which is the beginning and border of the state and realm of the sharifian king of Mecca. At their approach the Governor of the land comes out with all his people to receive the caravan, with such shouting and triumph as is impossible to express. They stay one whole day. This place abounds with fresh and clear waters, with streams falling down from the high mountains. Moreover, there are great stores of dates in this place, and meat in great store and very cheap, especially sheep, which they sacrifice.

Rested and refreshed, the caravan departs on its way next day. The first place they arrive worthy of mention is called Bedrihonem, where those little shrubs grow from which balm issues. . . . Arriving here at sunrise, all the pilgrims wash themselves from top to toe, men as well as women. Then all the men who are able to do so leave off their apparel, each one putting on a cloth about their privates and another white cloth upon their shoulders. These are thought to merit more than the others, but those who cannot manage it make a vow to sacrifice a ram. . . .

And so the caravan, marching, comes within two miles of Mecca, where they rest that night. In the morning at the break of day, with all pomp possible, they set forward toward Mecca. Drawing near, the Sharif issues forth from the city with his guard, accompanied with an infinite number of people, shouting and making a great triumph. In a fair field a bow shot outside the city, a great multitude of tents are pitched. In the midst stands the pavilion of the Captain. After meeting with the Sharif, and after salutations on both sides, they light from their horses and enter into the pavilion, where the King of Mecca deprives himself of all authority and power, committing it to the Captain, giving him full license and authority to command, govern, and minister justice during his abode in Mecca with his company. On the other side, the Captain, to requite the King's liberality towards him, gives him a garment of cloth and gold of great value, with certain jewels and other things. Then, sitting down together upon carpets and hides, they eat together and, rising thence with certain of the chiefs, and taking with them the garment and the gate mentioned before, they go directly to the mosque, attended on by but a few.

Inside, they order the old [covering] to be pulled down and put the new coverture upon the House of Abraham. The old vestment goes to the eunuchs who serve in the mosque, who after sell it to the pilgrims at four or five *seraphim* per pike's length. Happy does the man think himself who can acquire ever so little a piece of it, to conserve ever after as a most holy relic. They say that by putting the [cloth] under the head of a man at the hour of his death, all his sins are forgiven through its virtue. Also they take away the old door, setting in its place the new door. The old one by custom they give to the Sharif. After having made their prayers with certain ordinary and wonted ceremonies, the Sharif remains in the city, and the Captain of the pilgrimage returns to his pavilion.

OF THE SHARIF, THE KING OF MECCA The Sharif is descended of the Prophet Muhammad by Fatima, daughter of that good Prophet, and Ali, her husband, the Prophet's son-in-law. . . . To the eldest son the realm comes by succession. This realm has of royal revenues every year half a million of gold, or a little more. All who are of the Prophet's kindred, or descended of that blood (which are almost innumerable), are called sharifs, that is to say, lords. These all go clothed in green, or at the least have their turban green, to be known from the others. Neither is it permitted that any of those Christians who dwell or traffic in their country go clothed in green, neither may they have anything of green about them. For they say it is not lawful for unbelievers to wear that color, wherein that great friend and Prophet of God, Muhammad, was wont to be apparelled.

OF THE CITY OF MECCA The city of Mecca in the Arabian town is called Macca. . . . It is environed about with exceeding high and barren mountains, and in the plain between the mountains and the city are many pleasant gardens where grows a great abundance of figs, grapes, apples, and melons. There is also great abundance of good water and meat, but not of bread. This city has no walls about it and contains in circuit five miles. The houses are very handsome and commodious, and are built like the houses of Italy. The palace of the Sharif is sumptuous and gorgeously adorned. . . .

In the midst of the city is the great mosque, with the House of Abraham standing in the very midst thereof. The mosque was built in the time when their Prophet lived. It is four square and so great [now] that it contains two miles in circuit, that is to say, half a mile on each side. It is made in the manner of a cloister. In the midst, separate from the rest, is the House of Abraham. The galleries round about are in the manner of four streets, and the partitions which divide the one street from the other are pillars, some of marble and others of lime and stone. The famous and sumptuous mosque has ninety-nine gates and five steeples, from whence the [muezzins] call the people to the mosque.

OF THE HOUSE OF ABRAHAM The House of Abraham is also four square and made of speckled stone, twenty paces high and forty paces in circuit. And upon one side of this house within the wall there is a stone, a span long and half a span broad, which they say fell down from heaven before this house was built, and at which a voice was heard saying that wherever the stone fell, there should be built the House of God, wherein God will hear sinners. Moreover, they say that when this stone fell from heaven, it was not black as now, but as white as the whitest snow, but because it has so often been kissed by sinners it is therewith become black. All the pilgrims are bound to kiss this stone. . . .

The entrance into the House is very small, made in the manner of a window, and as high from the ground as a man can reach, so that it is difficult to enter. . . . There stand at the entrance two pillars of marble, one on each side. In the midst there are three [pillars] of aloeswood, not very thick, and covered with tiles of India of one thousand colours, which serve to underprop the terrazzo. It is so dark [inside] that they can hardly see within for want of light. Outside the gate five paces is the Well of Zamzam, the blessed well that the angel of the Lord showed to Hagar when she went seeking water for her son, Ishmael, to drink.

OF THE CEREMONIES OF THE PILGRIMS In the beginning we said how the Muslims have two feasts in the year. The one they call Pascha di Ramadan [Id al-Fitr], that is to say, the Feast of Fasting. . . . The other is called the Feast of the Ram [Id al-Adha], wherein all who are able are bound to sacrifice a ram, and this they [also] call Bine Bayram, that is, the Great Feast. Just as the caravan departs from Cairo thirty days after the Little Feast, so likewise they come hither five or six days before the Great Feast, so that the pilgrims may have time before the feast to finish their rites and ceremonies, which are these.

Departing from the caravan, and being guided by such as are experienced in the way, they go to the city twenty or thirty in a company, walking through a street which ascends little by little until they come to a certain gate whereupon is written on each side in marble stone, BAB AL-SALAAM, the

Gate of Peace. From this place the interior of the Great Mosque is clearly visible. It surrounds the House of Abraham, which they reverently salute twice, saying, "Peace to thee, ambassador of God." Proceeding on their way, they find an arch upon their right hand, whereon they ascend five steps, on which is a great void place made of stone: [before them] after descending another five steps and proceeding the space of a flightshot, they find another arch like the first, and this way from the one arch to the other they go and come seven times, saying always some of their prayers, which they say the afflicted Hagar said while she sought and found not water for her son, Ishmael. After this ceremony,* the pilgrims enter into the mosque and, drawing near to the House of Abraham, they go round about it seven times, always saying "This is the House of God, and of his servant Abraham." This done, they go to kiss the Black Stone mentioned above. After, they go to the Well of Zamzam and, in their apparel as they be, they wash themselves from head to foot, saying, "Pardon, Lord, pardon, Lord" . . . and in this wise washed and watered, everyone returns to his place of abode. These ceremonies everyone is bound to do once at least. But those who have a mind to outstrip the others, and to go into Paradise before the rest, do the same once a day while the caravan remains there.

WHAT THE CARAVAN DOES AFTER HAVING RESTED AT MECCA [After five days in Mecca], the night before the evening of their feast, the Captain with all his company sets forth towards the Mountain of Pardons, which they call Mount Arafat. This mountain is distant from Mecca fifteen miles. In the mid way there is a place called Mina, the Haven, and [a] little way from there are four great milestones, of which we will speak hereafter. Now first touching the Mountain of Pardons, which rather should be called a little hill: it is low, little, delightful, and pleasant, containing in circuit two miles and surrounded with the goodliest plain that ever with man's eyes could be seen. The plain likewise is compassed with exceedingly high mountains. This is one of the goodliest situations in the world. It seems Nature has shown all her cunning there, in making the place under the Mountain of Pardons so broad and pleasant.

On the side towards Mecca there are many pipes of water, clear, fair, and fresh, and above all most wholesome, falling down into tanks made for the purpose, where the people refresh and wash themselves and water their animals. The Muslims say that when Adam and Eve were cast out of Para-

*The order of the *sa'y* and *tawaf* rites are reversed here, probably by an uninformed copyist or translator. [Ed.]

dise by the angel of the Lord, they came to inhabit this little Mountain of Pardons. They had lost one another, they say, and were separated for forty years, but in the end they met at this place with great joy and gladness. They built a little house on the top of this mountain, which today they call the House of Adam.

THE OTHER CARAVANS The same day that the caravan of Cairo comes to this place, two [other] caravans come here also, one of Damascus, the other of Arabia. In addition, all the inhabitants for ten days' journey round about come, too, so that at one time there may be seen about two hundred thousand people and more than three hundred thousand animals. With all this company meeting together in this place the night before the feast, the three hosts cast themselves into a triangle, setting the mountain in the midst of them. All that night there is nothing to be heard or seen but gunshot and fireworks of sundry sorts, with such singing, sounding, shouting, hallooing, rumours, feasting, and triumphing that it is wonderful.

After this, on the day of the feast, they are all at rest and silence. They attend on no other thing than to offer oblations and prayers to God. In the evening, all those who have horses mount them and approach as near to the mountain as they can. Those who have no horses do the best they can on foot, giving the Captain of the Cairo caravan the chief place, the second to the Captain of Damascus, and the third to the Captain of Arabia. When all have approached, there comes a squire, one of the *santones,* mounted on a well-furnished camel. At the side of the mountain he ascends five steps into a pulpit for that purpose and makes a short sermon. He shows them how many and great are the benefits God has given the Muslim people, through the work of his beloved friend and Prophet Muhammad, who delivered them from the servitude of sin and idolatry they were drowning in before; and how he gave them the House of Abraham, where they could be heard, and the Mountain of Pardons, where they might obtain grace and remission from sins; adding that merciful God, who gives liberally all good things, commanded his secretary Abraham to build him a house in Mecca, where his successors might make their prayers to Him and be heard. At that time all the mountains in the world came together in this place, with enough stones to create it, except that little and low hill which, because of its poverty, could not discharge the debt. For this it became sorrowful, weeping beyond all measure for thirty years. And in the end eternal God had pity and compassion on the poor mountain, and said to it: "Weep no more, my daughter, for your bitter complaints have reached my ear; take comfort, for all those that shall go to visit the house of my friend Abraham will not be absolved from their sins, unless they first come to do you reverence and to keep their holiest feast in this place. This I have commanded to my people by the mouth of my friend and Prophet Muhammad." Then the preacher exhorts everyone to the love of God, to prayer, and to almsgiving.

The sermon is done at sunset. Then the pilgrims make three prayers—the first for the Sharif, the second for the Sultan and his host, and the third for the people, to which all with one voice cry, "Be it so, Lord. Be it so." Then having had the . . . [preacher's] blessing and saluted the Mountain of Pardons, they return to Mina the way they came. At the end of the plain stand the four milestones mentioned before, two on each side of the way, through which they say it is needful that everyone pass. And those who pass outside them are said to lose all the merit that in their pilgrimage they had earned. From the Mountain of Pardons to the milestones none dare look back, for fear the sins which he has left in the mountains return to him again.

Past the milestones everyone dismounts, seeking in this sandy field fifty or sixty little stones, which they gather and bind in a handkerchief and carry to Mina. There they stay five days, and during that time there is a fair, free of all customs charges. At Mina are three pillars, not together, but set in diverse places where, it is said, were the three apparitions which the devil made unto Abraham, Hagar, and Ishmael, their son. (Amongst the Muslims they make no mention of Isaac, as if he had never been born.) . . . The pilgrims during their abode here go to visit these three pillars, throwing the little stones which before they gathered, while they repeat the same words which they say that Ishmael addressed to the devil when he withstood him. . . . After five days, the Captain rises with all the caravan and returns to Mecca, where they remain another five days.

6

Joseph Pitts
England
ca. 1685

One day in the summer of 1678, when piracy on the high seas was as common as carjackings in Florida today, an Algerian rowing galley accosted an English fishing boat off the Spanish coast, captured its crew, and sank the vessel. Among those taken prisoner was a fifteen-year-old hand named Joseph Pitts.

A Presbyterian cabin boy without much education, Pitts was delivered to Algiers and sold into slavery. Over the next fifteen years, he served three owners. The first was merely cruel. The second, perverse, forced Pitts to change religions. The third, benign, took him to Mecca and set him free. Returning to Exeter still in command of his English, Pitts produced an account of this fifteen-year adventure. It is one of English literature's more curious travelogues: on the one hand, an exotic yarn of capture and escape on the Barbary Coast; on the other, an earnest Christian's effort to disavow his conversion to Islam. It is the ingenuous account of a common man whom fate made an expert witness. The longest section, omitted here, consists of an accurate guide to the fundamentals of Muslim religious practice. Other chapters provide a vivid window on the complex world of Mediterranean piracy and slavery. Inserted into all this, a tale within the tale, is an oddly sympathetic account of an English sailor's pilgrimage to Mecca.

These excerpts begin by sketching Pitt's life as a slave in Algiers, continue with passages depicting his itinerary to Mecca, and contain a few sections on the city and on the Hajj. It should be pointed out that Pitts's Mecca of the 1680s was either greatly reduced in style and comfort as compared wth the city in previous reports, or he was judging it by the standards of contemporary London. He remained in the city for four months and his account of it is credible and detailed. The selections conclude with a detailed description of his return to Egypt with the official Cairo caravan.

It will come as no surprise that Pitt's book is studded throughout with descriptions of enslavement. Slavery in his day was a booming, lucrative, and brutal business in which every Mediterranean culture engaged. To work its vast plantations in the New World, Portugal alone had extracted a million and a half slaves by 1650 from just one of its colonies, the present-day Angola. The English were equally active in the trade, from the Gold Coast to Maryland to Jamaica. The Spanish, French, and Dutch played large roles, too, in the Caribbean and South America. Superficially, all slavery looks alike. Pitts's description of the market in Algiers could almost stand for Norfolk, Virginia's. Yet the workings of the two systems were quite different. For one thing, slaves in Algeria were often European, while their owners, of course, were African. Turks, Arabs, Berbers, Christians, and Jews could all own slaves in Algiers, and many did so. Households, farmlands, palaces, public shops, even the local army and navy, depended on them. Moreover, the pirate ships that brought fresh captives into port were often run by European captains who, in exchange for a market and safe harbor, paid one eighth of their profits to the Dey, the Ottoman governor. The galley that captured Joseph Pitts, for instance, had a Dutch captain, an English mate, and thirty or forty oarsmen, mostly slaves. Pitts refers to the captain as a renegado.

The status of a slave in Muslim Algiers was radically different from that of a slave in the European system, too. The unskilled poor were treated worst, of course, since a slave's value rested on two things: potential for ransom and earning power. Ransom applied to slaves with family wealth, connections at home, or the skills to earn an income in Algiers. It was an occasional source of ready cash for owners. Because it put an end to further profits, however, slaves were more often hired out to work—in a shop, in a factory, in the military, or on a ship. With these low-paying jobs, a slave's earnings accrued to his "patroon." Pitts's first owner signed him on to a pirate ship, then collected his wages.

Slaves with skills—leatherworkers, ironmongers, and so on—were commonly set up in public shops. Their owners encouraged them to ply their trades, and the relationship became one of simple business. Many a Spanish blacksmith or an Italian cabinetmaker earned his freedom this way, paying part of his profits to his patron and saving another portion for his ransom. A skilled slave was worth too much to mistreat or hem in. A literate one with a head for numbers might well be sent to work at the Dey's palace, again to the mutual profit of slave and owner. Such a berth meant a life of ease and comfort, but it also reduced a slave's chances of release. Under his beneficent third owner, Pitts quit excelling in a Turkish school for fear that too much success might jeopardize his future liberty. On the one hand, he tells us, he "was in a much fairer way for honor and preferment in Algiers than I could expect ever to have been in England." On the other, he wanted his freedom.

Like the picaresque hero in a Henry Fielding novel, Pitts experienced a decade of captivity in Algiers that ran the gamut of mistreatment. His first owner *merely misused and occasionally whipped him. His second, a brute with a flair for melodrama, by personally beating Pitts most of one night, forced him with a stick to "embrace" Islam. Pitts makes it clear that this treatment was a rarity in Algiers, that the man's behavior was socially aberrant and personally compulsive.* It is no surprise to learn that a few months later the same man was beheaded in a failed attempt to overthrow the Dey. At this point in the story, Pitts's third owner, an elderly bachelor, turns up like an unexpected trump card and all but adopts him. He apparently planned to leave Pitts all his money and trusted him completely. He also carried him to Mecca for the Hajj.*

Pitts was devoutly Christian. His forced conversion filled him with anxiety and remorse and redoubled his desire to escape. Offered liberty on returning to Algiers, he took it, but slipping the bonds of Ottoman society was not simple. It took several more years of religious masquerading, a stint in the Turkish army, and clandestine assistance from two British consuls before Pitts managed to escape. Near the end, he wrestled with temptation: to take the easier route, to return to Algiers, collect his eight months' army pay and, perhaps in time, the estate of his ex-master. He describes this period of uncertainty as "a labyrinth of sorrows." A month later he finally took the leap, boarded a French ship at Smyrna, and returned to England, where he remained until his death, in the 1730s.

Pitts was the first (and for many years the only) Englishman to visit Mecca and write about it. He was not, however, the only European slave to make the journey. There are earlier records of similar adventures: an anonymous report by a Portuguese slave, written in code in the margins of an Arabic book in the Vatican Library, dated 1565; a 1612 account by a German youth named Hans Wild, captured by Turks in Hungary and taken on the pilgrimage as a servant. A few years later we hear from Marco de Lombardo, a Venetian boy captured at sea and sold into slavery in Egypt, then (like Pitts) appointed as an escort on the Hajj. All returned home with eyewitness accounts of the Muslim holy cities. These few surviving records give reason to assume that many more European captives performed the Hajj but wrote nothing about it or that their records have been lost. How many more? In Pitts's lifetime, Mecca was the least accessible spot on earth for a Western Christian. What was the ratio of authors to travelers there—one in a hundred, one in a thousand? What is the ratio of saved to lost accounts?

---

*Cervantes testified that he was not beaten once in his five years of captivity in Algiers. James Cathcart, an Irishman enslaved there a century after Pitts, mentions one execution of a Christian in ten years.

Pitts's book is by far the best informed of these curious memoirs. For the work of a man coerced into apostasy, it is amazingly evenhanded. His commitment to accurate reporting is so strong that he frequently neglects to express a grudge against the society that wronged him. An antipapist and a Puritan, he approved Islam for its lack of a priesthood. He makes no secret of his disbelief in non-Christian dogma, but he seems more determined to get Islam right than to knock it. This passion for factual information is a hallmark of his age, a period of expanding trade, when Europe was seized with a need to know the world it so profitably exploited, and a time of Islamic expansion, too, when the Ottoman Empire was literally at the gates of Western Europe.

European maritime expansion quickened an interest in all things foreign, and Islam, the West's old nemesis and neighbor, gained a lion's share of the attention during this period. With the spread of the printing press and the waning of the Spanish Inquisition, old works from Muslim Spain began to resurface. In 1542, a Latin translation of the Quran, one that Robert of Ketton had made in Toledo in 1143, appeared in Basel, with a Protestant preface by Martin Luther. In England, at Oxford and Cambridge, other old translations, dusted off, became the foundation stones of Oriental studies. By the time of Pitts's birth, there were twice as many European publications on Muslims as on all the tribes of Africa and the Americas combined. Even an unschooled author such as Pitts could read up enough on his subject to criticize, in footnotes, certain acknowledged authorities on Islam: "And since I came home, I have seen many books, some of which have treated of Algiers in particular, and others of the Muslim religion in general, which are stuffed with very great mistakes."

In 1704, when it appeared, his True and Faithful Account of the Religion and Manners of the Mahometans *was received well enough to go into several editions, one of them pirated. In the preface, Pitts apologizes for his unpolished prose and scholarship, then bases his right to speak on experience. "I question," he writes, "whether there be a man now in England who has ever been at Mecca." Of his book, he says, "I am sensible that I have not the abilities which are required in a person that writes such a history: Only I beg leave to say plainly, I have the most valuable qualification of the historian on my side, i.e., Truth."*

Pitts wrote a layman's version of plain-style English prose that nonetheless succeeds by delivering direct experience in a personal tone without euphemisms. The style was already being made popular by Daniel Defoe, who, about the time that Pitts's book appeared, was editing his much read periodical, the Review. *Defoe was obsessed with tales of shipwreck and exile, and he is generally credited with ghostwriting the best book about piracy of his time. He also created new amalgamations of all the subgenres of Western travel writing—the* itinerario, *the wonder book, the geography, the explorer's account, the travel liar's fiction. Defoe possessed a large collection of travelers' accounts in English, from which he drew new plots. It is almost inconceivable that he did not own Pitts's book. Certainly Pitts could not have missed Defoe.*

from A *True and Faithful Account*
by Joeseph Pitts

BEING TAKEN BY THE ALGERIANS When I was about fourteen or fifteen years of age, my genius led me to be a sailor and to see foreign countries, much contrary to my mother's mind, tho' my father seemed to yield to my humour. Having made two or three short voyages, my fancy was to range farther abroad, for which I sufficiently suffered, as in the sequel of my story will appear.

I shipped myself on Easter Tuesday 1678 with one Mr. George Taylor, master of the *Speedwell* of Lymson near Exeter, bound to the Western Islands, thence to the Canaries, and so home, had God permitted. We got safe to Newfoundland and, our business being ended there, with a fair wind we set sail for Bilbao. After we had been out about forty days from Newfoundland, coming near the Coast of Spain, which we knew was the place where Algerians used to hunt for poor ships that come from the westward, we looked out sharp for ships, avoiding all we saw, but especially did we look out in the morning at sunrise and in the evening at sunset. The day on which we were taken, our mate Mr. John Milton was early at the topmast head and cried out, "A sail!" The master asked him, "Where?" "At leeward," replied the mate, "about five or six leagues." And so, to be brief in my relation, about midday, being almost overtaken by them, the enemy being but about a mile's distance from us, our master said, "It will be in vain for us to make our flight any longer, seeing it will be but an hour or two e'er we shall be taken, and then probably fare the worse if we continue our flight."

As soon as the pirate came up with us, the captain being a Dutch *renegado* and able to speak English, bid us hoist our boat. [This] we could not do without much trouble [because] a few days before one of our men in

a great storm was washed overboard and I myself was so scalded with boiling water as to be disabled for working, so that we had but four men that
were able. Therefore, before we could make half-ready to hoist our boat, they
came aboard us in their own. I being but young, the enemy seemed to me as
monstrous ravenous creatures, which made me cry out, "O master! I am afraid
they will kill us and eat us." "No, no, child," said my master. "They will
carry us to Algiers and sell us."

We were the first prize they had taken for that voyage, tho' they had
been out at sea about six weeks. As for our vessel after they had taken out of
her what they thought fit and necessary for their use, they sunk her. For being
laden with fish, they thought it not worthwhile to carry or send her home to
Algiers.

About four or five days after our being thus taken, they met with another small English ship which also came from Newfoundland with five or
six men aboard. . . . And two or three days after that they espied another
small English vessel, with the like number of men aboard, laden with fish
and coming from New England. This vessel was . . . some leagues at wind-
ward of them, and as there was but little wind, they were out of hopes of
getting up to her. They therefore used [a] cunning device: [they] hauled up
their sails and hung our English king's colours and so, appearing man-of-
war-like, decoyed her down and sunk her also.

Two or three days after this, they took a fourth little English ship with
four or five men aboard, laden with herring, of which they took [the] most
part and then sunk her. And last of all they met with a small Dutch ship
with seven men, laden partly with pipe staves, which they also sank. . . . They
used a like stratagem to decoy her down: [they] put up Dutch colours. But
when the Dutchman came about half a league from him and perceived him
to be a Turk, he begun to loose up with all his sail but to no purpose. For
e'er it was night, he was overtaken.

A SLAVE IN ALGIERS Soon after our arrival at our undesired haven, Algiers,
we were carried ashore to the captain's house and allowed nothing but a little
bread and water that night. The next morning they drove us all to the Dey's,*
or King's, house. The Dey makes his choice and takes his *pengick,* that is,
the eighth of part of the slaves for public use and the same part of the cargo.
After which all were driven to the *battistan,* or marketplace, where Christians are wont to be sold. There we stand from eight in the morning till two

---

*Dey: commander of the Ottoman army at Algiers, who in Pitts's time shared authority
with a civilian ruler, the Pasha. After 1710, the Dey ruled alone. [Ed.]

in the afternoon and have not the least bit of bread allowed us during our stay there. Many persons are curious to come and take a view of us whilst we stand exposed to sale, and others who intend to buy, to see whether we be sound and healthy and fit for service. The taken slaves are sold by way of auction and the crier endeavours to make the most he can of them. When the bidders are at a stand, he makes use of his rhetoric: "Behold what a strongman this is! What limbs he has! He is fit for any work. And see what a pretty boy this is! No doubt his parents are very rich and able to redeem him with a great ransom." And with many such fair speeches does he strive to raise the price. After the bidders have done bidding, the slaves are all driven again to the Dey's house, where any that have a mind to advance above what was bidden at the *battistan* may. But then whatever exceeds the bidding in that place belongs not to the picaroons, or pirates, but goes to the Dey.

MY THREE OWNERS 'Tis usually reported among us here in England that when any Christians are taken by the Algerians, they are put to extremest tortures, so that they may be brought over to the Muslim faith. But I assure the reader it is a very false report, but they very seldom use any such severities on that account, tho' it was my hard lot be so unmercifully dealt with. They do not usually force any Christian to renounce his religion.

In Algiers, I have known some Turks who, when they have perceived their slaves inclined to turn [to the Muslim religion], have forthwith sold them. . . . For you must know that when a Christian slave turns Muslim, there can be no ransom for him, and it is looked on as an infamous thing for any patroon,* [within a few years of their conversion] to deny them their liberty and to refuse to set them out handsomely in the world. . . . For my part I remained several years a slave after my defection, suffered a great deal of cruel usage, and then was sold again.

My first patroon would, when exercising his barbarous cruelty upon me, press me to turn Musselman,† but all the while I did not believe that he was really willing I should do so. [He only did this so that] he might think that he discharged his duty in importuning me. [The] reason why I thought so is because I knew at that time he could hardly sustain such a loss, for not very long before he had bought a little boy of Dover who soon renounced his religion and died some years after. This cruel man I lived with about two

*patroon: patron, or slaveowner. [Ed.]

† Musselman: older, variant European spelling of Muslim, [Ed.]

or three months, and then he sent me to sea in one of the ships to attend upon the head gunner. . . .

We made, they said, a very indifferent voyage, for we took but one ship, a Portuguese, with eighteen slaves. We were out about two months, to my great ease and contentment. When we were returning to Algiers, my heart began to be heavy with the thoughts of entering again into my former misery, but there was no remedy but patience. But (bless be God) within a few days he sold me, and so I was out of the possession of that inhuman wretch.

My second patroon lived in the country and was called Handsome Abraham. He had several slaves, both Christians and Negroes. He [also] had two brothers in Algiers and a third in Tunis. The middle brother had designed to make a voyage to Tunis and to see his brother there and, it seems, I was bought in order to be given as a present to him. I was then clothed very fine that I might be the better accepted. On the ship there was another young Englishman with his patroon, bound also for Tunis, where he was to be redeemed by the [British] Consul at a moderate price. The next day my patroon's brother's son, taking pride to have a Christian to wait upon him, made me walk after him. I was ready and glad to do it, because I was desirous to see the city. [In] the streets, I met with a gentleman dressed like a Christian. . . . He looked earnestly upon me and asked me whether I was not an Englishman? I answered, "Yea." "How came you hither?" said he. I told him I came with my patroon. "What? Are you a slave?" said he. I replied, "Yes." "To what place do you belong?" continues he. "To Algiers," quoth I. But he was not willing to enter into any further discourse with me in the public street. He therefore [indicated to] the young man on whom I waited that he would be pleased at such an hour of the day to bring me to his house with a promise of a hearty welcome. The young man assured him he would, for being a drinker of wine and knowing the [store] of it in the gentleman's house, he was willing to go. . . .

My new master told me that [this] was the English consul which I was glad to hear. We went as appointed to the consul's house, where, when he came, I was directed up to his chamber (the young spark in the meantime eating and drinking in another room). The consul asked me many questions about my country, parentage, etc., and whether I could write and understood arithmetic. I told him I could do both tolerably. . . . Upon the whole, the Consul kindly told me, if I were left in Tunis, he would order matters to my satisfaction. But if my patroon designed to carry me back again to Algiers, I should acquaint [the consul] with it. In the meantime, he bid me, if I had the liberty, to come every day to his house, where I should be welcome. This worthy gentleman's name was Baker (I think Charles), brother to Thomas Baker, Consul of Algiers. . . .

[After my second owner died], l was in hopes that my patroona, or mistress, would now give me my freedom. But she would not and intended to sell me . . . in the country[side]. [If this had happened, I would], in all probability, have been a slave as long as I lived, for I don't see how I could possibly have made my escape. I therefore earnestly desired that I might be sold in Algiers, which was at length granted. According to custom, I was carried three days by the crier about the streets and was bought the third time by an old bachelor. My work with him was to look after his house, dress his meat, wash his clothes, and in short to do all those things that are looked on as a servant-maid's work in England.

I must own that I wanted nothing with him. Of meat, drink, clothes, and money I had enough. After I had lived with him about a year, he made his pilgrimage to Mecca, and carried me with him. . . . He seldom called me anything but son, and he bought a Dutch boy to do the work of the house, who attended upon me and obeyed my orders as much as his. . . . He desired me to mind my reading, in which I made a considerably proficiency, and would have me also learn to write. Understanding something of writing, I could strike the Turkish character beyond their expectations, and all in the school admired me for it. But I began to consider with myself that I should soon be a master of writing, as well as a pretty good accountant, and my patroon, being related to the then Dey, could easily get me promoted, as such usually are; and for this reason I laid aside my writing, fearing what the consequence might be. I often saw several bags of his money, a great part of which, he said, he would leave me. He would say to me, "Tho' I was never married myself, yet you shall in a little time, and then your children shall be mine" [and will inherit]. An offer was made to me of that nature, but, I bless God, it was no temptation to me. Had I been prevailed upon to alter my condition there, I tremble to think what the issue might have been. Many more kindnesses of this, my last patroon, I could relate, for which I cannot but say I had a great love for him even as a father. But still this was not England and I wanted to be at home. . . .

THE FOUR HAJJ CARAVANS There are four caravans which come to Mecca every year, with great numbers of people in each. There is first the Maghrib caravan, which comes from the west, from the Emperor of Fez and Morocco's country (from which parts they all go by land) and touches at Egypt, where they take in what provision will serve to Mecca and back again to Egypt. . . .

The second caravan goes from Grand Cairo in Egypt, which is joined by great multitudes, because it is better armed and they go with more safety under its protection. And it is also more pleasant, because they go everyone in order and each knows his place, so that there arise no quarrels or disputes at all on the road about precedence. With this caravan is sent the covering of the Bayt Allah, or House of God, of which I shall give a description by and by.

The third caravan is called Sham [Syrian] *carawan,* which brings those that come from Tartary and parts thereabouts, and also from all Turkey, Natolia, and the land of Canaan, without touching at Egypt.

The fourth is called Hind [Indian] *carawan,* which comes from the East Indies and brings many rich and choice goods, which are sold to all sorts of persons who resort to Mecca.

These four caravans jump all into Mecca together, there being not above three or four days' difference in their arrival, which usually is about six or seven days before the Feast of Sacrifice. . . .

ALGIERS When a ship is going for Alexandria, it is cried about the town of Algier, where I lived, that she will sail such a day, and then everyone that designs for Mecca that year joyfully embraces the opportunity of going so far by sea, because they thereby save both a great deal of trouble and cost, which they must be at if they were forced to go by land.

You must observe that no Turks who are in pay [public employment] dare to undertake this pilgrimage without leave from the Dey, and if they exceed a year in it, how much soever it be, when they return to Algier, they must be contented with one year's pay and lose all the rest.

That year I went from Algier to Mecca, we arrived at Alexandria in between thirty and forty days, which is reckoned to be a very good passage. In our voyage we espied a small vessel one morning, which we chased till almost night. We hung out French colours, and the chased vessel did the like but still shunned us, which made us continue our chase. When we came up with her, we found the men to be all Turks and Moors in a French vessel, who were brought from Malta and were designed to be carried to Leghorn and sold there. They told us that that very morning they were at an anchor at a certain place and most of the French crew went ashore in their boat, leaving only two men and a boy on board, upon which the slaves rose and killed the two Frenchmen and so became masters of the ship, [and] that therefore, upon our hanging out French colours, they were in a great consternation at the first, but when they knew we were Turks, they as much rejoiced as before they feared. Some of them, men, women, and children, came on board of us and would by no means be persuaded to return to the French vessel again. They steered directly for Tunis, where (we heard) they safely arrived.

At Alexandria we tarried about twenty days. . . .

THE RED SEA PASSAGE We were on this sea about a month. After we had sailed from Suez about twenty days, we came to a place where was buried ashore a marabout, i.e., a saint or one reputed eminently devout and religious, and perhaps some hundreds of years are passed since he was there interred. When we came here, one of the ship's crew, with the consent of the rest, made a little ship, about two feet in length, and went to everyone of the pilgrims (for you must observe that if any die on the journey before they come to Mecca, they are notwithstanding ever after termed by the honourable name of hajji), desiring them to bestow their charity in honour of the said marabout, and at such a time they liberally bestow some piece of money to the said end. They then took some small wax candles, with a little bottle of oil, and put them into the ship, together with the money they had received of well-inclined people (as they said, but I am apt to think they put in but a very small part of it, if any at all, but kept it to themselves). This being done, they all held up their hands, begging the marabout's blessing and praying that they might have a good voyage. And then they put the ship overboard into the sea, not in the least doubting of its safe arrival to the marabout, for the benefit of his sepulchre, tho' it be a desolate place and not at all inhabited where he is said to lie interred. Poor ignorant creatures! This marabout, they have a tradition, died in his voyage towards Mecca, and therefore his memory is most highly esteemed and venerated by them. The veneration they have for these marabouts is so great that if any person who has committed murder flees to one of the little houses which are built upon their sepulchres for sanctuary, he is as safe as if he were in a convent, for none durst touch him in order to fetch him thence.

A few days after this we came to a place called Rabigh,* about four days' sail on this side [of] Mecca, where all the hajjis (excepting those of the female sex) do enter into *ihram,* i.e., they take off all their clothes, covering themselves with two large white cotton wrappers. One they put about their

---

*Rabigh: a small seaport about halfway between Yanbu and Jibbs, and 124 miles northwest of Mecca.

middle, which reaches down to their ankles; the other they cover the upper part of the body with, except the head. And they wear no other thing on their bodies but these wrappers; only a pair of *jamjamiya,* i.e., thin-soled shoes (like sandals), the overleather of which covers only the toes, their insteps being all naked. In this manner, like humble penitents, they go from Rabigh till they come to Mecca to approach the temple, many times enduring the scorching heat of the sun till their very skin is burnt off their backs and arms and their heads swollen to a very great degree. Yet when any man's health is by such austerities in danger and like to be impaired, they may lawfully put on their clothes, on condition still that when they come to Mecca, they sacrifice a sheep and give it to the poor. During the time of their wearing this mortifying habit, which is about the space of seven days, it is held unlawful for them so much as to cut their nails or to kill a louse or a flea, tho' they see them sucking their blood; but yet if they are so troublesome that they cannot well endure it longer, 'tis lawful for them to remove them from one place of the body to another.

During this time they are very watchful over their tempers, keep a jealous eye upon their passions, and observe a strict government of their tongues, making continual use of a form of devout expressions. And they will also be careful to be reconciled and at peace with all such as they had any difference with; accounting it a very sinful and shameful thing to bear the least malice against any. They do not shave themselves during this time.

Next we come to Jidda, the nearest seaport to Mecca, not quite one day's journey from it, where the ships are unloaded. Here we are met by *dalils** i.e., certain persons who come from Mecca on purpose to instruct the pilgrims in the ceremonies (most of them being ignorant of them), which are to be used in their worship at the temple there, in the middle of which is a place which they call Bayt Allah, i.e., the House of God. They say that Abraham built it, to which I give no credit.

ARRIVAL AT MECCA As soon as we come to the town of Mecca, the guide carries us into the great street, which is in the midst of the town and to which the temple joins. After the camels are laid down, he first directs us to the fountains, there to take *abdast,*† which being done, he brings us to the temple,

---

**dalil:* "a guide, generally called at Mecca *mutawwif.*" (Sir Richard Burton, *Personal Narrative of a Pilgrimage to al-Madinah and Mecca*)

†*abdast:* "the Turkish word, borrowed from the Persian, for *wudu',* the minor ablution." (Burton, *Personal Narrative*)

into which (having left our shoes with one who constantly attends to receive them) we enter at the door called Bab al-Salaam i.e., the Welcome Gate, or Gate of Peace. After a few paces' entrance the *dalil* makes a stand and holds up his hands towards the Bayt Allah (it being in the middle of the mosque), the hajjis imitating him and saying after him the same words which he speaks. At the very first sight of the Bayt Allah the hajjis melt into tears. Then we are led up to it, still speaking after the *dalil;* then we are led round it seven times, and then make two *rakat*s. This being done, we are led out into the street again, where we are sometimes to run and sometimes to walk very quick with the *dalil* from one place of the street to the other, about a bowshot.* And I profess I could not choose but admire to see those poor creatures so extraordinarily devout and affectionate when they were about these superstitions, and with what awe and trembling they were possessed, insomuch that I could scarce forbear shedding of tears to see their zeal, tho' blind and idolatrous. After all this is done, we returned to the place in the street where we left our camels, with our provision and necessaries, and then look out for lodgings; where when we come, we disrobe and take off our *ihram* and put on our ordinary clothes again.

All the pilgrims hold it to be their great duty well to improve their time whilst they are at Mecca, not only to do their accustomed duty and devotion in the temple but to spend all their leisure time there and (as far as strength will permit) to continue at *tawaf,* i.e., to walk round the Bayt Allah, which is about four and twenty paces square. At one corner of the Bayt there is a black stone fastened, and framed in with silver plate, and every time they come to that corner, they kiss the stone; and having gone round seven times, they perform two *rakat*s, or prayers. . . .

This place is so much frequented by people going round it that the place of *tawaf,* i.e., the circuit which they take in going round it, is seldom void of people at any time of the day or night. Many have waited several weeks, nay, months, for the opportunity of finding it so; for they say that if any person is blessed with such an opportunity, that, for his or her zeal in keeping up the honour of *tawaf,* let him petition what they will at the Bayt Allah, they shall be answered. Many will walk round it till they are quite weary, then rest, and at it again, carefully remembering at the end of every seventh time to perform two *rakat*s. . . .

---

*This is the ceremony technically called *al-saʿy,* or running between Safa and Marwa. Burckhardt describes it accurately (*Travels in Arabia,* 174–75). (Burton, *Personal Narrative*)

THE TOWN AND ITS TEMPLE I shall now give you a more particular description of Mecca and the temple there.

First, as to Mecca. It is a town situated in a barren place (about one day's journey from the Red Sea) in a valley, or rather in the midst of many little hills. 'Tis a place of no force, wanting both walls and gates. Its buildings are (as I said before) very ordinary, insomuch that it would be a place of no tolerable entertainment were it not for the anniversary resort of so many thousand pilgrims, on whose coming the whole dependence of the town (in a manner) is, for many shops are scarcely open all the year besides.

The people here, I observed, are a poor sort of people, very thin, lean, and swarthy. The town is surrounded for several miles with many thousands of little hills, which are very near one to the other. I have been on the top of some of them near Mecca, where I could see some miles about, but yet was not able to see the farthest of the hills. They are all stony rock, and blackish and pretty near of a bigness, appearing at a distance like cocks of hay, but all pointing towards Mecca. Some of them are half a mile in circumference, etc., but all near of one height. . . .

There is upon the top of one of them* a cave, which they term *hira* [Arabic, *khira*], i.e., blessing; into which (they say) Muhammad did usually retire for his solitary devotion, meditations, and fastings. And here, they believe, he had . . . [the first] part of the *Quran* brought him by the angel Gabriel. I have been in this cave, and observed that it is not at all beautified, at which I admired.

About half a mile out of Mecca is a very steep hill, and there are stairs made to go to the top of it, where is a cupola, under which is a cloven rock. Into this, they say, Muhammad, when very young, viz., about four years of age, was carried by the angel Gabriel, who opened his breast and took out his heart, from which he picked some black blood specks, which was his original corruption, then put it into its place again and afterward closed up the part; and that during this operation Muhammad felt no pain. Into this very place I myself went, because the rest of my company did so, and performed some *rakat*s, as they did. . . .

As to Mecca itself, it affords little or nothing of comfortable provisions. It lies in a very hot country, insomuch that people run from one side of the streets to the other to get into the shadow, as the motion of the sun causes it. The inhabitants, especially men, do usually sleep on the tops of the houses for the air, or in the streets before their doors. Some lay the small bedding

---

*One of them: "now Jabal Nur." (Burton, *Personal Narrative*)

they have on a thin mat on the ground; others have a slight frame, made much like drink stalls on which we place barrels, standing on four legs, corded with palm cordage, on which they put their bedding. Before they bring out their bedding, they sweep the streets and water them. As for my own part, I usually lay open without any bed covering, on the top of the house. Only I took a linen cloth, dipped in water and, after I had wrung it, covered myself with it in the night; and when I awoke, I should find it dry. Then I would wet it again; and thus I did two or three times in a night.

Secondly, I shall next give you some account of the temple of Mecca. It has about forty-two doors to enter into it; not so much, I think, for necessity as figure, for in some places they are close by one another. The form of it [is] much resembling that of the Royal Exchange in London, but I believe it's near ten times bigger. 'Tis all open, and gravelled in the midst, except some paths that come from certain doors, which lead to the Bayt Allah and are paved with broad stones. The walks or cloisters all round are arched over-head and paved beneath with fine broad stone; and all round are little rooms or cells, where such dwell as give themselves up to reading, studying, and a devout life, who are much akin to their dervishes, or hermits. The dervishes are most commonly such as live an eremetic life, travelling up and down the country, like mendicants living on the charity of others, wearing a white woollen garment and a long white woollen cap (much like some of the or-ders of friars in the Romish Church), with a sheep or goat's skin on their back to lie on and a long staff in their hand. When they read, they com-monly sit down, putting their legs across and keeping their knees above the ground. They usually carry their beads about their arms or necks, whereas others carry them in their pockets. Many Turks, when they reform, give themselves up to a dervish sort of life. And for an instance, my second patroon had a younger brother who had lived a very debauched life; but on a sudden a great change seemed to be wrought upon him, insomuch that he let his beard grow, never shaving it, and put on his great green turban (which none presume to wear but such as are of the blood and race of Muhammad) and betook himself to the learning his *alif, ba, ta,* i.e., A, B, C. In a little time he attained to read very well, and spent a great part of his time in reading. Some of his old jolly companions would laugh at him for it, but he still kept on in this strict way of living, notwithstanding all their banters.

The Bayt Allah, which stands in the middle of the temple, is foursquare, about twenty-four paces each square and near twenty-four in height. 'Tis built with great stone, all smooth and plain, without the least bit of carved work on it. 'Tis covered all over, from top to bottom, with a thick sort of silk. Above the middle part of the covering are embroidered all round letters of gold, the meaning of which I cannot well call to mind, but I think they were some devout expressions. Each letter is near two foot in length and two inches broad. Near the lower end of this Bayt are large brass rings fastened into it, through which passes a great cotton rope, and to this the lower end of the covering is tacked. The threshold of the door that belongs to the Bayt is as high as a man can reach, and therefore, when any person enters into it, a sort of ladder stairs are brought for that purpose. The door is plated all over with silver, and there's a covering hangs over it and reaches to the ground, which is kept turned up all the week, except Thursday night and Friday, which is their Sabbath. The said covering of the door is very thick embroidered with gold, insomuch that it weighs several score pounds. The top of the Bayt is flat, beaten with lime and sand, and there is a long gutter or spout, to carry off the water when it rains, at which time the people will run, throng, and struggle to get under the said gutter, that so the water that comes off the Bayt may fall upon them, accounting it as the dew of heaven, and looking on it as a great happiness to have it drop upon them, but if they can recover some of this water to drink, they esteem it to be yet a much greater happiness. Many poor people make it their endeavour to get some of it and present it to the hajjis, for which they are well rewarded. . . .

This Bayt Allah is opened but two days in the space of six weeks, viz., one day for the men and the next day for the women. As I was at Mecca about four months, I had the opportunity of entering into it twice—a reputed advantage which many thousands of the hajjis have not met with; for those that come by land make no longer stay at Mecca than sixteen or seventeen days. . . . Those that go into the Bayt tarry there but a very little while, viz., scarce so much as half a quarter of an hour, because others wait for the same privilege; and while some go in, others are going out. After all is over and all that will have done this, the Sultan of Mecca, who is a sharif, i.e., one of the [family] of Muhammad, accounts himself not too good to cleanse the Bayt and therefore, with some of his favourites, doth wash and cleanse it. And first of all they wash it with the holy water, Zamzam, and after that with sweet water. The stairs which were brought to enter in at the door of the Bayt being removed, the people crowd under the door to receive on them the sweeping of the said water. And the besoms wherewith the Bayt is cleansed are broken in pieces and thrown out amongst the mob, and he that gets a small stick or twig of it keeps it as a sacred relic.

Every year the covering of this Bayt Allah is renewed in Grand Cairo, by the order of the Grand Seigneur [Sultan]; and when the caravan goes with the hajjis to Mecca, then is the new covering carried upon two camels, which do no other work all the year long. It is sent out of Egypt with a great deal of rejoicing and received into Mecca with wonderful joy, many people even weeping for joy, and some kissing the very camels that carry it, bidding them welcome again and again, reaching their hands up to the covering and then smoothing down their faces. This and a great deal more they do, to show what a veneration they have for this new covering, tho' not yet put on about the Bayt. Well may you think then what esteem they have for the Bayt Allah itself. . . . But to speak something further of the temple at Mecca, for I am willing to be very particular in matters about it, tho' in so being I should (it may be) speak of things which by some people may be thought trivial. The compass of ground round the Bayt (where the people exercise themselves in the duty of *tawaf*) is paved with marble about fifty feet in breadth, and round this marble pavement stand pillars of brass, about fifteen feet high and twenty feet distant from each other; above the middle part of which iron bars are fastened, reaching from one to the other, and several lamps made of glass are hanged to each of the said bars with brass wires in the form of a triangle, to give light in the night season. For they pay their devotions at the Bayt Allah as much by night as by day during the hajjis' stay at Mecca. These glasses are half-filled with water and a third part with oil, on which a round wire of brass is buoyed up with three little corks. In the midst of this wire is made a place to put in the wick or cotton, which burns till the oil is spent. Every day they are washed clean and replenished with fresh water, oil, and cotton. . . .

THE HAJJ PROCESSION The Feast of Sacrifice follows two months and ten days after the Ramadan fast. The eighth day after the said two months they all enter into *ihram,* i.e., put on their mortifying habit again, and in that manner go to a certain hill, called Arafat, i.e., the Mountain of Knowledge; for there, they say, Adam first found and knew his wife, Eve. . . .

It was a sight, indeed, able to pierce one's heart to behold so many thousands, in their garments of humility and mortification, with their naked heads and cheeks watered with tears, and to hear their grievous sighs and sobs, begging earnestly for the remission of their sins and promising newness of life, using a form of penitential expressions, and thus continuing for the space of four or five hours, viz., until the time of *salat maghrib,* which is to be performed about half an hour after sunset. . . .

After their solemn performance of their devotions thus at the mountain, they all at once receive that honourable title of hajji from the imam and are so styled to their dying day. Immediately upon their receiving this name, the trumpet is sounded and they all leave the hill and return for Mecca; and being gone two or three miles on their way, they there rest for that night. But after *salat,* before they go to rest, each person gathers nine and forty small stones, about the bigness of a hazel nut, the meaning of which I shall acquaint you with presently.

The next morning they move to a place called Mina. . . . Here they all pitch their tents, it being in a spacious plain, and spend the time of Id al-Adha, viz., three days. As soon as their tents are pitched and all things orderly disposed, every individual hajji, the first day, goes and throws seven of the small stones (which they had gathered) against a small pillar or little square stone building. Which action of theirs is intended to testify their defiance of the devil and his deeds, for they at the same time pronounce the following words, viz., *urjum al-Shaytan wa-hizbahu,* i.e., "stone the devil and them that please him." And there are two other of the like pillars, which are situated near one another, at each of which (I mean all three) the second day they throw seven stones,* and the same they do the third day. As I was going to perform this ceremony of throwing the stones, a facetious hajji met me. Saith he: "You may save your labour at present, if you please, for I have hit out the devil's eyes already."

You must observe that after they have thrown the seven stones the first day, the country people, having brought great flocks of sheep to be sold, everyone buys a sheep and sacrifices it; some of which they give to their friends, some to the poor which come out of Mecca and the country adjacent (very ragged poor), and the rest they eat themselves; after which they shave their heads, throw off *ihram,* and put on other clothes and then salute one another with a kiss, saying *Id mubarak,* i.e., "the Feast be a blessing to you."

These three days of the Id they spend festivally, rejoicing with abundance of illuminations all night, shooting of guns, and fireworks flying in the air; for they reckon that all their sins are now done away, and that they shall, when they die, go directly to heaven, if they don't apostatise, and that for the future, if they keep their vow and do well, God will set down for every good action ten, but if they do ill, God will likewise reckon every evil action ten; and any person who, after receiving the title of hajji, shall fall back to a vicious course of life, is esteemed to be very vile and infamous by them. Some have written that many of the hajjis, after they have returned

---

*The three pillars "mark the successive spots where the devil, in the shape of an old shaykh, appeared to Adam, Abraham, and Ishmael and was driven back by the simple process, taught by Gabriel, of throwing stones about the size of a bean." (Burton, *Personal Narrative,* II: 203)

home, have been so austere to themselves as to pore a long time over red-hot bricks or ingots of iron, and by that means willingly lose their sight, desiring to see nothing evil or profane after so sacred a sight as the temple of Mecca, but I never knew any such thing done.

During their three days' stay at Mina scarce any hajji, unless weak or ill, but thinks it his duty to pay his visit, once at least, to the temple at Mecca. They scarce cease running all the way thitherward, showing their vehement desire to have a fresh sight of the Bayt Allah, which as soon as ever they come in sight of, they burst into tears for joy. And after having performed *tawaf* for a while and a few *rakat*s, they return again to Mina. And when the three days of Id al-Adha are expired, they all, with their tents, etc., come back again to Mecca. . . .

MECCA After they are returned to Mecca, they can tarry there no longer than the stated time, which is about ten or twelve days, during which time there is a great fair held, where are sold all manner of East India goods and abundance of fine stones for rings and bracelets, etc., brought from Yemen, also of China ware and musk and a variety of other curiosities. Now is the time in which the hajjis are busily employed in buying, for they do not think it lawful to buy anything till they have received the title of hajji. Everyone almost now buys a *kafan,* or shroud, of fine linen to be buried in—for they never use coffins for that purpose—which might have been procured at Algiers, or their other respective homes, at a much cheaper rate, but they choose to buy it here, because they have the advantage of dipping it in the holy water, Zamzam. They are very careful to carry the said *kafan* with them wherever they travel, whether by sea or land, that they may be sure to be buried therein.

The evening before they leave Mecca, everyone must go to take their solemn leave of the Bayt entering in at the gate called Bab al-Salaam, i.e., Welcome Gate. And having continued at *tawaf* as long as they please (which many do till they are quite tired), and it being the last time of their paying their devotions to it, they do it with floods of tears, as being extremely unwilling to part and bid farewell. And having drank their fill of the water Zamzam, they go to one side of the Bayt, their backs being towards the door called by the name of *Bab al-Wida,* i.e., the Farewell Door, which is opposite the Welcome Door; where having performed two or three *rakat*s, they get upon their legs and hold up their hands towards the Bayt, making earnest petitions, and then keep going backwards till they come to the abovesaid Farewell Gate, being guided by some or other; for they account it a very irreverent thing to turn their backs towards the Bayt when they take leave of it. All the way as they retreat, they continue petitioning, holding up their hands, with their eyes fixed upon the Bayt till they are out of sight of it; and so go to their lodgings weeping. . . .

THE CARAVAN LEAVES MECCA Having hired camels of the carriers, we set out; but we give as much for the hire of one from Mecca to Egypt (which is about forty days' journey) as the real worth of it is, viz., about five or six pounds sterling. If it happen that the camel dies by the way, the carrier is to supply us with another, and therefore those carriers who come from Egypt to Mecca with the caravan bring with them several spare camels; for there is hardly a night passes but many die upon the road. For if a camel should chance to fall, 'tis seldom known that it is able to rise again; and if it should, they despair of its being capable of performing the journey or ever being useful more. 'Tis a common thing, therefore, when a camel once falls, to take off its burden and put it on another and then kill it, which the poorer sort of the company eat. I myself have eaten of camel's flesh, and 'tis very sweet and nourishing. . . .

The first day we set out from Mecca it was without any order at all, all hurly-burly, but the next day everyone laboured to get forward. And in order to do it, there was many times much quarrelling and fighting, but after everyone had taken his place in the caravan, they orderly and peaceably kept the same place till they came to Grand Cairo. They travel four camels in a breast, which are all tied one after the other, like as in teams. The whole body is called a caravan, which is divided into several *kitar*s, or companies, each of which has its name and consists (it may be) of several thousand camels, and they move, one *kitar* after another, like distinct troops. In the head of each *kitar* is some great gentleman or officer, who is carried in a thing like a horse litter, borne by two camels, one before and the other behind, which is covered all over with searcloth* and over that again with green broadcloth, and set forth very handsomely. If the said great person has a wife with him, she is carried in another of the same. In the head of every *kitar* there goes likewise a sumpter camel, which carries his treasure, etc. This camel has two bells, about the bigness of our market bells, hanging one on each side, the sound of which may be heard a great way off. Some other of the camels have round bells about their necks, some about their legs, like those which our carriers put about their fore horses' necks, which, together with the servants (who belong to the camels and travel on foot) singing all night, make a pleasant noise, and the journey passes away delightfully. They say this music makes the camels brisk and lively. Thus they travel in good order every day till they

*searcloth: cerecloth, that is, cloth coated with wax.

come to Grand Cairo. And were it not for this order, you may guess what confusion would be amongst such a vast multitude.

They have lights by night (which is the chief time of travelling, because of the exceeding heat of the sun by day), which are carried on the tops of high poles, to direct the hajjis in their march. They are somewhat like iron stoves, into which they put short dry wood, which some of the camels are loaded with. 'Tis carried in great sacks, which have a hole near the bottom, where the servants take it out as they see the fires need a recruit. Every *kitar* has one of these poles belonging to it, some of which have ten, some twelve, of these lights on their tops, or more or less. And they are likewise of different figures as well as numbers; one perhaps oval, like a gate; another triangular, or like an *n* or *m,* etc., so that everyone knows by them his respective *kitar.* They are carried in the front and set up in the place where the caravan is to pitch, before that comes up, at some distance from one another. They are also carried by day, not lighted, but yet by the figure and number of them the hajjis are directed to what *kitar* they belong, as soldiers are by their colors where to rendezvous; and without such directions it would be impossible to avoid confusion in such a vast number of people. Every day, viz., in the morning, they pitch their tents and rest several hours. When the camels are unloaded, the owners drive them to water and give them their provender, etc. So that we had nothing to do with them besides helping to load them.

As soon as our tents were pitched, my business was to make a little fire and get a pot of coffee. When we had eaten some small matter and drunk the coffee, we lay down to sleep. Between eleven and twelve we boiled something for dinner and, having dined, lay down again till about four in the afternoon, when the trumpet was sounded which gave notice to everyone to take down their tents, pack up their things, and load their camels, in order to proceed in their journey. It takes up about two hours' time e'er they are all in their places again. At the time of [the] two evening prayers, they make a halt and perform their *salat* (so punctual are they in their worship), and then they travel till next morning. If water be scarce, what I call an imaginary *wudu'** will do. As for ancient men, it being very troublesome for them to alight off the camels and get up again, 'tis lawful for them to defer these two times of prayer till the next day, but they will be sure to perform it then.

As for provisions, we bring enough out of Egypt to suffice us till we return thither again. At Mecca we compute how much will serve us for one day and,

*imaginary *wudu'*: "the sand ablution—lawful when water is wanted for maintaining life." (Burton, *Personal Narrative*)

consequently, for the forty days' journey to Egypt; and if we find we have more than we may well guess will suffice us for so long a time, we sell the overplus at Mecca. There is a charity, maintained by the Grand Seignieur, for water to refresh the poor who travel on foot all the way; for there are many such undertake this journey or pilgrimage without any money, relying on the charity of the hajjis for subsistence, knowing that they largely extend it at such a time.

Every hajji carries his provisions, water, bedding, etc., with him, and usually three or four diet together, and sometimes discharge a poor man's expenses the whole journey for his attendance on them. There was an Irish *renegado* who was taken very young, insomuch that he had not only lost his Christian religion but his native language also. This man had [later] endured thirty years' slavery in Spain and in the French galley, but was afterwards redeemed and came home to Algiers. He was looked upon as a very pious man and a great zealot by the Turks, for his not turning from the Muslim faith, notwithstanding the great temptations he had so to do. Some of my neighbours, who intended for Mecca the same year I went with my patroon thither, offered this *renegado* that if he would serve them on this journey, they would defray his charges throughout. He gladly embraced the offer; and I remember, when we arrived at Mecca, he passionately told me that God had delivered him out of a hell upon Earth, meaning his former slavery in France and Spain, and had brought him into a heaven upon earth, viz., Mecca. I admired much his zeal, but pitied his condition.

Their water they carry in goatskins, which they fasten to one side of their camels. It sometimes happens that no water is to be met with for two, three, or more days; but yet it is well-known that a camel is a creature that can live long without drinking; God in his wise providence so ordering it, for otherwise it would be very difficult, if not impossible, to travel through the parched deserts of Arabia. Every tent's company have their convenient place for easing nature, viz., four long poles fixed square, about three or four feet distance from each other, which is hung round with canvas. . . .

In this journey many times the skulking, thievish Arabs do much mischief to some of the hajjis; for in the night time they'll steal upon them, especially such as are on the outside of the caravan, and being taken to be some of the servants that belong to the carriers or owners of the camels, they are not suspected. When they see a hajji fast asleep (for it is usual for them to sleep on the road), they loose a camel, before and behind, and one of the thieves leads it away, with the hajji upon its back asleep. Another of them in the meantime pulls on the next camel, to tie it to the camel from whence the halter of the other was cut; for if that camel be not fastened again to the leading camel, it will stop, and all that are behind will then stop of course, which might be a means of discovering the robbers. When they have gotten the stolen camel, with his rider, at a convenient distance from the caravan and think themselves out of danger, they awake the hajji and sometimes destroy him immediately; but at other times, being a little more inclined to mercy, they strip him naked and let him return to the caravan. . . .

APPROACHING CAIRO When we came within seven days' journey of Cairo, we were met by an abundance of people more, some hundreds, who came to welcome their friends and relations. But it being night, it was difficult to find those they wanted, and therefore, as the caravans passed along, they kept calling them aloud by their names, and by this means found them out. And when we were within three days' journey of it, we had many camel loads of the water of the Nile brought us to drink. But the day and the night before we came to Cairo, thousands came out to meet us, with extraordinary rejoicing. 'Tis thirty-seven days' journey from Mecca to Cairo, and three days we tarry by the way, which together make up (as I said) forty days' journey. And in all this way there is scarce any green thing to be met with, nor beast or fowl to be seen or heard, nothing but sand and stones, excepting one place which we passed by night. I suppose it was a village, where were some trees and (as we thought) gardens. We travelled through a certain valley, which is called by the name of Attash al-Wayt, i.e., the River of Fire; the vale being so excessively hot that the very water in their goatskins has sometimes been dried up with the gloomy, scorching heat. But we had the happiness to pass through it when it rained, so that the fervent heat was much allayed thereby, which the hajjis looked on as a great blessing and did not a little praise God for it.

When we came to Cairo, the plague was very hot there, insomuch that it was reported there died sixty thousand within a fortnight's time. Wherefore we hastened away to Rosetta, and from thence to Alexandria, where in a little time there was a ship of Algiers ready to transport us thither.

The plague was hot in Alexandria at this time, and some persons infected with it being taken on board our ship, which was bound for Algiers, the plague reigned amongst us; insomuch that, besides those that recovered, we threw twenty persons overboard who died of it. And truly I was not a little afraid of the distemper and wished I were safe at Algiers, hoping that if I were got there I should escape it. But soon after we got ashore there, I was seized with it, but through the divine goodness escaped death. It rose under my arm, and the boil which usually accompanies the plague rose on my leg. After it was much swollen, I was desirous to have it lanced, but my patroon told me it was not soft enough. There was a neighbour, a Spaniard slave, who advised me to roast an onion and apply a piece of it, dipped in oil, to the swelling, to mollify it, which accordingly I did. The next day it became soft, and then my patroon had it lanced; and, through the blessing of my good God, I recovered. Such a signal mercy I hope I shall never forget, a mercy so circumstantiated, considering everything, that my soul shall thankfully call it to mind as long as I have any being; for I was just returned from Mecca when this mercy was dispensed to me. I do observe the divine providence plainly in it, and hope ever to make the best use of it.

7

Ali Bey al-Abbasi
Spain
1807

※❀※

Unlike Varthema and Joseph Pitts, the Spanish noble Domingo Badia y Leyblich was both European and a Muslim. He signed his books as Ali Bey al-Abbasi, spoke various Arabic dialects, and read the Quran; he was also fluent in Spanish and Italian and passionately devoted to the Enlightenment. His five-year round-trip journey between Europe and Mecca was, on one level, a scientific expedition, and he later lectured on his travels before the Institut de France. This blend of Western science with Islam is one of his most fascinating aspects. His political allegiance, however, remains an enigma.

Although he seems to have been an intelligence operative for some Western power, no one can say exactly whose interests he was serving. Most commentators imply that he was in Napoleon's pay, but he was probably engaged with Britain, too. Near the start of his journey, in 1802, he visited the botanist Sir Joseph Banks in London. As president of the African Association* and the Royal Society, Banks groomed and financed numerous other African explorers, including the famous Mungo Park and, later, Burckhardt, whose own Hajj record follows al-Abbasi's in this collection. Whether Britain benefited, scientifically or politically, from information supplied by al-Abbasi is not clear. We do know that the two men were friendly enough for him to leave a portrait of himself in Sir Joseph's study. Shortly after, he was on his way to Morocco and points east.

Al-Abbasi's two-volume account is an eccentric, meticulous record of the regions and great cities through which he passed. The following excerpts treat his stays in the principal centers of Morocco and northern Egypt. They conclude with longer passages concerning the Hijaz.

Al-Abbasi arrived in North Africa in grand-tour style, with a carriage and steward. This assumption of high privilege was natural to him; a person of lesser station could not have managed it. In Tangier, he endowed a fountain at the

---

*The Association for Promoting the Discovery of the Interior of Africa.

mosque and immediately succeeded in placing himself at the center of affairs. The Governor provided him a house, where he unpacked his instruments: thermometers, barometers, hygrometers, an achromatic telescope, chronometers, compasses, and sextants, paraphernalia for preserving specimens, chemistry equipment, and a camera obscura. In Tangier, he busied himself for weeks with problems of geology, topography, meteorology, and the successful prediction of an eclipse. By the time the royal court arrived in August, he was a personage. He met the Sultan and quickly won his favor.

The scholars of Fez, where he traveled next, did not impress this Enlightenment traveler. Their city had been a great center of learning in Ibn Battuta's time, but the present court philosophers were incurious, superstitious, and shallow. Weary of Fez, al-Abbasi traveled south under royal escort. In Marrakesh, the Sultan deeded him a villa, where he passed the idyllic months excerpted here. In the end, however, he overstayed his welcome. The causal facts are cloudy. Either the Sultan came to resent him, or chagrined astrologer intrigued against him. Or perhaps it is true, as some sources imply, that during his stay he had traded a scientific relationship with England for a political one with France and that he planned to found a colony between Morocco and Algeria. For whatever reasons, after two years of celebrity, al-Abbasi was abruptly expelled, forced onto a royal ship and hustled off to Libya pondering the fickleness of sultans.

With the sprawling Ottoman Empire coming unraveled at its edges, 1807 proved a hard year to make the Hajj. From Algeria to the Sudan, local tribes were rising against their deys and governors, and the land routes to Egypt were in chaos. Al-Abbasi docked long enough in Tripoli to visit the court and befriend the navy's Admiral. In Alexandria, he mingled with North African grandees and so obtained letters of introduction for the Hijaz. He went to Cairo next but kept his distance from its new pasha, Muhammad Ali, who after prolonged skirmishing had finally unseated the long established Mamluks and chased them upriver. Egypt's first modernizing ruler, Muhammad Ali was himself Albanian and an admirer of French engineering. He would have appreciated meeting a scientific Muslim from the West, but al-Abbasi's expulsion from Morocco made the traveler cautious. After a few weeks, he dismissed Cairo in an epigram: "The soldier tyrannizes. The people suffer. The great endure no evil. The machine runs on as it can." With Ramadan over, he joined a caravan of five thousand pilgrims and sailed from Suez to the Hijaz.

In Mecca, al-Abbasi presented his letters to Sharif Ghalib, fiftieth ruler in the old Qitada line and the wealthiest man in the territory. Because several of our authors comment on him, Ghalib's reign is important here. He had already governed Mecca for twenty years in a lucrative alliance with the Turks. He was oppressive with his people but evenhanded with the British. As the principal voice in the India trade at Jidda, he set the rates at which goods flowed west to Europe. Just now, however, Sharif Ghalib's regime (like so many others) was facing an internal revolution—this one based on an alliance between the Saudis, a preeminent tribal family from eastern Arabia, and the followers of a radical religious reformer named Muhammad ibn Abd al-Wahhab (died 1792). United by marriage, the goal of this secular-religious alliance was to free the whole peninsula from the Turks. Sa'ud al-Sa'ud, its current leader, or Amir, had already harried Mecca (1802) and Medina (1804) with tens of thousands of militant adherents. Now they were returning for the Hajj of 1807, and Ghalib and his Turkish troops were on the spot. Al-Abbasi had arrived at a critical moment, a turning point for the Hijaz. His is the first eyewitness account of the Saudis and their army of believers.

Sharif Ghalib accepted al-Abbasi's letters and permitted him to measure the Haram. It took courage to use his instruments, however, under the scrupulous gaze of forty-five thousand Wahhabi soldiers. These vigorous, rough-hewn puritans with their own strict version of Islam believed that science meant anathema and writing was for spies. Al-Abbasi, to his credit, remained unflustered. At Arafat, against his guides' advice, he conducted personal interviews among the rough battalions surrounding al-Sa'ud's tents.

Al-Abbasi's failed attempt to reach Medina rounds out these selections. It may interest readers to know, that a little later, in Aleppo, he crossed paths with the Swiss explorer Burckhardt, whose letters contain the only surviving description of the man: a Tunisian of average size with a long, thin head, black eyes, narrow beard, prominent nose, and feet that showed he had once worn European shoes. Al-Abbasi continued home through eastern Europe. Reaching Spain at the time of the French invasion, he declared himself for Bonaparte and held office under Napoleon's brother Joseph. When the French were expelled from Spain in 1813, he retreated to Paris and saw his book through publication. The two-volume set, with maps and plates, went quickly into English. In 1816, a deluxe edition appeared in Philadelphia.

Ali Bey al-Abbasi seems to have traveled by four rules: (1) Spread money liberally from the moment you enter a new region. (2) Always address the ruling class as your equals. (3) Speak your mind. (4) Depart with as many letters of introduction as possible. His adherence to these rules and to the privileges they brought allowed him to cut a wide swath through elite Muslim society. Throughout his travels, this haughty nobleman formed real relationships with real people. He neither smiled on what displeased him nor flattered those in power. Unlike many Europeans traveling east, he did not dismiss the Arabs as infantile, nor freight them with old Crusader propaganda. His four ground rules of travel won him protection, respect, and gifts. In the end, they may have cost his life as well. Al-Abbasi left for Mecca again in 1818 but died on the road in Syria, of dysentery or poisoning, perhaps at British hands.

from *The Travels of Ali Bey al-Abbasi*

AUTHOR'S NOTE After having spent many years in the Christian states, studying the sciences of nature, and the arts most useful to man in society, (whatever be his faith or the religion of his heart), I determined at last to visit the Muslim countries; and, while engaged in performing the pilgrimage to Mecca, to observe the manners, customs, and nature of the countries through which I should pass, in order that I might make the laborious journey of some utility to the country which I at last select for my abode.

AFFAIRS AT TANGER, 1803 Soon after my arrival at Tangier my situation became sufficiently agreeable. The first visit which was paid to me by the Qadi Sidi-Abderrahman Mfarrash; my prediction of the eclipse of the sun, which was to take place on the seventeenth of August, and of which I had traced the figure as it would be seen in its greatest darkness; the appearance of my carriages and my instruments, which arrived from Europe in a vessel; my presents to the Qadi, to the Caid, as also to the principal characters there; my liberality toward others; all these circumstances contributed to fix on me the general attention, and in a very short time I attained a decided superiority over all the strangers, and even over all the persons of distinction in the town. . . .

The cannon of the batteries of Tangier announced, on the fifth of October, the arrival of the Sultan Moulay Suleyman, Emperor of Morocco, who dismounted at the castle of the town called al-Kasbah. As I had not been yet presented to the Emperor, I did not go out, but remained at home waiting his orders, as I had settled with the Caid and Qadi; hence I could not witness the ceremony of his arrival.

The next morning the Caid apprised me that I might get the customary presents ready for the following day; I did so immediately, and on the morning of the appointed day I had an interview with the Caid and Qadi, to prepare for my presentation. The Caid asked me for the rest of the presents which I intended for the Sultan; I gave them to him, and we soon agreed upon the subject.

As it was Friday I went to the great mosque to make my noon prayers, as this was an indispensable duty; the Sultan was also to be there.

Soon after entering the mosque, a Moor came to me and told me that the Sultan had just sent one of his servants to let me know that I might repair to the Kasbah at four o'clock, in order to be presented to him.

Previous to the Sultan's arrival at the mosque, some Negro soldiers entered it, but without order; they were armed, but yet placed themselves promiscuously on either side, without observing rank or file.

The Sultan was not long behind; he entered at the head of a small retinue of grandees and officers, who were all so plainly dressed that we could not distinguish them from the rest of the company. The mosque was crowded; it contained about two thousand people. While I stayed there, I kept myself rather retired.

The prayer was performed as usual on every Friday, but the sermon was preached by one of the Sultan's *faqih*s,* who insisted with energy on the point that it was a great sin to cultivate any commerce with Christians, or to sell or give them any sort of food or nourishment; with many such topics.

As soon as the prayers were over, I had a passage opened for me by my servants and went out. About a hundred black soldiers were formed out of doors in a semicircle; a numerous assembly of spectators were around them. I went home, and a few minutes after, a servant of the Sultan came to bring me a personal order from his master, and to receive the usual presents.

At three o'clock in the afternoon, the Caid sent to me some men, in order to assist in carrying my presents, which consisted of the following articles:

20 English musquets, with bayonets
2 blunderbusses of a large size
15 pairs of English pistols
Several thousands gun flints
2 sacks of shot for hunting, and a complete hunting equipage
A barrel of the best English gunpowder

faqih: an expert in Islamic jurisprudence (*fiqh*). [Ed.]

Several pieces of rich muslin, both plain and embroidered
Some trinkets
A handsome umbrella
Sweetmeats and essences

The firearms were packed up in boxes, which were locked; all the other objects were placed on large dishes, covered with pieces of red damask, bordered with silver lace. The keys of the boxes, tied together with a large ribband, were placed on a dish.

I went up to the Kasbah, marching at the head of the men and servants who were carrying my presents. The Caid was waiting for me at the door, and paid me many compliments. We crossed a portico, under which a number of officers belonging to the court were assembled, and entered into a small mosque close by, where we performed our afternoon prayers, at which the Sultan also assisted.

After prayer we left the mosque, at the door of which a mule was waiting ready for the Sultan; it was surrounded with a great number of servants and officers of high rank belonging to the court. Two men in advance were armed with pikes or lances about fourteen feet long, which they held in a perpendicular direction. The retinue was followed by about seven hundred black soldiers, armed with musquets; they were closely grouped, but without regard to order or rank, and were surrounded by a great throng.

The Caid and myself placed ourselves in the middle of the passage, close to the two lancers. At our sides were the presents, carried on the shoulders of my servants and of the men who had been sent to me.

The Sultan came out soon after and mounted his mule; when he came to the center of the circle, the Caid and myself advanced a few steps; the Sultan stopped his mule. The Caid presented me; I made an inclination with my head toward him, putting my hand on my breast. The Sultan answered by a similar inclination, and said, "You are welcome." Then turning his head toward the crowd, he invited them to salute me. "Tell him," said he, "that he is welcome," and instantly all the crowd exclaimed, "Welcome." . . . I found this Sovereign very favorably disposed toward me, at which I was the more surprised, as I had as yet done nothing to merit it.

The Sultan asked me in what countries I had traveled, what languages I spoke, and if I could write them; what were the sciences which I had studied in the Christian schools, and how long I had resided in Europe? He praised God for having caused me to leave the country of the infidels, and regretted that a man like me had deferred so long his visit to Morocco; much satisfied that I had preferred his country to Algiers, Tunis, or Tripoli, he repeated me the assurance of his protection and friendship. He then asked me whether I had any instruments to make observations, and having answered him in the affirmative, he told me that he wished to see them, and that I might bring them to him. He had hardly uttered this word, when the Caid took me by the hand in order to conduct me home; but without stirring, I observed to the Sultan that it would be necessary to wait until the next day, as it was too late to prepare them for any observations. The Caid looked at me with astonishment, as no one dares to contradict the Sultan; but this Sovereign only said, "Well, bring them tomorrow." At what o'clock? "At eight in the morning"; I shall not fail, said I, and taking leave of the Sultan, I went away with the Caid.

TEA AT THE PALACE   The next day I went to the castle at the appointed hour. The Sultan was waiting for me on the same place with his principal *faqih* or mufti,* and another favorite. He was served with tea. . . .

The tea-things consisted of a gold sugar box, a teapot, a milk pot, and three cups of white china, gilt; they were all placed on a gilt dish. The sugar was put in the teapot, according to the custom of the country, a method not very convenient, as it compels you most frequently to take it either too much or too little sweetened.

The Sultan repeated to me several times indications of his regard to me. He desired me to produce my instruments, and examined them one after another with much attention, asking me an explanation of everything that was new to him. He showed great pleasure in what he saw, and commanded me to make some astronomical observations in his presence. To satisfy him I took two heights of the sun with my multiplying circle. I showed him several astronomical tables and logarithms which I had brought with me, in order to convince him that these instruments would be of no use to anyone who did not understand these books and many others. He was very much surprised at the sight of so many figures. I then offered him my instruments; his answer was that I ought to keep them as I only knew how to use them, and that we should have plenty of days and nights to amuse ourselves in contemplating the sky. I saw from these and the former expressions that his intention was to keep me near his person, and to attach me to his service; he added that he desired to see my other instruments. I proposed to bring them the next morning, and took my leave.

The next day I attended the Sultan, and went into his chamber; he was lying on a small mattress and cushion; his high *faqih* and two of his favorites

*mufti: doctor of Islamic law (Sharia). [Ed.]

were sitting before him on a small carpet. The moment he saw me, he raised himself upright, and ordered another small blue velvet cushion, like his own, to be brought for me; he had it placed at his side, and made me sit down.

After some compliments on both sides, I ordered my electrical machine and a camera obscura to be brought in. I presented these to him as objects of mere amusement, which had no scientific application. Having prepared these two machines, I placed the camera obscura near the window. The Sultan got up and went twice into the camera; I covered him with the baize all the while that he amused himself in contemplating the objects transmitted by it. That he permitted me to do so was a mark of his high confidence in me. He afterward amused himself with seeing the electric jar discharged, and had it often repeated; but what surprised him most was the experiment of the electric shock, which I was obliged to repeat a great many times, all of us holding ourselves by the hands in order to form the chain. He asked me many and various explications of these machines, as also of the influence of electricity.

I had sent the day before to the Sultan a telescope, and asked for it now, in order to adapt it to his sight, which I immediately did, and marked the exact place on the tube, after he had found the suitable distance.

I wore very long whiskers; the Sultan asked me why I did not cut them like other Moors; I told him that it was the custom in the East to wear them at full length. He answered, "Well, well, but this is not the fashion here." He had some scissors brought in and cut a little from his own; he then laid hold of mine, and showed me what I ought to cut and what to preserve; perhaps his first intention was to clip them himself, but as I did not answer he put down the scissors.

Continuing our conversation, he asked me whether I had a proper instrument for measuring heat. I promised to send one, and took leave, carrying along with me my instruments. I sent him the same day a thermometer.

In the evening being at home, and in company with some of my friends, a servant arrived from the Sultan and brought me a present from him. In delivering it to me, he fell on his knees, and laid before me something covered with a cloth wrought with gold and silver. The curiosity of seeing the Emperor of Morocco's present made me uncover it eagerly, and I found *two black loaves*. As I was by no means prepared for such a present, I could not, at the moment, make any conjecture of its meaning, and was for a time so much staggered that I knew not what to answer. But those who were about me began eagerly to wish me joy, saying, "How happy you are: what good fortune! You are now the brother of the Sultan; the Sultan is your brother." I then began to recollect that among the Arabians the most sacred sign of fraternity consists in presenting each other with a piece of bread; and both eating of it; and therefore these two loaves sent me by the Sultan were his token of fraternity with me. They were black, because the bread made for the Sultan is baked in portable ovens of iron, which gives this black color to their outside, but they are very white and very good within. . . .

AFFAIRS AT FEZ, 1804 Fez is surrounded by vast chains of walls, which are very old and in a state of utter decay. In this enclosure New Fez and a number of large gardens are comprised. On two of the elevations on the east and west of the town two strong castles very ancient are to be seen; they consist of some square walls about sixty feet in front. It is said that there are subterraneous passages which communicate between them and the town. Whenever the people revolt against the Sultan, cannon are planted on the castles with a hundred soldiers as their guard, though this would be but a miserable defense.

The town contains a great number of schools. The most distinguished are established at the mosques of Karaouyine and of Moulay Idris, in a small house and mosque called a *madersa,* or academy.

In order to form an idea of the manner of instruction, imagine a man sitting down on the ground with his legs crossed, uttering frightful cries or singing in a tone of lamentation. He is surrounded by fifteen or twenty youths, who sit in a circle with their books or writing tables in hand and repeat the cries and songs of their master, but in complete discordance. This will give an exact notion of these Moorish schools. As to the subjects which are treated here, I can assert that, though disguised by various names, *morality* and *legislation* identified with *worship* and *dogmas* are the sole topics; that is to say, all their studies are confined to the Quran and its commentations, and to some trifling principles of grammar and logic, which are indispensable for reading and understanding even a little of the venerated text. From what I have seen, I believe that most of the commentators do not understand [these subjects] themselves. They drown their meaning in an ocean of subtleties or pretended metaphysical reasoning and entangle themselves often in such a manner that they are unable to extricate themselves. They then invoke predestination, or the absolute will of God, and thus reconcile everything.

This learned class are eternal disputers *in verba magistri;* as their understandings are not strong enough to understand the thesis which they defend, they have no other foundation on which they can support themselves, but the word of the master or of the book which they cite, right or wrong. Setting out from this principle, they are never to be convinced, because no reason can be equal, in their minds, to the word of their master or the sentence of their book.

Several of the most learned men of Fez frequented much my little circle, and I have too often been witness of these tedious and endless disputes. Frequently I availed myself of my ascendancy over them to put a stop to their debates; but wishing to produce a greater and better effect, I undertook to inspire them with doubts both on their masters and their books. In fact, having gained this point, I opened a new career to the minds of these men, whose improvable talents had been paralyzed by a sort of spiritual stagnation.

Having thus prepared my plan, I often entered into a discussion with them, and when, after some arguments which they could not refute, I had put them to silence, they had no way of answering me but by presenting me with the book, and making me read the sentence which was in favor of their opinion. I asked them who wrote that? "Such and such a one." And what was he? "A man like other men." "After this acknowledgment I shall not estimate him more than another. When he ceases to be reasonable, I shall leave him as soon as he abandons good sense to hunt after sophistry."

This manner of speaking was so new to them that in the beginning they were struck dumb with astonishment, and alternatively looked at each other and at me. At last I accustomed them to reason, a thing which they had never thought of in the whole course of their studies. By degrees they left off their silly answers to which they had accustomed themselves. I observed, however, that these doctors fell into another inconvenience not less troublesome, and that was that they began to support themselves on my words, so that they only changed their colors; their tactics were still the same.

I repeated to them a thousand times that they should not maintain a point because *Ali Bey had said so* but that, before they began to dispute, they should examine with their own reason whether the thing was probable, whether it was possible, or had ever occurred, and then they might discuss it. At last I obtained this result; and I hope that the spark of light may in time produce good consequences among them.

The study of astronomy is confounded with astrology here, too. Everyone who looks into the skies to know the time of day, or of the new moon, is considered by the people as an astrologer or prophet, who can foretell the fate of the king, of the empire, and of individuals. They have some astrological books, and this talent is very much respected with them. It opens the road to high places at court, on account of the influence which the astrologers exert in public and private affairs. As I declared deadly war against astrology and alchemy, I was happy enough, by force of reasoning, to convince some of them of the ridiculous pretensions of astrologers and alchemists.

I had a very striking opportunity of proving that they confounded astronomy with astrology; when the chief of these astronomers of Fez entreated me to give him the longitude and the latitude of every planet, on the first day of the year, in order to form a calculation and to foretell whether the year would prove a good one or a bad one. I answered him with firmness, that the science of astronomy being almost a divine one, ought never to be prostituted to the reveries and quackeries of astrology; and treating divination with contempt, I convinced him that the arbitrary beginning of the year, in the various almanacs, has no connection with nature.* I finished my philippics by showing him by the Quran, that the practice of astrology is a sin. This sentence was confirmed by several doctors of [religous law], and I was proclaimed as one of their fellows.

AN ESTATE IN MARRAKESH The Sultan was highly satisfied with my arrival at Marrakesh; so were [Prince] Moulay Abd al-Salem and all my friends at court. Soon after my arrival, the Sultan sent me a quantity of milk from his table, as a sign of his affection; and Moulay Abd al-Salem did the same. Next day I waited on them, and received new tokens of their friendship and esteem, which seemed to increase daily.

Some days afterward, the Sultan made me a present of some considerable estates, which, independently of my own funds, enabled me to maintain the expenses which my rank required. I was at home when one of the Sultan's ministers was introduced, presenting me a *firman,* by which the Sultan made me an absolute donation of a villa called Semelalia, with estates belonging to it and consisting of lands, palm trees, olive tree plantations, kitchen gardens, etc. And besides this, a house in the town was attached to them, known by the name of Sidi ben Ahmad Dukkala.

The chateau and the plantations of Semelalia had been constructed by the Sultan Sidi Muhammad, father to Moulay Suleyman, who made of it his favorite habitation. The choicest fruit trees were planted there, and the gardens were in a very agreeable state. Abundant waters, brought to them from Mount Atlas, improved the charms of this estate, which was nearly a mile in extent. It was surrounded by walls. The large fields and

---

*no connection with nature: That is, no influence upon seasonal weather, the success of crops, or human events. [Ed.]

palm tree plantations were without the walls; and within them the pleasure garden, kitchen garden, and olive plantations had each separate individual enclosures.

The house in the city was large. It was built by Ben Ahmad Dukkala,
who was a favorite minister and who governed the empire a long while. A
part of the house and the baths were of a regular and handsome construction; but the remainder, though very spacious, was but of a mean appearance. These donations are still my property. . . .

As the Sultan was to go a few days afterward to Meknes, and wished to
make my stay in the empire as agreeable as possible, he desired that I should
proceed to Essaouira, or Mogador, to partake of a party of pleasure there.
He therefore ordered the three pashas of the provinces of Haha, Scherma,
and Sous, to join all their troops at Mogador.

During the ten days that I stayed there, the weather was very change-
able; I made, however, some excellent observations, by which I was able to
ascertain the latitude at 31° 32' 40" N and the longitude 11° 55' 45" W
from the Parisian observatory.

During these ten days the pashas of Haha, of Scherma, and of Sous,
who were here with their troops, gave me the spectacle of some horse races,
of sham fights representing their battles, and of some exercises with firearms,
in which they squandered a deal of gunpowder, and made much noise. On
one of these days they gave me a sumptuous dinner in one of the sultan's
mansions, situated in a wood on the mountains; at our return from it we
were accompanied by more than a thousand horsemen, who amused themselves with horse racing and sham fighting. We went afterward to a palace
which the sultan Sidi Muhammad had been constructing in the sand plain;
I found in one of its rooms a falcon, which had been hiding itself; I took it
along with me.

Some moments afterward, as we were crossing a shallow river, one of
the soldiers, who was not far from me, discovered a large fish about two feet
and a half long, which was stunned with the noise of the passage of the horses.
The soldier therefore found it easy to thrust his sword through it and presented it to me. It is impossible to describe the happy omens which the capture of the bird and of the fish afforded my companions. . . .

Having settled at Semelalia, I was taken with a terrible disease, which threatened my life; and in three months I relapsed five times, in a very serious
manner. Three months more I passed in a very weak state of health, and

during this period I was unable to make any observations whatsoever. I remained all this time at my mansion of Semelalia. I had no physician, as I did not wish to consult any of that country, and there were no European physicians. I was therefore obliged to prescribe for myself and to make use of such medicines as I thought proper, and of which, fortunately, I had a good choice. It was happy for me that my senses were preserved. When I could make use of my legs I made some astronomical observations. . . .

At the end of the month of August the storks commonly migrate for Sudan. I had three of them in my summer garden, with their wings cut; they were very quiet and tame. They always followed me when I dined in a pavilion or in an arbor. When their wings grew again to their original size, they continued to stay with me, and seemed to have no desire to emigrate. . . .

I also had in my garden four antelopes that were become very tame. The play of these animals, when they are at liberty, is really attractive; they jump and canter in an astonishing manner. My gardeners were always at war with them, because they destroyed the plants; but I took them under my protection, as the garden was large enough to make their consumption either of no importance, or hardly perceptible. As tame as the storks, they always came about me at dinner and supper; and these seven companions became my best friends.

As I wished to keep the circuit of my dominion free from all bloodshed, I gave strict orders not to fire off a gun, or to kill any animal, by any means whatsoever. My intention was to give the birds a sacred asylum. And I can say that the warbling of these many various kinds made a real earthly paradise of my Semelalia; so much so that when I walked within the limits of my territory, though without the walls, whole bands of partridges came about me, and the rabbits ran almost over my feet. I did my utmost to attract and tame all those animals, and they answered my friendly intentions more cordially than many men who call themselves civilized . . . One might fancy that the immunity of my residence became known to a class which is called unreasonable by man, for the antelopes came in bands of hundreds to the walls of Semelalia to play their tricks, and seemed to ask for admittance.

I formed a fine collection of plants, insects, and fossils at Semelalia. Among the insects I have some *aranea galleopedes,* of a very scarce kind, with regard to their size. The first of them I saw frightened me very much, as it was passing over my chest when I was sitting on my canopy. Among the fossils, the collection of the porphyries and of rolled pebbles from the Atlas is valuable.

As I had foretold that an eclipse of the moon would take place in the night of the fifteenth of January 1805, several pashas and other men of rank assembled at my house to observe it; but unfortunately the weather was so thick, chiefly during the night, and it rained so hard, with continual gusts of wind, that it was impossible to discover the least thing.

At length I declared that I should set off for Mecca, and had, upon this subject, several discussions with the Sultan, with Moulay Abd al-Salem, and with my friends, who all united to dissuade me from this journey. They observed that even the Sultan had never made it; that their religion did not require it to be made personally; and that I might hire a pilgrim, who, making it in my name, would confer on me the same merit as if I had performed it myself. All these objections, and others useless to mention, did not alter my determination. . . .

The day on which I took my leave of the Sultan, he renewed his entreaties for me to stay. He represented to me the fatigues and dangers of so long a journey, and at last, embracing me, we parted with tears in our eyes. My leave from Moulay Abd al-Salem was really affecting, and to my last breath I shall bear in my heart the image of this beloved Prince.

The Sultan made me a present of a very magnificent tent, lined with red cloth, and adorned with silk fringes. Before he sent it to me he had it put up in his presence, and twelve *faqih*s said prayers in it, in order to draw down on me the blessings of heaven and every possible success on my journey. He added to this present some leather bags to contain the necessary provision of water for the journey, which is a matter of great importance. . . .

A FAILED ATTEMPT TO TRAVEL EAST, 1805 On my arrival at Oujda, the chief and the principal inhabitants of the village told me that I could not proceed, as they had received that very day the news of a revolution which had broken out in the kingdom of Algiers, and that much blood had been shed between the Turks and Arabs at Tlemcen, to which I was going.

I asked the chief of the village to furnish me with an escort. He told me that he had not forces enough, but that he would try and arrange things to my satisfaction.

Two days after, the chief and the principal inhabitants of Oujda requested the Shaykh al-Boanani, who is the chief of an immediate tribe, to conduct me to Tlemcen. . . . Several days passed in useless negociations. The rebels approached to the walls of Oujda and fired several shots at the inhabitants, which killed two of them. My situation became worse and worse, for on the one side my means of subsistence were exhausted, and on the other I heard that my enemies at Marrakesh had endeavored to make me suspected in the eyes of the Sultan, on account of the prolongation of my stay at Fez. . . .

I observed a mysterious behavior in my conducting officers, and some signs of intelligence among them; but as they continued to treat me with the most profound respect, I could not make any remarks to them upon it, nor form any doubts as to the nature of their secret conversations. The tribes which lived on the road where I passed continued to show me every civility and provided me with victuals and forage. I assumed the right of using an umbrella;* and everyone treated me as a brother of the Sultan. But this state of things was not of long duration. . . .

SATURDAY, AUGUST 17 Today the great mystery of my officers was unveiled to me; for they apprised me that we were going to Larache instead of Tangier, as I had been told. This behavior displeased me very much; however, after some reflection, it seemed as indifferent to me to go to one place as to another.

After this discussion we proceeded at six in the morning toward the west. An hour after we turned to the north and northwest and got into a wood of very high holm oak, much intermixed with fern. We were out of this wood at twelve, after having made numberless windings in it. We crossed a small river, and entered Larache at one in the afternoon. . . .

Larache is a small town of about four hundred houses. It is situated on the north side of the steep descent of a hill, and its houses extend to the banks of the river, the mouth of which forms a port for large vessels. Those which do not exceed two hundred tons can get into the river, but they are obliged to unload in order to pass the bar. . . .

By order of the Sultan, the Pasha of the town, Sidi Muhammad Salani, assigned me the best house in the town; it was situated in the marketplace, near the principal mosque.

Notwithstanding these advantages, I could not make any lunary observations, as I dared not get on the top of the house. My longitude, however, was well established, by the eclipses of the satellites; and I found it to be at 8° 21' 45" W from the Parisian observatory. The latitude I computed to be 35° 13' 15" N; my magnetical declination 21° 39' 15" W. The climate was very mild, and the same as in Andalusia. . . .

In consequence of the violent journey from Oujda, I was taken ill for ten days. Some of my people and cattle were also indisposed and lame; however, we had none dead except one mule. I took some sea bathing, upon which

*a symbolic gesture usually reserved for royalty.

occasion I did not forget my collections, for I gathered several maritime productions.

A corvette from Tripoli was in this port, where it had laid several months. The Sultan ordered it to be fitted out at his cost, and the cabin in the stern was assigned to me for my passage to the East. I examined this vessel, which was in fact going to Tripoli, and I had the cabin fitted out properly for this long voyage.

Sunday, 13 December 1805, being fixed for my departure, I called in the morning on the Pasha and took leave of him. He received me with all possible demonstrations of esteem and consideration, and engaged me to delay my departure till three in the afternoon, in order to have the pleasure of being himself present at it. I could not but accept of so kind an offer. As my equipages had been brought on board, I went at the appointed hour to the port in order to embark myself with all my people.

I asked for the Pasha, and they told me that he was coming. In the meanwhile I waited the arrival of the boat. . . . The boat arrived, but the Pasha did not come. I therefore determined to go on board, when all of a sudden two detachments of soldiers came up to me on both sides, and a third detachment from the . . . lane. The two first ones laid hold of my people, and the third, surrounding me, ordered me to embark alone and to depart that very moment. I asked for the reason of so strange a treatment; they answered, *"It is the order of the Sultan."* I wished to speak to the Pasha, and they said bluntly, *"Embark."* This was enough to prove to me the bad intentions of the Sultan and the Pasha, who to the last moment had ordered all possible honors to be conferred on me as well by the troops as by the people, while they had been meditating a blow which was to affect me most deeply, as the fate and welfare of my people interested me as much as my own.

I went into the boat with a broken heart, hearing the cries of some of my people, and got down the river. My rage and despair was only interrupted by the passage over the bar of the river, where the motion of the water caused me a severe seasickness. Exhausted by this violent moral and physical exhaustion, I arrived, almost in a senseless state, at the corvette, which was lying at anchor at some distance from the bar. I was taken into the cabin, and went to bed.

In this manner I left the empire of Morocco. I suppress now the reflections which they excited; perhaps one day I may have an occasion to express them. . . .

CAIRO, 1806 Several Christian travelers have represented the streets of Cairo as being extremely dirty and of a dull appearance. I can certify that I have seen few cities in Europe whose streets were cleaner. The ground is extremely soft, without stones, and appears like a watered walk. If there are some streets narrow, there is a much greater number broad, although all of them appear narrower than they really are, on account of the projection of the first floors over the streets, as at Alexandria, which advance so far that in some narrow streets they are only a few inches distant from the houses in front of them. Notwithstanding, this form of the streets, in a country so hot, is very agreeable.

Far from the streets of Cairo exhibiting a dull appearance, they present as gay and agreeable a view as those of the large cities of Europe, on account of the number of shops and warehouses, and the immense multitude of people who parade them at every moment. The quarter of the Franks, or Europeans, situated in a hollow, is solitary, and separated from the great commerce, which may have given rise to this description. I do not deny that the abode of the Europeans at Cairo is disagreeable to them, shut up as they are in their quarter, and obstinately persevering in preserving the costume and the manners of their country. When they go out, the natives stare at them; and they walk as if they were scared. Can the Arabs be reproached for this conduct, when at London the civilized English may be seen doing the same thing, and insulting the poor stranger who may present himself in a coat two fingers longer or shorter than their own? . . .

The largest suburb of Cairo is Bulaq. The city being at some distance from the Nile, Bulaq is the port. It has some good buildings, and, by its position, is not likely to sink into neglect like Giza and Old Cairo. It is a large place, and the port is enlivened by a number of vessels which carry on a trade with the banks of the Nile that occupies many hands. The customs produce considerable sums. The road from Bulaq to Cairo is superb, since it has been repaired and embellished by the French.

In speaking of the commerce of Bulaq, it may be imagined that it is hardly the shadow of what it ought to be, since the insurrection of Upper Egypt, to which place the Mamluks with Ibrahim Bey and Osman Bey Bardissi have retired, makes Cairo lose all the trade of the interior of Africa. The revolutions in Barbary prevent the arrival or departure of caravans for Morocco, Algiers, and the whole of the western countries.

The wandering Arabs of the desert repair to the environs of Suez to rob the caravans, which convey effects from Arabia and the Indies that arrive by the Red Sea. The war with England suspends the commerce with the Mediterranean. These are the causes which have diminished the exterior commerce of Egypt.

The interior commerce is not more flourishing. The Mamluks reign over all Upper Egypt; Elfi Bey, in the province of Beheira; the Arabs of the province of Sharqiya are in rebellion; partial revolutions occur continually in the Delta; in short, it may be said that it is almost impossible to perform the least journey in Egypt without running the greatest risks.

When I see Cairo carrying on so great trade as it does under such fatal circumstances, I say Egypt is a great country. But what would it be under more favorable circumstances, and a tutelary government!

JIDDA TO MECCA, 1807 Being a little recovered, though very weak, I set out for Mecca on Wednesday the twenty-first of January, at three o'clock in the afternoon.

I traveled in a machine made of sticks and covered with cushions, of the form of a sofa or cabriolet, roofed with boughs upon arches, which they placed upon the back of a camel, and called a *shevria*. It was very convenient, as I was enabled to sit up or lie down in it, but the motion of the camel, which I felt for the first time in my life, completely exhausted me in the feeble state that I was in. My Arabs began to dispute before they left the town, and continued during a whole hour, shouting and stunning everybody. I thought they had finished; but new disputes and cries arose when we were outside the walls, which lasted another hour. At last a calm succeeded to the storm, and the camels being loaded, we set out upon our way at five in an easterly direction, across a large desert plain terminated at the horizon by groups of small detached mountains, the aspect of which gave a little variety to the picture.

At half-past eight in the evening we arrived at the mountains, which are composed of bare stone, and do not produce any vegetation.

The serene atmosphere, and the moon, which shone bright above our heads, rendered our journey very agreeable. My Arabs sang and danced around me. For my part, I was far from being at my ease; the motion of the camel was insupportable. At length, stunned by their noise, exhausted by fatigue, and my weak state, I fell asleep during two hours. When I awoke my fever was increased, and I vomited some blood.

My Arabs having fallen sleep, we lost our way; but discovering about midnight that we directed our course to Mocha, we changed it to the northeast, passing between woody mountains of a certain height, and having found our road again, we continued eastward until six o'clock in the morning, when we halted at a small hamlet called Hadda, where there was a well of briny water.

I could not exactly estimate the distance we had gone, but I think we were about eight leagues to the east of Jidda. . . .

At midnight, between Thursday and Friday the twenty-third of January 1807, I arrived through the favor of divine mercy at the first houses of the holy city of Mecca, fifteen months after my departure from Morocco.

There were at the entrance of the town several North African Arabs, who were waiting my arrival with little pitchers of the water from the Well of Zamzam, which they presented me to drink, begging me not to take it of any other person, and offering to supply my house. They told me secretly never to drink the water which the chief of the wells should offer to me.

Several other persons, who were also waiting, disputed between themselves which should have me for a lodger, for the lodgings are one of the principal speculations of the inhabitants. But the persons who were charged with providing everything for me during my stay at Jidda soon put an end to these disputes, by taking me to a house that had been prepared for me. It was situated near the temple, and the house inhabited by the Sultan Sharif.

Pilgrims ought to enter on foot into Mecca, but in consequence of my illness I remained upon my camel until I arrived at my lodging.

The moment I entered, I performed a general ablution, after which I was conducted in procession toward the temple, with all my people, by a person appointed for that purpose, who as he walked along recited different prayers in a loud voice, which we repeated altogether word for word in the same tone. I was supported by two persons, on account of my extreme weakness.

In this manner we arrived at the temple, making a tour by the principal street to enter at the Bab al-Salaam, or Gate of Health, which they look upon as a happy auspice. After having taken off our sandals, we entered in at this blessed gate, which is placed near the northern angle of the temple. We had already traversed the portal, or gallery, and were upon the point of entering the great space where the House of God, or Ka'ba, is situated, when our guide arrested our steps and, pointing with his finger toward it, said with emphasis, *"Shouf, shouf, al-Bayt Allah al-Haram."* "Look, look, the House of God, the Prohibited." The crowd that surrounded me; the portico of columns half-hidden from view; the immense size of the temple; the Ka'ba, or House of God, covered with the black cloth from top to bottom and surrounded with a circle of lamps or lanterns; the hour; the silence of the night; and this man speaking in a solemn tone, as if he had been inspired; all served to form an imposing picture, which will never be effaced from my memory.

We entered into the court by a path a foot high, bordering diagonally upon the northern angle of the Ka'ba, which is nearly in the center of the temple. Before we arrived at it, we passed under a sort of isolated triumphal arch, called Bab al-Salaam, like the gate by which we had entered. Being arrived at the House of God, we repeated a little prayer, kissed the sacred Black Stone brought by the angel Gabriel, named Hajar al-Aswad, or the Heavenly Stone; and, having the guide at our head, we performed the first tour round the Ka'ba, reciting prayers at the same time.

The Ka'ba is a quadrilateral tower, entirely covered with an immense black cloth, except the base. The Black Stone is revealed through an opening in the cloth. It is encrusted on the eastern angle. A similar opening to the former at the southern angle discovers a part of it, which is of common marble. On the northwest side rises a parapet about a leaning height, forming nearly a semicircle, separated from the building, called the Stone of Ishmael.

The following is a detail of the ulterior ceremonies which are observed in this religious act, such as I performed them myself at this period.

The pilgrims go seven times round the Ka'ba, beginning at the Black Stone, or the eastern angle, and passing the principal front, in which is the door; from whence turning to the west and south, outside of the Stone of Ishmael. Being arrived at the southern angle, they stretch out the right arm; when, having touched the angular marble with the hand, taking great care that the lower part of their garment does not touch the uncovered base, they pass it over the face and beard, saying, "In the name of God, the greatest God, praises be to God," and they continue to walk toward the northeast, saying, "Oh great God! be with me! Give me the good things of this world, and those of the next." Being returned to the eastern angle, they raise their hands as at the beginning of the canonical prayer, and cry, "In the name of God, the greatest God." They afterward say, with their hands down, "Praises be to God," and kiss the Black Stone. Thus terminates the first tour.

The second is like the first, except that the prayers are different from the angle of the Black Stone to that of the south; but they are the same from the latter to the former, and are repeated with the same forms during the seven rounds. The traditional law orders that the last rounds should be made in a quick step; but in consequence of my weak state we went very slowly.

At the end of the seventh, and after having kissed the Black Stone, they recite in common a short prayer, standing near the door of the Ka'ba, from whence they go to a sort of cradle called Maqam Ibrahim, or the place of

Abraham, situated between the Ka'ba and the arch Bab al-Salaam, when they recite a common prayer. They then go to the Well Zamzam, and draw buckets of water, of which they drink as much as they can swallow. After this they leave the temple by Bab al-Safa, or the Gate of Safa, from whence they go up a small street facing, which forms what is called the Hill of Safa.

At the end of this street, which is terminated by a portico composed of three arches upon columns, ascended by steps, is the sacred place called Safa. When the pilgrims have arrived there, they turn their faces toward the gate of the temple and recite a short prayer standing.

The procession then directs its course through the principal street and passes a part of the Hill of Marwa, the pilgrims reciting some prayers at the end of the street, which is terminated by a great wall. They then ascend some steps and, turning their faces toward the temple, the view of which is interrupted by the intervening houses, recite a short prayer standing and continue to go from the one hill to the other seven times, repeating prayers in a loud voice as they proceed, and short ones at the two sacred places, which constitute the seven journeys between the two hills.

These being completed, there are a number of barbers in waiting to shave the pilgrims' heads, which they do very quickly, at the same time saying prayers in a loud tone, which the former repeat after them word for word. This operation terminates the first ceremonies of the pilgrimage to Mecca. . . .

The day beginning to dawn when I had finished these first ceremonies, they told me I might retire to take a little rest; but as the hour for morning prayer was not far distant, I preferred to return to the temple, notwithstanding my weakness, which was increased by fatigue; and I did not return home until six o'clock in the morning, after prayers. . . .

A VISIT WITH THE SHARIF   I received an order in the afternoon to hold myself in readiness to present myself to the Sultan Sharif.

The chief [assistant] of the Sharifs came to conduct me to the palace. He entered, but I waited at the door for the order to go in. A moment after, the chief of the well, who was already my friend, came to meet me. We ascended the staircase, in the middle of which was a door that stopped our passage. My guide knocked at it, when two armed servants opened it. We continued to ascend; we traversed a dark gallery; and, after having left our sandals in this place, we entered into a fine saloon, in which was the Sultan Sharif (named Sharif Ghalib), seated near a window, surrounded by six persons who were standing.

After I had saluted him, he asked me the following questions:
"Do you speak Arabic?"*
"Yes, sire."
"And Turkish?"
"No, sire."
"Arabic only?"
"Yes, sire."
"Do you speak any Christian languages?"
"Some."
"Of what country are you?"
"Haleb, or Alep [Aleppo, Syria]."
"Did you leave it when young?"
"Yes, sire."
"Where have you been since?"
I related my history to him. The Sharif then said to him who was on his left, "He speaks Arabic very well; his accent is pure," and addressing himself to me, he cried, "Come near to me." I approached a little. He repeated, "Come near to me." I then went close to him. He said, "Sit down." I hastened to comply, and immediately he made the person upon his left sit down. "You have without doubt," said the Sharif, "some news from the Christian lands. Tell me the last you have heard." I related to him briefly the actual state of Europe. He asked me if I could read and write French. "A little, sire," I replied. "A little, or well?" "A little, and incorrectly, sire." "Which are the languages that you speak and write the best?" "Italian and Spanish." We continued this conversation during an hour. At length, after having made him my present, and delivered the *firman* of the Captain Pasha, I retired, accompanied by my friend the chief of Zamzam, who conducted me to my house. . . .

The Sultan Sharif of Mecca is the son of Sharif Mas'ad, his predecessor. Many years have elapsed since his family obtained possession of the Hijaz. The same custom prevails here as at Morocco upon the death of the Sultan, in regard to the obtaining of the throne, for the right of succession is not established.

The Sharif Ghalib is a man of sense, cunning, political, and brave, but completely ignorant. Led away by his passions, he is transformed into a vile egotist, so that there is not any species of vexation which he does not exercise upon the inhabitants, strangers, or pilgrims. His inclination for rapine

*The Sharif thought that I was a Turk.

147

is such that he does not even spare his most intimate friends or faithful servants, when he thinks he can obtain a sum from them. During my stay, I observed him commit an injury to a merchant of Jidda, who was one of his greatest favorites, which occasioned a loss of one hundred thousand francs to the latter. The imposts leveled upon commerce, as also upon the inhabitants, are entirely arbitrary and increase every day, because he invents new methods of stripping them of their money. He reduces the people to the last extremity, so that I did not find one person in the whole Holy Land who spoke well of him, except the merchant above mentioned.

Besides overloading commerce by arbitrary taxes, he injures the merchant and puts fetters upon him, because he himself takes an active part in commerce by means of his own ships. No private ship can be loaded or unloaded until his are completed; and as these are the largest, best built, and best manned, they absorb the greatest part of the trade of the Red Sea, to the ruin of the merchants, who find themselves reduced by these means to a state of slavery.

The English are looked upon as the best friends of the Sharif, on account of the direct interest he enjoys by his traffic with the Indies through their means, notwithstanding which he does not spare them, when he can oppress them. Last year an English ship loaded with rice put into Jidda. The captain, having landed, found this article very cheap in the country. He therefore resolved to go to another port, but the Sharif pretended that the captain ought to pay all the dues, as if he had landed and sold his cargo. After some very warm discussions, the captain was obliged to leave the port, in order to escape the rapacity of the Sharif. . . .

THE WAHHABIS One day a part of the army of the Wahhabis entered Mecca to fulfill the duties of pilgrimage, and to take possession of this holy city. It was by chance I saw them enter.

I was in the principal street, about nine o'clock, when I saw a crowd of men coming; but what men! We must imagine a crowd of individuals thronged together without any other covering than a small piece of cloth round their waist, except some few who had a napkin placed upon the left shoulder that passed under the right arm, being naked in every other respect, with their matchlocks upon their shoulders, and their large knives hung to their girdles.

All the people fled at the sight of this torrent of men and left them the whole street to themselves. I determined to keep my post, not being in the least alarmed, and I mounted upon a heap of rubbish to observe them better.

I saw a column of them defile, which appeared composed of five or six thousand men, so pressed together in the whole width of the street that it would not have been possible to have moved a hand. The column was preceded by three or four horsemen armed with lances twelve feet long, and followed by fifteen or twenty men mounted upon horses, camels, and dromedaries, with lances like the others; but they had neither flags, drums, nor any other instrument or military trophy during their march. Some uttered cries of holy joy; others recited prayers in a confused and loud voice.

They marched in this manner to the upper part of the town, where they began to file off in parties, to enter the temple by the Bab al-Salaam.

A great number of children belonging to the city, who generally serve as guides to strangers, came to meet them and presented themselves successively to the different parties, to assist them as guides in the sacred ceremonies. I remarked that among these benevolent guides there was not one man. Already had the first parties begun their turns round the Ka'ba and were pressing toward the Black Stone to kiss it, when the others, impatient no doubt at being kept waiting, advanced in a tumult, mixing among the first, and, confusion being soon at its height, prevented them from hearing the voices of their young guides. Tumult succeeded to confusion. All wishing to kiss the stone, precipitated themselves upon the spot, and many of them made their way with their sticks in their hands. In vain did their chiefs mount the base near the stone, with a view to enforce order: their cries and signs were useless, for the holy zeal for the House of God which devoured them would not permit them to listen to reason, nor to the voice of their chiefs.

The movement of the circle increased by mutual impulse. They resembled at last a swarm of bees which flutter confusedly round their hive, circulating rapidly and without order round the Ka'ba. By their tumultuous pressure they broke all the lamps which surrounded it with their guns, which they carried upon their shoulders.

After the different ceremonies round the House of God, every party ought to have drunk and sprinkled themselves with the water of the miraculous well, but they rushed to it in such crowds and with so much precipitation that in a few moments the ropes, the buckets, and pulleys were ruined. The chief, and those employed at the Zamzam, abandoned their post: the Wahhabis alone remained masters of the well and, giving each other their hands, formed a chain to descend to the bottom, and obtained the water how they could.

The well required alms, the House of God offerings, the guides demanded their pay, but the greater part of the Wahhabis had not brought any money with them. They acquitted themselves of this obligation of conscience by giving twenty or thirty grains of a very coarse gunpowder, small pieces of lead, or some grains of coffee.

These ceremonies being finished, they commenced shaving their heads, for they all had hair an inch long. This operation took place in the street, and they paid the barbers in the same coin that they had paid the guides, the officers of the temple, etc.

These Wahhabis, who are from Dir'iyya, the principal place of the reformers, are of a copper color. They are in general well made and very well proportioned, but of a short stature. I particularly remarked some of their heads, which were so handsome that they might have been compared with those of Apollo, Antinous, or the gladiator. They have very lively eyes, the nose and mouth well formed, fine teeth, and very expressive countenances.

When we represent to ourselves a crowd of naked armed men without any idea of civilization and speaking a barbarous language, the picture terrifies the imagination and appears disgusting; but if we overcome this first impression, we find in them some commendable qualities. They never rob either by force or stratagem, except when they know the object belongs to an enemy or an infidel. They pay with their money all their purchases, and every service that is rendered them. Being blindly subservient to their chiefs, they support in silence every fatigue and would allow themselves to be led to the opposite side of the globe. In short, it may be perceived that they are men the most disposed to civilization, if they were to receive proper instruction.

Having returned home, I found that fresh bodies of Wahhabis were continually arriving, to fulfill the duties of their pilgrimage. But what was the conduct of the Sultan Sharif during this period? Being unable to resist these forces, he hid himself, fearing an attack from them. The fortresses were provisioned and prepared for defense. The Arabian, Turkish, Maghribi, and Negro soldiers were at their posts. I saw several guards and sentinels upon the forts; several gates were walled up. All was ready, in short, in case of aggression, but the moderation of the Wahhabis, and the negociations of the Sharif, rendered these precautions useless.

PILGRIMAGE TO ARAFAT The grand day of the pilgrimage to Mount Arafat being fixed for Tuesday the seventeenth of February, I left the city the preceding afternoon, in a *shevria* placed upon a camel.

At two o'clock I passed the barracks of the Negro and Maghribi guards, which are situated at the northern extremity of the town. Afterward, turning to the east, I saw a large country house belonging to the Sharif and soon obtained a view of the celebrated Jabal Nur, or Mountain of Light. It was upon this spot that the angel Gabriel brought the first chapter of the Quran to the greatest of prophets. This mountain, which presents the appearance of a sugar loaf, rises alone above the others that surround it. There was a chapel formerly upon its summit, which was an object that the pilgrims visited, but the Wahhabis, having destroyed it, have placed a guard at the foot of the mountain, to prevent them from ascending and saying their prayers, which Abd al-Wahhab* has declared to be superstitious. It is said there is a staircase cut in the rock to facilitate the ascent. As it was situated a quarter of a league to our left, I only looked at it in passing with the crowd of pilgrims, but I took a sketch of it.

Upon turning the road to the east southeast about three o'clock, I saw a small spring of fresh water with stone basins; and shortly after I entered Mina, where the first thing I perceived was a fountain, in front of which is an ancient edifice said to have been built by the devil.

The town of Mina, called by some Muna, is composed of a single street, which is so long that it took me twenty minutes to pass through it. There are several handsome houses in it; but the greater number are in ruins and without roofs. There are several dwellings of dry stone about five feet high, which they let to pilgrims during the time of pilgrimage.

About four o'clock we pitched my camp upon the eastern side of Mina, in a little plain, where there was a mosque surrounded by a wall that resembled a fortification.

The country lies in a valley, between mountains of granite rocks that are perfectly bare. The road, which was very level upon a sandy bottom, was covered with camels, with persons on foot or on horseback and with a great number of *shevria*s, of the same form as my own.

A detachment of Wahhabis, mounted upon dromedaries, which I saw first at the foot of Jabal Nur, arrived, and encamped also before the door of the mosque. This was followed by several others, also mounted, so that in a short time the plain was covered. About sunset, the Sultan of the Wahhabis, named Sa'ud al-Sa'ud,† arrived, and his tents were pitched at the foot of a mountain, at a short distance from mine.

A caravan from Tripoli in Barbary, another from Yemen, a great number of Negro pilgrims from Sudan or Abyssinia, several hundred Turks from

---

*Muhammad ibn Abd al-Wahhab (died 1792), founder of their movement.

†Sa'ud al-Sa'ud: the third Saudi Amir (reigned 1803–1814), who extended the control of his predecessors into the Hijaz.

Suez, a great many Maghribi, who came by sea; a caravan from Basra, others from the East, Arabs from Upper and Lower Egypt, those of the country in which we were, and the Wahhabis were now all assembled and encamped together, or rather one upon the other, in this little plain. Here the pilgrims are obliged to camp, because tradition relates that the holy Prophet always did so when he went to Arafat.

The caravan from Damascus had not arrived; however, it had set out with troops, artillery and a great number of women to convey the rich carpet which is sent every year from Constantinople to the sepulcher of the Prophet at Medina. This present the Wahhabis look upon as a sin. The caravan was close to Medina when the Wahhabis went and met it and signified to the Pasha of Damascus, who that year was the acting Amir al-Hajj, that they could not receive the carpet which was destined for the sepulcher, and that if he wished to continue his journey to Mecca, he must first send back his soldiers, his artillery, and the women, so that by transforming themselves into true pilgrims, they would experience no impediment to the continuation of their journey. The Pasha, not willing to conform to these conditions, was desired to retrace his steps. Some pretend to say that the Wahhabis required a large sum of money from him, but others deny this fact.

On Tuesday the seventeenth of February 1807, the ninth of Dhu al-Hijja, at six o'clock in the morning, we all set out toward the southeast one-quarter east. At a short distance we passed a house of the Sharif; and at seven we arrived at Muzdalifa, a small chapel with a high minaret situated in a small valley. After leaving this, we defiled through a very narrow passage between the mountains and traversed a second valley to the southeast, which lay at the foot of Mount Arafat, where we arrived at nine.

Mount Arafat is the principal object of the pilgrimage of the Musselmen; and several doctors of Islamic law assert, that if the House of God ceased to exist, the pilgrimage to the former would be completely meritorious, and would produce the same degree of satisfaction. This is my opinion likewise.

It is here that the grand spectacle of the pilgrimage of the Musselmen must be seen—an innumerable crowd of men from all nations and of all colors, coming from the extremities of the earth through a thousand dangers, and encountering fatigues of every description, to adore together the same God, the God of nature. The native of Circassia presents his hand in a friendly manner to the Ethiopian, or the Negro of Guinea. The Indian and the Persian embrace the inhabitant of Barbary and Morocco. All look upon each other as brothers, or individuals of the same family united by the bands of religion, and the greater part speak or understand more or less the same language, the language of Arabia. No, there is not any religion that presents to the senses a spectacle more simple, affecting, and majestic! Philosophers of the earth! permit me, Ali Bey, to defend my religion (and the necessary existence of the Creation), as one defends spiritual things from those which are material, the plenum against a vacuum.

(Here, as I remarked in the narrative of my voyage to Morocco, is no intermediary between man and the Divinity. All individuals are equal before their Creator, all are intimately persuaded that their works alone reconcile them to, or separate them from, the Supreme Being, without any foreign hand being able to change the order of immutable justice. What a curb to sin! What an encouragement to virtue! But what a misfortune that, with so many advantages, we should not be better than the Calvinists.)

Arafat is a small mountain of granite rock, the same as those that surround it. It is about 150 feet high and is situated at the foot of a higher mountain to the east-southeast, in a plain about three quarters of a league in diameter, surrounded by barren mountains.

It is enclosed by a wall, and is ascended by staircases partly cut in the rock and partly composed of masonry. There is a chapel upon its summit, which the Wahhabis were then in the act of pulling to pieces in the interior. It was impossible for me to visit it, because individuals who follow the same rite as myself, that is to say, the Malikites, are forbidden to ascend the top, according to the instructions of the *imam,* the founder of the rite. It was therefore that we stopped when we were halfway up, to recite our prayer. At the foot of the mountain there is a platform erected for this purpose, called the Mosque of Mercy, upon which, according to tradition, the Prophet used to say his prayer.

Near the mountain are fourteen large basins which the Sultan Sa'ud has put in repair. They furnish a great abundance of excellent water, very good to drink, and which serves also for the pilgrims to wash themselves with upon this solemn day. The Sharif has a house close to the southwest side of the mountain. Toward the northwest there is a second platform for offering up prayers, which is situated about a quarter of a league from the first and is called Jemaa Ibrahim, or the Mosque of Abraham.

It was upon Mount Arafat that the common father of all mankind met Eve after a long separation; and it is on that account that it is called Arafat, that is to say, Gratitude. It is believed that it was Adam himself who built this chapel.

Ritual commands that after having repeated the afternoon prayer, which we did in our tents, we should repair to the foot of the mountain and await there the setting of the sun. The Wahhabis, who were encamped at great distances, with a view to obeying this precept, began to approach, having at their head the Sultan Saʿud, and Abu Noqta, their second chief. In a short time I saw an army of forty-five thousand men pass before me, almost all of whom were mounted upon camels and dromedaries, with a thousand camels carrying water, tents, firewood, and dry grass for the camels of the chiefs. A body of two hundred men on horseback carried colors of different kinds, fixed upon lances. This cavalry, I was informed, belonged to Abu Noqta. There were also eight or ten colors among the camels, but without any other customary appendage. All this body of men, almost naked, marched in the same order that I have formerly remarked.

It was impossible for me exactly to distinguish the Sultan and the second chief, for they were attired like the rest. However, I believe that a venerable old man with a long white beard, who was preceded by the royal standard, was Saʿud. This standard was green, and had, as a mark of distinction, the profession of his faith, *"La illaha ila Allah,"* "There is no other god but God," embroidered upon it in large white characters.

I distinguished perfectly one of Saʿud's sons, a boy about seven or eight years old, with long and flowing hair. He was brown like the rest and dressed in a large white shirt. He was mounted on a superb white horse, upon a sort of pannel without stirrups, according to their custom, for they are not acquainted with any other kind of saddle, and he was escorted by a chosen troop. The pannel was covered with a red cloth richly embroidered and spangled with gold stars.

The mountain and its environs were soon covered with Wahhabis. The caravans and detached pilgrims afterward approached it. Notwithstanding the remonstrances of my people, I penetrated among the Wahhabis to their center, to be able to obtain a nearer view of the Sultan. (Several of them with whom I conversed assured me that this was impossible, since the apprehension of a similar death to that which occurred to the unfortunate Abd al-Aziz,* who was assassinated, had occasioned Saʿud to multiply the number of his guard.)

I must allow that I discovered much reason and moderation among the Wahhabis to whom I spoke, and from whom I obtained the greater part of the information which I have given concerning their nation. However,

*Abd al-Aziz: the second Saudi Amir (reigned 1765–1803), who extended the control of his father, Ibn Saʿud, through the interior of Arabia.

notwithstanding this moderation, neither the natives of the country nor the pilgrims could hear their name pronounced without trembling and never pronounced it themselves but in murmurs. Thus they fly from them as much as possible, and shun conversation with them; in consequence of which I had to encounter and overcome the different scruples of my people who surrounded me whenever I wished to converse with any of them.

The Sultan Sharif had sent, according to annual custom, a part of his troops with four small pieces of artillery. It was reported even that he would come in person, but I did not see him.

It is customary also, that an imam of the Sharif should come every year and preach a sermon upon the mountain. The one that came this day was sent back by Saʿud before he commenced, and one of his own imams preached in his stead, but I was too far off to be able to hear anything. The sermon being over, I observed the Wahhabis make signs of approbation, and they cried outrageously.

I could easily have found means to introduce myself to Sultan Saʿud, which I very much desired, so that I might have known him perfectly; but as it would have compromised me with the Sultan Sharif, who would have attributed this simple action of curiosity to some political motive, I abstained from effecting it.

We waited upon the mountain for the period of the sun's setting. The instant it occurred, what a tremendous noise! Let us imagine an assemblage of eighty thousand men, two thousand women, and a thousand little children, sixty or seventy thousand camels, asses, and horses, which at the commencement of night began to move in a quick pace along a narrow valley, according to the ritual, marching one after the other in a cloud of sand and delayed by a forest of lances, guns, swords, etc., in short, forcing their passage as they could. Pressed and hurried on by those behind, we only took an hour and a half to return to Muzdalifa, notwithstanding it had taken us more than two hours to arrive in the morning. The motive of this precipitation ordered by the ritual is that the prayer of the setting sun ought not to be said at Arafat, but at Muzdalifa, at the same time as the night prayer, which ought to be said at the last moment of twilight, that is, an hour and a half after sunset. These prayers are repeated by each group or family privately. We hastened to say them upon our arrival, before we pitched our tents, and the day was terminated by mutual felicitations upon the happiness of our sanctification by the pilgrimage to Arafat.

THE RETURN TO MINA We set out the next day . . . at five o'clock in the morning, to go to encamp at Mina.

We alighted immediately after our arrival, and went precipitately to the pillar of the devil, which is facing the fountain. We had each seven small stones of the size of gray peas, which we had picked up expressly the evening before at Muzdalifa to throw against the pillar. Musselmen of the rite of Maliki, like myself, throw them one after the other, pronouncing after every one these words, *"Bismillah Allahu akbar!"* which interpreted are "In the name of God, very great God!" As the devil has had the malice to build his house in a very narrow place, not above thirty-four feet broad, occupied also in part by rocks, which it was requisite to climb to make sure of our aim when we threw the stones over the wall that surrounded it, and as the pilgrims all desired to perform this ceremony immediately upon their arrival, there was a most terrible confusion. However, I soon succeeded in accomplishing this holy duty through the aid of my people, but I came off with two wounds in my left leg. I retired afterward to my tent, to repose myself after these fatigues. The Wahhabis came and threw their little stones also, because the Prophet used to do so. We offered up the paschal sacrifice this day.

I must praise the moderation and good order which reigned amidst this number of individuals, belonging to different nations. Two thousand women who were among them did not occasion the least disorder; and though there were more than forty or fifty thousand guns, there was only one let off, which happened near me. At the same instant one of the chiefs ran to the man who had fired and reprimanded him, saying, "Why did you do this? Are we going to make war here?"

I met the eldest son of Sa'ud upon my way, in the morning. He was on horseback, at the head of a body of dromedaries, and arrived at Mina at the same time I did. At the moment of passing by my side, he cried to his company, "Come, children, let us approach." Then turning to the left, he galloped off, followed by his suite, to his father's tent, which was pitched as before at the foot of the mountain. Mine were situated opposite those belonging to the troops of the Sharif.

Having risen at break of day on Thursday the nineteenth to say my prayer, I perceived that my writing desk, books, papers, and some clothes had been stolen. My writing desk contained my chronometer, some jewels and other trifles, my great seal, and several astronomical observations and drawings.

My servants began to hunt on all sides, fearing the consequences of this robbery, because they had neglected to mount guard according to my desire; but being much fatigued on the preceding days, and the guard of the Turkish and Maghribi soldiers being close to my tents, they had been induced to take repose.

I finished my prayer, surrounded by my people; and when it was completely daylight, they discovered papers scattered over the mountain. They ran to the spot, and found my writing desk open, with the lock forced, and all my papers and books scattered about. The chronometer, jewels, and the tables of logarithms, which were bound, and which the thieves mistook for a Quran in the dark, were missing. . . .

A FAILED ATTEMPT TO REACH MEDINA I had a great desire to go to Medina to visit the sepulcher of the Prophet, notwithstanding the express order of the Wahhabis to the contrary. The thing was hazardous, but I succeeded in encouraging several Turkish and Arab pilgrims to undertake the risk of the journey with me.

As the Captain had his family at Yanbu, where the fleet was going to stay several days, we engaged with him that we would return within eight or nine, to which he consented. . . .

I sent for some dromedaries immediately, to enable us to traverse the country as quickly as possible, but with all my diligence, I was not able to set out before the next evening. I took with me nothing but a small trunk, with my instruments. Three servants alone accompanied me. I left the others, with my effects, on board the vessel. . . .

Two hours after we had set out, two Wahhabis coming from the mountains stopped my camels and asked me whither I was going. I told them to Medina. I received for answer that I could not continue my journey. A chief then presented himself, accompanied by two officers mounted upon camels, and interrogated me anew. The chief, believing me to be a Turk, threatened to cut off my head. I answered his questions very coolly, without being at all alarmed by his menaces. My answers were attested by my servants. In vain my imagination recalled to me at this moment the news which had circulated at Jidda, that all the Turks leaving Mecca had been strangled: my demeanor was in no degree less calm. They ordered me to give them my money; I gave them four Spanish piastres which I had in my pocket. They insisted upon having more. I declared to them I had not anymore, and told them they might search my effects if they pleased. They pretended that I had money hidden in my belt (an ordinary custom in the East). I said not. They insisted: I then threw my cloak upon the ground, and began to undress myself to satisfy them. They prevented me; but seeing the chain of my watch, they took it by force, and repeated their menaces. After having robbed me, they desired us to proceed, and indicated to the camel driver a spot very near, where we were to dismount and wait their orders.

Being arrived at the appointed spot, I immediately destroyed a case which contained the insects I had collected in Arabia, and threw it far from me, as also the plants and fossils collected in the journey from Yanbu. I swallowed a letter from Prince Moulay Abd al-Salem, which might have compromised me in the eyes of these fanatics. I gave to my house steward some piastres that I had in my little trunk, and remained perfectly quiet. My servants hid the tobacco they had under some stones, and we awaited their orders.

A moment afterward, two Wahhabis came to establish themselves near us, to keep us in sight. Happily this arrangement was tardy, for we were already disencumbered of everything that might have compromised us. I am persuaded that we owed these precious moments to the cupidity of these men, who had withdrawn to divide the booty, which they were at a loss to do equally among five persons.

Two more Wahhabis arrived two hours afterward, saying they were sent by the Amir, who demanded from me five hundred francs for my deliverance. I told them I had no money, and they withdrew.

Another Wahhabi soon after presented himself, with an order to conduct us to another place. We went with him behind a neighboring mountain, where I found the whole of my caravan equally made prisoners.

All my companions, who were surrounded by a strong guard, were pale, trembling, and unhappy concerning their fate. I seated myself beside the Arabs. The Turks were separated from us at a distance.

A Wahhabi arrived and announced that every pilgrim, whether Turk or Maghribi Arab, was to pay five hundred francs. At this demand all my unfortunate companions uttered cries and asked for mercy with tears in their eyes. As for myself, I said quietly that my answer had been already given, but I spoke in favor of my comrades.

The sun was nearly setting when a messenger came to inform us that the Amir had granted a diminution of the contribution, and that every pilgrim must pay two hundred francs. This produced fresh sorrow and tears among my fellow travelers, who had really no money.

At sunset they led us to a hollow, where they made us sit down in two separate groups. A great number of Wahhabis arrived soon afterward, which filled my companions with terror. I must own I was much afraid myself that I should soon witness a bloody scene, to which our poor Turks would furnish victims. I feared not for my own safety, because I was considered as a Maghribi Arab, and the Turks could not assert the contrary: however, I was not the less deeply afflicted for the uncertainty of the fate of these unfortunate people, who, had it not been for me, would never have undertaken the journey, and unfortunately I had not any influence or means to guarantee them from calamity.

An hour passed in this anguish, and some more soldiers arrived. They ordered us to mount and conducted us to another spot, giving us to understand that the Amir wished to examine each of us in private. We retraced our steps. The night was exceedingly dark. We passed Jidida, and shortly afterward halted for the remainder of this unhappy night.

The next morning, Friday the third of April, a little before sunrise, we were ordered to mount, and we continued our retrograde route, escorted only by three Wahhabi soldiers.

Two hours afterward I perceived an encampment composed of handsome tents. I thought we were going to be presented to the Amir, but I soon perceived that this assemblage of people consisted of the priests, servants, and slaves of the temple of the Prophet's sepulcher [in Medina], whom Saʻud had sent out of Arabia.

Being arrived at the encampment, they ordered us to fill our pitchers with water from a fine spring, and we continued our march.

Whilst we were getting the water, the servant who led my camel by the halter was so distracted with fright that he began to run, leading my camel, to put himself and me under the protection of the caravan of those belonging to the temple; but one of the Wahhabis ran immediately after us and, forcing the halter out of his hand, struck him to the earth and, after having kicked him a hundred times, conducted me back to the caravan without saying a word to me. We passed by Hamra, a village thinly peopled, as well as Jidida, in a better situation, surrounded with gardens and superb palm trees in the middle of an extensive valley, and at a short distance from a fine spring, where we filled our pitchers. This spring is hot, but it produces an abundance of excellent water.

We left the road half an hour afterward, when they made us alight among the mountains, where new discussions arose concerning the payment of the contribution, which lasted till three in the afternoon. The Wahhabis examined our effects and at length made each Turk pay twenty francs. They took a haʼik and a sack of biscuit from the Maghribis and seized upon three Spanish piastres which I had forgotten in my writing desk, as also the caftan belonging to my steward. They exacted fifteen francs from each camel driver. Mine refused to pay, and set out to speak to the Amir, from which moment I did not see him again. We were then informed of the positive order of Saʻud, which forbade any pilgrim to go to Medina, and were conducted back to the encampment of those belonging to the temple, who shortly after began to march with us escorted by other soldiers.

Thus terminated, happily I may say, this disagreeable event, though I had to regret the relinquishment of an interesting journey, and the loss of my watch, which served for my astronomical observations.

Five or six peals of thunder took place during the time the Wahhabis were collecting the contributions. It was about noon, and there was not the least cloud in the heavens.

In regard to this conduct of the Wahhabis, it must be observed that we knew as well as the Arabs the express order against going to Medina to visit the sepulcher. We therefore broke the order willfully. But I had determined to attempt the journey, hoping that chance might perhaps second me in my efforts in this enterprise. The Wahhabis, in stopping us, only put in execution the general order established.

The contribution they exacted was only a fine, which we had incurred in consequence of our infraction of the standing order, though the manner of collecting it was certainly rather harsh; but much may be said for uncivilized men. They took from me, it is true, my watch and other things, but why did they not take all I had?

These Arabs, though Wahhabis, and subjects of Sa'ud, are natives of the Hijaz, which has been newly subjected; consequently, they differ much from the brilliant Wahhabi youths of the East that I had seen at Mecca. Therefore, when they took my watch, etc., from me, I pardoned them willingly for these remains of the ancient vice of their country, and gave thanks to Abd al-Wahhab for effecting this reform, since they left me my other effects and my astronomical instruments. Their menace and bad conduct to the Turks are only the consequences of their resentment and hatred to that nation, the name of which alone suffices to rouse them to a fury. . . .

There was in this caravan, the new Qadi of Constantinople, destined to Medina, with whom I was in particular friendship during my stay at Mecca. I became acquainted at the same time with the Treasurer and the principal people employed in the temple at Medina.

They informed me that the Wahhabis had destroyed all the ornaments of the sepulcher of the Prophet, and that there remained absolutely nothing, that they had shut and sealed the doors of the temple, and that Sa'ud had taken possession of the immense treasures which had been accumulating for so many ages. The Treasurer assured me that the value of the pearls and precious stones was above all estimation.

The caravan had a safe passport from Sa'ud, to be respected during its journey; however, . . . it had been obliged to quit the road after leaving the Holy City, and a heavy contribution had been laid upon it; so much so that the agha, or Chief, of the Negroes had been obliged to pay for his share the value of three thousand francs, and the others in proportion. I learned also that the caravan of the Turks at Mecca had been robbed of everything immediately after its passage to Medina, and that they even took the provisions; so that it was doubtful whether these unhappy creatures escaped hunger and thirst in the midst of these deserts.

The same day, the fourth of April, at three in the afternoon, we took a west-southwest direction. In about an hour afterward I discovered the sea at a great distance, and after having marched the whole night, we arrived in sight of Yanbu at break of day. I proceeded to the head of my caravan, and entered the town at sunrise, on Sunday the fifth of April. I returned immediately on board the vessel, where I found my people very uneasy on account of the unpleasant news which had spread concerning me. Such was the end of this journey, which was unfortunate without doubt: notwithstanding this, my friends in misfortune, and myself, congratulated each other at being liberated so cheaply.

8

John Lewis Burckhardt
Switzerland
1814

※

More is known about this author than all our previous pilgrims put together. Burckhardt's family origins, unlike Varthema's and al-Abbasi's, are clear. Moreover, we understand why he performed the Hajj and to whom he reported. He was born in Lausanne in 1784 and grew up in Basel, steeped in culture and learning. Gibbon and Goethe were among his father's guests. When the French army overran Switzerland, however, the family went into exile, and Burckhardt was sent away to school. To this he owed a lifelong hatred for Bonaparte and a corresponding loyalty to Britain. He studied history and the new sciences at Leipzig and Göttingen. He read Greek and Latin and spoke French, German, and English fluently.

Burckhardt arrived in London in 1807 at twenty-three with an introduction to the same Sir Joseph Banks whom Al-Abbasi had visited five years earlier. As president of the African Association and of the Royal Society, Banks was England's chief patron of exploration. Their talk that winter centered on the Niger River question. Twelve years before, Mungo Park had come upon the river above Ségou and marched a hundred miles along one bank. Since then, nothing new was known about the river, most of interior Africa remained a blank, and the lucrative caravan routes that crisscrossed the continent were secret. (See Fig. 11.) One by one, Sir Joseph had sent four accomplished explorers to their death trying to chart the Niger from the west. To learn any more, he believed, they must approach the river from the opposite direction, moving southwest from Cairo through the Sudan, traveling with the Hajj caravans returning to Mali, through which the Niger flows. The key to reaching the river by pilgrim routes would be a sharp-eyed explorer capable of blending in with Muslims.

In May 1808, Burckhardt volunteered for the job. To reach Timbuktu or any town on the Niger's banks, it was agreed that he should travel disguised as an Arab trader. Since Muslims would be his constant companions, he was first to study their language and manners in Aleppo. The appointment would

162

run for eight years. Long terms were sensible. War, revolt, and raiders kept the Hajj caravan routes in an uproar, as al-Abassi's account makes clear. Already chastened by disaster, Banks hoped to give Burckhardt ample time. A small sum was placed in his name at Cairo to buy goods and camels for his journey. His passage from London to Malta was prepaid, and he received a first allowance of seventy pounds. Burckhardt proposed to spend any unused funds on Arabic manuscripts, shipping them to the British Museum.

Burckhardt made his way to Aleppo and stayed two years, often at the English consul's house, studying Arabic, translating Robinson Crusoe *for practice, and collecting manuscripts. During this time, he perfected a persona, Shaykh Ibrahim Al-Barakat,* to such a degree that he could argue Muslim law with local scholars. He traveled, too, through Syria, Lebanon, and Jordan, always in Arab dress, with little money, posting detailed reports to London on the true geography of the Hauran, on ancient Apamea beside the Orontes, on the first Hittite inscriptions at Hama, and on his discovery of the lost city of Petra.*

Banks was impressed by Burckhardt's work and trusted his instincts. When the explorer wrote from southern Nubia in 1813, proposing to cross the Red Sea and make the Hajj, Banks saw the logic. Rather than imitate a pilgrim returning from Mecca, Burckhardt was proposing to become one. Geographically, this meant traveling in the wrong direction for a Niger expedition, but the plan made sense. In March, with Banks's blessing, Burckhardt struck out for the Hijaz.

If al-Abbasi witnessed the arrival of the Wahhabis in Mecca, Burckhardt reported on their ebb. In the seven intervening years, Cairo's Pasha, Muhammad Ali, had garrisoned the Hijaz to drive them out. As the 1814 Hajj approached, his sixteen thousand troops were poised to strike. Burckhardt's meeting with the Pasha, excerpted here, posed the final test of his masquerade. Here we see the outline of every impostor's nightmare: a face-to-face confrontation with the powers that be. Burckhardt was at his most nimble in this encounter. He shrewdly took the Pasha's measure, effected his escape, and went on to perform the Hajj unhindered. In Mecca, he noticed everything: the casual talk of the local people, their proverbs and cooking, the taste of the water, the desert's geology, the town's infrastructure and economy. He found the revenues of the Haram to be substantial. It owned income-producing properties throughout the Near East, left in trust by pious Muslims, and it also received large donations every year from wealthy hajjis, especially the Indian governors. Some of these arrangements went back centuries, but Burckhardt was the first Westerner to examine them systematically.

---

*The last name, nearly the sound in Arabic of Burckhardt, was bestowed by neighbors in Aleppo.

The effects of long-term war on the Hijaz show through in these pages. Mecca, its population, and the safety of its roads all seem reduced and under pressure. Rifle fire echoes through the rites, and Arafat is thick with soldiers. Burckhardt, loathe to miss anything, walked to Arafat among the crowds, leading two donkeys, climbed Mount Mercy, and strolled through all the camps. The details of the sacred plain, the placement of the encampments, the general mood of the pilgrims, are precisely rendered in the handful of pages included here.

Burckhardt's achievement is all the more impressive in view of the martial backdrop all around him. As soon as the Hajj was over, war broke out, and thousands of homebound pilgrims were trapped in Mecca. Burckhardt himself took up residence in the Haram Mosque—banking that whoever won would still respect its laws of asylum. A few days later Muhammad Ali's troops triumphed decisively. By Burckhardt's count, five thousand Wahhabis were slaughtered in one day on the Bissal Plain. The remainder withdrew into the Nejd Desert. Only then were the pilgrims permitted to start home.

After the Hajj and a long illness in Medina, Burckhardt returned to Cairo. With Mecca behind him, he felt prepared to set out on his long-awaited Niger expedition. As he was now a well-traveled pilgrim, his Muslim credentials could not be doubted. Finally, in September 1817, the Niger caravan passed through town on its way to Mecca, and Burckhardt was able to arrange to travel back to West Africa with it in December. He was elated. In October, dysentery intervened. One week he was strolling the consular gardens, happily planning his crowning journey to the great river. The next week he lay on his deathbed. After nearly ten years of preparation for the Niger, he died in Cairo at the age of thirty-two. His grave lies south of the city's gates, facing the trailhead of the Niger caravans.

All of Burckhardt's seven books were published posthumously. When they finally appeared, one by one in the 1820s, they made him famous. His painstaking chapters on the Haram Mosque, which he treated as a city in itself, were issued separately, to wide acclaim. Their accuracy was such that Sir Richard Burton simply quoted whole sections in his own account of Mecca forty years later. Thomas Carlyle consulted Burckhardt, too, for his On Heroes, Hero-Worship, and the Heroic in History *(1841).* Washington Irving read him in composing *his two-volume* Mahomet and His Successors *(1849–50), the first book about the Prophet by an American.*

from John Lewis Burckhardt's
Travels in The Hijaz of Arabia

JIDDA My arrival in the Hijaz was attended with some unfavourable circumstances. On entering the town of Jidda, in the morning of the fifteenth of July 1814, I went to the house of a person on whom I had a letter of credit delivered to me at my departure from Cairo, in January 1813, when I had not yet fully resolved to extend my travels into Arabia. From this person I met with a very cold reception; the letter was thought to be of too old a date to deserve notice: indeed, my ragged appearance might have rendered anyone cautious how he committed himself with his correspondents, in paying me a large sum of money on their account. Bills and letters of credit are, besides, often trifled with in the mutual dealings of Eastern merchants, and I thus experienced a flat refusal, accompanied, however, with an offer of lodgings in the man's house. This I accepted for the first two days, thinking that by a more intimate acquaintance I might convince him that I was neither an adventurer nor impostor; but finding him inflexible, I removed to one of the numerous public khans in the town, my whole stock of money being two dollars and a few sequins* sewed up in an amulet which I wore on my arm. I had little time to make melancholy reflections upon my situation, for on the fourth day after my arrival I was attacked by a violent fever, occasioned, probably, by indulging too freely in the fine fruits which were then in the Jidda market, an imprudence, which my abstemious diet, for the last twelve months, rendered, perhaps, less inexcusable, but certainly of worse consequence. I was for several days delirious, and nature would probably have been exhausted had it not been for the aid of a Greek captain, my fellow passenger from Suwakin. He attended me in one of my lucid intervals and, at my request, procured a barber, or country physician, who bled me copiously, though with much reluctance, as he insisted that a potion, made up of ginger, nutmeg, and cinnamon, was the only remedy adapted to my case. In a fortnight after, I had sufficiently recovered to be able to walk about, but the weakness and languor which the fever had occasioned would not yield to the damp heat of the atmosphere of the town, and I owed my complete recovery to the temperate climate of Ta'if, situated in the mountains behind Mecca, where I afterwards proceeded. . . .

The present state of the Hijaz rendered travelling through it, in the disguise of a beggar, or at least for a person of my outward appearance, im-

*sequin: a gold piece, ducat, or dinar.

practicable; and the slow progress of my recovery made me desirous of obtaining comforts. I therefore equipped myself anew in the dress of a reduced Egyptian gentleman and immediately wrote to Cairo for a supply of money, but this I could hardly receive in less than three or four months. Being determined, however, to remain in the Hijaz until the time of the pilgrimage the following November, it became necessary for me to find the means of procuring subsistence until my funds should arrive. Had I been disappointed in all my hopes, I should then have followed the example of numbers of the poor hajjis, even those of respectable families, who earn a daily subsistence during their stay in the Hijaz by manual labour . . .

The Pasha, Muhammad Ali arrived in the Hijaz at the close of the spring of 1813 and was now resident at Ta'if, where he had established the headquarters of the army with which he intended to attack the strongholds of the Wahhabis. I had seen the Pasha several times at Cairo, before my departure for Upper Egypt, and had informed him in general terms of my travelling madness (as he afterwards jocularly termed it himself at Ta'if). . . .

The Pasha, however, had heard of my being at Jidda, through another person in his suite whom I had seen there and who had arrived at Ta'if; and hearing that I was walking about in rags, he immediately despatched a messenger, with two dromedaries, to the collector of customs at Jidda, Sayyid Ali Odjakli, in whose hands was the management of all the affairs of the town, with an order to furnish me a suit of clothes and a purse of five hundred piastres as travelling money, accompanied with a request that I should repair immediately to Ta'if with the same messenger who had brought the letter. In a postscript, Sayyid Ali Odjakli was enjoined to order the messenger to take me by the upper road to Ta'if, which leaves Mecca to the south, the lower and more usual road passing through the middle of that town.

The invitation of a Turkish pasha is a polite command; whatever, therefore, might be my reluctance to go at this time to Ta'if, I could not avoid, under the present circumstances, complying with the Pasha's wishes; and notwithstanding the secret aversion I had to receive a present at his hands instead of a loan, I could not refuse to accept the clothes and money without hurting the pride and exciting the resentment of a chief whose good graces it was now my principal aim to conciliate.* I likewise understood the mean-

*Some persons, perhaps, consider it an honour to receive presents from pashas; but I think differently. I know that the real motive of a Turkish [ruler] in making presents is either to get double the value in return (which could not be the case with me) or to gratify his own pride in showing to his courtiers that he deigns to be liberal towards a person whom he holds infinitely below him in station or worth. I have often witnessed the sneers of the donor and his people on making such presents, and their sentiments are sometimes expressed by

ing of the postscript, although Sayyid Ali was not aware of it, but on this point I flattered myself I should be a match for the Pasha and his people.

As the invitation was very pressing, I left Jidda in the evening of the same day on which the messenger arrived, after supping with Sayyid Ali, in company with a great number of hajjis from all parts of the world; for the fast of Ramadan had already commenced, and during this month everybody displays as much hospitality and splendour as he possibly can, particularly in the supper after sunset. Distrusting in some measure the Pasha's intentions, I thought it necessary to carry a full purse to Ta'if. . . . A person who has money has little to fear among Osmanlis, except the loss of it; but I thought that I might stand in need of what I had, either as a bribe, or to facilitate my departure from Ta'if. I was, however, fortunately mistaken in both these conjectures.

RESIDENCE AT TA'IF I arrived at Ta'if about midday, and alighted at the house of Bosari, the Pasha's physician, with whom I had been well acquainted at Cairo. As it was now the fast of Ramadan, during which the Turkish grandees always sleep in the daytime, the Pasha could not be informed of my arrival till after sunset. In the meanwhile, Bosari, after the usual Levantine assurances of his entire devotion to my interests and of the sincerity of his friendship, asked me what were my views in coming to the Hijaz. I answered, to visit Mecca and Medina and then to return to Cairo. Of my intention respecting Egypt he seemed doubtful, begged me to be candid with him as with a friend and to declare the truth, as he confessed that he suspected I was going to the East Indies. This I positively denied; and in the course of our conversation, he hinted that if I really meant to return to Egypt, I had better remain at headquarters with them till the Pasha himself should proceed to Cairo. . . .

In the evening Bosari went privately to the Pasha at his women's residence, where he only received visits from friends or very intimate acquaintances. In half an hour he returned and told me that the Pasha wished to see me rather late that evening in his public room. He added that he found seated with the Pasha the Qadi of Mecca, who was then at Ta'if for his health, and

---

the saying, "Look, he has thrown a morsel to this dog!" Few Europeans may, perhaps, agree with me in this respect, but *my* knowledge authorises me to form this opinion; and the only advice which I can give to travellers who would not lower themselves in the estimation of Turkish grandees is to be always ready, on similar occasions, to return the supposed favour twofold. As for myself, I had but seldom occasion to make presents during my travels; and this was the only one that I was ever obliged to accept.

that the former, when he heard of my desire to visit the Holy Cities, observed jocosely, "It is not the beard alone* which proves a man to be a true Muslim"; but turning towards the Qadi, he said, "You are a better judge in such matters than I am." The Qadi then observed that as none but a Muslim could be permitted to see the Holy Cities, a circumstance of which he could not possibly suppose me ignorant, he did not believe that I would declare myself to be one unless I really was. When I learnt these particulars, I told Bosari that he might return alone to the Pasha, that my feelings had already been much hurt by the orders given to my guide not to carry me through Mecca, and that I certainly should not go to the Pasha's public audience if he would not receive me as a Muslim.

Bosari was alarmed at this declaration and in vain endeavoured to dissuade me from such a course, telling me that he had orders to conduct me to the Pasha, which he could not disobey. I however adhered firmly to what I had said, and he reluctantly went back to Muhammad Ali, whom he found alone, the Qadi having left him. When Bosari delivered his message, the Pasha smiled and answered that I was welcome, whether Muslim or not. About eight o'clock in the evening I repaired to the castle, a miserable, half-ruined habitation of Sharif Ghalib, dressed in the new suit which I had received at Jidda by the Pasha's command. I found His Highness seated in a large saloon, with the Qadi on one hand and Hasan Pasha, the chief of the Arnaut soldiers on the other. Thirty or forty of his principal officers formed a half-circle about the sofa on which they sat, and a number of Bedouin *shaykh*s were squatted in the midst of the semicircle. I went up to the Pasha, gave him the "*Salaam Alaykoum,*" and kissed his hand. He made a sign for me to sit down by the side of the Qadi, then addressed me very politely, inquired after my health and if there was any news from the Mamluks in the black country which I had visited, but said nothing whatever on the subject most interesting to me. Amin Effendi, his Arabic dragoman, interpreted between us, as I do not speak Turkish and the Pasha speaks Arabic very imperfectly. In about five minutes he renewed the business with the Bedouins, which I had interrupted. When this was terminated and Hasan Pasha had left the room, everybody was ordered to withdraw except the Qadi, Bosari, and myself.

I expected now to be put to the proof, and I was fully prepared for it, but not a word was mentioned of my personal affairs, nor did Muhammad Ali, in any of our subsequent conversations, ever enter further into them than to hint that he was persuaded I was on my way to the East Indies. As soon as

*I wore a beard at this time, as I did at Cairo, when the Pasha saw me.

we were alone, the Pasha introduced the subject of politics. He had just received information of the entrance of the allies into Paris and the departure
of Bonaparte for Elba. Several Malta gazettes, giving the details of these
occurrences, had been sent to him from Cairo. He seemed deeply interested
in these important events, chiefly because he laboured under the impression
that after Bonaparte's downfall, England would probably seek for an aug-
mentation of power in the Mediterranean and consequently invade Egypt.

After remaining for two or three hours with the Pasha in private conversation, either speaking Arabic to him, through the medium of the Qadi,
who, though a native of Constantinople, knew that language perfectly, or
Italian, through Bosari, who was an Armenian but had acquired a smatter-
ing of that tongue at Cairo, I took my leave, and the Pasha said that he expected me again on the morrow at the same hour.

AUGUST 29 I paid a visit to the Qadi before sunset and found him with his
companion and secretary, a learned man of Constantinople. The Qadi, Sadiq
Effendi, was a true Eastern courtier of very engaging manners and address,
possessing all that suavity of expression for which the well-bred natives of
Istanbul are so distinguished. After we had interchanged a few complimentary phrases, I mentioned my astonishment on finding that the Pasha had
expressed any doubts of my being a true Muslim, after I had now been a
proselyte to that faith for so many years. He replied that Muhammad Ali
had allowed that he (the Qadi) was the best judge in such matters and added
that he hoped we should become better acquainted with each other. He then
began to question me about my Nubian travels. In the course of conversation literary subjects were introduced. He asked me what Arabic books I had
read and what commentaries on the Quran and on the law, and he probably
found me better acquainted, with the titles, at least, of such works than he
had expected, for we did not enter deeply into the subject. While we were
thus conversing, the call to evening prayers announced the termination of
this day's fast. I supped with the Qadi and afterwards performed the evening
prayers in his company, when I took great care to chant as long a chapter of
the Quran as my memory furnished at the moment; after which we both
went to the Pasha, who again sat up a part of the night in private conversation with me, chiefly on political affairs, without ever introducing the subject of my private business.

After another interview, I went every evening, first to the Qadi and
then to the Pasha, but notwithstanding a polite reception at the castle, I could
perceive that my actions were closely watched. Bosari had asked me if I kept
a journal, but I answered that the Hijaz was not like Egypt, full of antiqui-

ties, and that in these barren mountains I saw nothing worthy of notice. I was never allowed to be alone for a moment, and I had reason to suspect that Bosari, with all his assurances of friendship, was nothing better than a spy. To remain at Ta'if for an indeterminate period in the situation I now found myself was little desirable, yet I could not guess the Pasha's intentions with respect to me.

I was evidently considered in no other light than as a spy sent to this country by the English government to ascertain its present state and report upon it in the East Indies. This, I presume, was the Pasha's own opinion: he knew me as an Englishman, a name which I assumed during my travels (I hope without any discredit to that country) whenever it seemed necessary to appear as a European, because at that time none but the subjects of England and France enjoyed in the East any real security: they were considered as too well protected, both by their governments at home and their ministers at Constantinople, to be trifled with by provincial governors. The Pasha, moreover, supposed me to be a man of some rank, for every Englishman travelling in the East is styled "my lord"; and he was the more convinced of this by a certain air of dignity which it was necessary for me to assume in a Turkish court, where modesty of behaviour and affability are quite out of place. Afraid as he then was of Great Britain, he probably thought it imprudent to treat me ill, though he did nothing whatever to forward my projects. As far as he knew, I could have only the five hundred piastres which he had ordered for me at Jidda and which were not sufficient to pay my expenses for any length of time in Hijaz. Nothing was said to me either by him or Bosari of taking my bill upon Cairo, as I had requested him to do, but this favour I did not again solicit, having money enough for the present and expecting a fresh supply from Egypt.

To remain for any length of time at Ta'if, in a sort of polite imprisonment, was little to my taste, yet I could not press my departure without increasing his suspicions. This was manifest after my first interview with the Pasha and the Qadi, and I knew that the reports of Bosari might considerably influence the mind of Muhammad Ali. Under these circumstances, I thought the best course was to make Bosari tired of me and thus induce him involuntarily to forward my views. I therefore began to act at his house with all the petulance of an Osmanli. It being the Ramadan, I fasted during the day and at night demanded a supper apart; early on the following morning I called for an abundant breakfast before the fast recommenced. I appropriated to myself the best room which his small house afforded, and his servants were kept in constant attendance upon me. Eastern hospitality forbids all resentment for such behaviour; I was, besides, a great man, and on a visit to the Pasha. In my conversations with Bosari, I assured him that I felt myself most comfortably situated at Ta'if and that its climate agreed perfectly with my health, and I betrayed no desire of quitting the place for the present. To maintain a person in my character for any length of time at Ta'if, where provisions of all kinds were much dearer than in London, was a matter of no small moment, and a petulant guest is everywhere disagreeable. The design, I believe, succeeded perfectly, and Bosari endeavoured to persuade the Pasha that I was a harmless being, in order that I might be the sooner dismissed.

I had been six days at Ta'if but seldom went out, except to the castle in the evening, when Bosari asked whether my business with the Pasha was likely to prevent me much longer from pursuing my travels and visiting Mecca. I replied that I had no business with the Pasha, though I had come to Ta'if at his desire, but that my situation was very agreeable to me, possessing so warm and generous a friend as he, my host. The next day he renewed the subject and remarked that it must be tiresome to live entirely among soldiers, without any comforts or amusements, unacquainted besides, as I was, with the Turkish language. I assented to this but added that being ignorant of the Pasha's wishes, I could determine on nothing. This brought him to the point I wished. "This being the case," said he, "I will, if you like, speak to His Highness on the subject." He did so in the evening, before I went to the castle, and the Pasha told me, in the course of conversation, that as he understood I wished to pass the last days of Ramadan at Mecca (a suggestion originating with Bosari), I had better join the party of the Qadi, who was going there to the feast and who would be very glad of my company. This was precisely such a circumstance as I wished for. The departure of the Qadi was fixed for the seventh of September, and I hired two asses, the usual mode of conveyance in this country, in order to follow him.

As it was my intention to proceed afterwards to Medina, where Tussan Pasha, the son of Muhammad Ali, was Governor, I begged Bosari to ask the Pasha for a *firman,* or passport, authorising me to travel through all the Hijaz, together with a letter of recommendation to his son. In reply, Bosari told me that the Pasha did not like to interfere personally in my travels; that I might act as I pleased, on my own responsibility; and that my knowledge of the language rendered a passport unnecessary. This was equivalent to telling me, "Do what you please; I shall neither obstruct nor facilitate your projects," which, indeed, was as much, at present, as I could well expect or desire.

On the sixth of September I took my leave of the Pasha, who told me at parting that if ever my travels should carry me to India, I might assure the English people there that he was much attached to the interests of the India trade. Early on the seventh the Qadi sent me word that he should not set out till evening, would travel during the night, and hoped to meet me at Jabal Qora, midway to Mecca. I therefore left Ta'if alone, as I had entered it, after a residence of ten days. At parting, Bosari assured me of his inviolable attachment to my interest, and I blessed my good stars when I left the precincts of the town, and the residence of a Turkish court, in which I found it more difficult to avoid danger than among the wild Bedouins of Nubia. . . .

TA'IF TO MECCA Not far from Ta'if I overtook three Arnaut soldiers, each, like myself, mounted on an ass. At Ta'if they had exchanged their money, getting thirteen piastres of the Cairo mint for one Spanish dollar, which at Jidda was worth but eleven; they had, therefore, made a common purse of one thousand dollars and travelled from Jidda to Ta'if, whenever the road was secure, for the sake of the two piastres which they gained upon each dollar. They carried the money, sewed in bags, upon their asses; and having forgotten, perhaps, to leave out any cash for travelling expenses, they joined me, finding that my travelling sack was well stocked with provisions, and left me to pay for our joint expenses on the road whenever we stopped at the coffee huts. But they were good-humoured companions, and the expense was not thrown away.

In passing by Wadi Mohram, I assumed the *ihram,* as being now for the first time about to visit Mecca and its temple. . . . I arrived at Mecca about midday, when my companions went in search of their acquaintance among the soldiers and left me to shift for myself without knowing a single individual in the town and without being recommended to anybody but the Qadi, whom, as I have already said, I wished to avoid.

Whoever enters Mecca, whether pilgrim or not, is enjoined by the law to visit the temple immediately and not to attend to any worldly concern whatever before he has done so. We crossed the line of shops and houses, up to the gates of the mosque, where my ass driver took his fare and set me down. Here I was accosted by half a dozen *mutawwifs*, or guides to the Holy Places, who knew, from my being dressed in the *ihram,* that I intended to visit the Ka'ba. I chose one of them as my guide and, after having deposited my baggage in a neighbouring shop, entered the mosque at the gate called Bab al-Salaam, by which the newcomer is recommended to enter. The ceremonies to be performed in visiting the mosque are the following: 1. certain religious rites to be practised in the interior of the temple; 2. the walk between Safa and Marwa; 3. the [optional] visit to the Umra [mosque]. These ceremonies ought to be repeated by every Muslim whenever he enters Mecca from a

journey farther than two days' distance, and they must again be more particularly performed at the time of the pilgrimage to Arafat. . . .

MECCA I hired decent apartments in a quarter of the town not much frequented, called Haret al-Mesfala. I had here the advantage of several large
trees growing before my windows, the verdure of which, among the barren
and sunburnt rocks of Mecca, was to me more exhilarating than the finest
landscape could have been under different circumstances. At this place I
enjoyed an enviable freedom and independence, known only to the Qadi
and his followers, who soon after took their departure. The Pasha and his
court remained at Ta'if till the days of the Hajj. I frequented only such society as pleased me, and, mixing with a crowd of foreign pilgrims from all
parts of the world, I was not liable to impertinent remarks or disagreeable
inquiries. If any question arose about my origin (a circumstance that rarely
happened in a place which always abounds with strangers), I stated myself
to be a reduced member of the Mamluk corps of Egypt and found it easy to
avoid those persons whose intimate knowledge of that country might perhaps have enabled them to detect the falsehood. But there was little to be
apprehended even from the consequences of such detection, for the assumption of a false character is frequent among all Eastern travellers, and especially at Mecca, where everyone affects poverty in order to escape imposition
or being led into great expenses. During all my journeys in the East, I never
enjoyed such perfect ease as at Mecca; and I shall always retain a pleasing
recollection of my residence there, although the state of my health did not
permit me to benefit by all the advantages that my situation offered. . . .

Mecca may be styled a handsome town: its streets are in general broader
than those of Eastern cities, the houses lofty and built of stone, and the
numerous windows that face the streets give them a more lively and European aspect than those of Egypt or Syria, where the houses present but few
windows towards the exterior. Mecca (like Jidda) contains many houses three
storeys high. Few at Mecca are whitewashed, but the dark grey colour of the
stone is much preferable to the glaring white that offends the eye in Jidda.
In most towns of the Levant the narrowness of a street contributes to its
coolness, and in countries where wheel carriages are not used, a space that
allows two loaded camels to pass each other is deemed sufficient. At Mecca,
however, it was necessary to leave the passages wide for the innumerable
visitors who here crowd together, and it is in the houses adapted for the reception of pilgrims and other sojourners that the windows are so contrived
as to command a view of the streets.

The city is open on every side, but the neighbouring mountains, if properly defended, would form a barrier of considerable strength against an enemy. In former times it had three walls to protect its extremities; one was built across the valley, at the street of Ma'la, another at the quarter of Shubayka, and the third at the valley opening into the Misfala. These walls were repaired in 1413 and 1425, and in a century after some traces of them still remained.

The only public place in the body of the town is the ample square of the Great Mosque. No trees or gardens cheer the eye, and the scene is enlivened only during the Hajj by the great number of well-stored shops which are found in every quarter. Except four or five large houses belonging to the sharif, two colleges (now converted into corn magazines), and the mosque, with some buildings and schools attached to it, Mecca cannot boast of any public edifices and in this respect is, perhaps, more deficient than any other Eastern city of the same size. Neither *khans*, for the accommodation of travellers, or for the deposit of merchandise, nor palaces of grandees, nor mosques, which adorn every quarter of other towns in the East, are here to be seen, and we may perhaps attribute this want of splendid buildings to the veneration which its inhabitants entertain for their temple. This prevents them from constructing any edifice which might possibly pretend to rival it.

The mode of building is the same as that adopted at Jidda, with the addition of windows looking towards the street; of these many project from the wall and have their framework elaborately carved, or gaudily painted. Before them hang blinds made of slight reeds, which exclude flies and gnats while they admit fresh air. Every house has its terrace, the floor of which (composed of a preparation from limestone) is built with a slight inclination, so that the rainwater runs off through gutters into the street, for the rains here are so irregular that it is not worthwhile to collect the water of them in cisterns, as is done in Syria. The terraces are concealed from view by slight parapet walls, for throughout the East it is reckoned discreditable that a man should appear upon the terrace, whence he might be accused of looking at women in the neighbouring houses, as the females pass much of their time on the terraces, employed in various domestic occupations, such as drying corn, hanging up linen, etc. . . . All the houses of the Meccans, except those of the principal and richest inhabitants, are constructed for the accommodation of lodgers, being divided into many apartments, separated from each other, and each consisting of a sitting room and a small kitchen. Since the pilgrimage, which has begun to decline (this happened before the Wahhabi conquest), many of the Meccans, no longer deriving profit from the letting of their lodgings, found themselves unable to afford the expense of repairs; and thus numerous buildings in the outskirts have fallen completely into ruin, and the town itself exhibits in every street houses rapidly decaying. I saw only one of recent construction; it was in the quarter of al-Shubayka, belonged to a sharif, and cost, as report said, 150 purses. Such a house might have been built at Cairo for 60 purses.

The streets are all unpaved, and in summertime the sand and dust in them are as great a nuisance as the mud is in the rainy season, during which they are scarcely passable after a shower, for in the interior of the town the water does not run off, but remains till it is dried up. It may be ascribed to the destructive rains, which, though of shorter duration than in other tropical countries, fall with considerable violence, that no ancient buildings are found in Mecca. The mosque itself has undergone so many repairs under different sultans that it may be called a modern structure, and of the houses, I do not think there exists one older than four centuries. It is not, therefore, in this place, that the traveller must look for interesting specimens of architecture or such beautiful remains of Saracenic structures as are still admired in Syria, Egypt, Barbary, and Spain. In this respect, the ancient and far-famed Mecca is surpassed by the smallest provincial towns of Syria or Egypt. The same may be said with respect to Medina, and I suspect that the towns of Yemen are generally poor in architectural remains.

Mecca is deficient in those regulations of police which are customary in Eastern cities. The streets are totally dark at night, no lamps of any kind being lighted; its different quarters are without gates, differing in this respect also from most Eastern towns, where each quarter is regularly shut up after the last evening prayers. The town may therefore be crossed at any time of the night, and the same attention is not paid here to the security of merchants, as well as of husbands (on whose account principally, the quarters are closed), as in Syrian or Egyptian towns of equal magnitude. The dirt and sweepings of the houses are cast into the streets, where they soon become dust or mud according to the season. The same custom seems to have prevailed equally in ancient times, for I did not perceive in the skirts of the town any of those heaps of rubbish which are usually found near the large towns of Turkey.

With respect to water, the most important of all supplies (and that which always forms the first object of inquiry among Asiatics), Mecca is not much better provided than Jidda. There are but few cisterns for collecting rain, and the well water is so brackish that it is used only for culinary purposes, except during the time of the pilgrimage, when the lowest class of hajjis drink it. The famous Well of Zamzam, in the Great Mosque, is indeed sufficiently copious to supply the whole town, but however holy, its water is heavy to the taste and impedes digestion; the poorer classes besides have not permission to fill their waterskins with it at pleasure. The best water in Mecca is brought by a conduit from the vicinity of Arafat, six or seven hours distant. The present government, instead of constructing similar works, neglects even the repairs and requisite cleansing of this aqueduct. It is wholly built of stone, and all those parts of it which appear above ground are covered with a thick layer of stone and cement. I heard that it had not been cleaned during the last fifty years. The consequence of this negligence is that the most of the water is lost in its passage to the city through apertures or slowly forces its way through the obstructing sediment, though it flows in a full stream into the head of the aqueduct at Arafat. The supply which it affords in ordinary times is barely sufficient for the use of the inhabitants, and during the pilgrimage sweet water becomes an absolute scarcity; a small skin of water (two of which skins a person may carry) being then often sold for one shilling—a very high price among Arabs.

There are two places in the interior of Mecca where the aqueduct runs above ground; there the water is let off into small channels or fountains, at which some slaves of the Sharif are stationed to exact a toll from persons filling their waterskins. In the time of the Hajj, these fountains are surrounded day and night by crowds of people quarrelling and fighting for access to the water. During the late siege the Wahhabis cut off the supply of water from the aqueduct, and it was not till some time after that the injury which this structure then received was partially repaired. The whole length of the aqueduct is seven or eight hours. . . .

As soon as we pass the extreme precincts of Mecca, the desert presents itself, for neither gardens, trees, nor pleasure houses line the avenues to the town, which is surrounded on every side by barren sandy valleys and equally barren hills. A stranger placed on the great road to Ta'if, just beyond the turn of the hill, in the immediate neighbourhood of the Sharif's garden house, would think himself as far removed from human society as if he were in the midst of the Nubian Desert. But this may be wholly ascribed to the apathy of the inhabitants and their indifference for agricultural pursuits. Numerous wells, dispersed throughout the town, prove that water may be easily obtained at about thirty feet below the surface.

In Arabia, wherever the ground can be irrigated by wells, the sands may be soon made productive. The industry of a very few years might thus render Mecca and its environs as remarkable for gardens and plantations as it now is for absolute sterility. Al-Azraqi* speaks of gardens in this valley and describes different springs and wells that no longer exist, having probably

---

*al-Azraqi: Abu al-Walid Muhammad al-Azraqi, chronicler of Mecca (flourished 865). [Ed.]

been choked up by the violent torrents. Al-Fasi* likewise affirms that in his days the town contained no less than fifty-eight wells. But in the earliest times of Arabian history, this place was certainly barren, and the Quran styles it accordingly "the valley without seeds." Al-Azraqi further says that before houses were constructed here by the Qusayy,† this valley abounded with acacias and various thorny trees.

Nothing is more difficult than to compute exactly the population of Eastern towns, where registers are never kept and where even the number of houses can scarcely be ascertained. To judge from appearances, and by comparison with European towns in which the amount of population is well-known, may be very fallacious. The private habitations in the East are generally (though the Hijaz forms an exception to this rule) of one storey only, and therefore contain fewer inmates in proportion than European dwellings. On the other hand, Eastern towns have very narrow streets, are without public squares or large marketplaces, and their miserable suburbs are in general more numerously peopled than their principal and best streets. Travellers, however, in passing rapidly through towns, may be easily deceived, for they see only the bazaars and certain streets, in which the greater part of the male population is usually assembled during the day. Thus it happens that recent and respectable authorities have stated 200,000 souls as the population of Aleppo, 400,000 as that of Damascus, and 300,000 as that of Cairo. My estimate of the population of the three great Syrian towns is as follows: Damascus, 250,000; Hama (of which, however, I must speak with less confidence), from 60,000 to 100,000; and Aleppo, daily dwindling into decay, between 80,000 and 90,000. To Cairo I would allow at most 200,000. As to Mecca, which I have seen both before and after the Hajj and know, perhaps, more thoroughly than any other town of the East, the result of my inquiries gives between 25,000 and 30,000 stationary inhabitants for the population of the city and suburbs, besides from 3,000 to 4,000 Abyssinian and black slaves. Its habitations are capable of containing three times this number. In the time of Sultan Selim I (according to Qutb al-Din,‡ in 1526) a census was taken of the inhabitants of Mecca, previous to a gratuitous distribution of corn among them, and the number was found to be 12,000 men, women, and children. The same author shows that in earlier times, the population was much more considerable; for when Abu Daher, the chief of the

---

*al-Fasi: Muhammad ibn Ahmad al-Fasi, chronicler of Mecca (died 1429). [Ed.]

†Qusayy: founders of urban Mecca (ca. 390–410). [Ed.]

‡Qutb al-Din: Ottoman chronicler of Mecca (died 1582). [Ed.]

Qarmatians (a heretic sect of Muslims), sacked Mecca, in 926, 30,000 of the inhabitants were killed by his ferocious soldiers.

THE PROCESSION TO ARAFAT The Syrian and Egyptian caravans always arrive at fixed periods, generally a day or two before the departure of the Hajj for Arafat. Both caravans usually pass by Badr on the same day, or with an interval of one day only. The Syrian caravan coming from Medina, and the Egyptian from Yanbu, prosecute their route from Badr to Mecca, at a short distance from each other. On the fifth of the month of Dhu al-Hijja, or the twenty-first of November 1814, the approach of the Syrian caravan was announced by one of its scouts, who came galloping into the town to win the prize which is always awarded to him who brings the first tidings of the safe arrival of that caravan. The loud acclamations of the mob followed him to the Governor's house, where his horse expired the moment he dismounted. The news was the more important, as nothing had been heard of this Hajj caravan, and rumours had even been circulated of the Bedouins having plundered it on the road to the north of Medina. Two hours after, many other persons belonging to it arrived, and in the night the whole body came up and encamped, with the Pasha of Damascus at their head, in the plain of Shaykh Mahmud.

Early the next morning, the Egyptian caravan also arrived. The heavy baggage and the camels were sent to the usual place of encampment of the Egyptian Hajj, in the Moab Desert, but the *mahmal,* or holy camel, remained at Shaykh Mahmud, that it might pass from thence in procession next day through the town. Pasha Muhammad Ali arrived unexpectedly this morning from Ta'if, to be present at the Hajj and to inspect the cavalry which had come with the Egyptian caravan, a reinforcement that strongly excited his hopes of success against the Wahhabis. He was dressed in a very handsome *ihram,* having two large entirely white *cashmirene* shawls wrapped round his loins and shoulders. His head was bare, but an officer held over it an umbrella to protect him from the sun, while riding through the streets. On the same morning, all the hajjis resident at Mecca took the *ihram* at their own lodgings, with the usual ceremonies preparatory to their setting out for Arafat, and at midday they assembled in the mosque, where a short sermon was preached on the occasion. The hajjis who had come with the caravan had already taken the *ihram* at Asfan, two stations in advance of Mecca, but a great number of them, especially the servants and camel drivers, did not throw off their ordinary dresses and even appeared in them at Arafat, without causing either surprise or indignation. There is no religious police or inquisition here, and everybody is left to the dictates of his conscience, either to observe or neglect the precepts of the canonical law.

Great bustle prevailed this evening in the town. Everybody was preparing for his journey to Arafat; Syrian hajjis came to engage lodgings, to inquire about the state of the markets, and to pay their first visits to the Ka'ba. A number of pedlars and petty shopkeepers left the town to establish themselves at Arafat and to be ready there for the accommodation of the pilgrims. A number of camel drivers from Syria and Egypt led their unloaded camels through the streets, offering to let them out to the hajjis going to Arafat. The rate of hire this year was very moderate on account of the great number of beasts of burden. I engaged two of these camels, for the journey of four days to Arafat and back again, for three dollars.

On the eighth of Hajj, early in the morning, the Syrian Hajj passed in procession through the town, accompanied by all its soldiers and carrying the *mahmal* in front. All its baggage was left at Shaykh Mahmud, excepting the tents that were to be pitched at Arafat. Most of the hajjis were mounted in the *shubreya,** a sort of palanquin placed upon the camel. The great people, and the Pasha of Damascus himself, rode in *takhtruans,* a kind of closed litter or box carried by two camels, one before and the other behind, and forming a very commodious conveyance, except that it is necessary always to have a ladder by means of which one may mount or descend. The camels were decorated with feathers, tassels, and bells, but their heads, bent down towards the ground, showed how much they were fatigued by their journey. While these passed, the streets were lined by people of all classes, who greeted the caravan with loud acclamations and praise. The martial music of the Pasha of Damascus, a dozen fine caparisoned horses led in front of his litter, and the rich *takhtruans* in which his women rode particularly attracted attention.

Soon after the Syrians had passed, the Egyptian procession followed, consisting of its *mahmal,* or sacred ark (for each of the caravans carries one), and the *shubreyas* of the public officers who always accompany the Hajj. But not a single private pilgrim was to be seen in its suite. The good appearance of the soldiers who were with them, the splendour of the *mahmal* and of the equipage of the Amir al-Hajj, who was a commander of the Turkish horsemen, drew from Meccans many signs of approbation, such as had been given to those who immediately preceded them. Both caravans continued their route to Arafat without stopping.

---

shubreya: the *shevria* of Ali Bey al-Abbasi. [Ed.]

Before midday, all the hajjis who had resided for some time at Mecca likewise mounted their camels and crowded the streets as they pressed forward to follow the Hajj. They were joined by the far greater part of the population of Mecca, who make it a rule to go every year to Arafat, and by a similar portion of the population of Jidda, who had been assembled here for some time. During five or six days, the gates of Jidda, thus deserted by so many people, remain shut.

I left my lodgings on foot after midday with a companion and a slave boy mounted on two camels which I had hired from a Syrian driver, a native of Homs. It is thought meritorious to make the six hours' journey to Arafat on foot, particularly if the pilgrim goes barefooted. Many hajjis did so, and I preferred this mode because I had led a very sedentary life for some months. We were several hours before we could reach the outskirts of the town, so great was the crowd of camels, and many accidents happened. Of the half-naked hajjis, all dressed in the white *ihram,* some sat reading the Quran upon their camels, some ejaculated loud prayers, whilst others cursed their drivers and quarrelled with those near them, who were choking up the passage. Beyond the town the road widens, and we passed on through the valleys at a very slow march for two hours, to Mina Valley, in the narrow entrance of which great confusion again occurred. The law enjoins that the hajjis shall recite five prayers at Mina, Muhammad having always done so. That is to say, that they shall arrive there at noon, in time for the midday prayer and, remaining until the next morning, shall perform the prayers of *asr, maghrib, 'isha,* and that of the dawn on the ensuing day. The inconvenience, however, arising from a delay on the route has led to the neglect of this precept for some time past, and the Hajj now passes Mina, on its way to Arafat, without halting.

In advance of Mina, we had the mosque of Muzdalifa to our right, whither many pilgrims went to recite the prayers of *asr* and *maghrib,* but the caravan continued its march. Beyond Muzdalifa, we again entered the mountains by the pass called al-Mazumayn, on the eastern side of which we issued towards the Plain of Arafat. Here the pilgrims passed between the two pillars called Alamayn and, on approaching the vicinity of Jabal Arafat, dispersed over the plain in search of their place of encampment. I reached the camp about three hours after sunset, but the last stragglers did not arrive till midnight. Numberless fires were seen lighted on an extent of ground of three or four miles in length, and high and brilliant clusters of lamps marked the different places of encampment of Muhammad Ali Suleyman Pasha, and the Amir al-Hajj of the Egyptian caravan. Hajjis were seen in every direction wandering among the tents in search of their companions, whom they had lost in the confusion on the road, and it was several hours before the noise and clamour had subsided. Few persons slept during that night: the devotees sat up praying, and their loud chants were particularly distinguished on the side of the Syrian encampment; the merry Meccans formed themselves into parties, singing the jovial songs called *djok,* accompanied by clapping hands; and the coffeehouses scattered over the plain were crowded the whole night with customers.

The night was dark and cold, and a few drops of rain fell. I had formed a resting place for myself by means of a large carpet tied to the back part of a Meccan's tent. Having walked about for the greater part of the night, I had just disposed myself to sleep when two guns, fired by the Syrian and Egyptian Hajj, announced the approaching dawn of the day of pilgrimage and summoned the faithful to prepare for their morning prayers. . . .

THE STANDING DAY VIGIL   At sunrise on the ninth of Dhu al-Hajj, every pilgrim issued from his tent to walk over the plains and take a view of the busy crowds assembled there. Long streets of tents, fitted up as bazaars, furnished all kinds of provisions. The Syrian and Egyptian cavalry were exercised by their chiefs early in the morning, while thousands of camels were seen feeding upon the dry shrubs of the plain all round the camp. I walked to Mount Arafat, to enjoy from its summit a more distinct view of the whole.

This granite hill, which is also called Jabal al-Rahma, or the Mountain of Mercy, rises on the northeast side of the plain close to the mountains which encompass it, but separated from them by a rocky valley. It is about a mile or a mile and a half in circuit. Its sides are sloping, and its summit is nearly two hundred feet above the level of the plain. On the eastern side broad stone steps lead up to the top, and a broad unpaved path, on the western, over rude masses of granite with which its declivity is covered. After mounting about forty steps, we find a spot a little on the left, called the Place of Prayer of Our Lord Adam, where, it is related, the father of mankind used to stand while praying; for here it was, according to Muhammadan tradition, that the angel Gabriel first instructed Adam how to adore his Creator. A marble slab, bearing an inscription in modern characters, is fixed in the side of the mountain. On reaching about the sixtieth step, we come to a small paved platform to our right, on a level spot of the hill, where the preacher stands who admonishes the pilgrims on the afternoon of this day, as I shall hereafter mention. Thus high, the steps are so broad and easy that a horse or camel may ascend, but higher up they become more steep and uneven. On the summit the place is shown where Muhammad used to take his station during the Hajj; a small chapel formerly stood over it, but this was destroyed by the Wahhabis. Here the pilgrims usually pray two *rakat*s in salutation of Arafat. The steps and the summit are covered with handkerchiefs to receive their pious gifts, and each family of the Meccans or Bedouins of the tribe of Quraysh, in whose territory Arafat lies, has its particular spot assigned to it for this purpose. The summit commands a very extensive and singular prospect. I brought my compass to take a circle of bearings, but the crowd was so great that I could not use it. Towards the western extremity of the plain are seen the Basan Well and the [pillars marking the boundary of the Haram territory]; somewhat nearer, southwards, the Namira mosque, and on the southeast a small house where the Sharif used to lodge during the pilgrimage. From thence an elevated rocky ground in the plain extends towards Arafat. On the eastern side of the mountain, and close to its foot, are the ruins of a small mosque built on rocky ground where Muhammad was accustomed to pray, and where the pilgrims make four prostrations in memory of the Prophet. Several large reservoirs lined with stone are dispersed over the plain; two or three are close to the foot of Arafat, and there are some near the house of the sharifs. They [all] are filled from the same fine aqueduct which supplies Mecca, and the head of which is about one hour and a half distant, in the eastern mountains. The canal is left open here for the convenience of pilgrims and is conducted round the three sides of the mountains, passing by Adam's Place of Prayer.*

From the summit of Arafat, I counted about three thousand tents dispersed over the plain, of which two thirds belonged to the two Hajj caravans and to the suite and soldiers of Muhammad Ali, the rest to the Arabs of the Sharif, the Bedouin hajjis, and the people of Mecca and Jidda. These assembled multitudes were for the greater number, like myself, without tents. The two caravans were encamped without much order, each party of pilgrims or soldiers having pitched its tents in large circles, in the midst of which many of their camels were reposing. The plain contained, dispersed in different parts, from twenty to twenty-five thousand camels, twelve thousand of which belonged to the Syrian Hajj, and from five to six thousand to the Egyptian; besides about three thousand, purchased by Muhammad Ali from the Bedouins in the Syrian deserts and brought to Mecca with the Hajj, to convey the pilgrims to this place, previous to being used for the transport of army provisions to Ta'if.

The Syrian Hajj was encamped on the south and southwest side of the mountain; the Egyptian on the southeast. Around the house of the Sharif,

*At the close of the sixteenth century, according to Qutb al-Din, the whole Plain of Arafat was cultivated.

Yahya himself was encamped with his Bedouin troops, and in its neighbourhood were all the Hijaz people. Here it was that the two Yemen caravans
used formerly to take their station. Muhammad Ali and Suleyman Pasha of
Damascus, as well as several of their officers, had very handsome tents, but
the most magnificent of all was that of the wife of Muhammad Ali, the mother
of Tussan Pasha and Ibrahim Pasha, who had lately arrived from Cairo for
the Hajj with a truly royal equipage, five hundred camels being necessary to
transport her baggage from Jidda to Mecca. Her tent was in fact an encampment consisting of a dozen tents of different sizes, inhabited by her women,
the whole enclosed by a wall of linen cloth eight hundred paces in circuit,
the single entrance to which was guarded by eunuchs in splendid dresses.
Around this enclosure were pitched the tents of the men who formed her
numerous suite. The beautiful embroidery on the exterior of this linen palace, with the various colours displayed in every part of it, constituted an object
which reminded me of some descriptions in the Arabian tales of *The Thousand and One Nights*. Among the rich equipages of the other hajjis, or of the
Mecca people, none were so conspicuous as that belonging to the family of
Jelani, the merchant, whose tents, pitched in a semicircle, rivalled in beauty
those of the two pashas and far exceeded those of Sharif Yahya. In other parts
of the East, a merchant would as soon think of buying a rope for his own
neck as of displaying his wealth in the presence of a pasha; but Jelani has not
yet laid aside the customs which the Meccans learned under their old government, particularly that of Sharif Ghalib, who seldom exercised extortion
upon single individuals;* and they now rely on the promises of Muhammad
Ali, that he will respect their property.

During the whole morning, there were repeated discharges of the artillery which both pashas had brought with them. A few pilgrims had taken up
their quarters on Jabal Arafat itself, where some small cavern, or impending
block of granite, afforded them shelter from the sun. It is a belief generally
entertained in the East, and strengthened by many boasting hajjis on their return
home, that all the pilgrims on this day encamp upon Mount Arafat, and that
the mountain possesses the miraculous property of expansion, so as to admit
an indefinite number of the faithful upon its summit. The law ordains that
the position of the Hajj should be on Jabal Arafat, but it wisely provides against
any impossibility by declaring that the plain in the immediate neighbourhood
of the mountain may be regarded as comprised under the term *mountain*.

I estimated the number of persons assembled here at about seventy
thousand. The camp was from three to four miles long and between one and

*A statement contradicted by al-Abbasi. [Ed.]

two in breath. There is, perhaps, no spot on Earth where, in so small a place, such a diversity of languages are heard; I reckoned about forty and have no doubt that there were many more. It appeared to me as if I were here placed in a holy temple of travellers only, and never did I at any time feel a more ardent wish to be able to penetrate once into the inmost recesses of the countries of many of those persons whom I now saw before me, fondly imagining that I might have no more difficulty in reaching their homes than what they had experienced in their journey to this spot.

When the attention is engrossed by such a multitude of new objects, time passes rapidly away. I had only descended from Mount Arafat and had walked for some time about the camp, here and there entering into conversation with pilgrims (inquiring at the Syrian camp after some of my friends and among the Syrian Bedouins for news from their deserts), when midday had already passed. The prayers of their period of the day ought to be performed either within or in the immediate neighbourhood of the mosque of Namira, whither the two pashas had repaired for that purpose. The far greater number of hajjis, however, dispense with this observance, and many of them with the midday prayers altogether, for no one concerns himself whether his neighbour is punctual or not in the performance of the prescribed rites. After midday, the pilgrims are to wash and purify the body by means of the entire ablution prescribed by the law, for which purpose chiefly the numerous tents in the plain have been constructed. But the weather was cloudy and rather cold, which induced nine tenths of the pilgrims, shivering as they were already under the thin covering of the *ihram,* to omit the rite also and to content themselves with the ordinary ablution. The time of *asr* (or about three P.M.) approached, when that ceremony of the Hajj takes place for which the whole assembly had come hither.

The pilgrims now pressed forward towards the mountain of Arafat and covered its sides from top to bottom. At the precise time of *asr,* the preacher took his stand upon the platform on the mountain and began to address the multitude. This sermon, which lasts till sunset, constitutes the holy ceremony of the Hajj called Qutba al-Wukuf, and no pilgrim, although he may have visited all the holy places of Mecca, is entitled to the name of hajji, unless he has been present on this occasion. As *asr* approached, therefore, all the tents were struck, everything was packed up, the caravans began to load, and the pilgrims belonging to them mounted their camels and crowded round the mountain to be within sight of the preacher, which is sufficient, as the greater part of the multitude is necessarily too distant to hear him. The two pashas, with their whole cavalry drawn up in two squadrons behind them, took their post in the rear of the deep lines of camels of the hajjis, to which those of the people of the Hijaz were also joined, and here they waited in solemn and respectful silence the conclusion of the sermon. Further removed from the preacher was the Sharif Yahya, with his small body of soldiers, distinguished by several green standards carried before him. The two *mahmals,* or holy camels, which carry on their back the high structure that serves as the banner of their respective caravans, made way with difficulty through the ranks of camels that encircled the southern and eastern sides of the hill, opposite to the preacher, and took their station surrounded by their guards directly under the platform in front of him.*

The preacher, who is usually the Qadi of Mecca, was mounted upon a finely caparisoned camel which had been led up the steps, it being traditionally said that Muhammad was always seated when he here addressed his followers, a practice in which he was imitated by all the caliphs who came to the Hajj, and who from hence addressed their subjects in person. The Turkish gentleman of Constantinople, however, unused to camel riding, could not keep his seat so well as the hardy Bedouin Prophet; and the camel becoming unruly, he was soon obliged to alight from it. He read his sermon from a book in Arabic, which he held in his hands. At intervals of every four or five minutes he paused and stretched forth his arms to implore blessings from above while the assembled multitudes around and before him waved the skirts of their *ihram*s over their heads and rent the air with shouts of *"Labayk*

*The *mahmal* . . . is a high, hollow, wooden frame in the form of a cone, with a pyramidal top, covered with a fine silk brocade adorned with ostrich feathers and having a small book of prayers and charms placed in the midst of it, wrapped up in a piece of silk. (My description is taken from the Egyptian *mahmal.*) When on the road, it serves as a holy banner to the caravan, and on the return of the Egyptian caravan, the book of prayers is exposed in the mosque al-Hassanayn, at Cairo, where men and women of the lower classes go to kiss it and obtain a blessing by rubbing their foreheads upon it. No copy of the Quran, nor anything but the book of prayers, is placed in the Cairo *mahmal.* The Wahhabis declared this ceremony of the Hajj to be a vain pomp, of idolatrous origin, and contrary to the spirit of true religion, and its use was one of the principal reasons which they assigned for interdicting the caravans from repairing to Mecca. In the first centuries of Islam, neither the Umayyads nor the Abassids ever had a *mahmal.* Al-Maqrizi, in his treatise *On Those Caliphs and Sultans Who Performed the Pilgrimage in Person,* says that al-Zahir Baybars Bunbukdari, Sultan of Egypt, was the first who introduced the *mahmal,* about 1280. Since his time, all the sultans who sent their caravans to Mecca have considered it as a privilege to send one with each, as a sign of their own royalty. I believe the custom to have arisen in the battle banners of the Bedouins, . . . which I have mentioned in my remarks on the Bedouins, and which resemble the *mahmal,* inasmuch as they are high wooden frames placed upon camels. [Ed.]

Allahumma Labayk" (i.e., "Here we are, at thy commands, O God!") During the wavings of the *ihram*s, the side of the mountain, thickly crowded as it was by the people in their white garments, had the appearance of a cataract of water, while the green umbrellas, with which several thousand hajjis, sitting on their camels below were provided, bore some resemblance to a verdant plain. . . .

At length the sun began to descend behind the western mountains, upon which the Qadi, having shut his book, received a last greeting of *"Labayk,"* and the crowds rushed down the mountain in order to quit Arafat. It is thought meritorious to accelerate the pace on this occasion, and many persons make it a complete race, called by the Arabs, the Rush from Arafat. In former times, when the strength of the Syrian and Egyptian caravans happened to be nearly balanced, bloody affrays took place here almost every year between them, each party endeavouring to outrun and to carry its *mahmal* in advance of the other. The same happened when the *mahmals* approached the platform at the commencement of the sermon, and two hundred lives have on some occasions been lost in supporting what was thought the honour of the respective caravans. At present the power of Muhammad Ali preponderates, and the Syrian hajjis display great humility.

The united caravans and the whole mass of pilgrims now moved forward over the plain. Every tent had been previously packed up, to be ready for the occasion. The pilgrims pressed through the al-Alamayn pillars, which they must repass on their return, and night came on before they reached the defile called al-Mazumayn. Innumerable torches were now lighted, twenty-four being carried before each pasha, and the sparks of fire from them flew far over the plain. There were continual discharges of artillery; the soldiers fired their muskets; the martial bands of both the pashas played; skyrockets were thrown as well by the pashas' officers, as by many private pilgrims, while the Hajj passed at a quick pace in the greatest disorder, amidst a deafening clamour, through the pass of Mazumayn, leading towards Muzdalifa, where all alighted, after a two hours' march. No order was observed here in encamping, and everyone lay down on the spot that first presented itself, no tents being pitched except those of the pashas and their suites, before which was an illumination of lamps in the form of high arches, which continued to blaze the whole night while the firing of the artillery was kept up without intermission.

In the indescribable confusion attending the departure of the Hajj from Arafat, many pilgrims had lost their camels and were now heard calling loudly for their drivers as they sought them over the plain: I myself was among their number. When I went to the Mountain of Arafat, I ordered my camel driver and my slave to remain in readiness upon the spot where they then were till I should return to them after sunset; but seeing, soon after I quitted them, that the other loaded camels pressed forward towards the mountain, they followed the example, and when I returned to the place where I left them, they were not to be found. I was therefore obliged to walk to Muzdalifa, where I slept on the sand, covered only by my *ihram,* after having searched for my people during several hours.

part three

Nineteenth-Century Changes 1853 — 1908

In the last half of the nineteenth century, as Western interests consolidated their hold on world trade, Europe's influence over Hajj travel reached a new zenith. During this period, Britain ruled India, held the purse strings in Egypt, and dominated traffic in the Red Sea, effectively controlling the flow of goods between Suez and Bombay. Not as a joke did Richard Burton, the first author in this section, call Great Britain the largest Muslim empire in the world. Similarly, Russia absorbed a large swath of Ottoman lands along its borders, while Dutch and British shipping took the lead in longtime Muslim maritime zones like Southeast Asia and the China Sea. In all these regions, trade routes forged or appropriated by European powers were often popular as Hajj routes, too. Already in 1814, Burckhardt noted a growing contingent of Malay pilgrims visiting the Hijaz, some of whom considered themselves Dutch or British subjects. A century later, Joseph Conrad would convey their numbers in *Lord Jim,* a novel that begins with eight hundred hajjis of the Far East boarding a steamer for Mecca:

> They streamed aboard over three gangways, they streamed in urged by faith and the hope of Paradise, they streamed in with a continuous tramp and shuffle of bare feet, without a word, a murmur, or a look back; and when clear of confining rails spread on all sides over the deck, flowed forward and aft, overflowed down the yawning hatchways, filled the inner recesses of the ship—like water filling a cistern, like water flowing into crevices and crannies, like water rising silently even with the brim. Eight hundred men and women with faith and hopes, with affections and memories, they had collected there, coming from north and south and from the outskirts of the East, after treading the jungle paths, descending the rivers, coasting in praus along the shallows, crossing in small canoes from island to island, passing through suffering, meeting

strange sights, beset by strange fears, upheld by one desire. They came from solitary huts in the wilderness, from populous *campongs*, from villages by the sea. At the call of an idea they had left their forests, their clearings, the protection of their rulers, their prosperity, their poverty, the surroundings of their youth and the graves of their fathers.

By the 1860s, more than half of all hajjis came from European colonies around the world. As the following accounts indicate, the French, British, and Dutch all introduced controls on pilgrim travel at this time. They issued passports, visas, and health certificates to their subjects, then transported them to the Hijaz. With steamships circling the globe and with the completion of the Suez Canal in 1869, pilgrims from Jakarta to Cairo began arriving in Jidda on European vessels. By 1885, the trip from Beirut to Yanbu took seven days, and half of all Meccan pilgrims came by sea. Trains played a large part, too. The most important to our story was an Ottoman-financed line from Damascus to Medina. Finished in 1908, it carried millions of pilgrims in the next six years. Old hands at package touring, Hajj travel representatives throughout the Near East simply treated a line of rail cars as a faster caravan, charging pilgrims a lump sum for the round-trip journey, complete with lodgings in Mecca and Medina. Caravan traffic shrank as a result of all these innovations. By 1914, the only camel routes of consequence to hajjis were the few internal roads between Mecca, Medina, and the Red Sea. As Arthur Wavell's 1908–09 excerpts demonstrate, the Medina train struck a blow to the raid-based Bedouin economy, upsetting the balance of power in the Hijaz.

Modern transport raised disturbing cultural issues for pilgrims, too. In eastern Europe and much of Russia, the routes to new ports and terminals exposed traditional Muslims for the first time to societies outside the ambit of Islamic law and customs. Was the water in a train station in Baku clean enough for Muslim ablutions? Was the meat ritually slaughtered? Public drunkenness and unrestrained mixing of the sexes were likewise deeply disturbing to many rural pilgrims, as the 1885–86 excerpts here by Mohammad Farahani record. These were significant problems, yet the attractions of modern transport overrode them. Pilgrims flowed—Conrad's watery metaphor is a good one—in the direction of least resistance. Steam and rail increased the journey's speed and comfort, at the same time reducing cost and risk.

Finally, the European administration of Hajj travel profoundly affected pilgrim health and welfare. Repeated cholera epidemics early in the century led to modern quarantine stations on Hajj routes, installed at the insistence of an international body of observers convened *in Paris*. During this period, the colonial powers also began placing monetary conditions on their pilgrims, so that more and more often only travelers with sufficient means and a round-trip passage might leave a colonial port to start their journey. Although this step created resentment among hajjis it inadvertently reinforced Quranic law.* Responding to the world as they found it, the travel writers gathered in this section find a lot to say on all these matters.

Europeans affected the Hajj, but they did not advance into the Sacred Territory. Britain's first Vice-Consul to Jidda arrived in 1838; his Italian, French, and Dutch counterparts were there to greet him. Yet the city remained completely in the hands of the Sharif, who taxed every side of its lucrative trade in a facile alliance with the Turkish Pasha. Europeans might walk around the town, might occupy rented properties for years, but the gates leading to the Hijaz remained closed to them. A few miles past the eastern walls, in the steep ravines leading up to Mecca, *haram* law remained supreme. Muslims still took direction from the stone cairns bounding the territory. All men still donned the two white seamless cloths, and women put off veils and perfume. Here everyone obeyed special codes of behavior while non-Muslims went in fear of their violation. As our travel accounts continue to bear out, these laws remained inviolable for both cultures. No nonbeliever ever entered the Haram Territory and returned to write about it, except by deception. Moreover, despite a growing hold on the Near East, no Western nation ever gained a foothold in the Hijaz. The Sacred Territories remained exclusive.†

Orientalists trying to grasp Islam on paper also found the Hajj impregnable. Conditioned by their imperial milieu, convinced of Europe's moral superiority, these scholars were largely unprepared to deal with the pilgrimage, the feeling of the rites, the actual significance of Mecca. Leading European academics were still quick to treat "the Arab" as substandard. Joseph-Ernest Renan, to take one example, considered Arabic an inferior language, its sole value being to prepare the student for reading ancient Hebrew. Handicapped by received ideas forged in the Spanish Inquisition, nineteenth-century scholars like Silvestre de Sacy, Caussin de Perceval, and Edward Lane

---

*"Pilgrimage to the House of God is a duty to Allah for everyone who can afford to make the journey." (Quran III:97)

†"As for the unbelievers, Allah can surely do without them." (Quran III:97)

were loath to admit that complex social realities might exist outside Europe. Instead, they presented "the Arab lands" as monolithic, static, inferior, libidinous, and despotic, backward territories inhabited by minor populations requiring Europe's protection and tutelage. When, alternatively, they romanticized "the mysteries of the East," it was to possess them—as authors, authorities, privileged specialists. A despotic East and a mysterious East were two sides of one coin.

Beginning in the mid-nineteenth century, a number of Western travelers to Mecca writing in French, English, and German contested these long-established views, drawing instead on experience and travel. Of those who went to Mecca, Richard Burton remains the best known, but there were others.* Richard Burton, John Keane, and Arthur Wavell, the three Europeans presented here, all enjoyed a warm rapport with the Near East. Although writing for a British audience, they were not completely "of" Britain or very often in it. Burton, an exile by temperament, conceived his trip and wrote his book in India. Keane, born in Calcutta, ran away to sea in his youth. Wavell spent most of his adult life in Africa. None of these men suffered culture shock as a hajji or compared Mecca's mosque to the London stock exchange. Versed in Muslim manners, proficient linguists, they were young men with military backgrounds, adventurers shaping careers from an avocation, for whom Mecca was a place to make one's mark. In their view, Mecca had everything: romance, mystery, inaccessibility, and danger. Lying between India, Britain's richest colony, and Egypt, its location attracted interest among a readership in England avid for information about the world. And of course, the city was "forbidden." The Hajj-account genre gained new impetus in this period. By 1910, enough Europeans had visited Mecca and written up their trips to warrant a book on the subject, *Christians at Mecca,* by Augustus Ralli.

Works by these Western authors alternate here with accounts by an Indian princess and a Persian bureaucrat. The motives for such thoroughly Muslim books were naturally different from the European ones. The Begum of Bhopal (1864) is less concerned with the Hajj than with its high-handed and venal management by sharifs and pashas. By challenging corrupt Hijazi

---

*Léon Roches (1841), Georg Wallin (1845), and Christian Snouck Hurgronje (1885) are three examples. Of them, only Wallin performed the Hajj (but wrote nothing about it). Roches left an adventuresome account of his years as an undercover Muslim but was forced to leave Mecca before making the Hajj. Although Hurgronje fared likewise, his twin studies of Mecca and the Hajj remain the century's principal studies on these subjects. While of great interest, none of these men produced a pilgrim narrative.

institutions, she sought to improve the Hajj for her Indian subjects. Moham-mad Farahani's 1885–86 account of a trip from Tehran by land and sea has another goal, that of educating contemporary Persians to the changes brought about by modern transport and social engineers.

Both these Muslim travelers tried to improve matters for their people, and both books were somewhat official. The Begum governed a million people; the Shah of Persia commissioned Farahani's book. Although there is little to recommend them as literature, they are crucial for what they tell about the rapidly changing Hajj. Burton, Keane, and Wavell, on the other hand, left substantial narrations in their own right. Their more self-exposed narrations place a new emphasis on personal experience, and each one em-ploys ironic dialogue and painterly description to register and heighten new effects. As real-life encounters grew increasingly important for modern read-ers, authors like these supplied them, shedding new light on the men and women who undertook the Hajj.

9

Sir Richard Burton
Great Britain
1853

Richard Burton's Personal Narrative, published first in 1855, remains the only full-length Hajj account widely available in the West today. Insofar as our literature "has" a Hajj, we have it through Burton. His life story has been written half a dozen times, yet no two biographers quite agree on why he made the journey.

When Burton arrived in Mecca at age thirty-two, his role as explorer had already been formed by a seven-year stint in India and Sind as an East India Company soldier (1842–49). There, abundant linguistic skills and an instinct for anything "native" qualified him as a secret agent.* Traveling disguised as a merchant or a dervish, he experienced firsthand the life of Victoria's colonial Indian subjects. In this way, he served his nation's interests many times over and also made himself fluent in eight languages.

During a subsequent leave in Europe, Burton published four books on his travels. Although the editions sold poorly, they brought him notice in the tight-knit world of English exploration. Like Burckhardt (whom he revered), Burton was a natural ethnographer—curious, brave, indefatigable, with a sixth sense for cultures not his own. By 1851, his reputation was sufficient for him to propose to the Royal Geographical Society† a one-man expedition into Arabia.

Because it made him famous, most of Burton's biographers view his decision to make the Hajj as a smart career move. In fact, there were other motives. Besides studying languages in India and Sind, he had also experimented with numerous religions, been initiated into the Nagar Brahman caste, explored both Hindu Yoga and Tantric Buddhism, and even taken up Catholicism for a while

---

*Rudyard Kipling, in his novel Kim, based the shadowy character Colonel Creighton on Burton and his activities during this period.

†The African Association, which supported Burckhardt's journey (and al-Abbasi's, too?), was subsumed into the Royal Geographical Society shortly after the Society's founding in 1830.

in its Goan version. Burton was not, however, a deep religious thinker. He was a practitioner embarking on more or less seasonal theological forays, a seeker after what he called the gnosis. His first sustained exposure to Islam came through a Persian instructor, Mirza Husayn, who happened also to be the brother of the Agha Khan. Spiritual heads of the same Isma'ili sect that had inspired Nasir-e Khosraw eight centuries before, these men introduced Burton to mystical Shi'ism. Later he joined the Qadiriyya, one of the world's largest Sufi orders. By May 1847, he was already mulling over a pilgrimage to Mecca and, according to his letters, had begun "a systematic study of practical Muslim divinity, learned about a quarter of the Quran by heart, and become proficient at prayer." Furthermore, he wrote, "It was always my desire to visit Mecca during the pilgrimage season: written descriptions by hearsay of the rites and ceremonies were common enough in all languages . . . but none satisfied me, because none seemed practically to know anything about the matter."

In his proposal to the Royal Geographical Society a few years later, these largely personal motives go unmentioned. The point of the journey, so far as the R. G. S. directors understood, was to further scientific knowledge and to provide the East India Company with valuable information on Arabian trade routes. The fulfillment of the Hajj was scarcely mentioned, and Burton's Muslim interests not at all. Based on this carefully tailored proposal, the society became his backer.

In April 1853, Burton joined a steamer at Southampton for the thirteen-day cruise to Egypt. He went on board dressed as a Shi'ite Persian. In Alexandria, however, this first persona met with mixed success. Shi'ites were not quite "clean" in many Sunni Muslims' eyes, and Egypt was predominantly Sunni. Burton had not reckoned on the traditional ill will between these parties. So long as he persisted in the error, he was treated as only "a kind of Muslim, not a good one like themselves, but still better than nothing." In Cairo, he changed disguises and carefully recorded his subsequent elevation among Egyptians. Within a month, he had made himself over into an acceptable Sunni gentleman, an Afghan "Pathan" (Pashtun) born in India and a practicing doctor. This role provided the social access he was seeking. It also inspired one of the following excerpts, a humorous, Twain-like sketch of a usual day in the life of a medic on the Nile.

Burton dressed down to travel on the Hajj, adopting before he left Cairo a poor dervish's getup as protective coloration. When it came to obtaining official visas, however, his humble appearance created difficulties. British and Egyptian officials alike humiliated Burton, refusing him their precious transit stamps while never doubting what they saw before them—a penniless Hindi mendicant and, thus, a British subject. At one point Burton admits that as a British convert he might have "carried matters with a high hand," whereas, dressed as a native, "you must worm your way with timidity and submissiveness; in fact, by becoming an animal too contemptible for man to let or injure." By recording at length these humbling encounters, Burton cast new light on the officiousness of state-controlled pilgrim travel (a topic we have not heard the last of).

Burton's great contribution to the pilgrim literature concerns Medina, where he traveled next. Whereas Burckhardt's Meccan chapters were definitive, he had been too ill in Medina to leave his rooms. Burton therefore wisely devoted half of his first volume to the Prophet's City. This part of his record is a scholarly tour de force, presenting in detail the city's physical and spiritual geography, its major mosques, its history and trade, its markets, libraries, family life, rituals and legends. Much of this information had not appeared in Europe until now, and it displaced centuries of conjecture and false assumptions. Burton spent about a month in Medina. It is as though he had lived there half his life.

A caravan left for Mecca on September 1, "seven thousands souls on foot, on horseback, in litters, or bestriding the splendid camels of Syria." Burton crossed the desert with it, in the manner of Ibn Jubayr, riding in a shugduf. *His closest companions along the way, a handful of Medinese and a teenager from Mecca, play important reciprocal roles in this part of his narrative. He lent them small amounts of money, kept them amused, and cured their minor ills. In return, they looked after him in the Holy Cities. At home with the Hajj as only natives can be, they proved indispensable.*

The Syrian caravan reached Mecca only a day before the march to Arafat. During the Hajj, Burton correctly identified the Black Stone as an aerolite and measured the Ka'ba's perimeter with a tape, but his reports on the vigils at Arafat and Muzdalifa are oddly distracted. His descriptions of Mecca depend on Burckhardt. In fact, he transferred large sections of them to his pages, much as Ibn Battuta had done with Ibn Jubayr. The next week he was on his way to Jidda. It is a curious fact that the man who put Mecca on the map for English readers resided there for just eleven days.

Burton's pilgrimage was quickly hailed in the British press as an extraordinary act of daring. Certainly A Personal Narrative of a Journey to al-Madinah and Meccah *is the best of his two dozen travel books. Its successive chapters open like panels framing contradictory self-portraits: the outsider in England versus the inside man in Egypt; the proper British soldier versus the Eastern masquerader; the imperialist versus the dervish; the scholarly polymath versus the hell-for-leather traveler; and so on. With remarkable success, he persuades the reader to accept these many voices as belonging to one man. Although his mid-Victorian imperialist's tone wears badly on Burton's pages, the book contains other, more lasting accomplishments. It provides the first true, scholarly picture of Medina; it includes extracts of earlier travelers to Mecca (chiefly Varthema, Pitts, and*

*Burckhardt); and it overflows with personal encounters that illuminate, inter-
pret, and wryly satirize the lands he passed through. In all these ways, it supplies
a counter to the usual Western penchant for compressing the East into a voice-
less, monolithic symbol in opposition to "progress" and "civilization." Whereas
other nineteenth-century scholars reduced Islam to a set of Romantic, political,
or abasing terms, Burton gives us individual Muslims speaking their mind and
rendered in frank detail. At the same time, he offers a handbook for the hajji
masquerade.*

from *A Personal Narrative of a Journey to al-Madinah and Meccah* by Sir Richard Burton

A FEW WORDS CONCERNING WHAT INDUCED ME TO A PILGRIMAGE. In the
autumn of 1852, through the medium of my excellent friend, the late General Monteith, I offered my services to the Royal Geographical Society of
London for the purpose of removing that opprobrium to modern adventure, the huge white blot which in our maps still notes the eastern and the
central regions of Arabia. . . . The *experimentum crucis* was a visit to the Hijaz,
at once the most difficult and the most dangerous point by which a European can enter Arabia. I had intended, had the period of leave originally
applied for been granted, to land at Muscat—a favourable starting place—
and there to apply myself, slowly and surely, to the task of spanning the
deserts. But now I was to hurry, in the midst of summer, after a four years'
sojourn in Europe, during which many things Oriental had faded away from
my memory, and—after passing through the ordeal of Egypt, a country where
the police are curious as in Rome or Milan—to begin with the Muslim's
Holy Land, the jealously guarded and exclusive Haram. However, I being
liberally supplied with the means of travel by the Royal Geographical Society, thoroughly tired of "progress" and of "civilisation," curious to see with
my eyes what others are content to hear with ears, namely, Muslim inner
life in a really Islamic country, and longing, if truth be told, to set foot on
that mysterious spot which no vacation tourist has yet described, measured,

sketched, and photographed, I resolved to resume my old character of a Persian wanderer,* a dervish, and to make the attempt.

The principal object with which I started was this: to cross the unknown Arabian Peninsula, in a direct line from either al-Medina to Muscat or diagonally from Mecca to Makalla on the Indian Ocean. By what "circumstance, the miscreator," my plans were defeated, the reader will discover in the course of these volumes. The secondary objects were numerous. I was desirous to find out if any market for horses could be opened between central Arabia and India, where the studs were beginning to excite general dissatisfaction; to obtain information concerning the great Eastern wilderness, the vast expanse marked Rub' al-Khali (the Empty Abode) in our maps; to enquire into the hydrography of the Hijaz, its watershed, the disputed slope of the country, and the existence or nonexistence of perennial streams; and finally, to try, by actual observation, the truth of a theory proposed by Colonel W. Sykes, namely, that if tradition be true, in the population of the vast peninsula there must exist certain physiological differences sufficient to warrant our questioning the common origin of the Arab family. . . .

I have entitled this account of my summer's tour through the Hijaz, *A Personal Narrative,* and I have laboured to make its nature correspond with its name, simply because "it is the personal that interests mankind." Many may not follow my example; but some perchance will be curious to see what measures I adopted, in order to appear suddenly as an Eastern upon the stage of Oriental life; and as the recital may be found useful by future adventurers, I make no apology for the egotistical semblance of the narrative. Those who have felt the want of some "silent friend" to aid them with advice, when it must not be asked, will appreciate what may appear to the uninterested critic mere outpourings of a mind full of self.

On the evening of April 3, 1853, I left London for Southampton. By the advice of a brother officer, Captain (now Colonel) Henry Grindlay, of the Bengal cavalry . . . my Eastern dress was called into requisition before leaving town, and all my impedimenta were taught to look exceedingly oriental. Early the next day a "Persian prince," accompanied by Captain Grindlay, embarked on board the Peninsular and Oriental Company's magnificent screw steamer *Bengal.* . . .

ALEXANDRIA Having been invited to start from the house of a kind friend, John W. Larking, I disembarked with him. . . . Wonderful was the contrast

---

*The vagrant, the merchant, and the philosopher, amongst Orientals, are frequently united in the same person.

between the steamer and that villa on the Mahmudiya Canal! Startling the sudden change from presto to adagio life! In thirteen days we had passed from the clammy grey fog, that atmosphere of industry which kept us at anchor off the Isle of Wight, through the loveliest air of the Inland Sea, whose sparkling blue and purple haze spread charms even on North Africa's beldame features, and now we are sitting silent and still, listening to the monotonous melody of the East—the soft night breeze wandering through starlit skies and tufted trees, with a voice of melancholy meaning. . . .

The better to blind the inquisitive eyes of servants and visitors, my friend Larking lodged me in an out building, where I could revel in the utmost freedom of life and manners. And although some Armenian dragoman, a restless spy like all his race, occasionally remarked *voilà un Persan diablement dégagé,* none, except those who were entrusted with the secret, had any idea of the part I was playing. The domestics, devout Muslims, pronounced me an Ajami,* a kind of Muslim, not a good one like themselves but still better than nothing. I lost no time in securing the assistance of a Shaykh, and plunged once more into the intricacies of the faith, revived my recollections of religious ablutions, read the Quran, and again became an adept in the art of prostration. My leisure hours were employed in visiting the baths and coffeehouses, in attending the bazaars, and in shopping—an operation which hereabouts consists of sitting upon a chapman's counter, smoking, sipping coffee, and telling your beads the while, to show that you are not of the slaves for whom time is made; in fact, in pitting your patience against that of your adversary, the vender. I found time for a short excursion to a country village on the banks of the canal; nor was an opportunity of seeing *al-nahl,* the "bee dance," neglected, for it would be some months, before my eyes might dwell on such a pleasant spectacle again. . . .

A NEW DISGUISE After a month's hard work at Alexandria I prepared to assume the character of a wandering dervish; after reforming my title from *mirza*† to Shaykh Abdullah.‡ A reverend man, whose name I do not care to

*Ajami: a Persian as opposed to an Arab.

†*mirza:* the Persian "mister." In future chapters the reader will see the uncomfortable consequences of my having appeared in Egypt as a Persian. Although I found out the mistake, and worked hard to correct it, the bad name stuck to me; bazaar reports fly quicker and hit harder than newspaper paragraphs.

‡Shaykh Abdullah: Arab Christians sometimes take the name of Abdullah, Servant of Allah—"which," as a modern traveller observes, "all sects and religions might be equally proud to adopt." The Muslim Prophet said, "[T]he names most approved of God are Abdullah, Abd al-Rahman (Slave of the Compassionate), and such like."

quote, some time ago initiated me into his order, the Qadiriyya, under the high-sounding name of Bismillah Shah* and, after a due period of probation, he graciously elevated me to the proud position of a *murshid*,[†] or master in the mystic craft. I was therefore sufficiently well acquainted with the tenets and practices of these Oriental Freemasons. No character in the Muslim world is so proper for disguise as that of the dervish. It is assumed by all ranks, ages, and creeds; by the nobleman who has been disgraced at court, and by the peasant who is too idle to till the ground; by Dives, who is weary of life, and by Lazarus, who begs his bread from door to door. Further, the dervish is allowed to ignore ceremony and politeness, as one who ceases to appear upon the stage of life; he may pray or not, marry or remain single as he pleases, be respectable in cloth of frieze as in cloth of gold, and no one asks him—the chartered vagabond—Why he comes here? or Wherefore he goes there? He may wend his way on foot alone or ride his Arab mare followed by a dozen servants; he is equally feared without weapons as swaggering through the streets armed to the teeth. The more haughty and offensive he is to the people, the more they respect him, a decided advantage to the traveller of choleric temperament. In the hour of imminent danger, he has only to become a maniac, and he is safe; a madman in the East, like a notably eccentric character in the West, is allowed to say or do whatever the spirit directs. Add to this character a little knowledge of medicine, a "moderate skill in magic, and a reputation for caring for nothing but study and books," together with capital sufficient to save you from the chance of starving, and you appear in the East to peculiar advantage. The only danger of the "Mystic Path" is that the dervish's ragged coat not unfrequently covers the cutthroat, and if seized in the society of such a "brother," you may reluctantly become his companion, under the stick or on the stake. . . .

CAIRO I could find no room in the Wakala Khan Khalil, the Long's, or Meurice's, of native Cairo; I was therefore obliged to put up with the Jamaliya, a Greek quarter, swarming with drunken Christians and therefore about as fashionable as Oxford Street or Covent Garden. Even for this I had to wait a week. The pilgrims were flocking to Cairo, and to none other would the prudent hotel keepers open their doors, for the following sufficient rea-

---

*Bismillah Shah: "King in-the-Name-of-Allah." When a man appears as a faqir or dervish, he casts off, in process of regeneration, together with other worldly sloughs, his laical name for some brilliant coat of nomenclature rich in religious promise.

[†]*Murshid:* one allowed to admit *murids*, or apprentices. into the order. (It is doubtful that Burton attained to this level in his Sufi studies.) [Ed.]

sons. When you enter a *wakala,** the first thing you have to do is to pay a small sum, varying from two to five shillings, for the key. This is generally equivalent to a month's rent; so the sooner you leave the house the better for it. I was obliged to call myself a Turkish pilgrim in order to get possession of two most comfortless rooms, which I afterwards learned were celebrated for making travellers ill; and I had to pay eighteen piastres for the key and eighteen ditto *per mensem* for rent, besides five piastres to the man who swept and washed the place. So that for this month my house hire amounted to nearly four pence a day.

But I was fortunate enough in choosing the Jamaliya *wakala,* for I found a friend there. On board the steamer a fellow voyager, seeing me sitting alone and therefore as he conceived in discomfort, placed himself by my side and opened a hot fire of kind inquiries. He was a man about forty-five, of middle size, with a large round head closely shaven, a bull neck, limbs sturdy as a Saxon's, a thin red beard, and handsome features beaming with benevolence. A curious dry humour he had, delighting in "quizzing," but in so quiet, solemn, and quaint a way that before you knew him, you could scarcely divine his drift.

"Thank Allah, we carry a doctor!" said my friend more than once, with apparent fervour of gratitude, after he had discovered my profession. I was fairly taken in by the pious ejaculation, and some days elapsed before the drift of his remark became apparent.

"You doctors," he explained, when we were more intimate, "what do you do? A man goes to you for ophthalmia: it is a purge, a blister, and a drop in the eye! Is it for fever? Well! A purge and *kinakina* [quinine]. For dysentery? A purge and extract of opium. *Wa'llahi!* I am as good a physician as the best of you," he would add with a broad grin, "if I only knew the *dirhem-birhems,*†—drams and drachms—and a few break-jaw Arabic names of diseases."

Hajji Wali therefore emphatically advised me to make bread by honestly teaching languages. "We are doctor ridden," said he, and I found it was the case.

When we lived under the same roof, the Hajji and I became fast friends. During the day we called on each other frequently; we dined together and passed the evening in a mosque or some other place of public pastime. Coyly

---

wakala: a caravansary, or public hostel for traders and travelers. [Ed.]

†*dirhem-birhem:* The second is an imitative word, called in Arabic grammar *tabi'a,* as "Zayd Bayd," "Zayd and others"; so used, it denotes contempt for drachms and similar parts of drug craft.

at first, but less guardedly as we grew bolder, we smoked the forbidden weed hashish,* conversing lengthily the while about that world of which I had seen so much. Originally from Russia, he also had been a traveller, and in his wanderings he had cast off most of the prejudices of his people. "I believe in Allah and his Prophet, and in nothing else" was his sturdy creed; he rejected alchemy, jinnis, and magicians, and truly he had a most un-Oriental distaste for tales of wonder. When I entered the *wakala,* he constituted himself my cicerone, and especially guarded me against the cheating of tradesmen. By his advice I laid aside the dervish's gown, the large blue pantaloons, and the short shirt—in fact all connection with Persia and the Persians. "If you persist in being an Ajami," said the hajji, "you will get yourself into trouble; in Egypt you will be cursed; in Arabia you be beaten because you are a heretic; you will pay the treble of what other travellers do, and if you fall sick you may die by the roadside."

After long deliberation about the choice of nations, I became a "Pathan."† Born in India of Afghan parents who had settled in the country, educated at Rangoon, and sent out to wander, as men of that race frequently are from early youth, I was well guarded against the danger of detection by a fellow countryman. To support the character requires a knowledge of Persian, Hindustani, and Arabic, all of which I knew sufficiently well to pass muster; any trifling inaccuracy was charged upon my long residence at Rangoon. This was an important step; the first question at the shop, on the camel, and in the mosque is "What is thy name?" The second, "Whence comest thou?" This is not generally impertinent, or intended to be annoying; if, however, you see any evil intention in the questioner, you may rather roughly ask him, "What may be his maternal parent's name?"—equivalent to enquiring [of a Briton] in what church his mother was married—and escape your difficulties under cover of the storm. But this is rarely necessary. I assumed the polite, pliant manners of

---

*hashish: By the Indian called *bhang,* the Persians *bang,* the Hottentots *dakha,* and the natives of Barbary *fasukh.* Even the Siberians, we are told, intoxicate themselves by vapour of this seed thrown upon red-hot stones. Egypt surpasses all other nations in the variety of compounds into which this fascinating drug enters and will one day probably supply the Western world with "Indian hemp," when its solid merits are duly appreciated. At present in Europe it is chiefly confined, as cognac and opium used to be, to the apothecary's shelves. . . .

†Pathan: the Indian name of an Afghan, supposed to be a corruption of the Arabic *fat'han* (a conqueror) or a derivation from the Hindustani *paithna,* "to penetrate" (into the hostile ranks). It is an honourable term in Arabia, where "Khurasani" (a native of Khurasan), leads men to suspect a Persian, and the other generic appellation of the Afghan tribes "Sulaymani," a descendent from Solomon, reminds the people of their proverb *"Sulaymani harami!"*–The Afghans are ruffians!"

an Indian physician, and the dress of a small effendi (or gentleman), still, however, representing myself to be a dervish, and frequenting the places where dervishes congregate. "What business," asked the Hajji, "have those reverend men with politics or statistics, or any of the information which you are collecting? Call yourself a religious wanderer if you like, and let those who ask the object of your peregrinations know that you are under a vow to visit all the Holy Places in al-Islam. Thus you will persuade them that you are a man of rank under a cloud, and you will receive much more civility than perhaps you deserve," concluded my friend with a dry laugh. The remark proved his sagacity; and after ample experience I had not to repent having been guided by his advice. . . .

THE PHYSICIAN After lodging myself in the *wakala*, my first object was to make a certain stir in the world. In Europe your travelling doctor advertises the loss of a diamond ring, the gift of a Russian autocrat, or he monopolises a whole column in a newspaper, feeing perhaps a title for the use of a signature. The large brass plate, the gold-headed cane, the rattling chariot, and the summons from the sermon complete the work. Here, there is no such Royal Road to medical fame. You must begin by sitting with the porter, who is sure to have blear eyes, into which you drop a little nitrate of silver, whilst you instil into his ear the pleasing intelligence that you never take a fee from the poor. He recovers; his report of you spreads far and wide, crowding your doors with paupers. They come to you as though you were their servant, and when cured they turn their backs upon you forever. Hence it is that European doctors generally complain of ingratitude on the part of their Oriental patients. It is true that if you save a man's life, he naturally asks you for the means of preserving it. Moreover, in none of the Eastern languages with which I am acquainted is there a single term conveying the meaning of our "gratitude," and none but Germans have ideas unexplainable by words. But you must not condemn this absence of a virtue without considering the cause. An Oriental deems that he has the right to your surplus. "Daily bread is divided" (by heaven), he asserts, and eating yours, he considers it his own. Thus it is with other things. He is thankful to Allah for the gifts of the Creator, but he has a claim to the good offices of a fellow creature. In rendering him a service you have but done your duty, and he would not pay you so poor a compliment as to praise you for the act. He leaves you, his benefactor, with a short prayer for the length of your days. "Thank you," being expressed by "Allah increase thy weal!" or the selfish wish that your shadow (with which you protect him and his fellows) may never be less. And this is probably the last you hear of him. . . .

To resume. When the mob has raised you to fame, patients of a better class will slowly appear on the scene. After some coquetting about "etiquette," whether you are to visit them or they are to call upon you, they make up their minds to see you and to judge with their eyes whether you are to be trusted or not; whilst you, on your side, set out with the determination that they shall at once cross the Rubicon—in less classical phrase, swallow your drug. If you visit the house, you insist upon the patient's servants attending you; he must also provide and pay an ass for your conveyance, no matter if it be only to the other side of the street. Your confidential man accompanies you, primed for replies to the fifty searching questions of the servants' hall. You are lifted off the saddle tenderly, as nurses dismount their charges, when you arrive at the gate, and you waddle upstairs with dignity. Arrived at the sick room, you salute those present with a general "Peace be upon you!" to which they respond, "And upon thee be the peace and the mercy of Allah, and his blessing!" To the invalid you say, "There is nothing the matter, please Allah, except the health"; to which the proper answer—for here every sign of ceremony has its countersign—is "May Allah give thee health!" Then you sit down and acknowledge the presence of the company by raising your right hand to your lips and forehead, bowing the while circularly. Each individual returns the civility by a similar gesture. Then enquiry about the state of your health ensues. Then you are asked what refreshment you will take: you studiously mention something not likely to be in the house, but at last you rough it with a pipe and a cup of coffee. Then you proceed to the patient, who extends his wrist and asks you what his complaint is. Then you examine his tongue, you feel his pulse, you look learned, and—he is talking all the time—after hearing a detailed list of all his ailments you gravely discover them, taking for the same as much praise to yourself as does the practicing phrenologist for a similar simple exercise of the reasoning faculties.

The disease, to be respectable, must invariably be connected with one of the four temperaments, or the four elements, or the humours of Hippocrates. Cure is easy, but it will take time, and you, the doctor, require attention; any little rudeness it is in your power to punish by an alteration in the pill or the powder, and so unknown is professional honour that none will brave your displeasure. If you would pass for a native practitioner, you must finally proceed to the most uncomfortable part of your visit, bargaining for fees. Nothing more effectually arouses suspicion than disinterestedness in a doctor. I once cured a rich Hadramawt merchant of rheumatism and neglected to make him pay for treatment; he carried off one of my coffee cups and was unceasingly wondering where I came from. So I made him produce five piastres, a shilling, which he threw upon the carpet, cursing Indian avarice. "You will bring on another illness," said my friend, the hajji, when he heard of it. Properly speaking, the fee for a visit to a respectable man is twenty piastres, but with the rich patient you begin by making a bargain. He complains, for instance, of dysentery and sciatica. You demand ten pounds for the dysentery, and twenty pounds for the sciatica. But you will rarely get it. The Eastern pays a doctor's bill as an "Oirishman" does his "rint," making a grievance of it. Your patient will show indisputable signs of convalescence: he will laugh and jest half the day, but the moment you appear, groans and a lengthened visage and pretended complaints welcome you. Then your way is to throw out some such hint as "The world is a carcass, and they who seek it are dogs." And you refuse to treat the second disorder, which conduct may bring the refractory one to his senses. . . .

Whatever you prescribe must be solid and material, and if you accompany it with something painful, such as rubbing to scarification with a horse brush, so much the better. Easterns, like our peasants in Europe, wish the doctor to "give them the value of their money." Besides which, rough measures act beneficially upon their imagination. So the *hakim* of the King of Persia cured fevers by the bastinado; patients are beneficially baked in a bread oven at Baghdad, and an Egyptian at Alexandria, whose quartan resisted the strongest appliances of European physic, was effectually healed by the actual cautery, which a certain Arab shaykh applied to the crown of his head. When you administer with your own hand the remedy—half a dozen huge bread pills dipped in a solution of aloes or cinnamon water, flavoured with assafoetida, which in the case of the dyspeptic rich often suffice, if they will but diet themselves—you are careful to say, "In the name of Allah, the Compassionate, the Merciful." And after the patient has been dosed, "Praise be to Allah, the Curer, the Healer"; you then call for pen, ink, and paper, and write some such prescription as this:

A.*

In the name of Allah, the Compassionate, the Merciful, and blessings and peace be upon our Lord the Apostle, and his family, and his companions one and all! But afterwards let him take bees' honey and cinnamon and album Graecum, of each half a part, and of ginger a whole part, which let him pound and mix with the honey,

*A: a monogram generally placed at the head of writings. It is the initial letter of "Allah," and the first of the alphabet, used from time immemorial to denote the origin of creation. "I am Alpha and Omega, the first and the last."

and form boluses, each bolus the weight of a *miskal,* and of it let him use every day a *miskal* on the saliva. Verily its effects are wonderful. And let him abstain from flesh, fish, vegetables, sweetmeats, flatulent food, acids of all descriptions, as well as the major ablution, and live in perfect quiet. So shall he be cured by the help of the King, the Healer . . .

The diet, I need scarcely say, should be rigorous; nothing has tended more to bring the European system of medicine into contempt among Orientals than our inattention to this branch of the therapeutic art. When a Hindi or a Hindu "takes medicine," he prepares himself for it by diet and rest two or three days before adhibition, and [just] as gradually, after the dose, he relapses into his usual habits; if he break through the regime, it is concluded that fatal results must ensue. The ancient Egyptians, we learn from Herodotus, devoted a certain number of days in each month to the use of alteratives, and the period was consecutive, doubtless in order to graduate the strength of the medicine. The Persians, when under salivation, shut themselves up in a warm room, never undress, and so carefully guard against cold that they even drink tepid water. When the Afghan princes find it necessary to employ *chob-chini* (the ginseng,* or China root, so celebrated as a purifier, tonic, and aphrodisiac), they choose the spring season; they remove to a garden, where flowers and trees and bubbling streams soothe their senses; they carefully avoid fatigue and trouble of all kinds and will not even hear a letter read, lest it should contain bad news.

When the prescription is written out, you affix an impression of your ring seal to the beginning and to the end of it, that no one may be able to add to or take from its contents. And when you send medicine to a patient of rank, who is sure to have enemies, you adopt some similar precaution against the box or the bottle being opened. One of the pashas whom I attended—a brave soldier who had been a favourite with Muhammad Ali and therefore was degraded by his successor—kept an impression of my ring in wax to compare with that upon the phials. Men have not forgotten how frequently, in former times, those who became obnoxious to the state were seized with sudden and fatal cramps in the stomach. In the case of the doctor it is common prudence to adopt these precautions, as all evil consequences would be charged upon him, and he would be exposed to the family's revenge.

---

*ginseng: From M. Huc we learn that ginseng is the most considerable article of Manchurian commerce and that through China there is no chemist's shop unprovided with more or less of it. . . .

Cairo, though abounding in medical practitioners, can still support more; but to thrive, they must be Indians, Chinese, or Maghribis. The Egyptians are thoroughly disgusted with European treatment, which is here about as efficacious as in India—that is to say, not at all. But they are ignorant of the medicine of Hind, and therefore great is its name; deservedly perhaps, for skill in simples and dietetics. Besides which the Indian may deal in charms and spells—things to which the latitude gives such force that even Europeans learn to put faith in them. . . . As a Hindi I could use animal magnetism, taking care, however, to give the science a specious supernatural appearance. Hajji Wali, who, professing positive scepticism, showed the greatest interest in the subject as a curiosity, advised me not to practice pure mesmerism; otherwise, I should infallibly become a "companion of devils." "You must call this an Indian secret," said my friend, "for it is clear that you are no *mashaykh*,* and people will ask, 'Where are your drugs, and what business have you with charms?'" It is useless to say that I followed his counsel; yet patients would consider themselves my *murid*s (disciples) and delighted in kissing the hand of the *sahib nafas*,† or minor saint.

MEDINA: THE PROPHET'S MOSQUE   The Masjid al-Nabi, or Prophet's Mosque, is the second in al-Islam in point of seniority and the second, or, according to others, the first in dignity, ranking with the Ka'ba itself. It is erected around the spot where the she camel, al-Kaswa, knelt down by the order of Heaven. At that time the land was a palm grove and a *mirbad*, or place where dates are dried. Muhammad, ordered to erect a place of worship there, sent for the youths to whom it belonged, and certain Ansar or Auxiliaries, their guardians. The ground was offered to him in free gift, but he insisted upon purchasing it, paying more than its value. Having caused the soil to be levelled and the trees to be felled, he laid the foundation of the first mosque.

In those times of primitive simplicity, its walls were made of rough stone and unbaked bricks: trunks of date trees supported a palm-stick roof, concerning which the archangel Gabriel delivered an order that it should

---

mashaykh: a holy man. The word has a singular signification in a plural form, *"honoris causa."*

†*sahib nafas:* a title literally meaning the "master of breath"; one who can cure ailments, physical as well as spiritual, by breathing upon them—a practice well-known to mesmerists. The reader will allow me to observe (in self-defence, otherwise he might look suspiciously upon so credulous a narrator) that when speaking of animal magnetism as a thing established, I allude to the lower phenomena, rejecting the discussion of all disputed points, as the existence of a magnetic aura, and of all its unintelligibilities—pre-vision, levitation, intro-vision, and other divisions of clairvoyance.

not be higher than seven cubits,* the elevation of Moses's temple. All ornament was strictly forbidden. The Ansar, or men of al-Medina, and the
Muhajjirun or fugitives from Mecca, carried the building materials in their
arms from the cemetery al-Baqiyya‘,† near the Well of Ayyub, north of the
spot where Ibrahim's Mosque now stands, and the Apostle was to be seen
aiding them in their labours, and reciting for their encouragement,

> *O Allah! there is no good but the good of futurity.*
> *Then have mercy upon my Ansar and Muhajjirun!*

The length of this mosque was fifty-four cubits from north to south and sixty-
three in breadth, and it was hemmed in by houses on all sides save the western. Till the seventeenth month of the new era the congregation faced towards
the northern wall. After that time a fresh revelation turned them in the direction of Mecca, southwards, on which occasion the archangel Gabriel descended and miraculously opened through the hills and wilds a view of the
Ka‘ba, that there might be no difficulty in ascertaining its true position.

After the capture of Khaybar in 628, the Prophet and his first three
successors restored the mosque, but Muslim historians do not consider this
a second foundation. Muhammad laid the first brick, and Abu Hurayra
declares that he saw him carry heaps of building materials piled up to his
breast. The caliphs, each in the turn of his succession, placed a brick close to
that laid by the Prophet and aided him in raising the walls. Al-Tabrani relates that one of the Ansar had a house adjacent which Muhammad wished
to make part of the place of prayer; the proprietor was promised in exchange
for it a home in Paradise, which he gently rejected, pleading poverty. His
excuse was admitted, and Osman, after purchasing the place for ten thousand dirhems, gave it to the Apostle on the long credit originally offered.

This mosque was a square of a hundred cubits. Like the former building, it had three doors: one on the south side, where the Mihrab al-Nabi, or
the Prophet's Niche, now is; another in the place of the present Gate of
Mercy; and the third at the Bab Osman, now called the Gate of Gabriel.
Instead of a *mihrab,* or prayer niche, a large block of stone directed the congregation; at first it was placed against the northern wall of the mosque, and
it was removed to the southern when Mecca became the *qibla.*

*cubit: about nineteen and a half inches. [Ed.]

†Baqiyya‘: cemetery located to the east of the city of Medina, a major religious shrine and
historic landmark. It is the final resting place of many of the companions of the Prophet
Muhammad, as well as a number of his other important contemporaries. [Ed.]

In the beginning the Prophet, whilst preaching the *qutba,* or Friday sermon, leaned when fatigued against a post. The *minbar,* or pulpit, was the invention of a Medina man, of the Banu Najjar. It was a wooden frame, two cubits long by one broad, with three steps, each one span high; on the topmost of these the Prophet sat when he required rest. The pulpit assumed its present form about 709, during the artistic reign of al-Walid.*

In this mosque Muhammad spent the greater part of the day with his companions, conversing, instructing, and comforting the poor. Hard by were the abodes of his wives, his family, and his principal friends. Here he prayed, at the call of the *adhan,* or devotion cry, from the roof. Here he received worldly envoys and embassies, and the heavenly messages conveyed by the archangel Gabriel. And within a few yards of the hallowed spot, he died, and found a grave.

The theatre of events so important to al-Islam could not be allowed— especially as no divine decree forbade the change—to remain in its pristine lowliness. The first Caliph contented himself with merely restoring some of the palm pillars, which had fallen to the ground: Umar, the second successor, surrounded the *hujra,* or [his wife] Aisha's chamber, in which the Prophet was buried, with a mud wall; and in 638, he enlarged the mosque to 140 cubits by 120, taking in ground on all sides except the eastern, where stood the abodes of the "Mothers of the Muslims." Outside the northern wall he erected a *suffa,* called al-Batha—a raised bench of wood, earth, or stone, upon which the people might recreate themselves with conversation and quoting poetry, for the mosque was now becoming a place of peculiar reverence to men.†

The second *masjid* was erected 649, by the third Caliph, Osman, who, regardless of the clamours of the people, overthrew the old walls and extended the building greatly towards the north, and a little towards the West; but he did not remove the eastern limit on account of the private houses. He made the roof of Indian teak and the walls of hewn and carved stone. These innovations caused some excitement, which he allayed by quoting a tradition of the Prophet, with one of which he appears perpetually to have been prepared. The saying in question was, according to some, "Were this my mosque to Safa"—a hill in Mecca— "it verily would still be my mosque";

*al-Walid: Umayyad Caliph (reigned 705–715). [Ed.]

†Authors mention a place outside the northern wall called al-Suffa, which was assigned by Muhammad as a habitation to houseless believers; from which circumstance these paupers derived the title of Ashab al-Suffa, Companions of the Sofa.

according to others, "Were the Prophet's Mosque extended to Dhu al-Hulayfa,* it would still be his." But Osman's skill in the quotation of tradition did not prevent the new building being in part a cause of his death. It was finished on the first [of] Muharram, 650.

At length, al-Islam, grown splendid and powerful, determined to surpass other nations in the magnificence of its public buildings. In 707, al-Walid I,† twelfth Caliph of the Banu Umaya race, after building, or rather restoring, the noble Jami' al-Ammawi (Mosque of the Umayyads) at Damascus, determined to display his liberality at al-Medina. The governor of the place, Umar ibn Abd al-Aziz, was directed to buy for seven thousand dinars all the hovels of raw brick that hedged in the eastern side of the old mosque. They were inhabited by descendants of the Prophet and of the early caliphs, and in more than one case, the ejection of the holy tenantry was effected with considerable difficulty. Some of the women—ever the most obstinate on such occasions—refused to take money, and Umar was forced to the objectionable measure of turning them out of doors with exposed faces‡ in full day. The Greek Emperor, applied to by the magnificent Caliph, sent immense presents, silver lamp chains, valuable curiosities, forty loads of small cut stones for *pietra-dura,* and a sum of eighty thousand dinars, or, as others say, forty thousand *miskals* of gold. He also despatched forty Coptic and forty Greek artists to carve the marble pillars and the casings of the walls and to superintend the gilding and the mosaic work. One of these Christians was beheaded for sculpturing a hog on the

---

*Dhu al-Hulayfa: a place about five miles from Medina, on the Meccan way.

†al-Walid I: It is to this monarch that the Saracenic mosque architecture mainly owes its present form. As will be seen, he had every advantage of borrowing from Christian, Persian, and even Indian art. From the first he took the dome, from the second the cloister—it might have been naturalised in Arabia before his time—and possibly from the third the minaret and the prayer niche. The latter appears to be a peculiarly Hindu feature in sacred buildings, intended to contain the idol and to support the lamps, flowers, and other offerings placed before it.

‡The reader will remember that in the sixth year of the Hijra, after Muhammad's marriage with Zaynab, his wives were secluded behind the *hijab, purda,* or curtain. A verse of the Quran directed the Muslims to converse with them behind this veil. Hence the general practice of al-Islam: now it is considered highly disgraceful in any Muslim to make a Muslima expose her face, and she will frequently found a threat upon the prejudice. A battle has been prevented by this means, and occasionally an insurrection has been caused by it.

qibla wall; and another, in an attempt to defile the roof, fell to the ground, and his brains were dashed out. The remainder Islamized, but this did not prevent the older Arabs murmuring that their mosque had been turned into a *kanisa,* a Christian idol house.

The *hujra,* or chamber, where, by Muhammad's permission, Azrail, the angel of death, separated his soul from his body, whilst his head was lying in the lap of Aisha, his favourite wife, was now for the first time taken into the mosque. The raw-brick [perimeter wall] which surrounded the three graves was exchanged for one of carved stone, enclosed by an outer precinct with a narrow passage between. These double walls were either without a door or had only a small blocked-up wicket on the northern side, and from that day (709) no one, says al-Samanhudi, has been able to approach the sepulchre.* A minaret was erected at each corner of the mosque. The building was enlarged to 200 cubits by 167 and was finished in 710. When al-Walid, the Caliph, visited it in state, he enquired of his lieutenant why greater magnificence had not been displayed in the erection; upon which Umar, the Governor, informed him, to his astonishment, that the walls alone had cost forty-five thousand ducats.

The fourth mosque was erected in 805, by al-Mahdi, third prince of the Banu Abbas, or Baghdad caliphs—celebrated in history only for spending enormous sums upon a pilgrimage. He enlarged the building by adding ten handsome pillars of carved marble, with gilt capitals, on the northern side. In 817, al-Ma'amun made further additions to this mosque. It was from al-Mahdi's *masjid* that al-Hakim bin-Amri 'llah, the third Fatimid Caliph of Egypt, and the deity of the Druze sect, determined to steal the bodies of the Prophet and his two companions. About 1021, he sent emissaries to al-Medina: the attempt, however, failed, and the would-be violators of the tomb lost their lives. It is generally supposed that al-Hakim's object was to transfer the Visitation to his own capital; but in one so manifestly insane it is difficult to discover the spring of action. Two Christians, habited like Maghribi pilgrims, in 1155 dug a mine from a neighbouring house into the temple. They were discovered, beheaded, and burned to ashes. . . . In 1256, the fifth mosque was erected in consequence of a fire, which some authors

*After the Prophet's death and burial, Aisha continued to occupy the same room, without even a curtain between her and the tomb. At last, vexed by the crowds of visitors, she partitioned off the hallowed spot with a wall. She visited the grave unveiled as long as her father, Abu Bakr, only was placed behind the Prophet, but when Umar's corpse was added, she always covered her face, [Umar not being a relation].

attribute to a volcano that broke out close to the town in terrible eruption; others, with more fanaticism and less probability, to the schismatic Banu Husayn, then the guardians of the tomb. On this occasion the *hujra* was saved, together with the old and venerable copies of the Quran there deposited, especially the Kufic manuscripts, written by Osman, the third Caliph. The piety of three sovereigns, al-Mutasim (last Caliph of Baghdad), al-Muzaffar Shems al-Din Yusuf, chief of al-Yemen, and al-Zahir Baybars, Baharite Sultan of Egypt, completed the work in 1289. This building was enlarged and beautified by the princes of Egypt and lasted upwards of two hundred years.

The sixth mosque was built, almost as it now stands, by Qa'it Bey, nineteenth Sultan of the Circassian Mamluk kings of Egypt, in 1483: it is now therefore more than four centuries old. Al-Mutasim's mosque had been struck by lightning during a storm; thirteen men were killed at prayers, and the destroying element spared nothing but the interior of the *hujra*. The railing and dome were restored; niches and a pulpit were sent from Cairo, and the gates and minarets were distributed as they are now. Not content with this, Qa'it Bey established *waqf* (bequests) and pensions and introduced order among the attendants on the tomb. In the sixteenth century, Sultan Suleyman the Magnificent paved with fine white marble the *rauza,* or garden, which Qa'it Bey, not daring to alter, had left of earth, and erected the fine minaret that bears his name.

During the dominion of the later sultans, and of Muhammad Ali, a few trifling presents of lamps, carpets, wax candles and chandeliers, and a few immaterial alterations, have been made. The present head of al-Islam is, as I have before said, rebuilding one of the minarets and the northern colonnade of the temple.

Such is the history of the mosque's prosperity.

THE MOSQUE IN RECENT TIMES During the siege of Al-Medina by the Wahhabis,* the principal people seized and divided amongst themselves the treasures of the tomb, which must have been considerable. When the town surrendered, Sa'ud, accompanied by his principal officers, entered the *hujra,* but, terrified by dreams, he did not penetrate behind the curtain or attempt to see the tomb. He plundered, however, the treasures in the passage, and the ornaments sent as presents from every part of al-Islam. Part of these he sold, it is said, for 150,000 riyals, to Ghalib, Sharif of Mecca, and the rest

*Burckhardt has given a full account of this event in his history of the Wahhabis.

he carried with him to Dir'iyya, his capital.* An accident prevented any further desecration of the building. The greedy Wahhabis, allured by the appearance of the golden or gilt globes and crescents surmounting the green dome, attempted to throw down the latter. Two of their number, it is said, were killed by falling from the slippery roof,† and the rest, struck by superstitious fears, abandoned the work of destruction. They injured, however, the prosperity of the place by taxing the inhabitants, by interrupting the annual remittances, and by forbidding visitors to approach the tomb. They are spoken of with abhorrence by the people, who quote a peculiarly bad trait in their characters, namely, that in return for any small religious assistance of prayer or recitation, they were in the habit of giving a few grains of gunpowder, or something equally valuable, instead of "stone dollars."‡

When Abdullah, son of Sa'ud, had concluded in 1815 a treaty of peace with Tussan Pasha, the Egyptian general bought back from the townspeople, for ten thousand riyals, all the golden vessels that had not been melted down and restored the treasure to its original place. This I have heard denied; at the same time it rests upon credible evidence. Amongst Orientals the events of the last generation are, usually speaking, imperfectly remembered; and the Ulama are well acquainted with the history of vicissitudes which took place twelve hundred years ago, when profoundly ignorant of what their grandfathers witnessed. Many incredible tales also I heard concerning the present wealth of the al-Medina mosque: this must be expected when the exaggeration is considered likely to confer honour upon the exaggerator.

The establishment attached to the al-Medina mosque is greatly altered since Burckhardt's time, the result of the increasing influence of the Turkish half-breeds. It is still extensive, because in the first place the principle of divided labour is a favourite throughout the East, and secondly because the

---

*My predecessor estimates the whole treasury in those days to have been worth three hundred thousand riyals—a small sum if we consider the length of time during which it was accumulating. The chiefs of the town appropriated one hundredweight of golden vessels, worth at most fifty thousand dollars, and Sa'ud sold part of the plunder to Ghalib for one hundred thousand (I was told one third more), reserving for himself about the same amount of pearls and corals. Burckhardt supposes that the governors of al-Medina, who were often independent chiefs, and sometimes guardians of the tombs, made occasional draughts upon the generosity of the Faithful.

†I inquired in vain about the substance that covered the dome. Some told me it was tinfoil; others supposed it to be rivetted with green tiles.

‡stone dollars: The Bedouin calls a sound dollar *kirsh hajar,* or *riyal hajar,* a "stone dollar."

sons of the Holy Cities naturally desire to extract as much as they can from the sons of other cities with the least amount of work. The substance of the following account was given to me by Umar Effendi,* and I compared it with the information of others upon whom I could rely.

The principal of the mosque, or Shaykh al-Haram, is no longer a neuter. The present is a Turkish pasha, Osman, appointed from Constantinople with a salary of about 30,000 piastres a month. His *naib,* or deputy, is a black eunuch, the chief of the *aghawat,* upon a pay of 5,000 piastres. The present principal of his college is one Tayfur Agha, a slave of Esma Sultana, sister to the late Sultan Mahmud.† The chief treasurer is called the Mudir al-Haram; he keeps an eye upon the *khaznadar,* or treasurer, whose salary is 2,000 piastres. The *mustaslim* is the chief of the *katabs,* or writers who settle the accounts of the mosque; his pay is 1,500, and under him is a *nakib,* or assistant, upon 1,000 piastres. There are three shaykhs of the eunuchs, who receive from 700 to 1,000 piastres a month each. The eunuchs, about 120 in number, are divided into three orders. The *bawwabin,* or porters, open the doors of the mosque. The *khubziya* sweep the purer parts of the temple, and the lowest order, popularly called *battalin,* clean away all impurities, beat those found sleeping, and act as beadles, a duty here which involves considerable use of the cane. These men receive as perquisites presents from each visitor when they offer him the usual congratulation and for other small favours, such as permitting strangers to light the lamps or to sweep the floor. Their pay varies from 250 to 500 piastres a month: they are looked upon as honourable men and are, generally speaking, married, some of them indulging in three or four wives—which would have aroused Juvenal's bile. The Agha's character is [as] curious and exceptional as his outward conformation. Disconnected with humanity, he is cruel, fierce, brave, and capable of any villany. His frame is unnaturally long and lean, especially the arms and legs, with high shoulders, protruding joints, and a face by contrast extraordinarily large. He is unusually expert in the use of weapons, and sitting well "home," he rides to admiration, his hoarse, thick voice investing him with all the circumstances of command.

Besides the eunuchs, there are a number of free servants, called *farrashin,* attached to the mosque; almost all the middle and lower class of citizens belong to this order. They are divided into parties of thirty each and are changed every week, those on duty receiving 22 piastres for their services.

---

*Burton's host in Medina. [Ed.]

†Mahmud II, Ottoman Sultan (reigned 1808–39). [Ed.]

Their business is to dust and to spread the carpets, to put oil and wicks into the lamps which the eunuchs let down from the ceiling, and generally speaking, diligently to do nothing.

Finally, the menial establishment of the mosque consists of a Shaykh al-Sakka (chief of the water carriers), under whom are from forty-five to fifty men who sprinkle the floors, water the garden, and, for a consideration, supply a cupful of brackish liquid to visitors.

The literary establishment is even more extensive than the executive and the menial. There is a Qadi, or chief judge, sent every year from Constantinople. After twelve months at al-Medina, he passes on to Mecca and returns home after a similar term of service in the second Holy City. Under him are three muftis,* of the Hanafi, the Shafi‘i and the Maliki schools; the fourth, or Hanbali, is not represented here or at Cairo.† Each of these officers receives as pay about 250 piastres a month. The *ruasa,*‡ as the muezzins (prayer-callers) here call themselves, are extensively represented; there are forty-eight or forty-nine of the lowest order, presided over by six masters, and these again are under the Shaykh al-Ruasa, who alone has the privilege of calling to prayers from the *raisiyah* minaret. The Shaykh receives 150 piastres, the chiefs about 100, and the common criers, 60; there are forty-five *qutib*s, who preach and pray before the congregation on Fridays for 120 piastres a month; they are under the Shaykh al-Qutaba. About the same sum is given to seventy-five imams, who recite the five ordinary prayers every day in the mosque; the Shaykh al-Aimmat is their superior.

Almost all the citizens of al-Medina who have not some official charge about the temple qualify themselves to act as *muzawwir*s. They begin as boys to learn the formula of prayer and the conducting of visitors; and partly by begging, partly by boldness, they often pick up a tolerable livelihood at an early age. The *muzawwir* will often receive strangers into his house, as was

---

*Others told me that there were only two muftis at al-Medina, namely, those of the Hanafi and Shafi‘i schools. If this be true, it proves the insignificance of the followers of Malik [ibn Anas], which personage, like others, is less known in his own town than elsewhere.

†The Hanbali school is nowhere common except in Nejd and the lands eastward as far as al-Hasa. At present it labours under a sort of imputation, being supposed to have thrown out a bad offshoot, the Wahhabis.

‡*ruasa:* the plural of *rais,* a chief or president. It is the term generally applied in Arabia to the captain of a vessel, and in Yemen it often means a barber, in virtue, I presume, of its root— *ras,* the head.

done to me, and direct their devotions during the whole time of their stay. For such service he requires a sum of money proportioned to his guests' circumstances, but this fee does not end the connexion. If the *muzawwir* visits the home of his [client], he expects to be treated with the utmost hospitality, and to depart with a handsome present. A religious visitor will often transmit to his cicerone at Mecca and at al-Medina yearly sums to purchase for himself a prayer at the Ka'ba and the Prophet's tomb. The remittance is usually wrapped up in paper and placed in a sealed leathern bag somewhat like a portfolio, upon which is worked the name of the person entitled to receive it. It is then given in charge either to a trustworthy pilgrim or to the public treasurer, who accompanies the principal caravans.

I could procure no exact information about the amount of money forwarded every year from Constantinople and Cairo to al-Medina. The only point upon which men seemed to agree was that they were defrauded of half their dues. When the *sadaqa* and *waqf* (the alms and bequests) arrive at the town, they are committed by the *surrah,* or financier of the caravan, to the muftis, the chief of the *qutib*s, and the Qadi's clerk. These officers form a committee, and after reckoning the total of the families entitled to pensions, divide the money amongst them, according to the number in each household and the rank of the pensioners. They are divided into five orders:

The *Ulama,* or learned, and the *mudarrisin,* who profess, lecture, or teach adults in the Haram.

The imams and *qutib*s.

The descendants of the Prophet.

The *fukaha,* poor divines, pedadogues, gerund-grinders, who teach boys to read the Quran.

The *awam,* or *nobile vulgus* of the Holy City, including the burghers of the town, and the *mujawwirin,* or those settled in the place.

Umar Effendi belonged to the second order, and he informed me that his share varied from three to fifteen riyals per annum.

LITERARY MEDINA Al-Medina, though pillaged by the Wahhabis, still abounds in books. Near the Haram are two *madrasa*s, or colleges, the Mahmudiya, so called from Sultan Mahmud, and that of Bashir Agha: both have large stores of theological and other works. I also heard of extensive private collections, particularly of one belonging to the Najib al-Ashraf, or chief of the sharifs, a certain Muhammad Jamal al-Layl, whose father is well-known in India. Besides which, there is a large *waqf,* or bequest of books, presented to the mosque or entailed upon particular families. The celebrated Muhammad ibn Abdullah al-Sannusi* has removed his collection, amounting, it is said, to eight thousand volumes, from al-Medina to his house in Jabal Qubays at Mecca. The burial place of the Prophet, therefore, no longer lies open to the charge of utter ignorance brought against it by my predecessor.[†] The people now praise their *ulama* for learning, and boast a superiority in respect of science over Mecca. Yet many students leave the place for Damascus and Cairo, where the Azhar Mosque University is always crowded; and though Umar Effendi boasted to me that his city was full of lore, he did not appear the less anxious to attend the lectures of Egyptian professors. But none of my informants claimed for al-Medina any facilities of studying other than the purely religious sciences. Philosophy, medicine, arithmetic, mathematics, and algebra cannot be learnt here. I was careful to inquire about the occult sciences, remembering that Paracelsus had travelled in Arabia and that the Count Cagliostro (Giuseppe Balsamo), who claimed the Meccan Sharif as his father, asserted that about 1765 he had studied alchemy at Medina.[‡] The only trace I could find was a superficial knowledge of the magic mirror. But after denying the Medinese the praise of varied learning, it must be owned that their quick observation and retentive memories have stored up for them an abundance of superficial knowledge, culled from conversations in the market and in the camp. I found it impossible here to display those feats which in Sind, southern Persia, eastern Arabia, and many parts of India would be looked upon as miraculous. Most probably one of the company had witnessed the performance of some Italian conjuror at Constantinople or Alexandria, and retained a lively recollection of every manoeuvre. As linguists they are not equal to the Meccans, who surpass all Orientals excepting only the Armenians; the Medinese seldom know Turkish, and more rarely still Persian and Indian. Those only who have studied in Egypt chaunt the Quran well. The citizens speak and pronounce their language purely; they are not equal to the people of the southern Hijaz, yet their Arabic is refreshing after the horrors of Cairo and Muscat.

The classical Arabic, be it observed, in consequence of an extended empire, soon split up into various dialects, as the Latin under similar circumstances separated into the neo-Roman patois of Italy, Sicily, Provence, and Languedoc. And though Niebuhr has been deservedly censured for

---

*This shaykh is a Maliki Muslin from Algiers, celebrated as an *alim* (sage), especially in the mystic study al-Jafr. He is a *wali,* or saint.

[†]John Lewis Burckhardt, *Travels in Arabia,* II:174.

[‡]False claims. [Ed.]

comparing the Quranic language to Latin and the vulgar tongue to Italian, still there is a great difference between them, almost every word having undergone some alteration in addition to the manifold changes and simplifications of grammar and syntax. The traveller will hear in every part of Arabia that some distant tribe preserves the linguistic purity of its ancestors, uses final vowels with the noun, and rejects the addition of the pronoun which apocope in the verb now renders necessary. But I greatly doubt the existence of such a race of philologists. In al-Hijaz, however, it is considered graceful in an old man, especially when conversing publicly, to lean towards classical Arabic. On the contrary, in a youth this would be treated as pedantic affectation, and condemned in some such satiric quotation as

> *There are two things colder than ice,*
> *A young old man, and an old young man.*

THE DAMASCUS CARAVAN The Damascus caravan was to set out on the twenty-seventh of Dhu al-Qada (1 September). I had intended to stay at al-Medina till the last moment and to accompany the "Flying Caravan," which usually leaves on the second of Dhu al-Hijja, two days after that of Damascus.

Suddenly arose the rumour that there would be no Tayyara* and that all pilgrims must proceed with the Damascus caravan or await the Rakb. (This is a dromedary caravan, in which each person carries only his saddlebags. It usually descends by the road called al-Khabt and makes Mecca on the fifth day.) The Sharif Zayd, Sa'ad the Robber's only friend, had paid him [Sa'ad] an unsuccessful visit, [during which Sa'ad] demanded back his shaykh-ship, in return for a safe-conduct through his country: "Otherwise," said he, "I will cut the throat of every hen that ventures into the passes."

The Sharif Zayd returned to al-Medina on the twenty-fifth of Dhu al-Qada (30 August). Early on the morning of the next day, Shaykh Hamid returned hurriedly from the bazaar, exclaiming, "You must make ready at once, Effendi!—there will be no Tayyara—all Hajjis start tomorrow—Allah will make it easy to you!—have you your waterskins in order?—you are to travel down the Darb Sharki, where you will not see water for three days!"

Poor Hamid looked horror-struck as he concluded this fearful announcement, which filled me with joy. Burckhardt had visited and had described the Darb Sultani, the road along the coast. But no European had as

---

*The Tayyara, or Flying Caravan, is lightly laden and travels by forced marches.

yet travelled down by Harun al-Rashid and the Lady Zubayda's celebrated route through the Nejd Desert.

Not a moment, however, was to be lost: we expected to start early the next morning. The boy Muhammad went forth and bought for eighty piastres a *shugduf,* which lasted us throughout the pilgrimage, and for fifteen piastres a *shubreya,* or cot, to be occupied by Shaykh Nur, who did not relish sleeping on boxes. The youth was employed all day, with sleeves tucked up and working like a porter, in covering the litter with matting and rugs, in mending broken parts, and in providing it with large pockets for provisions inside and outside, with pouches to contain the gugglets of cooled water.

Meanwhile Shaykh Nur and I, having inspected the waterskins, found that the rats had made considerable rents in two of them. There being no workman procurable at this time for gold, I sat down to patch the damaged article, whilst Nur was sent to lay in supplies for fourteen days. The journey is calculated at eleven days; but provisions are apt to spoil, and the Bedawi camel men expect to be fed. Besides which, pilferers abound. By my companion's advice I took wheat flour, rice, turmeric, onions, dates, unleavened bread of two kinds, cheese, limes, tobacco, sugar, tea and coffee.

Hamid himself started upon the most important part of our business. Faithful camel men are required upon a road where robberies are frequent and stabbings occasional and where there is no law to prevent desertion or to limit new and exorbitant demands. After a time he returned, accompanied by a boy and a Bedawi, a short, thin, well-built old man with regular features, a white beard, and a cool clear eye; his limbs, as usual, were scarred with wounds. Mas'ud of the Rahla, a subfamily of the Hamida family of the Banu Harb, came in with a dignified demeanour, applied his dexter palm to ours,* sat down, declined a pipe, accepted coffee, and after drinking it, looked at us to show that he was ready for negociation. We opened the proceedings with "We want men, and not camels," and the conversation proceeded in the purest Hijazi.† After much discussion, we agreed, if compelled to travel by the Darb Sharki, to pay twenty dollars for two camels and to advance earnest money, to half that amount. The Shaykh bound himself to provide

---

*This *musafaha,* as it is called, is the Arab fashion of shaking hands. They apply the palms of the right hands flat to each other, without squeezing the fingers, and then raise the hand to the forehead.

†On this occasion I heard three new words: *Kharita,* used to signify a single trip to Mecca (without return to al-Medina); *ta'arifa,* going out from Mecca to Mount Arafat; and *tanzila,* return from Mount Arafat to Mecca.

us with good animals, which, moreover, were to be changed in case of accidents: he was also to supply his beasts with water, and to accompany us to Arafat and back. But, absolutely refusing to carry my large chest, he declared that the tent under the *shugduf* was burden enough for one camel and that the green box of drugs, the saddlebags, and the provision sacks, surmounted by Nur's cot, were amply sufficient for the other. On our part, we bound ourselves to feed the Shaykh and his son, supplying them either with raw or with cooked provender, and upon our return to Mecca from Mount Arafat, to pay the remaining hire with a discretionary present.

Hamid then addressed to me flowery praises of the old Bedawi. After which, turning to the latter, he exclaimed, "Thou wilt treat these friends well, O Mas'ud the Harbi!" The ancient replied with a dignity that had no pomposity in it—"Even as Abu Shawarib behaveth to us, so will we behave to him!" He then arose, bade us be prepared when the departure gun sounded, saluted us, and stalked out of the room, followed by his son, who, under pretext of dozing, had mentally made an inventory of every article in the room, ourselves especially included.

When the Bedawin disappeared, Shaykh Hamid shook his head, advising me to give them plenty to eat and never to allow twenty-four hours to elapse without dipping hand in the same dish with thcm, in order that the party might always be *malihin*—on terms of salt.* He concluded with a copious lecture upon the villainy of Bedawin, and on their habit of drinking travellers' water. I was to place the skins on a camel in front, and not behind; to hang them with their mouths carefully tied and turned upwards, contrary to the general practice; always to keep a good store of liquid; and at night to place it under the safeguard of the tent. . . . Towards evening time the Barr al-Manakha became a scene of exceeding confusion. The town of tents lay upon the ground. Camels were being laden and were roaring under the weight of litters and cots, boxes and baggage. Horses and mules galloped about. Men were rushing wildly in all directions on worldly errands or hurrying to pay a farewell visit to the Prophet's tomb. Women and children sat screaming on the ground, or ran to and fro distracted, or called their vehicles to escape the danger of being crushed. Every now and then a random shot excited all into the belief that the departure gun had sounded. At times we heard a volley from the robbers' hills, which elicited a general groan, for the pilgrims were still, to use their own phrase, "between fear and hope," and,

*Homer calls salt sacred and divine, and whoever ate it with a stranger was supposed to become his friend. By the Greek authors as by the Arabs, *hospitality* and *salt* are words expressing a kindred idea.

consequently, still far from "one of the two comforts."* Then would sound the loud *jhin-jhin,* of the camels' bells as the stately animals paced away with some grandee's gilt and emblazoned litter, the sharp plaint of the dromedary, and the loud neighing of excited steeds.

About an hour after sunset all our preparations were concluded, save only the *shugduf,* at which the boy Muhammad still worked with untiring zeal; he wisely remembered that he had to spend in it the best portion of a week and a half. The evening was hot; we therefore dined outside the house. I was told to repair to the Haram for the Farewell Visitation, but my decided objection to this step was that we were all to part—how soon!—and when to meet again we knew not. My companions smiled consent, assuring me that the ceremony could be performed as well at a distance as in the temple.

Then Shaykh Hamid made me pray a two-bow prayer and afterwards, facing towards the Haram, to recite [a] supplication with raised hands. . . .

Pious men on such an occasion go to the Prophet's tomb, where they strive, if possible, to shed a tear—a single drop being a sign of acceptance—give alms to the utmost of their ability, vow piety, repentance, and obedience, and retire overwhelmed with grief at separating themselves from their prophet and intercessor. It is customary, too, before leaving al-Medina, to pass at least one night in vigils at the Haram, and for learned men to read through the Quran once before the tomb.

Then began the uncomfortable process of paying off little bills. The Eastern creditor always, for divers reasons, waits [until] the last moment before he claims his debt. Shaykh Hamid had frequently hinted at his difficulties; the only means of escape from which, he said, was to rely upon Allah. He had treated me so hospitably that I could not take back any part of the five pounds lent to him at Suez. His three brothers received a dollar or two each, and one or two of his cousins hinted to some effect that such a proceeding would meet with their approbation.

The luggage was then carried down and disposed in packs upon the ground before the house, so as to be ready for loading at a notice. Many flying parties of travelers had almost started on the high road, and late in the evening came a new report that the body of the caravan would march about midnight. We sat up till about two when, having heard no gun and having seen no camels, we lay down to sleep through the sultry remnant of the hours of darkness.

*two comforts: success and despair, the latter, according to the Arabs, being a more enviable state of feeling than doubt or hope deferred.

Thus, gentle reader, was spent my last night at al-Medina.

I had reason to congratulate myself upon having passed through the first danger. Mecca is so near the coast that, in case of detection, the traveller might escape in a few hours to Jidda, where he would find an English vice-consul, protection from the Turkish authorities, and possibly a British cruiser in the harbour. But at al-Medina discovery would entail more serious consequences. The next risk to be run was the journey between the two cities, where it would be easy for the local officials quietly to dispose of a suspected person by giving a dollar to a Bedawi.

10

Her Highness Sikandar,
the Begum of Bhopal
India
1864

In these accounts we have heard before of royal pilgrim parties, their entourages and queens viewed from afar. The following, however, is the first Hajj report actually written by a regent. It reflects the importance of the Indian Hajj and underscores the growing universality of Islam. By 1850, 80 percent of the world's Muslims lived outside the Arab Near East.

Nawab Sikandar, the Begum of Bhopal, set sail for Mecca in late 1863, traveling with her uncle, her mother, and a retinue of several hundred people. Generations of Hindi rulers before her had traveled in state as pilgrims on the Hajj. They were among its most active supporters. At home, they financed ships to carry hajjis free of charge. In Mecca and Medina, they endowed the mosques and built hospices and schools for their Hindi pilgrims. In this sense, Sikandar's Hajj was not only an act of devotion. It was also an affair of state.

At the time of her pilgrimage, she governed a province of nine thousand square miles with a population of one million, the second largest of the Anglo-Indian principalities. Self-reliant, trusting little to officials, she showed great loyalty to Britain and opened many schools for boys and girls. Her friend and translator, Elizabeth Willoughby-Osborne, described Sikandar as a person of remarkable intellect and firmness, combining an aptitude for business with enormous energy. Unlike most of the Indian upper class, women in her family mixed in society, shunned the veil, and showed force of character. As her book makes clear, the Begum was not bashful.

She reached Jidda in January 1864 with a shipload of gifts to bestow on the Holy Cities. In the impoverished Hijaz, her wealth became a magnet for misfortune. Money chests were broken into on the docks. Ashore, a house she had reserved was sublet from under her. Next came the Turkish Pasha's tax collectors, who laid excessive dues on all her goods. The Begum met these rever-

226

sals with a volley of official letters that sets the tone for the rest of the account. Her train of eighty camels limped out of Jidda a week later. It was lightened several times along the way. The Pasha performed the official plundering; local Bedouin raiders did the rest. A low point occurred between Hadda and Mecca, where kidnappers briefly abducted Sikandar's mother.*

It was just the beginning. In Mecca, after performing her first rites, the Begum's life was threatened at a dinner party. Her host was the ruler of Mecca, Sharif Abdullah ibn Muhammad ibn Aun (reigned 1858–77) whose role as Guardian of the Holy Places entitled him to a quarter of all gifts sent from abroad. His numerous infractions of state decorum were the last straw for the Begum, who proved a stickler on protocol. Her pointed letters to him and to the Pasha and their factotums lay bare from a royal vantage the same local corruption noted by Burton. Yet the Begum's critique remains Muslim throughout. Despite a hand-in-glove relationship with Britain, she never suggests (as had the imperialistic Burton) that outside forces might one day be required to oversee the Hajj. Rather, she correctly faults the Sharif for rampant corruption and holds the Ottoman Turks responsible for not enforcing order on the roads.

Sikandar's jaundiced views of the Sharif are deserved but one-sided. He had his reasons for squeezing her wealthy delegation, and they were wholly economic. The lucrative Hajj caravans entering the Hijaz had shrunk from six to three in a hundred years, and the largest, from Istanbul via Damascus, was on its way to becoming mere ceremony. With the advent of steam, more and more pilgrims arrived for the Hajj by ship, and most came from the Begum's India. This sharply reduced the Sharif's overland tax base and lightened the purse assigned to him by the Porte† to protect the roads. Even the interior routes, on which the Begum hoped to travel to Medina, were losing more traffic every year to a safer sea route from Jidda to Medina's port of Yanbu. After reading of al-Abbasi's failed attempt in that direction, it is easy to imagine the outcome of such a trip, had the Begum chanced it The hard-pressed Hijazi tribes would surely have raided a seven-hundred-camel caravan led by a foreigner. The Sharif could not have guaranteed her safety, despite his vows (excerpted here). The Begum's final pages detail a baker's dozen reasons why the trip posed mortal dangers. In the end, she forfeited Medina.

---

*Leading a single rider away from a caravan at night, for later ransom, was a common Hijazi ruse, described by Joseph Pitts two centuries earlier (see p. 124).

†Porte: short for the Sublime Porte, a widely accepted French term for the "high gate" (*babiali*) of the Grand Vizier's offices in Istanbul, after which the Ottoman government was named.

Sikandar's book is dedicated to Queen Victoria, her co-regent. Originally written in Urdu and published in two copies (one for the Queen,* one for the Begum), it was subsequently translated into English by Willoughby-Osborne, wife of Bhopal's British political agent, and printed in London in 1870. (The imperial implications of this publication history are hard to miss.) The book's form is an official report partly told in letters, but its dryness is enlivened by the bizarre events the Begum describes. Her letter campaign sheds valuable light on the Hijaz pilgrim routes, not only their number and general disposition, but who controlled them, as well as the dangers a powerful foreigner faced in taking them. These excerpts also provide a rare glimpse into the wealthiest Meccan harems, including a passage on marriage customs that flies in the face of received opinion about Muslim women's rights. The Begum's account describes the clash of two discordant cultures. Although decorum is never broken, a battle of honor rages beneath the surface of this prose.

from *Pilgrimage to Mecca*
by The Nawab Sikandar,
Begum of Bhopal

ARRIVING AT JIDDA On the thirteenth of the month of Shaban, in the year of the Hijra 1280, corresponding to the twenty-third of January 1864 of Christ, having made in company with my fellow pilgrims a prosperous voyage from Bombay, I arrived at Jidda. Immediately after my arrival, the port admiral of the Sultan of Turkey came on board and said: "You cannot land today. After your arrival has been reported to the Sharif and the Pasha of Mecca, you may be able to disembark tomorrow at about eight or nine o'clock and enter the city."

Accordingly, on the twenty-fourth of January, at nine o'clock in the morning, the unlading of my luggage commenced; and accompanied by the

*The Queen took her relations with British India seriously. She later made herself fairly fluent in Urdu, with lessons from her favorite male servant, Abd al-Karim al-Munshci, a Hindi Muslim.

Nawab Kudsiah Begum,* Nawab Mian Faujdar Muhammad Khan,† and Dr. Thomson,‡ I proceeded to the house of Ahmad Arab, where the caravan of pilgrims was staying. Here Dr. Thomson left me and went to call on the Consul of Jidda. Ahmad Arab received me very hospitably, giving a dinner in my honour, at which all the ladies of his family were present. We remained there, however, only until six o'clock in the evening, Ahmad Arab having informed me that a princess had arrived from Egypt and would lodge at his house and that therefore I must vacate it for her. I had no alternative but to do this; and I was consequently obliged to seek an asylum elsewhere; this I found at a house called Khush Shamiyan (Happy Dwelling).

Abd al-Rahim, the head of the caravan, went and asked Ahmad Arab to tell him what the charge would be for the three or four hours we had spent in his house, and the latter replied that as we had done him the honour to remain but a short time, he would receive no payment. Whereupon I made him a present of some bales of cloth, some coins, etc.

After all, the Egyptian princess never came, having found quarters elsewhere, and not only had we been put to much inconvenience, but Ahmad Arab was in no way benefited.

While the goods were being taken out of the ship, Nawab Faujdar Muhammad Khan, who was present with the Kudsiah Begum, told her that her money chest had the cover broken and that the rupees were scattered about. "Those Bedouin thieves," he added, "are scrambling for them."

The Kudsiah Begum replied, "If the box is broken, the rupees are probably stolen. What is the use of your troubling yourself?"

On hearing this, I became anxious about my luggage and asked the people why they were opening the boxes. They replied, "That the custom dues might be paid."

I then wrote to Muhammad Baksh, Deputy Harbour Master of Jidda. . . . A letter came in answer from Shams al-Din, customhouse officer, saying: "Inasmuch as I am a servant of the Turkish government and there are fixed custom dues for this port, I have no power to take less than the prescribed rates; but in consideration of your Highness having honoured this empire with a visit, and of the letter you refer to from the Governor of

*Nawab Kudsiah Begum: Dowager Begum, mother of the Sikandar Begum.

†Nawab Mian Faujdar Muhammad Khan: uncle of the Sikandar Begum.

‡Dr. Thomson: Charles Thomson, Esq., M.D., Surgeon to the Bhopal Political Agency, who had been deputed by Her Majesty's Indian government to escort the Begum as far as Jidda.

Bombay, and of his friendship towards you, also out of regard for our common faith, I will only examine one of your ten cases; be pleased, however, to send a list of the whole of your Highness's goods, that I may certify to its correctness, and receive the customs according to the above-mentioned regulations. And further, inform me of the name of your agent here." . . .

THE ROYAL BAGGAGE I received the following account from [my agents] Mittu Khun and Abdul Karim: "Today, being the eighth of February, 1864, we disembarked the whole of your Highness's property with every care, under the direction of a person named Antonio de Silva. But the Custom House officer would not hear anything that was said and insisted upon opening all the bales and arbitrarily exacting the dues upon every article. The amount of trouble and annoyance we experienced is beyond description. He scattered all the things about; if a box chanced to be unlocked, well and good; if not, he broke it open. In short, he spoilt all the cases and their contents. As yet we have been unable to discover what the particular tax levied upon each article may have been; apparently not a single thing has been exempted from dues. When we are informed on the subject, we shall communicate with your Highness."

On hearing this, I passed an order directing a copy of this letter to be sent through Hafiz Muhammad Khan to the Sharif and Pasha. . . .

The Pasha and Sharif wrote that they were aware of Captain Mittu Khan being appointed to the charge of my property and that any representation made by him to them they would willingly attend to. They expressed regret at the conduct of the Custom House officer and said they had written to him on the subject and that his reply should be forwarded to me. . . .

AT EVE'S TOMB, JIDDA The Kudsiah Begum visited this tomb of our ancestor Eve and, according to her wont, distributed alms. But on turning to leave the place, some two hundred to three hundred beggars—men and women, old and young, boys and girls, followed her, shouting at and hustling her to the extent that she was well-nigh crushed to death and rendered senseless by their violence and importunity. It seems to be the established practice of these faqirs and inhabitants of the city to importune for alms and, on refusal, to make an attack all together—crowding, hustling, and even tearing the clothes off one's back. . . .

Every native of India who lands at Jidda has a dollar or half-dollar, according to his condition in life, extorted from him. There is no kindness of disposition among the inhabitants, but they are characterized by a large amount of cruelty and oppression. They consider it a meritorious act to oppress the natives of India—just as a heretic considers it a meritorious act to persecute the true believer. To steal their property or to maltreat them is looked upon as no offence at all. . . .

THE ROYAL CARAVAN, JIDDA TO MECCA I now proceed with the account of my march from Jidda. Sharif Abdullah of Mecca wrote to me as follows: "It is a long time since we first heard of your intended visit to the holy shrines. Praise be to God that you are on your way! The news has given me much pleasure, and as you will shortly reach Mecca, I have, with reference to the arrangements to be made for your reception, in accordance with your rank, sent to you my brother, together with an interpreter, and they will carry out all your wishes. Be so good as to look upon my relation as your sincere friend, and may you come with perfect ease and comfort to the House of God at Mecca!"

A similar letter came from the Pasha of Mecca with reference to sending his son, Suleyman Beg, to meet me.

After this I wrote to my agent, Abd al-Rahim, saying: "Hire, for the journey to Mecca, eighty camels, at the rate of one riyal each, but let me know if the hire be more or less." The agent accordingly hired camels for the various stages—viz.: from Jidda to Mecca, from Mecca to Mina, from Mina to Muzdalifa, from Muzdalifa to Arafat, and from thence by the same route back again to Jidda. . . .

At length the price of the camels having been settled by Abd al-Rahim, he took them off . . . to arrange about their distribution among the different members of the caravan; and about sunset, having mounted our *shugduf* camels,* we started from Jidda. . . .

THE DOWAGER'S ABDUCTION Between Jidda and Hadda (the first stage), I found the *istikbal*† waiting to receive me, and with it were Sharif Abdullah, brother of the Sharif of Mecca, and Suleyman Beg, son of the Pasha of Mecca, attended by Jafar Effendi. The latter said to me, "When the Sharif comes up and salutes you by saying *'Salaam alaykoum!'* ('Peace be with you!'), your Highness must reply, *'Alaykoum salaam!'* ('Upon you be peace!') Then he

---

*A *shugduf* camel carries two square panniers, or *shugdufs*, composed of a framework of wood, filled in with ropework. Each pannier holds one person.

†*istikbal:* literally, "meeting." It is the custom in the East for people of rank to be received at some distance from their destination by a deputation from the house of the host with whom they are to stay. In the case of royal personages, they are met by some member of the family accompanied by a large retinue; the procession in India on such occasions is very imposing. . . .

will say, 'Kif hal kyum?' ('How do you do?') Your Highness must reply, *'Tayib.'* ('Very well!')"

After this, the brother of the Sharif, riding on horseback, came up. The order of the procession was as follows: About fifty *sowar*s (horse soldiers) rode behind Sharif Abdullah, and about the same number of Turkish *sowar*s behind Suleyman Beg, son of the Pasha. The Sharif's brother was preceded by an Abyssinian seated on horseback, who wore a fur hat which appeared to me to be made of the skin of a shaggy sort of dog; he had two very small kettledrums in front of him and rode holding the reins in his mouth and using both hands for beating the drums. When the sun rose, I observed that an umbrella was held over the head of the Sharif's brother by an Abyssinian riding by his side. The horses were very handsome and well-bred and went along as quietly as if they were kids or lambs tied together; there was no neighing.

Suleyman Beg's escort was similar to that of the Sharif's brother, only he had but one kettledrum. They were both accompanied by torchbearers, and the torches were composed of a particular kind of wood, instead of rags soaked in oil, the ashes of which kept continually falling on the ground as the men moved along. The Sharif's brother rode by my side for some little distance, but when I told him that the Dowager Begum was coming up behind, he, together with Suleyman Beg, left me and went back to meet her.

We reached Hadda at seven o'clock in the morning, and on arrival, I heard the following account from Munshi Saraj al-Din: "In your Highness's caravan of pilgrims, which left Jidda for the great Mecca at seven o'clock in the evening . . . , was the camel ridden by Her Highness the Kudsiah Begum, and in the middle of the night, while on the road, it was seized by about twenty Bedouins, who began leading it away from the caravan in another direction, when Her Highness called out in a loud voice, '"I don't know where those people are taking my camel! They won't listen to or understand me, and none of my servants are with me. *Ari, Ari!* (Hullo, there!) Lead my camel along near the Sikandar's camels!' There was with Kudsiah Begum's camel a slave whom she had purchased for the pilgrimage, giving him his freedom, and he had joined her at Jidda. He was clinging round the neck of the camel, and would not let it go, when Budhu Khan, . . . one of your Highness's own orderlies, having heard the Kudsiah Begum's voice, ran back and began to deal such blows with the butt end of his musket at the three or four Bedouins who were leading off the camel, as well as at the ten or twelve others who were surrounding it, that he knocked several of them over. And when they saw that some of their companions were disabled, they left the camel and ran off. Budhu Khan had been joined, in the meantime, by Ghulam Husayn and Husayn Baksh, sepoys of the same regiment, and the three remained with Her Highness as escort."

The Kudsiah Begum herself gave a few more particulars of the occurrence and said that, as she never imagined the Bedouins who were leading off her camel to be robbers, she had entered into conversation with them, under the impression that they were escorting her, and had told them not to keep her camel by itself, but to lead it along with mine. It was not until she arrived at Hadda that she understood they were robbers.

Qasim Ali, an employee of the Bhopal state, reported to me as follows: "When I reached the outer gate of Jidda, the camel drivers, that is to say the Bedouins, began turning all the luggage topsy-turvy and ended with dispatching it in that state. After we had travelled about half a mile, one of the camel men seized a box full of goods and a bag containing a bill of exchange and other property belonging to some of the servants of Her Highness (the Dowager Begum). He ran off with these, leaving the camel behind him, the remainder of the caravan having gone on a long way ahead. We, therefore, being quite helpless, had no alternative but to return to Jidda. Arrived there, we procured a donkey from Abdl al-Rahim, and with three horse soldiers as escort we again set off, and reached here today. On our way we fell in with Mian Ida, who told us to inform your Highness that his camel men, after having unloaded the camels, had left him where we found him and that he was perfectly helpless."

On hearing this, I ordered a letter to be written to Jafar Effendi, requesting him to communicate with the Sharif of Mecca and to ask him what arrangements could be made for forwarding the goods. . . .

MECCA The city of Mecca the Exalted is very wild and desolate looking, and is surrounded by lofty hills, quite destitute of trees. These hills extend, I am told, to a distance of four or five marches on all sides of Mecca, and I found on the Amra Road that this was the case. The road runs between the hills, being in some places so narrow as to admit of only three or four camels going abreast, and in others wide enough for five or ten. . . .

There was a great deal of severe sickness, and the inhabitants of Mecca suffered considerably. Nine people in my suite were attacked with various complaints, such as dysentery, fever, and tumours in the leg. On the pilgrimage, I lost eight altogether, four of whom died on board ship and four at Mecca and Jidda. In the caravan that separated from me and went to Medina, a great many people died, some on land and some on board ship. Two persons also disappeared out of my suite and were never found again:

233

one was a woman whom we lost on the pilgrimage, and the other a water carrier who went to Medina. I do not know what became of them.

In the country round Mecca, there are neither lakes, rivers, nor streams; there are only springs, and in these no travellers are allowed to bathe without payment. People of the poorer classes are beaten and driven away from them, sentries belonging to the Sharif and Pasha being posted over them. The water is sold at the rate of half a *guirsh** a skinful. A chief or person of rank who is acquainted with the Sharif and Pasha can obtain a sufficient supply of water for the needs of his establishment. I had permission to receive as much as I wanted. There are magnificent baths in the city, those for men being separate from the women's. . . .

The foundations and walls of the buildings in Mecca are very strong, being composed of either bricks and mortar or stone, but the roofs and floorings are roughly constructed after this fashion: branches of the date palm are laid crosswise over the beams and rafters, and over them is spread a layer of earth, so that if any porous vessel containing water be placed on the floor, the drippings percolate through into the rooms below. Or should there be a pan of fire for cooking placed on the floor, the house is in danger of being set on fire. After rain it is common to see grass growing on the roofs. Every house has a kitchen, bathroom, and other offices of masonry, the remainder of the building being composed of mud. . . .

The custom of taking perquisites prevails to such an extent among all classes that if one only wants to hire a donkey for the pilgrimage, one has to employ an agent, and this man gets as commission from the owner of the animal upon the hire of it the sum of a *guirsh* or half-*guirsh*. On all occasions of buying and selling, the same custom prevails. It is usual to demand the price of an article the moment it is sold; one is not trusted for an instant.

It seemed to me that begging was held to be as honourable as working; and when travellers take their departure (from Mecca), they are besieged by nobles as well as plebeians who clamour obstinately and violently for [handouts].

Almost all the bad characters that have been driven out of India may be found in Mecca.

Imports from every part of the world are procurable, but the price of everything is dear.

Women frequently contract as many as ten marriages, and those who have only been married twice are few in number. If a woman sees her husband growing old, or if she happen to admire anyone else, she goes to the

---

**guirsh*: equal to one twentieth of a riyal, the Arab penny. [Ed.]

Sharif, and after having settled the matter with him, she puts away her husband and takes to herself another, who is perhaps young, good-looking, and
rich. In this way a marriage seldom lasts more than a year or two. . . .

The people who reside in the cities know something of religion, but
those who inhabit the mountainous regions are totally ignorant of it. . . .

A BANQUET The hour of my arrival at Mecca was the *'isha* (first watch of
the night), and the call to evening prayers was sounding from the different
mosques. I entered within the holy precincts by the Gate of Peace, and,
arriving at the House of Abraham, I stood and read the prescribed prayers.
After that, I performed the ceremonies of the Arrival Tawaf, and of running
at Safa and Marwa. It was then my intention to go to the house I had engaged, after I should have offered in sacrifice the animals brought for the
purpose, and have accomplished the ceremony of Halak Nisai [Ritual Hair-
cut], and have also visited the house of Abu Bakr, the *mutawwif,* where it is
customary for pilgrims to stay. If I should find my own house convenient, I
intended remaining there.

In the meantime, however, meeting Molvi Abd al-Kayum, I asked him
to conduct me to my house. He accordingly walked on before me; whereupon one of the four slaves of the Sharif of Mecca, who had accompanied
me from Hadda, ran after him and, striking him in the face, pushed him
against the wall. The Molvi called out in a loud voice, "Look, Madam! One
of the Sharif's slaves is beating me shamefully!" I said to the man, *"Bhai!"*
(literally, "Brother!") "Why are you beating the Molvi, who is one of my
people?" He replied, "You are to come to our Sharif's house and eat the dinner he has prepared for you." I answered, "The Sharif has not invited me; I
will come back when I have made my offerings." After this, I again proceeded
on my way, Molvi Abd al-Kayun walking before me, when a slave, who was
with Jafar Effendi, a very tall, powerful man, drew his sword and began to
attack the Molvi. The latter called out to me as before, and I remonstrated
with the man who had assaulted him, saying that the Molvi, in obedience to
my orders, was showing me the way to my house. The slave replied, "My
master the Sharif's feast, which cost him five thousand rupees, is all getting
spoilt, and his money is being wasted!" Jafar Effendi then said, "Your Highness had better go to the Sharif's; otherwise he will be very angry, and his
anger is certainly not pleasant." On hearing this, I bent my steps to the Sharif's
house, and arriving there, I found his brother, Abdullah, waiting for me,
who, after having made a *salaam* and inquired how I was, took his leave.

I made the prescribed offerings at his door and performed the ceremony
of Halak Nisai. On entering the house, I found a room in which a hand-

somely embroidered velvet carpet was spread, and in front of the room, on the top of an open portico, dinner was laid upon a tablecloth. The repast consisted of about five hundred specimens of Arabian cookery, some of the dishes savoury, some sweet. They said to me, "Eat your dinner." I excused myself by replying that I had had no invitation. Jafar Effendi said to me, "If you do not eat, the Sharif will be very displeased, and it would never do to offend him." Then, stooping down, he whispered in my ear, "When the Sharif is angry with people, he orders his head slaves to shoot them in the night, and *you* have to perform the *tawaf;* on this account, then, do not make the Sharif angry." After this, I said nothing more, but sat down and began to eat. The dew had fallen upon the food, making it as cold as ice, so that nothing had any flavour. Jafar Effendi and some Turks attend upon me at the meal. After it was over, night having set in, we passed it there. . . .

A LETTER FROM THE SHARIF "In accordance with the custom of this court and to show my friendship for you, I sent my brother to receive you with the *istikbal.* It is both right and proper that the remaining hospitable observances (which consist of an entertainment lasting three days) should be carried out; and as my servants knew that the custom was both an established and invariable one, they thought it superfluous to give you any notice, either of the entertainment or with regard to your staying in my house. This will account for your having heard nothing of the matter. I now, being acquainted with the custom of your country, find that I acted contrary to your etiquette; however, it was done unintentionally, so let bygones be bygones. Now, our friendship is established on a sure basis. It is no trouble to me to render you every assistance in my power; and although I do not see the necessity for informing you beforehand, every transaction between us shall be to our mutual satisfaction, in accordance with the request contained in your letter. The house is entirely at your disposal, and by occupying it you have inconvenienced no one; neither is any return expected for it; still, if you consider that it is not adapted to you, you must decide as you think best."

On receiving this, I wrote to the Deputy Commander-in-Chief (Naib Bakhshi) and told him to go to the Sharif and say from me "that his courteous reply had given me much pleasure; that adjoining the house I had rented there were five other houses, not government buildings, which I should be obliged by his obtaining for me, in order that privacy might be insured to me during my stay for the period of Ramadan, and that I would send the rent to him."

The [Deputy] wrote in answer that the Sharif had ordered the chief magistrate of the city to purchase the five buildings and make them over to me and that he had told him verbally if I did not like to remain in his house, he would not be hurt or annoyed at my leaving it; for he only desired my comfort, and wherever I could be most comfortable, there I had better remain. He added, "The pilgrimage is a sacred duty, but it is incumbent on everyone performing it to provide himself with a house suitable to his rank in life. I do not say that the Begum need necessarily remain in my house, but it is proper that she should select one adapted to the occupation of a personage of her great name and exalted dignity."

Notwithstanding the Sharif's persistent refusal to take any rent, he accepted it willingly enough when the time came for me to leave. . . .

I was now settled in Mecca and began to be occupied with my religious exercises.

After Her Highness the Nawab Dowager Begum had presented to the Sharif, the Pasha, and Shayba Sahib* the gifts she had brought for them from Bhopal, the fame of her liberality and great riches spread to such an extent throughout the whole city of Mecca that she was completely mobbed by faqirs, and the possibility of her performing the *tawaf* was entirely put an end to. I felt perfectly helpless and began to question the utility of having gone to Mecca for devotional ends. I accordingly requested the Sharif and Pasha to make over to me some of their Turks, to form part of my suite when I made the *tawaf* and so protect me from the violence of the faqirs. The Sharif, in compliance, ordered four Turks to attend me when performing the *tawaf.* They did this, and when they had safely escorted me home, they were going away after having made their *salaam,* but I judged from their demeanour that they expected a present, although they had not asked for one. I consequently ordered a present of eight annas† to be given to each man daily. They took it without any compunction and seemed in no fear of punishment at the result.

We were in the habit of wearing Turkish veils when going out on the *tawaf* and other expeditions, and the inhabitants of Mecca enquired of my people, "Which among those women was the Sikandar Begum of Bhopal?" Some of them were foolish enough to point me out, so to avoid a repetition of the annoyance, I issued an order to all my suite forbidding them, on pain of dismissal from my service, to cause me to be recognised, either indoors or out-of-doors, by anyone, be they inhabitants of Mecca, or strangers. . . .

*Shayba Sahib: The Keeper of the Keys of the Holy Places.

†anna: one shilling.

VISITING THE HAREM   The inhabitants of Mecca now began to say that I ought to pay visits to the Sharif and Pasha, they being the rulers of the country; and I accordingly made up my mind to send my prime minister to wait upon the Sharif. I wrote to the Naib Bakhshi and desired him to inform the Sharif and Pasha that after the ship with my retinue had arrived, I would, God willing, pay them a visit. . . .

[When the ship had arrived], I went on foot to the Sharif's house and learnt that he was sitting alone in one of his rooms. Three slaves met me and requested me to go into the [meeting hall], which I proceeded to do, they leading the way. At the first step of the staircase to the [hall], some slaves were stationed; three or four steps higher up, some female Georgian attendants; and at the same distance still higher up were some female Egyptians, servants of the mother and sisters of the Sharif. These women placed their hands under my arms and assisted me up the steps. Four or five steps higher up was one of the Sharif's wives and, at the same distance again, another wife. Then, beyond a door leading into a passage, at the place established by custom, being about halfway down the room, was the Sharif's mother. As each of the Sharif's wives met me, they first took my hand in theirs, and then putting their faces against both sides of my face and neck, they ended with kissing me lightly on my lips. The Sharif's mother did the same.

Nawab Faujdar Muhammad Khan, the Minister, Hafiz Muhammad Khan, and Captain Mittu Khan, who all accompanied me, were received in the gentlemen's apartments and were joined by the Sharif.

An hour afterwards some slaves came to me to say that the Sharif would, with my permission, come into the [room]. I replied: "It is the Sharif's own house," (meaning to say, "Of course, he can do as he pleases"). I was sitting with his mother and wives and conversing with the former, who spoke Arabic, Jafar Effendi's wife interpreting for us. The Sharif has seven wives, four of whom I saw. Of these, two were Georgians, very handsome and beautifully dressed, being, one might say, literally covered with diamonds from head to foot. Their heads were encircled with a wreath composed of jewels, and when the ladies moved or talked, the sparkling effect of these was very pretty. Underneath this diadem, they wore on their heads very small, fine handkerchiefs, such as English ladies carry in their hands; these were thickly embroidered with jewels and tied in a coquettish way. From their neck to their waist, they were adorned with gems in the same fashion. Altogether, in face, height, and beauty of limbs, these two Georgians were as perfect women as one could wish to see. The dress of one was composed of black satin and that of the other of lilac satin, embroidered with stars. The third wife was an Arabian and had regular features. The fourth was an Abyssinian.

Those wives only who have borne children to the Sharif are allowed to sit down in his presence, while those who have no family are compelled to stand with their hands put together.

When the Sharif came into the [hall], the four wives and the mother rose respectfully, and I, having marked their obeisance, advanced a few steps to meet him. After the Sharif was seated, I made my offering and then followed the usual complimentary speeches. Having enquired for my health, the Sharif asked: "How far is Bhopal from here?" I replied: "It is the Paradise of India—your Highness should pay it a visit." The Sharif laughed and said: "My home is the Ka'ba."* After this, the wives and mother, having again made their obeisance, sat down in the background.

Some Georgians and Africans who were in attendance now brought in cups of coffee and pomegranate sherbet, and others the rose water and incense. Just as it is the fashion in India to give attar† and rose water, so is it the custom in Mecca to fumigate the guests with sweet-scented incense.

The Sharif now said to me: "If your Highness will allow me, I will send for your uncle, the minister, and other gentlemen to come here." I replied: "I came here for the express purpose of paying a visit to the ladies of your Highness's family, and if the gentlemen come, they will go away. I had rather be with the ladies." The Sharif, however, persevered in his wish to send for them, so after a little while, I consented. The ladies accordingly withdrew, and some slaves were sent to fetch the gentlemen of my suite. The Sharif did not salute any of them, but they, having made their *salaam* and kissed his hand, sat down. After a few complimentary speeches, they all returned to the gentlemen's apartments. The Sharif remained sitting where he was. I should think his age was rather more than fifty. The ladies now came into the room again, and after remaining a little while longer, the Sharif took leave of me and returned to the gentlemen's apartments.

I then took leave of the ladies and went to another house to visit the Sharif's sisters. The party consisted of three sisters, four mothers, two sisters-in-law, and a number of other women. After the usual complimentary speeches, the Sharif's younger brother came and sat with us, and then coffee and sherbet were served. After the incense burning, I took my departure and returned to my own house. It is the custom at these visits for the men to embrace each other and for the women to do the same among themselves. . . .

---

*that is, the Sanctuary at Mecca.

†attar: a very strong perfume—such as oil of roses or sandalwood.

THIRTEEN REASONS TO AVOID MEDINA I wished to continue my pilgrimage to Medina, but before coming to any decision, I wrote to Mian Faujdar Muhammad Khan, saying that I had heard most appalling accounts of the state of the road to Medina, "which, if true, will deter me from going to that place, the pilgrimage to Medina not being obligatory." I am further induced not to go for the following reasons:

1. That all the camels being equipped with *shugdufs*, it is impossible for anyone to move a muscle when on them.

2. The roads are very bad.

3. I know no particulars regarding the route or the country through which it passes.

4. I know nothing of Arabic or of the language and customs of the Bedouins so cannot understand what they say or what they do.

5. I have very few troops with me.

6. I have not sufficient money to engage an escort of the Sharif's or Pasha's troops.

7. Even if I had, the officers have no fixed pay and would take all they could from me and are, I believe, capable of plundering my property.

8. The reputation of the Kudsiah Begum for wealth and liberality is now so widely known that she could not go *incognito*. If we could by any means get away quietly, the Bedouins would be very angry and would say: "This is the very Begum who could spend so much money at Mecca and yet is now travelling empty-handed, for fear we should plunder her on the way!"

9. The Bedouins demand [alms] at every step and, if they do not obtain money or food, frequently grossly insult or even kill one. Where am I to find money to satisfy all their demands?

10. The local authorities do not exert themselves to protect pilgrims. The Sharif takes two riyals from the Bedouins for every camel engaged; when he has collected a large number of pilgrims, he sends them off to Medina, caring only for the money he is to receive and nothing about the safety of the pilgrims.

11. The Sharif himself never goes with a caravan. His servants told me it is not [good] etiquette for him to do so. He sends a nephew or distant relative.

12. I have a great number of women and but few men in my suite. I should consequently require a large escort.

13. I have heard that the Bedouins frequently have disputes with the Turkish government, in which case caravans are obliged to remain at Medina two or three months.

Mian Faujdar Muhammad Khan's reply was as follows:

"What you write is quite true and most sensible; to go to Medina till the road is quite safe is to trifle with our lives. You are quite right not to go, for it is written in the venerable Quran, 'It is wicked to put one's life in danger.'

"It is laid down that all Muslims ought to go to Mecca, but it is not necessary to go to Medina. When our pilgrimage here is over, we should return to Bhopal."

Hakim Bakr Ali Khan also wrote:

"My opinion quite coincides with your Highness's; you should not go to Medina. You may come here again some day, when you may be able to go. The *molvis* and men learned in the law have decided that it is not necessary to go to Medina if the roads are unsafe. Imam Muhammad Ghazali* has even forbidden it."

I then wrote to Sharif Abdullah and Pasha Izat Ahmad, as follows:

"I have made many enquiries regarding the road to Medina; some people tell me there are four roads; others, that there are five or six. Some say the roads are open; others, that they are all closed. I believe, therefore, that none of them know anything about the matter. I shall feel much obliged by your sending me a list of the various routes, together with the names of the marches on each, and also by your informing me what roads are closed and what open."

In reply, Sharif Abdullah and the Pasha wrote:

"There are five roads to Medina, besides the Imperial Road, but only small caravans of forty or fifty camels go along most of them. The large caravans go either by the Imperial or Eastern Road.

*Muhammad al-Ghazali: a great Muslim theologian (1058–1111) whose works did much to inform and spiritualize the ritual obligations of his religion. [Ed.]

241

"It is to be hoped that, through the efforts of the Pasha of Medina, the Imperial Road will soon be clear of Bedouins."

I learnt from Muhammad Hasan, an Arab, the following particulars regarding the routes, etc., to Medina:

"About the fifteenth or twentieth Shawal, the first caravan leaves Mecca. It assembles at Wadi Fatima: owing to the scarcity of water, it goes in small parties to Safra Wadi (the seventh march from Mecca). Many stop one day and night at Rayek en route.

"At Safra Wadi, the caravan reassembles and marches together for two marches as far as Bir Sharoki, for fear of the Bedouins. From Bir Sharoki, they go in small parties to Medina, which is one march distant.

"In marching from Medina to Mecca, the same precautions are adopted.

"After the Hajj, two caravans go from Mecca to Medina; the first is called Tayyara, and goes with the Syrian caravan; the second starts about twenty days after and goes very slowly."

I wrote, as follows, to Miriam Bibi, of Aden,* whose orders all the Bedouins respect (twelve of the Bedouin chiefs being under Shaykh Sa'ad, who is her disciple):

"I have heard from the people at Mecca that the roads to Medina are closed because there is a dispute between the Bedouins and the Sultan of Turkey. I have also been informed that Shaykh Sa'ad, who is a great chief among the Bedouins, is your disciple. I write, therefore, to request that you will give me a letter to Shaykh Sa'ad to the effect that when my caravan goes from Mecca to Medina, he, or his son, or one of his near relatives, should accompany and escort it safely to Medina and back again to Mecca. I will handsomely reward him. Please send the letter for Shaykh Sa'ad to me, and I will forward it to him and receive his reply."

I wrote to Her Britannic Majesty's Consul at Jidda, as follows:

"I send herewith copies of all the reports I have received regarding the routes to Medina. Please give me your advice. I purpose going with the Egyptian and Syrian caravan to Medina and, having performed the pilgrimage, to go with the same caravan to Suez, from whence I hear I can proceed by steamer via Aden to Bombay. I cannot learn anything here about the route from Medina to Suez, which I believe is about twenty-seven marches. Will you kindly inform me whether supplies can readily be obtained, whether the road is safe, and also whether you can procure me an escort."

*Miriam Bibi: a spiritual leader of great regional power. [Ed.]

The Consul wrote in reply:

"There are hundreds of persons in Mecca who know far more about the routes than I do; as, however, you have asked my advice, I should recommend you to march to Jidda and to go from there to Yanbu by steamer; from Yanbu it is not many marches to Medina.

"I have learnt the following, regarding the Suez Road, from the people here. The road is bad, water is scarce, the distance great, and the expense will be enormous. It is six hundred British miles from Medina to Suez, and I should advise you *not* to go by that route: if, however, you are bent on going to Suez, your best plan would be this:

"From Medina to Yanbu by land, and thence to Suez by steamer. If you wish it, I will arrange to charter one of the imperial (Turkish) steamers for you. From Suez to Bombay you will, I fear, encounter difficulty, as there are only two or three of the Peninsular and Oriental Company's steamers ever there. In my opinion, it would be better for you to charter a steamer in Bombay to fetch you.

"The person who advised you to march from Mecca to Suez, and thence by steamer to Bombay, did so from interested motives.

"There is no doubt the Eastern Road from Mecca to Medina is the safest, but even on it men and animals suffer great inconvenience.

"This being a foreign country, I am unable to order an escort for you."

I received a letter from Shaykh Sa'ad in reply to the one sent him by Miriam Bibi; he wrote thus:

"I send my son Hazifah to you. He will do all you desire and convey you in all safety and comfort. I will do all I can to assist you. Pray treat my son, and the Arabs with him, with all kindness, because they will suffer much trouble and inconvenience. Your generosity is well-known.

"The camel men will receive every assistance from me, and my son will study your comfort in every way."

On further enquiry, I learnt that the marches are thus performed:

The caravan marches daily for seven *pahars** and halts for one. . . . In this manner Medina is reached in twelve days.

There is no water on the road. The Bedouins alone know the route and where any water is to be found.

There are many hills on the road to Medina, but all destitute of trees.

Whatever the pilgrims take with them the Bedouins seize, giving back only what they do not want.

**pahar:* a watch, equal to three hours.

Even the water which is carried on camels they sometimes seize. They will convey in safety to Medina any caravan with which they are pleased, but if they are annoyed, they leave the caravan and disappear among the hills; and the pilgrims, not knowing the road, wander about till they die from thirst and starvation.

The Bedouins, for five out of the twelve stages to Medina, acknowledge the Sharif Abdullah; for the other seven they look to Shaykh Sa'ad as their ruler.

But they only obey the orders of their chiefs so long as it suits them. No reliance is to be placed in them. They respect no promises and obey no orders, unless it pleases them to do so.

For these reasons I resolved not to go to Medina, as it would have been needlessly risking my own life and those of my suite.

John F. Keane
Anglo-India
1877—78

John Keane was born in Kipling's India. Son of a senior canon at Calcutta's
Anglican cathedral, he ran away to sea at twelve and worked as a sailor and
whaler, living (he writes) "a life of the wildest adventure . . . in every quarter of
the globe." He arrived in the Hijaz at thirty-two. His twin accounts of a year
there, in Mecca and Medina, are quirky gems of travel writing, good-humored,
nimble, surprisingly modern.

Keane had lived among Muslims all his life. Slower than Burton to cari-
cature a companion, disinterested in contrasting East and West, he writes as a
man completely at home in foreign quarters. Arriving alone in Jidda during
Ramadan, he quickly attached himself to the pilgrim suite of a visiting Hindi
amir. The ease with which he accomplished this transition is partly attributable
to his fluent Urdu. It also shows the social porosity of the Hajj and the way
members of one language group, regardless of race, might fall together. Keane's
stated aim was to give a short, inviting account of everything that interested him
in Mecca. He adopted the name Muhammad Amin (the last name rhymes with
Keane) and set out at once, riding with the Hindi caravan.

In Mecca, the Amir's entire suite lodged in a special ring of houses surrounding the Haram. Here Keane's windowed dormitory formed part of the
mosque walls facing the Kaʿba, providing a bird's-eye view of the whole arena.
Here he could watch the tawaf day or night and perform his prayers without
leaving his quarters. Judged by his lodgings, the wealth of Keane's protector must
have rivaled that of the Begum's in the last selection. It is not by chance that
many of the Hajj accounts during this period are by authors with strong attach-
ments to India. Not only was India Britain's wealthiest colony; it also supplied
the most pilgrims and produced the largest financial contributions to the Hajj.

After ten days spent mostly indoors, Keane began to ease into his surroundings, walking out one morning in a costume partly Indian, partly Arab. Neither
the clothes nor his white skin excited attention. In the early stages at any rate,

Keane foresaw no trouble in "entering Jidda an Englishman and leaving it a hajji." After so many accounts inflating the mortal dangers impostors faced here, it is refreshing to hear an Englishman state the truth—that Mecca itself provided a masquerader the best disguise imaginable: an international, racially diverse cosmopolis, organized around rites devised to downplay class and cultural distinctions. Keane experienced Mecca, not as a forbidden city but as a global convocation where strangers of every background blended in.

Keane was not Muslim in any lasting way. The ease of his entry into the Hajj world indicates a genuinely adaptable personality, humanistic rather than religious. In this sense, his book presents a case study in the malleability of identity without any apparent loss of self. In the following excerpts, Keane crosses from one culture to another by quick stages. During a first walk through the Haram Mosque, he compares his slight discomfort to the feeling of having disobeyed a sign to keep off the grass. A few weeks later, observing pilgrims surrounding the Ka'ba, he expresses his own version of religious awe. In a month, he remarks, "I was to all intents and purposes as honestly Muslim as any born Arab. I, in fact, acted the lie so well I believed it myself." Halfway through his second chapter, all traces of moral ambiguity dissolve. He finds himself "as much at home as if I had been a Muslim all my life."

Keane was not one to analyze contradictions. Instead, he gave himself the run of Mecca, plunging into pilgrim life. His book builds upon personal encounters. He formed friendships on the street, dined with his dormitory mess mates, and prayed punctiliously five times a day. He made the acquaintance of a local barber, too, and one day, in the course of being shaved, learned that an Englishwoman had been residing in Mecca for twenty years. This seemed so improbable that Keane arranged to meet the woman. So begins one of the stranger motifs in the pilgrim record, as two Britons, Keane and the Lady Venus (née Macintosh, of Devon), keep numerous rendezvous month after month in the Holy City.

Sometime after Ramadan, the Amir and his suite departed on a side trip to Jerusalem. Keane stayed behind and continued his solo walks around the town. Passing a crowded schoolyard one afternoon, he stopped to watch some children playing. One boy noticed his skin and called him a Christian. Keane's sketch of the ensuing fracas, excerpted here, is clear, even good-humored, but Keane sustained physical injuries and his confidence was shaken. He spent the next three weeks in the dormitory, recuperating, ingesting opium for pain, and hiding from the authorities.

No soldiers came. The Amir returned, and Keane recovered, returning to the streets and to his notebooks. Things ran smoothly, Mecca again became a protective backdrop, but he had learned to be more careful now, especially in his meetings with Lady Venus. In the weeks before the Hajj, he walked the moun-

tain trails above the city, taking stock of the human and animal populations, devoting a long chapter to each one. Understandably, he felt safer on the heights.

The schoolyard confrontation aside, Keane was able to relax on the Hajj to a degree that his predecessors could not. Unlike Burckhardt, al-Abbasi, and Burton, he does not seem to have been working for anybody, nor is his book an official report addressed to scientific or commercial backers. Keane performed the Hajj for his own interests and wrote about it for popular consumption. He moved freely in public, indulging a natural garrulousness even in the desert, climbing Mount Mercy with the crowds, reporting at length on a freak flash flood in Mecca—wandering, sampling, or sitting alone outside the mosque, a bag of bird-seed on his lap while clouds of pigeons flapped around him. From Ibn Jubayr to the Begum of Bhopal, pilgrims have usually described the Hajj as a physical ordeal. Keane is the first to represent it as enjoyable, on occasion even fun. None-theless, his record of Mecca ends on a dark chord. A deluge on the heels of the Feast of Sacrifice leaves the city awash in waste and, rather quickly, epidemics. Keane reports sixty-three deaths from cholera in one day.

Both Burton and Keane revealed the lives of particular pilgrims in ways that challenged the static tropes of mainstream Orientalism. Burton did this by imposing adopted personae (the itinerant doctor, the ragged dervish) on those he met, then recording and analyzing their reactions. Keane proceeded in a very different manner. There is little self-dramatization and almost no manufactured crisis or melodrama in his writing. Instead, he depends on the products of persis-tent, skillful loafing and social grace. When things go against him, he does not flee town; he hides in a closet until the trouble passes. (Samuel Beckett would have appreciated Keane.) He stumbles on his finds and, when they are people, usually befriends them. In his sketches and travels, he displays an eye for odd details: his image of pilgrims swimming their circuits around the Ka'ba is unique. While not an Arabist, the learning Keane possessed he marshaled rightly, and his record of the Hajj is comprehensive.

from John F. Keane's
Six Months in Meccah

ARRIVAL AT JIDDA . . . Many thousands of Muslims assemble at Mecca from all parts of the East during the pilgrim season, some of whom come in caravans across the Arabian deserts, while by far the greater number come by sea, giving employment to a number of English ships. During the season of which I am writing, 42,718 disembarked at Jidda.* It was at this place that I was enabled to attach myself to the train of a youthful Hindi amir,† whom I accompanied on pilgrimages to Mecca and other places in the Holy Land of Islam. . . .

Many of the wealthy pilgrims bring introductions to friends or countrymen resident in the Hijaz; with these introductions my patron was well provided, and thus we secured a tolerably peaceful reception. . . . To the gentleman acting as British Consul I gave my name and the addresses of friends in England, informing him of my intentions. He said much to dissuade me, telling me the roads were in an unsafe state and the country rather disturbed on account of the withdrawal of Turkish troops to the war in Europe; but I had already made up my mind on the subject and accordingly sold such of my clothes as would be unsuitable and provided myself with a native wardrobe; then, after a three-days' rest in Jidda, I entered into the preparations of our party en route for Mecca.

About noon on the third day, camels were hired from the Bedouins, . . . whom I now met for the first time, and of whom, notwithstanding . . . their wretched appearance at first, their haggling, and their shrill voices, I formed a favourable opinion and still believe to have their good points. . . .

JIDDA TO MECCA As we went through the gate, two fine soldierly looking Turkish sentries stood leaning on their rifles, smoking cigarettes, and seemed scarcely to notice even the camels passing them. Our party was composed of about fifty in all, men and women, and as only fifteen camels had been hired, ten with litters, and five pack-camels . . . and as each of these

---

*". . . The concourse at Mecca on the Great Feast-day was estimated to have exceeded 180,000 souls." (*The Times,* October 26, 1878)

†amir: properly, as in this case, a lord of the land under a ruler, and subject to feudal conditions.

carries only two persons, about twenty of our party had to walk by the camels, in company with a number of . . . [pilgrim beggars] who had attached themselves to us and who were accepted as a matter of course, receiving a great deal of charity. . . .

The kind of panniers, or litters, in which we sat or lay at full length when riding are known by the names of *shugduf* or *shubreya*. Inside the *shugduf* is a pocket for food, tobacco, and other little necessaries; outside, at the tail end and within easy reach, a wicker basket containing a bottle of water. Having mounted, that is to say, having, by the help of a ladder, ascended into this construction of bent boughs and old bags, resembling a rickety wigwam poised airily on the hump of a camel, the impression I laboured under was that we were instantly to plunge off in mad bounds across an exceedingly rough country (feeling at the same time pity for the poor beast under what I supposed could only have been an immense burden), spiced with momentary expectations of a spill. But on looking out, I found the road a perfectly level sandy plain, the camel crawling along at a slow walk, jolting more than the fastest pace of the hardest trotting horse; moreover, the platform on which you lay is on a level with the top of the animal's hump, and the whole structure of the *shugduf* so top-heavy that it requires the nicest adjustment of weight on either side to prevent the saddle, to which the *shugduf* is securely lashed (but which has no attachment whatever to the animal, merely adhering to its back in some mysterious way), turning a complete somersault—a thing which not unfrequently happens, for the art of balancing a *shugduf* is only acquired after long practice. Our camel driver threatened and abused us wildly for our awkwardness, my companion being as much a novice and as unaccustomed to this mode of travel as myself; however, we purchased peace at the price of a few dates and a little bread. I, for my part, spent one of the most wretched and apparently perilous nights I have ever had the misfortune to undergo, for the pitching and rolling of that desert ship could not find its equal afloat; so that I, old sailor as I was, became exceedingly sick, a thing which had not happened to me for many years while at sea.

The country over which we passed was a sandy plain, if anything, a slight ascent; our course, by the stars, nearly east; and the distance, I was informed, twenty-eight miles to Hadda, where we halted at daylight. Hadda is the stage, or halfway halting place, between Jidda and Mecca. Here there are about four or five square miles of cultivated ground, dotted over with groups of Bedawi huts. A stream of brackish water rises in the northeast and flows a mile or two over stone-built watercourses before losing itself in the desert. Around are what would be called the foothills of the approach to a range of mountains, the first outcropping of stone from the sandy plain, gradually increasing into rocky ridges and higher hills to the eastward. In the shade of a large shed-like caravansary we spent the day, praying, eating, and resting; but sleep could not be got, for some of the more devout pilgrims kept up the *talbiyya*, or pilgrim's prayer:

> *Labayk Allahumma, labayk!*
> *La sarika laka, labayk!*
> *Inna'l hamda wa'n niamata laka w'al-mulk*
> *La sharika laka, labayk!**

. . . I now found I could perform my ablution and prayer without attracting notice by any awkwardness on my part, audacious imitation giving me considerable help.

About an hour before sunset we got under way for Mecca; after this the road became a more decided ascent, the hills around being higher and more rugged as we passed through rocky defiles in which the moaning of the camels and the *labayk*s of the pilgrims were echoed and re-echoed with a truly weird effect. At daylight, when we seemed to have reached the summit of a rocky platform, the increased intensity of the *labayk*s and the dismounting of those ahead told that "the Mecca" was in sight. The distance we had come from Hadda was about twenty miles, and the course still easterly. The approach to Mecca by this road does not give a good view of the town. You arrive among collections of high stone buildings scattered over rocky slopes; then dismounting—for it is the proper thing to enter Mecca on foot if possible, women and invalids only being excepted—you find yourself passing along rather wide streets and between houses of some height; and as you continue on a downhill course, the streets become more narrow and dirty towards the centre of the city, where a house had been prepared for us in the walls of the Haram, or square enclosed for public worship, where is situated the Muslim Holy of Holies, the Ka'ba.

Now here was I, a veritable "Britisher," looking through a plain iron-barred window, estimating the dimensions of that Muslim pivotal point of the world—"Hub of the Universe," the Ka'ba, a shrine for which to die at

---

*"Here I am, O Allah! Here am I!
  No partner hast thou; here am I.
  Verily the praise and the beneficence are thine, and the kingdom:
  No partner hast thou; here am I."
(translation from *Burton's Pilgrimage*, third edition [London: W. Mullan and Son, 1879])

hundreds of thousands stint and pauper themselves in their old age, and towards which millions of eyes from all points of the compass turn with reverence five times daily. But my calculating mood was soon cut short, for having established ourselves on the premises, there was no escaping the forms and ceremonies appropriate to the occasion, which, tired and weary as I felt, kept me going the whole day. Besides the usual everyday five prayers and ablutions, we had to perform a two-prostration prayer in one part of the Haram and another in another part; to do the *tawaf*—i.e., walk, or rather trot, round the Ka'ba seven times, kissing the Black Stone let into a corner of the building, and touching another stone in it, at every circuit; to run seven times about one third of a mile through the streets repeating (after a guide hired for the purpose) proper prayers—this latter ceremony is called *sa'y* and is done in commemoration of Hagar's running up and down searching for water on the same spot. The street is in the middle of the city, skirting the Haram on the east and crossing the valley of Mecca indirectly from side to side. Lastly, the head must be shaved. And now I was at liberty to take off the pilgrim's garb. . . .

MECCA Right glad was I on this my first night in Mecca when we had said our last prayer and had laid down for the night to sleep, although the Amir and some thirty other true believers, packed head and tail in the same room, were snoring . . . Nor did I wake at the 2:00 A.M. meal—for this was the month of Ramadan, when all food must be eaten between sunset and sunrise—but my well-meaning friends took sufficient interest in my spiritual welfare to turn me out for the morning prayer, for which service I appeared properly grateful, exhibiting a great deal of cheerful alacrity in the shape of a cold-water wash before sunrise on a chilly morning and a quarter of an hour's gymnastic praying. One convenience was that the room in which we lived had three large recessed windows looking straight into the Haram, so that we could see the Ka'ba to which we prayed, and which is known as the Ear of God and by a dozen other flowery Eastern appellations, without going out. Neither the Amir nor any of his superior retainers went into the arcades surrounding the Ka'ba to pray except at noon on the Muslim Sunday, which falls on our Friday, and on a few other festive occasions. At first I always secured a place at these windows, not caring to show myself more in public than was necessary.

As this narrative is written chiefly for those who know little of Islam or Mecca, before going further I will explain what this pilgrimage is and endeavour to demonstrate my position in Mecca. I had often heard it said and myself believed that this great concourse of people which every year assembles at Mecca, ostensibly on a pilgrimage, really meets for a great mart or fair held there; but now having made the journey, I know that this is not the case. It is a true pilgrimage, the outcome of a belief in the tenets of a religion, the commands of the Prophet. I think I might truly say that a very small minority go for temporal gain. . . .

MY MASQUERADE All through I made assurance my strong suit and my acquaintance with India and hailing from Bombay my trump card; but if ever really cornered, as on one or two occasions, a little handplay, implying that I was a recent convert, would in every case call forth nothing but approval and commendation. To undertake an expedition of this kind was certainly a wild and unscrupulous thing, and I suffered many qualms of conscience and felt the veriest hypocrite; but having once entered into it, there was no drawing back, and the ordeal had to be gone through, though I often at first longed to declare myself a humbug. I remember once hearing a sailor say to another: "You have told that lie so often, Jack, you believe it yourself." I now found this to be no impossibility. It became my case to a nicety, and in less than a month I was to all intents and purposes as honestly Muslim as any born Arab among them. I, in fact, acted that lie so well I believed it myself! The name I had adopted, the Servant of the Prophet, though common in several forms in India, was objected to by the most correct of our party as not strictly orthodox, for said they, Was not Muhammad himself the servant of God? I thought this would be very inconvenient, as a cause of discussion bringing me into uncoveted notice, and added Amin to the name I had already adopted, then dropping "the servant," by an easy transition I became known as Muhammad Amin, a name which I supposed could not be objected to by any Muslims, no matter of what peculiar persuasion. Though I do not pretend but that I should be very much out of my depth were I to enter into any description of the discrepancies of belief existing among the various sects of the Muslims, still I do know more of Wahhabis than of the Wesleyans, and the Shafi'i is not altogether such a mystery to me as the Shaker; but I will spare the reader the infliction and myself the risk of exposure, having received probably much misinformation from so fertile a source as a Hindi one-sided education, and so I shall continue my narrative as the pilgrim Muhammad Amin, a Sunni Muslim of the "reasonable class." . . .

IN MECCA I was now settled in Mecca, living the ordinary everyday life of a pilgrim waiting for the "Great Pilgrimage." . . . After a week or ten days I found I could walk about the crowded bazaars without attracting notice, my fair complexion exciting no curiosity among the chequered masses, nor my ignorance of Arabic giving me any inconvenience where so many nationalities were gathered, speaking more languages than I will stay to enumerate here, only mentioning that you may jostle against a Tartar, Malay, Negro, and Turk round any Hindi tea stall. Nor does the style of your getup make any difference, except that it is advisable not to be too "swell" in order to avoid attracting beggars, but otherwise the Archbishop of Canterbury doing the *tawaf* in his mitre and robes would not occasion a passing remark and would be placed nowhere by twenty much more wondrously attired figures. . . .

END OF RAMADAN The worship round the Ka'ba in the great square was attended by larger numbers than I saw at any other time, notwithstanding that but few of the pilgrims had as yet arrived. I estimated that there could not have been less than thirty thousand assembled at the sunset prayer on the second day. It was an imposing spectacle to see those thousands of bearded, turbaned, hard, worldly men standing, circle widening upon circle, round their sacred Ka'ba, silently following the imam as he praised God and blessed Muhammad. Then as from one voice rises the great cry, "God is great!" stirring emotions that must be felt to be appreciated, and simultaneously all bow and prostrate themselves with their faces to the earth. I have often stood in my window recess going through these motions, unconsciously wrapt in the scene before me, every bright-coloured dress or brilliant turban a contribution to an extent of blended colour which the eye could not take in, each wave of prostration as it swept over this rainbow-tinted space making aurora-like transformations. In the twilight it was beautiful and impressive beyond most human displays. At this time the Ka'ba was opened, but I did not now venture to seek admission, though I did so on a future occasion. At the end of three weeks I began to know the ropes and find my way about pretty well. . . .

THE CITY AND ITS MOSQUE The town lies in a basin among steep hills of from five hundred to seven hundred feet in height and probably not more than twelve hundred to fifteen hundred above the sea. The whole of this valley, about one mile and a half long by one third of a mile across, is packed and crammed with buildings of all shapes and sizes, placed in no kind of order, climbing far up the steep side of the surrounding hills, with here and there an outlying house on the summit of some rock, looking as though crowded out and waiting for a chance to squeeze into the confusion below; a curious grey mass, flat topped, to a European eye roofless, half-plastered, for plaster in this climate is always either being put on or well advanced in coming off, but never to be seen in its entirety. The walls of the houses are composed of uncut stone and rubble from three to six feet thick, in very high buildings even thicker, but stone is used only for the sills of windows or jambs and arches of doorways, and very little brick is employed anywhere. Notwithstanding the substantial thickness of the walls, tottering ruins may be found by the sides of the most thronged thoroughfares in every part of the city. Many of the houses are of great height, large and factory-like, full of little windows; seldom two adjacent houses face the same way or are the same height; nothing resembling a row or street could by any stretch of imagination be extricated from such a chaos of masonry. It was impossible, even from my elevated point of view, to trace a hundred yards of open space between houses in any direction (many of the passages are boarded over, which to a certain extent conceals them), except on the outskirts of the town, where two or three suburbs straggle off up the less inclined outlets from the valley, and where the ground is not so thickly built over, though with the same systematic irregularity. The rule seems to be that no two things must be alike, an Eastern characteristic developed into a fixed law of non-uniformity in everything about Mecca, a town which—built as it is of fragments of the crumbling rock about, made to adhere with 30 percent of coarse lime together with the dusky crowds creeping in swarms about its dark lanes and streets, if such mere tortuous intricacies can be called so—suggests the simile of the giant anthill most strikingly, and indeed it applies better than any other description. There is a great sameness about all this detailed dissimilarity, from the midst of which the Haram stands out most prominently, at once fixing the attention, and indeed it is the main feature of Mecca. It is a large quadrangular open space, its longest direction northeast by east and southwest by west, enclosed within four arched colonnades or arcades, 190 yards on the longest sides by 127 yards on the shortest, close up to which, on the exterior, houses are built, except on the east side, where it is bounded by a street skirting the wall of the Haram. . . .

The measurements and numbers given were obtained at different times by a regular system, which I followed on every opportunity. I carried with me wherever I went a bamboo stick exactly a yard long, which I dropped or laid down carelessly as I moved about. No one would have suspected the zealous devotee crawling on his hands and knees at night round the holy Ka'ba was by way of a prayer mumbling the number of times he moved his stick. The height of buildings I got by measuring their shadows, which bore the same proportion to the object as my stick's shadow bore to three feet, provided I had a plain surface, as in the Haram. All the measurements given in feet may be relied on as tolerably accurate, and were noted down at the time. . . .

Observing and enquiring were now the only things which recalled me to my identity. I had become so accustomed to my surroundings, and accommodated myself to circumstances so rapidly, that in six weeks I was as much at home as if I had been a Muslim all my life. I formed friends, had little tiffs and jealousies with my companions in the household—we all having the same interests, and even eating out of the same plates. . . . My trencher mates were a blind *molvi**and a gentleman with only two fingers on his right hand, the only one with which a Muslim may take food. . . . After the evening meal, we all used to sit round a lamp in the middle of the room, eating sweets, smoking hookahs, and telling stories. I got to be very fond of the hookah; the smoke passes through a chamber full of water which takes up the more solid particles and condenses the steam from the tobacco and cools the smoke, which is always inhaled right into the lungs and has a very soothing effect, though somewhat painful to a beginner.

Sometimes I would tell a story, something in this style: The Amir begins by asking me, "You have been in many countries, Muhammad Amin?"

"Why not, your honour? Is not my work sailing?"

"I have heard there is a big fish in the sea, bigger than a ship?"

"I have seen many and hunted them in the sea to the south of India!" and so go on to give a long account of whaling to which all would listen most attentively, the Amir occasionally asking shrewd questions; or I would tell of a country where the sun does not set for six months, where there is hardly any land to be seen, all ice, ice, ice.

The Amir has said, "Good! Is there such a place in the world?"

"Yes."

"Good! If there is nothing but ice, for what do ships go?"

This is expected to be a poser, and the whole circle say, "Yes, yes," and look enquiringly at me.

"Oh, there is a big animal called a walrus, as big as two camels, having the body of an ox, the feet of a crocodile, the head of a tiger, tusks like an elephant, and tail of a fish; it is very fat, and we went to hunt them."

I can see incredulity on every countenance, and the Amir puts a final clencher with, "Good! and what can it get to eat to make it so fat?"

**molvi:* doctor of divinity.

"The fish in the sea!"

Here follow general laughter and exclamations of, "God! What a father of lies!"

I invented many wonderful stories to amuse them and found, here as everywhere, truth less credited than fiction. . . .

THE LADY VENUS Altogether I was not at all unhappy and remember many pleasant evenings with my Muslim friends, with whom I was, I believe, a bit of a favourite all round and looked upon as an agreeable harmless fellow, my punctilious observance of all religious duties making me much approved by the most devout. I often astonished even the blind *molvi* by my knowledge of divinity and the soundness of my principle—though I could neither read nor write much and had spent my whole life among men who were only Muslim by name. I made also a number of acquaintances outside; a chatty old barber to whom I went twice a week to get my head shaved, and who had been a "company's sepoy," I found very entertaining. He knew Bombay well and liked comparing notes with me, talking about those "Shaytan English," whom I could not help thinking he remembered kindly, though he of course joined me in my Muslim disapproval of them, expressing a little proper patriotic antipathy.

One day, when work and talk were rather slack, the old fellow casually remarked apropos of the previous conversation, "There is an Englishwoman in Mecca, the Lady Venus by name."

This was an eye-opener, though I took care not to show it, merely replying in an uninterested way:

"Praise be to God, how long has she been here?"

"Many years."

"Whose harem is she in?"

"Nobody's; she works at sewing and keeps herself, a *nawab* gives her a room in his harem house, and she does some little work for him. She is old."

"She is not an English lady. I think perhaps she is a half-caste."

"No, she is a real lady, sahib. Would you like to see her?"

"Yes, I will speak English to her and find out who she is." For I did not conceal any of my Christian accomplishments; instead, I rather bragged of them and got it believed I pretended to know more than I really did. Whether the old barber wanted to test me with a real Englishwoman or whether he did it in a kindly busybody spirit, I cannot say; there is no accounting for motives. At any rate, he arranged a meeting at his brother-in-law's house (a *molvi*) at two o'clock next day, saying he was certain to get the woman to come. The old fellow may have seen clean through me and expected a tip from one of us, and if so, he got one. You may be sure I had but one thing to think about that night. An Englishwoman in Mecca, been here many years—impossible! I have seen a gentleman driving an ox team in his swallowtails and once met a Cambridge B.A. before the mast in a whaler; but this seemed impossible even to me. Still I thought, "*I* am here, and I did not find it very difficult to get here either." . . .

AN INTERVIEW I slipped off my shoes, entered the room, and made my bow and "Peace be upon you," exchanged a few "Take-a-seats," "Don't-stirs," with the *molvi,* then subsided cross-legged on the floor opposite the woman. She evidently understood my real character, and it seemed a painful interview to her. We sat silently for some minutes, the motion of her hand to her eyes under the veil showing she was in tears.

At length the *molvi* spoke to her in Arabic, telling her to ask me some questions in English—as my name, age, country, employment—all of which I answered as I wished the *molvi* to believe; but when she asked, at his instance, how I came to Mecca, and I replied, "God put it into my head," which she interpreted, "God put it into his heart," I felt safe and talked more freely. After a time, by her advice, we talked in Hindi on general and safe topics of interest to us both. I found that she had been amongst Muslims since 1858 and satisfied myself, in the half-hour's conversation, that she was a real, educated Englishwoman. When she rose to go, I asked her in English if I might shake hands with her. She said: "No," and told me the part of the Haram in which she prayed, where I could meet her any day at noon. . . .

When I got home I found the Amir had suddenly made up his mind to start on a long-talked-of pilgrimage to Jerusalem in two days and that four of the party and myself were to be left to occupy the house till his return. . . . I never expected they would get away at all, and certainly they would not if they had waited till things were in order. However, camels had been engaged and came at the right time—nothing ready of course; still away they went, bundled everything handy onto the camels and started; found they had forgotten something, sent back for it; sent back for something else, and kept on sending back for things till they got too far away. One of the last things sent back for was the Amir's watch, a very valuable English gold one, which was found under the rug where he had been enjoying an opium sleep during the hubbub of the last two hours before starting. All my Hindi friends were addicted to opium and in any emergency used just to increase the dose a little and trust to Providence. . . .

A RENDEZVOUS During the last three days I had had no time to look for the Lady Venus, but the moment I was at liberty, I set out in quest of her. . . . Anyone familiar with the social habits of Muslims—the jealousy, conventional and affected, of the men and the formal restraint under which the women are held—will be surprised that I was able to walk in public with the lady without attracting notice in the way I did; but in Mecca the women are allowed great freedom. Many of the most ordinary precautions of the harem are relaxed, and it is quite the correct thing for the women of the wealthy to appear at public worship unattended, praying among the men, no part of the Haram being set apart for them as in every other mosque.

On the second day after the Amir's departure, I went to that part of the Haram she had mentioned as her place of prayer at noonday. . . . When the crowd had dispersed, I observed a little way off on my left a woman sitting alone. I thought this might be my friend and looked fixedly at her for a few minutes. She was evidently looking at me, and I thought I noticed a beckoning movement of the hands under her garments, so I rose and walked towards her. She then got up and went out of the Haram, and I followed her at a little distance. We had gone some quarter of a mile through the town in this way, she always looking back at me before turning a corner, when she stopped and let me come up to her. She at once addressed me in English, telling me to walk by her side and that we were going to a Hindi friend's, where we could talk undisturbedly as long as we liked.

Some two hundred yards farther on we passed through a narrow part of the street, where a Turkish sentry was posted; here she talked loudly in Arabic, and I answered her in the same, making a great display of such expressions as I was master of. Half an hour's walk brought us to a little shieling, into which we went and sat down. I found the old Hindi who dwelt in it very well disposed. He made tea, gave me a smoke of his hookah, excused himself, and left us to ourselves. What a talk we had! How we let loose our English tongues! Sometimes we laughed wildly, sometimes she cried. It must have been a strange pleasure to her to hear and talk her native language after so many years. I, who had only been a few weeks away from my kind, felt most foolishly elated, talked all kinds of nonsense, anything that came into my head, just for chattering's sake. We asked one another questions and asked others without waiting for answers.

We had three hours of this, and then the old Hindi came in, and we thought it time to be going. Before parting she raised her veil and showed me her face, which was as English as my own. We also shook hands and arranged that a boy Abdullah, a mutual acquaintance, should be our future means of communication. We then parted and went home by different roads. . . .

A REMINDER One day I was passing a large college on the outskirts of the town . . . when the students, about 150, of all ages from five to fifteen, were out playing. I stayed to look on at their various games, such as marbles —not unlike the English game, as far as I could see. One little group had an old pistol, snapping caps, and altogether I was much amused watching them when a little Hindi child near me shouted, "Oh, look at the Christian!" I shall never be able to guess what put it into that son of Iblis's head. Perhaps he had seen Englishmen in India and was struck with a fancied resemblance; or it may have been only for fun, though Eastern children are not generally given to unprovoked mischief. Up to this, nothing of the kind had happened to me, and as it was unexpected, it took me very much aback. It also collected all the young imps in the neighbourhood, who took up the cry; and one great hulking brute stepped up to me and said, in a blustering manner, "Christian dog, if you are a Muslim make the profession of your faith."

Now I am one of the most peacefully disposed of men. . . . "I would rather run a mile than fight a minute," yet all my life I have been getting dragged into fights. I suppose I must look like a fellow easily put upon, but I have a Bedawi aversion to dirt as an article of diet. This beggar riled me and I did not feel at all disposed to give an account of myself to him. No, I just took the fellow by the shoulders, turned him round, and administered a kick in the rear that must have made him see stars. Now, I do suppose I could not have perpetrated a more un-Islamic act. Instead of seizing the opportunity to deliver myself of profuse expressions of devotion and faith, as a Muslim does on the slightest provocation, I had offered to my very proper interrogator one of the greatest indignities possible to a Muslim—I had struck him with a shoe. It brought a yell of "Ya! Christian!" from its recipient, taken up by the whole crew. I had put my foot in it, had been taken off my guard, and now saw things could not be mended, so turned round and attempted to make a dignified retreat, when—*whirr!*—close past my ear flew a blue object (a pigeon I thought), but it lit a few feet ahead with a clatter that showed the kind of blue rock it was, and another followed, fetching me one on the skull, that would have settled the number of my mess but for the thickness of my too attractive headdress. These Meccan youths living, so to speak, on a stone heap, get, from constant practice, to be able to deliver a stone as straight and almost as hard as a pistol shot.

I looked round an instant and saw that the whole swarm had entered into the holy work of stoning a Christian to death, with a zeal worthy of first-century Jews. Stones were coming from all directions; I was getting some nasty blows and had to defend my face with my hands. My probable ignominious fate flashed across my mind—stoned to death by children, the disclosures that would follow, the example I should be held up as. Suddenly one on the knee and another in the small of the back brought me down; when up again I did not know which way to turn. A pretty little Arab child was struggling to heave a rock he could scarcely lift. I made a rush, seized the squalling brat in my arms, and a run up (rugby rules) of about twenty yards brought me to a long wall, to which I turned my back and held the kicking little wretch before me as a shield. This bewildered my tormentors for a moment; then on they came again, led on by my kicked friend to rescue young struggling Ibrahim, as I heard them call him.

Poor little Ibrahim! Even when torn nearly limb from limb, he looked a very pretty child, and I was sorry for him. The struggle was short and sharp; Ibrahim got terribly mauled, chiefly by his friends. I was somewhat of an old hand at a scrag and managed to keep from under the ruck, watched my chance, bolted off, and got about twenty yards' start before I was missed and the pack set out in full cry after me. A Turkish guardhouse was close at hand, into which I rushed, passed the sentry, and squatted down behind him out of breath, arms and legs aching with bruises, and completely blown; however, I was safe for the moment and had time to pull myself together for what had become a very serious affair. In the meantime a crowd of Arabs and Negroes were gathering outside and the word "a Christian!" was being passed, and the Turkish guards were giving me very black looks.

One of the soldiers went to bring an officer and returned in a minute or two with a young lieutenant, very spruce and civilised he looked; it was quite a relief to see him in his Paris-cut uniform. He came up to me and at once addressed me in French; but I had got myself all there by this time and artlessly replied, "I cannot speak Turkish," and proceeded on to declare that "Allah was great, all praise be to Allah! There is only one God, Muhammad is his Prophet," working myself up gradually till at last I rushed out of the guardhouse, saw an old friend—an Arab slave dealer, who in his negotiations with the Amir had smoked many of my cigarettes—seized his stick and went for the promising young crowd with "sons of burnt fathers" and a torrent of similar abuse. The men now all took my side, and the old slave dealer laughingly apologised for the excess of zeal in the rising generation, though he could not help admiring it, while even the Turkish sentry helped to disperse the boys with a parting stone, and the lieutenant showed me out into a back way by which I could go home without any chance of being further annoyed.

On my way home I strayed into a coffee shop to arrange my disordered robes, explaining that I had been thrown from my donkey which had bolted. After a smoke and a cup of coffee I began to feel a little more myself and limped off home, getting stiffer all the time from bruises about the back and limbs. I had luckily no marks on my face, so that I was able to lie down as soon as I got into the house without any awkward questions being asked. My chief fear now was that the affair would get noised abroad in quarters where it would lead to my having a visit paid me by some inquisitive gentlemen, whom I knew I should not be able to humbug, if once their suspicions were really aroused and they took to serious enquiries. . . .

To guard against this sort of thing I told my companions I was very sick (I really was in a good deal of pain), and that I would go and sleep in a little closet off the cooking room so as not to be disturbed by noise or visitors. Into this room about eight feet by four I moved my clothes and blankets and did not stir out of it till the Amir's return—about three weeks, during which there were many friendly enquiries for me. . . .

My assurance and indiscretion had all but done for me, and now I must appear to have gone to the other extreme. It was not so much caution kept me confined the whole time as the ball of opium, a small pill of which I took the first night and continued to take every day, increasing the dose as I found it affecting me. I only ate one meal a day, brought me by the [Amir's secretary] when he came to make up housekeeping accounts. He knew I was under opium and sympathised with me and could recommend nothing better, looking upon that drug as a specific for all maladies. I will not go into the "pains and pleasures of opium eating" more than to say the three weeks passed like three days. I was perfectly happy, everything appeared *couleur de rose*. . . .

OBSERVATIONS If, at this time, the congregation in the Haram had been shaken together, well mixed, and then one hundred taken out and analysed, different nationalities would have been found in about the following proportions:

Turks*	6
Arabs*	15
Hindis*	20
Malays*	5
Negroes*	10
Persians*	10
Maghribis*	15
Syrians*	6
Tartars	5
Bedawin	3
A nondescript rabble from China, the west coast of Africa, or Russia, and wild dervish-looking savages from God knows where	5
	100

*The[se] races . . . are mere general classifications and might be made subject to innumerable subdivisions, as under the head of Hindi I include all the Muslim races of India, and under the Turks, Maghribis, and Syrians, I have allowed the Egyptians to fall.

The settled Hindi population in Mecca, I was told, numbered thirty thousand. This may be an exaggeration, as my Arab informer would be likely to overrate the numbers to me, coming as I did from India. Still, the statement is possible, the Hindi element much exceeding, perhaps even doubling, the Arab, and the pilgrims from India almost equalling in number those from all other parts of the East, except the Bedawin and Arab population of the country round, which must be almost depopulated on the day of assembling at Arafat. Many Hindis are in official employ and hold lucrative, and a few even important, posts under the government. . . .

Blue-rock pigeons are to be seen here in large numbers such as are probably not to be met with elsewhere. I amused myself for some time by counting smaller flocks and comparing them with larger, so estimating the number to be seen at one time in the Haram, which could not have been less than between five and six thousand. They are so tame that they feed freely from the hand. The reason of this extreme fearlessness is that they are held to be almost sacred, more so than any other Meccan animal (unless, perhaps, the swallow). They are considered the property of the Haram, and are, I believe, never killed.* I have occasionally gone out into the Haram to feed these birds, after the manner of the pilgrims, who purchase baskets of mixed and damaged grain sold for the purpose. The moment you leave the pavement, you become the vortex of a revolving storm of pigeons, the air taking a leaden hue above and about you, while the view is completely obscured by the cloud of birds, and the grain is whisked out of your basket, and your clothes whirled about by the wind from their wings. The noise is deafening, and you are glad to empty your basket and escape. Or I have sometimes sat down in the middle of the turmoil and let the birds light on me and struggle over me, the ground for yards round paved two or three deep with their fluttering bodies; when the grain is finished, they disperse over the square or to the neighbouring bazaars. . . .

MECCA TO ARAFAT Friday, December 14, 1877, was the Day of Standing to Arafat. The pilgrimage coming off on Friday is called the Greater Pilgrimage and is attended by far greater numbers than in an ordinary year. On December 13, all the gathering of nations which had hitherto loaded almost to bursting the small valley of Mecca was shot out, discharged—I can give no better idea. In twenty-four hours this army of two hundred thousand strong, everyone his own general, everyone his own commissary, evacuated Mecca almost to a man, marched about eleven miles east, and camped on the Plain of Arafat, near Mount Arafat; this march must at least have been confused, but with every man doing his worst to make a rout of it (for it is intended to be figurative of Muhammad's flight from Mecca), confusion was no name for it. Our preparations had as usual been of the most casual and desultory character. The camels were at the door shortly after morning prayer, yet it was eleven o'clock before the tents, baggage, and provisions could be hurry-scurried together on to their backs. Some of the most important articles had been forgotten, such as water bottles, new pilgrim's garbs, etc., which had to be purchased at the last moment. . . . We mounted the camels at the door, and it took us two hours to get over the first mile through the streets, so closely were they thronged with camels; sometimes the *shugdufs* would get entangled and be torn nearly off; the inmates, if women, would scream and pray; if men, curse and pray, notwithstanding the guard which they are supposed to keep over their tongues on this so solemn an occasion;

*I heard no reason given for the special favour shown to these birds and suppose that they, sharing with all other Meccan creatures a common immunity from harm, have by their nature merely accommodated themselves in the way they have to the favourable circumstances.

and predominant over all rose the oft-repeated shrill Labayks, to which I added my quota of discordance, entering into the thing gleefully. In the narrow streets, the *shugdufs* would get jammed together, and no advance could be made for some minutes; but as the crush all tended in one direction, we were at last carried out of the town into the open roads and passed on with the current—one continuous stream of men and animals flowing out of Mecca towards Mina, a village some five miles east of Mecca, at which we arrived about 3:00 P.M. Two rooms had been engaged for us on the ground floor of a house near the middle of the village, facing the main road, passing through it to Arafat, and here we put up for the night. The road towards Mina had been a gradual ascent. We passed over one or two stone viaducts and some cuttings between the hills; altogether it was the best attempt at a made road I saw in the country. We also met with one or two reservoirs well supplied with water.

The village of Mina lies in a pass rather than a valley, some two or three hundred yards across and half a mile long, between two abrupt rocky ridges about two or three hundred feet in height. A good many low houses are built along the pass at the sides of the Arafat Road, which is about eighty feet wide. All along this street rows of provision, tea, or tobacco stalls had been set up, and the place for the time had become a fair. In one of the windows of our room I took up my post to watch the crowds passing in their uniform white dresses, for although the women do not wear the pilgrim's garb, they must dress in white. . . .

In the morning I did not get up till the stir of rolling up rugs and carpets awoke me. I found bright sunshine and the morning prayer long over. So taken up had my companions been with peacemaking and forgiving one another all grudges, as they were to be absolved from all past sins on that day, that I had been overlooked. So I said a great many "God-forgive-me's" with all due contrition and, after my ablution and prayer, joined in the general reconciliation that was going on. We fell on one another's necks, recalled and confessed all little petty offences one to another, certain of being forgiven in tears. I at first relied on my imagination for items, but my companions soon reminded me of numbers of ways in which I had offended them unconsciously or otherwise. They seemed sincere though and made very clean breasts of it themselves. I found where numbers of little articles had gone that I had missed from my bundle. This one had appropriated a penknife, another a pair of socks. I, of course, gave and forgave with the best grace possible. We were now supposed to be at peace with all the world of true believers and might with clear consciences appear at Arafat. Though the crowds had been pressing past all night, their numbers did not seem in the least diminished.

I remember feeling very uncomfortable on that morning, the morning of the day on which I was to acquire the honoured title of hajji and witness a scene which it is given to few Europeans to see (probably not more than one in a generation). I felt a sort of depression, as though I required to be brought up to the sticking point. Perhaps I had not quite got over the opium. I tried to wear this off by extra exertion in assisting at loading the camels; and while passing to and fro from the house, with bundles of gear, I twice fancied a woman in the yard tried to attract my attention, and the next time I passed I heard her pronounce my name. The Lady Venus at once dawned on me. I had been living in such stirring times lately that she had quite escaped my memory, and you may be sure my "Peace be upon you!" and "God be praised!" came from the bottom of my heart when she now appeared on the scene so opportunely. She told me that she was staying in the same house as myself, with a lady friend, who was treating her to a seat on a camel for the pilgrimage. She also said the boy Abdullah had been twice to my house in Mecca to inquire for me but had been told that I was gone to Jidda. We had not much opportunity to talk, but I hastily got her to give me a programme of the forthcoming events of the next three days, and we agreed to meet in the Haram on that day week. Coarse remarks soon began to be made by the men standing about, and we were obliged to part quickly. . . .

About 11:00 A.M. we reached the Plain of Arafat, a large sandy open, appearing to be somewhat below the level of the approach and occupying an area of some four or five square miles. In the northeast of the plain is Mount Arafat, a small hill, about two hundred feet high, composed of large masses of grey granite, at the base of quite a respectable little mountain, the Mount of Mercy.

We pitched our tents (one for the Amir and men, another for the Begum and women) about a third of a mile south of this hill. As soon as this work was completed, I took good bearings, marked the tents well, and went off alone to the top of Mount Arafat. The scene from here was—I shall not be surprised if it flits across my mind on my deathbed. The depression of the plain gives an amphitheatre-like appearance, and you could almost believe yourself on the stage of some mighty theatre, miles of audience before you and the sombre scenery of the black Mount of Mercy behind you. What a time and place for a sermon! We had all come out into the wilderness to hear a sermon on this day, and I had determined to hear it, so sat down on the hill to wait till noon, when the Lady Venus had told me it would begin.

As I looked down on the great throng, a grey rippling sea of black heads and white bodies extending from the sides of the hill, thickly clothed with men to a mile and a half off on the south and half a mile across, and remembered the distant countries from which they came and what brought them, it was impossible to help a feeling almost of awe. It set one thinking. Could all this be of no avail and all this faith be in vain? If so, it was enough to make a man lose faith in everything of the kind.

At noon I left my post on the top of the hill and pressed my way about to try and find where the preacher would stand and see what was to be seen. The practice among the pilgrims seemed to be to come up on the hill, say one or two prayers, remain a quarter of an hour or so, and return to the plain. At noon there was no general call to prayer, the pilgrims praying in parties near their tents and judging the hour for themselves. I said no noonday prayer myself, but spent the afternoon looking about on Mount Arafat.

On the top there is a small colonnade, an obelisk about fifteen feet high, and some low stone walls separating one little irregularity of the surface of the rock from another. Inside and outside these enclosures, and, in fact, all over the hill, the crowd was so great that it was very difficult to get from one place to another, even by climbing walls and jumping from rock to rock. On the sides of the hill are a number of platforms, built up or hewn out of the rock, and a winding road, cut from the bottom to the top, much of which is composed of steps in the rock. At the bottom of the hill is a gravelled terrace forming a road between the hill and a large reservoir of water at its base, and there is another of these built "tanks" (as they are called in India) about one hundred yards south of the first. The sides of both these tanks were occupied the whole day by pilgrims performing the "lesser" ablution. I only saw one man enter the water bodily, and he slipped off the stone edge, I think, as I noticed those near him laughing. Though I stayed on or about the hill until nearly time for afternoon prayer, I heard no sermon, saw no preacher, unless a very old and dirty Arab, not in pilgrim's garb, sitting with his legs across the top of a six-foot wall, haranguing the crowd in a voice that could not be heard ten yards off, was the orator we had all come so far to hear; but this I doubt. The probability is, seeing the crowd and noise was so great, the mufti and his sermon escaped me. . . .

RETURNING TO MECCA FROM ARAFAT It was piercingly cold next morning, and about two hours before daylight we started for Mina, being among the first of the great mass to get there. I said my morning prayer at Mina, using warm water for the ablution, and went off immediately after to Mecca on a donkey, in company with the boy Jack,* as I was anxious to reach the town, which had before been such a scene of life and bustle, in the deserted state I knew it would then be. There was nothing out of the way in this, and my haste to go before the morning meal was only put down to a little superfluous religious zeal, it being the proper thing to go into Mecca as soon as possible after the pilgrimage and perform the same rites as on your first arrival at the Holy City, discarding the pilgrim's garb.

The road to Mecca was not yet thronged by returning pilgrims, and the few who were on foot so early we soon passed on our donkeys, reaching Mecca shortly after sunrise. On the outskirts of the town a few coffee shops had already been opened, and we passed two or three groups of Bedawi and Negroes; but as we came more into the town, the streets were entirely deserted, not a living soul to be seen, all the shops being shut up and the house doors and windows closed. It had a most strange aspect, after the appearance which I had been accustomed to for months. As we approached the Haram, we came upon some beggars sitting and lying at the roadside, who had been in extremis or too feeble to join the pilgrimage: such as were alive, for some were actually dead, greeted us most piteously, imploring us for food—and a hungry time they must have had of it. It was not so with the dogs, as they had been making horribly free with the legs of the defunct. I soon got rid of a handkerchief of bread and dates I had brought as a snack for myself and prolonged the existence of one or two exhausted wretches. One of these held our donkeys while we went into the Haram.

I found only a party of half a dozen Maghribis who had returned straight from Arafat during the night and who were the only pilgrims that had been beforehand with me. Some of the Arabs who officiate in the Haram, and who had remained behind to change the cover of the Ka'ba, which is renewed at this time yearly, were giving the finishing touches to their work. This cover is sent from Cairo and is supposed to be made there by seven hundred virgins. After our prayers and *tawaf,* we did *sa'y* on our donkeys, which is allowable to the weak, and we easily reconciled it to our consciences, seeing we had made such haste to do it and might be supposed to be at least very tired. After this we roamed about the dismal streets, letting our animals go as they willed. There was a kind of fascination about the lonely, lifeless lanes and passages lately so thronged, and my companion seemed to share the feeling with me, for he made the original remark, which I quote from him and not anyone else: "It is like a city of the dead." While going along a

*Jack: a member of the Hindi Amir's suite, to whom Keane gives an English nickname.

narrow out-of-the-way passage I had not before been in, I came across an object that nearly brought me off my beast. Overhead, projecting straight out over the lane was a large black board, and painted on it in yellow these letters—LODGINGS. . . .

"Jack," I said, "let's go back." I felt as if I had seen a ghost. However, I recovered the shock sufficiently to note the locality for future investigation and returned thoughtful and meditative along the road, now thronged with returning pilgrims, to our headquarters for the time at Mina. When I got back, I was glad to get out of the pilgrim's garb, which I had found very inadequate against the cold of the night and the sun in the day, which struck painfully on my bare shaven head. . . .

AFTER THE PILGRIMAGE On the fourth day after the pilgrimage we returned to our old quarters in the walls of the Haram, and next day early I set out to look for LODGINGS. As I wended my way among turbaned and scimitared Syrians, Parthians, Moghuls, and Arabians, I began to think it must have been a dream, and when I came to the place and saw the veritable notice, I was almost as much surprised as on my first meeting it. There was a little tobacco shop opposite the house, to which I went and began making small purchases, getting up a dispute about the change of a rupee, at the same time taking stock of the premises opposite, for I fought rather shy of the place. I had just come to an amicable conclusion about my change, purposely making a mistake on the right side for the shopkeeper to put him in a good humour, and was asking him who lived in the house over the way, when a tall heavily-built man, whom I at first took for a fair-skinned Arab, slouched out of the door and came straight over to the shop, whistling merrily. That was enough.

"Good morning," said I.

"Well, I be d——. Do you speak English?"

"Yes."

"Good morning."

We stood for some moments looking at one another, and I thought I had taken the fellow's measure to be the right sort and was just on the point of opening out and declaring myself when he said:

"You are not an Englishman, are you?" with a gravity that gave me my cue.

I replied in the vilest Che-che* I could muster, "Oh yes, I am Englishman. I am speaking the English very well."

*Che-che: Anglo-Indian patois. [Ed.]

This and a happy unconscious air banished any suspicions of such a possibility he might have had for the moment. Though he said, "English-men turn Muslim and come here and see what we do and go back and write books. There are three here now with iron collars round their necks chained among the hills."

I did not tell him I thought that was a lie. He walked about with me the greater part of the morning, I talking broken English to him. He was a Cape of Good Hope Malay, one of an English-speaking Muhammadan community, who yearly send their half dozen pilgrims to Mecca. He had been living some years in Mecca, and said his people had been very ill treated when they began to come [on] the pilgrimage. The authorities had only allowed them to live in Mecca on condition that they spoke no other language than Arabic, of which few of them knew the meaning of more than a dozen words. If an Arab had heard them speaking any other language, he was at liberty to beat them, and they dared not retaliate. This was in the days of a strict old pasha of the good old school, who had administered the law of the Quran to the letter.

In evidence of this he pointed out to me what a number of beggars were to be seen minus a hand or a foot, the result of the said old pasha's summary justice. This lopping off of limbs is a great idea, by degrees practically incapacitating the old offender. However, such severity is seldom resorted to under the present milder regime. The Cape Malays have now outlived all prejudice, and my new friend told me that he was very comfortable in Mecca and making money. He had in his youth been to an English school, could read and write English well, and he confessed he missed his beer and potatoes. . . .

ANOTHER RENDEZVOUS Then came my meeting with the Lady Venus. This time we had arranged that she should, after the noonday prayer, walk backwards and forwards in the arcade under my window, where I was to sit and look out till we recognised one another. This was easily managed, and I went off under her guidance. The crowd was so great that we were able to keep close together without appearing to be in company till near the shop of a Hindi binder of Qurans, where she told me to wait while she went in. After waiting a few minutes, a little child came up to me and invited me into the shop, leading me through to a small room at the back, where I found her sitting alone: the child then left us to ourselves. We talked for a short time about our lucky meeting at Mina, about her health, which had been very bad during the last year, almost as bad as on her first coming to Mecca many years ago (I think she said twenty). She threw her veil back and exposed her face for some time—a scandalous impropriety which, if witnessed by anyone, the least I could have done would have been to declare her my wife or near relation on the spot. I had time to observe her features closely. She was rather short and appeared about forty. She must have been good-looking in her youth, nor was she by any means ill favoured now. She looked healthy, all things considered. Though her complexion was somewhat sallow, her skin was fair. She had an animated and pleasing expression. I can at this moment see her in my mind as distinctly as if she were before me in the flesh—the same sad, indulgent smile with which she greeted my little attempts at Anglo-Arabic jokes, saying: "Speak English, child."

I really felt the deepest pity for her, an Englishwoman existing in the way she had been doing for years, and I must confess to a very soft moment when I saw the poor creature smiling, with her eyes brimful of tears, before giving way and having a good cry, which relieved her. I had found in our very first tête-à-tête that any reference to her past had a painful effect and hesitated to broach the subject and so began to tell her about myself, my Christian name, why I had come to Mecca, and the like, in the hope of getting her to give some such account of herself, when a noise outside made her draw her veil, and a boy entered with some tea and sweetmeats sent by her friend, the master of the house. This took our attention for the moment, and we both had tea, and I asked the boy to get me a smoke: first, because I wanted a smoke; secondly, because when I had done, returning the hookah would be a good excuse for going out of the room and having a look round. This little interruption over, I asked her if she knew the Cape people. She said she had made friends with some of their women a year or two before and had sent letters by them to the Cape to a relation whom she had seen there on her way out to India and whose address she remembered, but had heard nothing of it since.

Having brought her to talk about herself, I now kept her at it and pumped her as dry as I could, but it was very hard work. As well as my memory serves me, she told me that her name was Macintosh, her father a doctor, and that she had lived in Devonshire in her youth, that she was at Lucknow at the time of the siege,* and had been taken from there by a leading rebel. She avoided going into particulars, so that I did not ascertain whether she went willingly or as a captive. She said she had lived a year or so in India with this man and that he had been hunted out of the country by the English, who set a price on his head, and had found refuge in Mecca,

*When the Indian Mutiny broke out in 1857, Lucknow's European community was besieged for several months, until rescued by British troops. [Ed.]

taking her with him, that he had died eight years before, leaving her in poverty, and that she now made a living by embroidering skullcaps, which she sold to the dealers in the bazaars.

A rich Hindi merchant, who occasionally received letters written in English from his son, who was managing his business for him in India and knew that he could get them translated by her, gave her a little room in his harem-house to herself. All this I got from her only in replies to my persistent questioning, till at last I was obliged to desist out of pure compassion, she seemed so cowed and bullied and was getting quite incoherent. After this I got her to repeat a few chapters of the Quran, pretending I wanted to learn the Mecca accent, so interesting her. I found, besides Hindustani, she could speak and read Persian and Arabic, though not Turkish. She regretted she was not in a position to be acquainted with any Turks, for whom she seemed to have some respect. She mentioned the names of a number of men living in Mecca who she said had been rebels or mutineers, also telling me the prices set on their heads by the English government, and appeared perfectly up in everything connected with the siege and relief of Lucknow. She also let drop that a young Frenchman had lived eighteen months in Mecca, and had died about six months before my arrival. . . .

FLASH FLOOD I think it was on the eighth day after the pilgrimage that the inundation occurred. Such a flood had not visited Mecca for seventeen years, on which occasion the water had risen seven feet in the Haram. This time the day opened very black indeed to the eastward, the clouds having a sandy, smoky appearance I had noticed before on one or two occasions when it had been followed by a heavy downpour of rain. These black days were very marked as a great and sudden change from the usual blue clearness of the sky. It did not begin to rain in Mecca till about 11:00 A.M., though it must have been raining for some time towards Mina and Arafat, for the stream from there into the valley of Mecca had overflowed, and already the streets at the east end and in the centre of the city were flooded with several inches of water. Still no serious inundation was anticipated, the flooding of the streets being the usual result of an ordinary shower, and the stalls in the bazaars stood at the sides of streets, down the centre of which people were wading in little torrents.

As soon as it began to rain, I returned to the house and saw through the window that it shortly after set in to blow hard from the east, accompanied by heavy tropical rain—not exceptionally heavy for the tropics, but much harder than would be likely [here]. As the rain continued, all our people and a number of friends not belonging to our party, dripping wet, came in for shelter and filled our two rooms. In the Haram a few inches of water quickly gathered, and the attendants were employed, as I had often seen them before, in keeping the pavement round the Ka'ba clear by sweeping the water down large holes in the pavement.

Another hour, and the rain still continued to come down as hard as ever, the wind blowing half a hurricane, flapping and bellying out the cover of the Ka'ba as though it would blow it away, which it certainly would have done had it not been new. At this time the Amir sent some of his underservants out to try and get a little of the water that flowed off the Ka'ba for us to drink, and as they went in and out, they told us that the water was rising rapidly in the streets and shortly afterwards came in and said it would soon be flowing into the Haram.

Some of us went out to see, I among the rest. The water had risen so suddenly and unexpectedly that there had been no time for the most ordinary precautions. Those who had seen it said it had come in like a wave from the direction of Mina; if so, and it had passed over the scene of the late slaughter, it must now be simply a poisoned flood. It was now flowing in turbid muddy streams, three or four feet deep, down all the streets.

Across every entrance to the Haram there is a raised stone parapet, apparently built for the purpose of keeping the water out during these floods. I took my stand on one of these and watched the strong steady stream flowing past laden with the floating wreck of the bazaars, cages of fowls, all kinds of fruit, flocks of bread loaves, empty baskets, the legs and tops of wooden stalls, dogs swimming about and being forced whining back wherever they attempted to land, Negroes and Arabs standing in the stream, seizing whatever was best worth picking up as it floated past.

Most of the shops were already flooded, and the water had risen so quickly that there had not been time to remove much of the stock, which was being floated out into the stream, the owners piling it back manfully. Such of the shops as were not already flooded were crowded by as many as could find standing room, as were all steps and isolated dry points.

The depth and strength of the stream continued to increase visibly, and it became a business of swimming for those who plunged in after salvage. The flood had not yet reached the Haram, where thousands had taken refuge and shelter under the arcades, but in a few minutes the water trickled under our feet down into the Haram behind us. The larger gates of the Haram were now shut, but these had little doors in them which were left open till the rush of water became so strong that it was found impossible to close some of them. This was about noon. I then went into the house out of the storm, put on dry clothes, and spent the rest of the day looking out of the window.

The rain showed no signs of easing, and the wind continued to blow with great violence, and in the same direction. The water was rushing into the Haram at every gate, the badly made and loosely jointed doors scarcely offering any obstruction and merely filtering it of the coarser debris. At this time a sailor might have described the Haram as taking in green seas fore and aft, except that the water was bright pea-soup colour.

About 2:00 P.M. the wind suddenly shifted to the west, taking the cover of the Ka'ba "flat aback," only giving it time for a couple of tremendous flaps and bangs before it settled into fluttering and bellying in the opposite direction. It continued to rain and the water to flow in until about 3:00 P.M., when the wind fell away with a few parting gusts, and the rain took off with one or two parting gushes of large drops.

After this, the water ceased to rise in the Haram and stopped flowing in from the outside very quickly. During the whole storm pilgrims had been performing the *tawaf* and kissing the Black Stone in greater numbers than usual at this time of day, and now, when the water was at its highest and the Black Stone immersed, many continued to swim round the Ka'ba and put their heads under to kiss the Stone. The temperature throughout the storm was uniformly cool, though not more than normally so, and it only remained overcast until sunset, the storm passing away to the north.

The whole of the large square was now turned into a lake, the water lying about three feet deep in the western arcades, six feet round the Ka'ba, and a few inches in the eastern arcades, showing that though the square looked a plain when dry, it was considerably inclined in these directions. There was great rejoicing among us when the water ceased to rise, for it was beginning to be feared that it would put out the lamps as it had done in the last great flood; and this is looked upon as unfortunate or ominous in some way. The water subsided almost as quickly as it had risen; by the time of sunset prayer it had retreated from the arcades on the three higher sides of the square, and at the evening prayer (9:00 P.M.) there remained only a couple of feet of water near the Ka'ba, and the arcades were left dry all round. . . .

THREE EPIDEMICS For many days after the flood the water in all the wells was brown and muddy and if left standing all night would not be more than half-settled in the morning. The taste of all the wells was altered, the ordinary water tasting like Zamzam, and the Zamzam itself much weakened. For a couple of days there was some moisture in the air, and bread left on a shelf uncovered for a few hours did *not* appear to have undergone a second baking and have a metallic ring from hardness. The worst result of the flood was the great amount of sickness that prevailed after it; cholera, smallpox, and typhus epidemics broke out and raged wildly together for about three weeks.

Muslim burial rites differ a good deal in different countries and of course vary with circumstances—from the dancing howling wakes of Egypt and Syria to the mere laying of the body straight and placing a few stones over it in the desert. In Mecca it is usual to take the bier to a part of the Haram near Abraham's Station, so that the soul may pass out of it through the door of the Ka'ba, and the noonday prayer is recited by the imam before interment of the body under a few bushes and a couple of feet of earth, with its face towards the Ka'ba. A coffin is never used by Muslims, though voluminous swathings and wrappings are, the graveclothes being sometimes made of fine material, white being the common mourning colour.

Within three days after the flood I noticed the number of funerals increasing; and at one time, about ten days after, the quantity passing through the Haram was so great as to form almost a continuous procession for an hour before noon. One day I counted sixty-three funerals.

No idea can be formed from this of the number of deaths which really occurred daily, as probably by far the greater majority of those who died had no friends or were not thought worth the trouble of carrying to the Ka'ba on the way to the burial ground. Men in the agonies of cholera might frequently be seen lying at the sides of the streets, and never a good Samaritan went near them. Smallpox and typhus cases, in all stages of the diseases, walked about in public, almost arm in arm, no one avoiding or seeming to think it the least out of the way. In one house I visited there were eight smallpox cases down at the same time, of which five died, and yet five other healthy men continued to eat and sleep in the same room!

If there is any foundation at all for our English notion about contagion, how Mecca escaped decimation does seem a miracle. Somehow I did not apprehend anything myself; I don't know why exactly, but I had not the slightest fear, though I certainly expected some of our party to be laid up, so many of us being crowded into the two rooms, which had become revoltingly filthy. Still, though we moved about amidst infected localities and among infected people in the most reckless manner, none of us were taken seriously ill. This was attributed to the Amir's energetic precautions, he having, regardless of expense, provided his whole household with a new and infallible charm. I wore mine round my neck till it got entangled with my beads, so I broke the string and threw it away, first opening it out to see what it was made of. It was a ball of bees' wax, about the size of a number 12 bullet, with a little pellet of paper inside on which something had been written; but it was now so crumpled and torn I could make nothing of it.

The run on the graveyards soon began to take the pilgrims off, and the town was getting less crowded, the pilgrims leaving by thousands; and we now began to make our preparations for starting with the first caravan to Medina.

12

Mohammad Hosayn farahani
Persia
1885—86

The helpless Iranian traveler is confused: What should he do? Where should he go? To which gang should he entrust himself? How can he renounce his baggage, clothes, food, and drink? How can he bear this amount of customs duties? How can he take refuge from these Russian thieves and Iranian swindlers? On whom can he rely? How can he flee?

—Mohammad Farahani

In contrast to the work of Keane or Burton, Mohammad Farahani's long, precise account of a Hajj from Persia is not a story of adventure. Nor does it focus on the author or even on the Hajj itself so much as on the regions crossed to reach Mecca from Tehran. The point of this account is fairly simple: to provide contemporary Persian pilgrims all the latest details necessary to travel safely through a radically transformed portion of the world. While the passages here do not pertain to Mecca, they appear in this collection because they provide a valuable view of Hajj travel as it entered modern times. A scholarly bureaucrat, Farahani wrote of Hajj travel as it was entering the machine age. He labored to acquaint Persian-speaking pilgrims with rail and steamer transport, and he sought to shed light on new Hajj routes, too, across western Asia to the Hijaz. Along the way, he educates them in that major development, the quarantine station, together with new international health standards recently adopted to combat decades of pilgrim epidemics. The themes Farahani opens up spread through most of the subsequent Hajj accounts.

Rail and steam combined during this period to make the journey from Asia to the Hijaz shorter, safer, and less costly than ever before. By 1870, India, Afghanistan, parts of the Caspian region, and the Caucasus were linked by rail. Meanwhile, at the western terminus of the great Hajj routes, the Suez Canal and Turkish and British steamships began providing pilgrims access to Jidda on a near mass-transit scale. By the time Farahani set out from Tehran, in 1885, the Black and Red Seas were in close communication. Although he traveled overland, it is by a very different route from that of the traditional Damascus or Baghdad caravans. (See Fig. 13.) After a coach ride to Qazvin, he conducts us on horseback (and later by steamer) to the railhead at Baku. There, in the social and moral free-for-all of an oil-boom Russian city, many Persian pilgrims received their first distressing blast of culture shock. Not since Ibn Jubayr, in the 1180s, had such numbers of hajjis been exposed to Christian lands on the way to Mecca.

On one level, Farahani's book is an effort to demystify new scenes for first-time pilgrims. On another, it serves as a vast collection of warnings about the journey. In addition to the traditional chasm between Russian Orthodox and Persian Shi'ite societies, thieves, con men, greedy customs agents, corrupt quarantine officers, rich camel brokers, and self-serving guides all pass under the wary eye of this author. At times, the entire stretch of land and sea between Tehran and Mecca seems peopled by nothing but innocent hajjis and a multitude of officials in charge of fleecing and plundering them—when, that is, the debauched wildcatters of Baku are not at work outraging their sense of decorum. In later excerpts, we see that Persian officials could, of course, be scoundrels, too.

The nineteenth century provided hajjis at least one danger more chilling than corruption. Cholera first occurred in Mecca in 1831, introduced by infected pilgrims from British India. Although a quarantine board was immediately established, the disease continued west. By 1845, it threatened Europe. As a result, the French attached médecins sanitaires *to their Near Eastern consulates. The Ottoman states and Britain responded too, and a first international conference on the disease was held in Paris in 1851. Despite these early precautions, a major epidemic swept Mecca in 1865, introduced by pilgrim ships from the Dutch East Indies. Fifteen thousand hajjis died in June. Sixty thousand more perished in Egypt; then the disease entered Europe through Marseilles. In November, cholera was reported in New York. Even at the time, these epidemics were correctly ascribed to the added speed and cramped conditions of steamships.* The slow-paced, open-air caravans, by contrast, made of the desert a natural quarantine.*

After the scourge of 1865, large, more efficient centers were rapidly set up at key points bordering the Hijaz, and pilgrims were made to pass through them coming and going. Here signs of the disease could be discovered, pilgrims and their baggage disinfected, then isolated for up to fifteen days while the disease ran its course. Health certificates were also required of every pilgrim entering Egypt from the Red Sea, and all ships submitted to inspection at Suez. In spite of

---

*Britain's rejection of widely agreed upon controls on the Hajj transport industry was another important cause of continued epidemics.

these efforts, John Keane was still recording epidemics at Mecca a decade later. For years to come, the system remained subject to corruption, as we shall see. On another tack, many pious Muslims resented what they saw as interference from the West, wrapping the Hajj in yet another layer of paperwork and ruined schedules. Despite much noncooperation, the huge effort gradually succeeded. After 1912, epidemic cholera vanished for good from the Hijaz, partly due to passport requirements, partly to the required show of sufficient cash to make the journey, and partly to fumigation and quarantine.

Farahani's descriptions of the quarantine sights are the first attempt in the literature to introduce Muslim pilgrims to modern hygiene. He addressed the reverse of the hygiene question, too: what happens when the non-Muslim world is not clean enough for pilgrims? By 1880, large numbers of Persian hajjis were traveling outside the borders of Islam for the first time. Without the protection of Islamic law, they felt exposed. Whereas Western nations were mainly preoccupied with bacterial contaminants, Muslims had their own concerns about purity. Clean water was crucial: to pray five times a day can require two or three ritual washings and the occasional bath or shower. Proper food, prepared according to Muslim law, was another concern. Farahani proved a reformer in most of these matters. He felt that Islamic law should guide, not obstruct, Hajj travel, and he did not shy from saying so in print.

Farahani wanted to offer useful, clearly stated information at a time when for many pilgrims the world seemed to be turning upside down. Religious interpretation was only one aspect of the problem. He unravels complex visa problems too, gives accurate distances between train stations, depicts each port precisely, and notes down necessary facts about climate, diet, architecture, currency, social customs, hostels, and market prices. Farahani traveled twice through the Suez Canal, minutely describing the ways in which its procedures affected pilgrims, and he clearly described the almost Kafkaesque quarantine stations at Tur and Sinai. By doubling back on the same itinerary, he was also able to register important differences as timetables changed and seasons varied. The result is a Guide Michelin *for the round-trip Persian Hajj, starting by coach from Tehran to Enzeli, thence by ship and train to Istanbul, down the Aegean to Alexandria, and through the Suez Canal to the Hijaz.*

Mohammad Farahani was a quick, accurate judge of human behavior, and he knew the value of an anecdote. As we read him today, his meticulous book provides keys to the Hajj in the first stage of a radical transition. Farahani was a thoroughly modern pilgrim; the only camel he rode on his three-thousand-mile journey was one that carried him from Jidda into the Hijaz. Although the world he described has largely vanished, its outlines seem strangely familiar even now.

from *A Shi'ite Pilgrimage to Mecca*, 1885 — 86:
by
Mirza Mohammad Hosayn Farahani

INTRODUCTION One of the manners and customs of our contemporaries is that for the sake of full and excellent style, even if they only have some trifling subject, they write so much prefatory matter that the subject disappears from view. A brief speech does not justify a lengthy prologue, and it is not necessary to have two thousand lines of preface for a book of a thousand lines. "Get to the point and leave the preliminaries behind." Modesty has thus induced this devoted servant, Mohammad Hosayn ol-Hosayni ol-Farahani, to write this short, simple preface during the reign of the august *Naser od-Din Shah*,* may God perpetuate his kingdom and his rule.

The idea of visiting the House of God occurred to me, so I brought up this matter with a wise mentor. He said concerning this point, "If you display any selfishness or circumspection, it will not be possible to attain such bliss."

I took to heart the saying "the lightly burdened shall be saved" and recalled that "unencumbered people travel quicker." I entrusted myself to God and determined to travel all alone.

Thus I started toward my goal with the blessing of the beloved king [Naser od-Din Shah]. . . .

DEPARTURE FROM TEHRAN Thursday evening, 16 July 1885, I went to the *tarantass* station and, three hours after nightfall, took a seat in a *tarantass* and departed. As for the fare of the coach, the livery has several classes of transport for passengers; the fare for each varies. One is for the *tarantass*,

The following excerpts maintain the Persian spellings from the 1990 American edition of Farahani's book, edited, translated, and annotated by Hafez Farmayan and Elton L. Daniel. Diacritical marks have been omitted. The footnotes, selected and on occasion simplified by the present editor, come from Farmayan-Daniel's edition. They are not Farahani's. [Ed.]

*Naser od-Din: The Shah of Iran from 1848 until his assassination in 1896; the Qajar Dynasty to which he belonged ruled Iran from 1786 to 1925. There is as yet no good biography of Naser od-Din. . . .

which has a folding top but does not have spring mountings or room for more than three people. The fare for the *tarantass* from Tehran to Qazvin, less the horse, is three *toman*s.* Another [vehicle for rent] is known as the troika, which does not have the folding top or springs and which seats three people. The fare for it, without the horse, is two *toman*s. Another [vehicle] is the droshky, which has a folding top, spring mountings, and room for three people. The fare for the droshky from Tehran to Qazvin, without the horse, is five *toman*s. Another is the calash, which has a folding top, springs, and seats four people. The fare for it to Qazvin is six *toman*s. Another is the diligence, which has springs, is covered over, resembles the droshky, and seats ten people. The fare for it, without the horse, from Tehran to Qazvin is ten *toman*s. . . .

GUARDHOUSES ON THE WAY   It is twenty-four *farsakh*s† from Tehran to Qazvin. Five guesthouses have been built along the way. The horses are changed at each place. It is four *farsakh*s from each guesthouse to the next. Three guard-houses have been erected between each of the guesthouses, so that there is a guardhouse every *farsakh*. The building for the guardhouse is also of neces-sity the home for the custodian. Some of the custodians have brought their wives and children to the guardhouses and live there. Others live alone. At each guardhouse which has running water near it, the custodians have planted tasteful flower beds, trees, and little gardens in front. . . . The guardhouses which do not have [running] water nearby have had wells dug beside them. The telegraph also has lines strung along the road by the stations.

BAKU, JULY 29   This city has very little water and very few trees. . . . In some of the houses are found a few flowers such as geraniums, storksbill, and evening stock. The climate is humid because of the proximity to the sea. It is not possible to sleep outdoors. Nevertheless, its soil is very dry and has no moisture because of the oil in the vicinity. The curious thing about this is that the people of Baku, despite their water and climate, are very plump and

---

toman: The toman (*towman*) was a coin, usually gold, first introduced in the Mongol period as the equivalent of ten thousand dinars; here, it is equal to ten silver *kran*s. The *kran* was . . . equal to twenty copper *shahi*s (about eight cents).

†*farsakh:* A traditional unit for measuring distance; since it reflected a distance one could travel in a fixed period of time, the actual length varied from 2.3 to 4.2 miles (3.7 to 6.7 kilometers). It is more or less synonymous with the *farsang* (or parasang in common English usage).

fair and in good physical condition. One of the customs of the people is that they eat [only] one meal a day. Their regular meal is confined to lunch. They do not eat dinner at night. They are awake most of the night visiting with each other.

OIL WELLS   On the outskirts of the city as far as the village of Balakhaneh, which is two *farsakh*s from the city, there are many oil wells, a few of which are state owned but most of which are privately owned. The main commerce in Baku now is the trade in oil which goes to Iran, Europe, and the Ottoman Empire. There are many people who for years have dug wells on their own and labored and have not yet struck oil and have suffered severe losses in the enterprise.* Usually those wells are dug down about eight *zar*ᶜ† where they strike oil. After striking oil, they set up canals and tanks near the well so that as soon as oil is struck, it gushes up all at once, comes out of the well, empties into the canals, and flows into the tanks. They take it out of those tanks, allow it to settle, and refine it in the factories. After the purification and refining, a third of it becomes kerosene [suitable] for burning and is sent to the provinces. The other two thirds are burned in place of coal in the ships and factories in that immediate area. The principle oil field is in Balakhaneh, where many factories have been built. Every day fifteen thousand poods‡ of oil are conveyed from there to the city. They also refine crude oil there and make kerosene.

ANCIENT FIRE TEMPLE IN THE VILLAGE OF SORAKHANI   Three *farsakh*s to the northeast of the city there is a village named Sorakhani where there has been a fire temple since ancient times. Some Zoroastrians and Hindus still come on pilgrimage there. Several Indians are always staying in this village. The fire temple is in the shape of an open square building in the middle of which there is a pit from which the fire comes out. There are chambers around it with a small opening between each chamber and the pit. There is a covering over the openings; whenever they want, they open the covering of the opening, touch a lighted match to the opening, and at once the gas is ignited like

---

*The extensive petroleum resources of the Baku area were known and exploited even in antiquity; the first modern drilling for oil there occurred in 1842. The industry had been opened up to private enterprise in 1872; this, plus the completion of the railway link in 1883, resulted in a considerable boom in prosperity for Baku. . . .

†*zar*ᶜ: a measurement of length equal to forty-one inches.

‡pood: a Russian unit of weight equal to about thirty-six pounds.

a lamp. It is the same everywhere in this village. Anyplace they want to ignite a fire, they dig down into the earth to a depth of one quarter to half a *zar‘*. They put an external flame, such as a match, to the dug-up earth and at once it is kindled and blazes like a fire. However, its heat is not very great. It has no smoke. It cannot be extinguished with water, but if a little earth is poured on it, it is extinguished. Sometimes the fire is ignited spontaneously without the ground being dug up or disturbed. If [people] want to take the fire to another spot, they place a leather bag opposite the excavated earth. When the bag is full of gas, they stop it up and move it. Anywhere a fire is needed, they put an iron pipe on the tip of the bag, touch an external flame to the tip of the pipe, and the end of the pipe is ignited and gives off light in the manner of a gas lamp. As long as there is some of that gas in the bag, it is lighted; after that, it will go out. In this village of Sorakhani, factories have also been set up for refining oil [using] the natural [gas] fire from the earth. There is also an oil field in the midst of the sea. . . .

ADMINISTRATION Most of the government employees in Baku are Russians. Outwardly, they act in such a way that everything [seems] completely orderly and free and no one bothers anyone else. But in actuality it can be said that it is utterly without order, and no one is secure in life, property, or his own affairs. One cannot spend a tranquil night in one's own home. There are many criminals, and few nights go by that there are not robberies in homes and [on] the streets or two or three people are not killed. If someone wants to travel by night from one quarter to another, he must first of all be [in the company of] five or six people—one or two people would not dare to go [alone] from one quarter to another. After a theft or murder takes place, and they complain to the government, nothing is done. As it is said, "They think the uncaptured thief is a king." Proof is required; it is not possible to prove it easily, so they are compelled to tolerate the loss of life and property.

CORRUPTION AND DEBAUCHERY One of the things which the people have implemented as a means of freedom and comfort is that whores and young male prostitutes are permitted to indulge in debauchery. If, for example, someone quarrels with his wife or young son, straightaway that woman or boy goes to the coffeehouses or the brothel and says, "By my own wish, I want to engage in debauchery." It never occurs to anyone to prevent them or to force them to leave there and not permit them to engage in debauchery. In reality, this is a kind of sanctuary. Thus one is not in control of his honor, and the men are [thus] extremely afraid of their own wives and juvenile children. As a result of feeling jealousy and disgrace at this having happened, men who have been afflicted by this situation have often taken opium and poison and died. I don't understand the meaning of this [sort of] freedom.

ETHICS AND RELIGION Generally, the middle and lower [classes] of Russians, insofar as [I] have seen, are very impolite, wicked, devious, coarse, rude, unjust, harsh, haughty to the peasants, and careless. The institution of marriage does not have much sanctity among these people. Usually when anyone desires someone, they have intercourse without informing father, mother, or monks. They pay no attention to the priests and their own canon law. They imagine the most fanciful things about our prophet Jesus, his family, the disciples, and religious law. They exceed all bounds in drinking wine; they know neither day nor night, right time nor wrong time, too much nor too little. Usually they are so drunk they are senseless. They do not know or understand anything about purity and modesty, which are the norms of humanity, but which are not understood by them at any level. There are few Russians who do not drink one *mann** of wine in a day. Their drink is usually wine. They do not have the sense or intelligence to make or drink any other beverage.†

FROM BAKU TO BATUM Having arrived in Baku on the afternoon of Wednesday the sixteenth, we left Baku at noon on Thursday the seventeenth of the month of Shavval [30 July], took a calash, and went to the train station.

There is a railroad from Baku to Batum.‡ It is called the *chemin de fer*. . . . The train goes daily from Baku to Tiflis and Batum. The Baku station

*Mann: unit of weight varying from 3 to 6 kilograms.

†In these paragraphs, Farahani may seem to be rather excessive in his criticism of the Russians. On the other hand, it should be remembered that Baku during the oil boom did have a wild life. The English travelers Hone and Dickinson, [in] *Persia in Revolution,* also wrote that Baku "is a Mecca of adventurers" where "an enemy may be disposed of . . . at a cost of five rubles" and where "prosperous citizens are kidnapped in broad daylight" and "the average number of murders per day is five." They also quote the famous rebel Shamel as saying, "Alexander the Great took a dislike to this district on account of its barrenness and he turned it into a place of exile for all the criminals of the world."

‡Once the Transcaucasian Railroad was opened to passenger traffic, it quickly became a popular means of connecting Iran with the Black Sea maritime routes since it alleviated the problem of making either an arduous overland trip across the rugged Caucasus or the longer detour via Tzaritzina and Taganrog. As Benjamin, *Persia and the Persians*, reported, "The Railway between Tiflis and Batum had been opened about ten days before our arrival in Tiflis. Otherwise, instead of riding comfortably from that city to Baku by rail in twenty-four hours, we should have been obliged to go over the route in springless troikas, over a rough, treeless road, traversing barren plains and mountains infested by brigands, and weeks would have been required to accomplish the distance."

is half a *farsakh* from the city. It is a very good building, spacious, and constructed with an upper and lower story. A guard and [some] workers are there. There are several counters. One is reserved for issuing and collecting tickets. One must first of all pay for and get a ticket at that counter. Another is reserved for carrying and taking delivery of baggage, of which each passenger may have one pood. . . . They allow baggage, samovar, water pipe, carrying case, and water vessel without charging a separate fee. . . .

There are thirty-six stations from Baku to Batum. . . . The stations are all different. Each one that is located in a principal town, where there are many travelers and passersby, has more rooms, buildings, and workers. From each station to the next in terms of time takes from twenty-two or twenty-three minutes to thirty-five minutes. In each station, [the trains] stop from two minutes to half an hour. . . .

There are four sentry posts between each station and the next. Each [serves] as the residence for one family. All along the way, at intervals of one verst, a sentry and custodian are standing. If they raise a green flag, it signifies that that section is safe and the coach goes along quickly. If they raise a red flag, that is a sign that the railway is in some disrepair and the coach must travel slowly and with caution. If they raise a red and black flag, it is a sign that the railway is in bad shape and the coach must stop until the obstruction is removed. At night, in place of these flags as signals, they light green and red lanterns in the same manner as described. The telegraph line is strung out all along the side of the railway. One is able to telegraph from any station to another station. They give information by telegraph about every section of the railway which is in disrepair. . . .

THE SITUATION ON THE TRAINS The employees of the coach, such as servants, etc., are usually Russians. If anyone is careless, these employees will steal his belongings with utter nimbleness and agility. If, after the theft, the individual complains to anyone, he will never get anywhere because in all the stations the passengers are continuously changing, some going and some coming, so no one can be caught. Thus the individual must be extremely watchful and protect his property. In the coach, men and women, Muslims and infidels, are mixed together. There is no way to avoid it. The status of everyone is equal. Everyone in every class who has obtained a ticket sits anywhere [he wants], and there will be no preventing it. In all the stations, most foods and drinks are found. Every station which is in a principal town has more foods, but the price of everything is expensive. In some stations, foods and fruits are brought for sale from the surrounding villages and are offered cheaply. . . .

THE PORT OF SUEZ The train arrived at Suez at the second hour of the night [before] Friday, . . . 19 August. The Suez station is in the center of the city, and at that time of night it was very crowded. Amid the crowd and throng, several Iranian landlords and coffee shop keepers appeared and invited the Iranian pilgrims to their own residences. I gathered from the situation that since the coffee men's homes had not been seen and the rate was not fixed, it might be a cause for dispute, and so I went in person and saw the residences, selected one, and ascertained its rates. They brought the baggage and belongings there. Some of the pilgrims also accompanied me. Other pilgrims had quarrels and disputes and were involved in distraint and consular litigation with the landlords and coffeehouse keepers.

THE CONSULATE AND SUBJECTS OF IRAN In Suez, there are seven or eight people of Iranian origin. The representative of the exalted government of Iran is a merchant by the name of Ahmad Afandi, whose father was a well-known merchant and a dignitary of Suez, and who is himself a man of property and wealth. He represents the governments of Iran, Austria, and Brazil. He displays the three flags [of these countries] on the rooftop of his house three days a week. [If] citizens of these three countries have any [legal] business, they have recourse to him. He is a man of considerable competence. Here it is again customary that the pilgrims have their passports endorsed. The Ottoman agent signs the passports of the Ottoman pilgrims, and the Iranian deputy and agent signs the passports for the Iranian pilgrims. They charge one and a half *majidis** per passport. . . .

THE QUARANTINE Another of the difficulties for the pilgrims at Suez is that the chief physician there on behalf of the Khedive must give health certificates to the pilgrims. As for the fee for writing the certificate, he charges . . . about one Iranian *kran*. However, it is not necessary that the physician see every pilgrim. That is, the object is to collect the fee. One person goes with the money and gets the health certificates for ten or twenty people. . . .

THE PORT OF JIDDA The steamship anchored beside the Jidda pier on Friday, . . . 27 August, at one hour past noon. Its entire trip from Suez to Jidda without any delay took sixty-eight hours. Because of the extreme crowding and cramped space on this steamship, three Arabs perished in the hold and several people had become ill.

*one and a half *majidis*: approximately twenty-five dollars. [Ed.]

The steamship was delayed at the Jidda pier for about three hours. No rowboat or launch came near it until the government quarantine doctor with the quarantine employees first boarded the ship, looked and searched around, and ascertained and verified that there was no serious contagious disease on the ship. Then they gave people permission to enter Jidda. Launches and rowboats came and transported people. They charged more than warranted for the rowboat fare. They said this [fare] is divided into three shares: the government takes one, the consul of each state takes one, and the oarsman one. In all places throughout the Ottoman Empire, exorbitant taxes are exacted from the oarsmen, but especially in Jidda.

THE QUARANTINE First of all, they bring the pilgrims in the launches and rowboats by the quarantine building, which is beside the sea and adjacent to the city. The people disembark, without baggage or belongings, at this guarded enclosure. They give everyone a printed certificate which is the quarantine permit, and they charge each person half a *majidi*. . . . In this same place, there is another enclosure where they inspect and stamp one's passport. For stamping the passport, they also charge each person half a *majidi* and several para. . . .*

Also in this enclosure, the representatives of the professional pilgrim guides are sitting on chairs from one end to the other, waiting to see under the guidance of which of them the pilgrim will place [himself]. After that, they never let go of one and don't grant one a moment's peace. They become one's guardian and provide one with tutorship. A detailed account of the pilgrim guides and their activities will be written in the proper place.

CUSTOMS Anyhow, after one pays the fee for the quarantine permit and the fee for stamping the passport, one then obtains a dismissal ticket, exits from this enclosure, and is free [to go]. As soon as one comes out, one seeks one's baggage and belongings (which had been placed in the rowboat and left at the quarantine house) at the pier among the rowboats beside the open square fronting the gate of the city. In the same square the pilgrims bring their own things and belongings from the rowboats to land. However, there is no way into the city unless one enters by the gate. They search all one's things at the customs house. If one has something dutiable, they

---

*para: the smallest denomination of Ottoman coinage.

collect the customary fee; otherwise, if they do not find any dutiable things, they will charge as much as they can squeeze out of people as "reward" for the customs officer.

The customs house closes on Friday one hour before noon. If one disembarks from the steamship then, there is no prohibition against entering the city but the baggage must be left in the square until the next day [when] they inspect the baggage and take it inside the city—except [in the case of] dignitaries who inform the consulates of their own government. The consulate, out of respect, obtains a permit from the customs chief that the belongings not be detained. Thus even on Friday one may enter the city with baggage and belongings. . . .

RESTING We went to an excellent house which the pilgrim guide's apprentice had indicated. We entered a carpeted room with cushions placed about and sat down tired and hungry until the curtain to a dining room was raised. A very elaborate dining tray had been placed on the floor in which were pilaf and other essentials. It was evident that the servant of the pilgrim guide had exhorted the owner of the house [to arrange] for provisions and ceremonies. We ate and thanked God. Very delicious foods appeared to gratify the palate, but later, when we paid an exorbitant gratuity to the owner of the house, the flavor of the foods was not so tasty! . . .

THE PILGRIM GUIDES After I went . . . to my own residence, Sayyed Mansur, who is one of the Shi'ite pilgrim guides, and whose servants had informed him that some of the pilgrims had arrived at Jidda, came posthaste by donkey from Mecca the Exalted to visit. He swore such oaths of close friendship that it seemed he was my slave or bondsman or an old friend whom for many years I had the favor of raising.

At this point, I must write a description of the circumstances concerning the professional pilgrim guides. In Mecca, there are about thirty Shi'ite and Sunni pilgrim guides appointed by the Sharif* of Mecca who have permits for leading pilgrimages. Usually they and their fathers have been pilgrim guides for generations. Each of them has seven or eight assistants and servants. Before the pilgrimage season [begins], they go to the

---

*At the time of Farahani's visit the Ottoman Sultan was attempting to increase his authority in the Hijaz at the expense of the Sharif. As Farahani indicates here, one of the most important (and lucrative) prerogatives of this office was the right to license individuals to transport pilgrims or to serve as pilgrim guides. . . .

cities which are transit points for pilgrims, such as An Najaf, Karbala, Baghdad, Bombay, Bushehr, Bandar 'Abbas, Rasht, Istanbul, and Odessa. They issue to everyone they locate who wants to go to Mecca the following invitation: "You are without information about the practices and activities there; you must have someone knowledgeable and a pilgrim guide; you will not find [anyone] better than me." Of course, the pilgrims are beseeching God that they might have a knowledgeable man who will work hard on their behalf. Another thing they do is to promise some of the 'akkam, hamleh-dars, and hajjeh forushes* (who are well-known and who come to Mecca every year): "I will give you one Levant dollar . . . for every pilgrim you bring for me." After making these preparations, they return to Mecca near the beginning of the pilgrimage season. For their part, these [men], with a view to making a profit for themselves, assure every pilgrim they see or know of the commendability of that pilgrim guide: "So and so the pilgrim guide is a marvelous man, good, very hard working, and not greedy. It's good for you to entrust your pilgrimage to him so that it will be a simple matter in every respect." The pilgrim is deceived and agrees. Another thing they do is to send one of their agents or servants to every port which is a point of entry for pilgrims to the Hijaz, such as Jidda, Yanbu, or Medina the Agreeable, in order to watch out for and to assemble the followers there. As soon as the pilgrim says one word about "my pilgrim guide is so and so," these agents and servants report to the respective pilgrim guide that "such and such a pilgrim is under your direction; take note [of him]." If the pilgrim is a notable, the pilgrim guide goes out a day's journey or two to welcome him and also invites him home one night to give him supper. Thus, the pilgrim is totally dependent upon the pilgrim guide and utterly at his mercy. If, for instance, he has any goods to sell, he is compelled to inform and seek the approval of his pilgrim guide, who arranges with the buyer to get half of the money for those goods.

*The 'akkam were servants hired to pack up baggage and handle other routine aspects of managing a caravan. The hamleh-dar was the actual organizer of the caravan who drew up contracts to transport pilgrims and then led the caravan to its destination. Islamic law permitted a Muslim who could not make the pilgrimage ritual to Mecca in person to hire someone to make the pilgrimage in his stead; an individual who contracted to make the pilgrimage for someone else in this manner was known as a hajjeh-forush (literally, "pilgrimage seller"). Since these individuals regularly made the pilgrimage (and thus could influence other potential pilgrims who would trust their experience), they could be used by the pilgrimage guides to recruit customers. . . .

If . . . the pilgrim wants goods from there for gifts or to buy for commerce, [the guide will] go to the seller [and say], "Let that pilgrim buy at a high price." At least half the profit goes to [the guide].

Or if, for instance, the pilgrim wants to go from Jidda to Sa'deyyeh* or Mecca, or to hire transport from Mecca to Medina or Yanbu, this, of course, must be with the assistance of the pilgrim guide. Thus this year everyone who went from Jidda to the Sa'deyyeh *miqat*† paid eighteen Levant dollars to hire camels. Of these eighteen Levant dollars, seven dollars is the fare for the camel that carries one. For every camel, the Pasha, the Sharif, the Consul, the pilgrim guide, and the camel broker‡ take eleven dollars.

If [the pilgrim] wants to rent a place to stay in Jidda or Mecca, the pilgrim guide has a role in that and will receive a share. If the pilgrim goes to Arafat and Mina, part of the charge for the beast of burden and the tent goes to the pilgrim guide.

If the pilgrim or someone in his party dies, a payment to the pilgrim guide is expected [for] the vows and prayers which are the special duty of the pilgrim guide. In the end, if the pilgrim is poor and has little money, he must certainly give at least two Levant dollars . . . as remuneration for the pilgrim guide. If he does not pay or does not have [the money], the matter will result in hostility, disputes, and petitions to the Sharif, the Governor, and the consuls. It will be collected by force, violence, or the imprisonment of the helpless pilgrim. If the pilgrim is wealthy and a dignitary, the pilgrim guide will try as hard as [he can] to collect from one to ten lira from him.

The earnings of the pilgrim guides during the pilgrimage season varies. It may be from two hundred *toman*s to three thousand *toman*s for himself, his associates, and his agents.

ARRIVAL OF NEW PILGRIMS   In the two or three days I was in Jidda, two ships arrived from Bushehr, Batra, and Baghdad. About a thousand Iranian pilgrims were on board them. The ship which came first anchored at the Jidda docks; the other ship followed it and came up beside the first ship with such

---

*Sa'deyyeh is a more modern name for Yalamlam, the place where pilgrims coming from the town of Ta'if and other areas to the southeast of Mecca, notably the Yemen, put on the ritual pilgrimage garments.

†Specified locations for donning the *ihram*. [Ed.]

‡The *mokharrej*, or camel broker, was an official licensed by the Sharif of Mecca to rent out camels and other mounts to pilgrims traveling between Mecca and Jidda. . . .

speed that it struck the anchored ship. The anchored ship was immediately wrecked. The captain, the workers, and the pilgrims were alarmed. They left the cargo and baggage and cast themselves into rowboats. Since the land was near, the ship did not sink, but in the excitement and confusion some of the pilgrims' belongings were lost. Upon investigation and inquiry, it was learned that these two captains had previously had a grudge against each other and had been trying to destroy each other. In the end, they collected indemnities for the wreck from the captain and owner of the ship [that had caused the accident]. . . .

FARES FOR PILGRIMS IN THE PROVINCE OF THE HIJAZ In order for the pilgrims to hire riding animals throughout the Hijaz—from Jidda to Sa'deyyeh and Mecca or from Mecca to Arafat or from Mecca to Medina and Yanbu— a camel broker is designated by the Sharif for each [national] group of pilgrims. That is, six people have been designated as camel brokers: one is the camel broker for the Iranian pilgrims; another is the camel broker for the Ottoman pilgrims; another is the camel broker for the people of Java; another is the camel broker for the Indian pilgrims; another is the camel broker for the North African pilgrims; and another is the camel broker for the Egyptian pilgrims. Their work is that they sit down together and take counsel and fix the hiring rates every year according to the situation. The hiring of riding animals by the pilgrims in every part of the Hijaz is with their knowledge, assignment, and assistance. For example, the camel brokers fix whatever rate they desire for the fare from Mecca to Medina, or from Medina to Yanbu or Jidda. Whatever the amount of the fare they determine is put into practice, and no one will disagree. For each camel, a fee is expected for the Sharif, the Consul, the pilgrim guide, and themselves and is added to the fare. The camel broker for the Iranians is an individual named Mohammad Kaboli, whom the late Hosam os-Saltaneh had bastinadoed. Every Iranian must hire riding animals with his advice and approval. All of these camel brokers have gotten very wealthy. . . .

THE POST-HAJJ QUARANTINE STATION AT MOUNT SINAI, NOVEMBER 1885 We were en route Tuesday, . . . 10 November. Wednesday, 11 November, at nine o'clock, the steamship anchored at the wadi of Mount Sinai, which was the quarantine site this year. When the captain first informed the quarantine officials, ten or twelve government rowboats came below the steamship and transported the pilgrims without charging a fare. Although the oarsmen took one and a half *guirsh* from the pilgrims as a gratuity, this was not in addition to a fare. On land, they went on foot. A government building had been constructed at the edge of the landing. Most of its rooms were like very spacious storage rooms or halls.

The employees of the quarantine are as follows: chief doctor, one person; doctors, two persons; inspector, one person; assistant inspector, one person; accountant, one person; official in charge of security, called the *mohafez,* one person; foot soldiers, two hundred persons.

These troops do not allow the pilgrims to wander around. As soon as all the people of a steamer have assembled in the open area in front of the building, they announce that the pilgrims must obtain tickets and enter the quarantine. The inspector, assistant inspector, and accountant are seated in one of the rooms. All the pilgrims must pay them one and a quarter Levant dollars per person and take tickets. They charged some of them who were not knowledgeable about the operation of the quarantine from one and a half to two Levant dollars for the tickets. They cheated in some other ways, too. For example, they took imperials, liras, and other gold money for less [than they were worth]. They gave printed tickets to each person, couple, ten people, or whatever. As soon as they had collected the money from all the pilgrims and given out the tickets, then the accountant stood at the door to the building with two soldiers and inspected the people's tickets. They entered the building group by group. In some of the rooms of this building, there is fumigating equipment present. . . . If people do not have a disease known to be contagious, they do not have to be fumigated.

THE FIELD TENTS At another door to the building by which the people exit, there is a vast plain. On that plain, four groups of military field tents had been pitched, so that each group was at an interval of about one *maydan** from the next. Each group had three rows of white tents, and each row had twenty-five tents. So all together, there were three hundred tents. In front of each group of tents, there were also six tents where shopkeepers stayed. There were two coffeehouses and four grocer's tents. They also have fruit and sell everything at exorbitant prices. Those six shopkeepers are Arabs. There is also a tent in each group for two Jewish money changers and two Armenian butchers. Live sheep can also be obtained but they are extremely expensive. Beside each group of tents there are also two iron water tanks. Each one has two or three spigots. They draw water from those spigots. The water is brought in continuously by government camels and poured into the tanks.

*maydan: Equivalent to one quarter of a *farsakh;* about a mile. [Ed.]

They give water, however much is desired, to the pilgrims for free. These four groups of tents are the collective property of the four steamers. Each steamer that comes to the quarantine must lodge all its passengers in one of these groups of tents. Variously, every five, seven, eight, or ten people will have one tent. There are thirty soldiers to take care of each group of tents. They watch out for the pilgrims' belongings at night, and by day they also insure that the people of one ship and group of tents do not mix with the group or people of another ship. Thus, after our arrival at the quarantine, two other ships came which were visible from afar, but we did not see the people of that ship nor did they see us. . . .

THE QUARANTINE To sum up, . . . this quarantine was set up by the Ottoman government's bureau of health in Istanbul. If there is no contagious disease, the period the pilgrims stay in the quarantine is forty-eight hours. If during the forty-eight hours someone dies [while] on land, the period will be renewed. However, its employees are [employed] by the Khedive of Egypt. The Sinai wadi is also part of the kingdom of Egypt. It seems that the service and fealty and obedience which the Khedive of Egypt renders to the Ottoman Empire is no more than using the moon and star flag and this matter [of the quarantine.] This quarantine in no way causes any loss or expense for the Ottoman Empire. Whatever they expend on it, they get back double from the pilgrims. Exorbitant sums go to the employees of the quarantine. When officials are posted to the quarantine, it is as if [they had been appointed] officials in charge of fleecing and plundering the pilgrims. One of the circumstances that makes this clear is that the authorities of the quarantine, especially the chief doctor, take something from the captains of the steamers so they won't cause any trouble: if someone dies during the two days stopped at the quarantine, they don't renew the period and do not delay the steamer.

Anyhow, since the spell of hot weather was broken and the land at this place was less humid and had wholesome water, it was not too hard on the pilgrims at the quarantine. Having arrived at the quarantine on Wednesday, . . . 11 November, and having been released from the quarantine on Friday, . . . 13 November, and having gone to the landing, government rowboats carried the pilgrims to the steamer for free. The steamer left one hour before sunset. . . .

IRANIAN CHARLATANS IN BATUM In this city, a hardship which is worse than the customs business for Iranian pilgrims is this. Several Iranian brokers stay there who have been rascals and rogues since way back. They are divided into two factions. Each faction has several followers, and they are occupied with robbing and vexing the pilgrims. The names of their leaders are as follows:

Tekran the Armenian, who is an Iranian by origin and sometimes has consular authority in Batum.

Hajji Gholam, who is an Iranian and has become one of the soldiers and employees of the customs house; Karbalai Mohammad Ali; Mashhadi Reza; and Mashhadi Ali Yazdi.

First of all, they insist that travelers and pilgrims are responsible for passport fees which are not customarily paid there, so that each person pays about two *tomans* passport fee. Secondly, [they get money for] every lodging rented by a traveler in Batum. If, for example, that lodging costs half a *toman,* they, by force or cajolery or sharp talk, hold a person responsible for paying [them] two *tomans*. Third, everything that one wants to buy there costs double its value since they have an understanding with the merchants and tradesmen. If a traveler wants to sell anything, they belittle his goods so much that he sells for half the value or no one will buy it at all. Fourth, if the broker for this helpless traveler belongs, for example, to Tekran's faction, the faction of Hajji Gholam tries to harm him or to steal his property. Or if he smuggles something past customs, this faction will reveal his delinquency and thus entangle him with imprisonment and fines. The helpless Iranian traveler is confused: What should he do? Where should he go? To which gang should he entrust himself? How can he renounce his baggage, clothes, food, and drink? How can he bear this amount of customs duties? How can he take refuge from these Russian thieves and Iranian swindlers? On whom can he rely? How can he flee?

Really, it is a strange situation. "These days a father doesn't know his own son." "It is like doomsday." "It is a day when a man flees from his brother." It is in this place that all the travelers are utterly distraught and upset. Since I did not have anything dutiable, I was at ease and merely observing [what was going on].

They tell the story about Shaykh Shebli,* that on one of his trips he was with a caravan. Bandits fell on the caravan, and the people were distraught out of

---

*Abu Bakr Dolaf osh-Shebli (861–945): a celebrated Sufi from Baghdad. . . .

grief and sorrow over the loss of property. They were weeping and lamenting. They saw the *shaykh* seated in a corner laughing. They said, "What reason is there for laughter?" He said, "The bandits stole whatever all these [people] had and thus they are upset and weeping. I didn't have anything for the thieves to steal. Therefore I am at ease and laughing!" "The lightly burdened shall be saved."

13

Arthur J. B. Wavell
Anglo-Africa
1908

꧅

Arthur Wavell at twenty-five was the first pilgrim author to describe the Damascus-Medina railway and the last Western pretender to write up the Hajj. His father was an army colonel. A cousin served as Viceroy to India.* Like others of his military family, Wavell trained at the Royal Military College, Sandhurst, then obtained a commission in the Welsh Regiment. He fought in South Africa, then served with British Intelligence in Swaziland and Botswana. Leaving the army in 1906, he purchased a farm near Mombasa, where he joined other early settlers in the colonial community later chronicled by Isak Dinesen. But whereas Dinesen wrote with affection of the Muslim workers on her coffee farm, Wavell went further. He learned Arabic, studied Islam, and in 1907 returned to England, bringing along a paid Swahili named Masaudi to accompany him on the Hajj.

In Marseilles, they procured black-market Turkish passports. With a third, Syrian companion, Abdul Wahid, they traveled by train to Genoa, then by ship to Egypt. Wavell assumed a Muslim guise along the way, shaving his head, doffing Western dress in Beirut, observing the arduous Ramadan fast in Damascus. In the following excerpts, he plays down the dangers of this imposture, performing his part with a wink, affecting a breezy tone, as if one generation's conundrums were mere incidentals to the next. Wavell viewed the Hajj with respect, but from a distance, treating it as a stepping stone to advance his new career as an explorer.

One day after Ramadan, the trio walked to the outskirts of Damascus, where the annual caravan was preparing to leave for Medina. Faced with this set piece in Hajj reporting, Wavell limits himself to a paragraph's description, returns to

---

*Archibald Wavell (1883–1950), British Commander in Chief for the Middle East (1938–41) and Supreme Commander of Allied forces in the Southwest Pacific (1942), of Allied forces in India and Burma (1942); Field Marshal and Viscount (1943); Viceroy of India (1943–47).

town, and a few days later buys three train tickets. For reasons never stated, his presence in Syria in the fall of 1908 exactly coincides with a major turning point in pilgrim travel: the completion after eight years of the Damascus-to-Medina pilgrim railway. This train was the crowning symbol of the Ottoman Porte's efforts to revive the caliphate. However cynical its resumption may have been, the new track represented a significant accomplishment, and it was a wholly Muslim affair, built by eight thousand Turkish soldiers over a period of eight years, financed by Muslim contributions from around the world, and owing nothing to European aid except for a handful of German engineers. Small wonder that a British intelligence officer of a trusted family should show up at the railhead for an unofficial peek. The new track slashed the thousand-mile journey from thirty to five days, and a third-class ticket cost three pounds. The train not only improved troop movements in a far-off province; it also introduced a new age in internal Hajj transportation. In the next five years, it carried more than a million pilgrims between the Near Eastern central lands and the southern deserts. Wavell was among the first to ride it.

The train improved a pilgrim's lot in many ways; it also disrupted the balance of power in the Hijaz. In a thumbnail summation excerpted here, Wavell shows what lay at stake for all the parties—urban Medinese, rural tribes like the Banu Ali, occupying Turks, and the pilgrims they all claimed to be protecting. He was quick to note the embattled condition of the Turkish garrisons. He knew by the thudding artillery that the train was nearing the city. At the time of his arrival in Medina, ten thousand troops with twenty cannon occupied the ramparts. Outside, twenty thousand Bedouins lay waiting. Wavell's description of a recent battle, in which a Maxim machine gun is used, should remind readers that by now the Hijaz was entering the age of modern warfare. Wavell and Masaudi volunteered to help defend the garrison; because they were pilgrims, their offer was declined.

Wavell's military interests did not divert him from other aspects of the town. He rightly points up the importance of Hajj traffic for the economy. In 1908, virtually every male adult in Medina earned most of his annual income by devoting a few months to the pilgrim service. Wavell also correctly registers Medina's peculiar power for the hajji: "At Mecca the feeling is one of awe and reverence," he wrote. "Here the personal element comes in."

In Jidda, where we meet them next, Wavell's party found the streets full of pilgrims clad "only in bath towels" (the ihram*). Setting out for Mecca on camels, they joined a steady stream of humanity flowing up into the hills. In Mecca, Wavell struck up an acquaintance with the Chief of the Zamzam Well. Other chance events offered a means to reflect on the little details of Hajj living, from cashing letters of credit in a city without banks to evading thieves along the roads.*

After the Hajj, most pilgrims were confined to Mecca for a week. When the Turkish troops finally returned from Arafat to guard the roads, the trio went down to Jidda, where they parted.

Muslim dietary laws in European settings, the flouting of the rules of quarantine—Wavell fills in many themes first touched on in Farahani's study. His tone is lighthearted, wry, intelligent, the voice of a capable Englishman bearing secrets of the East to London readers. He marshals theology easily, and his sense of humor is modern, ironic. His physical descriptions of Mecca are succinct, and he appears to have believed that producing a well-written travel book was in itself important. Because he traveled close to the ground with a pair of believers, Wavell was more able than most Europeans to convey the emotional power of the city. Clearly he did not share Masaudi's devotion, but he grasped it. For a Muslim, he writes, "Mecca is a place hardly belonging to this world, overshadowed by an almost tangible presence of the deity." Wavell had the sense to integrate this reflected spirituality into his writing. It adds a valuable dimension to his book. Almost a century later, he remains the last non-Muslim author to make the Hajj.

from A Modern Pilgrim in Mecca and a Siege in San'a by Arthur J. B. Wavell

PREFACE: CONCERNING MECCA AND MEDINA It would be strange indeed if the exclusive character of these cities had not excited in western Europe the liveliest curiosity concerning them. Before going further, let it be clearly understood that anyone who wishes to visit them may do so, after publicly professing Islam. It would be necessary to go before a *qadi* [judge], repeat certain formulae, and submit, in most cases, to one of the minor operations of surgery. This done, and a sufficiently long apprenticeship served to convince the local Muslim feeling that the convert's professions were sincere, there would be no objection to his making the pilgrimage. A long and drivelling correspondence between himself, the Foreign Office, and the Sublime Porte would probably end in the last named having exhausted all possible pretexts for further delay, giving him a special passport. This once obtained, the Ottoman government would be responsible for his welfare, and he would be enabled to travel to Mecca and Medina without running any special risk. He would probably be given an escort and otherwise looked after. He would generally be regarded as a legitimate object for curiosity, if not suspicion.

The only alternative to this unattractive prospect, if one wishes to see these places, is to go there in disguise.

The writer made the pilgrimage in the year 1908–09, partly out of curiosity, more particularly to accustom himself to Arab ways with a view to future journeys in disguise into the unexplored interior. The rank and reputation of a hajji, that is to say, one who has duly performed certain rites on the prescribed day at Mecca, is useful to the traveller in Muslim countries.

The following pages contain an account of the journey that I wrote on my return and did not originally intend to publish. It shows that the Hijaz is by no means the inaccessible country it is often supposed to be. Masaudi, I must explain, is a Mombasa Swahili whom I took to England on purpose to assist me in the enterprise, and Abdul Wahid is an Arab from Aleppo, established in Berlin, whom I signed on later. . . .

DAMASCUS As is usual in the East, the town is divided up into the Muslim, Jewish, and Christian quarters—the first of course being much the largest and richest. There is one tolerably decent hotel, where Europeans usually stay, and many hostelries for visitors of Eastern races. In one of the latter we installed ourselves, taking one large room. This hotel had been recommended to us by one of our companions in the train, but as it was by no means the best of its sort and rather expensive, we afterwards changed. We took our meals at various cafés. Food is seldom obtainable at hotels in these places.

It was now the twentieth day of Ramadan, and as we did not propose to start for Medina for about another month, it was worthwhile making ourselves comfortable. I felt that in view of what was before us, the time was none too long for me to get at home with Eastern life to the extent necessary. It was essential that I should have at my fingers' ends certain phrases, quotations, and greetings, with the appropriate answers to them, that I should be able to go through the various Muslim ceremonies, in and out of the mosque, without making mistakes, and get so far accustomed to wearing and arranging my clothes, and doing other things in the conventional way, that I should not in any ordinary circumstances be conspicuous. It is these multifarious customs and ceremonies that constitute the real obstacle to a European passing himself off as a Muslim born and bred—for they are common to Islam the world over, and a bad mistake would emphatically give him away. . . . It is in these matters, and not in the language or disguise, that the real difficulty is experienced. There are nearly as many white men at Mecca as there are men black or brown in colour. Syrian Arabs not infrequently have fair hair and blue eyes—as likewise have some of the natives of the Holy Cities themselves. I was once asked [by a European] what colour I stained myself for this journey. The question reveals the curious ignorance that lies at the bottom of the so-called race prejudices of which some people are so proud. . . .

It must not be concluded, however, that to travel successfully in disguise, it is necessary to be a good actor. The main thing is to keep one's eyes open and one's mouth shut. It is wonderful how easy it is to acquire foreign habits when one is really living in their atmosphere. The secret, I believe, is in playing a part as little as possible consciously and in trying to identify one's self as closely as may be with the assumed character, in private as well as in public. . . .

PREPARATIONS TO LEAVE DAMASCUS On the second day of the festival we witnessed the departure of the *mahmal* for Mecca. Prior to the completion of the railway, the pilgrim caravan used to start at this date. The journey to Medina took forty days, and meant hardship even to the rich, while the poor people who travelled on foot had a very rough time. The *mahmal* is an elaborately embroidered camel litter which, along with other presents from the city, is sent annually to the shrines as a mark of respect. A similar *mahmal* is sent from Egypt, and formerly there was one from Baghdad also, though of late years this has been discontinued for some reason. A great crowd assembles to see the *mahmal* off, and it is escorted for some distance by the Governor and principal dignitaries *en grande tenue.* The camel that has the honour of carrying it is of great size and, I believe, of the highest breeding. . . .

The time for our departure was now drawing near, and we began to make preparations for the journey. We bought the *ihram,* or white robes that we should require when entering Mecca and during the three days of the actual pilgrimage. We also bought the tent, mats, and saddlebags which would constitute our camp equipment, knives, forks, plates, and what cooking utensils we required; not forgetting water pipes and a good supply of tea and tobacco. These things can be bought much more cheaply in Damascus than in Medina. I deposited my money, now reduced to two hundred pounds, with our friend Abdullah [a local merchant], who gave me two cheques, one on his agent at Medina, the other on Mecca. In neither place are there any banks.

We had intended to start on the fifteenth of the month, but had to postpone our departure till the eighteenth owing to the trains being full up with troops sent to reinforce the garrison at Medina, which was reported to be hard-pressed. Trouble that had arisen with the Bedouin tribes during the Ramadan festival had swelled into a respectable war. Wild and improbable rumours about the desperate nature of the fighting were daily circulating in the town; but as the papers were not allowed to give details, even if they knew any, and the officials were not communicative, it was difficult to get at the truth. All that seemed certain was that the government troops had sustained a considerable defeat at the outset and that the city was in a state of siege. This was good news for me, because I felt sure that it would make my journey easier in many ways. In time of war and commotion, when people have much to occupy their minds, they are less apt to be inquisitive. Moreover, I am never averse to being where anything interesting is taking place, and consequently I was all anxiety to be off to the scene of action.

THE HIJAZ RAILWAY The Hijaz railway station is situated on the eastern side of the town some little distance out. It took us over an hour to drive there from our hotel. The train was due to start at eleven in the morning—European time—but we were warned not to be later than nine, as it was expected to be very crowded. There are two classes, first and third. Seeing that the journey was to take four days at the least, and we were fairly affluent, I was strongly tempted to travel first class, especially as the difference did not amount to very much. Our Damascus friends however strongly opposed this extravagance. They said that even the "very best people" went third and that it was nearly as comfortable. I gave up the idea when I found that it would probably involve their putting on a special carriage for me, for I naturally wished to make myself as inconspicuous as possible on arriving. I was thankful afterwards that I allowed myself to be persuaded. Our entry into Medina was quite sufficiently sensational as it was.

We got to the station in good time and secured our places, which we left Masaudi to guard while we took the tickets and registered the luggage. The tickets cost £3.10s each, not a great deal for a journey of over a thousand miles. As we had still two hours and a half to wait, we adjourned to a small café with our friend Abdullah, who had come to see us off. Later I walked back with him some distance towards the town, which opportunity he took to bestow upon me some excellent advice. "Remember," he said, "that the people of the Hijaz are not civilized as they are here; do not quarrel, or you will get into trouble. They are accustomed to make money out of the pilgrims, so do not be cheated, yet do not accuse them lightly of trying to rob you. Do not spend too much money at the beginning, as you may want it all. If you are attacked in the train, or with the caravan, by overwhelming numbers, do not try to fight; give up your things quietly, and no harm will befall you." He further admonished me to be punctual in the performance of prayer while on the pilgrimage, whatever I might be at other times, and to give some small sum in charity before starting. I further had to promise to pray a prayer of two *rakat*s on his behalf in the Prophet's Mosque at Medina. At parting he embraced me affectionately in the objectionable manner customary everywhere but in England.

On returning to the train, I found all confusion. The carriages consisted of plain wooden benches with a passage down the middle. These were in pairs facing one another with just room for two to sit on each. We had reserved four of them, but other passengers turning up had forcibly removed our things from two in spite of Masaudi's protests. Our carriage was now absolutely crammed, as likewise were all the others. There was no room for anything, and we were jammed up together with our belongings in a most uncomfortable way. Although we had still an hour to wait, we did not dare to leave again and sat in our places waiting for the train to start. As it was, many people arriving late were turned away for want of room. When, much to our relief, we did start, we were half an hour late.

Among those in our compartment were several Turkish officers in uniform, some Syrian pilgrims, and some very dirty Moroccans. Next to us on the other side of the carriage were two Turks, father and son, whose only luggage appeared to consist of a Gramophone. This ubiquitous instrument is very popular in the Hijaz, and many Arabic records for it are now to be obtained—among them even passages from the Quran! I have never lost an opportunity of pointing out the impropriety of this, having always entertained a strong objection to this invention of the Evil One.

We travelled through open cultivated country till night fell. The Jabal ash-Shaykh, a fine peak overlooking Damascus, well above the snow line, was still visible the following morning. In the course of the first day we passed several large stations, but by the morning of the second we had entered the desert and thenceforward few habitations were visible. The soil was brown and dry, with scanty herbage which thinned out more and more as the train passed on to the south. We had brought what food we required—mostly hard-boiled eggs, bread, and cakes, but what with the dust and the stuffy atmosphere we could hardly eat anything. Through the night we dozed at intervals, but sleep in our constrained position was difficult. The second day I had a bout of malarial fever, which lasted till we got to Medina and did not enhance my enjoyment of the journey. The kindness of our fellow passengers in this emergency was remarkable. Seeing that I was ill, they insisted on crowding together so that I could have room to lie down, as often as I would permit them to do so. The Turkish officers, who had a small charcoal brazier, cooked things for me when possible and gave me fruit, of which we had foolishly lost our own supply. We were able to repay them for this in some measure, as we had a Primus stove which made tea in a few minutes whenever anyone wanted any.

There was a small closed compartment at the end of the corridor that was occupied by an elderly Turk with his son, wife, and two daughters. I was sorry for the latter, for they were the only women on the train. They spent most of the time intoning what is known as the "Maulid," a poetical work describing the birth of the Prophet.

On the third day we arrived at a station at nine in the morning and did not leave till five in the afternoon. This was owing to the engine driver, who should have taken us on, not being there for some reason. Our own driver said he was dead tired and must have a sleep. As we heard that the track ahead was in a very dangerous condition, we made few protests and in fact were only too glad to get out and stretch our legs. This station, like most of them, consisted merely of a couple of tin huts and a tank. We soon had to take refuge in our carriage from the heat of the sun. The reddish sand of the Arabian and Syrian Deserts is not, however, nearly so trying to the eyes in bright sunlight as that of Egypt—nor does the country, being generally hilly, give the same idea of desolation as the Sahara.

The engine driver being at last sufficiently refreshed, we started again. Another long night passed, and we were traversing a country broken up into fantastically shaped hills and covered with huge boulders of weird forms. Some stood straight up on end like huge Cleopatra's needles. Others reminded me of Stonehenge, and for about an hour we passed through a plain covered as far as the eye could reach with rocks nearly resembling the "toad rock" at Tunbridge Wells. We were now in Arabia, and as we proceeded, the aspect of the country became ever wilder. High mountain ranges appeared on either side, and the great pinnacles of rock became more twisted and uncanny in appearance. The track wound through gloomy gorges over which huge rocks hung menacingly. About midday we reached Mada'in Salih. This is the boundary of the Hijaz Province, and beyond it no one not being a Muslim is allowed to pass. When the railway was being built, all the European engineers were discharged at this point and the work was carried on entirely by Turks and Arabs.

This place, which itself is simply a couple of tin shanties, is remarkable for the extraordinary rock dwellings, which from time immemorial have excited the wonder of travellers. These have been well described by the Arabian explorer Doughty* and several others. The huge isolated boulders which cover the country are here hollowed out and fashioned into caves with doors, very much like the rock temples of Abu Simbel in Upper Nubia. I was unable to examine them closely, but there are hundreds of them, and they appear to be beautifully made. According to the Arabian story, this place, as its name implies, was the town where dwelt the prophet Salih. As related in the Quran, the people of these cities, being hard of heart and refusing to listen to his preaching, besides killing his miraculous camel, were finally overwhelmed by a convulsion of nature like that which destroyed the Cities of the Plain on the occasion when Lot's wife came to such an untimely end. "The earthquake overtook them and the morning found them lying dead in their city."†

In the afternoon of this the third day we reached a good-sized village surrounded by date palms—the first habitations we had seen since leaving Syria. Here we stayed for an hour and were able to replenish our provisions and get some coffee. All the stations south of Mada'in Salih are fortified with trenches and barbed wire, and the whole scene reminds one of South Africa at the time of the war. There was fighting all along here while the railway was in course of construction, and the posts are still occasionally attacked by wandering tribes. We passed several wrecked engines that had run off the track owing to it not having been properly laid, and we were obliged to proceed very carefully. We were told that it was by no means unlikely that we should be attacked between this place and Medina—not by the belligerent tribes, but by bands of marauders whose object was merely robbery. We therefore looked to our weapons on restarting. We were due to arrive at Medina at noon the next day—Sunday.

Nothing happened during the night, and we were all much cheered by the reflection that it was the last we had to spend in that accursed train. I was also feeling much better, in spite, or perhaps because, of having had no medicine whatever. We were somewhat delayed, and it was not till one o'clock that the dull thudding of distant artillery fire told us that we were approaching our destination. The stations were now protected by considerable earthworks and had garrisons of a company or more. I did not particularly admire either the construction of these defences or the sites chosen for them.

*Charles Montagu Doughty (1843–1926): English traveler and author of *Arabia Deserta* (1888).

†Quran, VII.

A little later, through a gap in the hills, there appeared the needle-like mina-rets of the Prophet's Mosque—then, as we emerged on to the plain, the city itself.

One of our Turkish friends, standing with me on the footboard, pointed out several places with familiar names—the Mountain of Uhud, where the forces of the Prophet were defeated by the Quraysh, the tomb of his uncle Hamza, and the different gates. As we drew nearer, the rattle of musketry fire became audible, and as we steamed into the station, I half-expected to find a hand-to-hand conflict going on outside the booking office. The fighting, however, for the moment was on the other side of the town, and the station was not under fire. That morning, however, it had been, and consequently the crowd that usually assembles to see the train come in was absent—very fortunately for me as it turned out.

TURKISH-BEDOUIN RELATIONS Another digression is necessary here to explain the causes and conduct of this little war and how we came to pass in as we did, unmolested by the besiegers.

This part of Arabia being theoretically a province of Turkey, the Arab tribes inhabiting it are nominally Turkish subjects. Turkey being the most powerful Muslim country of the present day, her ruler claims the title of Commander of the Faithful, and on him devolves the guardianship of the Sacred Cities and the maintenance of order there. As a matter of fact, how-ever, apart from occupying Mecca and Medina and the coast ports, Turkey has little real authority in the Hijaz. The Bedouin remain, what they always have been, independent tribes, each community having its own country, rulers, laws, and customs. They are an intensely aristocratic race, setting great store by genealogy and noble descent; they despise the rest of the world, not excepting the so-called Arabs of the towns, who are usually of mixed blood, or the other Arabic-speaking peoples, such as the Egyptians and Syrians. It is certain that few other races can boast such pure breeding as the Arabs, or more honourable traditions. The best families have done no manual labour except fighting and brigandage since the creation of Adam.

These Arabs, known generically as the Bedouin, live in the desert; that is to say, their country is dry and arid generally, though fertile spots occur. They build no towns, but move from place to place. They despise all civi-lized customs and appliances—even houses. Their food is of the simplest, their dress a single cotton gown. Their favourite pursuit is war in some good cause or, failing that, robbery. They are excellent horsemen and camel mas-ters, very hardy, daring, and resourceful. In character, though brave, gener-ous, and hospitable, they are treacherous and consider things allowable in war that are decidedly not cricket. They are by no means fanatically religious, contrary to the received idea; they neither fast nor pray and in reality are only nominal Muslims.

The pilgrims consider them savages and have good reason to hate and fear them; so also have the inhabitants of the Arabian towns.

For many years past the Turks have found it less trouble to pay a certain sum of money to the shaykhs of the Bedouin tribes through whose country the pilgrim caravans have to pass, in return for immunity from attack, rather than to send large escorts with them. Though it may well be considered undignified for a civilized government to submit to such extortions in their own country, there is really no help for it. To occupy and police Arabia in such a manner as would make it a safe country for travellers would be at present about as practicable an undertaking as an invasion of the moon. Neither the Turks nor anyone else can hope to accomplish it. The character of the country, difficulty of transport, and scarcity of water would effectually settle a European army, and the Bedouin themselves are much more formidable opponents than the half-armed savages we destroyed in such numbers at Omdurman.* They are well armed with modern rifles (a good proportion being small bores), and judging by the amount of firing at long ranges round Medina, they have little trouble in obtaining ammunition. In fact, so far as I could see, no attempt is made to prevent traffic in either rifles or cartridges; they are sold in the open market both in Mecca and Medina.

It is impossible to do more than guess at the number of Bedouin Arabs in Arabia—seeing that three fourths of it is unknown. But I have been told that the Hijaz tribes alone, were they to combine, could put nearly one hundred thousand men in the field.

With the completion of the Hijaz railway,† the Turkish government made a precipitate and, in the circumstances, an ill-advised attempt to stop further payment of tribute for safe conduct to the tribes en route. This as a matter of fact did not amount to very much, as the part between Syria and Medina never gave the caravans any great trouble. The news, however, spread through Arabia and alarmed the more important tribes be-

*In 1898, under Governor General Horatio Herbert Kitchener. [Ed.]

†The deposed [since 1908] Sultan, Abd al-Hamid, was mainly responsible for this work. Subscriptions in aid of it were raised throughout the whole Muslim world. The railway reached Medina in the year I went there—1908. It is proposed to carry it on to Mecca; but there seems little prospect of this being accomplished for some time to come. The object in building it was in part to render the pilgrimage safer and easier, and in part strategical.

tween Medina and Mecca, and Medina and Yanbu. If they were not allowed to plunder and not paid to refrain from doing so—they would evidently be in a bad way.

When the first train arrived, it was the subject of much curiosity. At first they did not realize its significance. "Can this thing," they asked, "carry as much as a camel?" When, a few days later, they saw it disgorging hundreds of men and tons of baggage, they began to realize that something new had come into their very conservative country and to resent it accordingly. It was fairly obvious that this would soon make camel travelling a thing of the past, and with it all their profits derived from the hiring out of the camels and the tribute they had for so long extorted. Further, they observed with consternation that the train was by no means so easy to "stick up" as they had imagined it would be, and on hearing that it came all the way from Syria in four days, their amazement passed all bounds.

During the ensuing two months their shaykhs no doubt held many anxious consultations. Deputations waited on the Governor of Medina to protest against the railway on the ground that it would bring Europeans into the country. The Governor was authorised to promise them on the word of the Caliph himself that this should not happen. It was pointed out to them that arrivals by train could be scrutinised much more easily than formerly, in the days of caravans.

The one idea of the Bedouin was to stop the railway going any farther. But it was not at all easy for them to find a pretext on which they could reasonably object. The railway had been built and was to be continued by subscription throughout the whole of Islam. Enthusiasm for it ran high; it was regarded as a grand and patriotic undertaking and a triumphant refutation of the charge that the Muslim religion is decadent or lacking in vitality. It had received the blessing of the religious heads of all sects, and rich and poor alike had contributed their share with equal generosity.

The best thing to do, it seemed to the Bedouin, was to pick a quarrel on some other grounds and make things so hot for the Turks that for a time at any rate they would have something better to do than build railways. Opportunities for doing so were not wanting. Four miles east of Medina is situated the tomb of the uncle of Muhammad, Hamza, who fell at the battle of Uhud, a place of pious visitation by all pilgrims. The Ali (sons of Ali), a large and important tribe living and cultivating round the city, were charged with the policing of this road, and paid for doing so. At the end of Ramadan two men returning late at night were killed, presumably by robbers. The Governor sent a protest to the chiefs of the tribe and demanded payment of a fine. The effect of the answer he received was that they could no longer be responsible for the road and were not going to pay anything. Some further negotiations took place, but their demeanour was so truculent that it became obvious that they were "out for a row." On the third of Shawal* a force of about one thousand men with a Maxim was sent to disperse a large body of tribesmen that had assembled and was threatening the town. The Turks, supported by artillery fire from the walls, advanced boldly through the date plantations. Before long, however, they were completely outflanked by their more mobile enemy, and subjected to a galling fire from all sides. On their attempting to retreat, the Bedouin charged in their usual impetuous manner, captured the Maxim, killed a hundred men, and drove the rest back into the town in the wildest confusion. Since that day there had been several engagements on a small scale, but no serious fighting. The Turks had abandoned everything but the town itself and two forts lying outside the walls, which were strongly garrisoned. Reinforcements from Turkey and Syria were hurried forward, and included several batteries of artillery, which were distributed along the wall.

The Banu Ali on their side proclaimed a sort of holy war against the Turks, and invited all Arabia to assist them. They said they would not harm or interfere with the pilgrims, who should be free to come and go as usual, and to pass through their lines. Their quarrel was with the government and the government alone.

The assistance they asked for was soon forthcoming; fresh levies kept arriving from all quarters. For once in a way the tribes seemed in perfect agreement.

At the time of our arrival the Turkish troops in Medina may have mustered ten thousand, with twenty guns; the Arabs, upwards of twenty thousand, and were daily increasing.

MEDINA Medina is situated in an open plain at an altitude of about three thousand feet above sea level. On three sides the plain is bounded by mountains, from five to ten miles distant from the town, but to the south the country is open. The city itself in shape is roughly an oval, measuring about a mile at its greater diameter. It really consists of two towns joined together. The older one, which has a separate wall, contains the mosque and most of the dwelling houses and shops; the other is the more modern part, in which are situated most of the public buildings, markets, and barracks. It includes a large open space in which caravans assemble on arrival or before starting.

*Shawal: the month after Ramadan.

A smaller wall has been built on to the other to protect this quarter. There
are several gates, which are named after the places to which the roads issuing
from them lead: one, for instance, is called the Bab al-Sham, or Syrian Gate,
another the Mecca Gate, and so on. Water is supplied by a number of wells,
and is plentiful and good in quality. There are date plantations and other
cultivation almost completely surrounding the town, and extending for several miles. The railway station lies to the west of the town, about a quarter
of a mile from the outer wall. At the time I was there, it was not completed,
but some substantial stone buildings were then in course of erection, which,
by the way, being quite bulletproof, proved very useful during the fighting.
The cemetery known as the Baqiyya῾ is on the south side, abutting on to the
wall. Here are buried many of the most famous men in the history of Islam,
including several relations of the Prophet. During my stay it was almost
constantly under fire.

I should put the normal population of Medina, apart from troops
and pilgrims, at thirty thousand all told. Their occupations are almost all
in connection with the pilgrims, on whom they subsist almost entirely.
They work hard for the three months of the pilgrim season, and do nothing the rest of the year. There is a place for every one in the system. The
wealthier classes own houses, which they let for large sums. The younger
men are mostly employed as guides, and are often very generously rewarded
for their services. The shopkeepers of course do a roaring trade, and every
one, down to the porters and water carriers, makes a good thing out of the
visitors. . . .

JIDDA Non-Muslims are allowed to reside in both Yanbu and Jidda, provided that they do not go outside the walls. In the latter place there are a few
Christian and Jewish merchants, and most of the European powers are represented by consuls. They are, however, by no means safe from maltreat-
ment even here. The consulates are situated all together in the northernmost
quarter of the town.

Jidda is supposed to be one of the oldest cities in the world. It is a very
picturesque place, especially as seen from the sea, and, like Yanbu, it is in a
very dilapidated condition. The high, narrow houses seem tottering on their
foundations—the minarets of its mosques are all yards out of the plumb. A
slight earthquake shock would reduce both places to a heap of rubble. The
streets and markets, though dirty, are as nothing in that respect compared
with Yanbu. There are a number of good shops and several fairly respectable cafés. The climate, though hot, is not in itself unhealthy, and is far preferable to that of Mecca, which on a still day is a perfect furnace. Here at

Jidda the sea breezes keep the air moving and help to carry away the miasmas arising from the unsanitary condition of the streets and habitations. The water, like that of Yanbu, is scarce and brackish. Epidemic diseases of all sorts are unfortunately very prevalent.

The Oriental appearance of the place is accentuated at this season by the *ihram,* which nearly every one is wearing. It seems strange to see streets and cafés filled with people clad only in bath towels. At first I could not help feeling positively indecent, but the sensation soon wore off. . . .

JIDDA TO MECCA Besides our lot, [our camel man] had three other camels, which were carrying some Egyptians—a man and two women. He managed to bluff them into starting at eleven o'clock, just as the moon was rising, and then came to us to say that they would not be allowed to enter Mecca unless we came too, since his pass was for a certain number of camels, and if they did not all appear, he would be refused admittance. This was probably a lie, but as we could not very well make the Egyptians offload again, we had to make the best of it and go, too. I did not much mind; it was much more pleasant to ride through the warm, still night than in the daytime with the sun beating down on our shaven and defenseless heads. So we saddled up and joined the stream of camels still flowing silently eastward. Day and night it is the same, we seemed drifting into Mecca on a rising tide of humanity. When one considers that in the course of the month perhaps half a million people travel this road, besides nearly all the food and other stores they require, it is easy to realise the enormous number of beasts that must be employed.

The silence of the whole is strange and impressive. There is no longer any shouting, singing, or firing of shots. Most of the pilgrims are too awed by their surroundings to divert themselves thus, and the camels steal forward over the soft sand without a sound. It is difficult for an outsider to realize the true Muslim's feelings as he approaches Mecca. To him it is a place hardly belonging to this world, overshadowed like the Tabernacle of old by the almost tangible presence of the deity. Five times daily throughout his life has he turned his face toward this city whose mysteries he is now about to view with his own eyes. Moreover, according to common belief, pilgrimage brings certain responsibilities and even perils along with its manifold blessings. Good deeds in Mecca count many thousand times their value elsewhere, but sins committed there will reap their reward in hell.

In the early hours of the morning we passed between two white stone pillars, which mark the boundary of the Sacred Territory, and thenceforward we were treading consecrated ground. Nothing within may be hunted, or killed at all except for food. All wanton destruction of life is forbidden.*

After passing the line, a special prayer [the *talbiyya*] is repeated at intervals, at times in chorus. . . . The last words . . . are repeated many times over in a sort of wailing key and taken up again and again at different points along the line.

In our half-clad condition we found the early morning air very chilly and were glad when the sun rose. As it got light, Ibrahim, [a hajji] who had made the pilgrimage before, pointed out to me the Jabal Nur (Mountain of Light), a high conical peak surmounted by a sort of beacon, which I am told is really a tomb. This is one of the famous hills overlooking the city. About eight o'clock we passed a few stone houses some distance to the left, which we were told belonged to Mecca, and accordingly we read the prayer appropriate to the first sight of its buildings. Each of us was provided with a book containing all these prayers in their proper order, to be recited on different occasions, such as on assuming the *ihram,* the first view of the city, passing the gate, catching sight of the Ka'ba, and so on. . . .

Though I must confess to having felt a little nervous, I had only to glance round to see that most of my fellow pilgrims were more frightened still. As we approached the town, their excitement became quite painful to witness. For about an hour we travelled on, passing only a few small huts and an occasional Bedouin tent, till I began to wonder where on earth Mecca could be hidden. Suddenly we turned to the left and saw in front of us a great hollow surrounded by high stony hills, one of them crowned by a large, formidable-looking fort, another by a mosque, and the rest by other buildings that I was at the time unable to identify.

Mecca in fact lies at the edge of the rough mountainous country which extends far into the interior of Arabia. The town is situated in a deep, narrow valley, so completely hidden on the seaward side that one sees no sign of it till almost arrived at the gate. This valley runs approximately northeast and southwest, and seems to extend for a considerable distance. . . .

MECCA We spent the next few days very pleasantly in exploring Mecca. There was much to see and do, and the crowded markets were a never-failing source of interest and amusement. Mecca is a very much bigger place than Medina: its normal population apart from pilgrims is said to be seventy thousand, though

---

*In the state of *ihram* the pilgrim is forbidden to take life of any kind; even insects, with the exception of scorpions and one or two others dangerous to human beings, are protected. All loud talking and squabbling are likewise prohibited.

I should have put it myself at a much higher figure. It must be remembered, however, that the pilgrims there during the week of the Hajj may number upwards of five hundred thousand and that for most of them house accommodation has to be provided, so that the number of buildings composing the city is greatly in excess of what would normally be required. The streets are, generally speaking, wide and clean, and the houses are nearly all three or four storeys high—sometimes more. The principal markets are roofed, as in Damascus, and though they do not compare with those of that place in number or variety, there are nevertheless some very good shops. The merchants cater almost entirely for the pilgrims, most of whom like to take away with them some memento of their visit. There are no local industries whatever, and I quite failed to find anything that could be considered characteristic of the place itself. Goods are imported hither from all parts of the Orient—silks from Syria, carpets from Turkey and Persia, brass work from India and Egypt—and all these things go down well enough with most of the pilgrims, but are the despair of the traveller who knows he could buy the same things better and cheaper in many much more accessible places than Mecca. Besides, the resident merchants, traders from all parts of Islam bring their wares to Mecca at this season, and are always certain of finding a ready market and doing a profitable business.

The government of Mecca is peculiar. It is really a semi-independent province of Turkey, under the rule of a sharif who is invariably chosen from certain families descended from Ali and Fatima. This sharif is considered to be an independent monarch: he lives in a palace, maintains a corps of guards, and has theoretically absolute powers within his own narrow dominions. He is treated with the same ceremony as the Sultan of Turkey or any other Eastern potentate. The lineage of the sharifian families is supposed to be pure and irreproachable. In them one ought to see the Arab as he was in the days of the Prophet, before the Muslim conquests had introduced the foreign element which in these days is so apparent in most of them. The present Sharif is a man of about fifty, of medium height and good build. He has straight, regular features, a long, grey beard, and a rather dark complexion. . . .

CHIEF OF THE ZAMZAM WELL We made several friends in the course of the first week, mostly old acquaintances of Abdul Wahid. Among them was an officer in a Baghdad regiment, who introduced us to . . . Abd al-Rahman. The latter was an elderly man, a native of Mecca, who had charge of the special water carriers that dispense the water from the sacred well and the army of attendants who hand it round in the Haram. . . .

This particular job was apparently a perquisite of Abd al-Rahman's family, and had been so for generations. He was a person of some considerable consequence and proved a very useful acquaintance. He ordered a place to be kept for us in the Haram alongside himself and his friends, our mats being spread in the shade of the colonnade by day and outside in the evening. This was a great convenience, especially on Fridays, when most people have to come hours too early in order to get a place in the shade; otherwise they have to sit in the open square, which, at midday, is rather trying. We, however, could turn up any time we liked and make certain of finding a good place kept for us by Abd al-Rahman's obsequious retainers—all of which we got gratis but for the inevitable bakhsheesh. Abd al-Rahman invited me to his house, which overlooked the Haram, and I twice went to tea with him there. He was very hospitable, and before leaving I had to write my name in his visitors book, the collection of autographs being one of his hobbies. He turned out to be a misogynist and, what is much more unusual in the East, a bachelor. The fiendish temper of his only sister, who kept house for him, was responsible, he told me, for his dislike of women in general. He had, it seemed, no sympathy whatever with the new constitution or with parliaments of any sort. He had the profoundest admiration for Abd al-Hamid, and much preferred the old regime, to which he hoped and expected that his country would shortly return. We got on rather well together because on most of these points—I mean his political views—I was able to agree with him. On my second visit to him, however, his questions regarding my family and other affairs became so extremely embarrassing that I decided to decline future invitations, feeling that my talents for invention were unequal to further strain upon them. . . .

AN OLD ACQUAINTANCE We had been in Mecca about a week when Masaudi ran across an old acquaintance. This was a boy of about thirteen, Kepi by name, who, with his father, a certain Shaykh Muhammad, had travelled in the same ship with us from Mombasa to Port Said early in the year. They were then going on by way of Yanbu to Medina, where they proposed to stay till near the time of the pilgrimage. Shaykh Muhammad had died on entering Mecca, about a month previous to our own arrival, and Kepi had been left in a destitute condition. He had, however, found out some fellow countrymen, who had given him enough money to subsist on, and he lived in hopes of finding some party of pilgrims to take him back to Zanzibar. There are, by the way, a certain number of Swahilis and Arabs from that coast living in Mecca. Of course I was careful to avoid meeting any of them, but Masaudi, having once been recognized, could not help doing so. He accordingly went round with Kepi to call on their Shaykh, and thenceforward saw a good deal of them. He explained that he had come there with two rich Arabs, one a Baghdadi and the other from Muscat, with whom he was living; but being in the position of a servant, he could not invite people to the house. As Kepi was a relation of some Mombasa friends of mine, I thought I would do a kind action by taking him with us when we went. Masaudi informed him that his Muscat patron, hearing of his misfortunes, had decided to return him to his own country, and would give him a weekly allowance in the meantime. Kepi of course was delighted, and at once volunteered to come to us as a servant during our stay; but Masaudi told him that we had already too many retainers. He knew me by sight, so could not be allowed into the house till we were actually leaving. As a matter of fact, if Kepi had had a little more Arabic and common sense, he would have applied to any rich pilgrim for assistance, which in nine cases out of ten would have been amply forthcoming. Any act of real charity performed on the pilgrimage, more especially in Mecca itself, is believed to cover a great multitude of sins, and most people are on the lookout for genuine cases worthy of their generosity. Orphans, moreover, are always objects of compassion among the Arabs. . . .

OF BANKS AND MONEY I had some trouble in getting my cheque cashed. The merchant to whom I had been referred declined to honour it on the ground that, owing to some trouble that had occurred, he had no further business relations with Abdullah Waridi [on whom the cheque was drawn]. On receiving, some time previously, the latter's notification that he was drawing on him, he had written on the subject and was waiting an answer. In the meantime he declined to do anything. Fortunately a letter from Abdullah, containing a draft on another merchant, arrived before my supplies were exhausted; but it might easily have been very awkward. I decided that it was less risky on the whole to carry one's money in cash.

There are no banks in the Hijaz, owing to an absurd belief that the business of a banker is forbidden by the Quran. There is no justification for this, and the idea has long been combated by reasonable people. The prohibition in the Quran is against usury, and obviously was never intended to apply to reasonable rates of interest on deposits of money in business affairs. The odd thing is that anyone might start a bank provided only that he paid no interest at all! It is not giving the money to the bank that is considered immoral, but receiving profit on it. Stranger still, they cannot see that the business of a money changer, of whom there are many hundreds in Mecca and Medina, involves exactly the same thing. The money changers make their profits by giving short change; thus in changing a dollar for rupees they take a few *pice* as commission, and I believe their business is often very profitable. . . .

THE PILGRIMAGE At about five o'clock we ourselves donned the *ihram* after making our *niya,* or formal vow to perform the pilgrimage. Our luggage and servants had been sent on in the morning, and we hoped to find all in readiness on our arrival.

We mounted our donkeys, fine big animals well over eleven hands, I should say, and rode out accompanied by the [cameleer] we were employing, Jaffa by name, his son, and the three Persians who had been occupying the rooms above our own suite. Progress was slow at first, owing to the narrowness of the way; but on leaving the town, the road broadened out, and we got along faster and were able to canter part of the way. The road rises gently between low stony kopjes; it is paved in some places, but elsewhere not even metalled. We reached Mina shortly after dark and found Jaffa, our cook, awaiting us on the road.

We were conducted to our tents, which we found had been pitched a short distance beyond, on the outskirts of the great encampment, not far from the blaze of torches that indicated the quarters of the Sharif. We dined in comfort and afterwards listened to a reading by the leader of our Persian acquaintances, who was a descendant of the Prophet and by way of being a learned man. Strictly speaking, we ought to have gone to the mosque of Mina for the *'isha* prayer, but few people do so nowadays. One would run a very good chance of losing one's self, for one thing, and this is none too safe a place after dark. We turned in early, knowing that the next day would tax all our endurance.

We struck camp at dawn and sent the servants and tents forward with the camels. I never expected to find them again; but Jaffa, our cameleer who had now taken charge, seemed quite confident about it. We ourselves went into Mina and waited a couple of hours in a café there before going forward. We finally started about eight o'clock. The road leaving the village runs due east and is on the average about half a mile wide, except in two places where it passes through defiles and narrows down to a couple of hundred yards. After riding for about an hour, we halted at one of the many refreshment booths pitched at intervals along the road and had some breakfast.

To do justice to the extraordinary scene would require a descriptive skill that I do not possess. The best idea of what it is like will be gained by considering that at least half a million people are traversing these nine miles of road between sunrise and ten o'clock this day, that about half of them are mounted, and that many of them possess baggage animals as well. The roar of this great column is like a breaking sea, and the dust spreads for miles over the surrounding country. When, passing through the second defile, we came in sight of Arafat itself, the spectacle was stranger still. The hill was literally black with people, and tents were springing up round it, hundreds to the minute, in an ever widening circle. As we approached, the dull murmur caused by thousands of people shouting the formula *"Labayk Allahuma, labayk!"* which had long been audible, became so loud that it dominated every other sound. In the distance it had sounded rather ominous, suggestive of some deep disturbance of great power, like the rumble of an earthquake.

Mount Arafat is a hill about four hundred feet in height, pyramidical in shape, and strewn with great boulders. At the base of it are the springs which feed the conduit leading to Mecca. On the summit there is a paved platform surmounted by a stone beacon. The surrounding country is rough and mountainous, especially to the east, but Arafat itself stands isolated in the middle of a level, scrub-covered plain. The camp is formed round the hill on the flat and covers many square miles.

Thanks to the excellence of Jaffa's arrangements and the punctuality with which his orders had been carried out, we found our tents almost at once. Their position was on the very border of the camp—the best place, for many reasons—and several of our acquaintances were congregated in the same neighbourhood. Everyone was in the best of spirits, and there was nothing in their demeanour to denote that the assembly had any religious significance. It was more suggestive of a gigantic picnic party than anything else.

We rested an hour in the shade of our tent and then ascended the hill to pray the customary two *rakat*s on the platform on top. The whole of the pilgrimage was now assembled, and the view from the summit gave an idea of the vast number present. It was curious to reflect that the day before, this hill was silent and deserted, as it would be again tomorrow, and as it would remain till each succeeding year brought round the Day of Arafat. In fact, it would be almost impossible for any small party to get here at all on any other day, so infested with robbers is this part of the country.

The hour of the midday prayer arrived while we were on the summit. A salute of sixty-three guns was fired, numerous bands struck up, and the crowd cheered themselves hoarse. There were in all three six-gun batteries present and two mountain guns carried on mules.

Descending the mountain, we inspected some large tanks filled by the springs, in which many people were bathing. The water was very dirty, and the flanks of the hill, where many thousands of the poorer pilgrims were seeking shelter among the rocks, were in a horribly dirty condition. It is not surprising that infectious diseases spread rapidly amid such surroundings; the astonishing thing is that cholera, once started, does not make a clean sweep of the whole pilgrimage.

A market had been established, where food of various sorts was being sold, and there were also a number of refreshment tents where drinks and so on were obtainable. We strolled about for some time; but finding the midday sun on our bare heads rather trying, we returned to lunch in our tent. . . .

RETURNING TO MINA We had now to dress ourselves in the best clothes we possessed, and we were all provided with new suits for the occasion in accordance with the accepted custom. This is done partly in honour of the festival, and partly because the new-made hajji is believed to start with a clean "defaulter sheet," all his previous sins and errors being completely remitted, and the new clothes are held symbolical of his spiritual condition. The completion of the Hajj is therefore the appropriate moment for making new resolutions, breaking off old habits, and so on.

I had white cloth robes, a black *jubba,* and gold sash, with a dagger; Masaudi was somewhat elaborately attired in the *kanzu* of Zanzibar, a regimental mess waistcoat (pattern obsolete, needless to say, as it was several years since I had paid about ten pounds for it), and a gold-embroidered *joho*—a garment peculiar to Muscat and its former dependencies. Abdul Wahid looked peculiarly bilious in a yellow caftan he had bought in Damascus.

Our donkeys having been brought, we rode back to Mina, starting just before sundown. We had not gone far when Masaudi took a toss, which somewhat marred the beauty of his appearance, and was immediately followed by Abdul Wahid, that being his seventh in the three days. The wretched donkeys were dead beat, and could hardly keep their feet even at a walk. When we started to canter, I fell off. The Arabian donkeys are given neither saddle nor stirrups, but a pile of cloths, often elaborately embroidered, is strapped across their backs, which is really much more comfortable, but difficult to hold on to, especially when compelled by one's costume to ride side-saddle.

We reached Mina just as the salute of guns was announcing the hour of the *'isha* prayer. Twenty-one guns are fired by each battery at each of the five daily prayers during the days of the festival. Being very tired, we turned in directly after dinner.

Our tent was a large one, about fifteen feet in diameter. The three of us—Abdul Wahid, Masaudi, and myself—slept with our feet toward the pole and our heads outwards—like spokes of a wheel. In the middle we had collected what little luggage we had brought out and a few other odd belongings. The principal thing was a brown bag containing about five pounds in gold, a beautifully bound Quran I had bought for thirty shillings two days before leaving for Arafat, a string of amber beads, and a couple of spare pistols. We seem to have slept heavily that night, for when Masaudi, the first to awake, looked round next morning, the bag was gone, and so were several other things, including his beautiful new turban. Some tracks in the sand and a round hole in the fly of the tent remained to show how the thief had come upon us. There was of course nothing to be done, but the incident serves to illustrate the daring of these robbers. To break into a tent where three armed men are sleeping in the middle of a well-guarded camp and abstract their belongings is no mean feat. As a matter of fact we probably came well out of it, for had one of us stirred while the thief was in the tent, a knife thrust would probably have prolonged his sleep to the Day of Judgment. This is how people who live in such places acquire the habit, as many notice, of remaining quite motionless when they are waking from sleep until they have become completely conscious of their surroundings. It is unsafe to touch an Arab of the desert in order to wake him. Of course, had we been so fortunate as to catch the thief in the act, he would have been shot on the instant. We had frequently been warned of these dangers, and never slept without weapons ready to hand.

On our way out we had passed a party of nineteen thieves chained together on their way to Mecca. Of these six were shot, and the remainder had their right hands cut off. This latter method of punishment is sometimes considered barbarous by Europeans, but is endorsed by all reasonable people in these countries. Violent remedies are necessary when dealing with dangerous diseases.

part four

The Early Twentieth Century
1925—33

The five accounts in this section are all by Western converts to Islam. They overlap the crucial years between Abd al-Aziz ibn Sa'ud's conquest of Mecca (1924) and the establishment of the Saudi state in 1932. By chance, these pieces also alternate between those with a special interest in regional politics and others of a less public nature. Of the three men of action, Eldon Rutter (1925) wrote well-observed passages about Ibn Sa'ud while Muhammad Asad (1927) and St. John Philby (1931) were the king's intimates. Two other travelers left more private memoirs—one highborn, wealthy, and well educated (Lady Evelyn Cobbold, 1933), the other a hard knocks cameleer from the Australian outback (Winifred Stegar, 1927).

Each of the authors in this section had different reasons for becoming Muslim. Winifred Stegar married an Indian who swept her off her feet, then off to Mecca. Muhammad Asad embraced Islam as an alternative to bourgeois Occidental values. Philby, a Christian agnostic, converted to live more fully in Arabia, while Lady Cobbold, a landed Briton, had no other religion than Islam. All five wrote at a time when relations between Europe and the Muslim lands were close and when Europe might almost be called post-Christian. In addition, since at least 1900, Muslims had been immigrating to Europe in large numbers, first to fill a low-wage labor vacuum and, after 1914, to help fight World War I.* By 1925, Islam was not the stranger it once had been in western Europe. Western converts, while still distinctly odd, no longer carried the stigma of apostasy that had haunted Joseph Pitts in the eighteenth century. Letters from Philby's friends in 1930, when he became a Muslim, imply that the more surprising side of his decision lay simply in being concerned enough with one's religion to want to change it.

*During WWI, in France alone, two hundred thousand Algerians were "requisitioned" for war-related labor.

Readers may wonder, *How reliable a reporter can a convert be?* The assumption, in Richard Burton's time in Europe, was that nonbelievers were more credible. Today as well, disinterest seems to guarantee a more scientific view on any subject. This may apply in the field of particle physics, but it does not hold true with regard to Mecca. Both Ibn Jubayr and the Begum of Bhopal, while deeply devout, could be scathing about the Hajj when it was called for. Faith did not automatically reduce their capacity to be objective; it may have increased it. Western observers, on the other hand, were sometimes more involved with their disguises than with the Hajj. Almost invariably, they inflated the risks of the journey, while their access to local information was badly compromised by fears of discovery. An unspoken question, *What are you doing here?* hovers over these interlopers' texts, whether by Burckhardt (1814) or Wavell (1908). With few exceptions, the observers were neither very impartial nor more complete in their accounts than the converts who followed them a few years later. They were often fair writers, but in any real sense they were not pilgrims. They shed light on a unique experience, yet it was an experience only a Muslim could have. Even when they performed the *tawaf,* they literally were going through the motions. Burton, who remained a kind of Muslim all his life, had the grace to admit this. Contrasting himself to other hajjis circuiting the Ka'ba, he wrote:

> I may truly say that, of all the worshippers who clung weeping to the curtain, or who pressed their beating hearts to the stone, none felt for the moment a deeper emotion than the hajji from the far north . . . but to confess the humbling truth, theirs was the high feeling of religious enthusiasm, mine was the ecstasy of gratified pride.

Contrast the remarks of the Austrian convert, Muhammad Asad:

> And there I stood before the temple of Abraham and gazed at the marvel without thinking . . . and out of some hidden, smiling kernel within me there slowly grew an elation like a song.

The disappearance of non-Muslims from these pages coincides with the completion of Europe's colonization of the world. So long as that process continued, from the sixteenth through the nineteenth centuries, Mecca remained one of a few forbidden cities Western travelers made it their business to "discover." (Tibetan Lhasa, Moroccan Smara, Malian Timbuktu, Beijing's Forbidden City, and Ethiopian Harrar were others.) By 1925, however, the frontiers of exploration lay elsewhere. After four centuries, Mecca returned to being an exclusively Islamic subject. For Muslims, of course, it always was.

Historical Background

THE MANDATE PERIOD Most of the authors in this section were concerned with Middle Eastern politics and the impact of European strategy on the region. After all, World War I and its treaties altered the shape of the Middle East forever. And they changed the Hajj as well.

After the Ottomans joined the war on the German side in 1914, the Triple Entente of Britain, France, and Russia entered into numerous veiled accords concerning the future division of the Ottoman Empire. The Constantinople (1915) and Sykes-Picot (1916) Agreements and the 1917 Balfour Declaration promised prospective chunks of Ottoman land to each ally once the war ended. In addition to these advance bookings east of the Bosporus, France and Britain took steps to exploit some very real ethnic divisions between the Turkish Porte and its Armenian, Kurdish, and Arab territories. They not only encouraged regional leaders to rebel against the Turks; they plied them with arms, money, and promised independence.

By the middle of World War I, Britain's chief Arab rebel leader was none other than Sharif Husayn ibn Ali of Mecca (1908–24). In March 1916, Husayn inaugurated a revolt against the Turks by firing a rifle at their garrison from his palace window near the Haram Mosque. The subsequent uprising spread through the Hijaz and continued during the war with British backing. While not much more than a sideshow in the Allies' eastern war, the Sharif's revolt remained strategically important to British policy, for it linked the ruler of Mecca to the Allied cause, and so won approval from millions of Muslims despite the fact that the Ottoman Porte had sided with Germany. Here we see the only viable government in the Hijaz being made increasingly a pawn in the strategic diplomatic games of Great Britain and the Ottomans. Any local political unity in Arabia was thereby compromised as greater powers sought new allies for their struggle. As for the Hajj, Husayn's Arab Revolt affected it most directly in 1916, when his troops, assisted by British arms and T. E. Lawrence's flair for explosives, blew up the railroad lines as far north as Ma'an. The train's disappearance rocked the new economy of the Hijaz and stunted the growth of Medina, as we shall see. It did not, however, permanently reduce Hajj attendance in Mecca. Once the war ended, a renewed flow of pilgrims reverted to sea and land travel. Even interior camel routes enjoyed a new lease on life in the 1920s. Such were the deep attractions of the Hajj.

THE MANDATE SYSTEM At the end of the war, Allied promises of Arab independence were brushed aside at the treaty tables. Instead, the core of the Ottoman Empire was diced into six new political entities called mandates. (See Figs. 14 and 15 to compare the region's political boundaries before and after World War I.) The mandates were colonies with a sunset clause—undeveloped, fledgling states to be placed under the tutelage of more "advanced" nations until they were "able to stand by themselves under the strenuous conditions of the modern world."

The paternalistic mandate system put a League of Nations face on naked colonialism. Behind its façade, France and Britain were able to guard their own strategic interests (oil, trade, communications with India) simply by bankrolling and administering the region for an infinitely extendable "preparatory period." By 1923, new borders had appeared on the map; Transjordan, Iraq, and Syria acquired names; and Arab "regents" from the Meccan sharifate were imported as figureheads to rule them.* Egypt and Palestine did not require the full charade: they were directly administered by British commissioners, but it hardly mattered. Policy in either case was soon being set by Europeans, using a network of high commissions taking orders from London or Paris. One of our authors, St. John Philby, was Britain's chief representative in Iraq (1921–24).

SAUDI RESURGENCE Meanwhile in Arabia, a second crucial chapter of the story was unfolding. In the years before World War I, deep in the northeastern Nejd Desert, Abd al-Aziz ibn Sa'ud, inheritor of the Sa'ud-Wahhabi alliance, had begun reconquering ancestral territory. Ibn Sa'ud was a tall, decisive tactician with sufficient charisma to carry out his plan—the complete unification of Arabia under one banner. His chief adversaries were Amir Muhammad ibn Rashid, a local Nejdi lord and a Turkish ally, and the British-backed ruler of Mecca, Sharif Husayn. Whereas Ibn Rashid and Husayn were already allied with non-Arab powers, Ibn Sa'ud drew to his side an indigenous band of resurgent Wahhabi tribesmen who had begun, around 1912, to sell their belongings and settle together in farm-based spiritual communes

---

*This use of Meccan rulers was a veiled Allied ploy to garner Muslim support around the world for the new mandates; it also gave members of the Hashimite line new job opportunities after the fall of their sharifate in 1925.

throughout the Nejd. Ibn Sa'ud, their hereditary leader, placed himself at their head almost at once. By judicious gifts of land, he acquired an army.

The first goal of these Brothers, or Ikhwan, was to restore Islam to as many Bedouin as possible, to fix the people's attention on Muslim values, and to break their allegiance to local chiefs and shaykhs. In this way, with surprising speed, thousands of semi-nomads developed a loyalty beyond their tribes. They also acquired a livelihood that, for the first time in these records, excluded looting pilgrim caravans. Rather, they pledged their rifles to Ibn Sa'ud, who used them to consolidate a kingdom. In return, the Ikhwan communes received farm tools, arms, mosques, books, livestock, and stables. The communes with their strong social emphasis on unitarian Islam broke down clan jealousies, providing the people a new identity, and put a brake on intertribal warfare. By 1917, a quarter of a million Bedouin men, women, and children had moved from desert tents to several hundred mud-brick settlements around the Nejd. Among them were sixty thousand men of fighting age, ready to respond at a moment's notice. They overwhelmed Amir Ibn Rashid, and the Saudis claimed his lands.

World War I had freed the Hijaz from Turkish control. Now, Ibn Sa'ud set out to solve his family's other problem, control of the two Holy Cities by the sharifs. To most outside observers, Sharif Husayn's postwar position appeared secure. Hopeful British and French diplomats had placed his sons on the thrones of three mandates,* and his claims to kingship of the Hijaz were being honored. In reality, however, he was bottled up in Mecca, and Ibn Sa'ud's armies were entering the Hijaz. In September 1924, three thousand Wahhabi warriors swept down on Ta'if (overlooking Mecca) and sent a clear message: The centuries-long cold war between Arabia's two most influential families, the sharifs and the Saudis, was about to be decisively concluded. Husayn abdicated a few days later, and Ibn Sa'ud's army entered Mecca without firing a shot. The next year he became King of the Hijaz.

Ibn Sa'ud was crowned near Mount Safa in 1925. With the recent abdication of Sharif Husayn and the collapse of the Ottoman caliphate the year before, Muslims were left without a symbolic world representative for the first time in memory. Lacking this powerful organizing symbol, the Middle East was ripe for the tide of nationalism then sweeping through it. Pan-Islam, the vision of a larger community beyond one's region, had fueled a millennium of major bids for a single sovereign to whom all Muslims would look. In 1925, that long tradition was left without a reasonable figure to

---

*It is a curious fact that during this period not only regional sovereigns but Western nations, too, were desperate for partnership and recognition in Mecca.

represent it. Although the timing of Ibn Saʿud's victory gave it added reso-
nance around the Muslim world, he was never a likely candidate for caliph.
The world accepted his revolution because he won, but his puritan-style
Islam was too strict for most Muslims.

THE SAUDI REFORMATION OF THE HAJJ Under Husayn's long, venal rule, the
Hajj service system reached new extremes of unbridled profiteering. With
Ibn Saʿud's appearance, it faced a regime bent on ending corruption. Particularly in Mecca, the headstrong, doctrinaire Wahhabi army demanded
adherence to Quranic law. It is as if these Nejdi reformers had taken a page
from the wish list of the Begum of Bhopal. Determined to curtail excess in
every form, they ended public graft and exorbitant duties, lowered prices on
food and pilgrim lodgings, and secured the roads from Jidda and Medina.
But their uncompromising approach offended many. Again and again in the
following excerpts, we see the Wahhabis enforcing a stricter, remoralized
Islam, stamping out Ottoman excess, pulling down saints' shrines, banning
tobacco, music, alcohol, dancing. Ibn Jubayr's old demand that the Hijaz
be cleansed by the sword was not too extreme for the average Wahhabi soldier.

The mass of pilgrims endured these extreme measures in exchange for
fair prices and safety on the roads. The Muslim world as a whole, however,
abhorred their violence and strictness. Even after 1929, when Ibn Saʿud
demobilized the Wahhabis, he was some years repairing the damage done to
his name outside the country. A strong alliance with Britain, the discovery
of oil in his kingdom, and continued, scrupulous attention to the management of the Hajj are reasons often given for the accommodation by neighboring Arab governments of Saudi rule. One might, however, ask, *What*
neighboring Arab governments? Thanks to the mandate system and World
War II, only Saudi Arabia among the ten core sites of the Middle East
emerged after 1945 with a durable, indigenous regime. Severe, conservative,
and inward looking, it nonetheless functioned and benefited its people. It
was about to be enriched beyond their dreams.

Our image today of Saudi Arabia as a wealthy, modernizing state does
not apply to the interwar period. Ibn Saʿud's new country was impoverished.
It had no roads, no national currency, and no communications system. The
modest receipts of the Hajj remained its chief source of revenues through
the 1930s. During the Great Depression, Britain augmented this income
with small annual subsidies of sixty thousand pounds. Not until the 1950s
would large amounts of capital be dedicated to modernization. Meanwhile,
reforming the Hajj was a slow process accomplished in many stages over

decades. The groundwork, however, was laid almost at once. In November 1926, Ibn Saʿud issued a decree setting out the first comprehensive Hajj regulations. Its forty articles granted his regime the right to license and oversee all pilgrim guilds. The duties of guides, water bearers, greeters, and camel brokers were thus defined, and boards and committees set up to supervise their activities. Fixed rates for services were published and distributed abroad. Step by step, the pilgrim service system would be reshaped along these lines into a public utility industry. Despite a hiatus during the Great Depression, the Hajj under Ibn Saʿud grew and prospered rather than falling to putative French or English protection in the 1930s. Ironically enough, it was the French and British Empires, not the Hajj, that were on their way to virtual extinction. Meanwhile, European consuls and representatives remained confined to Jidda, on the coast.

14

Eldon Rutter
Great Britain
1925

⁂

In May 1925, Eldon Rutter was in Cairo making arrangements for the pilgrimage. By then, he had already met Nur al-Din Sharqawi, a young Meccan willing to go with him, and together they had assembled some equipment for the trip: a small camera, a compass, a pocket aneroid barometer, shaykh's robes, a set of saddlebags, a few books in Arabic, and a revolver. This much was in order when, a few days prior to leaving, the Meccan died. Rutter set out alone to take his chances.

It was not a good time for any pilgrim to visit the Hijaz. Arriving in Suez by train, Rutter found no other traveler in the port. Abd al-Aziz ibn Saʿud had secured Mecca eight months earlier, and roads were in dispute throughout the region. The last time Wahhabis had taken the city, in the days of Ali Bey al-Abbasi, every hajji had been forced to leave the country. Now the difficulty was to get in. Villages from the mountains to the coast were under siege or in revolt against Sharif Husayn, and Ibn Saʿud's high-handed zealots patrolled the roads. So great were the dangers in 1925 that weeks before Rutter's departure from Suez, the Egyptian religious senate had temporarily dissolved the obligation to make the Hajj.

For an Englishman intent on taking notes, the risks in such a setting were compounded. Medina, Yanbu, and Jidda remained in the Sharif's hands, and they bristled with weapons. Rutter skirted these hot spots, taking a tertiary route—one that has gone unrecorded in these pages. He sailed with a Red Sea dhow from Massawa in Eritrea to al-Ghawm, a small port near the Yemeni border. Even this remote depot was occupied by sharp-eyed Saudi guards looking for any excuse to show their authority. Their numbers grew approaching Mecca. To avoid interrogation, Rutter changed traveling companions four times, choosing the risks of anonymity over false comfort.

The people of the Hijaz were friendly, however, and Rutter met with warm receptions in many towns. At al-Birk, for example, he was welcomed by the local muezzin, then entertained by a solicitous Serbian Muslim from Mecca:

After the banquet, we carried a couple of [rope beds] from Umar's hut, and placed them on a little raised space in the open air without. Sitting here, we could dimly see the inky sea on the one hand, and on the other the dark outline of the hills with the moon's bright disk hanging low above them among the glittering stars. Soon we were joined by another party who brought out their bedsteads from the next hut. . . . [As I dropped off to sleep], the dozing but watchful Umar rose to his feet, and produced a pillow and a blanket, which he insisted upon helping me adjust—and so I slept till dawn.

The passages excerpted in this section come from Rutter's long account of Mecca. He was the first competent writer to witness the Hajj under Ibn Sa'ud, and he rose to the challenge. He gamely remained in town about eight months, longer than any traveler after Burckhardt, and his portrait of the city is exhaustive. No sooner has he arrived than his guides sweep him off to the mosque for Friday prayers. There he reports on the water-bearer's trade and catches a first glimpse of Ibn Sa'ud circuiting the Ka'ba. Later Rutter visits Ibn Sa'ud's tent at Mina, where, like Ali Bey before, he uses the occasion to produce a sketch of the new ruler. In a pivotal excerpt, Rutter is stopped in the street by an old acquaintance. Their chance encounter quickly leads to an audience with Abd al-Aziz himself, then with various powerful dignitaries. These meetings shed valuable light on the city's workings. A few of Rutter's canny observations on Meccan culture appear here, too, part of a large body of information presented in chapters with titles like "The Meccan's Daily life."

The half-clad, camel-borne Wahhabis, with their ringleted hair and flashing rifles, pass like a scouring wind through Rutter's pages. After centuries of corrupt sharifs, decadent Turks, and surly Egyptian pashas, these iconoclastic and preemptive Brothers understandably sent nervous tremors through the Hijaz. Arabians call them the Mudayyina, Those Given Up to Religion. As Rutter makes clear, their sharp swords cut two ways. On the one hand, they castigated smokers as Satanists and pulled down saints' shrines in every village. On the other, they dealt directly with graft and corruption, rooting out superstition and unfair charges on the Hajj. Poorer pilgrims (the vast majority of hajjis) benefited from Sa'ud's new, fixed prices at the wells, in the markets, and on the caravans, but as Rutter shows, they found his Ikhwan intimidating.

Rutter's work contains so much first-rate material that one's first wish is simply to republish the whole book. His erudition is always related to the experience before him, and he is full of understanding for Arab ways. Historically speaking, his book forms the third and final section of a century-long report on the Saudi bid to take over the Hijaz. The story begins with Ali Bey al-Abbasi's initial sightings of the Wahhabis in 1807, continues in Burckhardt's record of their rout by Muhammad Ali in 1814, and is completed here with Rutter's view of their triumphant return in 1924. It seems a shame that such a fine travel book should have slipped into near oblivion so quickly. Except for what can be gleaned from his pages, little is known about the author's life.

from *The Holy Cities of Arabia*
by Eldon Rutter

HISTORICAL NOTE It is probable . . . that Mecca and Medina never attained to a greater height of prosperity than in the later years of the Turkish Empire—during the reign of the Sultan Abd al-Hamid. Abd al-Hamid was a wonderful exponent of the power of advertisement, and he saw to it that his public paid for his advertising. The Hijaz Railway, from Damascus to Medina, was constructed with funds supplied by every country in the Islamic world. The printing presses of Constantinople worked at high pressure upon the printing of the Quran and books of prayers in many Muslim languages; and to this day, from Java to Morocco, it is a Muslim's pride to possess a Stambuli Quran. Pictures of the Holy Places, drawn with such startling perspective that they compelled attention, were strewn about the world, from Algeria to China, from Serbia to Sumatra. All this activity aroused great enthusiasm among the Muslims, and was the means of enormously increasing the numbers of hajjis at the annual pilgrimage, and also the numbers of the permanent population of the Holy Cities. There are now in Mecca, and still more noticeably in Medina, streets of houses which, as is obvious from the descriptions published by J. L. Burckhardt, did not exist in the early part of last century. Since the fall of imperial Turkey the population of the Holy Cities has again shrunk, and many houses are in ruins.

The Islamic world never reposed any confidence in Sharif Husayn. In spite of his white beard and his piety, he was never able to create that atmosphere of power which emanated from the [Sultan]. Husayn was the puppet of unbelievers; not their opponent and diplomatic equal.

Mecca has several times been almost deserted of inhabitants, and the pilgrimage has been completely stopped by wars, sometimes for several years.

The Haram, whose very name means "Sanctuary," has more than once been the scene of bloody strife. As late as 1916, when the Arabs joined the Allies, some of the Sherifal troops attacked, with rifle fire, a party of Turks who took refuge in the Great Mosque.

MY MECCAN HOST AND GUIDES Abd al-Shukur . . . was frequently my companion in my walks about Mecca and its neighbourhood. His knowledge of his native town was not profound, as he could not read, but he was seldom at a loss to supply an answer to a question concerning it. His age was probably a year or two over fifty, and his shoulders were slightly bowed with the weight of those years. His father, an Indian, had settled in Mecca and married an Arab wife, and Abd al-Shukur now owned a small house on the slope of Jabal Hind.

My new friend had never been outside Mecca, excepting to go to Ta'if. He had never been to Jidda; he had never been to Medina. This is a very common condition among the Meccans: hundreds of them have never been outside that rock-walled pit, save to go the half-day journey to Arafat for the annual pilgrimage.

Abd al-Shukur now took a pinch of tobacco from his little tin box, and rolling a cigarette, he offered it to me.

"God bless you!" I said, "but I am a Wahhabi."

"Good!" said he, with a smile. "Then you may smoke in the house as the Mudayyina* do, but not in the street. That is to say, the act of drinking smoke is not unlawful. The unlawful is for a man to let people see him drinking smoke. Is that not so? That is to say, the unlawful . . ."

I took the cigarette, and lighted it.

"For the sake of friendship between me and between you," I said.

"Known!" he said, "and we are your servants."

"What happened when the Mudayyina came into Mecca?" I asked him.

"There came four men wearing the *ihram* and riding camels, and they passed down the streets, which were deserted, and cried out the promise of security, and that the people of Mecca—the neighbours of God—were under the protection of God and of Ibn Sa'ud. And all of us had locked and barred our doors. And in the second day there came two thousand of the Mudayyina, *ihram*ed and carrying rifles and swords, all mounted on *diluls*. Then they all performed the *tawaf,* and went out again to al-Abtah, the place of their camp. After a few days they broke into the palace of Sayyidna (King Husayn), and

*Mudayyina: Literally, "Those Devoted to Religion," and the name preferred by them then and now. [Ed.]

tied up a donkey in his sitting place. And on the donkey's head they put the turban of Sayyidna. After that they drove the donkey, and he wearing the turban, out into the streets, and went round the city with him in front of them. Then they kicked the jewelled Stambuli coat of Sayyidna, and his jewelled state umbrella, into the marketplace with their feet, and sold them for five piastres (about sixpence)."

"Did you see this?" I asked him.

"No!" replied Abd al-Shukur. "Thus we heard."

At this moment there entered the room a thin and simple-looking youth with a bronze-coloured skin and handsome eyes. He was probably seventeen years of age. Over his white *thobe* he wore a pink silk jacket, and on his head a yellow turban.

"*Salaam Alaykoum,*" he said in greeting, and going to the old man, he kissed the back of his hand and put his forehead to it for a moment.

"This," said the old man, "is my son. His name is Abd al-Fatah," and addressing his son, he added, "this is Hajj Ahmad Effendi, the guest of Abd al-Rahman. It is upon you to serve him well."

"Welcome!" said Abdul Fatah, his eyes shining with cordiality as he attempted to kiss my hand.

I smiled at the youth (he afterwards became my constant attendant in Abd al-Rahman's house), and asked him where he had been when the Wahhabis entered Mecca.

"I? I was with the harem in this house," he said without a blush. "*Wallah!* [By God!] I dressed in the clothes of a woman, with a veil over my face, and a *malaya*. My appearance was like a woman's exactly. If the Mudayyina had broken open the door, there was I, one of the harem."

"White upon you,* O Abdul al-Fatah!" said Abd al-Rahman, who now entered the room.

The portly *mutawwif* seated himself comfortably, with his back against a cushion; and taking a tobacco box from the fold of his belt, he commenced to roll a cigarette.

It being Friday, the Muslim Sabbath, all my companions wore clean clothes; and now, as we sat talking, the sound of the *adhan* broke in upon us. The minaret of Bab al-Umra was only a few feet away from the back of Abd al-Rahman's house, and its topmost gallery overlooked part of our roof. Many a time from that minaret in after days the resonant voice of the blind muezzin, Abd al-Ghafar, or of another, went swelling and echoing over the housetop—waking me before dawn as I lay in the cool silence under the stars.

---

*"White upon thee" may be translated by the colloquialism "Good for you!" i.e., "Bravo!"

Having performed ablutions, we all descended to the Haram; and choosing a convenient place under the cloisters, we performed the *sunna* prayer of two prostrations, and then sat to meditate, repeat parts of the Quran, or observe the congregation, until the chanting of the beginning of the congregational prayer.

Prayers being over, many of the congregation proceeded to perform *tawaf.* Among these, I observed a broad figure, over six feet in height, dressed in a yellow *mishlah* and carrying a black umbrella as a protection from the sun. He compassed the House with long deliberate strides, and at his heels pressed a motley crowd of Bedouins. This was Abd al-Aziz ibn Saʿud, the lord of the desert and invader of the Hijaz.

Before we returned to the house, Abd al-Rahman introduced me to one Sayyid Hasan, who, he said, was to be my *zamzami;* that is to say, he was the person who would give me a drink of Zamzam water whenever I might want it, particularly at prayer times.

This old man was the hereditary lord of a tiny stone-walled cavern in the wall of the Haram. A small but heavy wooden door a few yards from the Bab al-Daudiya—through which we usually entered the Haram—gave access to this cave, and here before his cavern door old Hasan was usually to be found at any hour of the day—either chanting the Quran in a low voice, or sleeping in a high one.

He was a short and stocky little man with a thin grey beard. His yellow turban was always immaculate, both as to cleanliness and folding. A man of over sixty years, his face was lined and furrowed in all directions, and his eyes were a trifle dim. He always exhibited an extremely pleasant manner and delighted to pour out for the hajjis, not only a draught of Zamzam water, but a copious stream of historical information concerning Mecca. His cavern, some ten feet square, was situated beneath the house of the Chief Judge of Mecca, which abutted upon the Haram. The Judge's house possessed windows, above the door of Hasan's cave, which looked into the mosque from beneath the roof of the cloisters. Within the old man's cavern, the roof of which was arched and little more than seven feet above the ground at its highest point, were two stone tanks, some four feet long by two feet broad and three feet deep. These tanks held Zamzam water. They were situated against the wall at the farther end of the cave, and on either side were stacks of clay water jars. Several empty tins for dipping water were scattered about on the damp floor, and in one corner was a pile of the little shallow white-metal basins in which Hasan offered the nectar to the thirsting hajjis. The only means of ventilation in this chamber were the door and two tiny holes in the right-hand wall, which latter admitted a little air from the passage

334

outside Bab al-Daudiya. The cavern had a musty smell, like that of most water-sodden caves, and was always in semi-darkness.

In this dank place Sayyid Hasan, like some wizard, would dole out the precious water to his assistant, a flat-footed pleasant-faced minion of middle age, name Jafar. Jafar, with the water bottle held on his left hip and a couple of little metal bowls in his right hand, would then issue from the cave, seeking whom he might relieve of thirst.

Only Hasan's personal friends, among whom I was eventually counted, ever dared to set foot over the damp threshold of that dismal but exclusive chamber. A hajji who exhibited sufficient financial proof of his regard for the old man, however, might even, an he would, bathe himself completely in holy Zamzam water within the cave. . . .

The office of "waterer" to the hajjis is pre-Islamic in origin, and is hereditary. There is nothing to prevent a hajji from going to the well itself, where there is usually at least one water drawer who will pull up a bucketful of water for him. The water coming fresh from the well, however, is warm, and therefore is less palatable than when it has been cooled. The *zamzamis* pour it into their porous jars, where it quickly becomes cool. Each *zamzami* has one or more wooden stands outside the cloisters opposite his cave, in which he places his jars full of water. Nobody is ever forbidden to drink from these, but their owner naturally expects a gratuity from those who can afford to give it. The *zamzamis* or their "youths" constantly offer a bowl of their coolest water to better class hajjis, whenever they see one sitting near. The gratuity is usually given after the conclusion of the Hajj, when the pilgrim is about to depart from Mecca. The *mutawwifs* often go out on the Jidda Road, either on foot or mounted on asses, in order to meet the pilgrim caravans. On these occasions they usually take with them a jar of Zamzam water, from which they offer a drink to any of their own hajjis who may be in the caravan. Some of them even send the water in *qirbas* to their agents in Jidda for this purpose. . . .

MY MUTAWWIF Abd al-Rahman, one of the principal *mutawwifs* of the Palestinians, usually had a thousand hajjis or more for whom to provide quarters during the pilgrimage season. The Wahhabi invasion, however, had this year left him without a single hajji save myself. *Mutawwifs* with large numbers of hajjis hire houses in different parts of the city in which to accommodate them. Many of the Malay hajjis like to lodge near the Haram, and are willing to pay highly for that privilege. Consequently, a man whose house is near the Haram will rent it to a *mutawwif* of Malays, and accommodate his own hajjis in hired houses in a cheaper quarter. Abd al-Rahman yearly let his house (with the exception of the top floor and the roof, which he occupied with his family) to a Malay *mutawwif* for three months. For this he received forty pounds, which was over ten pounds more than the rent which he paid annually for the whole house. . . .

One day Abd al-Rahman, growing confidential, showed me his death register—a book which each *mutawwif* keeps by order of the government. In it are entered the names and addresses of pilgrims who die while in a *mutawwif*'s care, together with a list of the deceased's effects. The latter are handed over to the government to await the claim of the dead person's relatives. Abd al-Rahman had had twenty-seven deaths among his thousand hajjis of the previous year, he smilingly informed me, and on looking down the list, I found that nobody among that departed company had left more than a couple of pounds in cash, while most of them appeared to have died in circumstances of complete destitution. This struck me as curious; as, unless they came to Mecca expressly to die there, they would presumably have possessed at least sufficient means to enable them to return to Palestine. Many poor wretches beg their way to Mecca, but such do not lodge with *mutawwifs*. It is true, however, that many old people, when they feel themselves to be approaching dissolution, go to Mecca in order to die there, and be buried within the sacred limits of the Haram. . . .

IBN SAʿUD AT MINA Later, as we sat in the tent, I asked Abd al-Rahman to come with me to join the crowd of Bedouins and Meccans and hajjis who were streaming from all parts of the valley towards the tent of Ibn Saʿud, in order to offer him their congratulations upon the conclusion of the Day of Arafat, and the arrival of the Feast of Sacrifice. This proposition he deprecated, saying, "We know nothing of the Mudayyina, nor do we want to know them." Eventually, however, he said he would go with me to the Amir's tent, and himself remain outside while I entered. Accordingly we made our way to the cope-stoned earthen platform where the tents of the Sharif of Mecca were formerly pitched at this season. Over the tents which now stood there flew the green flag of Nejd. Before the entrance of the reception tent stood two black slaves, cloaked and kerchiefed like Bedouins, and armed with Arab swords adorned with massive silver hilts. The visitors streamed into the tent in batches, shook hands with the Sultan, and wishing him a blessed feast, passed out at the further side. A few of them kissed him on the forehead, the shoulder, or the back of the hand. Abd al-Rahman left me at the tent, and I mingled at once with the crowd of callers and endeavoured to look as though I belonged to a party of Bukharans who were among them.

Upon entering the tent, I could at first see very little save the jostling crowd. Soon these dispersed to the sides of the tent, or went out of the further exit, and I saw at the opposite end a number of Bedouins and Meccans sitting upon chairs and benches arranged in a semi-circle around the side of the tent. In the centre of the curve, flanked by three or four of his military amirs, sat Abd al-Aziz ibn Sa'ud. He wore no finery, nor carried any weapon. Over a white linen *thobe* he wore a simple *mishlah,* or cloak, of yellow haircloth, and on his head a red-and-white cotton kaffiya, surmounted by a black hair-rope *iqal* bound with silver wire. His feet were bare, as he had shed his sandals at the edge of the carpet. He sat with an amiable smile on his face, and wearing black spectacles in order to lessen the effect of the sun glare. He rose to take the hand of each of his visitors in turn, and returning our salutations and congratulations briefly and smilingly, he then immediately turned his attention to the next comer. This lion of many desert battles, and sovereign lord of more than half Arabia, invariably rises to receive his visitors, whether prince or dervish. On this occasion, there being so large a number of visitors, the names were not announced to him.

Ibn Sa'ud was at that time (July 1925) some forty-five years of age. Although considerably over six feet in height, he is well and even gracefully proportioned. The features of his long Arab face are large and strong, the mouth somewhat coarse and thick-lipped, the eyes a trifle on the small side. His beard and moustache—the latter cropped short, the former in length a hand's breadth in the Wahhabi style—are inclined to sparseness. He speaks remarkably well, in an easy well-modulated tone, and uses slight, graceful gestures of the hands. Like many other people of energy, he is frequently very abrupt with his minions when they make mistakes or get in his way. Abd al-Aziz is not himself a religious fanatic, but he is an ambitious statesman; and in the latter capacity he does not scruple to make use of religious fanaticism for the purpose of attaining the objects of his ambition. For years he has made it his business to instil into the simple minds of the illiterate Bedouin doctrines which will, at a word from himself, cause them to act with an insane disregard of themselves. His personal ambition is boundless, but is tempered by great discretion and caution. He is a relentless enemy while opposition lasts, but in the hour of victory is one of the most humane Arabs in history.

As for his system of rule—he keeps his own counsel even among his relatives, and essentially his rule is absolute. As an instance of his diplomatic play with democracy, I may mention that in Mecca there is an Advisory Council and also a Municipal Council. Half the members of these are appointed by Ibn Saʿud himself, and the remainder are, or were at that time, elected by public ballot. The election being over (and no elected member would be allowed to take his seat unless Ibn Saʿud approved of him), the Sultan proceeds to appoint a chairman who holds the casting vote, and thus brings the number of his own nominated members into the majority. Needless to relate, neither of these bodies can enact any law or bylaw, or spend more than a few pounds, without the previous sanction of the ruler. However, the composition of the councils being what it is, they seldom vex His Highness by presenting to him measures to which he refuses his sanction.

This despot is known among his Bedouin subjects as al-Imam (the Leader), as al-Amir (the Commander, or Prince), and as al-Shuyukh (which word is the plural of *shaykh*). Among the Ikhwan, or Brotherhood of the Wahhabis, he is usually spoken of as al-Imam, by which they mean "Leader of all the Muslims who are worthy of the name." These intolerant puritans have never recognised any *khalifa** save the ruling member of the House of Saʿud. The sultans of Turkey were looked upon by them as the leaders of schism. . . .

A CUSTOM Until quite recently a curious custom prevailed among the women of Mecca. During the period when the Hajjis were encamped at Mina, the women left alone in their houses in the deserted city would dress in male attire, with turbans on their heads and sticks or daggers in their hands, and after dark would issue forth in companies of from four or five to a score. Thus dressed and armed, and without their veils, they would patrol the silent lanes of the deserted city, singing a rhymed song which is too obscene to be set down here. If they met any man in the course of their rambles, they would yell their song at him, and all of them hammer him the while with their sticks or their hands. This pretty custom was abolished by order of Sharif Husayn. . . .

THE MOSQUE AT MINA At each of the five hours of prayer, a small cannon was discharged five times near the tents of the Sultan. At sunset, after stoning (in company with Abd al-Rahman) all three of the devils, I went to the mosque of al-Khayif. This building is very similar in form to the Masjid

---

*The *khalifa* (or caliph) is God's vice-regent on Earth, the successor in leadership to the Prophet, the commander of all the Muslims in the world. He must be an independent sovereign prince, of religious life, and one who rules according to the precepts of the Sharia or Islamic law. The failure of the later Ottoman sultans to conform to the latter condition (by their adoption of the Napoleonic code) would have disqualified them from holding the position of *khalifa,* were it not for the fact that, as in the West so in the East, might frequently transcends right.

Namira at Arafat. It differs from it in that al-Khayif has two minarets, while Namira has no minaret at all. In the centre of the open quadrangle is a small dome which covers the spot where the Prophet used to pray. Beside this stands the smaller minaret; the larger one surmounts the gateway, which is in the northern wall. We found the place crowded with hajjis, who walked or sat about in the walled quadrangle, apparently unaware of its grim secret; for beneath the ground at the western end of this mosque, as Abd al-Rahman told me on a later day, lie several great vaults. In the years when the plague strikes Mecca these vaults are opened, and thousands of bodies are stacked in them—"like your books," said Abd al-Rahman, pointing to a pile of books stacked on the floor of my room. He himself had helped to "stack" the poor wretches who perished in the plague of 1906.

The mosque al-Khayif is kept closed all the year except during the Feast of Sacrifice. . . .

STONING THE DEVILS We remained two more days at Mina, and on each day we threw seven stones at each of the three pillars, or Satans. Each of these objects is surrounded by a low circular parapet, which forms a receptacle into which the stones fall. After the completion of the Hajj, these stones are gathered up and carried on donkeys to Mecca, where they are strewn like gravel upon the ground within the Haram. It is said that the fanatical wild men of the desert sometimes discharge their guns at the "devils" and yell curses at them, but personally I did not observe any such excesses.

The ceremony of the stoning at Mina is supposed to commemorate the circumstances of Abraham's meeting with the devil in this valley on his return from a pilgrimage to Arafat. . . .

These legends are said to have been current among the pagan Arabs, who worshipped a number of idols in the Valley of Mina, and stoned the devils there, as the Muslims do to this day. The Muslim *ulama* affirm that the stoning is intended as a symbol, by the performance of which the pilgrim may strengthen his contempt for the devil and all his works. . . .

Soon after midday on the twelfth of Dhu al-Hijja, we loaded our camel, which had been led in by its owner during the night, and proceeded on foot by its side down the street of Mina, in order to stone the devils for the last time. This duty having been completed, we mounted into the *shugduf.* All my companions, save Abd al-Rahman, had gone into Mecca on foot before dawn. The Wahhabis were in great force, filling the whole of the rock-bound road. Above the horde flew their noble standards—some green, others red— surmounted by shining gilded points, and bearing in white letters the great and simple dogma—THERE IS NO GOD BUT THE GOD.

All was of the East. The little stone houses, a few of them with *mashrabiya* casements; little shops open to the wind and the sun; no wheeled cart; no glazed window; no machines. Nothing but men of the East and camels, and donkeys, and little shops where primitive, unmanufactured products were sold. In distance I was perhaps fifty miles from the outskirts of modern civilisation, but in time I was separated by a thousand years. . . .

THE MOON Talk has died down for a moment. Out of the shadows to westward a breeze comes across the valley, stirring the lote, palm, and tamarisk trees. My gaze falls on young Hasan's face. He is watching the low-hanging moon. A nice youth, Hasan—cordial and kind. Yusef and Shafik are bubbling their *shishas* [water pipes] and emitting slow streams of smoke from their mouths—contemplatively. Abd al-Rahman rolls a cigarette with care. Sabri hums a tune, no louder than the wind. Suddenly Hasan speaks.

"Which is the brighter," he says to me; "your moon in Damascus, or this our moon?"

Everybody awaits my reply with lazy interest. Shafik makes as though to speak, but thinks better of it.

"The moon is one," I replied. "This moon which we see here is the same moon which the Syrians see, and the Egyptians, and the Indians, and all the world."

Hasan looked serious, but would make no comment. He was unconvinced: I had given him no proof.

"We had two hajjis from al-Sham [Syria] in the past year," said Shafik, between the whiffs of his *shisha,* "and while they were with us, there happened an eclipse of the moon. The call to prayer was chanted for the prayer of eclipse,* and the two Shamis went to the Haram with the other people in order to pray. When they arrived at the Haram, the one said to the other, 'Then is our moon in al-Sham eclipsed, O my brother?'

"'No, *wallah!*' said the other. 'The prayer is for the moon of Mecca.'

"'Good!' said the first man. 'Then I do not intend to pray just because the moon of Mecca is eclipsed. That is the Meccans' matter. I am a Shami, and if our moon in al-Sham is not eclipsed, by the life of thy beard I do not pray.' And upon that he left the Haram."

Our company all laughed at this, excepting Hasan. He had evidently not yet fathomed the matter. At the outset, I think, Shafik was the only one-

*Salat al-Khusuf—a special prayer decreed to be performed when the moon is eclipsed.

moon man. All the rest had been for plurality. But they were quicker to understand Shafik's attitude and opinion than was Hasan.

I liked Hasan, and I thought I would try to convince him of the moon's unity. To attempt to convince a bigoted Muslim by science without religion was hopeless.

"In the Enlightening Book,"* I told him, "we find [a] chapter [named] *'The Moon.'* Had there been more than one moon, would not this have been called 'A Moon' or 'The Moons'?"

Hasan smiled a sudden glorified smile of perfect belief.

"True!" said he. "*Wallah,* true, Hajj Ahmad!"

Then he commenced to chant from memory chapter 'The Moon':

"'The last hour approacheth, and the moon is split asunder. . . .'"

AN UNEXPECTED ENCOUNTER One day I went with Abd al-Shukur to the scene of a fire which had broken out in a little street between the Zugag al-Hajar and Souk al-Layl. . . .

Having observed the scene for some minutes, I left Abd al-Shukur, who wished to go to al-Layl market, and crossing the Mudda'a, made my way homeward through the quarter of al-Garara.

As I walked up the dark straggling alley, I suddenly heard a familiar voice cry "Sallah al-Din!"

Now this word represented the other half of my name. It had been conferred upon me by a well-meaning old shaykh . . . as a reward for my industry in mastering some of the mysteries of jurisprudence and Quranic commentary.

The voice gave me a sudden shock, and almost simultaneously the sight of its owner's face confirmed my apprehension. The next moment I was shaking the hand of one named Husni, a native of Aleppo, who had known me as an Englishman in Egypt. I had not seen him for some weeks preceding my departure from the banks of the Nile, and had thought him to be in Damascus, whither it was then his purpose to proceed. He was now accompanied by a dark-skinned Arab wearing the Bedouin dress.

Husni was rather an interesting character. I had met him in the previous year at Cairo. . . . His father had taken him from Aleppo to India when he himself was but a tiny child. From India they had travelled, by stages, to China; and at Hong Kong, Husni's father had become connected with the local agent of a line of steamers owned by an Indian Muslim. During the

*Enlightening Book: the Quran.

fifteen years of his residence in Hong Kong, Husni had acquired a knowledge of both the Hokien and the Cantonese dialects. Finally he and his father had returned to their native Syria. Husni, however, was an inveterate wanderer. He had visited every town in North Africa and Asia Minor, and had also been to Mecca and Medina. He and I subsequently met frequently, and I found him an entertaining companion. He liked to hint that he was a potential kingmaker, and he corresponded with several Islamic societies in India and elsewhere.

This was the man who now greeted me in Mecca.

I returned his salutation with guarded enthusiasm, endeavouring to cool his ardour with the intention of telling him privately that I had done him the honour of adopting his nationality for the time being. But in the next moment he had turned to his companion, the Bedouin.

"This one," said he effusively, "is one of the greatest of the English, and a Muslim."

As he heard the word "Inkilizi," Husni's companion looked serious and careful.

"But are you of a truth an Inkilizi?" he asked, regarding me earnestly.

"Inkilizi!" said Husni in a tone of finality.

"Ay, yes!" I replied. "I am an Inkilizi."

"But a Muslim—of course," he persisted.

Again Husni anticipated me with his effusive exaggeration.

"Muslim! This one is of the learned!" he cried with conviction.

"Naturally—a Muslim," I assured the Bedouin.

At that his gaze grew less intent. "*Alhamdulillah!*" exclaimed he, as we turned to walk up the street.

"But say not thus to others than ourselves, O Sallah al-Din!" said Husni. "The ignorant ones do not understand. You have told them?"

"No," I replied. "They understand that I am of the people of Syria."

"*Wallah,* it is better so!" said he. "Neither will we tell it."

Nevertheless, the fact that there was an Englishman in Mecca was known, soon after that, to some of the minions of Ibn Sa'ud. Going one day to the printing press in order to purchase a copy of the Wahhabi newspaper, *Umm al-Qura,* I found the editor, a Syrian, there. With exaggerated politeness he said that "one" had pointed me out to him and told him about me, and would I like to meet the Sultan? To this question I replied with a prompt affirmative. I thought it probable that they had decided to subject me to a verbal examination, as Muhammad Ali did in the case of Burckhardt. In such case my best plan was to meet them more than half way. In the result, however, I was never questioned at all, from which I conclude that my practice satisfied any observer who knew of my true identity.

Each, in his own heart, knows the significance of his intentions, whether good or bad. As for me, my sole object in assuming disguise was that I might be inconspicuous. This matter of inconspicuousness is very important in a country largely inhabited by religious fanatics and robbers. Many Persians and other followers of the Shi'ites, or schism, call themselves Kurds, Bukharans, or Circassians when making the pilgrimage, for there is more ill feeling between these schismatics and the Sunnis (orthodox Muslims) than there ever is between Roman Catholics and Protestants [now]. In the Hijaz, the Shi'ite fraternity is held in great contempt. Occasionally, too, Sunnis whose avarice is stronger than their vanity assume the character of persons in a much lower order of society. This enables them to escape with a lesser degree of imposition at the hands of *mutawwifs* and others, who adjust their charges to the station of the hajjis.

The Syrian told me that Ibn Sa'ud would be "sitting" in the Hamidiyya on the following afternoon, and invited me to meet him there. Accordingly I went with him, an hour before sunset, to the office of the government. The reception room is on the first floor and its windows overlook the Haram gate called Bab Umm Hani. Upon mounting the stairs to the upper landing, I found half a dozen of Ibn Sa'ud's Bedouin escort sitting there on benches. As we entered the room, the Sultan, who was sitting on a large divan with his back to the window, rose and extended his hand. At the same moment the Syrian told him who I was—"Sallah al-Din al-Inkilizi."

Abd al-Aziz motioned me to a seat beside him on the divan, and all resumed their seats. There were merely some four or five of his employees in the room. This was in the days before the fall of Jidda. After that event, the word had only to go round that the Sultan was "sitting" in the Hamidiyya for half the leaders and place hunters of Meccan society to crowd into the government building in order to make their flattering speeches and recite their poems of praise.

Ibn Sa'ud, having politely enquired as to my "state," now launched forth into a long harangue about 'Isa,* Muhammad, and religion generally. After a couple of minutes I felt I had had more than enough of that, so in order to change the subject, I told him that I thought of writing an account of his ca-

---

*'Isa: Jesus. [Ed.]

reer. This appeared to please him exceedingly, and he smilingly expressed his appreciation of my suggestion, saying that he was greatly obliged to me.

Soon afterwards, having read through and approved the manuscript of the editor's leading article for the forthcoming number of his paper, Ibn Sa'ud rose, and with a word of farewell resumed his sandals and went out. At this time he was using a light motorcar which had recently been brought by sea. He now took up his position in the backseat of his car, the chief of the escort sat in front with the driver, the rank and file of the escort ranged themselves along the footboards, and away they all went to the house of al-Sagaf in al-Abtah.

I subsequently visited Ibn Sa'ud several times at his palace in the Abtah. On one of these occasions he told me that his concerns were three—"Firstly, Allah; secondly, my beloved . . . Muhammad; thirdly, the Arab nation." On his return from Bahra on the Jidda Road, where he had been in conference with a British mission concerning the boundaries between his territories and those of Transjordan and Iraq, he told me that an excellent understanding had been arrived at, and that he was exceedingly pleased with the result of the conference; particularly with the fact that certain disputed territories in the Wadi Sirhan, north of al-Jawf, had been ceded to him.

On one occasion I told him the Meccan tale that the white turban cloth worn by the Ikhwan in place of the *agal* was in reality carried so that it might serve as their burial shroud in case of sudden death on the field of battle. This made Ibn Sa'ud laugh, and he told me that they wear it because they think it is the correct headdress for one given up to religion. Pointing round the circle of grim-faced rascals who had that morning ridden in from the East, and who now sat before him, he said, "These have all killed men, and lived by the raid. But now they are Mudayyina, and they wear the turban cloth in order to distinguish themselves from the others." His air of kind approval and of pleasure in the contemplation of them as he made these remarks was very charming. One felt that he understood his rabble infinitely better than anybody else could possibly understand them. They, on their part, looked fixedly at their captain, watching his every expression, with a sort of hard yet half-bashful admiration struggling to sweeten the habitual sourness of their stern visages. They were of the tribe or community of Ghatghat,* the most fanatical and violent of all the Nejd Ikhwan. When-

---

*I designate the Ghatghats a tribe or community because the communities of the Ikhwan are in most cases composed of elements from a number of tribes. The Ghatghats are drawn chiefly from the tribes of Cahtan and Atayba.

ever, as frequently happened, a party of the Ikhwan came to blows with the Meccan crowd, the Ghatghats were invariably in the thick of the fray. In its grammatical origin the word *ghatghat* means "to boil audibly" (of a cooking pot) or "to rage and roar" (of the sea). The Nejd Ghatghats live up to their name.

When the news arrived that the British government, or the government of Transjordan, had occupied Ma'an and Aqaba, Ibn Sa'ud took the occasion of my visiting him to indulge in a defiant speech. "Let the Europeans come with their guns, and their armoured cars, and their aeroplanes," said he; "we will retire into our deserts, and then if they try to follow us, we will turn upon them." I told him I did not imagine that the European governments wanted anything from his deserts, and that they respected him for upholding his own rights and those of the Arabs.

"*Alhamdulillah!*" exclaimed he, looking round the circle of faces with a beaming countenance.

A number of mysterious Syrians arrived in Mecca at various times, by devious routes. At this time Syria was in revolt, and the French were smashing up Damascus with artillery. One of Ibn Sa'ud's Syrian employees told me that his master had been repeatedly begged to go to the assistance of the Druzes and Syrians, and help them to drive the French out of Syria. His opinion was that the Sultan would have had no hesitation in attacking the French, provided that he could have relied upon Great Britain's neutrality. At this time, however, [the sieges of] Jidda and Medina were fully occupying his attention. . . .

During one of my visits to Ibn Sa'ud, the Shaybi* came in to discuss the arrangements for some repairs which were necessary to the roof of the Ka'ba. He kissed the imam's shoulder, and seated himself. In the course of the session of the *majlis*[council], he learnt of my nationality, and upon the break-up of the meeting he took me by the arm and invited me to visit him at his house. This I did on a subsequent day. . . .

A CLAIRVOYANT CHIEF Another person with whom I became acquainted in Mecca was an educated man of considerable charm—Sharif Pasha Adnan, the chief of the sharifs, and one of the candidates for the amirate of Mecca before Ibn Sa'ud made plain his intention not to give any important position to any member of the sharifs. Sharif Pasha's favourite theme concerned

---

*Shaybi: The Shayba clan, appointed by Muhammad in perpetuity, remain traditional custodians of the Meccan mosque. Rutter's Shaybi was the Keeper of the Keys. [Ed.]

the material development of the Hijaz. He saw no reason why there should not be railways and motorcar roads all over the country. "Were we to practise irrigation," said he, "the country of the Arabs, with Allah's blessing, would become like Egypt and Syria, and one might travel from Mecca to Jidda without seeing the sun—by reason of the shade trees which would grow by the way." He would extract petrol from the earth—had it not been found at al-Wajh?—copper, quicksilver, iron, and many other minerals also. The Bedouins would abandon their roving life, and till the ground, and . . . and so on.

IBN SAʿUD'S CORONATION Upon a Friday, after the midday prayer, I mounted the crumbling stone stairs of the Fakhriya school, which stands beside the Abraham Gate, in order to visit an acquaintance who was employed as a schoolmaster there. As we sat sipping tea beside a window looking into the Haram, we were surprised to observe a sudden rush of people towards Bab al-Safa. They were evidently attracted by something which was happening near that gate.

Rising, we descended the steps and passed into the Haram. Making our way towards Bab al-Safa, we came upon a great press of Meccans and Bedouins. In the midst of them was one of the Haram preachers, perched upon a little wooden platform or pulpit, apparently addressing the multitude. Elbowing our way into the crowd, we were able to see Ibn Saʿud sitting in a prepared place near the gate. The preacher was addressing to the Sultan a speech of adulation. Presently he made an end, and then several of the sharifs, the Shaybi, and other prominent Meccans in turn, took the Sultan's hand and acknowledged him King of the Hijaz. Ibn Saʿud received these advances with his usual cordial smile, and upon the conclusion of the ceremony he rose, and accompanied by his armed guards, made his way slowly through the crowd towards the Kaʿba and proceeded to perform the *tawaf*. Having completed this, and prayed two prostrations in the Maqam Ibrahim, he left the mosque and went to the Hamidiyya, where he held a general reception.

Instead of following the crowd to the Hamidiyya, I seated myself in the cloisters with my companion. The sun had lost something of its summer savagery, and the air was cool. Suddenly one of the old guns in the Fort of Jiyad boomed, and was immediately followed by another on Jabal Hindi. The troops of the garrison were saluting the new King. A hundred and one times the peace of the city was broken.

15

Winifred Stegar
Australia
1927

Winifred Stegar's Hajj account was composed in her eighties, a few years before she died. The memoir in which it appears is less concerned with Mecca than with the arduous trip that brought her there. Her record proves the proverb that a Hajj begins with the first step from one's door. In its central chapters, Stegar narrates a journey across half the world as she, her husband, Ali, and three young children trek west from Australia by cart, train, and freighter over the Indian Ocean to the Hijaz. This account is representative of the difficult, often prosaic lives of millions of hardworking men and women who have scrimped and saved, sometimes for decades, until in middle life they become pilgrims—people detached and called away from daily life by sheer devotion, frequently at great expense and risk. This is not careerist travel writing. Stegar did not observe these people; she married one; she became one herself. In that sense, her book is not a literary product. Set down for pleasure in old age, it is a feat of memory, a summing up.

Stegar's life was unique from start to finish. A green-eyed Caucasian foundling born in China, she was raised by Catholic Sisters who named her Win (for winsome) Strange. She lived in their care until she was sixteen, when an epidemic swept the church mission. For the next three years, she clung to a clerical job in a cotton factory. In a chapter called "A Knock at the Door," she encounters an English seeker named Alice Blake, a devotee of Tibetan Buddhism. This chance meeting at age nineteen drew Stegar into her first pilgrimage, a mountain trek to a Buddhist lamasery, where she stayed seven months. Accompanying Blake back to Beijing, she next took a job in a silk factory. Here she had her own office and learned accounting. Here she met her future husband, Ali, a dapper, magnetic Hindi Muslim with a taste for cream silk suits and gold-fringed turbans. His family was well-off. He had studied at Oxford.

When Ali chose Stegar over an arranged marriage, his father disinherited him, leaving the couple just enough cash for two tickets to Australia. "To me it

seemed a fine idea," Stegar writes. "What had we to lose? We were both young
and strong, and even in that strange land we ought to be able to earn our keep."
They settled down in the hardscrabble Northern Territory, in a land Stegar compares to the Dead Sea. Ali joined a group of Hindi and Syrian cameleers, freight-
ing goods on long trips through the desert. Gradually the couple acquired their
own livestock; Stegar balanced the books and on occasion traveled with her husband. It was a hard existence, but, she adds, "I had eaten my fill of lonely years
before I met him, so I thrived on this rough, romantic life." For fourteen years,
they lived at Oodnadatta, South Australia, and Alice Springs, in the Northern
Territory. Then one night Ali brought up the Hajj, telling her that he must go
and that his only worry was where and with whom to leave her while he traveled. The mere suggestion of leaving her made Stegar furious. She insisted on
coming along and taking the children. A few weeks passed before Ali gave in.

   The following excerpts track the family from Australia to India, then
through the Red Sea to the Hijaz. They depict the tedium of such a journey, with
its flashes of trouble and painful turning points: the officious inspectors at quarantine stations, the decision to leave two sons behind, the difficult choice to take
along a daughter. We ride with them on a Hajj train from Lucknow, where
every station is bedecked with flowers. We see what conditions were like aboard
a typically overcrowded pilgrim steamer more broken down than Conrad's Patna.
Grueling experiences like these remain common for thousands of hajjis even now.
Subsequent excerpts provide a realistic view of the Jidda-Mecca caravan by a
hajja who had lived too long with camels to romanticize them. The landscape
they pass through she registers as mythic—Abraham's wells, the mines of Solomon,
are on the way. In her depiction of the pilgrims on the night before they entered
Mecca, we see the devotion of the travelers as they wait at the border to a sacred
world.

   Stegar's book presents the realities of travel as endured by a scrappy survivor without connections or much money. Cast in the simplifying accents of a
woman thinking back decades, it first appeared in 1969. "If it should seem at
all disjointed," she remarks, "just sigh and say, 'Oh, but she was eighty-seven
when she wrote it.'" Winifred Stegar's whole life was a journey.

from Winifred Stegar's
Always Bells

OODNADATTA, AUSTRALIA. 1926 Though I made light of the [Hajj] journey, I knew it would not be child's play. I had met so many pilgrims in my younger days and listened to so many stories that I had quite a grim idea of the future journey and of the very real dangers. For me there was a danger in addition to those usually encountered by pilgrims. I had never become an expert in the recital of the prayers. They were long and many, and the language used was Arabic, with all the different gestures at their appointed place. Keen eyes would be watching if there was any suspicion of my being an infidel, and it would mean my life and Ali's also for profaning the Holy Land of the Hijaz. I admit I was a coward at heart and deeply afraid, but I was more afraid of letting him go alone and remaining behind with the anguished fears that I might never see him again. That would be too much to face; if there was danger for him then my place was beside him. . . .

LUCKNOW We were to join the first pilgrim train of the season at Lucknow. When we arrived there, we found it would not arrive till the next day, which meant that we must sleep overnight on the asphalt of the platform. . . . The gaslight flickered, making weird shadows over the many sleepers, and the night was noisy with the raucous coughing of aged travellers. And all night vans and pedestrians came in, adding to the great throng, all intent on catching the first pilgrim train of the season. Pariah dogs on the ceaseless hunt for food circled about among the sleepers, afraid of none, for no one hurts them.

With the cool, damp dawn—for it had rained the night before— women began to twine flowers round pillars and posts. Many sat in groups making garlands with great mounds of flowers before them. Blossoms were hung from the vaulted roof over trestles, doors, and windows—even the wheelbarrows were decked. One wondered where all the roses and jasmine could have come from. . . .

Just before noon the old train rolled in—I call her old because she was decrepit with her years. Her whistle seemed the strongest thing about her. The paint on the carriages had long gone, the engine was rusty, and when she let off steam, it sounded as if she were coughing with a galloping consumption. But through her rust there came a powerful rumble; maybe she was stronger than she looked. Or perhaps it was skittishness from the feeling of all the flowers that wreathed her humps and smokestack.

Every knob, door, and handle of the carriage dangled flowers, every crack or cranny was used to hold a flower. The uproar was deafening, pilgrims bidding relatives farewell, vendors shrieking, children crying, the old engine sending off intermittent blasts like a foghorn at sea.

The passengers swarmed into the carriages, many so eager to get in first that they pushed themselves in through the windows. The doors were choked with bodies as they shoved together.

Ali secured a seat for me and the children. Then more decorating began. Women scrambled in and decked the passengers' necks with garlands. I and mine received far more than our share; I felt that these darling women knew I was both strange and scared almost sick. They literally buried me in flowers up to my chin and I had to rescue the children to get them breathing space from the blossoms. Yes, it was a day in my life to remember. I, the abandoned baby, left to die in a Chinese temple garden, was today a queen in a royal garment of rose and jasmine. . . .

A full hour later the engine gave out three wheezy blasts. The onlookers moved back from the platform edge. The vendors stopped shrieking, and as one body the mass on the platform turned to the east. The wheels moved as the thunder of *"Allahu akbar!"* shook the rafters—the salute to God as the train pulled out into the open, the engine still hoarsely blasting and the rickety carriages swaying with the prayers and movement of a thousand Muslim passengers on their sacred journey to Mecca. . . .

PREPARATIONS AT KARACHI Ali had arranged with a wealthy family, whom he had known in earlier days, to take charge of our sons whilst we were away. Janey, my girl, was only four and, I felt, too young to leave, yet it was more than possible she would be far safer left behind in Karachi. I was torn both ways, and it did not add to my confidence that all pilgrims were required to make their wills and leave them with the authorities before embarking. . . . One dear old man never got the chance—he was murdered and robbed almost within sight of the gates. There was quite a lot of robbery with violence going on out in the city. Ali insisted I always bolt the door during his absences, not that I could see that there was anything in our room worth stealing. There were a few items of the children's clothing, three rugs, my daughter's big doll, some dried peas, some whole-meal flour, curry, and spices, with a gallon tin of ghee, which is really melted butter.

I eyed those dried peas gloomily. They were to be the bulk of our fare on the ship. Every passenger must carry his own supplies. We would be allowed three gallons of water and fifteen pounds of wood for cooking, a head—no allowance for children. That limited water supply hit us hard in the Red Sea.

Ali finally, after a lot of trouble, secured the tickets, which rose in price with the demand. Then our names had to be changed for the duration, so that they would be strictly Muslim. Ali's name was right, but Janey's and mine were wrong. As for my new name, I didn't wear it long enough to get it shop soiled, for it was changed again not long after.

It was in Karachi that Ali's brother rejoined us. Lubu was of the thoughtful, introspective type; you really felt the calm assurance of the man and knew that he would stand beside you firmly in a crisis. He was always good to me, but at heart I wondered what he really thought of his unpredictable sister-in-law. . . .

THE MEDICAL EXAMINATION The day came for us to board the ship. One-horse gharries were to carry us to the wharf. I thought that we would be going straight on board, but the pilgrim authorities had other ideas. In relays we were carried to a sandy patch on the beach, on which was one long, cool shed made of bamboos and thatched roof, with great crocks of cool drinking water within. This fine shed was solely for the male pilgrims; in it they would be medically examined in cool comfort.

The rest of us, four hundred women, were led to the roofless ruins of an old building of which but three walls remained. By now it was midday, and without hats or other shelter we were lined round the three walls, Janey back to the wall beside me. When it was considered we were in position, a lady doctor, a Eurasian, came across the sand to us, followed by her ayah bearing an inkwell with red and black ink, pens, and paper.

I could not help wondering what our sex had done that we might not enjoy the comfort of shelter and cool water as did the men. Before we had left the home of Ali's parents, I had contracted malaria, and attacks came on every second day at about the same hour. Standing by the old wall, I felt the first cold shudders of the usual attack coming on; also in the midday sun my prickly heat was torturing me.

The lady doctor swept in upon us, in white linen coat and skirt with topee and silk puggaree complete. She was, I judged, in her late thirties. For a minute she stood still and eyed us off, then snapped out a command like a whiplash, to the effect that we must lift up our shirts and expose chests and stomachs. Then she slapped each sweaty stomach with the back of her hand, one after the other. I gasped. I knew this was wrong. If there was any contagious disease she was spreading it to all. Apart from this, the women of

351

India are extremely modest. If any had malformations she was exposing them, and in Indian eyes, this thing was a gross indignity. The women showed they felt it as such, their dark eyes looking helplessly round them.

The few who resisted had their heads banged on the brick wall behind them, to the accompaniment of moans, shrieks, and sobs. I was aghast at the vicious, sadistic cruelty of the doctor—all done in the name of medical examination.

By this time my malaria had taken firm hold and I was shaking like an angry jelly. Rapidly, with ayah following, the doctor circled the building, coming now to the third and last wall. Four women down from where Janey and I were standing, a tiny little mother from the Punjab was literally crouching in terror of she hardly knew what.

Blind with fear, she did not seem to grasp the doctor's vicious order of "Up with your shirt!" The poor thing only crouched lower against the wall, her face wrapped between her hands and her chador. With a wrench the doctor tore at the woman's shirt. My sight was hidden for a moment; the next I saw, the doctor had her by the neck and was banging her head mercilessly on the wall behind her. The woman fell sobbing to the ground. The ayah said something to her mistress, but was answered with a slap that sent her bangles and anklets jangling.

The doctor came to Janey. "Up with her shirt," she snapped at me.

"No you don't! You keep your dirty hands off my child! Don't you dare to touch her!" I had barely got the words out before she reached down for the child's garment, but Janey, terrified, slipped behind my legs and evaded her. "You," she snapped turning back on me, "up with your shirt—don't be all day. I've no time to waste if you have."

"No, doctor, I won't. What you are doing is not examining, but spreading disease."

"How dare you say such a thing? I can have you punished for that, but I don't want trouble, so pull up your shirt at once."

"Never! Your filthy hands shall never touch me!"

It was at this point that she made the mistake of tearing at my shirt herself, and I saw red. I sprang on her with all my strength and rage; she fell with me on top of her. One wrench and away came a hunk of her silk blouse. I wrenched and tore her clothing in a delirium of rage. It's years ago now, but I can still quiver with the unholy joy of ripping that woman's garments to bits.

Oh yes, she squealed and wriggled, but I was the stronger; I rolled on her and kept her down. The ayah came to her mistress's aid and, forgetting she held the double glass inkwell, she let it run all over us. That once white costume of my enemy was now a mass of dirt, mingled with black and red ink, giving the effect of gallons of gore. Her screams and my angry gasps were added to by a choir of screeching women. If you have ever heard four hundred women scream, then you have heard something. The uproar brought the men and doctors running from their hut. The doctor and I were torn apart and upended. It was too soon; I was not half-finished with all I meant to do to her. I was too shaky to stand alone, and someone plumped me into a chair. A squad of police moved into position. The male pilgrims were ordered to stand back, and doctors demanded an explanation from me. I opened my mouth to answer, then with a shudder of disgust dropped to the ground a handful of hair I was still clutching.

Those men were aghast as I described the so-called medical examination, the brutality the women had experienced, the bashing of their heads against the wall, the viciously slapped faces. Then and there they questioned many of the women, some of whom showed their sore heads. Someone snapped out a command and the police moved forward and two of them took the lady doctor into custody. It was, I heard later, the end of her doctoring.

Poor Ali had been watching, indeed he had been one of the group who had interfered and dragged the doctor from my clutches. Poor man, he was terribly upset.

"You've done it now," he whispered hoarsely to me. "The very least you'll get is jail. Oh, it's the end of us—dear God, the bitter end."

More gentlemen hurriedly arrived; they were the pilgrimage officials. I felt ready to die; indeed I wished I was dead, what with malaria, prickly heat, a violent headache, and tension. Why could not I faint and so find release like other women? And beyond all the bodily discomfort was what I had done to Ali. No pilgrimage now for him. I had torn that precious thing from him—my man would hate me forever. Oh yes, death at that moment would have been infinitely sweet.

I grew conscious that strange words were being addressed to me. They were saying that the authorities could not be grateful enough to me for exposing the woman, and much more in the same strain. Then they called a carriage and in a few minutes Ali, Janey, and I were being driven to a sumptuous hotel, where we were given the use of a bathroom and bedroom, followed by a truly gorgeous lunch—but not till after one doctor had given me a sedative and a stiff dose of quinine. Later we were taken to the wharf, but before that, with many more gracious words and thanks, the pilgrimage authorities asked me to virtually take charge of the four hundred women on board and to report on how they fared, because on other voyages there had been rumours of ill treatment. I was too bewildered to do more than agree, but, thinking over it later, I thought a husband, three children, and four hundred women were quite a load for one pair of shoulders. . . .

THE FREIGHTER ISTOPHAN "Are you very tired, little one?" Ali asked me tenderly as he took Janey from my shoulder.

"Oh, Ali, where have you been all this time? Yes, very tired, let's go to our cabin."

"Here, wait on a minute, who said anything about a cabin? Do you think this is a P. & O. liner?"

"But—but—why haven't we got a cabin?" Then a wild hope arose. "Aren't we going on this ship?"

"Of course we are going on this ship, why not? But no one on board has a cabin except the Captain and his officers."

"But where do we sleep and dress?"

"Don't worry your little head; I've got a beautiful spot for us. It's three decks down, right on top of a hatch."

"But that must be very near the bottom of the ship." . . .

AT SEA The ship was fairly steady, but I guessed by the throbbing and vibration of my rug wall that we must be very close to the engine. It was also very dark. The one little hurricane lamp swinging below the iron stairs gave only a dim light. Neither was it by any means quiet down there. At times the noise was appalling, what with the raucous coughing, spitting, and shouting of the pilgrims. Every inch of the third deck round my hatch was filled with passengers, both male and female. To reach the stairs, you had to hurdle over the sleeping or lounging bodies. Each pilgrim had seized himself just room to lie down and pack his gear at his feet.

Our cooking arrangements left much to be desired. On either side of the top deck was a sheet of heavy iron, clamped to the deck, and on this were seven little spaces, about eighteen inches long by eight inches wide, each walled with two bricks and quite open to the sky. You built your little wood fire in one of these spaces and rammed your pot on it the best way you could, for there were no bars to hold it. Only one person could cook at a time in each space. If you allow one hour to cook a curry and make bread, then remember that some thousand others were awaiting their turn to use the fourteen tiny fireplaces, you can understand why we always seemed hungry, for my Ali was not of the pushing type. I had a few extra little things in stock for Janey, such as tins of milk, some biscuits, and a few dates. But for this the child might have suffered.

There were other things, too, not as well arranged as might be. On the top deck, at the stern, were two red ship's tanks some six feet square, one embellished with a man's head wearing a turban, the other with a woman's in a chador.

A door was cut in the side of each, a great hefty creaking thing of solid iron, and within, on the bottom, lay a trough similar to those used for feeding pigs. In this you relieved yourself. A lascar cleaned them out each evening.

Shut within, it was an inferno, especially when we reached the Red Sea. The same tanks were also the bathing place. The women were provided with a bucket tied to a long rope, which you let down into the sea and hauled up full of water. Then, shut in the smelly tank, you ladled the water over yourself with a jam tin—that is, if you were prepared to take such a bath, and believe me, you were, even though the salt dried on you and stung. The men had things a bit easier in that they had an old pump with a hose attachment which sucked up the water from the ocean. I loathed the trips up to the top deck—the heat, the smell, and the rust from the tank roof getting in your hair.

The *Istophan* had a sister ship; they had been built long years ago as convict hulks and later they had sunk. After being in the water several years, they had been salvaged and sold cheaply. An enterprising man decided they would do for the pilgrim trade, so new engines had been installed and the hulls patched up with brown paper or some such thing.

All the upper ironwork on the *Istophan* was riddled with rust holes. Four small boats dangled above the upper deck; I hoped that they, like the engines, were trustworthy, but there were times—quite often, in fact—when I speculated as to how eleven hundred passengers, not to mention the crew, could be fitted into them. There were no such luxuries as life belts, neither was there any boat drill. If you got the wild idea of a constitutional, then you had to do it leapfrog fashion, for nowhere was there any empty deck. I don't remember what the ship's tonnage was, but I'm sure she was no bigger than an Australian coaster.

That very first night on board my prescribed duty of looking after my sister women's interests began. I felt the urgent need of a breath of fresh air and climbed down off my hatch, almost falling over an aged and bearded pilgrim who had made his residence at the edge of my footplate.

Scrambling over sleeper after sleeper, I came at last to the foot of the stairs, then stopped in surprise. On the floor right under them lay two very young girls asleep. Huddled on the very edges of their rugs stood five sheep, meat for the lascar crew, and that bilgewater Ali had spoken of was seeping into the edge of their bedding and washing through an adjacent fowl house. The fowls were the Captain's perquisites.

I looked round, but there was not another inch of either dry or wet space. Something had to be done about the girls. I climbed the other stairs, but there was no room anywhere. Right up to the very top deck under the stars it was the same. Oh well! Girding myself up for battle, I hauled on my *shalwar* strings. The fore part of the deck was cut completely off from the stern end by a solid iron grille with a small gate let into it, which could only be approached by climbing a few stairs. This heavy, high grille was the remains of protection provided in the convict days against mutiny. The wind was rough and the ship not as steady up here as down below. I rattled on the gate till at last an officer appeared.

"What the hell are you doing here? Get down below where you belong," he barked.

"Would you please listen to me for a minute?" I said courteously.

"Well, what is it?"

In a few words I told him about the plight of the young girls lying in the bilgewater.

"Well, it's not my fault. Nothing to do with me. Why didn't they camp on one of the upper decks? And now you get below."

"Not till you come and do something about it," I said quietly.

"I tell you it's not my business, and now are you going down below, or must I make you?"

"Look here, Mr. Officer, I happen to be representing your owners. These people are passengers, and your wages come from them. Will I have to report that you gave no care to the people in your charge?"

"It's not my business—anyway, they are little better than cattle. To be on board should be enough for them."

"Look, young man, I happen also to be one of them. Are you deliberately insulting me?"

I don't know what reply he would have made, but just then another officer stepped up asking, "What is the trouble?"

I quickly explained. He unlocked the gate and came with me right down to the third deck, saying as he did so, "It's really difficult, memsahib, but I'll come and have a look."

We found the girls asleep as I had left them.

"Poor little devils," he said pityingly as he stared down at them. "They should not be here, but at home with their parents. Wait here." And he leapt over the pilgrims till he reached a small door leading from number 3 deck into what looked the forward part of the ship, only it wasn't. It was a small cupboard affair some six or seven feet square, which seemed to be a holdall for ropes, chains, and so on, with a couple of deck brooms added. In a few minutes, disregarding his white clothing, he had shot the stuff out and made room for the girls.

"This ought to do them," he said. I thanked him and he left, saying, "I leave you to fix them up." Then, turning back, he said, "I overheard you say something about representing the owners—was that true?"

"Well, yes, I suppose it is, in a way. I was asked by the pilgrimage officials to report on the treatment of the women on this ship."

"I see," he said thoughtfully, then said, "Would it be possible to forget Mr. Harvard's rudeness up above? He didn't really mean it; he was feeling a bit sore because the old man had just been grilling him for something or the other."

"Sir, your kindness and cooperation have washed the memory out. You have made those girls comfortable—or at least they will be when I've finished with them."

"Fine. Good night."

I heard the history of the girls later. They and an elder brother had come down from Peshawar, sent by their parents to join the pilgrimage to Mecca. All had gone well till two days before the ship was to leave; then the brother was knocked down and killed by a heavy lorry. But before he died, he told the girls that their parents must not be disappointed; they must continue the journey alone—truly an ordeal for two young country girls totally unused to crowds or cities. The elder girl was perhaps sixteen years old and her sister a couple of years younger.

It's an odd thing, but many aged people will try to be represented at the Hajj by younger relations, thinking thus to find favour with Allah. . . .

I remember one day I had been lying dozing with Janey beside me in the stench of heat, tobacco, and bilgewater, and awoke to look straight up into a full forty pairs of down-staring eyes. It was too much. In a second some devil within me caused me to make a series of the most hideous grimaces I could possibly screw my face into. There came a startled calling of "Allah!" then I heard racing footsteps above gone to find Ali and tell him that his woman was having fits. Poor lad, he came tearing down those stairs, anxiously inquiring what it was all about.

Indignantly I told him, but did he sympathize? Not a bit of it. He turned a heavy barrage on me for daring to make faces at the poor innocent onlookers. For a few minutes there was wordy shrapnel flying—again to the great interest of the spectators upstairs. Finally, worn out with heat and frustration, I began to cry. Now usually when we had our little spats, we would kiss and make up, so, weary of fighting, I said I was sorry, that I would not make faces at them again—and I held up my arms and face for his forgiving kiss. He gasped, looking upward, "Oh Lord, no!" and with a shudder he was gone and up those stairs as if someone was chasing him. Of course I should have known better. The very first instruction you get from the *molvi*s, or priests, is that once you set foot on the ship, both men and women are sexless, just one kind of humanity before Allah. Not even one little innocent kiss can be allowed. All women's face coverings must come off, because they proclaim sex. No longer were there married couples in the sexual sense. A whitewashed wall was not more chaste than we. . . .

The water in our petrol tin was hot and brackish. The bilgewater smelt worse, and oh, how those pilgrims coughed! The raucous noise never ceased. One thing I noticed was that Ali's brother, Lubu, seemed to have taken the two young girls under his protection. If ever there was a good man, Lubu was one. I had told him of the girls in the broom closet, and he saw how they were likely to suffer through the scanty cooking arrangements. I saw him often take and share his own scant pot of curry with them.

Those little fires on the top deck were never out. Those who could not get near them in the daytime tried to cook at night, and there was always a crowd of cooks and would-be cooks about them. On windy days the flying sparks made me uneasy; the thought of our overcrowded ship catching fire was too horrible to contemplate. . . .

JIDDA   The sea around Jidda is surely the bluest [I have] ever seen. It was midday when we dropped anchor in the bay, and the colours of water and sky, yellow sand and white buildings, were dazzling. From the shore, winding a mile or more out to sea, was a line of white posts to mark the channel, along which the usual lateen boats were starting to race towards us. The water was so clear that we plainly watched the sharks circling us. Maybe the fish were used to the incoming ships and were waiting for garbage to be flung overboard. . . .

Ibn Sa'ud had decreed that every pilgrim landing on shore should pay a tax of seven rupees. This had not been charged before, though, learning the cause of the tax, Ali and I felt it was fair enough. Ibn Sa'ud had taken it upon himself to protect the pilgrims this year from the Bedu. They are usually called Bedouins in books, but as far as I could make out, they were called

Bedu—actually it sounded more like "Budoo"—in their homeland. In other years these men came down from the hills, preying upon the pilgrims with robbery and violence. It was considered a sin to retaliate against them, since they are regarded as direct descendants from the Prophet's mother. Ibn Sa'ud, attempting to curb some of this cruelty and brutality, told the Bedu to refrain from molesting the travellers and he would provide free supplies for them during the Hajj. This proclamation was the cause of the extralarge pilgrimage that year. There were several other ships in the bay, bringing pilgrims from all over the world. We met people from Malaya, Java, Africa— even Thursday Island.

Thinking it over, I cannot see that His Majesty was at all out of pocket by the deal. Seven rupees multiplied by tens of thousands comes to quite a lot; in addition, he placed a half-rupee tax on every date tree in his domin- ion. Moreover, at the great sacrifice, when thousands of beasts were slaugh- tered, he claimed all hides and skins, which were sent away in shiploads to America—or so I was told.

Naturally there was no escape from the seven-rupee tax, and everyone had to pay up and like it. Once passed through the door on the city side, our various agents took over again by arrangement with the authorities, so many pilgrims in the charge of each agent. It was their duty to find us accom- modation in the city, and later camels, and to arrange all matters of travel.

We had to hand over our passports to the agent in charge of our group; he was supposed to keep them till the Hajj was over and we embarked again. Some of the rooms allotted us had as many as twenty people in them, and each person paid one rupee. Ali and I were singularly lucky in that we got a small room to ourselves at the top of a five-storey house.

We had to buy wood and water, also foodstuffs. Water, . . . was at that time very scarce in Jidda, with the population swollen to at least three times its normal size by the influx of pilgrims. It was carried on donkeys by means of four petrol tins, two to each side of the beast. It also cost a rupee a tin, and was hard to get even at that. Sometimes it took Ali a whole day to get hold of a tin. . . .

DEPARTURE FOR MECCA The days raced by. All too soon for me it was time to move on again. We found our camels beside the town hall, in a scene of sheer bedlam—choking dust, shouts, arguing agents and camel drivers, camels loose and camels held in check.

Don't ever tell me of love between camel and owner. The camels loathe their drivers, their passengers, and anything connected with them. They snarl and show their filthy black teeth at all and sundry. I have been amongst camels the greater part of my life, have known them from their birth to their death. That animal scorns the human race.

In this batch there were old beasts and young ones, many of the latter tossing their loads sky-high, for with such a mighty influx of pilgrims thousands of beasts not yet properly broken were pressed into service. If you have never heard a thousand or so camels squealing in rage as they are being loaded, then you have something yet to hear. . . .

It was sundown when, finally mounted on our animals, we passed through the city wall and out into the great desert beyond. Once clear of the wall the beasts were stopped and everyone dismounted and prepared for prayers. These were barely finished when there came a sudden rush to hoosh down the camels and take refuge beside them with covered heads from a great red wall of choking sand advancing on us, but it only lasted a few minutes, then was gone.

Two pilgrims rode on each camel; there was an arrangement of two string beds, one hanging on each side of the animal, with his hump running up between them. They were very lightly fastened and one passenger, the first up, had to balance himself on the hairy hump till the other party arrived; otherwise one bed went earthwards and the other aspired to heaven. I learnt my lessons of ascent and descent the hard way.

The camels could not be properly hooshed down because of these beds. Some agents had short ladders to help pilgrims mount, but of course they were a drop in a bucket for such a crowd. The usual way to mount was to place your foot on the camel's neck, then leap backwards onto your bed contraption. The first time I did it, as I reached the creature's neck, he snarled angrily and looked back at me. I missed the hump in my fright and shot back to earth. Ali said he was sure that scream was heard back in Australia.

Over and covering both beds was erected a beehive cover of jute, its centre prop in a direct line with the animal's neck. On this upright stick you lashed your red crock water bottle. Your spare gear rode at the back of your pillow. When weary you could lie down full stretch. This then was your home—a home on a camel's back. In assigning pilgrims to the camels, the drivers tried to match the weight on either side; thus Janey and I rode on one side and Ali on the other. Two fat men would be allotted to a stronger beast, probably a bull camel, and lighter weights to lighter camels.

The long camel trains ran snake-like, tied tail to nose, maybe thirty or forty to a string. Two drivers walked alongside with sharply pointed sticks.

It was a frightening land we travelled through—stark, bare, inhospitable with its collars of dead volcanoes and naked mountains dotted with black basalt boulders, a land of hunger and fear—yet perhaps today, since oil has been given to it, the people may be better off. I certainly hope so. The emaciated Arabs who ran out begging to the camel trains were terrible to see. All the long night the beasts plodded almost silently along, and Ali and Janey slept soundly. It grew very cold towards morning, a peculiarity of that land, where you can scorch by day and freeze by night. At dawn there was a break of ten minutes for prayers, then on again till midday. It was good to "get on shore," as I called it, to buy some wood and make curry and bake chapatis. But there were days when we did no cooking at all, but had to subsist on a handful of dates. . . .

ARRIVAL IN MECCA It was good to sit under the date palms when we were camped at some oasis. Sometimes you could buy the dates straight from the tree, oozing with their creamy juice, and eaten thus they are delicious. Those trees seem to be as useful to the Arabs as the bamboo is to the Chinese. I saw that the date stones were kept and crushed into a brownish flour, then fed to the camels. The Arabs also fed their beasts on long plaits of grass coiled into rings, but where that grass came from, I cannot say, for I can almost swear I never saw a blade growing anywhere during the whole trip, though in Jidda I had seen grass bunched like carrots and sold as a vegetable. . . .

As we travelled, the land took on a weird familiarity; to my eyes it was strange, but to my mind it was not. Trained at a Christian mission in China, I had a vivid memory of the stories of the Old Testament, and it gradually seemed to me that I was living with Abraham and almost back in his days. For in that desert the days of Abraham were still present, and his name was everywhere.

Jewish and Christian traditions placed many of these Old Testament sites farther north, but those we were shown also had long traditions behind them, and certainly it was easy to visualize the prophets and patriarchs wandering through this ancient land. One morning, casually pointed out to us, were the old gold diggings which provided most of the gold for Solomon's temple. There was still gold there, we were told, but none might work it lest it bring trouble from the greed of invaders. Again, our track winding across a small plateau, to the right lay a narrow stony valley, awesome, stark, and forbidding. This, we were told, was the place where God fed Elijah by means of birds. . . .

The map tells me that Mecca lies forty odd miles from Jidda; I don't know how that can be, for memory tells me it took us a good ten days to reach it. The camels were hooshed down early one afternoon. We were told that we were close to the Holy City, but that we could not go in till morning. The news ran through our hosts like a wild breeze, then an awesome silence fell as each pilgrim paused to realize the great fact. They seemed to all but hold their breath. The silence was broken then by a concerted shout of *"Labayk!"* That was what it sounded like to me, but I have been told it really has three syllables— *"Lab-bay-yak."* It is an all-encompassing word of praise and gratitude and submission to the divine will.

That night the *molvis* prayed and instructed the faithful till nearly dawn. We were told we must not fight amongst ourselves, covet, or wish harm to anyone. We must enter the city clean of heart and clean in action. No oils or scents were to be used at ablutions. Should we break any one of these laws, we must sacrifice an extra sheep or goat. Should anyone harm us we must not retaliate, even if it meant our death, always remembering that the ground we walked upon was holy in Allah's sight. I fell asleep at about midnight, and when I woke in the dawning, Ali was still at his devotions on his prayer rug.

Most of our Indian pilgrims were very old; some even tottered on crutches and sticks. We all knew that hundreds of our company would not return again to their homeland, and many of them did not even wish to, for they deemed themselves doubly fortunate if their weary bodies could lie down in eternal rest in this, their Holy of Holies. So very many were weak and ill, coughing their lungs away, but still deep in the rheumy old eyes was the glint of a peace their souls longed for, a gleam of joy at something at last attempted but yet by no means done. For this coming to Mecca was not by a long way the end of their journey; it would not give them the right to wear the green turban of the hajji. The grand culmination would not come for many weeks yet.

A short while after dawn—fasting, of course, [for it was Ramadan]— we mounted our camels again. As the light grew stronger, we were descending what looked like a steep basin. The mountains ringed the depression in the earth all around; and then as the sun rose, we saw the city far down below us—saw right into the heart of the Great Mosque itself. Racing up the mountainsides were the houses of Mecca. We caught glimpses as we went down of the large black Ka'ba, the five minarets with their onion domes, and the gilded dome over the Zamzam waters.

16

Muhammad Asad
Galicia
1927

๛

*Muhammad Asad was a traveler of large spiritual energy whose adventures, books,
and diplomatic service spanned seventy years. Born in Lwów in 1900, a descendant of rabbis and lawyers, Asad studied history and philosophy at University of
Vienna, then joined a circle of artists and intellectuals at Café des Westens in
Berlin. In 1921, he left a desk job with the United Telegraph news agency and
went to Jerusalem. There, as special correspondent to the* Frankfurter Zeitung,
he sent home popular despatches later published as a book, The Unromanticized
East. *After extensive travels in Syria, Iraq, Iran, Afghanistan, and Asia, Asad
returned to Germany in 1926. He was twenty-six, a well-known journalist.*

The pages excerpted here, from his 1954 memoir, The Road to Mecca,
*touch on three pivotal events after his return: his marriage to a German painter,
Elsa Weiss, their conversion to Islam in Berlin, and their subsequent pilgrimage
to Mecca. As the reader will see, it was in the Hijaz that his first wife's untimely
death changed Asad's trajectory forever. He was not to return to the West for
many years.*

The Road to Mecca *is full of good travel writing, yet this is not a travel
book at all. It is a conversion narrative, constructed to convey the largely psychological process by which a European Jew of some refinement gradually and whole-
heartedly transferred his allegiance to Islam and to Muslim culture. As its title
suggests, the book takes the Hajj as the emblem of this journey. Although its evo-
cations verge on the rhetorical at times, the book as a whole succeeds in ways that
a handful of excerpts may not convey. It is a favorite text throughout the Muslim
world.*

*Asad's growing disaffection with the West was a powerful catalyst in his
conversion. He was a seeker, a student of Freud with a strong, modernist urge to
make life cohere rationally and spiritually. Islam offered an ideological center
and a compelling reason to travel, too. It also provided an alternative to the
totalitarianism and increased anti-Semitism then sweeping Europe. Arabia in*

particular appealed to Asad, and he appealed to Arabians. Ibn Saʿud himself befriended him. No doubt the King saw utility in a man who spoke Arabic and the languages of Europe, one with an open channel to the journals of the West, and Asad was clearly proud to know the King. Later he wrote occasional articles about him for the German press, and once he went on a secret Saudi mission to Kuwait, but his real value to Ibn Saʿud appears to have been as confidant. As with Philby (and many others) later, we see here a remarkable regent surrounded by lesser intellects, reaching out from his isolation to passing strangers. If Asad had political value to the King, it remains a secret.

Asad stayed in Arabia for six years, traveling in every corner of the kingdom, indulging his passion for the desert. From there, he continued east. The notion of the Muslim world as a vast, intercommunicating zone, with Mecca as a major crossroads, did not die out in the fourteenth century. Throughout Asad's pages, travel and professional life are linked in ways that recall the career of Ibn Battuta. While en route to China, Asad stopped for a time in India. There, by an accident of his Austrian citizenship, he was interred through World War II in a prisoner of war camp as an involuntary guest of the Indian government. Following the war, he was invited by the philosopher Muhammad Iqbal to help lay the groundwork for a Pakistani nation. After Pakistan's independence in 1947, he went on to serve the new government as head of the Middle East Division. He married again in 1952, to Pola Asad of Boston, who became instrumental in helping him to write and publish many works. Reflections on all these experiences are contained in The Road to Mecca, *written in English and published in 1954.*

In addition to autobiography, Asad wrote books on the principles of Islamic government and Muslim law. His views were drawn from a sound knowledge of tradition refreshingly unencumbered by dogma. He became an advocate of Muslim women's rights (at his insistence, Pakistan's constitution allows for the election of a woman as prime minister), and in his essays on the Sharia legal system he consistently argued for mercy and understanding over cold justice. In the early 1980s, his disillusionment with intolerant extremists, and with the spreading effects of the Iranian revolution in particular, forced him to move, first to Portugal, then to Spain, where Asad lived in self-exile from the Muslim world. Muhammad Asad, born Leopold Weiss, died February 22, 1992. He is buried in the Muslim cemetery in Granada.

from The Road to Mecca
by Muhammad Asad

THE STORY OF A STORY The story I am going to tell in this book is not the autobiography of a man conspicuous for his role in public affairs; it is not a narrative of adventure—for although many strange adventures have come my way, they were never more than an accompaniment to what was happening within me; it is not even the story of a deliberate search for faith— for that faith came upon me, over the years, without any endeavour on my part to find it. My story is simply the story of a European's discovery of Islam and of his integration within the Muslim community.

I had never thought of writing it, for it had not occurred to me that my life might be of particular interest to anyone except myself. But when, after an absence of twenty-five years from the West, I came to Paris and then to New York in the beginning of 1952, I was forced to alter this view. Serving as Pakistan's Minister Plenipotentiary to the United Nations, I was naturally in the public eye and encountered a great deal of curiosity among my European and American friends and acquaintances. At first they assumed that mine was the case of a European "expert" employed by an Eastern government for a specific purpose, and that I had conveniently adapted myself to the ways of the nation which I was serving; but when my activities at the United Nations made it obvious that I identified myself not merely "functionally" but also emotionally and intellectually with the political and cultural aims of the Muslim world in general, they became somewhat perplexed. More and more people began to question me about my past experiences. They came to know that very early in my life I had started my career as a foreign correspondent for Continental newspapers and, after several years of extensive travels throughout the Middle East, had become a Muslim in 1926; that after my conversion to Islam I lived for nearly six years in Arabia and enjoyed the friendship of King Ibn Saʿud; that after leaving Arabia, I went to India and there met the great Muslim poet-philosopher and spiritual father of the Pakistan idea, Muhammad Iqbal. It was he who soon persuaded me to give up my plans of travelling to Eastern Turkistan, China, and Indonesia and to remain in India to help elucidate the intellectual premises of the future Islamic state which was then hardly more than a dream in Iqbal's visionary mind. To me, as to Iqbal, this dream represented a way, indeed the only way, to a revival of all the dormant hopes of Islam, the creation of a political entity of people bound together not by common descent but by their common adherence to an ideology. For years I devoted myself to this ideal, studying, writing, and lecturing, and in time gained something of a reputation as an interpreter of Islamic law and culture. When Pakistan was established in 1947, I was called upon by its government to organize and direct a Department of Islamic Reconstruction, which was to elaborate the ideological, Islamic concepts of statehood and community upon which the newly born political organization might draw. After two years of this extremely stimulating activity, I transferred to the Pakistan foreign service and was appointed Head of the Middle East Division in the Foreign Ministry, where I dedicated myself to strengthening the ties between Pakistan and the rest of the Muslim world; and in due course I found myself in Pakistan's Mission to the United Nations at New York.

All this pointed to far more than a mere outward accommodation of a European to a Muslim community in which he happened to live: it rather indicated a conscious, wholehearted transference of allegiance from one cultural environment to another, entirely different one. And this appeared very strange to most of my Western friends. They could not quite picture to themselves how a man of Western birth and upbringing could have so fully, and apparently with no mental reservations whatever, identified himself with the Muslim world; how it had been possible for him to exchange his Western cultural heritage for that of Islam; and what it was that had made him accept a religious and social ideology which—they seemed to take for granted—was vastly inferior to all European concepts. . . .

RETURNING TO THE WEST. 1926 It was in 1926, toward the end of the winter, that I left Herat [Afghanistan], on the first stage of my long homeward journey, which was to take me by train from the Afghan border to Marv in Russian Turkistan, to Samarkand, Bukhara, and Tashkent, and thence across the Turkmen steppes to the Urals and Moscow.

My first (and most lasting) impression of Soviet Russia—at the railway station of Marv—was a huge, beautifully executed poster which depicted a young proletarian in blue overalls booting a ridiculous, white-bearded gentleman, clad in flowing robes, out of a cloud-filled sky. The Russian legend beneath the poster read: THUS HAVE THE WORKERS OF THE SOVIET UNION KICKED GOD OUT OF HIS HEAVEN! ISSUES BY THE *BEZBOZHNIKI* [Godless] ASSOCIATION OF THE UNION OF SOVIET SOCIALIST REPUBLICS.

Such officially sanctioned antireligious propaganda obtruded itself everywhere one went; in public buildings, in the streets, and, preferably, in the vicinity of houses of worship. In Turkistan these were, naturally, for the most part mosques. While prayer congregations were not explicitly forbidden, the authorities did everything to deter people from attending them. I was often told, especially in Bukhara and Tashkent, that police spies would take down the name of every person who entered a mosque; copies of the Quran were being impounded and destroyed; and a favourite pastime of the young *bezbozhniki* was to throw heads of pigs into mosques, a truly charming custom.

It was with a feeling of relief that I crossed the Polish frontier after weeks of journeying through Asiatic and European Russia. I went straight to Frankfurt and made my appearance in the now familiar precincts of my newspaper. It did not take me long to find out that during my absence my name had become famous, and that I was now considered one of the most outstanding foreign correspondents of central Europe. Some of my articles—especially those dealing with the intricate religious psychology of the Iranians—had come to the attention of prominent Orientalist scholars and received a more than passing recognition. On the strength of this achievement, I was invited to deliver a series of lectures at the Academy of Geopolitics in Berlin—where I was told that it had never happened before that a man of my age (I was not yet twenty-six) had been accorded such a distinction. Other articles of more general interest had been reproduced, with the permission of the *Frankfurter Zeitung,* by many other newspapers; one article, I learned, had been reprinted nearly thirty times. All in all, my Iranian wanderings had been extremely fruitful . . .

BERLIN. 1926 It was at this time that I married Elsa. The two years I had been away from Europe had not weakened our love but rather strengthened it, and it was with a happiness I had never felt before that I brushed aside her apprehensions about the great difference in our ages.

"But how can you marry me?" she argued. "You are not yet twenty-six, and I am over forty. Think of it: when you will be thirty, I will be forty-five; and when you will be forty, I will be an old woman . . ."

I laughed: "What does it matter? I cannot imagine a future without you."

And finally she gave in.

I did not exaggerate when I said that I could not imagine a future without Elsa. Her beauty and her instinctive grace made her so utterly attractive to me that I could not even look at any other woman; and her sensitive understanding of what I wanted of life illumined my own hopes and desires and made them more concrete, more graspable than my own thinking could ever have done.

On one occasion—it must have been about a week after we had been married—she remarked: "How strange that you, of all people, should de-

367

preciate mysticism in religion . . . You are a mystic yourself—a sensuous kind of mystic, reaching out with your fingertips toward the life around you, seeing an intricate, mystical pattern in everyday things—in many things that to other people appear so commonplace . . . But the moment you turn to religion, you are all brain. With most people it would be the other way around . . ."

But Elsa was not really puzzled. She knew what I was searching for when I spoke to her of Islam; and although she may not have felt the same urgency as I did, her love made her share my quest.

Often we would read the Quran together and discuss its ideas; and Elsa, like myself, became more and more impressed by the inner cohesion between its moral teaching and its practical guidance. According to the Quran, God did not call for blind subservience on the part of man but rather appealed to his intellect; he did not stand apart from man's destiny but was *nearer to you than the vein in your neck;* he did not draw any dividing line between faith and social behaviour; and, what was perhaps most important, he did not start from the axiom that all life was burdened with a conflict between matter and spirit and that the way toward the Light demanded a freeing of the soul from the shackles of the flesh. Every form of life denial and self-mortification had been condemned by the Prophet in sayings like *"Behold, asceticism is not for us"* and *"There is no world renunciation in Islam."* The human will to live was not only recognized as a positive, fruitful instinct but was endowed with the sanctity of an ethical postulate as well. Man was taught, in effect: you not only *may* utilize your life to the full, but you are *obliged* to do so.

An integrated image of Islam was now emerging with a finality, a decisiveness that sometimes astounded me. It was taking shape by a process that could almost be described as a kind of mental osmosis—that is, without any conscious effort on my part to piece together and "systematize" the many fragments of knowledge that had come my way during the past four years. I saw before me something like a perfect work of architecture, with all its elements harmoniously conceived to complement and support each other, with nothing superfluous and nothing lacking—a balance and composure which gave one the feeling that everything in the outlook and postulates of Islam was "in its proper place." . . .

MEDINA. 1932 Darkness has fallen over the courtyard of the Prophet's Mosque, broken through only by the oil lamps which are suspended on long chains between the pillars of the arcades. Shaykh Abdullah ibn Bulayhid sits with his head sunk low over his chest and his eyes closed. One who does not know him might think that he has fallen asleep; but I know that he has been listening to my narrative with deep absorption, trying to fit it into the pattern of his own wide experience of men and their hearts. After a long while he raises his head and opens his eyes:

"And then? And what didst thou do then?"

"The obvious thing, O Shaykh. I sought out a Muslim friend of mine, an Indian who was at that time head of the small Muslim community in Berlin, and told him that I wanted to embrace Islam. He stretched out his right hand toward me, and I placed mine in it and, in the presence of two witnesses, declared: 'I bear witness that there is no God but God and that Muhammad is his Messenger.'* A few weeks later my wife did the same."

"And what did thy people say to that?"

"Well, they did not like it. When I informed my father that I had become a Muslim, he did not even answer my letter. Some months later my sister wrote, telling me that he considered me dead . . . Thereupon I sent him another letter, assuring him that my acceptance of Islam did not change anything in my attitude toward him or my love for him; that, on the contrary, Islam enjoined upon me to love and honor my parents above all other people . . . But this letter also remained unanswered."

"Thy father must indeed be strongly attached to his religion . . ."

"No, O Shaykh, he is not; and that is the strangest part of the story. He considers me, I think, a renegade, not so much from his faith (for that has never held him strongly) as from the community in which he grew up and the culture to which he is attached."

"And has thou never seen him since?"

"No. Very soon after my conversion, my wife and I left Europe; we could not bear to remain there any longer. And I have never gone back . . ."†

"LABAYK, ALLAHUMMA, LABAYK . . ." How many times have I heard this cry during my five pilgrimages to Mecca. I seem to hear it now. . . . It hums and throbs and pounds like the pounding of sea waves against the hull of a ship and like the throbbing of engines: I can hear the engines throb and feel

---

*This declaration of faith is the only "ritual" necessary to become a Muslim. In Islam, the terms Messenger and Prophet are interchangeable when applied to major prophets bearing a new message, like Muhammad, Jesus, Moses, Abraham.

†Our relationship was resumed in 1935, after my father had at last come to understand and appreciate the reasons for my conversion to Islam. Although we never met again in person, we remained in continuous correspondence until 1942, when he and my sister were deported from Vienna by the Nazis and subsequently died in a concentration camp.

the quiver of the ship's planks under me and smell its smoke and oil and hear the cry *"Labayk, Allahumma, labayk"* as it sounded from hundreds of throats on the ship which bore me on my first pilgrimage . . . from Egypt to Arabia over the sea that is called the Red, and nobody knows why. For the water was grey as long as we sailed through the Gulf of Suez, enclosed on the right side by the mountains of the African continent and on the left by those of the Sinai Peninsula—both of them naked, rocky ranges without vegetation, moving with the progress of our voyage farther and farther apart into a hazy distance of misty grey which let the land be sensed rather than seen. And when, in the later afternoon, we glided into the open width of the Red Sea, it was blue like the Mediterranean under the strokes of a caressing wind.

There were only pilgrims on board, so many that the ship could hardly contain them. The shipping company, greedy for the profits of the short Hajj season, had literally filled it to the brim without caring for the comfort of the passengers. On the decks, in the cabins, in all passageways, on every stair-case, in the dining rooms of the first and second class, in the holds which had been emptied for the purpose and equipped with temporary ladders: in every available space and corner human beings were painfully herded together. They were mostly pilgrims from Egypt and North Africa. In great humility, with only the goal of the voyage before their eyes, they bore uncomplainingly all that unnecessary hardship. How they crouched on the deck planks, in tight groups, men, women, and children, and with difficulty managed their household chores (for no food was provided by the company); how they always struggled to and fro for water with tin cans and canvas canteens, every movement a torture in this press of humanity; how they assembled five times a day around the water taps—of which there were too few for so many people—in order to perform their ablutions before prayer; how they suf-fered in the stifling air of the deep holds, two stories below the deck, where at other times only bales and cases of goods travelled: whoever saw this had to recognize the power of faith which was in these pilgrims. For they did not really seem to feel their suffering, so consumed were they with the thought of Mecca. They spoke only of their Hajj, and the emotion with which they looked toward the near future made their faces shine. The women often sang in chorus songs about the Holy City, and again and again came the refrain: *"Labayk, Allahumma, labayk!"*

At about noon of the second day the ship siren sounded: this was a sign that we had reached the latitude of Rabigh, a small port north of Jidda, where, in accordance with an old tradition, the male pilgrims coming from the north are supposed to put away their everyday clothes and don the *ihram*, the pilgrim's garment. This consists of two unsewn pieces of white woollen or cotton cloth, of which one is wound around the waist and reaches below the knees, while the other is slung loosely around one shoulder, with the head remaining uncovered. The reason for this attire, which goes back to an injunction of the Prophet, is that during the Hajj, there should be no feeling of strangeness between the faithful who flock together from all the corners of the world to visit the House of God, no difference between races and nations, or between rich and poor or high and low, so that all may know that they are brethren, equal before God and man. And very soon there disappeared from our ship all the colourful clothing of the men. You could no longer see the red Tunisian tarbushes, the sumptuous burnooses of the Moroccans, or the gaudy *jallabiya*s of the Egyptian fellahin: everywhere around you there was only this humble white cloth, devoid of any adornment, draped over bodies which were now moving with greater dignity, visibly affected by this change to the state of pilgrimage. Because the *ihram* would expose too much of their bodies, women pilgrims keep to their usual garments; but as on our ship these were only black or white—the black gowns of the Egyptian and the white ones of the North African women—they did not bring any touch of color into the picture.

At dawn of the third day the ship dropped anchor before the coast of Arabia. Most of us stood at the railing and gazed toward the land that was slowly rising out of the mists of the morning.

On all sides one could see silhouettes of other pilgrim ships, and between them and the land pale-yellow and emerald-green streaks in the water: submarine coral reefs, part of that long, inhospitable chain which lies before the eastern shore of the Red Sea. Beyond them, toward the east, there was something like a hill, low and dusky; but when the sun rose behind it, it suddenly ceased to be a hill and became a town by the sea, climbing from its rim toward the centre, with higher and higher houses, a small delicate structure of rose and yellow-grey coral stone: the port town of Jidda. By and by you could discern the carved, latticed windows and the wooden screens of balconies, to which the humid air had in the course of years imparted a uniform grey-green colour. A minaret jutted up in the middle, white and straight like an uplifted finger.

Again the cry, *"Labayk, Allahumma, labayk!"* was raised—a joyful cry of self-surrender and enthusiasm that swept from the tense, white-garbed pilgrims on board over the water toward the land of their supreme hopes.

Their hopes, and mine: for to me the sight of the coast of Arabia was the climax of years of search. I looked at Elsa, my wife, who was my companion on that pilgrimage, and read the same feeling in her eyes . . .

And then we saw a host of white wings darting toward us from the mainland: Arabian coastal boats. With Latin sails they skimmed over the flat sea, softly and soundlessly winding their way through fords between invisible coral reefs—the first emissaries of Arabia, ready to receive us. As they glided closer and closer and, in the end, flocked together with swaying masts at the side of the ship, their sails folded one after another with a rush and a swishing and flapping as if a flight of giant herons had alighted for feeding, and out of the silence of a moment ago, there arose a screeching and shouting from their midst: it was the shouting of the boatmen who now jumped from boat to boat and stormed the ship's ladder to get hold of the pilgrims' baggage; and the pilgrims were so filled with excitement at the sight of the Holy Land that they allowed things to happen to them without defending themselves.

The boats were heavy and broad; the clumsiness of their hulls contrasted strangely with the beauty and slimness of their high masts and sails. It must have been in such a boat, or perhaps in a somewhat larger one of the same kind, that the bold seafarer Sindbad set out to run into unasked-for adventures and to land on an island which in truth—oh horror!—was the back of a whale ... And in similar ships there sailed, long before Sindbad, the Phoenicians southward through this same Red Sea and on through the Arabian Sea, seeking spices and incense and the treasures of Ophir ...

And now we, puny successors of those heroic voyages, sailed across the coral sea, skirting the undersea reefs in wide curves: pilgrims in white garments, stowed between cases and boxes and trunks and bundles, a dumb host trembling with expectation.

I, too, was full of expectation. But how could I foresee, as I sat in the bow of the boat, the hand of my wife in my hand, that the simple enterprise of a pilgrimage would so deeply, and so completely, change our lives? Again I am compelled to think of Sindbad. When he left the shores of his homeland, he—like myself—had no inkling of what the future would bring. He did not foresee, nor desire, all those strange adventures that were to befall him, but wanted only to trade and to gain money; while I wanted no more than to perform a pilgrimage: but when the things that were to happen to him and to me really happened, neither of us was ever again able to look upon the world with his old eyes.

True, nothing so fantastic ever came my way as the jinns and the enchanted maidens and the giant bird Roc that the sailor from Basra had to contend with: but, nonetheless, that first pilgrimage of mine was destined to cut deeper into my life than all his voyages together had done to him. For Elsa, death waited ahead; and neither of us had any premonition how near it was. And as to myself, I knew that I had left the West to live among the Muslims; but I did not know that I was leaving my entire past behind. Without any warning, my old world was coming to an end: the world of Western ideas and feelings, endeavors and imageries. A door was silently closing behind me, so silently that I was not aware of it; I thought it would be a journey like all the earlier journeys, when one wandered through foreign lands, always to return to one's past: but the days were to be changed entirely, and with them the direction of all desire.

By that time I had already seen many countries of the East. I knew Iran and Egypt better than any country of Europe; Kabul had long since ceased to be strange; the bazaars of Damascus and Isfahan were familiar to me. And so I could not but feel, "How trivial," when I walked for the first time through a bazaar in Jidda and saw only a loose mixture and formless repetition of what elsewhere in the East one could observe in far greater perfection. The bazaar was covered with planks and sackcloth as protection against the steaming heat; out of holes and cracks thin, tamed sun rays shone through and gilded the twilight. Open kitchens before which Negro boys were roasting small pieces of meat on spits over glowing charcoal; coffee shops with burnished brass utensils and settees made of palm fronds; meaningless shops full of European and Eastern junk. Everywhere sultriness and smells of fish and coral dust. Everywhere crowds of people—innumerable pilgrims in white and the colorful, worldly citizens of Jidda, in whose faces, clothes, and manners met all the countries of the Muslim world: perhaps a father from India, while the mother's father—himself probably a mixture of Malay and Arab—may have married a grandmother who on her father's side descended from Uzbeks and on her mother's side possibly from Somalis: living traces of the centuries of pilgrimage and of the Islamic environment which knows no colour bar and no distinction between races. In addition to this indigenous and pilgrim-borne confusion, Jidda was in those days (1927) the only place in the Hijaz in which non-Muslims were allowed to reside. You could occasionally see shop signs in European writing and people in white tropical dress with sun helmets or hats on their heads; over the consulates fluttered foreign flags.

All this belonged, as it were, not yet so much to the mainland as to the sea: to the sounds and smells of the port, to the ships riding at anchor beyond the pale coral streaks, to the fishing boats with white triangular sails—to a world not much unlike that of the Mediterranean. The houses, though, were already a little different, open to the breeze with richly moulded façades, carved wooden window frames, and covered balconies, thinnest screens of wood that permitted the inmates to look out without hindrance into the open but prevented the passerby from seeing the interior; all this woodwork sat like grey-green lace on the walls of rose coral stone, delicate and extremely harmonious. This was no longer the Mediterranean and not yet quite Arabia; it was the coastal world of the Red Sea, which produces similar architecture on both its sides.

Arabia, however, announced itself already in the steely sky, the naked, rocky hills and sand dunes toward the east, and in that breath of greatness and that bare scarcity which are always so strangely intermingled in an Arabian landscape.

JIDDA TO MECCA. 1927 In the afternoon of the next day our caravan started on the road to Mecca, winding its way through crowds of pilgrims, Bedouins, camels with and without litters, riding camels, gaily caparisoned donkeys, toward the eastern gate of the town. Off and on motorcars passed us—Saudi Arabia's earliest motorcars—loaded with pilgrims and noisy with their Klaxon horns. The camels seemed to sense that the new monsters were their enemies, for they shied every time one approached, frantically veering toward house walls and moving their long necks hither and thither, confused and helpless. A new time was threateningly dawning for these tall, patient animals, filling them with fear and apocalyptic forebodings.

After a while we left the white city walls behind and found ourselves all at once in the desert—in a wide plain, greyish-brown, desolate, dotted with thorny bushes and patches of steppe grass, with low, isolated hills growing out of it like islands in a sea, and hedged into the east by somewhat higher, rocky ranges, bluish-grey, jagged of outline, barren of all life. All over that forbidding plain there plodded caravans, many of them, in long processions—hundreds and thousands of camels—animal behind animal in single file, loaded with litters and pilgrims and baggage, sometimes disappearing behind hills and then reappearing. Gradually all their paths converged onto a single, sandy road, created by the tracks of similar caravans over long centuries.

In the silence of the desert, which was underlined rather than broken by the plopping of the camels' feet, the occasional calls of the Bedouin drivers and the low-toned singing of a pilgrim here and there, I was suddenly overcome by an eerie sensation—so overwhelming a sensation that one might almost call it a vision: I saw myself on a bridge that spanned an invisible abyss: a bridge so long that the end from which I had come was already lost in a misty distance, while the other end had hardly begun to unveil itself to the eye. I stood in the middle: and my heart contracted with dread as I saw myself thus halfway between the two ends of the bridge—already too far from the one and not yet close enough to the other—and it seemed to me, for long seconds, that I would always have to remain thus between the two ends, always above the roaring abyss—when an Egyptian woman on the camel before mine suddenly sounded the ancient pilgrim's cry, "*Labayk, Allahumma, labayk!*"—and my dream broke asunder.

From all sides you could hear people speaking and murmuring in many tongues. Sometimes a few pilgrims called out in chorus, "*Labayk, Allahumma, labayk!*"—or an Egyptian fellah woman sang a song in honor of the Prophet, whereupon another uttered a *ghatrafa,* that joyful cry of Arab women: a shrill, very high pitched trill which women raise on all festive occasions—like marriage, childbirth, circumcision, religious processions of all kinds, and, of course, pilgrimages. In the knightly Arabia of earlier times, when the daughters of chieftains used to ride to war with the men of their tribe in order to spur them on to greater bravery (for it was regarded as extreme dishonour to allow one of these maidens to be killed, or, still worse, to be captured by the enemy), the *ghatrafa* was often heard on a field of battle.

Most of the pilgrims rode in litters—two on each camel—and the rolling motion of these contraptions gradually made one dizzy and tortured the nerves, so unceasing was the pitching and rocking. One dozed exhausted for a few moments, was awakened by a sudden jolt, slept again, and awoke again. From time to time the camel drivers, who accompanied the caravan on foot, called to their animals. One or another of them occasionally chanted in rhythm with the long-drawn-out step of the camels.

Toward morning we reached Bahra, where the caravan stopped for the day; for the heat permitted travel only during the night.

This village—in reality nothing but a double line of shacks, coffee shops, a few huts of palm fronds, and a very small mosque—was the traditional halting place for caravans halfway between Jidda and Mecca. The landscape was the same as it had been all the way since we left the coast: a desert with isolated hills here and there and higher, blue mountains in the east which separated the coastal lowlands from the plateau of central Arabia. But now all this desert around us resembled a huge army camp with innumerable tents, camels, litters, bundles, a confusion of many tongues—Arabic, Hindustani, Malay, Persian, Somali, Turkish, Pashto, Amharic, and God knows how many more. This was a real gathering of nations; but as everyone was wearing the all-leveling *ihram,* the differences of origin were hardly noticeable and all the many races appeared almost like one.

The pilgrims were tired after the night march, but only very few among them knew how to utilize this time of rest; to most of them traveling must have been a very unusual enterprise, and to many it was the first journey of their lives—and such a journey, toward such a goal! They had to be restless; they had to move about; their hands had to search for something to do, even if it was no more than opening and retying their bags and bundles: otherwise one would have become lost to the world, would have entirely lost oneself in unearthly happiness as in a sea . . .

This seemed to have happened to the family in the tent next to mine, apparently pilgrims from a Bengal village. They hardly exchanged a word, sat cross-legged on the ground and stared fixedly toward the east, in the direction of Mecca, into the desert that was filled with shimmering heat. There was such a faraway peace in their faces that you felt they were already before the House of God, and almost in his presence. The men were of a remarkable beauty, lean, with shoulder-long hair and glossy black beards. One of them lay ill on a rug: by his side crouched two young women, like colourful little birds in their voluminous red-and-blue trousers and silver-embroidered tunics, their thick black tresses hanging down their backs; the younger of the two had a thin gold ring in one nostril.

In the afternoon the sick man died. The women did not raise a lament as they so often do in Eastern countries: for this man had died on the pilgrimage, on sacred soil, and was thus blest. The men washed the corpse and wrapped it in the same white cloth which he had worn as his last garment. Thereafter one of them stood before the tent, cupped his hands to his mouth, and called out loudly the call to prayer: "God is the greatest, God is the greatest! There is no God but God, and Muhammad is God's Messenger! . . . Pray for the dead! May God have mercy upon you all!" And from all sides the *ihram*-clad men flocked together and lined up in rows behind an imam like soldiers of a great army. When the prayer was over, they dug a grave, an old man read a few passages from the Quran, and then they threw sand over the dead pilgrim, who lay on his side, his face turned toward Mecca.

MECCA Before sunrise on the second morning the sandy plain narrowed, the hills grew closer together; we passed through a gorge and saw in the pale light of dawn the first buildings of Mecca; then we entered the streets of the Holy City with the rising sun.

The houses resembled those in Jidda with their carved oriel windows and enclosed balconies; but the stone of which they were built seemed to be heavier, more massive than the light-coloured coral stone of Jidda. It was still very early in the morning, but already a thick, brooding heat was growing. Before many of the houses stood benches on which exhausted men were sleeping. Narrower and narrower became the unpaved streets through which our rocking caravan moved toward the centre of the city. As only a few days remained before the festival of the Hajj, the crowds in the streets were very large. Innumerable pilgrims in the white *ihram,* and others who had temporarily changed again into their everyday clothes—clothes from all countries of the Muslim world, water carriers bent under heavy waterskins or under a yoke weighted by two old petroleum cans used as buckets, donkey drivers and riding donkeys with tinkling bells and gay trappings, and, to make the confusion complete, camels coming from the opposite direction, loaded with empty litters and bellowing in various tones. There was such a hubbub in the narrow streets that you might have thought the Hajj was not a thing that had taken place annually for centuries but a surprise for which the people had not been prepared. In the end our caravan ceased to be a caravan and became a disorderly tangle of camels, litters, baggage, pilgrims, camel drivers, and noise.

I had arranged from Jidda to stay in the house of a well-known *mutawwif,* or pilgrim's guide, by name of Hasan Abid, but there seemed to be little chance of finding him or his house in this chaos. But suddenly someone shouted, "Hasan Abid! Where are you pilgrims for Hasan Abid?"—and, like a jinn from out of a bottle, a young man appeared before us and, with a deep bow, requested that we follow him; he had been sent by Hasan Abid to lead us to his house.

After an opulent breakfast served by the *mutawwif,* I went out, led by the same young man who had received us earlier, to the Holy Mosque. We walked through the teeming, buzzing streets, past butcher shops with rows of skinned sheep hanging before them; past vegetable vendors with their goods spread on straw mats on the ground; amidst swarms of flies and the smell of vegetables, dust, and perspiration; then through a narrow, covered bazaar in which only clothiers had their shops: a festival of colour. As elsewhere in the bazaars of western Asia and North Africa, the shops were only niches about one yard above ground level, with the shopkeeper sitting cross-legged, surrounded by his bolts of cloth of all materials and colours, while above him there hung in rows all manner of dress articles for all the nations of the Muslim world.

And, again, there were people of all races and garbs and expressions, some with turbans and others bareheaded; some who walked silently with lowered heads, perhaps with a rosary in their hands, and others who were running on light feet through the crowds; supple, brown bodies of Somalis, shining like copper from between the folds of their togalike garments; Arabs from the highlands of the interior, lean figures, narrow of face, proud of bearing; heavy-limbed, thickset Uzbeks from Bukhara, who even in this

Meccan heat had kept to their quilted caftans and knee-high leather boots; sarong-clad Javanese girls with open faces and almond-shaped eyes; Moroccans, slow of stride and dignified in their white burnooses; Meccans in white tunics, their heads covered with ridiculously small skullcaps; Egyptian fellahin with excited faces; white-clad Indians with black eyes peering from under voluminous, snow-white turbans, and Indian women so impenetrably shrouded in their white *burqa*s that they looked like walking tents; huge Fulani Negros from Timbuktu or Dahomey in indigo-blue robes and red skullcaps; and petite Chinese ladies, like embroidered butterflies, tripping along on minute, bound feet that resembled the hooves of gazelles. A shouting, thronging commotion in all directions, so that you felt you were in the midst of breaking waves of which you could grasp some details but never an integrated picture. Everything floated amid a buzz of innumerable languages, hot gestures, and excitement—until we found ourselves, suddenly, before one of the gates of the Haram, the Holy Mosque.

It was a triple-arched gate with stone steps climbing up to it; on the threshold sat a half-naked Indian beggar, stretching his emaciated hand toward us. And then I saw for the first time the inner square of the sanctuary, which lay below the level of the street—much lower than the threshold— and thus opened itself to the eye like a bowl: a huge quadrangle surrounded on all sides by many-pillared cloisters with semicircular arches, and in its centre a cube about forty feet high, draped in black, with a broad band of gold-embroidered verses from the Quran running around the upper portion of the covering: the Ka'ba . . .

This, then, was the Ka'ba, the goal of longing for so many millions of people for so many centuries. To reach this goal, countless pilgrims had made heavy sacrifices throughout the ages; many had died on the way; many had reached it only after great privations; and to all of them this small, square building was the apex of their desires, and to reach it meant fulfillment.

There it stood, almost a perfect cube (as its Arabic name connotes) entirely covered with black brocade, a quiet island in the middle of the vast quadrangle of the mosque: much quieter than any other work of architecture anywhere in the world. It would almost appear that he who first built the Ka'ba—for since the time of Abraham the original structure has been rebuilt several times in the same shape—wanted to create a parable of man's humility before God. The builder knew that no beauty of architectural rhythm and no perfection of line, however great, could ever do justice to the idea of God: and so he confined himself to the simplest three-dimensional form imaginable—a cube of stone.

I had seen in various Muslim countries mosques in which the hands of great artists had created inspired works of art. I had seen mosques in North Africa, shimmering prayer palaces of marble and white alabaster; the Dome of the Rock in Jerusalem, a powerfully perfect cupola over a delicate under-structure, a dream of lightness and heaviness united without contradiction; and the majestic buildings of Istanbul, the Suleymaniye, the Yeni-Valide, the Bayezid mosque; and those of Bursa in Asia Minor; and the Safavid mosques in Iran—royal harmonies of stone, multicolored majolica tiles, mosaics, huge stalactite portals over silver-embossed doors, slender minarets with alabaster and turquoise-blue galleries, marble-covered quadrangles with fountains and age-old plantain trees; and the mighty ruins of Tamerlane's mosques in Samarkand, splendid even in decay.

All these had I seen—but never had I felt so strongly as now, before the Ka'ba, that the hand of the builder had come so close to his religious conception. In the utter simplicity of a cube, in the complete renunciation of all beauty of line and form, spoke this thought: "Whatever beauty man may be able to create with his hands, it will be only conceit to deem it wor-thy of God; therefore, the simplest that man can conceive is the greatest that he can do to express the glory of God." A similar feeling may have been responsible for the mathematical simplicity of the Egyptian pyramids—although there man's conceit had at least found a vent in the tremendous dimensions he gave to his buildings. But here, in the Ka'ba, even the size spoke of human renunciation and self-surrender; and the proud modesty of this little structure had no compare on earth.

There is only one entrance into the Ka'ba—a silver-sheathed door on the northeast side, about seven feet above ground level, so that it can only be reached by means of a movable wooden staircase which is placed before the door on a few days of the year. The interior, usually closed (I saw it only on later occasions), is very simple: a marble floor with a few carpets and lamps of bronze and silver hanging from a roof that is supported by heavy wooden beams. Actually, this interior has no special significance of its own, for the sanctity of the Ka'ba applies to the whole building, which is the *qibla*—that is, the direction of prayer—for the entire Islamic world. It is toward this symbol of God's oneness that hundreds of millions of Muslims the world over turn their faces in prayer five times a day.

Embedded in the eastern corner of the building and left uncovered is a dark-coloured stone surrounded by a broad silver frame. This Black Stone, which has been kissed hollow by many generations of pilgrims, has been the cause of much misunderstanding among non-Muslims, who believe it to be a fetish taken over by Muhammad as a concession to the pagan Meccans. Nothing could be farther from truth. Just as the Ka'ba is an object of reverence but not of worship, so too is the Black Stone. It is revered as the only remnant of Abraham's original building; and because the lips of Muhammad touched it on his Farewell Pilgrimage, all pilgrims have done the same ever since. The Prophet was well aware that all the later generations of the faithful would always follow his example: and when he kissed the stone, he knew that on it the lips of future pilgrims would forever meet the memory of his lips in the symbolic embrace he thus offered, beyond time and beyond death, to his entire community. And the pilgrims, when they kiss the Black Stone, feel that they are embracing the Prophet and all the other Muslims who have been here before them and those who will come after them.

No Muslim would deny that the Ka'ba had existed long before the Prophet Muhammad; indeed, its significance lies precisely in this fact. The Prophet did not claim to be the founder of a new religion. On the contrary: self-surrender to God—*Islam*—has been, according to the Quran, "man's natural inclination" since the dawn of human consciousness; it was this that Abraham and Moses and Jesus and all the other prophets of God had been teaching—the message of the Quran being but the last of the Divine Revelations. Nor would a Muslim deny that the sanctuary had been full of idols and fetishes before Muhammad broke them, just as Moses had broken the golden calf at Sinai: for, long before the idols were brought into the Ka'ba, the true God had been worshipped there, and thus Muhammad did no more than restore Abraham's temple to its original purpose.

And there I stood before the Temple of Abraham and gazed at the marvel without thinking (for thoughts and reflections came only much later), and out of some hidden, smiling kernel within me there slowly grew an elation like a song.

Smooth marble slabs, with sunlight reflections dancing upon them, covered the ground in a wide circle around the Ka'ba, and over these marble slabs walked many people, men and women, round and round the black-draped House of God. Among them were some who wept, some who loudly called to God in prayer, and many who had no words and no tears but could only walk with lowered heads . . .

It is part of the Hajj to walk seven times around the Ka'ba: not just to show respect to the central sanctuary of Islam but to recall to oneself the basic demand of Islamic life. The Ka'ba is a symbol of God's oneness; and the pilgrim's bodily movement around it is a symbolic expression of human activity, implying that not only our thoughts and feelings—all that is comprised in the term *inner life*—but also our outward, active life, our doings and practical endeavors, must have God as their centre.

And I, too, moved slowly forward and became part of the circular flow around the Ka'ba. Off and on I became conscious of a man or woman near me; isolated pictures appeared fleetingly before my eyes and vanished. There was a huge Negro in a white *ihram,* with a wooden rosary slung like a chain around a powerful, black wrist. An old Malay tripped along by my side for a while, his arms dangling, as if in helpless confusion, against his batik sarong. A grey eye under bushy brows—to whom did it belong?—and now lost in the crowd. Among the many people in front of the Black Stone, a young Indian woman: she was obviously ill; in her narrow, delicate face lay a strangely open yearning, visible to the onlooker's eye like the life of fishes and algae in the depths of a crystal-clear pond. Her hands with their pale, upturned palms were stretched out toward the Ka'ba, and her fingers trembled as if in accompaniment to a wordless prayer . . .

I walked on and on, the minutes passed, all that had been small and bitter in my heart began to leave my heart, I became part of a circular stream— oh, was this the meaning of what we were doing: to become aware that one is a part of a movement in an orbit? Was this, perhaps, all confusion's end? And the minutes dissolved, and time itself stood still, and this was the centre of the universe . . .

Nine days later Elsa died.

She died suddenly, after less than a week's illness which at first had seemed to be no more than an indisposition due to heat and the unusual diet, but later turned out to be an obscure tropical ailment before which the Syrian doctors at the hospital of Mecca stood helpless. Darkness and utter despair closed around me.

She was buried in the sandy graveyard of Mecca. A stone was placed over her grave. I did not want any inscription on it; thinking of an inscription was like thinking of the future: and I could not conceive of any future now.

Elsa's little son, Ahmad, remained with me for over a year and accompanied me on my first journey into the interior of Arabia—a valiant, ten-year-old companion. But after a time I had to say good-bye to him as well, for his mother's family finally persuaded me that he must be sent to school in Europe; then nothing remained of Elsa except her memory and a stone in a Meccan graveyard and a darkness that was not lifted until long afterward, long after I had given myself up to the timeless embrace of Arabia. . . .

ARAFAT REMEMBERED Not far from here, hidden from my eyes in the midst of this lifeless wilderness of valleys and hills, lies the Plain of Arafat, on which all the pilgrims who come to Mecca assemble on one day of the year as a reminder of that Last Assembly, when man will have to answer to his Creator for all he has done in life. How often have I stood there myself, bare-headed, in the white pilgrim garb, among a multitude of white-garbed, bare-headed pilgrims from three continents, our faces turned toward the Jabal al-Rahma—the Mount of Mercy—which rises out of the vast plain: standing and waiting through the noon, through the afternoon, reflecting upon that inescapable day "when you will be exposed to view, and no secret of yours will remain concealed" . . .

And as I stand on the hillcrest and gaze down toward the invisible Plain of Arafat, the moonlit blueness of the landscape before me, so dead a moment ago, suddenly comes to life with the currents of all the human lives that have passed through it and is filled with the eerie voices of the millions of men and women who have walked or ridden between Mecca and Arafat in over thirteen hundred pilgrimages for over thirteen hundred years. Their voices and their steps and the voices and the steps of their animals reawaken and resound anew; I see them walking and riding and assembling—all those myriads of white-garbed pilgrims of thirteen hundred years; I hear the sounds of their passed-away days; the wings of the faith which has drawn them together to this land of rocks and sand and seeming deadness beat again with the warmth of life over the arc of centuries, and the mighty wingbeat draws me into its orbit and draws my own passed-away days into the present, and once again I am riding over the plain—

Riding in a thundering gallop over the plain, amidst thousands and thousands of *ihram*-clad Bedouins, returning from Arafat to Mecca—a tiny particle of that roaring, earth-shaking, irresistible wave of countless galloping dromedaries and men, with the tribal banners on their high poles beating like drums in the wind and their tribal war cries tearing through the air: *"Ya Rawga, ya Rawga!"* by which the Utayba tribesmen evoke their ancestor's name, answered by the *"Ya Awf, ya Awf!"* of the Harb and echoed by the almost defiant, *"Shammar, ya Shammar!"* from the farthest right wing of the column.

We ride on, rushing, flying over the plain, and to me it seems that we are flying with the wind, abandoned to a happiness that knows neither end nor limit . . . and the wind shouts a wild paean of joy into my ears: "Never again, never again, never again will you be a stranger!"

My brethren on the right and my brethren on the left, all of them unknown to me but none a stranger: in the tumultuous joy of our chase, we are one body in pursuit of one goal. Wide is the world before us, and in our hearts glimmers a spark of the flame that burned in the hearts of the Prophet's companions. They know, my brethren on the right and my brethren on the left, that they have fallen short of what was expected of them, and that in the flight of centuries their hearts have grown small: and yet, the promise of fulfilment has not been taken from them . . . from us . . .

Someone in the surging host abandons his tribal cry for a cry of faith: "We are the brethren of him who gives himself up to God!"—and another joins in: *"Allahu akbar!"*—"God is the greatest!—God alone is great!"

And all the tribal detachments take up this one cry. They are no longer Nejdi Bedouins reveling in their tribal pride: they are men who know that the secrets of God are but waiting for them . . . for us . . . Amidst the din of the thousands of rushing camels' feet and the flapping of a hundred banners, their cry grows up into a roar of triumph: *"Allahu akbar!"*

It flows in mighty waves over the heads of the thousands of galloping men, over the wide plain, to all the ends of the earth: *"Allahu akbar!"* These men have grown beyond their own little lives, and now their faith sweeps them forward, in oneness, toward some uncharted horizons . . . Longing need no longer remain small and hidden; it has found its awakening, a blinding sunrise of fulfilment. In this fulfilment, man strides along in all his God-given splendour; his stride is joy, and his knowledge is freedom, and his world a sphere without bounds . . .

The smell of the dromedaries' bodies, their panting and snorting, the thundering of their innumerable feet; the shouting of the men, the clanking of the rifles slung on saddle pegs, the dust and the sweat and the wildly excited faces around me; and a sudden, glad stillness within me.

I turn around in my saddle and see behind me the waving, weaving mass of thousands of white-clad riders and, beyond them, the bridge over which I have come: its end is just behind me while its beginning is already lost in the mists of distance.

17

Harry St. John Philby
Great Britain
1931

※

Of the travelers in this section who knew King Abd al-Aziz ibn Sa'ud, only the British author and explorer St. John Philby lived and worked at court for decades, took his daily meals with the King, and on occasion played a role in the new state's evolution. In the same period, he also found time to explore and map three quarters of the country. An ex–British civil servant, a friend of the King, and a convert, Philby depicts events in Mecca from a point of view unique in this collection. He performed the Hajj as a privileged resident, traveling with the royal cavalcade, sometimes on camels, at other times by car.

Harry St. John Bridger Philby was born in Ceylon in 1885, the second of four sons to an English coffee grower and an Irish mother from Colombo. When blight struck the fields in the 1880s, his father drowned his losses in alcohol. The mother and children removed to London, where they lived a peripatetic existence for several years before she opened a boarding house in Queen's Gate. Philby won scholarships to Westminster School, in the shadow of the abbey, then to Trinity College, Cambridge. On completing a course in modern languages, he was accepted into the Indian civil service and arrived in the Punjab in 1907, already versed in French, German, Persian, and Urdu.

Like Richard Burton, Philby was shaped and made gregarious by a nomadic youth. As civil servants, both men moved with ease between the native and British worlds of the Raj. Philby, however, was the more successful. Between 1909 and 1915, he took up Arabic, was posted as a subdistrict officer to Sargodha, married, became District Commissioner and later Chief of the British Language Board. Philby was brilliant, hotheaded, and determined to distinguish himself in service. When World War I began in Europe, he found himself sidelined thousands of miles away. His great ambition, he wrote, was "to take some part in the war, coupled with work among the Arabs." A few months later he was sent to Iraq to serve Sir Percy Cox, Chief Political Officer of the Indian Expeditionary Force.

In 1917, Cox sent Philby to Ibn Sa'ud's camp near Riyadh to try to resolve the enmity between the eastern desert tribes and the Sharif of Mecca. Ibn Sa'ud was slow to warm to British tactics, but he took to Philby right away. A forthright civil servant, fluent in Arabic, schooled in Muslim ways, Philby brought a native's knowledge of Europe to the Amir's isolated camp. And he was intrepid. Simply to reach the Saudi base in the Nejd, he had crossed the unmapped wastes of central Arabia, a trip that later earned him the Royal Geographical Society's Founder's Medal. Philby, it proved, could ride most Bedouin into the ground, and his wanderlust was boundless. At the end of his visit, he asked the King's permission to trek overland to Jidda, across a thousand miles of territory barred to travel by Sharif Husayn. This chance to irk his enemy Husayn appealed to Ibn Sa'ud, and he provided Philby with local guides and good camels.

Present-day Saudi Arabia is about the size of Western Europe. When Philby arrived there, less than a quarter of its surface had been charted. When he finished his great journeys of the 1950s, the national map was more or less complete. None of the famous names associated with Arabian exploration—Niebuhr, Burckhardt, Seetzen, Burton, Doughty, Blunt, Musil, or Thesiger—covered half so much territory. The dotted lines on the map (see Fig. 16) mark the principal network of Philby's Arabian travels, much of it accomplished in his sixties. After World War II, when the car's role in desert travel became apparent, it was Philby who insisted on bouncing down thousands of miles of camel tracks in a Land Rover. The routes of Arabia's modern highways were first surveyed this way.

We have already seen how travelers from Ibn Battuta to Ali Bey al-Abbasi used Muslim rulers and institutions to further a personal passion for exploration. Philby did the same, availing himself of the King's largesse to mount dozens of expeditions in the next thirty years, usually into unknown territory. Between 1918 and 1955, Philby was the principal source of Arabian cartography for the Royal Geographical Society, the British Foreign Bureau, and Ibn Sa'ud. While his Bedouin companions shook their heads (and sometimes their rifles), the tireless Philby routinely climbed peaks on both sides of every track to improve his maps. His notebooks, preserved at the R.G.S. in London, record every alteration in landscape and compass direction, each animal, snake, and insect sighted, every rock specimen crated and shipped to the British Museum. His longest journey, an eight-month return trek between Mecca and Mukalla in 1936, began with a summer bouncing through the Hijaz in cars and ended the following winter with Philby, carless and alone, trudging on foot and muleback through freezing mountains above eight thousand feet. Returning from each new foray, he routinely wrote a book about his exploits.

The following excerpts begin with an account of Philby's conversion, followed by selections from his record of the 1931 Hajj. Philby, who attended the pilgrimage every year for the next decade, was well placed to summarize the effects of the Depression on Hajj travel. As he notes, visiting pilgrims fell from a high of 130,000 to 40,000 in 1931 and to half that many two years later, while the government's revenues dropped correspondingly from five million pounds to less than two million. Here we see the degree to which the Saudi economy still relied on pilgrim receipts and duties. The loss brought on by this crisis caused the value of the local coinage to fall steeply. It is no coincidence that in 1932, Philby turned his attention to desert exploration. Although he was there as a businessman, the cash to do business was simply not in the country. Hajj receipts did not pick up until 1935.

from *Arabian Days: An Autobiography* and *A Pilgrim in Arabia* by Harry St. John Bridger Philby

THE PEACE OF ISLAM. SUMMER 1930 Hitherto, with my journalistic work and other writing to keep me busy during the preparatory stages of the commercial venture, and my rather special position in the counsels of the King and his government, I had been fairly content with life at Jidda, but I was beginning to realize that the prospect of spending the rest of my days there was not particularly attractive. At the same time I fully appreciated that in the then circumstances of the country, there was little chance of any great expansion of my sphere of activity in Arabia, as Ibn Saʿud could not afford, even out of friendship for me, to create a precedent which might have awkward consequences thereafter. His considered policy was to maintain friendly and cordial relations with all European countries, and especially with Great Britain, while protecting his realm rigorously from European penetration and the economic and political exploitation that would almost inevitably follow in its train, as they had done pretty well all over the world and, since the war, in various parts of Arabia itself. I could not but approve of that policy, and fully understood that I myself must submit to its consequences. . . .

Be all that as it may, I had fallen in love with Arabia, and the problem that confronted me from 1925 onwards was whether I was prepared to go all the way with the Arabs, or whether it would not be wiser after all to return whence I had come, and try once more to fit into the scheme of things for which my birth and education seemed to have designed me. It was not an easy choice to make in cold blood. I was still young enough to contemplate a political career in England without jeopardizing the business interests which I had established in Jidda. On the other hand I still had plenty to learn and teach the world about Arabia, and it seemed a pity not to stay on and complete the work, to which I had put my hand long since and for which I had such special qualifications. I never really hesitated in my decision, but I took my time in making it, as I knew that, once made, it would be irrevocable. Ibn Sa'ud, for his part, had known for some time what was in my mind, but had scrupulously refrained from pressing or even encouraging me to a step which he regarded as lying entirely between myself and my conscience, though his considerate attitude left me in no doubt that he would welcome me into his fold with open arms if I came to it of my own free will. And in the end it was an accident which precipitated my decision.

Towards the end of July 1930, and during the first few days of August, Jidda had been sweltering under a long spell of its foulest weather, with temperatures running up to ninety-three degrees and ninety-five degrees and a humidity almost unbearable. I had been working rather hard to get some chapters of my book on Indian politics finished, and one afternoon, early in August, my head went down on the table like a log and the world seemed to be turning somersaults about me. I suppose it was an ordinary fainting fit, but being unaccustomed to that sort of thing, I thought it was a stroke, and managed to crawl to a sofa, where I lay for some hours in a stupor. On recovering from that, I confess I felt a bit alarmed, but my mind seemed to be working normally, and I began to consider what I should do in the circumstances. It was then that I made my decision.

The King was spending the summer at Ta'if, having come down to Mecca from Riyadh for the pilgrimage and visited Jidda to meet Ryan* and receive his letters of credence as Minister. Fu'ad Hamza, now Deputy Foreign Secretary in succession to Abdullah Damluji, who had left the country, was at Mecca, and I rang him up to tell him what had happened, and to ask him to tell the King that I had now finally made up my mind regarding the matters we had discussed and wished to visit him at Ta'if to arrange the necessary details. Within a matter of hours the King was on the telephone himself, speaking to me from Ta'if and expressing his pleasure that I had at last made up my mind to come into the fold of the faithful. He went on to

*Sir Andrew Ryan, first British Envoy and Minister Plenipotentiary to the court of Ibn Sa'ud. [Ed.]

say that he was immediately sending Fuʿad Hamza to me with a document which I was to sign, after careful perusal, in token of my acceptance of Islam. This was required for the satisfaction of the ecclesiastical authorities at Mecca, whither I would be conducted the following evening by Fuʿad Hamza himself and the Finance Minister, Abdullah al-Suleyman, to perform the rites of Umra, or the Lesser Pilgrimage, after which I would be welcome at Taʾif. These preliminaries occupied less than twenty-four hours from the moment of my telephoning to Fuʿad, and on the afternoon of 7 August 1930, making to my staff the excuse that I had to meet the Finance Minister in Wadi Fatima to discuss some business matters, I got into my Arab garments and drove off in my green Ford car—out of the old life into the new.

It happened to be a day of good augury, the birthday of the Prophet Muhammad himself. . . . At Hadda I was met by my distinguished sponsors and, after a siesta and tea, performed the prescribed ablutions in a tent and emerged from it in the garb of an ordinary pilgrim. After the sunset prayer, in which I joined my co-religionists for the first time, and an early dinner, I drove with Fuʿad Hamza and Abdullah Suleyman through the cool gloaming of a desert evening, passing through the Alamayn pillars on the boundary of the Sacred Territory and by other spots familiar enough to me in my reading, but now seen vaguely in the darkness for the first time, until we came to Abdullah Suleyman's villa in the Jarwal quarter of Mecca itself. From there, after a very short delay for coffee and refreshment, I proceeded with the Finance Minister's own chaplain to the Haram, the Great Mosque of Mecca, to go through the ceremony of the circumambulation of the Kaʿba and the rest of the ritual of the Lesser Pilgrimage under his guidance. It was an impressive and even awe-inspiring experience, but my main immediate impression of the scene and the ceremony was that it was all very familiar and intimate, like something vaguely remembered from a forgotten past. I seemed to be living in a dream, and I was content to relax in an orgy of intellectual and spiritual self-surrender—at least for that one unforgettable night—without concern for the consequences of my action, which was bound, I knew full well, to give rise to a good deal of comment and criticism. As I wrote later to a very good friend, I had, in taking this step, sacrificed neither my sanity nor my sincerity, but it was Ryan who found the best formula for my justification. "Mecca and Islam," he was reported to have said, "will give Philby the background which he has needed so badly ever since he quarrelled with the government." I certainly did seem to have now some sort of positive ideal or objective to work for henceforth, and I felt like some disembodied spirit restored by accident or miracle to its proper environment. For the first time for many years I felt strangely at peace with the world.

THE MECCAN PILGRIMAGE: PREPARATIONS By the end of the third week in April 1931, the last batch of pilgrim ships—from Egypt and the Sudan, from Morocco and Syria, from India and the Far East—had arrived in Jidda, and a disappointingly meagre concourse of some 40,000 visitors from overseas had gathered at Mecca, to be swelled during the few remaining days by perhaps twice that number of pilgrims from Nejd and Yemen and of local Hijazis.

The number of pilgrims from abroad during the preceding five years had varied between 80,000 and 120,000; and the drop in 1931 was mainly due to the worldwide economic depression which marked that and subsequent years. In 1932 the number fell further to 30,000 and in the following year to only 20,000. This represented the trough of the depression, for in 1934 the attendance from abroad rose to 25,370 and since then there had been a slow but steady improvement until the present war set back the clock once more. For the decade preceding the war the average number of foreign pilgrims visiting Mecca each year may have been about 35,000. Before this period the influx of pilgrims from Malaya and the Dutch East Indies alone frequently exceeded 50,000 souls in a year; and it was particularly this element which dwindled to meagre proportions owing to the subsequent slump in the prices of the commodities they produce—sugar and rubber in particular.

The new moon of 19 April had not been seen in the Hijaz, and news of its actual sighting that evening was anxiously awaited from the newcomers from far afield in desert and mountain. The actual day of the central ceremony of the pilgrimage—the Standing by Jabal al-Rahma in the vast Plain of Arafat on the ninth day of the lunar month of Dhu al-Hijja—could not be fixed in the absence of such information; and it was not till Thursday, 23 April, the fifth day of the month, that the prevailing uncertainty was relieved by the production before, and certification by, the ecclesiastical authorities of the necessary evidence. The moon had indeed been seen on the evening preceding 19 April and the ninth day of Dhu al-Hijja would thus fall on Monday, the twenty-seventh. Plans could now be made for the great exodus to Mina and Arafat, and those who would be early on the scene—to make holiday under the stars until the great Standing—began moving out from Mecca after the Friday prayers of the twenty-fourth.

That same evening the actual pilgrimage celebrations began with the customary royal banquet at the palace, to which between six hundred and seven hundred guests had been bidden, including Amanollah Khan, ex-king of the Afghans; Prince Ahmad Saif al-Din, grandson of Sultan Abd al-Aziz of the House of Osman; the Afghan Minister at Cairo and other representatives of the reigning Afghan King, Nader Khan; Sir A. K. Ghaznavi of the

Bengal Executive Council; and others too numerous to mention, representatives of practically every country and community professing the faith of Islam. . . .

THE HAJJ PROCESSIONAL The next day saw the exodus of white-clad, bareheaded pilgrims to Arafat in full swing. . . . The long broad street that leads from the Great Mosque through the city eastward past the historic cemetery of al-Maʻala and the royal palace in Maʼabida was all day long a scene of unceasing and ever-increasing activity as the long trains of litter-bearing camels, often four or five lines abreast, got under way, moving slowly but steadily to their destination some nine or ten miles distant. Between the files of those travelling in this manner small bands of pilgrims on donkeys threaded their way at a somewhat faster pace in and out of the motley rout. And yet the broad fairway had room enough for the legions that went on foot, old and young, men, women and children, generally in companies sporting multicoloured banners to serve as rallying points for the various groups both on the road and ultimately on the Plain of Arafat, now rapidly becoming a city of tents. These banners and the sun covers of the litters added a touch of gay colour to the otherwise white and brown mass of bodies and pilgrim robes that passed seemingly without end along the road. Here and there a valiant group of new arrivals from the East, intent on performing the ceremonies connected with first entry into Mecca, stemmed the eastward stream with such speed as they could make in the circumstances to reach the Haram, as the Great Mosque of Mecca is called. And every now and then a privileged motorcar with a pass signed by the King's own hand—for all motor traffic in the city had been suspended by order for the two days of the main exodus—snorted or purred in the throng, carefully feeling its way eastward or westward according to the errand of its occupants. As the day advanced towards evening, the throng of camels, donkeys, pedestrians, became ever more thick, and the shades of night fell upon a city still pouring forth its denizens in an endless stream.

THE EXODUS TO ARAFAT The flood continued with undiminished volume the next day, the traditional date for the exodus and known as Yawm al-Tarwiyya.* Only the King and his entourage sat still, going about their normal work till the hour fixed for their departure in the early afternoon.

---

*Yaum al-Tarwiyya: the day before the exodus to Arafat, when pilgrims traditionally supplied themselves with water enough to journey to and from the desert during the Hajj, literally, Watering Day. [Ed.]

"It is like a campaign," said the King, "this pilgrimage business." And so it was for him. From every part of the now-extended theatre of activities reports of progress and events were brought to him for his orders or attention: perhaps a motorcar trying to evade the restrictions on movement in force within the city or on the road to Arafat, or now a car capsized by some chauffeur's folly and needing succour for its damaged passengers, or again some member of the royal family or high official requiring transport, and so on. No matter was too small for the King's personal attention, which was throughout concentrated on the determination to make everything as successful as conditions would allow. And all the time he never moved from his place at headquarters which had been temporarily connected up by telephone with Mina, three miles distant, the advanced base whither the royal family had already gone overnight by car to be accommodated in a large but simple palace constructed during the preceding two months or, rather, greatly extended in comparison with the humble building of the earlier years.

I was to ride with the King but, owing to a last-minute hitch and the consequent late arrival of my riding camel, I actually made the journey to Mina by motorcar with the Minister of Finance, and thus had an opportunity of seeing the new route prescribed for all motor vehicles in order to leave the main road free for camels and pedestrians. The Nejdi camel still appears to have a rooted objection to the noisy lumbering motorcar, though his Hijazi brother has long reconciled himself to the latter's intrusion and competition.

The motor track follows the valley to the south of Mina which carries the splendid masonry aqueduct of Queen Zubayda at a high level along the flank of the low hills on the left hand as we went up. A car or two we found embedded in the occasional ugly patches of sand to be negotiated on this route, and another vehicle had apparently overturned owing to its too great speed over rocks hidden in the deep sand. Its more or less injured occupants were couched in its shade awaiting relief. Otherwise we reached Mina without incident after doubling back from the end of the spur dividing the two roads. The King was alone at the moment in the great newly built reception chamber adjoining the Mina palace, the camels of his bodyguard being couched around, while the various members of the royal family occupied the blocks of tents placed at their disposal.

Mina, a deserted and derelict village for 350 days of each lunar year, had suddenly come to life. Every one of its not numerous houses was fully occupied by pilgrims paying exorbitant rents—often as high as thirty or forty pounds for the few days of the festival. Its vast valley between low black hills had blossomed into a city of tents, and its single road, passing through the village and the middle of the valley, was thronged with pedestrians and caravans going through to Arafat, where many pilgrims prefer to spend the night in contrast to those of the Hanbali persuasion, for the most part people from Nejd, who, following as always the actual practice of the Prophet, spend the first night at Mina for the afternoon, sunset, and evening prayers of that day and do not move forward till after the sun has risen a spear's length above the horizon the following morning.

Dinner was served for the royal party in a huge tent near the palace, and after the meal I strolled through the camp and village—no easy matter in the ever-moving throng of camels and people. The moon lent enchantment to the scene, and I noticed that the three "devils" set up at intervals in the village—each a low masonry pillar within a circular masonry wall of modest dimensions—had been newly whitewashed against their customary lapidation during the holidays following the pilgrimage. The petty shopkeepers of Mina seemed to be doing a brisk business in the unconsidered trifles that pilgrims must have on such an occasion—souvenirs, foodstuffs, and water.

I had my bed laid out near the main road on the edge of the great platform adjoining the palace, and as I dozed off to sleep under the stars with no covering but my pilgrim garments, the ghostly train passed by unceasingly on the way to Arafat. The air buzzed all night with the querulous murmuring—half bray and half bleat—of camels and the fussy grinding of cars. No less than three hundred motor vehicles composed the fleet destined to take the royal family to its destination—its women and slaves and children even down to the less than year old Talal, the baby of the King's fifty-odd children.

On such occasions in the East there is no such thing as recognized hours of sleep. Many indeed slept, including myself, but our slumbers did not diminish the din, to which I awoke again about 3:00 A.M. for the dawn prayer in the great reception room. It would still be long before sunrise, and the King, according to his wont, having slept but little, was engrossed in his sacred readings, while we sat round drinking coffee and tea. . . .

As the light of day began to intrude upon the dust haze of the valley from behind the black hills, there was a stirring among the camels at the palace door. In another moment we were all in the saddle, and as the King's party moved down the valley, converging trains soon swelled the cavalcade to magnificent proportions. Not less than ten thousand camels rode behind the King that morning, the morning of the Hajj, and noiselessly enough though roughly the cavalcade swept down the valley like an untamed flood as the sun rose slowly but surely and at length peeped down over the crest of the black hills on to a haze of hanging dust. On past the solitary minaret of

Muzdalifa we swept and through the narrow valley of the Mazumayn to the *bazan* water tanks, where the Zubayda aqueduct swings across the road. And then we came to the two pillars marking the boundary of the Sacred Territory of Mecca. Beyond it lies the secular, or neutral, ground of Wadi Arina, in which is the mosque of Namira, a vast whitened enclosure with crenellated walls but without a minaret. Here in the neutral area, whose further border towards the Plain of Arafat is marked with other boundary pillars, we drew rein to halt, according to the Prophet's practice, till the early afternoon. Tents had been put up in advance, and we were soon tackling a frugal though not unwelcome breakfast, after which repose and, if possible, sleep were the order of the day. Not far ahead Jabal al-Rahma, the Mount of Mercy, which is the central feature of the Arafat Plain, stood out conspicuous with the whitened pillar on its summit over a canopy of dust haze marking the visible tent city which had sprung up overnight for the accommodation of the pilgrims. All around us was the sand valley of Arina with scattered tents, while vast crowds of pilgrims, mostly African blacks from far afield, centred on the Namira mosque and its bounteous wells. The day warmed to its work, exuding heat in the forenoon only to dissipate it in due course with gentle breezes which struck delightfully cool on our scantily clad bodies grouped in the grateful shade of tents. Water was plentiful, and even ice was in evidence from the royal palace.

For a brief space the King slept, and soon after noon we were summoned to his tent for the midday meal of mutton and rice and other simple things, after which we walked across the stretch of sand, now like fire to the bare feet and necessitating the use of sandals, to the Namira mosque, where the vast assembly of waiting worshippers made access to our places before the pulpit and *mihrab* not a little difficult. . . .

The sermon was preached by Shaykh Abdullah ibn Hasan, the chief ecclesiastic of Mecca, who mounted the steps of the simple pulpit, camel stick in hand, and proceeded to set forth in some detail the ordinances of the Prophet regarding the pilgrimage. The congregation from time to time gave vent to tears or tearful demonstrations as the memories of the Prophet's Farewell Pilgrimage of A.D. 632—almost exactly thirteen hundred years ago—were brought freshly to mind. Close by me an aged Indian lay convulsed in sobs, and one began to feel in common with one's fellow worshippers something of the solemnity of an occasion, designed to keep alive in the hearts of men the story of an inspiration which had reached its climax on this very spot so many centuries ago in the perfection of a faith which in the interval has spread far beyond the borders of Arabia to be a guiding light to millions upon millions in Asia and Africa and even in Europe. . . .

The sermon at Namira . . . was followed by the noon and afternoon prayers, combined in accordance with the Prophet's practice and led by Shaykh Abdullah from his place before the *mihrab,* or niche oriented towards Mecca. The congregation then dispersed and swarmed out of the mosque in a sort of *sauve-qui-peut.* We returned to our tents, and there the King was visited by various Indian and other pilgrims desirous of saluting the Prince of the Faithful. They were provided with coffee and food, and soon after 1:00 P.M. the King was in the saddle with his bodyguard, moving to the culminating ceremony of the Standing on Arafat.

The royal bodyguard was at this time entirely composed of His Majesty's henchmen from Nejd, some two hundred or three hundred strong—a sturdy, tough-looking body of men, all clad like the other pilgrims in the white garments of the *ihram* but differentiated from them by the fact that they carried rifles and cartridge belts, swords, and daggers. Latterly it has been considered more consonant with the King's dignity to have an escort of "regular" troops trained on the European model and instructed in the arts of saluting and heel clicking. During the pilgrimage, however, even regular troops have to discard their uniforms and wear the *ihram,* so that the scene has not changed except to the experienced eye, which easily detects the (generally) town-bred soldier from the desert-born janissary. Even so and in spite of the presence of the official royal escort the old bodyguard has not disbanded itself and is always to be found somewhere near the King's body, to guard it against all harm.

The Mount of Mercy, whose chief feature is a low granitic hummock about 100 to 150 feet high marked by a white pillar, is in fact a ridge with three low peaks, whose sand-covered slopes descend to form a semicircular enclave bounded on the outer side by the masonry of the Ain Zubayda Aqueduct. Outside this hill mass to west and south lay the Plain of Arafat with its temporary city of tents. All this area to the border of Wadi Arina is "Standing" ground, but a low mass of rocks on the south side of the arena above described is regarded as the spot on which the Prophet "stood" for the ceremony on the occasion of his Farewell Pilgrimage. Here accordingly is the traditional "Standing" area of the people of Nejd, and into this space they duly gathered in their thousands and tens of thousands from about 2:00 P.M. onwards, when the King and his party with the green Wahhabi standards unfurled in their midst took up their positions. Every man remained mounted on his camel facing not towards the hill (which is, however, permissible) but towards the *qibla,* the Meccan Ka'ba. Among the crowd were also the covered litters of women screened from male gaze. Thus bareheaded and in the scant pilgrim robes with never an umbrella to disgrace the scene (though they were common enough among the non-Nejdi elements on the plain), the huge throng remained through the afternoon from 2:00 P.M. to sunset reciting the prayers prescribed for the occasion, an endless prayer for the forgiveness of God and the remission of sins. At the head of the Nejdi group, bareheaded like the rest, stood the King, flanked by his brothers and sons, reading from the little "book of words" published by his order for the guidance of the congregation.

In other parts of the vast field, which I seized the opportunity to visit during the afternoon, there seemed to be more of a festival air. Groups of people remained in their tents rather than face the downward rays of the sun—fierce enough in the circumstances, though a cool dry breeze did much to mitigate the severity of the ordeal even in the open. The poorer folk had brought along a few palm fronds with them, which they rigged up with sacking to form small tents and shelters, while the Negroes from Africa grouped themselves on the flanks of the hill and along the Zubayda channel whence they got water in plenty to drink and for their ablutions.

This African element, collectively known as *Takruri,** though it comprises many different tribes of the Dark Continent—as widely separated, for instance, as the Sudan and Nigeria—is of considerable interest. . . .

Most of these Takruris spend several years on their journey from their homes to Mecca, generally working their way across the African continent and often spending several years on the cotton plantations of the Sudan. I once met a man and wife who had started out with a single child and had a family of six on the completion of their pilgrimage—their journey up to this point having taken fourteen years. But the most venerable Takruri pilgrim of my experience was a sturdy old man who claimed to be 120 years old and to have spent no less than seventy years on the road from Lagos to Jidda, where I met him in 1930. His whole life had been spent in the study of Islamic religion and philosophy, and his long journey had involved considerable sojourns at various centres of learning on the way. By careful cross-examination I elicited from him the interesting fact that he had been in Khartoum in the year of General Gordon's death at the hands of the Mahdi's force.[†]

*Takruri: "derived from the verb *takurrar,* 'to multiply, to renew, to sift, to purify, to invigorate,' i.e., their religious sentiments, by study of the sacred book, and by pilgrimage." (John Lewis Burckhardt, *Travels in Nubia,* p. 406)

[†]General Gordon: Charles George Gordon (1833–85), British soldier and administrator, was governor of the Egyptian Sudan (1877–80). In 1885, while attempting to crush Arab

Altogether there was a striking absence of all ceremonial in the proceedings at Arafat. People seemed to do much what they liked, the fact that they were pitched on the plain during the prescribed hours being satisfaction of the obligation connoted by the term "Standing."

The Egyptian contingent had a ritual of its own, as one might expect. During my wanderings I noticed a large gathering of men and women—obviously folk of some substance—lined up in rows behind a chorus leader with their backs turned on Mecca and their faces to the Mount of Mercy as they repeated in unison the sentences intoned by the leader and waved their handkerchiefs towards the hill as they did so. This was obviously a ritual surviving from the days of the *mahmal,* and nobody seemed to worry about their strange proceedings for the Wahhabi legions—positively legions—were on the other side of the hill, well out of sight. Elsewhere the "Standing" crowds held services of their own in little groups of twenty or thirty persons in the shelter of their large tents or awnings or merely sat or lay about drinking tea or even sleeping out the weary hours of the ordeal till sunset.

Perhaps in Turkish or sharifal times, when the Standing took the form of an organized service and the various stages of the sermon on the mount were punctuated by gunfire or other devices, the ceremony may have been more spectacular or imposing, but one had only to turn to the Nejdi arena to realize that a new spirit had come into the Arafat celebrations—a conviction of the essential purpose of the pilgrimage and of the human duty of humility and endurance that alone make it "acceptable" to God.

In due course, though very slowly, the blazing sun relented of his fierceness as he sank towards the crest of Jabal Thaur over against Mecca. The disc sank till it became invisible behind the line of the black hills. The prayers melted into a palpable silence, after which came a faint rustling, and in a moment, the sun having set, the great cavalcade was once more in motion for the return journey. So far as I can remember, no writer has previously emphasized the fact that the Arafat ceremony is essentially a festival of the camel. As I moved forward with the royal cavalcade and cast my eyes over the scene, it was the camel that chiefly impressed me. All over the immense plain, suddenly in motion towards the valley leading back to Mecca, it was the lines and phalanxes of camels that caught my eye. There must have been some fifty thou-

---

resistance to British rule, he died in the siege of Khartoum. The Mahdi was Muhammad Ahmad (1844–85), a Muslim religious leader in the Anglo-Egyptian Sudan. In 1881, Ahmad declared himself Mahdi, a divinely guided restorer of the faith. His army of followers captured the Sudanese capital, Khartoum, but he died soon after.

sand of them at least, and all moving forward together at the silent, hurried pace characteristic of the chief carrier of Arabia. It was, indeed, a goodly scene, and as the dusk increased and the dust rose from the padding feet, our legions seemed to lose reality and to become as it were a ghostly, heavenly host, moving so silently, so mysteriously in the dim limbo of a twilight illuminated by the moon above with Mars and Jupiter ahead and Sirius, Betelgeuse, and Capella in their train. For all the light of the moon it soon became impossible to see anything clearly in that moving mist with the white-shrouded bodies of men raised high aloft on their giant steeds. Past stunted shrubs and thorny acacia bushes we brushed, and as the valley narrowed between the darkening hills, we swept past litter-bearing caravans and groups of walking men and women—nay, even groups seated, resting on the ground as if conscious by instinct that that celestial host would pass over them without harm. It was amazing how, though we could scarcely see more than a few paces ahead, the camels instinctively avoided all obstacles in their path, human or otherwise, which rapidly receded through our phalanx to the rear.

THE RETURN TO MECCA Passing into Meccan territory through the boundary pillars, we marched up the valley and through the Mazumayn Pass, where there suddenly burst upon us a fairy scene as of some huge city with its myriad lights, great arc lamps in regular lines and smaller lanterns perched on posts. There had been no trace of this city at our passing in the morning. It had grown up suddenly in the valley since dusk. This was Muzdalifa, where we were to spend the night according to the Prophet's practice. The King's party moved towards the left flank of the valley and halted on a slope of sand not far from the mosqueless minaret. The motor vehicles had introduced an element of disorder and confusion into the scene and certainly made the night hideous enough, but there were apparently no accidents, and the royal household was in due course accommodated in the tents set up for its use.

Motor cars were tending to become an increasing element in the pilgrimage scene. At the time of which I write, the privilege of using them was still confined to the royal family and officials on duty, but in 1933 permission was granted to a wider circle, while in the following year all restrictions were removed, and the number of motor vehicles taking part in the ceremony was not less than four hundred. Since then the number has steadily increased, and foreign pilgrims who can afford the luxury have now little to complain of in the matter of comfort.

All around was the murmuring of camels and the cries of men calling to their missing companions—a veritable orchestra of discord. How anybody found anyone else in that mushroom city of a night, which none had seen nor was to see by day—for we would be on the move again long before sunrise—was a mystery to me.

The King himself camped in the open on rugs spread over the sandy slope, and in due course a noble meal of mutton and rice on a dozen portentous trays was spread out on a long carpet for our refreshment. We ate with a will, and after us the rest of the escort; and then the King ordered his henchmen to go forth and bring in the wayfaring pilgrims, who came in their hundreds, eager, famished, to feed at the royal table and, as I noticed in many cases, to put by in the corner of their grizzled robes some provender for the morrow. And they went their way rejoicing with full bellies and loud thanks. We slept.

I woke again seemingly in the middle of the night to the sound of grinding cars and groaning camels. The King was a few paces off, engrossed in his religious reading, and soon, though I was still heavy with sleep, we lined up for the dawn prayer about 3:00 a.m. We then mounted and moved off to the minaret of Muzdalifa, where we halted, though remaining mounted, for about half an hour for a ceremony of prayer and thanksgiving prescribed by the Prophet for those reaching this point on their return journey. The minaret was hung with great arc lamps, and groups of pilgrims seemed to be gathered about it and even on the squat tower by its side. Others groped about in the sand of the valley, which is Wadi Muhassir, to collect the forty-nine pebbles larger than a peanut needed for the coming lapidation of the "devils." We had incidentally collected ours from the ground where we had camped for the night—it would seem that they may be collected from anywhere in the Muzdalifa neighbourhood, though Wadi Muhassir is the place prescribed by tradition—and had duly made them fast in a corner of our towels.

Later, however, I noticed at Mina that many of the pilgrims, unmindful of the special virtue of stones gathered at Muzdalifa according to the Prophet's injunctions, were groping about in the gritty streets of the village for the requisite missiles. It may readily be imagined that fifty thousand pilgrims hurling forty-nine pebbles apiece at the effigies of Satan, which will be explained in due course, succeeded in adding substantially to the rubble heaps of Mina, which in the course of centuries should grow into mounds of considerable size—but for a putative miracle resulting, as is commonly believed, in the spontaneous disappearance of each year's contribution of execration before the next instalment becomes due.

As the light of day slowly grew upon us, the arc lamps were removed from the minaret, and our prayers over, we resumed our advance up the valley towards Mina. Here or hereabouts our camels suddenly shied at something on the path, which proved to be a camel that had fallen and died by the way.

I also observed one stretcher on which a sick or injured person was being carried, but I may say here that all through the proceedings up to this point and indeed up to my return to Mecca the same morning, I had noticed no other sign of any casualty in the vast throng—perhaps a hundred thousand pilgrims in all.

Moving through the gradually lessening gloom, we came to Mina, where the King immediately exchanged his camel for a horse and proceeded forthwith up the street of Mina to the Aqaba [Pillar] for the obligatory lapidation of the "Great Devil." Most people had dismounted to follow him, but I did so on my camel, which I only left when the crowd became too dense as we neared our destination. Completing the last hundred yards on foot, I arrived at the Aqaba to find an amazing crowd gathered below, pelting [it] with the pebbles brought from Muzdalifa, seven pebbles each on this occasion. The people seemed seized with a sort of frenzy as they plied their hands in the joyous task with the formulae of execration on their lips, and it was quite impossible to approach near enough to cast my pebbles at the object of the common wrath. My missiles probably alighted on the unheeding heads of those in front.

For the moment that was the end of the ceremony for me, as I found the King's brother Abdullah mounting a car to return to Mecca for the next stage of the pilgrim rites and was lucky enough to find a place with him. In less than half an hour I was back in my own house enjoying a light breakfast before facing the Meccan ceremonies which would complete and consolidate my Hajj. The essential conditions of the Hajj proper are (1) to assume the *ihram* which I had done some thirty-six hours before; (2) to "stand" at Arafat, which had also been safely accomplished; and (3) to stone the "Great Devil" immediately on return from Arafat and proceed to Mecca to perform the *tawaf* (circuit of the Ka'ba) and *sa'y* (the running between Safa and Marwa) and to have a shave and haircut. Having completed the threefold ceremonies of the third requisite, the pilgrim resumes ordinary clothes and is finally released from all the obligations of *ihram*. By performing only the first two of these conditions (and leaving the third to another time), he similarly becomes free of all restrictions with the sole exception that intercourse with women is forbidden until he has fulfilled the third condition also. Those who are not accompanied by their womenfolk often defer the Meccan ceremonies till the end of the three days of the Mina holiday.

THE CEREMONIES AT MECCA Though it was but little past 6:00 A.M. when I got back to Mecca, the main street was already overflowing with returning pilgrims, who must have omitted the Muzdalifa stage of the ritual and travelled, walking or camel borne, all night to get there in time. The Haram area was crowded, and the Masaʿa, or track between Safa and Marwa, which the main street cuts obliquely, was thronged with urgent, surging crowds running, walking, pushing, praying, this way and that.

Having refreshed myself and rested awhile, I drove back to the Haram soon after 7:00 A.M. to get through the *tawaf* and *saʿy* before the sun was far enough up to make things hot. I drew up at the Bab Ibrahim, the main door of the south frontage of the Great Mosque, and entered through a crowd of beggars anxiously assuring me of their hopes for the "acceptance" of my pilgrimage and in turn accepting without ceremony the mites that I drew from my pocket. . . .

The weathered and rain-stained *kiswa* of last year had now been rolled up a dozen feet, exposing the solid basalt masonry of the building, massive square-cut blocks of unequal size bound together with a strong greyish mortar. The silver umbo of the Black Stone projected naked from its corner, for all the world like the hawsepipe of a steamer; and on the side between the corner (east) and that of the Yemeni Stone, on the south, the new garment, made in its Meccan factory, had already been let down by a party of workmen on the roof to take the place of the old. In its shining blue-black glossiness of velvety silk, with a splendid band of gold arabesque two thirds of the way up, it stood out in striking contrast with the washed-out drapery that still clung to the other three sides, to be replaced as fast as the men could work. And even as I watched, the great sheet of new drapery for the main (northeast) front was let down with a rush to bury momentarily under its skirt the crowd of pilgrims pressing forward with prayerful invocations to the raised lintel of the great silvered door, which was at this time open under the guardianship of members of the Banu Shayba family—the hereditary Holders of the Key of the Kaʿba by divine decree—for the admission of those who could pay the price. When the four pieces of the *kiswa* are in place, they are duly dressed and joined up by workmen lowered from the roof on a platform operated by a wooden crane and pulley—the last item of the proceeding being the filling of the gap of the *kiswa* over the Kaʿba doorway by the rich *burqa*, or veil of silk and gold-lettered arabesque.

For the moment my business was the performance of the *tawaf*, the sevenfold circuit of the Kaʿba beginning with the kissing or salutation of the Black Stone: "In the name of God, God is great." Two uniformed policemen stood on duty at this spot to regulate the ever-increasing pressure and keep the stream flowing. To do this, they had to use their canes and fists freely enough, and the scene round this, the most sacred spot in the Islamic world, was one of amazing commotion and confusion, which suggested to a European mind thoughts of traffic regulation, barriers, and turn-stiles. But a little thought was enough to convince me that nothing of the kind was either feasible (though practicable enough if desired) or desirable. It would go against the basic principles of Islam which, though essentially a democratic and socialist creed, does prescribe and inculcate one element of individualism, which at certain moments—and only at those moments—makes the human ego all-important above the claims of society, race, and even family. Each Muslim, man, woman or child, is personally responsible for the achievement of his own salvation at all costs. That is not only his responsibility but his bounden duty to be performed without regard to the consequences to himself or others. . . . At such moments spiritual energy transcends the intellectual, and those who believe in the basic doctrines of Islam can scarcely wish it otherwise. . . . What matter then if the pilgrim occasionally loses control at the sublime moment of his ecstasy? What matter if he crowds and crushes when a little self-restraint, universally practised, would create a steady and unimpeded flow at the physically narrow centres of exaltation and self-realization? Barriers and turnstiles would perhaps throw back the press to other points of ingress and egress, but after all, nothing can alter the physical configuration of the Meccan valley, while the gradual progress of modernization is already sufficiently advanced to ensure improvements where they are needed without jeopardizing the symbolism of a historic faith. . . .

In due course the seven circuits were accomplished, and I was back where I had begun—at the Black Stone. Nearer approach being physically impossible without acute discomfort, I again saluted the holy emblem from afar and pushed my way through the outer fringes of the circling crowd to the Place of Abraham, or as near it as I could get, for the customary two-bow prayer in celebration of the *tawaf* duly performed. After this the usual practice is to stand before the door of the Ka'ba and as near to it as possible—indeed right up against the wall with arms upraised upon the *kiswa* itself in an attitude of despairing imploration—and to murmur such petitions for the betterment of one's lot in the present and in the inexorable hereafter as one may desire to make. Owing to the press, I omitted this step in the proceedings and refreshed myself with a draught of water from the historic and sacred Well of Zamzam, offered to pilgrims according to custom in metal cups into which it is poured from pear-shaped earthen pots by the *zamzamis* (water carriers), whom I duly rewarded in suitable proportion to the special occasion, a shilling for perhaps half a pint of the blessed beverage, which, I may take this occasion to remark, has been almost universally and quite unjustly maligned by those who have written of the Meccan ceremonies before me. There is indeed a brackish taste in this water, but of the slightest, and when cold, as it always should be if left awhile in the porous earthen pots, I have always found it a pleasant and refreshing drink—mildly beneficial to the internal machinery of the body and, surely, the most historic and sacred of all earth's waters. I frankly do not understand the aspersions of Burton, Wavell, Eldon Rutter, and others, and for the benefit of the ignorant, I may add that the well is now (and has for some considerable time been) protected from all possible contamination by the building which completely covers it.

This precaution was certainly necessary, for cases have been known of persons committing suicide by jumping into the well in the mistaken belief that its water would shrive them for immediate admittance to Paradise. Many pilgrims bring with them the winding-sheets in which they intend to be buried in due course, to wash in this Zamzam water, though not actually, of course, in the well. . . .

The last few drops in my second cup were sprinkled over my head and face by the *zamzami,* and I girt up my loins for the "running." Issuing from the Haram by the Safa Gate, I joined the throng proceeding to the head of the Masaʿa, or drome—an old mound now built up with several broad steps of basalt and granite and adorned with a comparatively modern arched superstructure. In former times those standing on this mound could see the Kaʿba towards which the opening formulae of the "running" are addressed with hands uplifted. Now the intervening houses and the Haram wall prevent the actual view. The formulae pronounced, one descends for the "course." The throng of "runners" going and coming in dense gangs or smaller groups or singly without order or method was terrific. One had to make one's way through the press as best one could, dodging here and dodging there to avoid the heavier phalanxes. For the first hundred paces one proceeds at a walk to the crossways formed by the cutting of the Masaʿa street by the Ghashashiya Road and its continuation along the eastern wall of the Haram to the Hamidiya, or government headquarters. At this point a pilaster set in the wall of the Haram marks the beginning of the section to be covered, according to ancient practice, at the pace known as *harwala,* a sort of shuffle run. In former times, as in our more spacious days of motors, this crossing carried the main highway of the city, and the shuffle run was doubtless designed as a very necessary aid to traffic. A green pillar on the right-hand side of the Masaʿa, built into a shop wall, marks the end of the *harwala* section, whose whole length is 53 paces. Here one resumes at a walk for the remaining 306 paces of the course, now a broad street covered over and lined with shops on both sides, to the mound of Marwa, similar to that of Safa and similarly furnished with broad steps and an arched superstructure. The whole of the Masaʿa, roughly 380 yards in length, has during the reign of the present King been cobble paved—a great improvement on the old regime of flying dust and uncleanable, accumulated filth and rubbish which used to make a real penance of the "running."

During the course the pilgrim repeats the prescribed formulae of the occasion, and at Marwa he turns towards Safa, standing on the steps with upraised hands, to repeat further formulae, after which he descends to return to Safa. Seven times in all, four from Safa to Marwa and three in the reverse direction, one does this course, and at the end of the seventh lap the ceremonies of the great pilgrimage are duly completed, all except the shaving or the haircutting according to choice or tenets, to aid in which an army of barbers throng the Marwa end of the Masaʿa and appear to do a flourishing business. I preferred to do my own hair trimming at home, and having done my course of 2,660 yards—it was now about 9:00 A.M. and getting warm—I was glad enough of my car to take me thither. In all respects my first pilgrimage was duly and faithfully completed, and during the coming days of festival my friends and acquaintances would wish me its "acceptance" and all the blessings implied thereby. I had now duly become a hajji, a title little used in Arabia itself, where most men may be assumed to perform the pilgrimage some time or other in their lives, though it is stated—with some appearance of truth—that there are or have till quite recently been greybeard, lifelong residents of Mecca itself who have never performed this essential rite! It seems incredible, but things have changed since the bad old days of Turk and sharif, when the main functions of the Meccan were to make the pilgrimage as onerous as possible for the stranger within his gates, while he himself avoided the very real dangers and troubles of the pilgrim way.

MINA I remained quietly at home through the heat of the day, and it was not till mid-afternoon that I drove out again in my car to Mina, where I found the King almost alone in his great new audience chamber. Throughout the Muslim world outside the limits of the Meccan territory this day, the Id al-Adha, or the Festival of the Sacrifice in commemoration of the story of Abraham, is celebrated rather than the actual day of Arafat itself. . . .

As for Mecca, the ceremonies which I have already described seem to break up the day in such a way that the usual sunrise service of the festival is either not held at all or held only for the benefit of a small congregation. As far as I am aware, there was no such service in the Haram itself, though those who deferred the *tawaf* and other Meccan ceremonies doubtless forgathered in the Mina mosque of Khayif. I missed, moreover, the actual ceremony of the sacrificing in the morning, and my personal sacrifice was offered by proxy the following day; but I may add that during these three days at Mina I neither saw nor by other less agreeable processes became aware of the great slaughter on which others have written with so much critical emotion—nor even saw the slaughter place now wisely removed to a reasonable distance from the main camps of the pilgrims and divided therefrom by the picturesque encampment of the human scavengers of the Holy Land—the Takruri colony of African residents and visitors to whom nothing comes amiss that is edible. I certainly saw a few severed sheeps heads lying about where perhaps they should not have been, but otherwise there was neither stench nor offensive sight of sun-grilled putrefactions. The medical authorities have unquestionably done this part of their work exceedingly well, and their reward this year was the smallest death rate on record for the pilgrimage up to date. And the flies, of which we hear so much! Where were they? Certainly not on pilgrimage, as stands to reason—they would come some days later no doubt, when the pilgrims would have made good their departure. But there would be no one for them to worry or infect. The place would be deserted, as it had been till but a few days ago. And to round off the tale of the blessings of Mina—what joy it was to sleep out in the open under that brilliant sky with no protection against the mosquito and no mosquito to molest one's slumbers! . . .

All day long, and particularly during the grateful coolth of the early mornings and the evenings, the streets of Mina were thronged with a dense multitude moving this way and that. Through it at intervals a heavy motor water van made its deliberate way, clearing a path before it with a broad spray of water mixed with some disinfectant fluid, laying the dust and slaying the germs in a single operation. At one point in the broader part of the street and about midway between the two "devils" a small Petter engine had been installed with an Aquatole chain-pump equipment over a large subterranean cistern (fed at intervals by another water-cart). Round this pressed all day a crowd of the thirsty poor with tins and cans of every shape and size, into which a municipal functionary, presiding aloft at the gushing water outlet, tirelessly and good-humouredly baled the life-giving liquid—sometimes into the tins and sometimes, to the general amusement, over the heads and bodies of the crowd below. . . .

Eastward of the valley beyond the great concourse of pilgrim tents sat Ibn Saʿud in his hall of audience, disposing of the affairs of state, receiving reports and passing orders for the governance of his realm. A telephone connected him with Mecca and Jidda; a branch post-and-telegraph office brought him news from far and wide; the headquarters of the medical administration was housed in the local hospital to keep him in touch with the vital statistics so necessary to the world's welfare, for the Meccan pilgrimage is the cynosure of a wider audience than Arabia or its pilgrims. Even the Foreign Office was present in full force in attendance on the King. Business as usual was the order of the day, but concentration on the main business of the pilgrimage did not exclude attention to other matters. . . .

And so, on the third day of the festival towards sunset, the last stones were flung and the ceremonies of the great pilgrimage were over. The "devils" were left in peace for another year; and the crowd poured forth from Mina down the valley, an endless stream of men, women, and children, walking or riding, tired but happy, and above all cleansed from the sins of the past— the heavy burden that all had carried in jeopardy until these days.

A woman of the Bedouin, veiled from the gaze of man and modestly muffled in garments that hid her form, trotted gaily through the slowly wending crowd of those who walked and those who rode in litters. Without saddle or bridle she sat back on the lean rump of her dromedary, and I mused, as my car carried me home through the pilgrim streams, that I had seen in her and her surroundings the spirit of Arabia coursing through the veins of Islam.

18

Lady Evelyn Cobbold
Great Britain
1933

Lady Evelyn Cobbold had already been a Muslim for many years when she went to Mecca. As a child spending winters in Algiers, Cobbold learned Arabic early, played with Algerian children, and became, as she put it later, "a little Muslim at heart." While she was still a girl, these visits ended. Gradually she forgot her Arab friends, the prayers they had taught her, their language. Then (she writes) years later,

> *I happened to be in Rome staying with some Italian friends, and my host asked me if I would like to visit the Pope. Of course I was thrilled, and clad all in black with a long veil, I was admitted into the august presence with my host and his sister. When His Holiness suddenly addressed me, asking if I was a Catholic, I was taken aback for a moment and then replied that I was a Muslim. What possessed me I don't pretend to know, as I had not given a thought to Islam for many years. A match was lit, and then and there I determined to read up and study. . . .*

Lady Cobbold was the eldest daughter of the seventh Earl of Dunmore. Her husband of thirty-eight years, the High Sheriff of Suffolk, died in 1929. She set out for Mecca in February, at the age of sixty-six, sailing alone from Cairo to Jidda, a widow, well traveled, at ease in the Middle East. Aboard the same ship were the Pasha of Meknes, "a magnificent Moor," with an entourage of seventy, and Sir Andrew Ryan, returning to his post as Britain's Minister in Saudi Arabia. In Jidda, Cobbold was hosted by Dora and St. John Philby—an incidental pleasure of her account is the view it provides of the life the Philbys were leading at this time. Through her diarylike entries, we glimpse the social activities of Jidda's small, isolated European community:* night drives in Ford sedans

---

*"There are very few European women here and possibly thirty men, living a great part of the year in intense heat and damp." (Cobbold, *Pilgrimage to Mecca*, p. 19)

for picnics and dips in the Red Sea; luncheons with Dutch bankers; meals at the new British legation with the Ryans and their guests, the Turkish, Italian, Persian, and Bolshevik ministers; and visits at the New Hotel with the Hamiltons, Twitchells, and Longriggs—prominent names in the early history of oil.

With the Hajj weeks away, the roads leading into the Hijaz ran with pilgrims. Passing by them on her outings rankled Cobbold. She had not come to Arabia to dine, yet she could not leave Mecca without permission, since current policy required prospective European pilgrims to remain in Jidda for one year. Interestingly, Cobbold lays the blame for this probation on her literary predecessors, travel writers who had lied their way into Mecca, then returned home to write up the Hajj as a daring adventure. A more general distrust of Europeans shaped the new probation, too, for wherever they appeared in the Near East, the result was a loss of Muslim territory. As Cobbold remarks in another passage:

> *Even as I write this, the Berbers [of Morocco] are being driven from their last stronghold in the Atlas Mountains by the French armies, and a chapter of a great race will finally close, a race noted for the independence and valiant qualities of its men and the beauty of its women, and which has gone down fighting to the last against an enemy vastly superior in numbers and supplied with every modern equipment and instrument of destruction.*

Her stay in Jidda was punctuated by politely probing visits from various members of the royal court. Ibn Saʿud's Finance Minister, Fuʿad Hamza, followed by the King's son Amir Faysal, Viceroy in Hijaz, came to Philby's house to vet the English hajja. Cobbold hired a tutor to help perfect her accent, while Philby worked on her behalf, dashing back and forth to Mecca to put her case before the King. Three weeks later Ibn Saʿud ended her probation. In a rented car with an Arab driver, a Sudanese cook, and one of Philby's guides, she struck out for Medina.

Throughout her journey, Cobbold was universally mistaken for a fair-skinned Turk, an impression she rarely contradicted. On her way to Medina, she passed through the desolate lands of the Banu Harb, a tribe much feared for their pilgrim raids over the centuries, now reduced to begging by the road. She also sighted the first Hajj buses on record, loaded with pilgrims bumping through the desert. In Medina, she visited the Prophet's Mosque and spent considerable time with local women. The town was much reduced since Wavell's visit in 1908, a fate she blames on British policy and the destruction of the Hijaz Railway. In Medina, Cobbold met a French-speaking Turkish widow whose husband had died in 1917, when Sharif Husayn's troops and T. E. Lawrence destroyed the railway bridge outside Maʿan.

Cobbold's praise for Ibn Sa'ud's programs may strike readers as overly admiring. Yet records show that the Hajj was infinitely safer under the King than it ever had been under the sharifs. Way stations with free dispensaries now dotted the same routes where disease, starvation, and death by thirst had been common for centuries. Hotels with special accommodations for women and children were also springing up in Jidda, Yanbu, and the Holy Cities, and fair prices had been set on rented quarters. Ibn Sa'ud instituted civic improvements, too. He prohibited importing slaves, set up welfare programs for destitute women, and hospitals with surgeons schooled in Paris. In Cobbold's record, as in Philby's, the King seems to be everywhere. The morning after her return to Mecca, she enters the mosque to find him serving as royal janitor, washing the interior of the Ka'ba with a pail of water and a broom. Listening to traditional storytellers in the markets, she notes that by 1934 the tale of Ibn Sa'ud's life and times had entered popular legend.

As a Muslim woman on the Hajj, Lady Evelyn enjoyed more social freedom than her male counterparts. Because Arabian culture strictly segregates the sexes, travelers like Burckhardt and Wavell were mostly cut off from conversing with Muslim women at home or in public. By contrast, Cobbold moved freely between the harem and all-male assemblies. Her special status as a non-Arab Muslim widow and as a guest with well-placed acquaintances inside the country gave her broad social access in the Hijaz. Throughout her trip, she traveled as a single woman, crossing long stretches of desert, visiting Bedouin families as she pleased.

This first Hajj account by an English woman also contains the first recorded trip by car from Mina to Arafat. Cobbold traveled widely all her life. At home, she enjoyed a reputation as a first-class shot and a deerstalker. She wrote two travel books, Pilgrimage to Mecca *in 1934, and, the following year,* Kenya: Land of Illusion. *She died, at the age of ninety-five, in 1963.*

from Lady Evelyn Cobbold's
Pilgrimage to Mecca

JIDDA. FEBRUARY 26, 1933 We arrive at Jidda after four days' voyage on summer seas, and the view from the bay is enchanting. A white and brown town giving the idea of a fortress, as it is enclosed on three sides by a high wall, its minarets stand out against the sky, its quaint carved wooden windows bulge over the narrow streets. Beyond the golden desert rise the low foothills of the Arabian mountains, losing themselves in the distance to the heights far away which reach eight thousand feet and more. The sea is a marvellous blue; inside the lagoons it becomes turquoise in the shallow water threaded by streaks of purple caused by seaweed.

I come a stranger to this land, hoping to get permission to visit the sacred places of Arabia, and the Philbys have most kindly offered to receive me as a guest in their house. It is perhaps unnecessary to mention that Mr. Philby is a Muslim and the trusted friend of King Ibn Sa'ud, besides being the well-known explorer who twice crossed Arabia from sea to sea and traversed the terrible Rub'al-Khali a year ago.

My hostess fetches me in a launch flying a green flag with white lettering in Arabic LA ILAHA IL-ALLAH, MUHAMMAD AL-RASUL'ALLAH—("There is but one God. Muhammad is a messenger of God"). It is the flag of Abd al-Aziz Ibn Sa'ud, Sovereign Lord of this land, and I feel indeed I am in Arabia.

The launch has nearly a mile to go, as the coral reefs and shallows make it dangerous for vessels to come close to the shore, and I am amused at the dexterity of our youthful steersman, an Arab child of ten years, who stands upright to see better while guiding the wheel entirely with his bare toes within the coral reefs. He brings us safely to the steps, where we land to pass through the customhouse, and shortly after we enter the Philbys' large stone house facing the quay. . . .

FEBRUARY 28 The King is away at Riyadh, his capital in Nejd, sixteen days' camel ride from here, so I fear he will not get the letter his Minister in London wrote him for some time. (Before leaving England, I had an interview with His Excellency Shaykh Hafiz Wahba, Minister of Saudi Arabia, and confided to him my desire to visit the Sacred Cities; he most kindly wrote to His Majesty on the subject. If I succeed in accomplishing my pilgrimage, I feel it will be largely owing to his help.) Till that letter reaches the King, I must possess my soul in patience, and my time is pleasantly spent bathing in the warm sea within the coral reefs, for fear of sharks, or in motor drives in the desert.

When the late King Husayn reigned over the Hijaz, the Europeans, who were suffered to reside in Jidda, were never allowed beyond its walls, and life must have been well-nigh intolerable, depending on one's house roof for a breath of air, where one was always at the mercy of the ubiquitous mosquito and its malaria-envenomed sting. Under the aegis of the present King the embargo has been lifted, and every evening, when the sun loses some of its fierceness, the whole world of Jidda leaves the city walls and goes into the desert for exercise and air. There are no roads, but the numerous Fords make their way through the sand and scrub and seldom let us down. There are a few sand grouse and hares to be shot and a lovely creek in which to bathe.

When the moon is full, we go at night to swim in the silvered sea, so salt that it is difficult to sink, and we picnic under the magic moon, whose white radiance lights the desert. I wander along the beach collecting the beautiful shells and red coral that strew the shore. These Arabian nights will live long in my memory.

We pass many pilgrims on their way to the Holy Cities, some in motors, some swaying on camels, and the very poor on foot. The men are clothed in their *ihram* (or two towels) and bareheaded. The women going to Medina are in black or colours, while those on the road to Mecca are in their pilgrim white. Some of the poor pilgrims from far countries take years on their way. My host related how he was one day motoring on the Medina Road and, seeing a man, his wife, and boy trudging wearily through the hot sand, with all their worldly goods packed on their heads and backs, stopped his car to give them a lift as he was travelling a short way on their road. What was his surprise when they gratefully lifted their bundles into the car to find three small babies in them, born during the years of tramping towards their goal.

MARCH 1 I find life in Jidda very different from that of any Eastern city I have visited before. It is so purely Arab. There are no drinking booths, no shops, excepting its bazaars, which only supply the needs of its Arab population. Cinemas, Gramophones, the manifold necessities that make up the complicated life of civilisation, are unknown.

The architecture of its houses is most attractive. They are built of stone procured from quarries in the desert close by; but wood is largely used in the quaintly carved shutters, doors, and balconies and is mostly teak, imported from Java, as there are no trees in this land.

The Philbys' house, Bayt al-Baghdadi, is one of the largest and finest in the town, with a roof garden extending round two sides, on which flowers are carefully cultivated in pots, mostly large pink periwinkles, which are perpetual flowering, seeding themselves, and very effective.

On a raised platform in one corner is a bedstead, where my host sleeps when in Jidda. He also has a house in Mecca, where he stays alternate weeks. There are several bathrooms, mostly round stone cupolas with marble floors and domed roofs pierced with holes, elaborately carved in arabesque designs, which fascinate me. The floors have deep holes to let the water away, and as we are provided with tin baths, we upset them down the holes when finished with.

There are loggias built over part of the roof garden, in which we take refuge from the sun, and the view looking west over the sea is enchanting. Jidda has no green vegetation of any description, but the amazing blues of the sea supply colour to the landscape, and the sunsets are often dreams of beauty. . . .

MARCH 2 Today we drove along the desert track which points the way to Mecca. Practically no rain has fallen this winter, but the camels find pasturage in the thorny scrub that manages to survive in the arid soil.

An American engineer has proved that irrigation could make this land fertile. Two years ago he sank a small artesian well on the edge of the foothills, where they meet the plain, and now this small plot is green with burseed and corn.

Arabia covers more than one million square miles, of which barely one fifth is cultivated; it may contain mineral wealth, but the feeling of its people is against all foreign interference, and up to now they have neither the capital nor the expert knowledge to develop its possible resources themselves.

Shortly after passing the well, we turn back to Jidda, as we are nearing the forbidden territory, on the confines of which two tall stone pillars mark the entrance, and none but the true believer may venture to pass within.

How I envy the pilgrims we meet on their way to Mecca, while we return to the social life of Jidda, which would be very pleasant if one were not aware of the mysterious city of Islam hidden in the hills only a few miles from us. Why do we always long for the unattainable, for the blue bird which hovers just beyond our reach?

We return to Jidda and dine at the New Hotel, which was opened for the pilgrims a few days ago and where the American engineers, who have come to try and obtain the oil concessions from the King, are now staying.

Their wives, Mrs. Hamilton and Mrs. Twitchell, welcome us and give us an excellent dinner, and the party includes Mr. Longrigg, the English representative of the Iraq Oil Company, who is also here trying to get the concession. Rivalry does not appear to spoil the friendly relations existing between all parties, even when Mr. Longrigg discovers broken glass in his coffee cup! After dinner we played bridge, and on breaking up the party at midnight, the moon looked so enticing that several of us went for a drive in the desert to the creek and had a bathe. . . .

MARCH 4 My host left for Mecca early this morning to take part in the Friday midday prayer; he wore ordinary Arab clothes, consisting of the aba over a white robe and, on his head the kaffiya bound by the *iqal.* The pilgrimage this year begins officially on the fourth of April. As the Arabs count by lunar months, it falls eleven days earlier each year, and for the next decade the Muslims can count on a comparatively cool period both for the fast of Ramadan and the pilgrimage.

This evening I hear that the King has received his Minister's letter from London and is favourably considering my request. I am advised to write a letter to the King's son, the Amir Faysal, Viceroy of the Hijaz, giving him details of myself and family: Also the Undersecretary for Foreign Affairs is coming to Jidda for a few days and wishes to see me.

MARCH 5 His Excellency Fu'ad Hamza called this afternoon; he is a Syrian, fair, speaking excellent English. After a short talk, when he showed himself exceedingly kind and helpful, he returned to Mecca with my letter to the Viceroy—so now I await my fate, which is in the King's hands. I am asking a great favour, as the King has decided to allow no European Muslim to enter the forbidden ground until he has spent at least a year of probation in Jidda. Unfortunately more than once a European has entered Mecca professing himself a Muslim, only when writing up his experiences to enhance his reputation by allowing the world to think he was performing the pilgrimage at the risk of his life, and the Arabs naturally resent this abuse of their hospitality. . . .

MARCH 8 My host has returned from Mecca and tells me it now only remains for the King to give his decision, whether or not I shall be permitted to enter the Holy Cities, and in the meantime the Viceroy, who is making a short stay in his palace outside the town, will pay a visit to my hostess on Friday. This is an honour only conferred on a Muslim household, and a small party, including the British Minister and Lady Ryan, are invited to meet him.

The King himself refuses to give audience to European women, making an exception in the case of my hostess. . . .

MARCH 9 The Amir Faysal arrived punctually at five o'clock (eleven by Arab time, which counts from the sunrise at 6:00 A.M.). It was impressive to see his tall figure enter the doorway clad in a brown and gold *aba* over a flowing white robe and the picturesque headdress of the Nejd, the *kaffiya* of diaphanous white bound round his head by black and gold cords—called the *iqal*—while beside him stood his small son, dressed exactly like his father. They were followed by some of the ministers. The Amir is slender and exceedingly graceful in his movements and, like most Nejd Arabs, has an air of distinction and good breeding. Through his mother he is a direct descendant of Abd al-Wahhab, the great founder of the Wahhabi sect, who perhaps might be described as the Puritans of Islam. His small son won all our hearts. Little Abdullah had never before entered a European household or met European women, yet his dignity and self-possession never failed him. At a gesture from his father he left his side and seated himself on a divan among us. He wore sandals bound round each big toe with a piece of embroidery, and as he drew his small feet under him, he resigned himself to a conversation carried on with difficulty, as our Arabic was not fluent. He told us he loved riding camels and horses, but seemed slightly offended when I asked him if he ever rode a donkey. Already at the age of ten years, this child has left the women's quarters and holds his own little court.

MARCH 10 One of the excitements of Jidda is the day the English boat *Toledo* calls, bringing the mails and also groceries and newspapers. This only occurs once a fortnight, and it is most unfortunately arranged that the Italian boat arrives on the same day. All the morning anxious eyes are fixed on the horizon, and as soon as the English vessel is sighted, that is generally about 10:30 A.M., the little world of Jidda go out in their launches and forgather on board to read their letters. Often an early lunch of cheese sandwiches and beer is partaken of while all the news is discussed. The small steamer is one's link with the outside world; when we leave her and she passes out of sight on her way to Port Sudan, we know we are once more shut off from all knowledge of what is happening on our globe for two whole weeks.

This afternoon, Mrs. Andresen, a Dutch lady, took us to visit some ex-slaves who were housed free by the charity of a rich merchant. The rooms opening into a courtyard were spotlessly clean—two women sleep in each room, they earn enough to keep themselves by laundry work and odd jobs. Most of them were from the Sudan and appeared happy and contented. There was a well in the centre of the courtyard, and a few trees and flowers grew about; a cat, some goats, and pigeons were also inmates. One old lady was pointed out who had nearly died of starvation. She was too proud to let them know she had been unable to find work and went without food for four days, when she collapsed. The other women came to her rescue on discovering her condition, and she was again a hale and hearty old lady when we saw her.

They entertained us with tea, cigarettes, and biscuits; the cigarettes they rolled with the tips of their henna-stained fingers, and while we were there, two most attractive ladies came to visit them. There are several of these homes in the town, where ex-slaves and destitute women take refuge. . . .

MARCH 12 Today the news has come through that I am permitted to do the pilgrimage to Mecca and visit Medina. I had for so long lived in alternate fits of hope and despair that I can scarcely credit that my great wish is at last to be fulfilled. Preparations for my journey are in the hands of my host, who is returning to Mecca and, notwithstanding his many preoccupations, is giving up much time and trouble arranging for my comfort and the many details that require consideration; while I prepare to get ready my pilgrim dress, which consists of a black crêpe skirt, very full, and a cape and hood in one, to be worn over ordinary dress when I visit Medina, also a black crêpe veil entirely obscuring my features; but for Mecca I shall be entirely in white, no colour allowed in any garment. As the official days of pilgrimage at Mecca do not begin till 4 April, I arrange to go first to Medina. . . .

MEDINA. MARCH 15 We started for Medina after the dawn prayer. I had hired a car for the twenty days of pilgrimage, with an Arab driver who knew the road and was accompanied by Mustafa Nazir, a very urbane personage lent me by Mr. Philby, who combined the duties of equerry and courier and proved invaluable. Also a nice old Sudanese, father of the cook, who had come from Dongola to do the pilgrimage and wanted to kiss my feet when I offered him a lift to Medina.

It was a lovely dawn, the sun rising over the hills soon after we left Jidda in a splendour of conflagration making the shadow of rock and bush stretch blue as indigo to the west. We sped northward through mile after mile of flat desert, where grew a few thorny bushes and a shrub with a yellow flower like a cistus. The road was marked by the whitened bones of dead camels that strewed the path of countless thousands of pilgrims who had trod that way for over a thousand years. No living thing was to be seen, except now and then some sand grouse and, once, a flight of flamingoes. . . .

Our first halt was at Rabigh, where we entered the forbidden territory, and passports were examined. Here we took an hour's rest; a third of our journey was accomplished, but the worst of the road was ahead. Rabigh is a seaport which, during the Hijaz war, largely took the place of Jidda as the port for Mecca for the landing of the pilgrims, but the town is two miles from the sea, and the mud-brick houses are scattered over a flat plain without any attempt at order. Near the marketplace is a collection of open-fronted booths, roofed in with rushes or palm fronds, where the pilgrims can sit at ease or lie full length to sleep on rude couches. There were already several of them stretched in slumber on their *serirs,** where they will spend the hot hours ahead, leaving again in the cool of the evening. . . .

A few of the Bedouin girls crowded round the car, trying to sell me baskets of plaited grass of brilliant colours and other primitive articles which they make specially for trade with the pilgrims. When I refused to buy, they were not in the least put out, but ran off to try their blandishments on the slumbering hajjis. . . .

While I rested, the car was supplied with water and benzine, two absolute necessities of which it was impossible to carry enough for the journey. Also Mustafa was able to smoke his beloved narghile in some secret recess where the police could not sniff the forbidden fumes, and our driver, Suleyman, who had often been this way before, chatted with his many friends. . . .

Here among these hills were human inhabitants who evidently found life a difficult problem, judging from their emaciated appearance: it was heartrending to see the children who were living skeletons.

They ran beside the slowly moving car, imploring help with a menacing persistence that to my mind boded ill if we should have a breakdown; their shrill voices held a curse when I ignored their appeal for alms.

There was something very forbidding about these Bedouins; the women being veiled, one only saw their sullen eyes, but the men were sinister figures with scowling faces. They belonged to the tribe of Harb, which has always lived by pillage, and it was from them that the sharifal army was largely recruited by Husayn, the Sharif of Mecca who was crowned King of the Hijaz after he defeated the Turks, driving them out of Arabia, only in his turn to be driven out a few years later by Ibn Sa'ud the ruler of Nejd.

The present King has succeeded in putting an end to this desert brigandage, and in consequence this tribe has lost its chief means of livelihood; at the same time they dare not do mischief, for fear of the King's swift retribution. . . .

serir: a string bed, the Eastern *chaise-longue* [Ed.]

415

On leaving the Medina Gate at Jidda and several times on the way, our passports were examined by the Wahhabi police, who patrol the pilgrim route and keep it safe for those who use it (as was never done before, when the poor pilgrim was often robbed of all his possessions and left to die).

The 250 miles from Jidda to Medina took us fifteen hours to accomplish, and I take off my hat to the little Ford that gallantly carried us through those sandy wastes: only once did Mustafa and the old Sudanese have to get out and push, when we stuck in a particularly deep drift. Besides the pilgrims on camels, we met many on foot, toiling slowly through the scorching desert with water jugs in their hands, clad in their *ihram* and, as they were bareheaded, many carried umbrellas.

Ten days is the usual time it takes a camel to accomplish the journey between Medina and Jidda and three weeks for the pilgrim on foot, who generally travels at night, resting in the heat of the day at one of the numerous caravansaries, where he can obtain food, water, coffee, tea, and a rush couch on which to sleep.

Also we occasionally met an omnibus carrying intending pilgrims and luggage tightly packed, cooking utensils and water jugs tied on anywhere, and the noise and clatter must have been most trying as they bumped over the rough ground. . . .

We halted once again when two policemen stopped us with flashlights and, after the Arab greeting of peace, warned us that it had rained for three days and the road was underwater. We thanked them and proceeded by another sandy track, which also led us to water. Our driver got out and waded in it to his knees, but returned to say that the bottom was hard and he thought the Ford could do it. The little car did not fail us, and after another hour we saw lights in the distance. They were the lights of Medina al-Munawara, the Illumined City. . . .

MARCH 17 This morning I was engaged in writing up my diary when I heard that some ladies were below waiting to see me. On being told they belonged to the family of an old friend in Damascus, I was glad to welcome them; and after unveiling and getting rid of their cloaks and hoods, they distributed themselves on the divans. There were five of them, the wife of my friend in Damascus, a very attractive personality with a sweet expression, her sister with two young daughters, and another lady of a cheerful frame of mind whose gay laugh infected us all. My hostess, the wife of the gentleman in whose house I was a guest, had already greeted me, and she returned to help me entertain them with tea and later with the unsweetened Mocha coffee.

On removing their outer garments of the inevitable black silk or satin, these ladies were dressed in full trousers hanging in folds that fit tight below the calf of the leg and are very becoming to slim figures. They are generally made of striped silk or cotton, and a tight-fitting bodice with long sleeves is worn above, and over the whole hangs a loose transparent dress of white gauze. A piece of coloured silk is wound round like a turban on the head, with one end hanging down to the shoulder. Their hair hangs in two long plaits down their backs, very often twisted with gay ribbons or ropes of seed pearls. Powder and rouge is unknown—but they all have their eyes blackened with kohl—which they tell me softens the glare of the sun; as a rule they have lovely teeth and carry themselves well.

They were very interested in hearing of my country and the lives we women live and asked me innumerable questions about our emancipation and our right to enter Parliament and share in the government of our land. Also they enquire when and why I had become a Muslim, and on my admitting that I could read and write Arabic, I was taken to the texts hanging on the walls and asked to read them. Luckily I was able to do so. . . .

ANOTHER STORY Later in the evening, in the corner of the market, or the open square, you may see a small crowd gathered in the twilight to listen to the storyteller.

This ancient profession has always been popular in the East, though the cinema and theatre have almost driven it out of modernised cities like Algiers or Cairo; but I remember seeing groups of eager Moors listening to the entrancing tales of the storyteller in the Jemaa al-Fna at Marrakesh, and here in Medina I find him again. He may be relating the "Stealing of the Mare" or portions of *The Thousand and One Nights* or the thrilling tale of "Antar the pre-Islamic Hero-Poet," but always he stops short at the most exciting moment, leaving his hearers to await with what patience they can for the continuance of the tale on the ensuing evening. . . .

Nowadays the repertoire of the storyteller has been added to by an epic of modern times: the heroic deeds of the present King of Arabia. The life of Abd al-Aziz Ibn Sa'ud makes a wonderful theme which the storyteller seizes on with avidity.

By the light of the campfires in the desert or the flare of the torches in the coffeehouse, the audience listen spellbound to the thrilling tale of the young Prince banished from his country when eleven years old, his father having lost the throne of Nejd; of how he spent eight years' exile in Kuwait, the seaport on the Persian Gulf, homesick for the mountains of his native

land, and how when barely nineteen years of age he returned with forty kins-
men to his country and by one of the most daring feats in the annals of war
he recaptured Riyadh, the capital of his lost kingdom, and seized the reins
of power; of how in time he fought and vanquished the Ottoman troops,
the powerful Amir Ibn Rashid, Lord of Ha'il, and the late King Husayn of
the Hijaz.

The storyteller proceeds with his narrative of this modern saga, more
wonderful than any fairy tale of old: of how this intrepid Prince has shown
a genius for government equal to his genius in battle; of how he harnessed
the desert tribes in a friendly brotherhood, the Ikhwan, and put an end to
brigandage and lawlessness in perhaps what was the most lawless country in
the world and now reigns supreme over Arabia from the Persian Gulf to the
Red Sea, holding the custody of the Sacred Cities of Mecca and Medina,
which constitutes him the real Protector of Islam.

The Amir Ibn Rashid was killed in battle, and the survivors of the family
were taken to the King's Palace at Riyadh, where they now live surrounded
by comfort, and all honour and deference paid them, but they are very carefully guarded and virtually prisoners in all but name. Sharif Husayn fled to
Cyprus and eventually died at Amman, the capital of Transjordania, where
Abdullah his son reigns as Amir. . . .

MARCH 21 On [19 March] I received a message asking me to visit the new
hotel, built to house the pilgrims. A pleasing feature in this country is the
increased care taken for the safety and well-being of these poor people, who
in the past suffered from every danger that can beset the path of a wayfarer
in the desert. Robbery and violence were rife: death from hunger and, more
especially, thirst lay in wait. Now there are stations with wells, rest houses,
and dispensaries, where all medical aid is given free at regular intervals on
the pilgrim routes; and hotels are being built for their accommodation not
only in the Holy Cities but at the ports of Jidda and Yanbu, where they land
at Mesajid and at Mina on the way to the final pilgrimage at Arafat. A general committee has been appointed by the government to see that these are
kept clean and in good repair and to fix the number of persons for each room
and [see that] special accommodation is available for the women.

For the richer pilgrims there are always houses at their disposal to rent,
to accommodate themselves and the large suite that generally accompanies
a great man.

The hotel I am invited to inspect is for the gentleman who does not
require the luxury and trouble of a house, but wants comfort and privacy
for himself and his family. It is to be called the Grand Hotel or its equiva-

lent in Arabic, and the manager wishes to hear from me how it compares with the hotels of London and Paris.

I entered an open courtyard, from which rose three tiers of galleries leading into numerous bedrooms. The courtyard formed a kind of entrance hall with many *kursis** about, on which the guests can squat and drink tea or coffee and play chess, a very favourite game in the Near and Middle East. An inner court provided a dining room. A wide stone staircase ascended to the bedrooms, which each contained an iron four-poster with a mattress, pillow, and sheet, also a mosquito net, and a table with a looking glass, brush, and comb; while on the ground stood large ewers, which being porous, kept the water cool. A splash of vivid colour beside the door were the soft slippers awaiting the pilgrim feet. What more can man desire? The four-posters were the only [western style] bedsteads in Medina.

I congratulated the manager on it all, especially on his forethought in providing a brush and comb, which he replied was most important for all the pilgrims' beards. No doubt equally important were the slippers for the tired feet. The hotel will open in a few days.

Later on in the afternoon, after the siesta, I started out to return the visit of the Lady Fatima and her family, accompanied by Mustafa, as it would not have been considered correct for me to walk alone in public any more than our grandmothers could have done so in the days of Queen Victoria. . . .

My host, leaving Mustafa drinking coffee in the reception room, led me up a steep narrow staircase with painted banisters to the flat roof of the chambers that encircled the courtyard. Here were the ladies' quarters, and very charming they were, with the roof garden massed with roses and pink oleanders growing in great pots of glazed green pottery. Here Fatima welcomed me, and her husband returned below to entertain Mustafa and a few male guests who had assembled, while I made acquaintance with the ladies who had been invited to meet me.

They were a gay crowd, and we laughed and chatted over small incidents that amused us at the moment; indeed, the surroundings were so full of charm that I was prepared to laugh at any and everything that came my way, for sheer gaiety of spirit.

To my astonishment I discovered one little Turkish lady who spoke French fluently. She told me that her father had been attached to the Turkish embassy in Paris before the war. She had married an officer in the Otto-

---

*A wood and string platform for lounging.

man army, who lost his life when the railway bridge near Ma'an on the Hijaz Railway was blown up in 1917, and she was now married to a gentleman of Medina. I asked her if she ever thought with regret of the gay life of her youth in Paris, and other Continental cities where her father had been posted during his career, but she assured me that she was perfectly content, and could not be happier than in her present home with her husband and three children, while she goes occasionally, when funds permit, to visit her family on the Bosporus. After drinking tea and eating quantities of delicious little cakes made of honey and almonds mixed with a small amount of flour, I quite reluctantly took leave of them, as the time for the sunset prayer drew near. . . .

MARCH 22 I paid my respects to the Amir this morning shortly after sunrise, arriving in my car accompanied by Mustafa. We were received by officials and shown into a large hall opening to the sky in the centre and raised on one side by a high step. There are divans below this dais, on which were seated several picturesque figures awaiting audience. The Amir entered a moment later and led me to the raised platform, which also had divans on three sides and where I sat cross-legged on his right hand. He is a tall man, thin, old, and very dignified, wearing a black and gold *aba* over his white robe and a red and white checked *kaffiya* of transparent material bound by the *iqal*. After I had thanked him for all he had done to make my visit to Medina easy, he replied how pleased he was to welcome me to the Holy City and hoped that my pilgrimage would strengthen my faith in Islam. He then asked me if I knew Mr. Philby (Hajji Abdullah Philby) and what position he held in England, and I felt the cold breath of suspicion was on us both, which does not surprise me when one thinks of the names of Burton, Burckhardt, and others who penetrated into the Haram disguised as Muslims; and what remains to Islam but to protect what is most sacred to her faith.

An attendant brought round glasses of hot sweet milk, which I managed to drink under my veil; then followed black unsweetened coffee and cakes, and shortly after, I bade farewell to my host, as the audience hall was filling up with ministers and others desiring interviews; it looked as if his morning would be a busy one. . . .

MARCH 23 Leaving Medina at eight o'clock (Arab time), we travelled through the hot hours until we reached Mesajid shortly before sunset, where we watered the car and refreshed ourselves with tea. Once more we sped on our way along the riverbed, which is the only road through the mountains, and we saw the wretched inhabitants stretch out their skinny arms imploring help.

I am told these are the robbers who once preyed on the pilgrims, and now the tables are turned indeed, as they thankfully receive alms from those who in the old days they so shamefully looted and mishandled.

When the mountains assume the blue shade of approaching night, we find ourselves once again on the open plain and halt for the evening prayer. As there is no water available, we rub our hands with the desert sand, turn our faces to Mecca, recite the opening chapter of the Quran and do the four prostrations required. After that we eat our supper of cold chicken with the desert for a table and the stars for lamps.

We proceed southward on our journey past the silent camels, past pilgrims walking wearily who hold out their jugs for us to replenish till Mustafa warns me there will be nothing left for us. I find my eyes closing, my head nodding; at last I can no longer hold out; the car stops; we spread our blankets on the ground; I see the Southern Cross before me, the Milky Way reveals a million worlds, Jupiter, Saturn, and others blaze the night; my head touches the pillow and I am asleep. . . .

MARCH 27 Three hours after the sunrise I am once more in the Haram, accompanied by Mustafa, but already when leaving the cloisters the marble pathway through the quadrangle is hot to my stockinged feet, and I gladly keep myself veiled as a protection against the sun. There is a great crowd round the Ka'ba, and I hear that Ibn Sa'ud, clad in his *ihram,* is inside, washing the floor with water from Zamzam, afterwards sprinkling it with attar of roses, the famous brew distilled by the scent merchants of Mecca from the roses that grow in profusion at Ta'if. . . . I try to mount the silver steps of the pulpit, to get a view of this unique ceremony performed by the warrior King of Arabia, but the soles of my feet are burnt in the attempt, so I reluctantly give it up and visit the famous well, Zamzam, over which is built a Moorish kiosk whose twilight interior is half underground. The well is surrounded by a parapet and iron railings, while two Arabs continually haul water from the deep, to fill the waiting jars from which goblets are replenished, as every pilgrim drinks from Zamzam, and it is in demand in many private houses for its medicinal attributes. . . .

MINA. MARCH 28 This afternoon, accompanied by my host and Mustafa, I motor to Mina and Arafat to see about accommodation for the pilgrimage, as it is incumbent that I remain at Mina for three nights. On leaving Mecca, we go north and pass the King's palace on the outskirts of the city, a very imposing pile of grey granite which he built himself, the large arch of the middle entrance showing a court full of mimosa and palm trees.

Shortly after we leave the palace behind us, we meet a large number of camels bringing pilgrims from Nejd, those fierce warriors, the redoubtable Ikhwan. Their women are carried in baskets like large cages or beehives slung on each side of the camel's hump and completely covered in by matting pierced with tiny holes like the veil I wear on pilgrimage. As they had been travelling for three or four weeks, one trusts they are allowed more air when in the desert. We turn east and make our way through a deep ravine which was blasted through the solid rock by the late King Husayn; his one good deed, so the Meccans say, but perhaps that is rather unkind! Before this corridor was made, it must have been an extremely dangerous route, more especially for the camels, and many pilgrims had died while trying to cross the steep slippery rocks. . . .

On emerging from this deep ravine, we soon arrive at Mina, a little desert town where the pilgrims stone the devil on returning from Arafat. There I visit the Pilgrim Hotel and come to the conclusion that a tent in the foothills will be preferable, hot though the weather is, as I cannot get a room to myself owing to the great demand.

In the sandy waste behind the one long street that is Mina there stands the mosque of al-Khayif. It is very old and has some fine stone arcades, also a dome beneath which the Prophet prayed during his last pilgrimage. The mosque is only open for the Festival of Sacrifice, and during these three days it is crowded day and night, and the *adhan* once again sounds from its two minarets. When the pilgrimage is over, the tents folded, and the multitudes gone, the mosque is left silent in its desert solitude.

We motor along a dry riverbed, and the hills become steeper, great ridges of mountains appear to the north and east; on their lower slopes these are clothed with green and grey thorny shrubs, many of them emitting an aromatic smell as you crush through them. Among the scant vegetation is a bush named *basham* by the Bedouins. It is the balm of Gilead, and during the summer months incisions are made in the bark and the soft gum collected in bags. It is then used as an ointment for treating wounds, having healing properties. Legend has it that the plant was introduced by King Solomon, to whom the Queen of Sheba presented it.

We have passed the two stone pillars which mark the boundary of the Sacred Territory and see long vistas of limitless desert and hills stretching into the heart of Arabia. The car can go no farther; we turn to the left and pull up beneath Mount Arafat, a steep rock with numerous praying places on its terraces, and topped by a granite column. . . .

The water from the mountains is collected here in huge tanks and flows through a deep aqueduct into a gorge and eventually to Mecca, a distance of some twenty miles, and this mighty work, over a thousand years old, which today supplies the city with its water, still stands, a lasting monument to the skill of the workmen of those days and the initiative of the Queen who built it.

We leave our car and climb to the first terrace, where is a small clearance called the Praying Place of Adam, where it is rumoured man first prostrated himself to God. Here, many pilgrims are resting, and from behind the boulders, more appear; the hill is alive with men and women from the Yemen, who have taken many months to arrive, trudging from their southern desert through the eternal sand, the womenfolk looking like witches, with their quaint straw hats ending in a sharp, conical peak. . . . I thought many of the women showed refinement and beauty, and they moved with the freedom and untrammelled grace that one often finds among the mountain dwellers.

They descend to stare at the car and huddle away terrified; never before have they seen a motor, and it takes a long time to persuade them it is harmless.

GOLD AND OIL Does this land hold nothing but rock and sand, or does it hide in its grim fastnesses a mineral wealth? In old days the gold mines of Ophir were renowned throughout the whole world, and surely their treasures are not exhausted. Perhaps the fear of foreign exploitation and the history of alien aggression in other Islamic countries deter this people from realising their own resources. They have kept their land free and their Holy Cities safe. The Hijaz has lived on its pilgrims for centuries, but now the pilgrims become fewer each year. Once they numbered two hundred thousand or more; but lately, owing to world depression, they are scarcely one hundred thousand, and Arabia suffers. When in Jidda, I heard of possible oil developments. American and English were both endeavouring to obtain concessions. . . .

APRIL 3 All night the camels were being loaded; never do the grunts and gurgles cease. Sleep is out of the question; apart from the universal din and excitement there is a tense feeling of expectation which tends to make one restless.

I rise early and thread my way to the mosque through the kneeling beasts to do a final *tawaf* before my pilgrimage. It is still dark, the dawn is an hour ahead when my *mutawwif* and I enter the Haram and join the crowd circumambulating the House of God. Many are in a state of frenzy and calling loudly while supplicating. Having finished the *tawaf*, I sit on a step to watch the strange scene. The niche that holds the sacred Stone is guarded by two soldiers armed with ropes and sticks. The maddened pilgrims fight to kiss it; a battle ensues, the soldiers hitting right and left, endeavouring to keep order. Shortly a friend joins me; we watch the endless scuffle, and I remark that nothing would induce me to try to kiss the Stone, upon which she promptly tells me she means to do so. I implore her not to attempt it. Just then a tall young man comes up and is introduced to me as her brother; he also endeavours to dissuade her; she seizes my hand, and as I don't like to refuse, we fight our way towards the niche with her brother and my *mutawwif* as our protectors. It is impossible to get near. We are pushed aside by excited Bedouins mad to kiss the Stone, and I thankfully retire whole and undamaged, while her brother brings back a rather battered lady to me, saying the Arabic equivalent for "I told you so." . . .

APRIL 5 I had brought an English book with me on my pilgrimage, knowing our progress must be slow in that great procession. The book was *Passages from Arabia Deserta* by that mighty traveller Doughty, and during a stop I opened it, and from under my veil I was soon absorbed in reading when a voice from a neighbouring car asked, "Is that an Arabic book?" Suleyman answered quickly that of course it was Arabic and whispered to me to close the book, which I refused to do. Again the voice spoke: "Can you swear by all we hold holy it is Arabic and a book for the Muslims?" Before the alarmed Suleyman could answer, I turned and held the book out to the anxious enquirer, saying, "This is an English book and I am an English Muslim, and I am here on pilgrimage by permission of the King." After a few seconds of astonished silence he returned the book to me saying *"Alhamdulillah!"* . . .

A few miles brought us to Muzdalifa, where stands a mosque in ruins, then on through arid hills till we arrive at the tall pillars marking the end of the Sacred Territory. Beyond lies the great Plain of Arafat, which is now thronged with tents, camels, and pilgrims. As we approach, the dull murmur caused by the many pilgrims shouting the formula *"Labayk Allahumma, labayk!"* which had long been audible, now became so loud it dominated every other sound. There were over a hundred thousand men and women, all now accomplishing the aims of a lifetime, the great pilgrimage, which probably has meant to most of them travelling many thousand miles, enduring great hardships, and spending all their savings. Surely no other city in the world could boast of a huge population abstaining from all sexual intercourse for a given time on account of its religion. . . .

My host invites me to remain in his tent, and I gratefully accept and have my mattress and cushion spread where I can get a good view of everything going on. I unveil; the heat is terrific, and every few minutes I drink tea or eat pomegranates brought me from Ta'if. My host, who is one of the

King's ministers,* has many friends to visit him, who with the perfect manners of the Arab show no surprise at finding me sitting there.

After introductions all round, we enter into conversation, and I try to tell them of the life and sport in Britain and wish my Arabic were more fluent to converse on the many subjects of mutual interest. Shortly before midday, we eat; I have my special dish brought, while they sit round a large tray. No knives and forks are used; we wash our hands with the water that is brought and poured over them into a basin with a perforated lid; then we wipe them dry with the towels provided.

After this I wander to the bell tent behind, to see how my hostess and her party are faring without their narghiles, as smoking would be out of the question today. They are bearing up, and Mustafa's mother is sound asleep. One of the younger ladies is reading them a *sura* from the Quran, which they all listen to with great intentness, occasionally breaking in with pious ejaculations. I sit among them for a while, but the heat is much worse here than in the large open tent, so I return shortly to its comparative coolness.

Shortly afterwards we do the ceremonial washing for the midday prayer, consisting of washing the face, feet, and hands to the elbow and carefully rinsing the mouth and nose, but where water is not available, it is permitted to wash the hands in sand.

A carpet is spread for me pointing to the Ka'ba of Mecca, and I pray the four *rakat*s prescribed. When I have finished, my host leads the prayers for the men, who also do four prostrations, after which we all join in the *"Labayk Allahumma, "*which we repeat again and again. Then a chapter from the Quran is read and very beautifully intoned.

There is excitement in the camp; the camel corps of Ibn Sa'ud, the puritan troops mounted on tall *diluls*, are clearing a road for the King, who is on his way to Jabal al-Rahma. As he passes in the car, I get only a brief glimpse of the ruler who, by his force and magnetic personality, has won a position hitherto unknown in Arabia, where power to command cannot be held by royal descent alone. . . .

The King is followed by many picturesque figures, among them not the least being Van der Pol, the Dutch banker who embraced Islam some years ago and whom I had already met at the British legation at Jidda. He rides past in his *ihram* with bare head in the blazing sun, mounted on a magnificent camel, its saddle of crimson and gold glittering in the sunlight, while three other riders equally splendidly equipped follow him. Van der Pol now lives in Algeria, and every year he comes to perform the pilgrimage.

*Philby did not hold an official post in Ibn Sa'ud's court. [Ed.]

We see the imam silhouetted against the sky on the top of Jabal al Rahma. In olden days he sat a camel, but now he stands beside the tall pillar while he preaches this "sermon on the mount." His voice cannot carry to where we are, so we pray the *asr* prayer and again [chant the] Labayk; then as the sun sets and the King departs, the tents are taken down, everything packed and put on camel or car in an incredibly short time. The great pilgrimage is over, and all who have assembled in the Plain of Arafat are now entitled to bear the name of hajji till their dying day. . . .

In time we reach Muzdalifa, where we wait for a few hours; our cars draw up on a slight rise, and after praying we spread our blankets under the stars and sleep. Midnight sees us on the road again, each of us armed with seven small stones which we have picked up in the desert to throw at the "great devil" at Mina. On arriving at the little town, we leave our cars, as all must walk to the stoning place. Mustafa's mother is again asleep at the back of the car, and no amount of shaking seems to rouse her, so we leave her stretched across the seat. Evidently she sleeps her pilgrimage through, as I have never met her doing *tawaf* in the mosque. She is an old lady, and no doubt deputises one of her sons to do it for her. Abu Bakr brought her from Jidda, so with two sons doing pilgrimage, between them they should manage the ceremonial while she slumbers.

It is barely a mile to the stoning place, but in the night it is slow work making our way through the crowds, especially for the poor ladies of the harem, who never walk. . . .

Mustafa's mother was still asleep on returning to the car, so we deposited her in the little house at Mina while we drove back to Mecca, arriving as the day broke, when we went direct to the Mosque to perform our *tawaf* at the Ka'ba and say the dawn prayer of two *rakat*s, after which we returned to the house we had left two short days ago. It felt like a century. Daylight was streaming in as I wearily ascended the stairs, followed by Suleyman carrying my suitcase. I had lost Mustafa in the mosque. On entering my rooms, I hastily discarded my pilgrim clothes and went to bed, but the sun was already blazing when I fell asleep.

APRIL 6. TAWAF OF DEPARTURE I wake to find a smiling slave congratulating me on the end of the pilgrimage. Immediately after the ceremonial washing, we all don our best clothes and, smothered in black silk cloaks and veils, we again repair to the mosque to perform the *tawaf* and also *sa'y* (the seven runs) at al-Masa'a. The Haram is crowded—no sleeping pilgrims. They have discarded their *ihram*s; all are circuiting the Ka'ba or prostrating themselves in prayer in their beautiful new clothes. The sonorous voice of the *mutawwif*s, the ecstatic cry of the pilgrims, the murmuring of the prayers, fill the Great Mosque like the muttering of thunder.

The Ka'ba is now covered with a new carpet wrought of silk and wool, and the band of gold writing that circles it about fifteen feet from the top is legible from a considerable distance, as the characters are in the largest style of Eastern calligraphy and are over two feet deep. It is said that in olden days all the Quran was interwoven into it. . . .

Some years ago it was thought that the old handweaving of the "carpet" could be superseded by machinery, and a loom was brought from Manchester at great expense, but it was not a success, and they reverted to the ancient process of handweaving. . . .

I again sleep in my eyrie under the stars, but my pilgrimage is finished, and I long to see green fields, grey skies, to hear the splash of rain, to escape from the pitiless sun.

Tomorrow starts the Feast of Sacrifice, and no one is allowed to leave till it is over, without the King's permission.

There are now a hundred thousand pilgrims encamped round Mina in tents, in their *shugdufs* and *shubreyas* on the ground, while their couched camels are tethered in the hills. Would the King miss one small pilgrim? I can but send in my request.

APRIL 7 Mustafa sends me word that the King has given me permission to depart; I am still on the roof when I get the gracious message, and I hastily put my things together, descend the rickety ladder, and bid farewell to my hostess and all the little ladies, servants, and slaves. My car is at the door, and my host and his sons beside it. I thank them for all the kindness and hospitality shown me and enter the motor with Mustafa and a small slave armed with the key of the house in Mecca, as I must go there to collect my possessions.

The car slowly picks its way among the tents and hajjis, all now feasting, dressed in their coloured robes, their *ihrams* discarded. Savoury smells of cooking float on the air, together with the groans of camels, shrill voices of children, and shouts of friends seeking each other in the crowd. The scene holds an abstracting charm of colour and movement in the sunlit valley, and it is good to look on the happy faces, to watch their quiet content.

As we proceed to leave the crowd behind, the road gets lonelier, and presently we only meet a few Bedouin with camels on the trek to Mecca.

We enter a silent city, its little shops are shuttered, its houses locked and empty; only the pigeons and dogs are left. On arriving at the house that has sheltered me during these marvellous days, I run upstairs to prepare for my journey, while Mustafa goes to the mosque and Suleyman collects eggs and bread for us to eat.

Mustafa tells me he will return in an hour; he goes down the stairs; I hear the door slam and am left in the great void which a short time ago was crowded with humanity. I busy myself with a cold-water bath, which eventually makes me feel hotter than ever! Then I finish my packing and wait for Mustafa with what patience I can; I am now longing to get away.

I have brought two books with me on pilgrimage, an Arabic Quran and *Arabia Deserta,* to which I have already referred. I open the latter and try to fix my attention on the quaint Elizabethan style, which to my mind is the charm of the book, but Doughty was too sturdy a Christian, or perhaps too bigoted, to perceive any truth in Islam, and the whole of his writing breathes such animosity that I shut the volume, feeling it sacrilege to read it in my present surroundings. I settle myself at the shuttered window, where through the pierced carving I can look down into the empty street for a sign of Mustafa, and opening my Quran at random, I am soon immersed in the beautiful *sura* [entitled] "Light." . . .

I am quite oblivious to my surroundings when I hear footsteps outside my door. For nearly three hours I have been shut within the great silent house a prisoner, and it is indeed with relief that I welcome the sight of Mustafa and Suleyman. The former tells me the reason of his delay is that he had trouble with the police, who asked him his business in Mecca when every self-respecting pilgrim is at Mina. The latter, with the help of the little slave, has collected the food required for our belated lunch, which we hastily eat, as I would like to reach Jidda before dark.

Before leaving Mecca, I once more go to the Haram to do my *tawaf* and to al-Masaʿa for *saʿy.*

Even now, with Mecca empty and the whole Islamic world celebrating the Feast of Sacrifice at Mina, I find some devoted pilgrims performing the *tawaf* of the Kaʿba, and it is a boast of the Meccans that there is not an hour of the day or night, year in, year out, when Bayt Allah has not got its meed of worshippers.

At Safa in my haste I slip on one of the steep steps and fall backwards, saving myself with my left hand and spraining my wrist.

Mustafa binds it up tightly, but it is too painful for me to continue, so I ask him to complete my seven runs, of which I had only done four.

After bidding good-bye to the little slave, who is returning to Mina on a donkey with the key, I enter my car, and accompanied by Mustafa, we drive through the silent streets, the deserted bazaars, till we reach the green gates of the city. We show our passports, but the Wahhabi police refuse to let us go through. My heart sinks; I ask Mustafa if it is possible that the King forgot to give the order to pass us, but he answers that he heard the King's message sent by telephone. It never occurred to me, nor I believe did it ever cross Mustafa's mind, that the permission to depart had been accorded to me alone and of course to Suleyman, my chauffeur. Mustafa regarded himself as responsible for my safety and had been so constantly with me during my pilgrimage that he and I never questioned the possibility that he would not accompany me back to Jidda.

Meanwhile there is nothing for it but to wait while the police telephone to the King at Mina for orders. I leave the car, as the sun is still hot, and take refuge in an adjoining café, where the proprietor sits alone telling his beads. He is intoning the ninety-nine attributes of Allah; in the dim silence the droning voice is like the faint humming of bees. The dusky quiet of this interior is very soothing after the fierce glare outside, but I wonder vaguely why my host is not at Mina, for his café is deserted. He hastens to supply us with caravan tea (red or green to your liking), which is so welcome in this sun-parched climate, while he mentions that we are the only human beings that have come his way for three days. He has a look of peace and great dignity, and Mustafa tells me that he is a sayyid, a descendant of the Prophet.

In Islam, where snobbery is unknown, a man may trace his descent from the noblest tribes for a thousand years or more yet earn his living in any humble but honest manner; and the descendants of Muhammad, himself one of the princely house of Quraysh, are often to be found among the very poor.

While my host is helping us to tea, a little maid comes shyly in and slips to her father's side. Her orange robe lights up the dim interior, and her small brown face is wreathed in smiles as she peeps at me from behind her parent, who gently lifts her on his knee. We soon make friends, and she chatters gaily away free from self-consciousness, her great dark eyes dancing, her slim little hands gracefully gesticulating in true Arab fashion as she relates the history of her day's doings.

After nearly an hour the telephone rings, and the message comes through that I am allowed to leave, but alone; Mustafa remains behind, and he is under arrest for attempting to go with me. We bundle his luggage out of the car, and I bid farewell to a very unhappy Mustafa, who, however, has his narghile to console him, if the police will ever allow him to smoke.

part five

The Jet Age Hajj
1947—90

Until the twentieth century, pilgrim travel followed a tradition almost as old as the Hajj itself. For a thousand years, people wanting to make the pilgrimage did so simply by showing up in the right month at one of several stations outside Mecca and engaging a local guide to take them in. Those coming from a distance attached themselves to an annual caravan, paid its leader something for food and protection, and proceeded overland as time allowed. As readers of these accounts now know, the pace of the overland pilgrimage hardly changed between Ibn Battuta's journey in 1326 and Richard Burton's in the 1850s.

In the next hundred years, it changed forever. Motorized transport led the way. Greater forces followed. By 1960, the airplane, petrodollars, and a forty-hour work week had increased the numbers of hajjis geometrically and stripped away the trappings of the medieval Hajj. The prescribed rites remained unaltered, but gone for good were the camels, the moonlit marches, the caravansary. In their place came paved roads, parking lots, and buses, airports, transportation terminals, and many more pilgrims. In 1933, when Evelyn Cobbold went to Mecca, the Hajj population was less than 100,000. After decades of unchecked growth, it has leveled off in the 1990s at around 2 million.

In spite of enormous pressures, the Hajj has survived and expanded for two reasons. First, the experience is still attractive worldwide: in a faith based on participation, the Hajj remains its largest participatory rite. Second, the extraordinary increase in pilgrims since 1950 has been matched by unparalleled growth in the Saudis' economy, enabling them to enlarge the pilgrim sites.

Early Stages of Hajj Development,
1950—75

The floor space in the Haram Mosque had been expanded only a few times before 1950. The first addition, in 638 C.E., came in response to a rapid early adoption of Islam abroad and to the arrival of thousands more pilgrims every year in the Holy City. Gates, lanterns, ceilings in the surrounding halls, teak decoration, pillars, ornaments, and inscriptions were added by stages in the next century, but no further expansions took place until the mid-700s, when the need for more space reached another critical level. The walls of the mosque were set back once again in 918, bringing the total available space to nearly 100,000 square feet. And that was all: unlikely as it seems, no significant enlargement of the Meccan sanctuary occurred for the next one thousand years. Instead, a long succession of Fatimid (961–1171), Ayyubid (1169–1250), Mamluk (1250–1517), and Ottoman (1517–1922) rulers confined themselves to renovation and cosmetics. It is true that in 1572, Sultan Salim ordered a complete reconstruction of the building, replacing the wooden roof with plaster domes, but the area of the mosque was not much changed.

When expansion started again, in the 1950s, it was based as before on a crying need for more space. In the first five years after World War II, the number of visiting pilgrims from other countries tripled, to 150,000. To accommodate this increase, the mosque required immediate attention. The first work centered on the Masaʿa corridor between Mount Safa and Mount Marwa, where the rite of *saʿy* takes place. The course received a second floor to serve more pilgrims. Both levels were widened and split into two lanes to prevent collisions, and massive domes were placed over the Safa and Marwa hills. Sixteen additional gates, new stairways, and basement-level prayer halls appeared, too, and the exterior walls were faced with marble.

In 1959, a second building phase began, including a large southern portico, better access to the Masaʿa area, and improved storm drainage. In 1961, a northern portico was added. The Kaʿba itself was renovated, too, and area for the *tawaf* was greatly expanded. A third story, actually the roof-top of the mosque, now became a major prayer place. By 1965, the total surface area of the mosque had grown to more than 656,000 square feet, accommodating 400,000 people. This is the facility that Saida Miller Khalifa, Jalal al-e Ahmad, and Malcolm X describe in the following excerpts. The mosque was then six times larger than in 1950.

By the mid-1950s, oil profits were transforming Mecca from a city dependent on pilgrimage receipts to an administrative and banking center. The ten million pounds sterling derived from pilgrims in 1954 was "a drop in the ocean of oil money," wrote one traveler. The city was becoming more modern, too. All of a sudden, construction seemed its principal industry, with paved roads, homes, and office buildings spreading through the hills. Electric power flowed to streets and houses. Shah also noticed an abundance of large American cars throughout the city.

The automated Hajj came into its own after World War II. Internally, the Arabian Transport Company was already ferrying a majority of pilgrims to Arafat in 1947. By 1960, most overland pilgrims arrived from outside the Hijaz by bus too. Ten years later the roads from Iraq, Jordan, and Yemen were being paved, and the country's first four-lane highway was in place, between Jidda and Mecca. By 1975, the number of both private cars and trucks had doubled. This huge increase was correctly read as the precursor of an automotive nightmare. Already the Rush (al-Nafra) between Arafat and Muzadalifa, a distance of a few miles, took four or five hours to cover. To reduce these new pressures, a complex highway system was developed, crisscrossing Mina Valley with numbered roads. Mile-long traffic tunnels were gouged through Mecca's granite hills, and beltways were laid around the city.

Like cars and trucks, airplanes received their trial run in the 1930s, but World War II forestalled real development until the 1950s, when a small fleet of state-owned aircraft began opening routes throughout the Middle East. This service was globalized within ten years. The popularity of air travel proved so great that by 1974, 50 percent of all visiting pilgrims—450,000 people—passed through the Jidda airport, most arriving on charter flights arranged by pilgrim agents around the world. That year the airport, with two parallel runways, received four hundred jumbo jets in a single twenty-four-hour period at the peak of the season. A new, much larger terminal with a separate Hajj facility was already under construction north of the city. When it opened, it was the largest airport in the world.

Certainly air travel has sharply reduced the adventure of coming and going for jet age pilgrims, but it has also made attending the rites more practical, economical, and democratic. It may well have intensified them, too, by bearing pilgrims away from home in a matter of hours and depositing them quickly in a heightened religious atmosphere. After all, the essence of the Hajj is expressed as a ritual act of mass acculturation. *Haram* law literally strips away social difference, turning people from every corner of the earth into a participatory community, and perhaps the faster this occurs, the more penetrating the experience. Of course, one is free to walk to Mecca, and a very few still do, but the Hajj infrastructure has turned away irrevocably from the old ways.

Recent Hajj Developments, 1975—95

Saudi Arabia grew oil rich in the 1960s, but the kind of wealth required to modernize a poor, isolated desert nation did not begin to flow into the country until after the worldwide oil crisis of 1973, when the stage-by-stage nationalization of Aramco's holdings finally made Saudi Arabia the chief beneficiary of its own production.* Even then it took a few more years for profits to enter the treasury. Only in 1978 would oil receipts begin to grow geometrically, generating vast amounts of cash and preparing the way for a more ambitious expansion of the pilgrim sites.

It was overdue. For most of the 1970s, foreign hajjis had fluctuated between 700,000 and 900,000. In 1983, they exceeded 1 million for the first time, and an astonishing number of Saudi pilgrims joined them—1.5 million by official count—bringing the high-season population to 2.5 million. Mecca was then a city of about 400,000. That year, accommodations, transportation, water, food, and medical assistance, indeed the entire Hajj service infrastructure, were taxed past their limits. Not surprisingly, planning sessions began the next year.

A multibillion-dollar expansion program finally commenced in 1989. In a series of sweeping changes to the mosque, three-story additions went up on the western side, outer courtyards were greatly extended, prayer halls were added on the basement and first floors, and the building's total area grew to more than 1 million square feet—enough room for 1 million wor-

---

*Aramco was the Arab American Oil Company, initially a subsidiary of Standard Oil Company of California (Socal), with whom Philby allied Ibn Saʿud in 1933 in the first concession agreement for Saudi oil. Over the years, American joint shareholders included Socal (later Chevron), Texaco, Standard Oil Company of New Jersey (later Exxon), and Socony-Vacuum Company (later Mobil Oil). In the 1950s, Aramco emerged as a powerful multinational corporation controlling not only exploration and extraction of Saudi oil but also its refinement, marketing, and pricing. The Organization of Petroleum Exporting Countries (OPEC) was founded as a counter to Aramco in 1960. OPEC wrested control of world oil prices in 1973, during a protest embargo against President Nixon's new annual 2.2-billion-dollar U.S. support package to Israel. Aramco was nationalized by the Saudi government that year.

shipers. Two minarets were added, too, making a new total of nine, while the sun-drenched rooftop level was tiled with heat-resistant marble. Escalators were installed; the whole building was air-conditioned. Fifty thousand new lights, including a few thousand chandeliers spaced through the porticos, and banks of stadium lighting on the roof, now saturate the mosque from dusk till dawn. When I performed the Hajj in 1990, all these projects were under way. When I returned in 1996, most had been completed. The mosque, which can hold 1.25 million worshipers, is the largest open-air arena in the world.

Needless to say, the Hajj's outward appearance has altered radically since the 1930s. Automobile headlights and high-pressure sodium-vapor searchlights now join the dotted campfires on the plain. Mina Valley, two miles wide by a distance of five miles, is entirely covered in a transitory city of canvas tents during Hajj week, creating stunning views from the hillsides, especially at night. The Hajj is fully televised inside the country, and segments, often hours long, are broadcast live throughout the Muslim world.

security, safety, and the modern Hajj

It is hard to imagine what spies and pretenders would be doing on the pilgrimage today or how they would manage to enter Mecca. By the early 1950s, security in the Sacred Territory was already being tightened and modernized. As Idries Shah observed,

> Matters of identity, documentation, and quarantine are so well attended to that I felt enormous relief that I was not trying to get past this and other posts under false pretenses. . . . I am quite certain that difficulties today are immensely greater than they were during the time of Turkish suzerainty. Saudi Arabia has all the modern methods of detention and control at her disposal; and she uses them.*

Security in Mecca has been a matter of concern throughout the Hajj record, but the word has meant different things in different periods. In our own time of rising political violence and international terrorism, the Saudis have on occasion had more to fear from internal disruption than from impostors or foreign agitators. Despite a monolithic family rule, things have

*Idries Shah: from *Destination Mecca*, (Octagon Press, 1969), an account from the early 1950s.

not always been peaceful. On one infamous occasion, Mecca was made the staging ground for a violent grass-roots attempts at revolution. On November 20, 1979, a band of five hundred latter-day Ikhwan led by a revolutionary Utayba tribesman named Juhaiman opened fire from the Haram minarets and laid siege to the mosque for two weeks. Juhaiman's aim was to embarrass the Saudi rulers in their role as protectors of the Holy Sites, creating the groundswell for a revolution. Although this failed, the Muslim world was shocked by streams of blood and rifle fire across the sacred colonnades, and critics in Iran and elsewhere interpreted the event to their advantage. Determined to shore up their claim as custodians, the Saudis have greatly strengthened security during the Hajj, but violence remains a matter of concern, as amply demonstrated in 1990, when over fourteen hundred pilgrims died in a bomb-blasted tunnel in Mina Valley.

In the interests of day-to-day physical safety during peak season, the Saudis have stabilized today's Hajj population at around two million, a figure that stops just short of swamping the intake and control of foreign visitors. The numbers no longer multiply each year, due to a strictly enforced quota system that assigns a fixed number of pilgrim visas to Saudi embassies and Hajj agents around the world. So many hajjis, and no more, may represent each country in the rites. In holding down the number of visiting pilgrims, the quota system has also helped the Saudis to reduce the number of indigent pilgrims who used to remain in Mecca after the Hajj, often becoming wards of the state. The system has buttressed internal security, too, by allowing Saudi officials a means to limit foreign pilgrims who, in violation of *haram* law, mount political demonstrations during the Hajj. Iranian pilgrims, for example, were more or less banned for a period after demonstrations in Mecca in 1987 and 1989 led to bloodshed. Iraqis were also refused at the border for a period following the 1991 Persian Gulf War.

Arranging for one's Hajj today means negotiating a bureaucratic trail of visas and permits. Pilgrims seeking permission to enter Saudi Arabia must now attach a check to cover their transportation to Mina Valley, the use of a tent there for a few days' stay, and, if they like, a round-trip journey to Medina. In Mecca, a range of lodgings are available, some more expensive than others, most rent-controlled, while many pilgrims continue to camp out on the streets. Prepaid guides help with arrangements and continue to lead pilgrims through the rites. Light and a fan in each tent, medical services, and water (no small matter in the desert) are provided free. Today food prices are fixed during the Hajj, Vaccinations are required, and a pilgrimage passport is mandatory. In addition, applicants must present a round-trip ticket and, in some instances, a minimal warranty deposit at the border.

Between the impact of jumbo jets, bureaucratic processing, and increased numbers, the Hajj today is a qualitatively different experience from before. Especially in the cul-de-sac of Mecca, cars and a seasonal fourfold increase in the urban population can create havoc. Today's pilgrims face a new challenge: how to conduct a spiritual rite in a state of gridlock created by hundreds of thousands of buses, trucks, and taxicabs. There are times when the whole point of the *haram* law, a peaceful atmosphere, seems undermined by bumper-to-bumper traffic, eye-stinging fumes, and screeching brake drums. Subway trains have been discussed for years, but nothing has come of it. Starting in the 1980s, pedestrian tunnels from Mecca to Mina were installed, and a miles-long shaded walkway now runs from Mina to the Plain of Arafat. But the car, the bus, and the truck still reign supreme.

Half the books excerpted in this section were written by Western converts; half are by Muslims from the Middle East. Together they provide a useful time line for gauging the enormous changes in Mecca after World War II. Their authors are as at home in cars and airplanes as Ibn Jubayr once was on ships and camels. Born on wheels, they tend to measure distance in hours, not in days or weeks, and the Jidda airport is a set piece in their writings.

To varying degrees these are all insider accounts. Most are also mediating records, addressed to outsiders as well as Muslims in the dual tradition first employed by Ali Bey al-Abbasi in 1807. The general tone of the following accounts is more popular than those found in Part Four. Jalal Al-e Ahmad's diarylike entries (1964) are the very opposite of polished prose, while Malcolm X's autobiography assumes the tone of a confidential whisper. Hamza Bogary's narrative (published in 1983) is intimate, Saida Miller Khalifa's account (1970) devout yet offhand.

The economics of these travelers differs from that in the imperial heyday, too. We find no private fortunes here and little if any support from foundations such as helped Burckhardt and Burton on their way. An impecunious Idries Shah elicited his invitation to Mecca from a Saudi prince. Jalal Al-e Ahmad traveled modestly. Malcolm X borrowed the airfare from his sister. Even Hamza Bogary, who lived in Mecca, was engaged as a teenage guide to earn some cash. As for me, I sold my share in a fishing boat to meet expenses, then wrote my book on a publisher's advance.

19

Hamza Bogary
Mecca
ca. 1947

꥟

Hamza Bogary published The Sheltered Quarter *in 1983. It is a short book about growing up in Mecca, presenting youth's usual trials and joys as experienced there by a teenager in the 1930s and 1940s. Few cities on Earth changed more than Mecca in the forty years between Bogary's youth and the publication of this lightly fictionalized memoir. Except for the streetlamps he read by as a boy, the author looks back on a premodern city and on a story that might have occurred anytime in the past four centuries. His descriptions of school and family life resemble closely what we know of a male student's rounds in eighteenth-century Mecca. The book is a Meccan bildungsroman, calling up those final days before the oil boom that transformed Saudi Arabia and the Hajj.*

The excerpts brought together here present two journeys. In the first, a boy of ten or twelve accompanies his mother and a redoubtable Aunt Asma to Medina. As the trip unfolds, we see how simply a caravan could form. The Bogary family's long ride to Medina took twelve days. Although the raiding tribes of the Hijaz had by then been subdued, "Auntie" Asma's nightmare encounter with "the Terror of the Night" attests to the gruesome risks faced by pilgrim travelers within her lifetime. In this same selection, we also glimpse the vestiges of traditions already being suppressed by the prevailing Wahhabi puritanism of the day. Once again, much of this conflict is embodied in Bogary's aunt, a local shaman and fortune-teller who hires singing ascetics (a dying breed) to bless her journey, then hears the ghosts of martyred soldiers drumming in the desert. With examples like these, Bogary draws attention to the irrational clash between spiritualism, music, and religion that has troubled Semitic reformers for millennia.

Our second excerpt concerns a long day's trip to Mina during the Hajj. As Arthur Wavell has already pointed out, the inhabitants of Mecca are by no means exempted from making the pilgrimage every year. They have to go forth with the rest, so that for two days the city is practically deserted. Philby, too, hints at the special case of performing the Hajj for resident Meccans, but Bogary takes us much

441

further in this direction. He is that invaluable thing in a reporter, a born and active participant in the culture he describes. In some cases, he preserves aspects of the Hajj that are otherwise unrecorded. His recollection of the women's torch-lit Qays festival, held when most male pilgrims were out of town, shows us Mecca's version of a seriocomic rite that once mitigated sex-segregated societies around the world. Of special interest, too, is Bogary's seasonal employment in the Hajj service industry, a common source of pocket money among Meccan scholars and a practice that continues today.

Hamza Muhammad Bogary was born in Mecca in 1932. As a young man, he completed his university studies in Cairo, then started to work for the nascent Saudi radio and television system, rising to Director General of Broadcasting in 1962. He also served as Deputy Minister of Information and later helped to co-found King Abd al-Aziz University in Jidda. Bogary published stories and es-says in periodicals. The Sheltered Quarter *appeared when he was fifty-two. It is based on his own experiences in Mecca during the Great Depression and World War II. Although a dramatization of the work has yet to appear on Saudi tele-vision, the many domestic insights in his story have about them a certain serial potential—creating a Meccan version of* Upstairs, Downstairs *that cuts across classes and age groups in Bogary's neighborhood. Published a year before Bogary's death, the book appeared at the last possible moment to bear witness to a way of life that had already vanished.*

About five years after his camel ride to Medina, the government started expanding its national airline, Saudia. In 1952, it purchased six used Convair Skymasters from TWA and some Bristol air freighters from Britain. These be-came the core of an in-country system that was already flying pilgrims from Mecca to Medina in the middle 1950s. The popular flights reduced Bogary's twelve-day trek to a two-hour hop over killing deserts. Soon after, Saudia began to fly abroad. In the early 1960s, the airline established international routes through-out North Africa, the Middle East, and India. By 1970, air travel had opened the Haram Territory to the major Muslim populations of the world, bringing the Hajj within reach for millions of people. Forty percent of foreign hajjis ar-rived by air that year, about 150,000 people.

Later accounts in this section reflect the pervasive effects of mass air travel, but Bogary's book is sublimely free of hindsight. Rather than the voice of a media mogul, we have a naïf narration that in some ways resembles Huckleberry Finn. *The period described here sits just the other side of the brink we call modern. Today it seems, like Twain's Mississippi, many centuries away.*

from *The Sheltered Quarter:*
A Tale of a Boyhood in Mecca
by Hamza Bogary

A JOURNEY FROM MECCA TO MEDINA As soon as the necessary legal period
after my uncle's death had expired,* during which she had been prohibited
from going out or traveling, my mother decided to take me on a visit to
Medina and the Prophet's shrine. As usual, my mother consulted Auntie
Asma, who decided to accompany us on the journey. As camels were the
only accommodative form of transport, Auntie Asma decided to locate a
family in our quarter which was intent on visiting the holy shrine and append
our camel to their caravan. Our first inquiry met with success, and we planned
to join a large family intent on traveling in a caravan of five camels; but for
some inexplicable reason Auntie Asma had by this time lost interest in the
scheme. Her search started all over again until she located another caravan
whose time of departure coincided with her own. Since both Auntie Asma
and my mother conformed to the traditions and customs of the time, Auntie
Asma, in accordance with custom, brought a man to our house on the day
we were due to depart. At first I couldn't make out what he was supposed to
do, particularly as he withdrew to one of the remoter rooms in the house.
After he had settled down and accepted tea, he began chanting, while Auntie
Asma directed her movements between the window overlooking the street
and the long corridor that terminated in the room in which the man was
chanting. As I grew accustomed to it, the voice appeared more pleasing, and
I was able to recognize the words he was chanting, all of which either related
to our anticipated voyage to Medina or were prayers invoking peace on the
Prophet. When I eventually found the courage, I asked Auntie Asma to explain the relationship between her frequent visits to the window and the room
in which this stranger to the house was chanting. Those familiar with the
customs of the time will know that the ceremonial chanter was the *muzahhid,*
the resonance of whose voice induced people to discredit earthly things and
generated in them a longing to visit Medina. Auntie Asma's frequent alter-
nations between the window and the corridor were to ensure that no one

---

*Bogary refers to his stepfather as an uncle. Under Sharia law, a period of one hundred days
is required to determine whether a woman has become pregnant by her deceased husband.
[Ed.]

who disapproved of such unorthodox religious practices would hear the *muzahhid*'s melodious voice.

Later, on coming of age, I was to ask God forgiveness for the many unorthodox religious practices I had followed while under the guidance of my mother and Auntie Asma. But I have never forgotten, and never will, and I hope to be forgiven for this, the beauty of the *muzahhid*'s voice as he chanted—"God's prayers and peace on you, Prophet."

That afternoon our camel driver, Atiyya, led out our camel while I sat in the *shugduf* between the two women. Our first few anxious moments were spent earnestly praying against the devil, for we were unaccustomed to the dizzy heights of a camel's back and expected at any moment to fall. But after traveling for a short distance, we grew calmer; our camel was even tempered, and we appeared to be in no immediate danger. Our feeling of confidence was enhanced when we caught sight of the rest of the caravan on the outskirts of Mecca. What I hadn't counted on was that the *muzahhid* would be waiting for us there, oblivious to possible observation, bidding us farewell with melodious chants and wishing the pilgrims acceptance by God and his Prophet.

Although I was to journey often through those same plains and hills, the smell of the caravan at twilight was never sweeter to me than during those initial twelve days of travel between Mecca and Medina. Suhail and I, who were the only two boys undertaking the journey, would romp around behind the camels before night fell and we were constrained to take our places in the *shugduf*. Trailing the camels, running through the dry grasses, and observing flying locusts was to us an experience comparable to the best adventures of youth. Of course, we all suffered the occupational hazards of caravan travel, the inescapable mosquito bites, bruises on our sides from sleeping on the backs of camels, but these were small things to pilgrims on their way to visit the best of all mankind.

During the course of the journey Auntie Asma was to tell me about "the Terror of the Night." It was he who would intercept caravans at nightfall and, on the pretext of offering friendly advice to the drivers, would lead them astray and ultimately to their death. A characteristic decoy of his was to set up illusory cafés in the desert stretches, the lights of which would attract the drivers in the same way as a lost Bedouin will head toward a mirage in the expectation of finding water. The caravans would never be seen again, and nothing survived of the people, camels, and goods they were conveying.

Auntie Asma was full of stories about those who had met their deaths at the hands of the notorious Terror of the Night. As a safeguard, she remained awake while the caravan was in motion, ready to warn the drivers, lest they be lured astray and all of us lost.

It must have been when we were between al-Safra and the Nar Valley that, one evening, I heard Auntie Asma's protracted, frantic screams ring through the last vestiges of the night. "The Terror of the Night! The Terror of the Night! Don't be misled by him; he comes to lie!" Startled out of sleep, I almost jumped off the camel in fright. Without effect my mother and the camel driver tried to calm her down, but all the while she continued screaming "the Terror of the Night." And what a commotion! She continued until the drivers brought the caravan to a halt, made our camel kneel, took the trembling Auntie Asma down, and poured a jug of water over her head. Having regained her composure, she was then in a state to listen to them and learn that her imagined "Terror of the Night" was only the figure of the café owner where we had put up the previous night. He had pursued us on a camel after discovering that one of our party had left a blanket on a chair in the café. Anxious, lest on our discovery of the missing item we had suspected that it was he who had stolen it, he had followed us to return it to its rightful owner.

After that Auntie Asma's obsession with the Terror of the Night diminished, but her imagination proved irrepressibly fertile in the collection of exciting narratives she was to have in store for me.

We had been traveling for eight nights, and, after eight stations, our caravan arrived at Badr.* No one anticipated any improbable occurrence that evening, and, arriving just before sunset, the camels were made to kneel by one of the shacks along the road, mats were spread on the sand, and preparations for our meal began as usual. Our supper consisted of a kind of *tharid* made of dry bread we had carried with us from Mecca, cooked with a small quantity of dry meat and water. After supper, Auntie Asma untied her clothes bundle, took out a few requirements, and then sat alone at a distance from the hut. There she began her cosmetic ritual, first of all combing her hair and then proceeding to rub coconut oil mixed with herbs on it. Satisfied with the remedial arrangements for her hair, she then placed a triangular strip of white cloth over it and tied the two attached strings at the back of her head. This white cloth was called a *shanbar*. She then wrapped her braid in a handkerchief called a *mahrama* and covered her head with a white shawl with em-

---

*Site of an early Muslim victory over the Quraysh, at the junction of a road between Mecca and Syria, 624 C.E. [Ed.]

broidered ends called a *mudawwara*. And, as a final act of embellishment, she penciled her eyebrows and applied kohl eyeliner to her eyelids. One would have thought she was making herself up for a wedding.

When the others were preparing to retire for the night, Auntie Asma led me by the hand toward the desert. When we were sufficiently far away from the encampment, she sat down on a small dune and motioned me to take a place next to her. As the night deepened, she began those gestures which were to develop into a quiet dance and then by degrees into a frenzied one. It seemed to me that she was dancing to a tune coming to us from far away, a drum or tambourine beat. She continued whirling while I sat terrified on the sand, wondering whether Auntie Asma had lost her mind or whether I was dreaming. Only after she was exhausted and the night was waning did she return to her place and rest. Taking my hand, she walked me back to the caravan. Mother showed no surprise at our late arrival, seeing the perspiration that beaded Auntie Asma. I was curious to know at once the nature of this dance, but my mother signaled to me to wait until Auntie Asma had gone to sleep; then she would explain all to me. She asked me first of all whether I had heard drums, to which I replied that I had heard reverberant noises whose source I couldn't identify. In reply she explained to me that these notes came from the drums of the warriors at Badr, martyrs who had fallen in that battle, and that at certain times of the year when the moon is full, their drums are heard again sounding in the desert. According to my mother, Auntie Asma was one of the few who knew when and where to intersect with this phenomenon. And this explained why she had refused to take the first caravan, for its arrival at Badr would have failed to coincide with the return of the martyred drummers. She then requested that I keep the incident secret, as the more orthodox expressed misgivings about the existence of those drums and had people refrain from dancing to their beat.

I can't properly recall now whether my reactions to what I had heard were negative or positive. But I did continue to give the matter thought until I was considerably older and had come to read the ode of Dhu al-Rumma* that speaks of jinn playing tunes in the desert: "The soft humming of the jinn by night on the desert fringes." Poor deluded Dhu al-Rumma and Auntie Asma; they knew nothing of the movement of sand in the desert and the undulating drifts that the wind mapped out at night.

After the fevered pitch of her dance, Auntie Asma grew calm. She ceased to express anxiety, and her face showed the same serene countenance as those

---

*Dhu al-Rumma (696–735): foundational Umayyad poet famous for verse about the desert. [Ed.]

of the other women who, in the days to come, would sit in the circle of the *zar** held in our house in Mecca. I was to see that same expression later on in the faces of young European women and men whom I saw on weekends, New Years, weddings, and whenever they grew excited by the beat of drums and flute. If I had wished to discourage those young people, I could have done so by informing them that the primitive African tribes I had met in the course of my travels arrived at the same psychological state of gratification after a night of dancing to rhythmic drums—and to songs that were not so very different from those of the Badr or the Latin Quarter. Man is probably as much a rhythmic musical animal as he is a thinking one.

Not that Auntie Asma's newfound serenity stopped her from telling her customary exciting stories or from making decisions that had the air of being sudden but which were in fact studied with care. It was for my benefit alone that she told the story of the people of al-Furaysh. "Al-Furaysh," she explained, "is a village situated between al-Mesajid and Abyar Ali. And today the Meccans still refer to someone who overcharges as being from al-Furaysh, a custom that derives from these people being the last highway robbers on the road to Medina. So even if the pilgrims had escaped the brigands at Mastura or al-Safra, they still had to confront those of al-Furaysh." Although I never attributed lies to Auntie Asma, I did wonder at her telling me about the Bedouin whose head she had crushed, many years ago, against the bottom half of the tent pole, after she had caught him scouting while they were camping at al-Furaysh. She had hit him impulsively on the head with the nearest object at hand, a picture that had me imagine her brawny armed, although nothing in her appearance suggested the likelihood of such strength.

Her last decision before our entry into Medina, the City of Light, after having completed the detailed proceedings required by the police at the Anbariyya Gate, was to order the camel driver to pull our camel out of the caravan and to go in the opposite direction from the others. On reaching the area to the south of the Prophet's Mosque, we realized the wisdom of that move. Having ordered the camel driver to stop, she untied a knot in her head shawl and took out a folded letter. Then, alighting from the camel, she proceeded to saunter into the vestibule of a large palace. She returned

---

zar: the term applies to spirit possession as a cause of physical illness; to the evil spirit itself; to the exorcism process, usually involving dance and music; and (as here) to the company that attends the exorcism. In traditional Mecca, this was almost always a woman's occasion—part festivity, part curative ceremony. The word's Ethiopian origin links the practice to similar psychotherapeutic meetings popular throughout much of Africa. [Ed.]

for us shortly, and it was there that we took up residence for our stay in Medina.

Adopting my usual method of gesturing with my finger when I wanted to inquire about something I didn't understand, I asked my mother to explain the incident. I learned that Auntie Asma, with characteristic foresight, had visited a notable of our quarter, a property owner in Medina, to ask of him permission for us to use one of his houses during our sojourn. As his properties stood empty for most of the year, being in demand only at the time of religious festivals, he readily consented to her request and provided her with a letter to present to the guard at the house. He had granted us the use of the upper sitting room overlooking the date grove, the waterwheel, and small fountain. All of these were new discoveries for me. I had never before seen a fountain, nor heard of a waterwheel. I knew of the latter only through the story of "The Peacock That Stood Beside the Waterwheel" in *The Rashida Reader.** For the record, it was this visit which had generated my infatuation with Medina and resolutely determined me to go there each year once I gained my independence.

On the last day of our sojourn, after paying the Farewell Visit to the holy shrine together with a large number of fellow pilgrims, Auntie Asma fainted, or at least that is what I presumed at the time. Her cloaked body went down in front of the railing surrounding the holy shrine. Her sudden fall shook the grillwork that protected the tomb and caused an uproar that soon had worshipers and the mosque guards in attendance. Auntie Asma just lay there, her hands clasped to the railing, while those nearest to her tried to lift her up. Throughout the incident, I found myself repeating the *hawqala*†—"There is no power or might except in God"—and reciting the Fatiha‡ over and over, asking God inwardly not to let Auntie Asma die here, far from her home and the rest of her family.

When at last she attempted to stand, I thanked God for granting my supplications and for protecting us from a possible tragedy. I was not aware at the time that what had taken place was nothing more than dramatics on the part of Auntie Asma. She had conceived of staging a fainting fit in order to come into contact with the railing surrounding the holy tomb. She her-

---

*The Raschida Reader: a popular children's collection of the time.

†*hawqala:* any of numerous verses from the Quran uttered in difficult situations to ward off evil. [Ed.]

‡al-Fatiha: the "opening," first chapter of the Quran, a short strophe memorized by all Muslims. [Ed.]

self told me later that she was renowned for collapsing there and that she could never contemplate returning to Mecca without first resting her hand on that green grille. . . .

THE HAJJ Without exception, all of the families in Mecca at this time undertook the pilgrimage year after year. They all had some involvement with the pilgrimage or the pilgrims, as agents, vendors, or participants in the ceremony for its own sake. How easy it was at that time—all you had to do was to pray one prescribed prayer or another in the Holy Mosque, then go to al-Mudda'a, where you would find a file of cameleers and donkey drivers waiting for you, crying out "Ride for hire!" and advertising their conveyance. For a few piastres you would find yourself mounted on the back of one of them, alone or riding behind someone else if you so desired. You would thus be on your way to Arafat if you had delayed until the ninth day or to Mina if you were performing the pilgrimage of the Prophet. On the ninth day of the pilgrimage there was scarcely a male to be found in Mecca, excepting the night watchmen and the *khullaif** thieves, as we called them. This band of thieves was insignificant in comparison with the pilgrimage thieves. The latter were notorious for sneaking into the pilgrims' tents on the evening of Yawm al-Tarwiyya, after everyone had retired for the night on the evening prior to reaching the Arafat station. From time to time you would hear intermittent cries of "Thieves, thieves!"—and then you would see the torchlit forms of the guides running in pursuit of their elusive suspects, without knowing who they were or where they had gone. The night would always be dark, that wonderful invention, electricity, not having been heard of yet, while torches and lanterns were confined to projecting over a limited radius.

On these particular nights, those who had stayed behind, largely the women who had elected not to undertake the pilgrimage that year for one reason or another, would gather together in an open space in the quarter, usually the Utaybiyya Quarter, to celebrate the Qays festival until late at night. Crowds of women, unaccompanied by men, would be seen there shouting and chanting folk songs pertaining to this particular festival.

Although it is accepted that God has delivered us from this heresy, nonetheless our women in the earlier part of the last century were anxious to attend that festival in order to participate in the songs and to mitigate the loneliness of their staying behind in Mecca. As a child, it came about that

---

Khullaif: thieves who remain in Mecca when the Hajj empties the town, to take advantage of the situation. [Ed.]

on several occasions I had the opportunity to attend these Qays festivals. I helped carry the torches, walking in front of the women as they danced holding wooden swords in their hands. Although Mother never actually participated in the dance, she watched the festival and carried a bag full of candied fruits and nuts, into which she repeatedly dipped her hand, and you could see her jaws moving constantly.

Although the last Qays festival occurred a long time ago, the ambiguous nature of its ceremony left a permanent indelible impression on me. Various mythic elements were interwoven into this women's festival, all of them associated with how they had discovered a male intruder in their midst, wearing female clothes, carrying a sword, and convinced that his identity wouldn't be discovered. As always, the unpredictable happened, and the culprit was discovered and punished, either by slapping or with the instrument of his wooden sword, and was further disgraced by the shame of his exposure in front of his family and relatives immediately after the feast. The matter invariably ended with the chief of the quarter heaping ridicule and rebuke on the offender and demanding that he solemnly swear that he would never commit such an aberration again.

Even before I had taken up the responsibilities of a teaching profession, the Qays celebration had long lost its appeal for me. The desire to participate in the activities of the pilgrimage assumed a strong affection. One opportunity open to me, and those like me, was to participate in guiding pilgrims at the Holy Mosque, as did dozens of boys of my age, either as helpers to the agents or as single operators hunting down those without Bedouin guides or those who wished to make additional circumambulations outside of the hours prescribed by the agents. This was a form of employment common to many of my generation. Participation in the Hajj festival in this way contributed toward our subsistence throughout the remaining months of the year. Even teachers took a part in it, offering their services to one of the agents. This category of teacher was regarded by people as being of a higher order than the freelancers who lay in wait at the many entrances to the Holy Mosque for pilgrims or those making the Umra.

After examining most aspects of the tradition, I decided to adopt a different course, though one which was still connected with the pilgrimage and its celebration. I decided to work for the leading agent of our quarter as the secretary to his organization, bookkeeping, recording the names of the pilgrims, their steamship, and the possessions they left in trust, as well as supervising the number of writs authorized for "substitutes," that is, listing the names of those absent for whom the pilgrimage was to be made, the sums devoted to this purpose, and whether or not sacrificial animals were to be a part of the ceremony. We also kept a record of their general expenses, which included the rental of housing, camel litters, tents, and campsites at Mina, the meals provided for pilgrim guests, which were most often a banquet on the night of arrival from Jidda, and food supplied during the course of the pilgrimage, which included the farewell dinner after each group had made the final circumambulation in preparation for their departure.

The writs regarding "substitutes" formed an additional source of income, shrinking or expanding in accordance with the conscientiousness of the agent. The less honest would lock the money in their steel boxes without endeavoring to give any of it to anyone but themselves. Others would pick out some of the substitute documents for pilgrims, especially the richer ones—and from them give generously to themselves, their families, and their top employees, distributing the rest to their servants, neighbors, and some inhabitants of the quarter. Some of the writs would incur deficits less than the amounts designated and thus contribute a profit to the agents. This was regarded as acceptable legal practice as long as the pilgrimage had been carried out in the name of the intended pilgrim who had not been able to perform the pilgrimage. If, for example, he or she had died and missed the opportunity of performing the pilgrimage and therefore it devolved upon his or her relatives and heirs to either perform the pilgrimage for the deceased or hire someone else to do so.

As it turned out, I didn't undertake the pilgrimage that year as a surrogate pilgrim, for this, according to the books of jurisprudence, is disallowed for one who has not performed the rite. This did not prevent me, however, from taking one of the documents in the name of my mother, who, it had been decided, would make the pilgrimage in the agent's caravan. In my naïveté, I decided to show one of these credit letters to the *ustadh*,* who, far from expressing interest, looked at me intently before saying in a dry, disinterested tone: "I do not make the pilgrimage for anyone else, nor have I any need to do so."

At the time I had not realized that those who accepted writs were generally simple folk with barely enough to live on, and not the sophists or the rich.

The day of ascent to Mina was an industrious one. The preparations made for it were not unlike those utilized for a military expedition, with the detailed regulations representing the accumulated experiences of over a thousand years. Preceding the caravan came the camels belonging to the "native Meccans," then the agent's family, who were mounted on four camels, then

---

ustadh: a professor or learned man; in this case, the narrator's principle instructor. [Ed.]

my own family. The camel litters, or *shugdufs*, of the native Meccans were distinguished from those of the other pilgrims in that the former were covered with smooth rugs, while the latter were covered with gunnysack. The former sported brightly colored railings in addition to having the fringes dyed red, while the other litters were of bare wood without the enhancement of any aesthetic detail. Even the camels chosen for the native Meccans seemed to be larger and of a more dignified bearing than those of the other pilgrims.

Once the *shugdufs* had been fastened to the camels, the latter were arranged in a long column, with the camel drivers strategically distributed so that the halter of the leading camel was taken by the oldest and most experienced cameleer. The other drivers were spread out along both sides of the caravan, each of them responsible for several camels, while two walked at the rear. Since the caravan was made up of Egyptian pilgrims, their native ululations were heard as soon as the leading camel was set in motion, to be followed by singing and chanting until we had left the houses of Mecca behind, heading eastward on the road to al-Masha'ir, or the Holy Places outside of Mecca.*

The practical reason for the strategic distribution of camel drivers was the fear that an assailant might have the temerity, when the congestion increased, to split off a portion of the caravan by detaching the guide rope, thus separating the rear of the caravan from the front. The rear section could thus become lost for hours or possibly days without anyone knowing its fate. This was a common occurrence, unless an experienced person noticed quickly and set up a cry: "Brigands, O camel drivers, brigands!" This would then lead to the reunion of the separated halves.

Those of us who operated as employees of an agent, whom we called Amm, equipped ourselves with a Bedouin bag, in place of the elegant attaché cases carried by businessmen today, and a belt worn over the gown. We also carried a curved cudgel, given to us by our employer, with which to defend ourselves in case of emergency.

Although I walked most of the way to Mina and Arafat, I was so intoxicated by the mission that I was oblivious of the fatigue induced by walking so far. I persisted in walking despite Mother's calling out from time to time: "Get onto the *shugduf*, son, and have a rest. Are you a camel driver?" But I resisted her entreaty as I enjoyed walking with the cameleers and the servants. I asked the head camel driver how many times he had made the pilgrimage and about his experiences. He had a lively memory, rich with

*Mina, Arafat, and Muzdalifa. [Ed.]

accounts of the terrors that he and the pilgrims had endured either on the pilgrimage to Mecca or when visiting Medina.

One of the most disturbing things he related was the phenomenon of those camel drivers who used to conspire with the brigands against the pilgrims instead of rightfully defending them. He told me of how he had lost a son during a raid in which the visiting pilgrims resisted with force instead of surrendering. They fought the raiders at one of the stations on the road to Medina, using staves, stones, and whatever came to hand, with the result that the thieves were defeated, leaving two dead, one of them his son. After this the camel driver reformed his ways and began to defend his caravan if need be, instead of handing it over to the hungry Bedouin and marauding cutthroats. He had an extraordinary ability to talk incessantly, as though his narrations were a prerecorded tape or as though he were reading from the written page. His stories followed on without any interruption, and, judging by the avidity with which he chattered, it was clear that he rarely found so receptive an ear.

At intervals, he would take off toward the rear to check on his camels and their riders, issuing instructions to his team of drivers to watch a certain camel because it was unreliable or to treat another gently because it was ailing. He kept a constant count of the camels, and only when satisfied that everything was proceeding as it should would he return to the head of the caravan and resume talking where he had left off. He would invariably begin his stories with the same sentence: "Once when we were on a visit to Medina" or "One time we were on a pilgrimage" and proceed from there. If I had possessed the facilities at the time, I would have recorded all of his stories and published them. They were a remarkable mixture of the comic and terrifying and included a great deal of information about camels, the maladies to which they were susceptible, their life span, the stations on this or that route which provided water and those that provided none, incidents of death by thirst, the constant fighting between al-Safra and al-Furaysh tribes along the way to Medina, the tribes most notorious for raiding the caravans, and the most illustrious and courageous cameleers of his day.

During the narration of these stories, one or more wayside beggars would appear, armed with a long stick, to the end of which was nailed an empty tomato-paste can which rattled. This he would raise in front of one of the litters, calling out, "O pilgrims, may God accept your pilgrimage." From time to time one would hear the clatter of a coin as it struck the brandished can. Upon this the beggar would move on to the next camel and the next . . .

Mother was determined to treat me as a juvenile on the occasion of the big feast day at the end of the pilgrimage. Collecting together a number of small children from the encampment, she produced a bag of candied fruits and nuts which she threw over me and laughingly sang out: "They went on a pilgrimage and came back." The children grabbed the scattered pieces, while the agent and his family laughed and shouted at this singular sight. The game ended with her draping a *qilada* round my neck, resembling a necklace and composed of dried dates sold during the pilgrimage season for this very purpose. They are sold also before the sacred feast at the end of Ramadan for the making of *dibyaza.** It seems unnecessary for me to relate here how this substance is formed, for most of the Meccan families and some of those in Jidda are still expert in its composition, despite its unpopularity with the present generation.

The nights spent at Mina were truly happy ones, full of jubilation, in which we strolled about the Arab bazaar, observing the itinerants and the women "who had not made the pilgrimage simply from a desire to obtain merit with God." The atmosphere exalted one, as did the various evening celebrations, such as gathering round a Quranic reciter seated on an agent's bench or around a group of Arab tribesmen chanting and dancing as though at a wedding. All of this was an important part of the sights of Mina.

*dibyaza: a sweet, thick drink made of dates, apricots, sugar, nuts, and water. [Ed.]

20

Jalal Al-e Ahmad
Iran
1964

※※※

Jalal was more honest about himself than many other writers. Ira-
nian writers are afraid to admit to their own weaknesses. Jalal . . . .
had the courage to confront the moral problems of his own life.
                                                        —Reza Baraheni

Lost in the Crowd* *is the personal diary of a three-week journey to Medina,*
then Mecca, composed on the spot in 1964 by one of Iran's most controversial
authors. In this brief book, Jalal Al-e Ahmad pays minute attention to the physi-
cal facts and social effects of Hajj travel, harking back to Naser-e Khosraw nine
centuries before. A professional writer, he patterned his book on Khosraw's and
knew it well.

Born into an influential religious family in 1923, Al-e Ahmad fell out as
a student with his Shi'ite cleric father, turned away from inherited traditions,
and had not performed a prayer in twenty years when he left for Mecca. Instead,
he launched a career as a teacher, author, and cultural observer, becoming one
of Iran's chief social critics in the years after World War II. For over two de-
cades, he published important novels and stories with contemporary settings, as
well as academic journal articles and popular essays on Persian society.

Al-e Ahmad understood the injurious effects of institutionalized Shi'ism
on his country. He wrote trenchantly of its failures to educate and lead. At the
same time, he was critical both of modernization and of the westward-leaning
monarchy of Muhammad Reza Pahlavi. He argued, for example, that Albert
Camus's novel The Plague *was an allegorical interpretation of a cultural illness*
brought on by modern mechanization. This disease he variously translated as

---

*A plain translation of the Persian title *Khasi dar Miqat* would read *A Chip of Wood, or a*
Piece of Straw [Khasi], at the Sacred Rendezvous, or Crossroads. *Miqat* signifies the stations*
marking the Haram area outside Mecca.

"Westoxification," "Western poisoning," and "Occidentosis," and he warned against importing it into Iran. The Shah was far from pleased by this critique, but Al-e Ahmad went further, putting on notice the entire political spectrum of Iran. In his most influential essay Westruckness, *he emphasized the importance of traditional Muslim values in the lives of most Iranians, quite apart from the hidebound Shi'ite hierarchy. As for the Shah's political opposition, he warned that* all *of Iran's parties were committing suicide by couching their programs in secular language that did not speak to the nation's deeply religious peasant majority. Al-e Ahmad raised this point again and again on his trip to Mecca, stating in a final passage that he had written his book as an answer to Iranian intellectuals who "spurn these events and walk among them gingerly and with distaste."*

Al-e Ahmad's own religious views remain in conflict throughout the book. He presents his reasons for making the Hajj as entirely personal. He went to Mecca accompanying his sister, two brothers-in-law, and a great-uncle, all devout Shi'ites, and his minute attention to their condition, moods, and needs occupies about half the diary entries. He clearly saw himself as their protector. A second motive, he repeatedly confides, was to learn more about his brother's death in Medina thirteen years earlier. This search for a lost family story becomes a theme, then a controlling metaphor, for the book. "I came looking for my brother," he writes in conclusion, "and all those other brothers—rather than in search for God." For a man of Al-e Ahmad's makeup, a self-described personal pilgrimage would have seemed a sentimental self-indulgence. It is the people in his path that mattered to him, whether family or strangers.

Lost in the Crowd *is a completely circumstantial Hajj account. Its approach is the very opposite of the rigorously impersonal Farahani, our last Iranian traveler. Here no detail is too intimate to record, no subject off-limits. An uncle's diarrhea, a woman's glance, the incipient madness of a fellow traveler, are all set down with equal weight among Al-e Ahmad's own intense reactions, elations, and complaints. As the book goes on, its unrelenting particularity, its insistently human frame of reference, become in themselves a kind of credo: that the daily events of a noble occasion demand full attention, that how individuals behave on the Hajj is more meaningful than any amount of philosophizing. Al-e Ahmad loved the oddness, the excitement and compression of the Hajj, just as he abhorred its grand disorder. He has kind words for those with open hearts, even when they happen to be clerics, but he detests hypocrisy and meanness. He berates the sanctimonious and scoffs like Diogenes at received opinion. Morality with Al-e Ahmad must come embedded in the details. Nothing is quite as it appears. Everything demands closer inspection.*

Al-e Ahmad saw the Meccan mosque in the second phase of its expansion. Building out in all directions from an eighteenth-century Turkish colonnade,

Abd al-Aziz's son, King Sa'ud, and his architects were preparing a ritual arena large enough to hold seven hundred thousand people. This work took years. In the spring of 1964, Al-e Ahmad found the whole eastern side of the building joined to the city by a continuous network of scaffolding. The mataf, *the track for making one's turns around the Ka'ba, was marbled now, while the Masa'a, the long runway for the* sa'y *rite between Safa and Marwa, had been "transformed to a huge two-level cement passageway." Al-e Ahmad's journal adds all sorts of "firsts" to the Meccan record: Hajj air tours, motels, garages, ice houses, miniskyscrapers, mechanized slaughterhouses, refrigerator trucks, and neon lighting. He describes the Hajj airport at Jidda in full swing, with its medical clinic and pilgrim dormitories. As one might imagine from his attacks on Western culture, all this modernity did not agree with him.*

Al-e Ahmad's curiosity is athletic and free of categories. Out on a stroll in the scorching April heat, he will follow strange-looking pipes across an unknown street and wind up describing, then criticizing, the Medina water system. His horrified description of the slaughterhouse at Mina presents the sacrifice as Ibn Battuta must have seen it. Throughout his stay, he is constantly chatting up strangers in broken Arabic, conversing on benches and in ice-cream stalls with soldiers and students and pilgrims in the crowd. From this close registration of chance encounter, Al-e Ahmad frequently wrings a complex mediation. His night bus ride to Mecca turns metaphysical, as do later passengers on the pilgrim rites. At other times, his observations resist summation. They sit on the page, sufficient to themselves. In this book, more than in any of his prior writing, Al-e Ahmad the existentialist may be seen struggling to reclaim the vocabulary of a lost religious past. The diary, with its informal, staccato prose, freely associative, mildly obsessive, neatly captures the cross-rhythms of the modern Hajj.

from Jamal Al-e Ahmad's
Lost in the Crowd

JIDDA. FRIDAY, APRIL 10, 1964 We started at five in the morning from Mehrabad airport. We got here at eight-thirty (seven-thirty local time), having had breakfast on the plane without tea or coffee. Bread, a piece of chicken, and an egg, in a box bearing the airline's logo. The hajjis-to-be, however, were unsure at first. Was it edible or not? Had it been killed according to religious law? I missed whatever it was that removed their doubts. It may have been our guide, who took such an interest in helping the flight attendants distribute the food that one would have thought he was paying for it himself. After the meal we each got an orange, again with the guide's help. . . .

Sitting next to me was a swarthy old man submerged in himself, somewhat frightened. It was his first flight. He was snapping at people. I helped him position the little tray so his food could be served. "Yes," he said, "thanks, but I know how this works." We talked a little then. A retired police major. His children had married, and he and his wife were alone. Now he was going to go into the presence of God and offer thanks. He was frightened, however. "Is Arafat as strenuous as they say?" I told him it was my first pilgrimage, too.

There are eighty-five in our group. Twenty or thirty merchants, about fifteen Mazanderani, five or six sayyids,* akhonds,† maddas,‡ and preachers, and about ten villagers from the Arak area who speak only Turkish. There are twenty women. In my group, there is my sister and her husband, Javad, another of the husbands of my sisters, Mohaddes, and my father's uncle. We are a little group unto ourselves in this crowd. Our guide is from our area. He was one of my father's§ followers. I had persuaded the others that we ought to let him take us. He had been a gable builder. This was my reciprocation for the devotion someone once extended to my father. The guide's job belongs to him, along with his son, a cook, and the cook's assistant. I don't think we'll lack anything with this arrangement.

JIDDA. NIGHT, SAME DAY. When we deplaned this morning, we came directly to this building in the "Hajj village" beside the airport. It's an enormous structure of three or four corners with squinches, three or four stories high. It has spacious balconies, open windows on all sides, and rooms designed to

---

sayyid—a descendant of the Prophet Muhammad, as used here, it can also be simply an honorific title, especially in Arabic. [Trans.]

†*akhond:* a lesser member of the Shi'ite religious leadership. He performs everyday religious functions, such as leading the prayers in the smaller mosques, and so on; the term, synonymous with *mulla,* has a pejorative connotation. [Trans.]

‡*madda:* one who sings songs and recites poetry about the imams on special Shi'ite anniversaries, such as the ninth and tenth of Muharram (when Imam Husayn [son of Ali and Fatima; grandson of Muhammad] was martyred) and at funerals. He may be merely a gifted performer, with no religious or scholarly credentials. [Trans.]

§The author's father was a Shi'ite clergyman. [Trans.]

trap and circulate the wind. You drink water and perspire. There is so much wind in the room, you'd think you were right at the peak of Tuchal.* Luckily, the morning we arrived, I packed my Tehran clothing away in the suitcase. I purchased an Arab *dishdashah*† for eight Saudi riyals—one riyal equals eighteen Iranian *qeran*s—and a pair of Javanese elastic slippers for two riyals. The shirt was delightful, like a cone of sugar cubes. Yet I split open the two sides of it with a knife so I could sit and stand. But the shoulders are so tight it feels like someone is hugging you all the time. But I'm getting off the track. I was talking about the Hajj village. It has four floors. We are on the third floor (each side on each floor has six or seven facets. It's an irregular trapezoid). The state owns it. They [pilgrims] come here from the airport for a little break until it's time to go to Jidda, en route to Mecca or Medina, depending on whether they arrive early or late in the season. They say the hajjis are sometimes detained for up to three days. I think we'll be leaving tonight, however. In the meantime, I pass the time with this notebook, waiting for our departure. . . .

THE HAJJ VILLAGE   The hajjis in our group seem unhappy about being idle. They have been unpacking and repacking their luggage since this morning. Maybe they're paying the price of their idleness at home, where their wives undoubtedly took care of everything, and with such precision. All the suitcases have covers of canvas and tarp cloth, with straps, locks, and ropes tied around them. They take the prayer mats out one by one and roll them into the suitcases. "No, that's not it. It just doesn't look right." Then they start over. This is the quest of the Hajj, and of the windswept plain! Every one of these people left his livestock, his cash register, or his desk just yesterday. They're getting an experience, in any event. Even though it takes the plane only three hours to bring you to Jidda from Tehran, and you don't get a chance to spend a year getting here by mule or camel from Mazlaqan or Suleqan, they make up for it by detaining you the same amount of time it would take to make the trip by camel in this Hajj village, to give you a chance to pack and unpack your bundles. Even more interestingly, they are Turks from Arak. One of them, who had not yet taken off his leather waistcoat (in spite of this humid early-evening heat) had just gone out this afternoon and bought a *dishdashah* to wear over it. His shoulders were held in awkwardly and tightly. Although his Persian was not good, I had joked with him in the

*Tuchal: a mountain in the Elburz range of northern Iran. [Trans.]

†*dishdashah:* the long gown worn by the Arabs of the Arabian Peninsula. [Trans.]

afternoon: "I hope you didn't catch cold?" One of our companions from Isfahan said: "Hajji, he's sewn his money into his leather coat." (We are already practicing calling each other Hajji.) More interestingly, it's money he's already converted at the market right here in the courtyard of this Hajj village. I've seen four people so far asking about the currency conversion rate from our *qeran*s to Saudi riyals, fearing they might be cheated. It's obvious that they've never even made a pilgrimage to Qom, and now? They've traded their *toman*s for riyals in Jidda. The money changers know Persian, Turkish, Urdu, and Javanese, to the extent necessary to do business.

The air is miserably humid. The body stays wet all the time, and the bones will surely ache tonight. If you can sleep, that is, with legs exposed, and an even more exposed chest and neck area. No matter what, one must get used to it for the days of *ihram*. And these ceiling fans go continuously. What would we do if they didn't? When the wind stopped at sunset, we ourselves turned on the fans. According to what they say, we will be traveling tonight. I went in the afternoon to visit the other corners and floors of the building. In front of the balconies around the building were clusters of flags of various nations and the names and emblems of this or that guide: Turkish, Persian, Iraqi, Syrian, and Moroccan. Guards continually walked the path going around the building. All of them young, wearing khakis, berets, revolvers, and carrying clubs, watching. . . .

I also visited our caravan's infirmary. It was on the second floor of this Hajj village, in a large, well-appointed, respectable room, with a proper pharmacy, a doctor, and two officious-looking orderlies. They've been on duty since the beginning of this week. There are seventy-two on the Iranian health staff. Twenty-two of them are physicians, and some of these are women. Up until the time of my visit they had had 449 patients. The complaints: air sickness, heat stroke, and diarrhea (caused by eating rancid yogurt, according to the doctor). Of this group, there were thirty Nigerians, three Afghanis, several Sudanese, Turks, and Yemenis, and an Egyptian. The infirmary's doors are open to everyone. Some of the physicians' staff are now in Medina, some in Mecca, and they will all assemble in Mecca on Ayd-e Qorban,* following the hajjis step by step. These are things I jotted down which were passed on to me by one of the infirmary's physicians. . . .

MEDINA. SATURDAY, APRIL 11 We arrived here at eight-thirty in the morning. The greetings from officials at the gate and the flower gardens in the

---

*Ayd-e Qorban, or the Feast of the Sacrifice, is usually called *Id al-Adha* (Persian *Ayd-e Azha*). [Trans.]

public squares made a happy welcome for us, for we had been on the bus since eleven the night before. My feet swelled up from sitting on the seats so long, and they're still swollen. I've never felt such pain in my life. I suspect it's the result of running around with exposed legs. Anyway, the only thing I've got on beneath this *dishdashah* is a pair of shorts. Fortunately, I thought to buy a blanket in Jidda. If I hadn't, I'd have fallen on my face after the first step. It hurts a lot between my shoulders right now, like colic. I haven't coughed yet, though I have some Ipesandrine. "Oh! Look at you! You've come on the Hajj, and you're this preoccupied with yourself? You really must forget these old traveling pharmacies. And definitely yourself as well."

We waited for the bus last night from eight o'clock until ten. I wrote by the dim overhead light, and the others griped at one another continually about space. We finally did get under way. I think it was even later than eleven o'clock. Such joy! At one point I noticed that we were back in the center of Jidda, in order to pay the highway toll and be counted (no doubt) and this sort of chicanery. Then we went back and got onto the road for Mecca in that same vicinity of the Hajj village. When was this? At exactly twelve-fifteen. I didn't last past one o'clock. I wrapped up tightly in my blanket and dozed off. I woke up suddenly at three o'clock, because of a mechanical breakdown. I woke up again at three-thirty, again because of a mechanical breakdown. We stayed awake then until we reached the village of Badr at five in the morning. The bus stopped every ten minutes. Then it would lurch ahead. Each time, the driver would get underneath it and tinker with the motor. Then he would run back up and pump the gas pedal—and he pounded it so hard you'd have thought he was driving nails with it. One slam after another, continuously. He had two or three drivers in our group, and no matter how much they tried to help him, he refused. Arab blockheadedness. The carburetor wasn't drawing fuel. The guy would go suck gas out of the tank with a hose and pour it into the carburetor. Then we would go for five minutes and stop again. It was a fiasco. The people became loud and agitated, the women whining and swearing, especially cursing everything Arab. It reached a point where I intervened once or twice, yelling at this one or that one, "Why have you lost control of yourself this way?" Other passing vehicles stopped occasionally to sympathize or help, but the driver was stubborn, or else unauthorized or in danger of being docked part of his pay. That is, the one who helped would be certain to report that "so-and-so was stalled in the middle of the road; I stopped to help him," and so on . . . It was six-thirty when we left Badr. We had washed our faces, prayed, drunk *barrad* tea, and eaten American corn bread. The bus had been repaired, and we had no further problems. We didn't stop again until we got to Medina.

My uncle kept on complaining, however; the old fellow couldn't handle it. . . .

It is now past noon. There is no word yet, however, from the other travelers in our group, and no word of my sister, who is with her husband on the next bus. Our guide says that Saudi officials do not allow any bus to venture out into the sun after nine in the morning. They must wait until sunset—and this is further evidence of an orderly system—but it is mostly on account of the buses, which would overheat in the sun and cause company losses. The house where we are staying is of recent construction, outside the city, near the date gardens, in a neighborhood called *Darb al-Jana'iz.* You can look into the middle of Baqi‘ cemetery* from the northern window. They bring our water in a tanker. Every half cubic meter costs one Saudi riyal. . . .

SUNDAY, APRIL 12 . . . Today I didn't set foot outside the house. I slept from eight to eleven in the morning, in order to compensate for the lack of sleep these two or three days. I was in such a state that at night I didn't hear what anyone said. I couldn't focus my attention. The day before that I couldn't focus my memory; that is, I couldn't find words. I'm trying to drink less water. The heat is such, however, that you perspire away whatever you drink. It's such a pleasure, this perspiring after drinking one's fill, and the kidneys are amazingly comfortable! (Again I'm preoccupied with myself!) Last night I no sooner laid my head down than it was four in the morning and a new group of hajjis came in and made a commotion in the house. They turned on the lights and everyone got up. Then we cleansed ourselves and went to the Prophet's Mosque. The greatest damage from these years of not praying was the loss of the mornings, with their delicate coolness, and the energetic activity of the people. If you get up before sunrise, it's like getting up before Creation, every day witnessing anew this daily transformation from darkness to light, from sleep to wakefulness, from stillness to motion. I was feeling so good this morning that I said hello to everyone, didn't feel like a hypocrite when I prayed, nor that I was doing my ablutions out of imitation. Yesterday and the day before I still couldn't believe this was me performing a religious rite just like everyone else. I remember all the prayers and the short and long verses from the Quran I memorized as a child. Arabic words, however, weigh heavily on my mind and tongue, excessively so. I can't pronounce them quickly. In those days I could read them off like

*Baqi‘ cemetery: Baqiyya‘. See note p. 211

a litany with no problems. I realized this morning, however, that Arabic has become a heavy burden on my conscience. In the morning when I said "Peace be upon you, O Prophet," I had a sudden start. I could see the Prophet's grave and the people circumambulating. They were climbing all over one another to kiss the Shrine. The police were continually scrambling to prevent forbidden behavior . . . I started crying and abruptly fled the mosque . . .

This house we have is newly built, made of cement bricks. They are a little larger than red earthenware bricks, and they used them to fill the foundation. Only the lower level has been completed and finished. What remains is the second floor and half the third floor, where the bricks are visible, the wiring is hanging out of the walls, and there is no running water. Again, there is a bit of water in the pipes in the morning and the evening. Yesterday when I was taking a shower, there was an uproar from my traveling companions. Water was seeping out of the shower room under their belongings. I had to interrupt my shower. There is a corridor running the length of every floor between the rows or rooms. The shower and the toilet are on opposite sides of the hallway, the toilet at the midpoint, and the shower at the end. The toilets, however, are not yet clogged, and that's something to be thankful for. There are three identical housing complexes. They belong to a man named Sayyid Umar the Abyssinian (but he isn't black). Two of them have been rented by two Iranian guides at seven hundred riyals apiece for the duration of the Hajj. The third one is vacant. . . .

This morning a young black man, a member of the Nakhawalah* clan (according to Mohaddes, they are date growers), came to see our guide. He had known my brother, who died here in Medina thirteen years ago. He was the late Borujerdi's† representative here . . . The young man was looking for a job as someone's surrogate on the Hajj. I didn't know what this meant. I asked. Our guide said it was a hajji hired in this locality on behalf of someone's father, mother, or relative, to make the trip from Medina to Mecca to observe the rituals. What was his price? He said, "They pay up to five hundred, but if two hundred fifty is satisfactory, that's all right." He

---

*Nakhawalah: a Shi'ite sect found in Medina and Jidda. They are holdovers from the days when the Shi'ites contributed to the conquest of western Arabia. Most of the other early Shi'ites have since converted to the Shafi'i school of Islam; the Nakhawalah, who did not, became a despised group which was compelled to follow the lowest of trades. [Trans.]

†Borujerdi's: referring to Ayatollah Muhammad Husayn Borujerdi, the Iranian scholar and clergyman who had become the leading religious dignitary of the Shi'ite world by the time of his death in 1961. [Trans.]

was talking about Saudi riyals. I remembered that last night our group's preacher had spoken favorably about this at the close of his sermon, saying, "If your father and mother are remiss [with respect to their religious obligations] and so on, . . . there are people here who will act on their behalf for a small price to release them from this great obligation . . ." Last night I had thought he was making suggestions in order to fill his own belly. Now it seems that this is a business for the Nakhawalahs, a Medina Shiʿite minority. My brother had been an agent for them. He continued this for no more than two years. They buried him in that same graveyard. I'm going to find his grave tomorrow. This preacher in our group is originally from Hamadan. He's been forbidden to preach [in Iran] for political reasons. I know him from the Tuesday night *rowzeh*s* in my father's house. . . .

TUESDAY, APRIL 14 . . . The stupefaction of our retired police major has now turned to terror. He is a morose man with no conception of a good disposition. He's done so much running around in the sun the last few days that he's losing his senses. No matter how much we try to get him to take off his city clothing and loosen his tie, to put on a *dishdashah* or a mantle and a night cap . . . In any case, it would make no difference if he did as those around him do. He has kept up a stiff demeanor right along, as if he were at his administrative post, and he's always bringing up Arafat and Medina and the terror of living in a tent. A man who's spent his life protecting the high walls of houses and prisons is now going to live in a tent? With no walls or doors? I spent an hour last night consoling him and so on. One of his roommates told us that according to a woman in his family, his wife in Tehran had told him that if any problem or any reason to do so should arise, he must drop the whole thing at once and go home. It appears that we must expect new developments.

Among those four or five preachers, *rowzehkhan*s,† and mullas, there is a sayyid in our group from Borujerd; he's hot to find supporters for some mosque they're building in Tehran; I don't know the name of it. He has acquired a following of four or five merchants, and every day they pray together in their room. They have asked us indirectly two or three times why we don't join their prayer. Mohaddes, who follows no one. Uncle, who is not up to it. And Javad, who's strung out all over the place. By

---

rowzeh: an impassioned verse account of the tragedy at Karbala. *Rowzeh*s are used to excite the emotions of the listeners by preachers prior to a sermon. [Trans.]

†*rowzehkhan*: one who specializes in the recitation of *rowzeh*s. [Trans.]

process of elimination, I'm the last one left in our family. He is one of those who think that five extra minutes of prostrations will take him three miles closer to the throne of God. Worse than that, he insists that I go listen to his talk to the villagers following the *maghrib* prayer. I finally went last night. Up on the roof. He did such a job of spoiling the delicate air with the same old nonsense about *shakkiyat,** *ghusl,†* *tathir,‡* and *nejasat§* that it made me sick at my stomach. These things ought not to be said even to the dummies of Mazandaran. Anyway, how long must religion be tied to the handle of *aftabeh,*** and be confined to the realm of "cleansing uncleanness"? Or be a menace to an old fool like me? Do these people hear the highest responsibility of religion? The guy doesn't even have the decency to refrain from immediately raising the subject of the unallowability of a mustache the minute you come near him. Worse than him is the hired mourner in our group, who's evidently deranged. He is in the habit of asking, "Why don't you beat yourself about the head and shoulders?" That's like saying "Why don't you jump off the roof?" when I talk about the tragedy. Praise be unto the preacher in our group, who speaks in terms of history and *hadith,††* and reasonably. He has begun a discussion of the historical period in which the Ka'ba was built and the customs of the Hajj were established. For the villagers. It is useful in any case, if his sermon finally gets around to the Karbala desert situation. He brings tears to the people's eyes, but not with images of tragedy and martyrdom. His words are warm. His own heart has broken. I have explained why. . . .

AFTERNOON OF THE SAME DAY The retired police major is not doing well. We put an ice pack on his head and forced him to lie down. I think he is one of those who are accustomed to solitude; he doesn't know what to do with himself now in the midst of a group. This trip is such that if you are overly concerned with etiquette, you'll have a very difficult time. And we just got

---

shakkiyat: uncertainties. [Trans.]

†*ghusl:* cleansing. [Trans.]

‡*tathir:* purification. [Trans.]

§*nejasat:* uncleanness. [Trans.]

***aftabeh:* a long-spouted water can or ewer used in ablutions. [Trans.]

††*hadith:* also called a "tradition," a *hadith* is an accepted account of something said or done by the Prophet Muhammad, his companions, or one of the imams. *Hadith*s have the status of Scripture in the determination of precedent in Islamic law. [Trans.]

the old fellow's thick winter coat off him today! I don't think he will make it to the end of the trip. Besides him, our own uncle's blood pressure has gone up; it has reached two hundred mm. I still don't understand those numbers. His nephew, who is also Javad's brother, is a member of our own infirmary staff. He came today to take him to the infirmary, and he asked him, "Why did you come?" Now he is quite uncomfortable. He won't even consider food. He can't walk, but we can't be slowing down for him all the time. . . .

Javad sold two of his carpets today for 370 Saudi riyals. He was delighted. He says he made a 150-*toman* profit. They were coarsely woven carpets made for everyday use. When I figure things, I realize I seem to be one of the poorest in the group. I saved one month's salary from the spoils of one or two of these silly books, and set out with four or five thousand *toman*s for the Hajj. That's very inexpensive.

Our situation is such in this house that you wouldn't think we had come for a journey, or at least not for a special kind of journey. We have a common room for prayers and *rowzeh*s in this house. . . . We have a room for the ladies for arguing and chattering, which goes on constantly. We also have a sick room. I went to ask about the condition of the retired major; I saw there were also two other people sleeping on the opposite side of the room. One had diarrhea, the other a cold. My sister said he was afflicted by the heat. I found some vitamin C among my belongings and took it to him. When I gave it to him, he said he thought he had some of his own, and he did. We agreed that he should suck two of them before nightfall so he would feel better. But then I'm feeling pretty bad myself. I've had a headache since noon. Is it possible to remain isolated in the midst of the crowd until the end of the journey? We have been content within the nobility of our own family until now. But later . . . (My condition is clearly not good.) It's easy to be among the people and not be a part of them. I have followed in the shadow of the group up to this very moment. They are all rich and capable! Yet they're so poor in experience it's frightening. They've lived in such poverty that they can't stand any change in routine. I try to get them motivated, but I know it's useless. One's sense of loneliness becomes more acute in a group like this. . . .

WEDNESDAY NIGHT, APRIL 15 It seems that we'll be leaving for Mecca on Friday, wearing the *ihram*. Today Ahmad ibn Wa'il came looking for us. He had been my brother's agent, or his local guide. He had been with him until the moment of his burial. He's black, tall, and powerful, fifty years old, and a clown. He didn't know what had been the cause of my brother's death. He had been out visiting one night, and the next morning his wife told him to get himself over there, but by that time it was too late. He said the Nakhawalah number five thousand, engaged in farming, butchering, buying and selling, and this sort of thing. He is one of them himself. My nephew had sent a letter to him through Javad, who found it this morning and took it over. He brought him to lunch at noon. When we started eating, I saw that he was not. I asked why. He said he wouldn't touch anything until we promised to come for lunch tomorrow. Arab custom. We promised. His purpose in coming, however, had been more to find clients for his services as a surrogate hajji than to seek out old acquaintances, thinking we would praise and recommend him to our guide or our fellow travelers. Javad said he would be happy with three hundred *tomans*. A good price for the dead relatives of the gentlefolk who are with us. He said the population of Medina is sixty thousand. It has three ice companies, two of them in the same gardens I visited. . . .

I went looking for one of the gardens in the Medina area—to the east of where we are staying—to bathe at the water pumps. I knocked on the door, holding a one-riyal bill. A young man came, wearing shorts and holding an *aftabeh*.

"Hello. I came to bathe."

He smiled. Then, "Come in."

I held out the bill. He didn't take it. "Why not?" I said. I realized that he was Shi'ite. "Are you Nakhawalah?" I asked. He said yes. He was not black, however. He knew a bit of Persian. Like all those living in the shrine area, he knew a few words of all the foreign languages. I then discovered that he had known my brother. He asked about his son. He was of the age that they might have been playmates. His name was Abbas. Then he guided me to the fixtures that brought water from the well. They were four inches across, and beneath the spray of water there was a shallow little cement pool. I got his permission to use soap and washed my entire body thoroughly. The date trees in the garden were young. Rue and sweet basil were planted beneath them. The soapy water drained through a gutter behind a wall that separated one part of the garden from another. Even as I delighted in the cool water, I felt sorry for the date trees which will be injured by the nitrous, soapy water. Also for the pomegranates, lush, blooming, and short, growing in clusters below the date palms or in the middle of the plots, giving wonderful coloration to the lifeless, monotonous green of the date palms.

The pump worked constantly, the water came up continuously, and I squatted. Under four inches of water, it was as though I had dived into the ocean. After I came out, I hung around in the gardens until the sunset call to prayer arose from the tops of the minarets in the Prophet's Mosque. . . .

THURSDAY, APRIL 16 I set out at six-thirty in the morning. The blisters on my feet finally got better. I ate a few bites of twice-sifted bread and drank some tea in the doorway to the tearoom on the floor below. Our guide came and sat next to me, confiding that the fellow had gone mad. He was talking about the retired police major. Yesterday he had personally seen him playing with himself when he had come upon him unobserved. It turns out that they had confined him yesterday in one of the lower rooms, which is a storeroom, when this happened. That night he had gone looking for the "supervisor" of the hajjis and asked to be sent back. I thought he wanted my opinion. He didn't wait, however. Continuing, he said, "Yes, when he returned, it was learned that he had broken dishes, scattered the rice, urinated on the door and walls of the room, and other things." The others had swarmed in on him, tied up his hands and feet, rolled him in the dirt, and reported him to the police that night. The police had come and put him in a temporary prison. (We had heard a commotion from the roof where we sleep, but had paid no attention to it.) He had gone to get him out of prison himself and sent him to Jidda the same night to be sent back to Tehran. He boasted that he had gotten a taxi to Jidda for 250 Saudi riyals and had sent one of his employees along with him also. I said it seemed that they had been very hasty and harsh, and certainly, before that, very nosy about his affairs. In any case, however, what choice was there?

"The Hajj is just like the Plain of Judgment," he said. "No one thinks of anyone else." He couldn't let a lunatic like that run loose all day among our women. And so on. I said it was over now. . . .

To the west of Medina, Mount Sala seemed to be blocking the city. As I passed its wide slope on which there were dwellings and streets in every corner, there was a carpet of plastic hoses, each one a different color, green, yellow, red, and blue, carrying water from one side of the street to the other, from this house to that house. They were very long, more than fifty yards, like translucent colored snakes, showing the passage of water and bubbles inside. If the hoses crossed a street used by carts, for two or three yards they turned into iron pipes, and then became plastic again. The city's water circulation system obviously leaves something to be desired. The hoses run to spigots which come out of the ground at every intersection, each hose leading to a house. Beside each spigot there were three or four hoses waiting for a turn, with only the small orifice of one of them drawing water. As I went down to the west, the traffic diminished. I now passed another city full of trees, date palms, and pomegranates. All the date palms were young. All were situated behind the mountain, cut off from Medina, but a part of the city. . . .

We learned that within three years the hajjis would be taken from Medina to Mecca in trucks. Now they use buses with the roofs removed,* and passengers sit comfortably in seats. We took a nap after eating lunch and then left. We went together to visit the Qoba mosque,† south of Medina, closer than Uhud. The mosque is said to have been built on a foundation of piety. It is a large, wide mosque with one minaret. There is a colonnade [*shabestan*] on the side facing the *qibla,* and the other three sides have porticoes; there is also a wide courtyard. We passed new construction everywhere along the road south of the Prophet's Mosque (city expansion is blocked on the west by Mount Sala, and on the east by the graveyard, and also on the north in the direction of Uhud, which is still a shrine area) or new gardens. And such pomegranates, with their blossoms, and minarets, atop newly built mosques with modern designs, all in cement—but white. The city is under construction, with new streets, trenches for pipes, streetlights, and half-finished structures. . . .

SATURDAY, APRIL 18. MECCA We got to Mecca at four-thirty in the morning. We left Medina last night at eight-thirty. Our vehicle was a bus—one of those red ones—whose top had been removed. The passengers took their places in the bus at five in the afternoon. Then there was a very long wait, until eight o'clock, when Javad came and called me. I got stuck with a bad seat, on the third row, next to my uncle. I was the third person in a two-person seat. The driver was a good man. His bus was in good condition, and our

*One of the ritual dress requirements for the performance of the Hajj rites is that nothing be worn on the head. Some pilgrims therefore refuse to ride in vehicles with covered tops. [Trans.]

†Qoba [Quba] mosque: located about three miles southeast of Medina at the site of the Prophet Muhammad's first stopping place after completing the Hijrah; mentioned in the Tawbah Sura of the Quran, VIII and IX. [Trans.]

guide was claiming that he had greased his palm. And so we came directly here, with only one stop, in Rabigh, and another one at the beginning of the trip, at the Haflah mosque, where we made ourselves *muhrim.** In the dark of the night, with no water and no privy. We performed the ritual purifications in the light of the bus's headlights. We had already put on the *ihram* garments in Medina, followed by the mosque rituals, getting back on the bus, and riding on and on and on. The sky and stars overhead were very low, the sky was amazingly close, Scorpio was right in front of us, and the wind blew in our faces constantly (some fifty to sixty miles per hour). We were huddling all the time. Then there was the job of looking after my uncle, an old man who was continually nodding off and in danger of hitting his head on the back of the seat in front of him. Never have I spent a night so awake, and so mindful of nothingness. Under the cover of that sky and that infinity, I recited every poem I'd ever memorized—mumbling to myself— and looked into myself as carefully as I could until dawn. I saw that I was just a piece of straw that had come to the *miqat,* not a person coming to a rendezvous. I saw that time is an infinity, an ocean of time, and that *miqat* exists always and everywhere, and with the self alone. A rendezvous is a place where you meet someone, but the *miqat* of time is just such a meeting with the self. I realized how beautifully that other atheist, Bastami,[†] had put it when he told that hajji bound for the House of God at the gates of Nishapur, "Put your sack of money down, circumambulate *me,* and go back home." I realized that traveling is another way of knowing the self, of evaluating it and coming to grips with its limitations and how narrow, insignificant, and empty it is, in the proving ground of changing climes by means of encounters and human assessments.

SAME DAY, AT BAYT AL-HARAM It appears that even the Ka'ba will have been rebuilt with steel-reinforced concrete by next year, just like the Prophet's Mosque. Not only has the Masa'a between Safa and Marwa been transformed to a huge two-level cement passageway; they are already busy putting in a new rectangular two-story outer colonnade, thereby destroying the one built by the Ottomans. They've already taken out one side of the old outer colonnade, the one facing the Masa'a, and will undoubtedly destroy its other parts within a year or two. It's true that the space available for circumambulation

---

*muhrim: term applied to someone who is in the state of ritual purity required for entry into the Mecca shrine areas for the Hajj. [Trans.]

†Bastami: Beyazid Bastami (died 874), a well-known early Sufi mystic. Al-e Ahmad's use of the word *atheist* here is ironic. [Ed.]

will be wider and that a larger crowd—three or four times the size of the current one—will be able to circumambulate the Ka'ba, but the problem is that they will still be using these cement slabs attached to reinforced-concrete pillars, and building upward with them . . . With beautiful hard rock close at hand, they still use this cement and these cement forms. Apparently, the only thing left of the old outer colonnade will be two or three minarets. They've covered the circumambulation track around the Ka'ba with marble, and those in the covered colonnades as well. There were more people doing the run between Safa and Marwa than there were making the circumambulation. As soon as the sun gets hot, the circumambulation virtually ceases. (I'm now sitting on the upper level of the outer colonnade, writing.) From up here the Ka'ba is just half the size I had imagined. That individual who was architect of this new outer colonnade was evidently unaware that when you destroy proportion, you change architecture. The Ka'ba is still the same size, but they've made the outer corridor twice as wide, and twice as high. How about destroying the Ka'ba itself and making it higher and larger? Out of reinforced concrete, no doubt? (A tall, fat, swarthy man carrying an umbrella just passed, saying "Hajji, sir, mention me in your journal, too— Qandahari of Mashhad."

"Sit down," I said, although there was a hint of mockery in his voice. It seems that this sort of activity is distastefully ostentatious in this setting, although so far I myself have seen two or three others writing on paper, notepads, or what have you. I must be more careful after this. Out in public and writing?) . . .

Mecca has more mountains around it than Jerusalem, and the city is largely made of stone. So much granite! No wonder the pre-Islamic Arabs had crammed so many statues into the House! Bayt al-Haram sits in a depression right at the bottom of the drainage area between the mountains. The water of Zamzam is a kind of reservoir for the rainwater that runs off these granite mountains and collects in that channel. The streets go up and down, mostly following the valleys, with homes on both sides, going up the sides of the mountains, and you find another flank of the mountain in every corner, with another neighborhood and another street. The streets have neon lighting, and there are multicolored miniskyscrapers along the streets, with garish colors in the new windows, such as bright green and burgundy . . . Very primitive, and it badly defaces the city. There are enough garages and motels to satisfy anyone, and then shops, shops, and more shops. They've torn down everything all around Bayt al-Haram in order to build a square which is not yet completed, and dirt is piled up all around in heaps and pits. Hajjis come and go in the midst of the remaining construction equipment.

To build something in this city, there's no need to dig and pour a foundation. No matter how high a building is to be, it may be laid right on a natural stone base and raised from there, except in the depression in the city's center, where Bayt al-Haram is located. It's really in the middle of a big bowl that has a flat layer of sand on the bottom. They've dug a thick foundation there for the new colonnade, and the reinforced concrete forms are still in place. The entire eastern side of Bayt al-Haram is joined to the city by a continuous network of wood and iron construction scaffolding. . . .

MECCA. SAME DAY, SATURDAY This *saʿy* between Safa and Marwa stupefies a man. It takes you right back to fourteen hundred years ago, to ten thousand years ago (it isn't hopping, it's simply going fast) with its jogging, the loud mumbling, being jostled by the others, the self-abandon of the people, the lost slippers—that will get you trampled underfoot if you go back for one moment to recover them—the glazed stares of the crowd, chained together in little groups in a state not unlike a trance, the wheelchairs bearing the old people, the litters borne by two people, one in front and one behind, and this great engulfing of the individual in the crowd. Is this the final goal of this assembly? And this journey? Perhaps ten thousand people, perhaps twenty thousand people, performing the same act in a single instant. Can you keep your wits in the midst of such vast self-abandon? And act as an individual? The pressure of the crowd drives you on. Have you ever been caught in the midst of a terrified crowd fleeing from something? Read *self-abandon* for *terrified,* and substitute *wandering aimlessly* and *seeking shelter* for *fleeing.* One is utterly helpless in the midst of such a multitude. Which one is really an individual? And what is the difference between two thousand and ten thousand?

Each of the Yemenis, filthy, with tangled hair, sunken eyes, and a rope tied around the waist, looks like another John the Baptist risen from the grave. The blacks, heavy, tall, and intense, froth on the lips, moving with all the muscles of their bodies. A woman with her shoes under her arm runs crying like someone lost in the desert. Whatever they are, they don't seem to be human beings to whom one may turn for help. A strong, smiling young man collides with someone and moves on, like a fool in a frenzied bazaar. An old man, panting, is unable to continue, but he is swept on by colliding bodies. I realized I could not watch him be trampled by the people. I took his hand and guided him to the rail in the middle of the runway that separates those coming from those going back. A group of women (there were twelve, fifteen of them) wearing the white *ihram* garments had marked the backs of their necks with violet flower designs, and each held onto another's *ihram* by the waistband. They were moving in one line toward the circumambulation.

You see the ultimate extent of this self-abandon at the two ends of the Masaʿa, which are a bit elevated, and at which you must turn around and go back. The Yemenis jump and spin every time they get there, say salaam to the Kaʿba, then start again. I realized I couldn't do it. I began to cry and fled. I realized what a mistake that infidel Bastami made by not coming to throw himself at the feet of such a crowd, or at least his selfishness . . . Even the circumambulation fails to create such a state. In the circumambulation around the House, you go in one direction shoulder to shoulder with the others, and you go around one thing individually and collectively. That is, there's an objective and a system. You're a particle in a ray of being going around a center. You are thus integrated, not released. More important, there are no encounters. You're shoulder to shoulder with the others, not face-to-face. You see selflessness only in the rapid movement of the bodies of people, or in what you hear them saying. In the *saʿy*, however, you go and come, in Hagar's same wandering manner. There's no aim to what is being done. In this going and coming, what's really disturbing is the continual eye contact. A hajji performing the *saʿy* is a pair of legs running or walking rapidly, and two eyes without a self, or that have leaped out of the self, or been released from it. These eyes aren't really eyes, but naked consciousnesses, or consciousnesses sitting at the edge of the eye sockets waiting for the order to flee. Can you look at these eyes for more than an instant? Before today, I thought it was only the sun that could not be regarded with the naked eye, but I realized today that neither can one look at this sea of eyes . . . and fled, after only two laps. You can easily see what an infinity you create in that multitude from such nothingness, and this is when you are optimistic, and have just begun. If not, in the presence of such infinity you see you are less than nothing. Like a particle of rubbish on the ocean, no, on an ocean of people, or perhaps a bit of dust in the air. To put it more clearly, I realized I was going crazy. I had an urge to break my head open against the first concrete pillar. Unless you do the *saʿy* blind. . . .

Then there are these huge cloths they spread out underfoot! First they soak them with water from the Zamzam Well, then they spread them out beneath the hajjis' feet, end to end, over the House of God's marble carpet and over the hot sand (the marble carpet over the mosque floor is not yet completed), both to prevent the hajjis from burning their feet and to bless the cloth as a commodity for the next life. Apart from the *ihram*, which each keeps, the hajji's greatest souvenir is his burial shroud.

I then went up on the eastern roof and kneeled to pray in a place at the roof's edge overlooking the entire House and the surrounding area. The call to prayer came at six-twenty, later than the usual Medina time. As the call arose, the crowd circumambulating the Ka'ba, moving to the center from the edges, began to quiet down and form circular ranks. By the time the words *"Allahu akbar"* were heard, the entire mosque population was in concentric files. The last circumambulators lined up instantly, but there was still a flurry of activity in that corner where the Black Stone sits in one of the Ka'ba's walls as I began my prostrations. By the time I raised my head again, the entire mosque population was lined up, from one end of the porticoes and rooftops to the other, the greatest number of human beings anywhere who are gathered in one place in response to a command. This assembly must have some meaning! A meaning higher than this dealing, marketing, tourism, discharge of obligation and ritual enactment, economy, government, and a thousand other inevitable things! When the prayer reached the second salaam, from that corner in front of the Stone there was a sudden explosion of people rushing to kiss it. Then the prayer ranks broke, and the circumambulating began anew. At first the ranks nearest the Ka'ba arose and began circling; then those behind them followed a stately rippling motion, moving away from the center. The gentlemen who built these new arched porticoes were aware of the grandeur of their task, but it's a pity. And God save us from all these molded reinforced-concrete structures. Despite this, when finished, it will be the largest uncovered temple on earth, with two new monstrous minarets competing for height.

As I descended the steps, I suddenly realized my foot was burning painfully. I withdrew into a corner and bent over to find the cause of the burning and saw that there were new blisters. Then I looked at my shins and saw that they were covered with strange red blemishes, which continued higher up. I hiked up my *ihram*. It was on my chest and belly too, as well as my arms. Because of my bad liver and this hot sun. As I straightened up to leave, I caught a woman lifting her eyes, looking me over. . . .

SUNDAY, APRIL 19 This Meccan mountain sun is dangerous; it brought back my dry cough. Every day I take a drop of Ipesandrine. So many of the Iranian hajjis are bald! The old men, of course. Especially the villagers. One of them is a very quiet old man who hides his baldness beneath a stocking cap and avoids the others like an ailing fowl. He lives in the corridor night and day. I paid him no heed in Medina, but here I can't help it. Yesterday, when I went to get a drink from my canvas water bottle which I hang in the window that opens on the corridor, I saw him. We were all having lunch. He, however, had placed a bowl of ice water in front of himself and sat alone, arms around his knees, smoking a cigarette, like a scolded child. You would think he came on the Hajj to mourn. I sat beside him and told him these things. It turned out he was from Tafresh, alone, with no friends in the group and no one from his province. Worst of all, he had diarrhea. I called among the women to my sister to see if anyone had some mild food for him. Then I said to him, "Hajji, dear, everyone gets diarrhea. This climate is bad. I am still on a restricted diet myself; diarrhea isn't contagious," and this sort of nonsense. Now he has come and joined the group. Really, the incident with that police major has made me apprehensive. At least this Tafreshi knows he is bald and protects his head from this fiendish sun. The others don't know this much. Their heads are blistered, just like the effects of erysipelas. I saw another one at the infirmary with a swollen head. Instead of a bandage, they had wrapped a turban around it and sent him back. The sun shines and the wind blows on all these heads. I have now gradually become a full-time doctor and secretary for our group, dispensing salt tablets, vitamin C, Ipesandrine, and the like and, most often, bandages. Every time the good people return from circumambulation and *sa'y,* it is as if they have just returned from the battle of Khaybar—some part of them is injured. They all know I have bandages. So much skin had peeled off a Mazandarani's big toe that I put three Band-Aids on it. Today I wrote my second letter as group secretary, for that fussy Mazandarani. He has an interesting name as well, Haj Ba'uch. What does that mean? He did not know. His letter consisted of two lines of news of the journey and then two pages of greetings to about fifty people. . . .

Three times so far I have seen young men holding the hands of their brides—almost embracing them—during circumambulation. A Hajj honeymoon? I say they were brides because of their beautiful, intricately designed, flowered or silver embroidered veils or because of their jealously protective men. I also saw pregnant women two or three times, almost due, doing the circumambulation the same as the others, without any precaution or fear. The hajjis, however, are extremely solicitous. . . .

SAME DAY I've been on a restricted diet ever since leaving Medina. Tea, compote, and yogurt. I adopted the latter in Mecca, but it's too bad it's so sour. The compote I had for lunch was from Japan, something like peaches or apricots. The mango juice was from India. Everything is from somewhere. They bring food here from all over the world. It's no joke. All these people, and such a market! Perhaps one may say that the Hajj rites provide an occasion to liquidate surplus for all the factories of the world. The good people traveling with us are all busy buying things. Now they are inspecting their purchases, comparing prices, and exchanging information on what is available where and which merchants have bargains and which don't. Tea, tamarind, cloth, red rubies, snake skins (for the well-to-do), robes, black chadors, perfume, *mumena'i* (which is pure pitch from oil wells), watches, men's shirts, socks, shoes, and a lot of other things . . . All of them from some corner of the world. . . .

MONDAY, APRIL 20 This morning I began buying things, too. A market like this gets a person into the mood to buy things. I think most of the things people buy as souvenirs are bought in this very manner, as a reaction to the frenzy of the bazaar. Then when they return to their own country, they label each purchase as a souvenir for some family member, relative, friend, or acquaintance. I bought two Arab head scarves, three bamboo canes, several bundles of aloe branches, and four ballpoint pens. "What did you buy?" asked my good fellow travelers. They liked the pens, and several people went to buy some of them. They didn't like the bamboo, however. No one said anything, but the reason was understandable. After all, the lance that struck Ali Asghar's* throat was made of bamboo. Can one write a Mecca travel diary and not go into the events at Karbala?

The movement toward Mina began today. The streets are unbelievably crowded. And how these drivers honk their horns! . . .

NIGHT, SAME DAY. ARAFAT We started out in a truck at nine in the morning, and we got there at eleven, although we had been waiting to leave since five. This "mechanized" primitivity is something else. Leaving Mecca and reaching the Plain of Arafat was a supreme effort in every way. A person learns the meaning of religious expressions here. Waiting, waiting, waiting, as in the past. The saving grace is that in such a situation I immerse myself in this little notebook, sequestering myself behind its paper doors—no matter what happens. Then we left and traveled thirteen or fourteen miles in three hours. The truck was constantly braking, with the hajjis continually falling all over one another and shouting. (Javad called me to get on top of the truck, over the driver's cab, so I did. I didn't know why at first. The wind blew under my *ihram* garments, and I was badly chilled.) We would take off suddenly at full throttle and two steps later the blaring of horns, the squealing of brakes,

*Ali Asghar: the infant son of Imam Husayn, who was killed along with his father at Karbala. [Trans.]

and then the angry shouts of hajjis falling all over one another. The women had been seated in front of the truck, the men behind. When the brakes were applied, everyone was dumped together, and such pandemonium. Then we reached a desert, one *farsakh* by two *farsakh*s. There were tents erected everywhere, ropes crisscrossing and a crossroads in the middle. There was a mosque on one street, on another stores, bakeries, and butcher shops. The entire plain was without electrical power. In the light of kerosene lanterns large and small, hanging and setting, meat carcasses hung on large tripods in front of stores and tents, and there were coffeehouses open for business. A store owner was asleep on the counter, bakery ovens were still wet on the outside, and the Bedouins were asleep right alongside the main road among their goats and sheep, which had blue feet and henna-dyed backs and necks.

There were tents, tents, tents. Here, even the police and the armed soldiers were dressed in *ihram,* but they patrol with rifles on their shoulders. Only the traffic police are allowed to wear their uniforms, guiding the Bedouin drivers with motions of their nightsticks. There are also boy scouts helping people locate their tents. We are relatively comfortable, and we are now in our tent. Everyone is worried about his place, about the carpet, about dinner, and everything else. It turns out we are at the foot of a mountain. It is cold, and everyone is talking about Mount Mercy, which we saw at a distance as we were arriving, with the moving flickers of hand lanterns on its flanks and peak. Too bad it's so cold, and my fatigue and cough won't let me; otherwise I would go out and spend an hour mingling with the crowd. The devil take this bronchitis, which by now is tracheitis. For tonight I will note that they call the place Arafat because Adam and Eve found each other and got acquainted on that mountain after their expulsion from Paradise. . . .

SAME DAY. When we got here last night, we were spreading out our lightweight bedding when I saw a large insect walking on the blanket. It resembled a beetle. I killed the poor thing, and all at once I realized I shouldn't have. Killing God's creatures dressed in *ihram*! But it was too late. Mohaddes, who took one end of the blanket so we could shake him off, said that it was dangerous. May it rest in peace, God willing! Then we ate dinner and went to sleep. And such a cold night! I wrapped the towel of my *ihram* around my body beneath the blanket and lay down, coughing, with the help of fifteen drops of Ipesandrine.

As for this Arafat, it is a desert, like a plain surrounded on three sides by mountains, on the road to Ta'if. An elevated plain, with a concave surface and cooler than the surrounding area, to some extent a grassland, especially at the base of the mountains. It is to the east of Mecca. The bottom of the concave surface is covered with fine sand, resembling that of the sea, with seashell fragments, or something bright, shiny, and cream colored. Even at the top of the heights and between the rocks on the mountains. When we got here last night, a cool breeze began to blow. I saw a bush resembling heather today on top of the rise. Then the sheep and goats were grazing on the heights of the area in groups, in addition to the livestock that was lingering with the people among the tents. It seemed as if they wanted to let the sheep feed on grass once more before sacrificing them. (Yesterday—8 Dhu al-Hijja—was Yawm al-Tarwiyya, or the Day of Washing.) I saw this business of coming to Arafat in a throng as being originally a kind of *sizdahbedar,* like a picnic. The side we are on is at the base of a mountain, and the tents of all the Iranians and Shi'ites are over on this side, grouped together. . . .

First thing in the morning they, mostly Bedouins and Yemenis, began slaughtering animals. Carcasses being skinned or gutted are hanging by their tents on frames, with little piles of sheep guts, intestines, and skin and a pungent smell in the air. I don't know what we would do if this sun weren't so hot that it dries anything in half an hour. . . .

I put out a cigarette in the sand the way one does at the seaside. It has become very hot, and I have taken the towel from my shoulder and replaced it with a white cambric shawl. Last night there were perhaps five hundred thousand kerosene lanterns burning in the desert. Only a few official health facilities and the mosque had electricity. The four main streets are asphalt, two or three miles. The rest of the roads are dirt, meaning sand. It turns out that one simply cannot leave the tent in the afternoon. I thought I would read the Quran awhile. Now I am at the end of the *sura* of the cow. I was making notes on my problems in the margins of the Quran's pages when I saw that my companions couldn't stand to see it. It seems that I ought to stop it. Some restrictions must be preserved in any case.

WEDNESDAY, FEAST OF THE SACRIFICE, APRIL 22 Yesterday afternoon at four o'clock the people began leaving for Mina, beginning with those on foot, the Bedouins, the nimble footed, and those with no baggage. We stayed until nine. We ate dinner on a carpet of sand, outside the tents, beneath the sky, when our belongings were in the truck, the other people had gone, and the feeling of this one day of Bedouin life in the open spaces was coming alive. The tents—now that the people aren't here to separate you from the environment with their trampling—are quite beautiful. They erect the tents for the Arafat rites two or three days beforehand in anticipation of the arrival of the hajjis, and then after the pilgrims leave, they remain up for two or three more days until they come and collect them. I walked among them. They are like capsized ships, the guy lines their oars, and they are in sand instead of water. . . . The remains of this Bedouin picnic consisted of campfire ashes, the remains of carcasses, and little piles of bones. There is no sign of a dog or a cat. What would happen if we stayed here one or two more days?

Last night was the most difficult we have had on this journey. We rode on top of the same truck from nine until ten-thirty, dressed the same way in *ihram* garments, in the same cold. We went back by the same route until we reached a pass that was full of buses, automobiles, and trucks. Scattered campfires flickered in the darkness; there was the smell of livestock, and the sound of the herd's footsteps, like a continuous thumping sound behind a wall at a dark meeting where you are sitting and waiting, along the edge of the pass. We slept on rocky ground. The women stayed in the truck, the men on the ground at the foot of the mountain. The four of us had one travel carpet, which we spread out beneath ourselves, and we stretched out in pairs, each sharing half the blankets, which we pulled up to our shoulders. My back was up against a thornbush, and there beside me were my uncle, Mohaddes, and Javad, in that order. Our traveling companions searched for small rocks in the darkness or by lamplight, for use in tomorrow's stoning of Satan. From time to time a flock passed below us, without a sound, as if they were all asleep, with only the striking of their hooves to indicate that they are alive. Sometimes there was the clop of a camel's hoof passing among the flock. Until morning there was the *hee-haw* of the shepherds and the tossing and turning of the other travelers, the cold that came into the unprotected *ihram*s, my coughing, and my uncle's complaining. My thoughts concerned the conditions for perpetuating the ecstasy of a tradition. I know that on such a night one must try to perceive the significance of the coming dawn. One thinks and then it becomes clear, just when the world becomes clear; it is like the experience of that old woman who waited and swept for forty days in her home expecting a visit from Khizr* and on the final day didn't see

*Khizr, or al-Khadhir: "the Green One," a famous figure in Arab folklore. He is said to have discovered and partaken of the fountain of youth, and thereby become immortal. Legends say that he wanders about in a green cloak, carrying out God's commandments and protecting people from misfortune. [Trans.]

him. At the last moment, fatigue, the cold, and sleeplessness had so over-whelmed me that I didn't even want to get up, even to look inside myself in the darkness of the last of the night. Self and other were quite intermingled, and the borders unclear. In that dark pass of Mash'ar al-Haram, even the distinctions between human and animal were blurred. I asked myself as I lay there, "Wasn't this the goal of the call? Isn't this also the thing you said *labayk* to? What does it mean to get beyond self?"

The pleasant aroma of coffee assailed my nostrils. Several steps away from us a "Bedouin" family was making coffee on its morning campfire. Such an aroma arose from it into the dark air that you might have thought it was a smell that could lift you into heaven. Javad got up. I heard him saying hello and exchanging courtesies in his broken Arabic, and the sound of cups and boiling coffee. I was in such bad shape, however, that I couldn't even get up and take part in that coffee banquet. I thought that for the one who has been reared and trained for this life, and who knows all its ways, there is even poetry about nights in such a desert, and hot coffee at its dawn. This is not only a renewer of strength for himself, but there is also even a share for me in its aroma, and God knows why I came from that side of the world on this journey.

SAME DAY, SAME PLACE We left Mash'ar al-Haram at five in the morning. We came a mile until the road was blocked. This took two hours. No exag-geration. We had to go through another narrow pass. Everyone was in a hurry. If one yard's space appeared among the vehicles, they gave it full throttle, then a sudden braking, and the ninety people in the truck were so piled to-gether I couldn't stand the sight of it. I jumped down off the top of the truck and began walking among the multitude of pedestrians. I knew the direc-tion of the Shi'ite tent area. I had directions. Now I was one among the many. We gradually moved ahead of the line of vehicles, where hajjis were packed together waiting. Waiting, waiting, waiting, for the road to open, for the commotion to die down, for the heat of the sun to subside, for there to be water in the faucets, for the privy to be empty, for food to be ready, and a thousand other fors. On this journey you continually go from one rendez-vous to the next. But time is so meaningless that it has no structure. . . .

I first passed behind a high cement wall, a slaughterhouse. Then I col-lapsed on a straw mat at the first temporary coffeehouse along the road, beneath a thatch awning. I had a bit of bread with tea and continued. At the base of the mountain I passed a water tower under construction and turned onto one of the streets, passing among the tents. The crowd of pilgrims was intermingling in groups, with the leaders bearing emblems to show the way.

They passed swarming among the tents with the kind of fear and urgency I used to see as a child in the Tehran bazaar on ʿAshura.* Everyone was saying *labayk,* and wearing white. For the first time today I realized how many varieties there are even of the color white. Dirty white, cream, blue-white, milk white, shiny white, dark white, and so on. The people were making a huge uproar, and there was a lot of extra activity generated by the fear of getting lost! As we went, I felt that we were climbing. The road became narrower, and I said to myself that surely we were approaching the *jamarat* area. There were residential dwellings here and there, built on naked boulders, with walls, balconies, doors, and water faucets. People stood watching on the rooftops. Or pilgrims? As we were climbing, the road suddenly ended, and it became apparent that an unguided group had come to a dead end. I was terrified for a moment by the pressure of the crowd. Alone in an unfamiliar crowd, everyone speaking a different language. The Tower of Babel fallen into a tiny cobblestone street. I climbed up on a carved stone wall; from a half yard above the heads of the crowd, I called out to every Iranian pilgrim that this street was a dead end, that they must go back, and to help pass the word to the back of the crowd. They began doing this. Then in Arabic: *"Awqifu! Ma bishariʿ!"* Several times.

The crowd crushed an old man so hard against the cobblestones of the wall that he passed out. We lifted him up to the top of the wall, where the local people brought water to bring him around. Fear of getting lost, fear of unfamiliar places, the desire to see things, and the desire to participate in the acts and rituals of the Hajj make a strange, totally unfamiliar amalgamation of every hajji. Totally agitated and without self, a particle in a flood. All the preliminaries are there for you to forget your will. My own *ihram* came open three times. Not only the towel over my shoulders, even my *izar.*† I understood then why pilgrims bring so much baggage with them, plus wallets, iceboxes, and so on. I lost my field notebook with the pencil inside it during all this. On the way back I looked everywhere in the temporary stores, but couldn't find a notepad. I bought a pencil, however, for six piastres. . . .

A WORD ABOUT THIS SLAUGHTERHOUSE It's a huge area surrounded by a wall with two entrances. There are large pits dug and prepared in groups,

---

* ʿAshura: the tenth day of the lunar month of Muharram, the day when Imam Husayn and his followers were martyred at Karbala in the year 680. [Trans.]

† *izar:* the lower half of the *ihram,* covering the body from the navel to the knees. [Trans.]

with mounds of earth scooped out of the pits and piled up higher than the walls, visible from the outside. All the ground is covered with carcasses, goats, sheep, and camels; there are no cattle to be seen. The muscles quiver on freshly killed carcasses. Children, knives in hand, play with their remains. One's feet are constantly stepping in blood and entrails, and I held up the hem of my *ihram* as I walked. One individual wearing the *ihram* was making a film with a sixteen-millimeter camera. Two or three employees of the Office of Health and Security were with him.* Everyone was standing around holding dull knives. They decapitated a goat and threw the head to one side. A young boy came and drove the point of a knife into the goat's throat, and the goat went into violent convulsions as the blood spurted out of its throat. It was clear that the boy was experienced and knew what to do to make the carcass dance. I don't know where he thrust the knife to make the convulsions greater. In any case he knew something that I did not know. A camel lying on the ground jerked twice— from one end to the other—by the time I got to him, and that was all. The blood coming out of a hand's-width gash in his neck was frothy, looking like fluffy light purple soapsuds on the ground. Such a huge carcass! A man had thrust a dagger into its neck above the sternum right where it stood, in the tuft of hair at the base of the neck. He made a hand's-width slash downward, and when the animal tried to turn its head, he struck it in the nose with his fist. The animal roared and tried to run, but its legs were hobbled. It fell on the ground. It tried to get up, but the blood spurted out, it couldn't, and it slowly, slowly collapsed. It lowered its neck gradually until its head touched the ground. When I got there, it was gasping; this stopped a moment later. Then two jerks, and that was the end. This is the most terrifying facet of this motorized primitivity. I almost passed out two or three times. I remembered the first time I visited the anatomy hall at the medical school. I had stopped to look with blind, adolescent courage. I rationalized to myself that this day of killing—and of animals—was perhaps originally a way to prevent the killing of people. If we go back to Abraham's sacrifice of his son . . . this is true. It can be rationalized, in any case, but a slaughterhouse of this type is a scandal. Seeing it once is the best possible advertisement for vegetarianism. If they had had just one scene from this slaughterhouse in the film *Mondo Cane,* they would have made a fortune. . . .

---

*I heard that the same year a group of Indonesians made a film of the Hajj rituals, as well as a French group. The French film was shown on French television. My brother saw it in Paris and told me about it. [Author]

I saw three blacks—a woman, a man, and a child—who had claimed a camel. They were cutting the red flesh away from the bones piece by piece. The animal's large white ribs were just like long stalks of rhubarb.

In another place a young man holding a knife stood up from inside the rib cage of a fallen, half-stripped camel so suddenly that I was stopped in my tracks. It startled me. Groups of live sheep and goats stood waiting in the midst of this filth, with the occasional huge camel. The goats were chewing their cud, the sheep napping. Only the goats sensed what was happening; they were very upset and kept bleating. The police at the slaughterhouse entrance would not allow new groups to enter before the others already inside had been killed.

As I see it, they satisfy two or three primitive human urges with this huge sacrifice. One was mentioned previously: sacrificing animals instead of human beings. Sheep instead of Ishmael. Kill animals in order to refrain from killing human beings. It is also the best possible practice in the use of knives, in shedding blood, seeing blood. Women, men, and children, knives in hand, take such delight in carcasses, for procuring provisions or simply for the thrill of it. Several times I saw people cutting up carcasses just for fun, and such a gleam of delight in their eyes. You'd think they were all studying anatomy, or exulting in victory after some heroic deed. Finally, this is itself a form of exercise. Standing and bending, skinning the carcasses, dallying with them, and so on. We get no other exercise on the Hajj except walking and pelting the pillars. This primeval picnic needs two or three vigorous activities in any case, and this is the third and last of them. . . .

It's clear that for years and years to come, the Hajj rites will continue, because they provide visits to shrines, tourism, business, entertainment, and experience for every villager who leaves his farm and has no other opportunity to see the world and have the experiences of a journey. If, however, we were able to make this pilgrimage suitable, not for a man of the twentieth century, but for a man of the fourteenth century, one could hope that the Hajj would be a stage of development and an experience in the lives of the people of the Muslim nations. If not, as it stands now, the Hajj is mechanized barbarism. That's all. My hand is aching. . . .

JIDDA AIRPORT. THURSDAY, APRIL 30 Now that we've boarded, it's a four-engine propeller-driven craft. They claimed we'd return by jet. There was no place for myself and three or four other people who came aboard last. They had to bring us into a little compartment behind the cockpit used as a resting place for the crew. There is a table in the middle with two long benches on each side. It was hard to get in. Its disadvantage is the sound of the motor right in your ear. You can't sleep; neither can you do anything while awake. I must again take refuge in this notebook. What would have happened on this trip if I hadn't had the companionship of this notebook? We will be airborne three hours and thirty-five minutes, they announced. The aircraft vibrates a lot. The nuts and bolts of the seats were loose. I tightened two of them with the screwdriver in my pocketknife. They tore my clothes. . . .

The way I see it, I've come on this trip mostly out of curiosity, the same way I poke my nose into everything, to look without expectations. Now I've seen it, and this notebook is the result. This was an experience, too, in any case—or perhaps a very simple event. Every one of these experiences and events was simple and uneventful. Although it was quite ordinary, it was the basis of a kind of awakening, and if not an awakening—at least a skepticism. In this way I am smashing the steps of the world of certainty one by one with the pressure of experience, beneath my feet. And what is the result of a lifetime? That you come to doubt the truth, solidity, and reality of the primary axioms that bring certainty, give cause for reflection, or incite action, give them up one by one, and change each of them to a question mark. At one time I thought my eyes saw through all the world's illusions. Now that I belong to one corner of the world, if I fill my eyes with images from all other corners of the world, I will become a man of the entire world. I think it was Paul Nizan who wrote in *Aden-Arabie* that "a man is not merely a pair of eyes. If, in your travels, you cannot change your position in history just as you change your geographical position, what you have done is futile." Along the same lines I realized that a man is an aggregation of life and culture mixed together, with certain capabilities and circumscribed ties. In any case, a man is not merely a mirror, but a mirror in which specific things are reflected, even that Hamadan pilgrim who's still wearing his sheepskin vest. But then, a mirror has no language, and you want to have only a language. Is this not what separates the eye in the head from the eye of the heart? When I assess the matter, I can see that with the eye of my heart I don't even know myself and the familiar life of Tehran, Shemiran, and Pachinar.* So what image have I given in the mirror of this notebook? Wouldn't it have been better if I had done the same thing a million other people did this year who came on the Hajj? And those millions of millions

*Shemiran is an upper class district in northern Tehran. Pachinar is an old district in southern Tehran. [Trans.]

of other people who've visited the Ka'ba during these fourteen hundred or so years and had things to say about it, but said nothing and took the results of the experience with them selfishly to the grave? Or simply discussed it with their sisters, mothers, children, and families for four days and then nothing? Isn't it really better if we let the experience of every event rot like a seed in the center of its fruit? Instead of eating the fruit and planting the seed? Obviously, with this notebook I have given a negative answer to this sincere question. And why? Because Iranian intellectuals spurn these events and walk among them gingerly and with distaste. "The Hajj?" they say. "Don't you have anywhere else to go?" Ignoring the fact that this is a tradition that calls a million people to a single place every year and prevails upon them to engage in a single ritual. Anyway, it was necessary to see, to be there, to go, and to witness, to see what changes there have or have not been since the time of Naser-e Khosraw.

In any event, whether it be a confession, a protest, heresy, or whatever, I mainly came on this trip looking for my brother—and all those other brothers—rather than to search for God. And God is everywhere for those who believe in him.

21

Malcolm X
United States
1964

꧁꧂

*Yes, I'm an extremist. The black race here in North America is in
extremely bad condition. You show me a black who isn't an extremist, and I'll show you one who needs psychiatric attention.*

—Malcolm X

*After a throwaway youth as a ghetto hustler, after seven years in jail for theft
and another twelve preaching the dogma of a race-based cult, Malcolm X came
into his own. His public adoption of mainstream Islam, a year before his death,
was central to this process. He considered the Hajj a turning point. He went to
Mecca twice in his last months.*

*Malcolm Little was born in Omaha, Nebraska, in 1925. His father Earl
Little, an itinerant Baptist preacher, was an ardent follower of Marcus Garvey's
Universal Negro Improvement Association and president of its local chapter.
Malcolm's mother, Louise—half-Scottish, half-Grenadan—followed Garvey, too.
A self-educated Jamaican, Garvey led the largest organization in the history of
the African diaspora, with two million members by 1924. His success disturbed
a young lawyer named J. Edgar Hoover, the newly appointed FBI director, and
Garvey was falsely indicted on charges of mail fraud.*

*Malcolm was born the year Garvey went to prison. Three months later,
fifty thousand Klansmen marched through Washington D. C. For blacks, it was
a frightening and apocalyptic period. The fourth of eight children, Malcolm grew
up in a poor household permeated by liberation theology. Black pride, racial
separatism, the Negro nation were Garveyite watchwords. His half-sister Ella
Collins later remarked that "progressive programs and ideas were in Malcolm's
natural makeup. He inherited it."*

*Malcolm's adult attraction to the Nation of Islam, starting in 1948, was
a logical outcome of this early background. The group's leader, Elijah Muhammad*

Poole, promised to help his followers escape injustice and racial exploitation by bringing their community under genuine black control. A weapon of protest, a means of self-definition, the Nation specialized in rebuilding wasted lives. This vision of racial oppression as a condition to be combated inspired Malcolm X, and he labored tirelessly in Elijah's cause throughout the 1950s. Spurred by his eloquence as a speaker, enrollment grew from a few hundred to forty thousand blacks in a few years. Thirty-eight NOI "temples" were founded by 1959, from New York to Los Angeles and Atlanta, and Malcolm had a hand in almost all of them. There were schools and small businesses, too, a national newspaper, real estate holdings, and thirty radio stations.

   Malcolm's much-publicized break with Elijah Muhammad in 1963 removed a final barrier to the freedom of self-expression he had lived for. Now he came to understand the Nation's shortcomings. Despite an extensive infrastructure, the NOI was not much of a religion. As the novelist James Baldwin pointed out, its homespun "Islam" built up black pride by demonizing whites as a race of devils. It mixed powerful insights with harebrained myths, and it deified its founder, a heretical transgression for believing Muslims. The NOI wrapped itself in Islamic symbols but ignored or reconfigured traditional practices. Members did not fast during Ramadan or go to Mecca. Their liturgy only vaguely resembled Muslim prayer. More damaging for a black-power group in the early 1960s, Elijah withheld from his membership the concept of jihad, of the fight fought in defense of rights and freedom. This idea, so misconstrued by Muslims and non-Muslims alike, has played a key role in traditional Islam. After his Sunni conversion in 1964, Malcolm gravitated to it quickly. In jihad, and in the Hajj as well, he found the framework for a global liberation movement. It reached him like an echo of Marcus Garvey.

   The following excerpts are drawn from the final chapters of Malcolm X's bestselling autobiography, written with Alex Haley. They convey the transformation at work in the last year of his life. An honored guest on the flight from Cairo, he is invited into the cockpit by the captain. Hours later, in a major reversal, Saudi officials detain him at the Jidda airport, where he is regarded as an oddity by all and issued a court summons. The next day, however, we find him released into the custody of a Saudi architect—coincidentally, the man in charge of renovating the Great Mosque. These passages are followed by an extract from a letter Malcolm wrote from Mecca after the Hajj. It testifies to significant changes in his thoughts about race in the United States. Malcolm's subsequent political networking in Mecca shows us the Hajj as an annual Muslim version of a UN General Assembly. In the last selection, Faysal ibn

Abd al-Aziz makes his third appearance in these records, this time not as Viceroy or Prince but as King.

By orthodox standards, Malcolm X barely qualified as a Muslim when he first went to Mecca. His Hajj deepened his religious practice. It also helped legitimize him as a leader. Indeed, events suggest that this was part of the purpose for his journey. Weeks before leaving for Mecca, Malcolm founded a new organization in Harlem named Muslim Mosque, Incorporated. It is at this point in the autobiography, a paragraph after describing the new mosque, that he mentions the Hajj for the first time. "There was one further major preparation that I knew I needed. I'd had it in mind for a long time—as a servant of Allah." It is worth pointing out here that only a real Muslim may found a mosque and that the surest way to be recognized as one by other Muslims is to make the Hajj. Viewed in its proper sequence, Malcolm's first trip to Mecca was more than a personal quest in pursuit of vision. It was also a quest for wider validation, for what his recent biographer, Lewis DeCaro, Jr., has called "religious authenticity in the Muslim world." It is a theme we have seen at work in these accounts since the Middle Ages.

Pilgrims bring to Mecca what they find there. Malcolm brought a lifelong hunger for racial equity. A few nights among the tents in Mina Valley led him to announce that "it takes all of the religious, political, economic, psychological, and racial ingredients, or characteristics, to make the Human Family and Human Society complete." Set against life in Harlem, Malcolm's Hajj was a brief stroll through a social paradise. Its heightened spirit, sacred laws, and democratic dress enabled him to experience equality on a scale unimaginable before. He enjoyed a few days of the racial ease he had dreamed of, and he came home buoyant, prepared to improvise. "Malcolm was free," his friend the entertainer, Ossie Davis, later recalled. "No one who knew him before and after his trip to Mecca could doubt that he had completely abandoned racism, separatism, and hatred." Most photographs from this period show him smiling, an expression rarely caught in prior years. He had shed what he called his "old hate and violence image." Enthusiasm overflows these pages. He displayed new detachment, too, and was able to joke about himself. "I used to parrot Elijah's views," he quipped in a speech at Harvard University. "Now the parrot has jumped out of the cage."

Our first author, Naser-e Khosraw, much like Malcolm X, transformed a dissolute and restrictive past into a powerful role as a reformer while on the pilgrimage. Both men went to Cairo, and then to Mecca, to study for the Muslim ministry. Returning home, Khosraw survived an attempted assassination for his new beliefs and escaped to the mountains. Malcolm, by contrast, died in a hail of bullets on February 21, 1965, while addressing a few hundred followers in Harlem. The Nation is widely blamed for his death, and most of Malcolm's last

*statements concur with this. He knew that NOI factions in Chicago and New
York were determined to end his influence, and he understood their vindictive
mentality; he had helped shape it. Malcolm bore no illusions about his position.
"If I'm alive when this book comes out, it will be a miracle," he told Haley. He
died a few weeks before its publication.*

*Malcolm X has been called the man who almost changed America. In the
years after his death, he became a small industry. He has been purveyed in hip-
hop culture as a militant icon, a charismatic leader, and the angriest man in the
United States. Spike Lee's 1992 Hollywood film reestablished Malcolm's charismatic image around the world. Meanwhile, academic scholars with new agen-
das have variously psychoanalyzed him, placed his development in a Trotskyite
or pan-African frame, lionized his heroism, exposed his apparent sexism, and
generally reread his inner life as a set of choices. For them, and for non-Muslims
in general, the determining factors in Malcolm's life were historical, political,
and racial forces. His profoundly religious nature, his almost mystical combination of militancy and submission, is largely ignored. Yet when Malcolm came to
dictate his own story, he told the tale in religious terms. Others have felt obliged
to explain him socially or psychologically, but in Malcolm's eyes his fate was the
work of God. He experienced life as a drama of salvation, and by and large that
is how he told it. Popular culture has enshrined him as a secular figure because
that is an easy way to deal with him. Unfortunately, it omits from the picture
the forces that guided him. Returning from Mecca, he changed his name to
al-Hajj Malik al-Shabazz, the name continued by his wife and children. On
his death certificate, in the box marked "business or industry," someone correctly
inscribed the word* Islam.

from The Autobiography of
Malcolm X

CAIRO AIRPORT. APRIL 1964 The literal meaning of Hajj in Arabic is to set
out toward a definite objective. In Islamic law, it means to set out for [the]
Ka'ba, the Sacred House, and to fulfill the pilgrimage rites. The Cairo airport was where scores of Hajj groups were becoming *muhrim*, pilgrims, upon
entering the state of *ihram*, the assumption of a spiritual and physical state

of consecration. Upon advice, I arranged to leave in Cairo all of my luggage and four cameras, one a movie camera. I had bought in Cairo a small valise, just big enough to carry one suit, shirt, a pair of underwear sets, and a pair of shoes into Arabia. Driving to the airport with our Hajj group, I began to get nervous, knowing that from there in, it was going to be watching others who knew what they were doing, and trying to do what they did.

Entering the state of *ihram,* we took off our clothes and put on two white towels. One, the *izar,* was folded around the loins. The other, the *rida,* was thrown over the neck and shoulders, leaving the right shoulder and arm bare. A pair of simple sandals, the *na'l,* left the anklebones bare. Over the *izar* waistwrapper, a money belt was worn, and a bag, something like a woman's big handbag, with a long strap, was for carrying the passport and other valuable papers, such as the letter I had from Dr. Shawarbi.*

Every one of the thousands at the airport, about to leave for Jidda, was dressed this way. You could be a king or a peasant, and no one would know. Some powerful personages, who were discreetly pointed out to me, had on the same thing I had on. Once thus dressed, we all had begun intermittently calling out *"Labayk! Labayk!"* ("Here I come, O Lord!") The airport sounded with the din of *muhrim* expressing their intention to perform the journey of the Hajj.

Planeloads of pilgrims were taking off every few minutes, but the airport was jammed with more, and their friends and relatives waiting to see them off. Those not going were asking others to pray for them at Mecca. We were on our plane, in the air, when I learned for the first time that with the crush, there was not supposed to have been space for me, but strings had been pulled, and someone had been put off because they didn't want to disappoint an American Muslim. I felt mingled emotions of regret that I had inconvenienced and discomfited whoever was bumped off the plane for me and, with that, an utter humility and gratefulness that I had been paid such an honor and respect.

Packed in the plane were white, black, brown, red, and yellow people, blue eyes and blond hair, and my kinky red hair—all together, brothers! All honoring the same God Allah, all in turn giving equal honor to each other.

From some in our group, the word was spreading from seat to seat that I was a Muslim from America. Faces turned, smiling toward me in greeting. A box lunch was passed out, and as we ate that, the word that a Muslim from America was aboard got up into the cockpit.

*Dr. Mahmoud Youssef Shawarbi, Egyptian scholar, author, and UN adviser, helped Malcolm X with his pilgrim visa in New York.

The captain of the plane came back to meet me. He was an Egyptian; his complexion was darker than mine; he could have walked in Harlem, and no one would have given him a second glance. He was delighted to meet an American Muslim. When he invited me to visit the cockpit, I jumped at the chance. . . .

JIDDA The Jidda airport seemed even more crowded than Cairo's had been. Our party became another shuffling unit in the shifting mass with every race on Earth represented. Each party was making its way toward the long line waiting to go through customs. Before reaching customs, each Hajj party was assigned a *mutawwif,* who would be responsible for transferring that party from Jidda to Mecca. Some pilgrims cried, *"Labayk!"* Others, sometimes large groups, were chanting in unison a prayer that I will translate: "I submit to no one but thee, O Allah. I submit to no one but thee. I submit to thee because thou hast no partner. All praise and blessings come from thee, and thou art alone in thy kingdom." The essence of the prayer is the oneness of God.

Only officials were not wearing the *ihram* garb, or the white skullcaps, long, white, nightshirt-looking gown, and the little slippers of the *mutawwif,* those who guided each pilgrim party, and their helpers. In Arabic, an *mmmm* sound before a verb makes a verbal noun, so mu*tawwif* meant "the one who guides" the pilgrims on the *tawaf,* which is the circumambulation of the Ka'ba in Mecca.

I was nervous, shuffling in the center of our group in the line waiting to have our passports inspected. I had an apprehensive feeling. Look what I'm handing them. I'm in the Muslim world, right at the fountain. I'm handing them the American passport which signifies the exact opposite of what Islam stands for.

The judge in our group sensed my strain. He patted my shoulder. Love, humility, and true brotherhood was almost a physical feeling wherever I turned. Then our group reached the clerks who examined each passport and suitcase carefully and nodded to the pilgrim to move on.

I was so nervous that when I turned the key in my bag, and it didn't work, I broke open the bag, fearing that they might think I had something in the bag that I shouldn't have. Then the clerk saw that I was handing him an American passport. He held it, he looked at me and said something in Arabic. My friends around me began speaking rapid Arabic, gesturing and pointing, trying to intercede for me. The judge asked me in English for my letter from Dr. Shawarbi, and he thrust it at the clerk, who read it. He gave the letter back, protesting—I could tell that. An argument was going on, *about* me. I felt like a stupid fool, unable to say a word, I couldn't even understand what was being said. But, finally, sadly, the judge turned to me.

I had to go before the Mahgama Sharia, he explained. It was the Muslim high court which examined all possibly nonauthentic converts to the Islamic religion seeking to enter Mecca. It was absolute that no non-Muslim could enter Mecca. . . . No courts were held on Friday. I would have to wait until Saturday, at least.

An official beckoned a young Arab *mutawwif*'s aide. In broken English, the official explained that I would be taken to a place right at the airport. My passport was kept at customs. I wanted to object, because it is a traveler's first law never to get separated from his passport, but I didn't. In my wrapped towels and sandals, I followed the aide in his skullcap, long white gown, and slippers. I guess we were quite a sight. People passing us were speaking all kinds of languages. I couldn't speak anybody's language. I was in bad shape.

Right outside the airport was a mosque, and above the airport was a huge, dormitory-like building, four tiers high. It was semidark, not long before dawn, and planes were regularly taking off and landing, their landing lights sweeping the runways or their wing and taillights blinking in the sky. Pilgrims from Ghana, Indonesia, Japan, and Russia, to mention some, were moving to and from the dormitory where I was being taken. I don't believe that motion picture cameras ever have filmed a human spectacle more colorful than my eyes took in. We reached the dormitory and began climbing, up to the fourth, top tier, passing members of every race on earth. Chinese, Indonesians, Afghanis. Many, not yet changed into the *ihram* garb, still wore their national dress. It was like pages out of the *National Geographic* magazine.

My guide, on the fourth tier, gestured me into a compartment that contained about fifteen people. Most lay curled up on their rugs asleep. I could tell that some were women, covered head and foot. An old Russian Muslim and his wife were not asleep. They stared frankly at me. Two Egyptian Muslims and a Persian roused and also stared as my guide moved us over into a corner. With gestures, he indicated that he would demonstrate to me the proper prayer ritual postures. Imagine, being a Muslim minister, a leader in Elijah Muhammad's Nation of Islam, and not knowing the prayer ritual.

I tried to do what he did. I knew I wasn't doing it right. I could feel the other Muslims' eyes on me. Western ankles won't do what Muslim ankles have done for a lifetime. Asians squat when they sit; Westerners sit upright in chairs. When my guide was down in a posture, I tried everything I could to get down as he was, but there I was, sticking up. After about an hour, my guide left, indicating that he would return later.

I never even thought about sleeping. Watched by the Muslims, I kept practicing prayer postures. I refused to let myself think how ridiculous I must have looked to them. After a while, though, I learned a little trick that would let me get down closer to the floor. But after two or three days, my ankle was going to swell.

As the sleeping Muslims woke up, when dawn had broken, they almost instantly became aware of me, and we watched each other while they went about their business. I began to see what an important role the rug played in the overall cultural life of the Muslims. Each individual had a small prayer rug, and each man and wife or large group had a larger communal rug. These Muslims prayed on their rugs there in the compartment. Then they spread a tablecloth over the rug and ate, so the rug became the dining room. Removing the dishes and cloth, they sat on the rug—a living room. Then they curl up and sleep on the rug—a bedroom. In that compartment, before I was to leave it, it dawned on me for the first time why the fence had paid such a high price for Oriental rugs when I had been a burglar in Boston. It was because so much intricate care was taken to weave fine rugs in countries where rugs were so culturally versatile. Later, in Mecca, I would see yet another use of the rug. When any kind of a dispute arose, someone who was respected highly and who was not involved would sit on a rug with the disputers around him, which made the rug a courtroom. In other instances it was a classroom.

One of the Egyptian Muslims, particularly, kept watching me out of the corner of his eye. I smiled at him. He got up and came over to me. "Hel-lo—" he said. It sounded like the Gettysburg Address. I beamed at him, "Hello!" I asked his name. "Name? Name?" He was trying hard, but he didn't get it. We tried some words on each other. I'd guess his English vocabulary spanned maybe twenty words. Just enough to frustrate me. I was trying to get him to comprehend anything. "Sky." I'd point. He'd smile. "Sky," I'd say again, gesturing for him to repeat it after me. He would. "Airplane . . . rug . . . foot . . . sandal . . . eyes . . ." Like that. Then an amazing thing happened. I was so glad I had some communication with a human being, I was just saying whatever came to mind. I said "Muhammad Ali Clay—" All of the Muslims listening lighted up like a Christmas tree. "You? You?" My friend was pointing at me. I shook my head, "No, no. Muhammad Ali Clay my friend—*friend!*" They half-understood me. Some of them didn't understand, and that's how it began to get around that I was Cassius Clay, world heavyweight champion. I was later to learn that apparently every man, woman, and child in the Muslim world had heard how Sonny Liston (who in the Muslim world had the image of a man-eating ogre) had been beaten in

Goliath-David fashion by Cassius Clay, who then had told the world that his name was Muhammad Ali and his religion was Islam and Allah had given him his victory.

Establishing the rapport was the best thing that could have happened in the compartment. My being an American Muslim changed the attitudes from merely watching me to wanting to look out for me. Now, the others began smiling steadily. They came closer; they were frankly looking me up and down. Inspecting me. Very friendly. I was like a man from Mars.

The *mutawwif*'s aide returned, indicating that I should go with him. He pointed from our tier down at the mosque, and I knew that he had come to take me to make the morning prayer, always before sunrise. I followed him down, and we passed pilgrims by the thousands, babbling languages, everything but English. I was angry with myself for not having taken the time to learn more of the orthodox prayer rituals before leaving America. In Elijah Muhammad's Nation of Islam, we hadn't prayed in Arabic. About a dozen or more years before, when I was in prison, a member of the orthodox Muslim movement in Boston, named Abdul Hamid, had visited me and had later sent me prayers in Arabic. At that time, I had learned those prayers phonetically. But I hadn't used them since.

I made up my mind to let the guide do everything first and I would watch him. It wasn't hard to get him to do things first. He wanted to anyway. Just outside the mosque there was a long trough with rows of faucets. Ablutions had to precede praying. I knew that. Even watching the *mutawwif*'s helper, I didn't get it right. There's an exact way that an orthodox Muslim washes, and the exact way is very important.

I followed him into the mosque, just a step behind, watching. He did his prostration, his head to the ground. I did mine. *"Bismillah ar-Rahman, ir-Rahman—"* ("In the name of Allah, the Beneficent, the Merciful—") All Muslim prayers began that way. After that, I may not have been mumbling the right thing, but I was mumbling.

I don't mean to have any of this sound joking. It was far from a joke with me. No one who happened to be watching could tell that I wasn't saying what the others said. . . .

LATER THE SAME DAY I kept standing at the tier railing observing the courtyard below, and I decided to explore a bit on my own. I went down to the first tier. I thought, then, that maybe I shouldn't get too far; someone might come for me. So I went back up to our compartment. In about forty-five minutes, I went back down. I went further this time, feeling my way. I saw a little restaurant in the courtyard. I went straight in there. It was jammed, and babbling with languages. Using gestures, I bought a whole roasted chicken and something like thick potato chips. I got back out in the court-yard, and I tore up that chicken, using my hands. Muslims were doing the same thing all around me. I saw men at least seventy years old bringing both legs up under them, until they made a human knot of themselves, eating with as much aplomb and satisfaction as though they had been in a fine res-taurant with waiters all over the place. All ate as One, and slept as One. Everything about the pilgrimage atmosphere accented the Oneness of Man under One God. . . .

I had just said my Sunset Prayer; I was lying on my cot in the fourth-tier compartment, feeling blue and alone when out of the darkness came a sudden light!

It was actually a sudden thought. On one of my venturings in the yard full of activity below, I had noticed four men, officials, seated at a table with a telephone. Now, I thought about seeing them there, and with *telephone,* my mind flashed to the connection that Dr. Shawarbi in New York had given me the telephone number of the son of the author of the book which had been given to me [in New York]. Omar Azzam lived right there in Jidda!

In a matter of a few minutes, I was downstairs and rushing to where I had seen the four officials. One of them spoke functional English. I excit-edly showed him the letter from Dr. Shawarbi. He read it. Then he read it aloud to the other three officials. "A Muslim from America!" I could almost see it capture their imaginations and curiosity. They were very impressed. I asked the English-speaking one if he would please do me the favor of tele-phoning Dr. Omar Azzam at the number I had. He was glad to do it. He got someone on the phone and conversed in Arabic.

Dr. Omar Azzam came straight to the airport. With the four offi-cials beaming, he wrung my hand in welcome, a young, tall, powerfully built man. I'd say he was six foot three. He had an extremely polished manner. In America, he would have been called a white man, but—it struck me, hard and instantly—from the way he acted, I had no *feeling* of him being a white man. "Why didn't you call before?" he demanded of me. He showed some identification to the four officials, and he used their phone. Speaking in Arabic, he was talking with some airport officials. "Come!" he said.

In something less than half an hour, he had gotten me released, my suitcase and passport had been retrieved from customs, and we were in Dr. Azzam's car, driving through the city of Jidda, with me dressed in the *ihram* towels and sandals. I was speechless at the man's attitude, and at my own physical feeling of no difference between us as human beings. I had heard for years of Muslim hospitality, but one couldn't quite imagine such warmth. I asked questions. Dr. Azzam was a Swiss-trained engineer. His field was city planning. The Saudi Arabian government had borrowed him from the United Nations to direct all of the reconstruction work being done on [the] Arabian holy places. And Dr. Azzam's sister was the wife of Prince Faysal's son. I was in a car with the brother-in-law of the son of the ruler of Arabia. Nor was that all that Allah had done. "My father will be so happy to meet you," said Dr. Azzam. The author who had sent me the book!

I asked questions about his father. Abd al-Rahman Azzam was known as Azzam Pasha, or Lord Azzam, until the Egyptian revolution, when President Nasser* eliminated all "Lord" and "Noble" titles. "He should be at my home when we get there," Dr. Azzam said. "He spends much time in New York with his United Nations work, and he has followed you with great interest."

I was speechless. . . .

THE HIGH COURT I learned during dinner that the Hajj Committee Court had been notified about my case, and that in the morning I should be there. And I was.

The Judge was Shaykh Muhammad Harkon. The court was empty except for me and a sister from India, formerly a Protestant, who had converted to Islam and was, like me, trying to make the Hajj. She was brown skinned, with a small face that was mostly covered. Judge Harkon was a kind, impressive man. We talked. He asked me some questions having to do with my sincerity. I answered him as truly as I could. He not only recognized me as a true Muslim, but he gave me two books, one in English, the other in Arabic. He recorded my name in the Holy Register of true Muslims, and we were ready to part. He told me, "I hope you will become a great preacher of Islam in America." I said that I shared that hope, and I would try to fulfill it.

The Azzam family were very elated that I was qualified and accepted to go to Mecca. I had lunch at the Jidda Palace [Hotel]. Then I slept again for several hours, until the telephone awakened me.

It was Muhammad Abd al-Azziz Magid, the Deputy Chief of Protocol for Prince Faysal. "A special car will be waiting to take you to Mecca, right after your dinner," he told me. He advised me to eat heartily, as the Hajj rituals require plenty of strength.

*Nasser: Gamal Abdel Nasser (1918–70), first President of the Republic of Egypt (1956–70.)

I was beyond astonishment by then.

Two young Arabs accompanied me to Mecca. A well-lighted, modern turnpike highway made the trip easy. Guards at intervals along the way took one look at the car, and the driver made a sign, and we were passed through, never even having to slow down. I was, all at once, thrilled, important, humble, and thankful.

Mecca, when we entered, seemed as ancient as time itself. Our car slowed through the winding streets, lined by shops on both sides and with buses, cars, and trucks, and tens of thousands of pilgrims from all over the earth were everywhere.

The car halted briefly at a place where a *mutawwif* was waiting for me. He wore the white skullcap and long nightshirt garb that I had seen at the airport. He was a short, dark-skinned Arab, named Muhammad. He spoke no English whatever.

We parked near the Great Mosque. We performed our ablution and entered. Pilgrims seemed to be on top of each other, there were so many, lying, sitting, sleeping, praying, walking.

My vocabulary cannot describe the new mosque that was being built around the Ka'ba. I was thrilled to realize that it was only one of the tremendous rebuilding tasks under the direction of young Dr. Azzam, who had just been my host. The Great Mosque of Mecca, when it is finished, will surpass the architectural beauty of India's Taj Mahal.

Carrying my sandals, I followed the *mutawwif.* Then I saw the Ka'ba, a huge black stone house in the middle of the Great Mosque. It was being circumambulated by thousands upon thousands of praying pilgrims, both sexes, and every size, shape, color, and race in the world. I knew the prayer to be uttered when the pilgrim's eyes first perceive the Ka'ba. Translated, it is "O God, you are peace, and peace derives from you. So greet us, O Lord, with peace." . . .

My feeling there in the House of God was a numbness. My *mutawwif* led me in the crowd of praying, chanting pilgrims, moving seven times around the Ka'ba. Some were bent and wizened with age; it was a sight that stamped itself on the brain. I saw incapacitated pilgrims being carried by others. Faces were enraptured in their faith. The seventh time around, I prayed two *rakat*s, prostrating myself, my head on the floor. The first prostration, I prayed the Quran verse "Say he is God, the one and only"; the second prostration, "Say O you who are unbelievers, I worship not that which you worship. . . ."

As I prostrated, the *mutawwif* fended pilgrims off to keep me from being trampled.

The *mutawwif* and I next drank water from the Well of Zamzam. Then we ran between the two hills, Safa and Marwa, where Hagar wandered over the same earth searching for water for her child, Ishmael.

THE PROCESSION TO ARAFAT Three separate times after that, I visited the Great Mosque and circumambulated the Ka'ba. The next day we set out after sunrise toward Mount Arafat, thousands of us, crying in unison: *"Labayk! Labayk!"* and *"Allah Akbar!"* Mecca is surrounded by the crudest-looking mountains I have ever seen; they seem to be made of the slag from a blast furnace. No vegetation is on them at all. Arriving about noon, we prayed and chanted from noon until sunset, and the *asr* (afternoon) and *maghrib* (sunset) special prayers were performed.

Finally, we lifted our hands in prayer and thanksgiving, repeating Allah's words: "There is no God but Allah. He has no partner. His are authority and praise. Good emanates from him, and he has power over all things."

Standing on Mount Arafat had concluded the essential rites of being a pilgrim to Mecca. No one who missed it could consider himself a pilgrim.

The *ihram* had ended. We cast the traditional seven stones at the devil. Some had their hair and beards cut. I decided that I was going to let my beard remain. I wondered what my wife, Betty, and our little daughters, were going to say when they saw me with a beard, when I got back to New York. New York seemed a million miles away. I hadn't seen a newspaper that I could read since I left New York. I had no idea what was happening there. A Negro rifle club that had been in existence for over twelve years in Harlem had been "discovered" by the police; it was being trumpeted that I was "behind it." Elijah Muhammad's Nation of Islam had a lawsuit going against me, to force me and my family to vacate the house in which we lived on Long Island.

The major press, radio, and television media in America had representatives in Cairo hunting all over, trying to locate me, to interview me about the furor in New York that I had allegedly caused—when I knew nothing about any of it. . . .

LETTERS FROM MECCA I wrote to Dr. Shawarbi, whose belief in my sincerity had enabled me to get a passport to Mecca.

All through the night, I copied similar long letters for others who were very close to me. Among them was Elijah Muhammad's son Wallace Muhammad, who had expressed to me his conviction that the only possible salvation for the Nation of Islam would be its accepting and projecting a better understanding of orthodox Islam.

And I wrote to my loyal assistants at my newly formed Muslim Mosque, Inc., in Harlem, with a note appended, asking that my letter be duplicated and distributed to the press.

I knew that when my letter became public knowledge back in America, many would be astounded—loved ones, friends, and enemies alike. And no less astounded would be millions whom I did not know— who had gained during my twelve years with Elijah Muhammad a "hate" image of Malcolm X.

Even I was myself astounded. But there was precedent in my life for this letter. My whole life had been a chronology of—*changes.*

Here is what I wrote . . . from my heart:

"Never have I witnessed such sincere hospitality and the overwhelming spirit of true brotherhood as is practiced by people of all colors and races here in this ancient Holy Land, the home of Abraham, Muhammad, and all the other prophets of the Holy Scriptures. For the past week, I have been utterly speechless and spellbound by the graciousness I see displayed all around me by people *of all colors.*

"I have been blessed to visit the Holy City of Mecca. I have made my seven circuits around the Kaʿba, led by a young *mutawwif* named Muhammad. I drank water from the Well of Zamzam. I ran seven times back and forth between the hills of Mount Safa and Marwa. I have prayed in the ancient city of Mina, and I have prayed on Mount Arafat.

"There were tens of thousands of pilgrims, from all over the world. They were of all colors, from blue-eyed blonds to black-skinned Africans. But we were all participating in the same ritual, displaying a spirit of unity and brotherhood that my experiences in America had led me to believe never could exist between the white and the nonwhite.

"America needs to understand Islam, because this is the one religion that erases from its society the race problem. Throughout my travels in the Muslim world, I have met, talked to, and even eaten with people who in America would have been considered 'white'—but the 'white' attitude was removed from their minds by the religion of Islam. I have never before seen *sincere* and *true* brotherhood practiced by all colors together, irrespective of their color.

"You may be shocked by these words coming from me. But on this pilgrimage, what I have seen, and experienced, has forced me to *rearrange* much of my thought patterns previously held, and to *toss aside* some of my previous conclusions. This was not too difficult for me. Despite my firm convictions, I have always been a man who tries to face facts, and to accept the reality of life as new experience and new knowledge unfolds it. I have always kept an open mind, which is necessary to the flexibility that must go hand in hand with every form of intelligent search for truth.

"During the past eleven days here in the Muslim world, I have eaten from the same plate, drunk from the same glass, and slept in the same bed (or on the same rug)—while praying to the *same God*—with fellow Muslims, whose eyes were the bluest of blue, whose hair was the blondest of blond, and whose skin was the whitest of white. And in the *words* and in the *actions* and in the *deeds* of the 'white' Muslims, I felt the same sincerity that I felt among the black African Muslims of Nigeria, Sudan, and Ghana.

"We were *truly* all the same (brothers)—because their belief in one God had removed the 'white' from their *minds,* the 'white' from their *behavior,* and the 'white' from their *attitude. . . .*"

THE MUSLIM FROM AMERICA Prince Faysal, the absolute ruler of Arabia, had made me a guest of the state. Among the courtesies and privileges which this brought to me, especially—shamelessly—I relished the chauffeured car which toured me around in Mecca with the chauffeur-guide pointing out sights of particular significance. Some of the Holy City looked as ancient as time itself. Other parts of it resembled a modern Miami suburb. I cannot describe with what feelings I actually pressed my hands against the earth where the great prophets had trod four thousand years before.

"The Muslim from America" excited everywhere the most intense curiosity and interest. I was mistaken time and again for Cassius Clay. A local newspaper had printed a photograph of Cassius and me together at the United Nations. Through my chauffeur-guide-interpreter I was asked scores of questions about Cassius. Even children knew of him, and loved him there in the Muslim world. By popular demand, the cinemas throughout Africa and Asia had shown his fight. At that moment in young Cassius's career, he had captured the imagination and the support of the entire dark world.

My car took me to participate in special prayers at Mount Arafat, and at Mina. The roads offered the wildest drives that I had ever known: nightmare traffic, brakes squealing, skidding cars, and horns blowing. (I believe that all of the driving in the Holy Land is done in the name of Allah.) I had begun to learn the prayers in Arabic; now, my biggest prayer difficulty was physical. The unaccustomed prayer posture had caused my big toe to swell, and it pained me.

But the Muslim world's customs no longer seemed strange to me. My hands now readily plucked up food from a common dish shared with brother Muslims; I was drinking without hesitation from the same glass as others; I was washing from the same little pitcher of water; and sleeping with eight or ten others on a mat in the open. I remember one night at Muzdalifa with nothing but the sky overhead I lay awake amid sleeping Muslim brothers and I learned that pilgrims from every land—every color, and class, and rank; high officials and the beggar alike—all snored in the same language. . . .

It was the largest Hajj in history, I was later told. Kasem Gulek, of the Turkish parliament, beaming with pride, informed me that from Turkey alone over six hundred buses—over fifty thousand Muslims—had made the pilgrimage. I told him that I dreamed to see the day when shiploads and planeloads of American Muslims would come to Mecca for the Hajj.

There was a color pattern in the huge crowds. Once I happened to notice this, I closely observed it thereafter. Being from America made me intensely sensitive to matters of color. I saw that people who looked alike drew together and most of the time stayed together. This was entirely voluntary; there being no other reason for it. But Africans were with Africans. Pakistanis were with Pakistanis. And so on. I tucked it into my mind that when I returned home I would tell Americans this observation; that where true brotherhood existed among all colors, where no one felt segregated, where there was no "superiority" complex, no "inferiority" complex—then voluntarily, naturally, people of the same kind felt drawn together by that which they had in common. . . .

Constantly, wherever I went, I was asked questions about America's racial discrimination. Even with my background, I was astonished at the degree to which the major single image of America seemed to be discrimination.

In a hundred different conversations in the Holy Land with Muslims high and low, and from around the world—and, later, when I got to black Africa—I don't have to tell you never once did I bite my tongue or miss a single opportunity to tell the truth about the crimes, the evils, and the indignities that are suffered by the black man in America. Through my interpreter, I lost no opportunity to advertise the American black man's real plight. I preached it on the mountain at Arafat, I preached it in the busy lobby of the Jidda Palace Hotel. I would point at one after another—to bring it closer to home; "You . . . you . . . you—because of your dark skin, in America you, too, would be called 'Negro.' You could be bombed and shot and cattle-prodded and fire-hosed and beaten because of your complexions."

As some of the poorest pilgrims heard me preach, so did some of the Holy World's most important personages. I talked at length with the blue-eyed, blond-haired Husayn Amini, Grand Mufti of Jerusalem. We were introduced on Mount Arafat by Kasem Gulek of the Turkish parliament. Both were learned men; both were especially well read on America. Kasem Gulek asked me why I had broken with Elijah Muhammad. I said that I preferred not to elaborate upon our differences, in the interests of preserving the American black man's unity. They both understood and accepted that.

I talked with the Mayor of Mecca, Shaykh Abdullah Eraif, who when he was a journalist had criticized the methods of the Mecca municipality—and Prince Faysal made him the Mayor, to see if he could do any better. Everyone generally acknowledged that Shaykh Eraif was doing fine. A filmed feature *The Muslim from America* was made by Ahmed Horyallah and his partner, Essid Muhammad, of Tunis's television station. In America once, in Chicago, Ahmed Horyallah had interviewed Elijah Muhammad.

The lobby of the Jidda Palace Hotel offered me frequent sizable informal audiences of important men from many different countries who were curious to hear the "American Muslim." I met many Africans who had either spent some time in America or who had heard other Africans' testimony about America's treatment of the black man. I remember how before one large audience, one cabinet minister from black Africa (he knew more about worldwide current events than anyone else I've ever met) told of his occasionally traveling in the United States, North and South, deliberately not wearing his national dress. Just recalling the indignities he had met as a black man seemed to expose some raw nerve in this highly educated, dignified official. His eyes blazed in his passionate anger, his hands hacked the air: "Why is the American black man so complacent about being trampled upon? Why doesn't the American black man *fight* to be a human being?" . . .

Two American authors, best-sellers in the Holy Land, had helped to spread and intensify the concern for the American black man. James Baldwin's books, translated, had made a tremendous impact, as had the book *Black Like Me,* by John Griffin. If you're unfamiliar with that book, it tells how the white man Griffin blackened his skin and spent two months traveling as a Negro about America; then Griffin wrote of the experiences that he met. "A frightening experience!" I heard exclaimed many times by people in the Holy World who had read the popular book. But I never heard it without opening their thinking further: "Well, if it was a frightening experience for him as nothing but a make-believe Negro for sixty days—then you think about what *real* Negroes in America have gone through for four hundred years."

INTERVIEW WITH FAYSAL One honor that came to me, I had prayed for: His Eminence, Prince Faysal, invited me to a personal audience with him.

As I entered the room, tall, handsome Prince Faysal came from behind his desk. I never will forget the reflection I had at that instant, that here was one of the world's most important men, and yet with his dignity one saw clearly his sincere humility. He indicated for me a chair opposite from his. Our interpreter was the Deputy Chief of Protocol, Muhammad Abdal-Azziz Magid, an Egyptian-born Arab who looked like a Harlem Negro.

Prince Faysal impatiently gestured when I began stumbling for words trying to express my gratitude for the great honor he had paid me in making me a guest of the state. It was only Muslim hospitality to another Muslim, he explained, and I was an unusual Muslim from America. He asked me to understand above all that whatever he had done had been his pleasure, with no other motives whatever.

A gliding servant served a choice of two kinds of tea as Prince Faysal talked. His son, Muhammad Faysal, had "met" me on American television while attending a northern California university. Prince Faysal had read Egyptian writers' articles about the American "Black Muslims." "If what these writers say is true, the Black Muslims have the wrong Islam," he said. I explained my role of the previous twelve years, of helping to organize and to build the Nation of Islam. I said that my purpose for making the Hajj was to get an understanding of true Islam. "That is good," Prince Faysal said, pointing out that there was an abundance of English-translation literature about Islam—so that there was no excuse for ignorance, and no reason for sincere people to allow themselves to be misled.

22

Saida Miller Khalifa
Great Britain
1970
꧁꧂

Sonya Miller, a British sculptor and calligrapher, became a Muslim in London in 1959. The following year, taking the name Saida, she traveled to Canada, where she met her husband, Yusry Khalifa, an Egyptian university professor. The couple moved to Cairo in 1967. Miller Khalifa's book The Fifth Pillar of Islam *is a short, informal narration of their Hajj together in 1970. Like Lady Cobbold's earlier account, it alternates reflections on Islam and the days of the Prophet with more personal sections detailing her journey. It is in these latter passages that she makes a unique contribution to the pilgrim record by providing a plainspoken, representative account of the Hajj as performed by modern Muslim women by the millions.*

Miller Khalifa takes her readers straight into a type of harem peculiar to the Hajj. And a very different place it proves to be from the hackneyed stereotypes of French painters. Nor does her harem make one think of the chambers visited by the Begum of Bhopal or Lady Cobbold, for those were family quarters in the private homes of local rulers. Miller Khalifa, by contrast, applies the term hareem* *to a transient collection of female pilgrims inhabiting quarters rented from their guide. This accidental delegation of several dozen women, thrown together in Jidda, taking shape in Mecca, transposed to a second dwelling in Mina Valley and, finally, to a tent in Arafat, represents a typical arrangement repeated thousands of times on every Hajj.*

Women have always been present on the Hajj, and influential. In 1970, they comprised about one third of all pilgrims. The hajjas depicted in Miller Khalifa's pages share three things: Islam, their nationality, and a talent for friend-

---

*The Arabic root that links this word to *haram* confers the meaning of a protected area on two types of sacred territory: the land on which a mosque stands and that part of a dwelling reserved for the women and children of a family. [Ed.]

ship. One, Hajja Wadida, elderly, infirm, traveling alone, is thrust upon the Khalifas by her son at the Cairo airport. Another, a Gambian grandmother with four children in her care, manages quite well without the usual male protector. At the other end of the female entourage stands their guide's mother-in-law, the severe and somewhat comical Turkish Tyrant, whose role gives an interesting twist to the complex business of guiding pilgrims in a sex-segregated society. In this family, the lady of the house flies over from Cairo every year to double as a female mutawwif, *leading the hajjas among their clients on the Hajj while her son-in-law guides the males.*

Miller Khalifa has read the principal accounts of her predecessors. In her prologue, she offers a brief review of this literature as recapitulated by Captain Burton, and she occasionally quotes Philby and others in her text. Aware how far the Hajj has progressed in health and safety, she recognizes, too, that certain technological improvements have introduced their own new difficulties. One of these is traffic. In a passage not included here, the Khalifas traveled half the night by bus to cover the five-mile route from Arafat to Muzdalifa. "It was hot, but my window was jammed shut," she writes, "and I could not move my feet an inch. Ahead, behind, and to our right stood vehicles crammed with the faithful." Any recent pilgrim will recognize this sketch. In years to come, the Hajj would set world records for the size and duration of its traffic jams.

A section of twenty photos accompanies Miller Khalifa's text. In them, one makes out Datsun pickups, Volkswagen bugs and camper vans, public buses with luggage racks, a single donkey cart, and not one camel. In Jidda, the Khalifas stayed in a newly constructed pilgrim village, too. They traveled on paved, four-lane highways between Jidda, Mecca, and Medina and paid no pilgrim tax. In the 1950s, the new King, Sa'ud, had abolished it. "Let the hajjis come," he announced; "I will pay the tax." Thirty years before, of course, his father had largely relied on Hajj receipts for a national budget.

The Khalifas moved to Cairo around the time of the 1967 June War (the Six-Day War). Naturally, Hajj attendance reflected this regional upheaval. In its aftermath, the numbers of Egyptian pilgrims dropped by half, to about ten thousand, and did not recover fully for five years. This was largely due to the eight-year closure of the Suez Canal, another outcome of the war, which also increased the burden on those too poor to afford an airline ticket. Yet even at the worst of times, applications for Egyptian exit visas remained high despite official restriction of their numbers. Partly to counter complaints of favoritism, President Nasser instituted a pilgrim's lottery in 1969. This is the "public ballot" described in Miller Khalifa's opening pages.

from *The fifth pillar*
by Saida Miller Khalifa

PREPARATIONS FOR PILGRIMAGE It was 1970 and my third year in Egypt. Ever since my arrival, I had been wondering how and when I would be able to go on pilgrimage with my husband.

The 1967 war with Israel had left us all in a state of shock; the tragic loss of life, the deprivation of the Suez Canal, and above all the crushing defeat were blows from which it would take Egypt years to recover. As far as the pilgrimage was concerned, pilgrims could no longer travel by ship, now that the canal was out of action, and Suez, main port of embarkation for Egyptian hajjis in the past, was out of bounds for civilians. Now the journey had to be made by plane, so the numbers of pilgrims had to be limited, and the amount of foreign currency available was restricted.

Somewhat paradoxically, despite the hardship of the journey in the old days of the caravan, the demands made by officialdom prior to departure were few. Nowadays the situation is reversed; the journey is made incomparably easier, but the setting out on it is far more difficult, with so many forms to fill out and signatures and stamps to obtain from various officials.

The Egyptian government announced that a public ballot would be held in the city zones and country districts for all those wishing to go on the Hajj. However, any applicants who received invitations from relatives, friends, or the pilgrim-guides-cum-travel-agents known as *mutawwifs* who could subsidize them during their stay in the Hijaz would be exempted from what came to be known as the Toss.

In 1969, we had entered our names for the ballot but were unsuccessful, so the following year Yusry wrote to a Saudi whose name had been recommended to him. This invisible benefactor (for we never saw him) obliged us by sending an invitation. Now we had only to be officially notified before starting our preparations to leave.

That year, about thirty thousand Egyptians had applied to go, a number too great for the local air traffic to handle, despite the fleet of extra planes rented from foreign countries. The number of names drawn in the Toss was around seventeen thousand, so many were disappointed. We were very fortunate in not having to rely on the Toss.

The happy news that we would be leaving in February for Saudeya, as Saudi Arabia is known throughout the Arab world, reached us after months of anxious waiting. As soon as the kindly official at our local police station notified us of our departure date, Yusry and I hurried to buy the special clothing and camping equipment needed. . . .

A shop in the centre of town fitted me out with three long-sleeved, ankle-length cotton gowns. I bought two white, one green, later wishing I had bought more white because of the relative lack of washing and ironing facilities for the huge number of hajjis in Mecca and Medina. Another reason for extra white dresses is the Egyptian tradition of wearing a fresh, new white dress and veil for the return journey and her arrival home. White knitted cotton stockings and a long length of fine white veiling completed my outfit, and we left with the good wishes of the entire shop staff. Next, shoes. Alas! Like many another woman, I later found that my new white sandals were too small! Luckily, an old pair of summer shoes proved serviceable enough and better able to withstand a lot of wear and tear.

For Yusry's *ihram*, we drove to Old Cairo, where certain little shops located in narrow winding lanes specialize in the fringed towelling, strong leather money belts, and open sandals required. In the same area, canvas water bags can be bought that provide deliciously cool water for thirsty wayfarers in desert areas where no ice is available. The thick canvas is porous enough to allow a little water to seep through, the droplets being cooled by the passing breeze. Like the traditional goatskins, these water bags take up little space when empty. . . .

Later, in town, we bought a small Primus stove, a couple of lightweight saucepans, a frying pan, a kettle, some plastic mugs and plates, and a few other items for cooking and eating. A handbook on the pilgrimage advised taking a quantity of tinned food. I also washed and dried some rice, storing it in time for the journey. This proved a most useful addition to our subsequent diet of canned fish, vegetables, and cheese.

Not everyone knew of our proposed trip, but those shopkeepers in whom we confided when buying necessary items always earnestly requested us to pray for them when we reached the Ka'ba, Islam's most sacred place. Egyptians are for the most part deeply religious, and to go on the Hajj is a wish cherished in very many hearts.

The official side of our preparations entailed several visits by Yusry to our local police station to obtain the official permits and to the specially organized air-travel offices. We also called in at the local health centre for the statutory inoculations against smallpox, typhoid, and cholera. The nurse there took a justifiable pride in the delicacy of her needlework and wished us a blessed journey.

Now it was time to pack our gear. We stowed food and a few extra clothes in a couple of suitcases and bundled up the camping equipment in an old green rug which Yusry knew would be useful later.

Had we been setting out from Cairo a hundred years ago, our food supplies would of course have been more extensive, bearing in mind the long journey by boat and camel. We would have laid in stores of tea, coffee, loaf sugar, rice, dates, biscuits, oil, vinegar, lanterns, and cooking pots. Several water skins would have been necessary and most likely a small tent, as well, which would in those days have cost a mere ten shillings. All these would have been packed into a hamper made of palm sticks and a huge wooden box, while the clothes would have been put into saddlebags. I can picture our loaded camel, hamper, box, and saddlebags hanging from his sides, with perhaps a cot placed on top of the load.

In both past and present, the final item bought or acquired by the pilgrim could be a shroud, later to be dipped in Zamzam water. . . .

CAIRO AIRPORT Cairo mornings are usually fine, but I remember that February morning as particularly lovely, with the airport buildings and the planes all shimmering in the sun. Egyptian families are generally very close, and arrivals and departures of family members are occasions when everyone who can gathers at the point of departure or arrival. Our family is no exception, and the farewell deputation included two of my sisters-in-law and Yusry's three brothers, all of whom we hold dear.

Not only relatives but friends and neighbours love to bear the departing pilgrim company. The fellahin, for instance, think nothing of several days' trip to speed the traveller on his way, and groups of them from the country will cheerfully spend days and nights at the airport waiting for him to arrive. Sometimes a few of their group will bring along pipes and drums to enliven the proceedings.

A huge marquee of multicoloured appliquéd cloth had been set up adjoining the main building to accommodate departing pilgrim passengers. Helpful officials were everywhere at hand, and we found ourselves clear of passport and customs formalities in almost no time. Relatives and friends crowding the visitors' balcony were waving and calling down to white-clad figures below.

Just as we were about to go through to the departure lounge, a hand was laid on Yusry's arm. He turned to be hailed by a young ex-student of his, whom he later told me he had not seen for about ten years. Two ladies were with this young man; one was young, the other, an elderly hajja. In urgent tones, because there wasn't much time, the young man explained that he was unable to accompany his mother to Mecca. Could we look after her?

Yusry agreed at once, but I must admit I was taken by surprise at this unexpected request! I found out later it is quite usual for relatives to ask someone else to look after a member of the family making the pilgrimage alone, although generally this is arranged beforehand. Women pilgrims in particular are advised against making the Hajj alone; indeed the Prophet usually forbade women to do so unless accompanied by a male relative. The reasons for this will perhaps become clear as my story unfolds. In fact, the physical strains imposed by the journey, the carrying of loads, possible troubles over transport or argument with men over payments, the chance of accidents or sickness, and the importance of keeping one's footing when in the midst of great crowds are all occasions when a woman is liable to require a man's care and protection. The Prophet also recommended that a woman travelling a long distance should be accompanied by a male relative.

Of course, all this was new to me then, and I was trying to get used to the idea of having this hitherto-unknown companion travelling with us.

However, I tried not to show my apprehension when our hajja's tearful daughter-in-law grasped my hand and begged me to "take care of Mother." I assured her we would, feeling sorry for the poor lady who looked quite lost, now that the moment had come to leave her family. The next minute I couldn't help smiling at my kindhearted husband, who was rummaging hopefully in the hajja's capacious handbag in search of vital documents for her, while the lady herself just stood gazing in a state of childlike wonder at the official behind the desk.

Then, formalities completed, we sat in the cafeteria sipping the local coffee from tiny cups. It is served in a way similar to Turkish coffee but is less thick, and as a rule Egyptians prefer it less sweet.

The cafeteria was filling up with white-clad hajjis. A loudspeaker was broadcasting religious songs accompanied by vigorous drumbeats. Paperback copies of the Quran were handed out free to those who wanted them. At the next table a solitary hajji sat quietly smoking. Poor Hajja Wadida, for that was her name, began to cry silently. Was the prospect of this journey into the unknown without her family too overwhelming? I patted her hand sympathetically. Unfortunately my Arabic was too inadequate to be of much comfort to her, so we could only sit smiling and nodding at each other. . . .

IN FLIGHT I glanced out of the window. A silver wing obscured the view, but I caught a glimpse of tawny desert far below. I thought of earlier pilgrims about whom I had read. How astonished they would have been, those wayfarers of past centuries, if, as they rode or plodded the weary miles of caravan routes through desert wastes and lonely valleys, they could have known that one day in the future great silver metallic birds would carry passengers and cargo speedily through the skies. And those pilgrims too frequently herded together in certain ramshackle, unseaworthy craft whose rapacious owners cared nothing for the safety and comfort of their passengers. What a wonder to them would have been the swift comfortable flight with ample food and drink that today we take so for granted!

I looked at Hajja Wadida sitting beside me. Her eyes were closed; her lips were moving in prayer. Perhaps she was nervous about flying, as she had told me this was her first flight. Hoping to reassure her a little, I took her hand and was rewarded with an answering pressure and a smile. . . .

THE MUTAWWIF Perhaps at this point the function of the travel agent, the *mutawwif,* in the pilgrimage season should be made clear. First, his employment is purely seasonal, that is, during the pilgrimage months only, the last two months of the Arabic lunar year. Second, the *mutawwif* forms a link between government and pilgrim, enjoying a special fee in return for handling passports, customs clearance, accommodation, and transport; third, he is qualified to act as a guide throughout the religious rites with which very many may be unfamiliar. *Mutawwif*s generally lodge their clients in private houses which may be rented for the season, or in their own. Hotels, especially those near the city centres, are so expensive as to be beyond the reach of most.

Frequently a *mutawwif* will specialize in dealing with pilgrims of one nationality. It may be, for instance, that he is married to a wife from outside Saudi Arabia and prefers to look after her fellow countrymen, being already familiar with their language and some of their ways. The cheapest accommodation is of course to share a room with others, which usually results in the sexes being segregated. The women's rooms are called *hareem,* a word deriving from *haraam,* the forbidden (that is, to men other than the husbands, fathers, brothers, or sons of the female occupants).

Due to the ever-increasing number of pilgrims every year and the relative smallness of the cities of Jidda, Mecca, and Medina, no one is permitted to stay too long in any of these cities, or to leave them until official permission is granted.

The passport of each hajji is handled by his *mutawwif* throughout the different stages of the journey. Numerous *mutawwif*s are honest and sincere men; some unfortunately are not. However, one should not expect them all to be paragons of virtue merely because they live in the vicinity of the Holy Places. They have their faults, like everyone else. . . .

JIDDA AIRPORT But now, barely an hour after my arrival in Jidda, I was suddenly faced with an unexpected setback. As is well-known, no one is allowed to enter the Sacred Cities unless he or she is a genuine Muslim. But Yusry and I had completely overlooked the fact that nowhere in my British passport was it stated I was a Muslim. What was worse, there was no official Egyptian declaration to this effect either. We had thought, erroneously, that my official clearance in Cairo would be sufficient—but it was useless to claim this with the Saudi immigration officials—how were they to know I was a bona fide Muslim? We waited, sitting on a bench, while a couple of men from immigration discussed what was to be done. In the end, they decided the English hajja must take an oath the next day before the supreme-court judge to prove she had adopted the faith correctly.

I looked at Hajja Wadida, who clearly was again on the verge of tears. Poor soul! No doubt she was already regretting having been entrusted to our keeping, since this seemed to involve too much frustrating waiting about on her part. Like all the faithful, she was anxious to be on her way to the Ka'ba, the focal point of Islam.

As we waited, a couple of planeloads of Indonesian hajjis streamed in, looking exotic, with their fine, delicate features, dark Western-style suits, and little black skullcaps. A few of the men already wore the *ihram,* and most of the *hajja*s were in their national dress, graceful and dignified, later to be changed for their *ihram.*

At last, having given the name of the *mutawwif* with whom we would be staying in Mecca, we were allowed to leave the building. By this time we were hot and tired. The weather was warm after the temperate Egyptian winter. We collected our baggage, plus Hajja Wadida's unbelievably heavy suitcase, and stumbled through to a wide courtyard which was enclosed by a low quadrangle three stories high. Here were located the offices of the numerous *mutawwif*s and the free hostel for hajjis. Hot and footsore, Hajja Wadida and I stood in the midst of the throng of pilgrims, most of whom were standing surrounded by their piles of luggage. Just then, a short bespectacled hajja darted from the crowd to be greeted with delight by Hajja Wadida. It seems they were old friends. However, they had only exchanged a few sentences when a brace of diminutive young porters appeared, oddly dignified despite their ragged work clothes of saronglike skirts and cotton vests. Bulky turbans wreathed their heads, and wide, metal-studded leather money belts were buckled round their slim waists. "Belonging to [Hajj] Thakafy?" they asked cheerfully. *"Aiwan"*—yes—we replied thankfully. Yusry joined us. He had gone off with a small guide to find our *mutawwif*'s representative in the hope that we could collect our passports and leave for Mecca. But my problem was delaying us, so it seemed best to spend the night in the hostel. . . .

ARRIVAL IN MECCA The taxi, having first dropped off our Sudanese fellow pilgrims, drew up at a narrow side turning. Yemeni porters took over our baggage. We walked a short way between tall old houses whose owners sat by their doors. One or two street venders displayed trays of assorted goods resting on the ground. The porters turned in at a narrow door flanked by two slender green pillars, beside which, on the typical high bench lined with carpeting we had seen in Jidda, a man was lounging. This was our *mutawwif,* in whose house we would be staying during our time in Mecca. Hajj Thakafy stood up, a smile on his finely chiselled features as he welcomed us. We went in and climbed several flights of steep old stairs, glimpsing shadowed rooms from the landings, until we reached a small room under the rafters. The walls were pale blue, the ceiling of wood.

Facing us, reclining rather like a Matisse odalisque in a long, flowered dress, was a large, moon-faced woman, smoking a hubble-bubble* of ornate design. As the occupant of the single bed, who was every inch the person in authority, rose to greet us, I was aware of a circle of white-clad *hajjas* sitting around the room, on the floor, incongruously putting me in mind of ladies-in-waiting around their queen.

"Ahlan wasahlan! Ahlan wasahlan!" ("Welcome! Welcome!") The moon-faced one boomed out the traditional welcome of the Arab world, which actually means, "We are your family and you are now in a valley (where there is protection and abundance)," thereby showing the richness of meaning in certain Arabic phrases.

I shook hands all around, the lady of the house (I learned later she was the mother-in-law of our *mutawwif* and the undisputed authority abovestairs) said she hoped I would be happy with her. I suspect that, had my stay with the Turkish Tyrant (as I privately dubbed her) been during our second pilgrimage, I would have been happier, because by then I knew better what to expect, and I knew also that none of the little incidents of communal living should be taken seriously. As it was, the combination of my ignorance of the language, living in a confined space with a roomful of ladies whom I did not know, having to share one small washroom, and feeling myself to be constantly under a kind of invisible restraint from the Turkish Tyrant's somewhat overpowering rule meant I was living under a considerable strain at

*hubble-bubble: a waterpipe, hookah, or *shisha.*

first. The fact that the lady was rather given to shouting when put out did not help matters, and naturally in my ignorance I made mistakes.

It was not until we had exchanged these pleasantries that I realized we would all be living together, about twelve hajjas crammed into one little room. As it happens, it is almost impossible not to have crowded living conditions while on the Hajj, and more recently returned pilgrims have described houses so full as to necessitate hajjis sleeping in the washrooms at times. At least our rooms were clean, and the washrooms were sluiced down every day. But it does take a little time to become adjusted. . . .

LIFE IN THE HAREEM Worn out after the tremendous experience of the previous day, I slept like a log. I woke to the twittering of the hajjas round me as they rolled up their slender mattresses and folded the cotton coverlets to be stacked neatly in a corner of the roof, which, like most Middle Eastern roofs, was flat. The Turkish Tyrant was reclining on her bed, supervising the tidying-up operations in stentorian tones. Noticing the newcomer was awake, she invited me to sit beside her. Our conversation began by being quite cordial. In a moment or two, however, it became apparent that her remarks were not fully understood and her questions not adequately answered. By degrees, the moon face took on a crimson hue, the voice rose to a bellow. No doubt, like thoughtless people the world over, the Turkish Tyrant imagined she would make herself understood by shouting! In vain, a kindly hajja pointed out that I was English and therefore did not understand everything the *sitt hajja* (the lady of the house) said. The crimson face merely grew darker.

At this awkward moment, to my relief, a diversion was provided by the formidable lady's grandchildren, who started to squabble in a corner. Upon these two young heads, the infuriated roar was now turned. Subsequently I discovered that as soon as she sensed any potential opposition was about to collapse, the roar would change, rather like that of a tigress after a meal, to a kind of cajoling singsong, the volume of which still tended to drown any other conversation. I do not know whether it was because of the sheer force of her personality or something else, but it seemed to be only when the Turkish Tyrant was asleep, rosy moon face covered by a handkerchief, that the conversation of the circle of hajjas became louder than pianissimo.

Amusingly, even when the *sitt hajja* meant to be kind, she was alarming. Once, just as she was about to commence saying the noon prayer, she noticed I was sitting with my back against the wall. She had been standing quite still in preparation for the prayer when suddenly she let out a yell: "O Hajja Saida! Why don't you use a cushion!" I almost jumped out of my skin.

The Turkish Tyrant's daughter, Amira, had a much gentler nature. Slim and small boned, she moved with an easy seductive grace. Her small head with its delicate features and long, heavy-lidded eyes had something of the enchanting Queen Nefertiti about it. In fact, mother and daughter were Cairenes, the mother flying every pilgrimage season to Saudi Arabia to help look after their hajji guests.

Of course, in their position of authority and knowing considerably more than many pilgrims about the rites, the two ladies in whose care we hajjas were felt they should advise us on correctness of dress and conduct. They were quite right to do so, my only reservation being the, to me, unnerving manner in which the advice was given! . . .

In Hajji Thakafy's house, every corner was occupied, the house alive with voices and movement.

On the upper floor, we of the Egyptian *hareem* were settling down more comfortably together. Our number included two elderly hajjas, one of whom found walking an effort because of her bad legs, but nevertheless she bravely carried on for as long as she could. Most of the group were mothers or grand-mothers; several, sad to say, were widows. However, there were two very young hajjas, one recently married, whose husband was sharing a room below with other men. The two youngest naturally preferred sitting together, with Amira's schoolgirl daughter making a third and enjoying a few jokes while the rest of us chatted more sedately. At breakfast time, Amira would join us, and after the main meal of the day, she again made part of the circle. Amira would sit gracefully on the carpet cross-legged, pouring the tea, a liquid amber without milk, into tiny glasses kept polished crystal clear. She always found a second glass for me, a gesture that rather touched me as if she realized the comfort it brought the strange English hajja. Then the Turkish Tyrant would call for her *shisha* and puff away merrily until the charcoal embers glowed and the water bubbled, making a cheerful background noise for the conversation.

When annoyed, the Tyrant would roar at Amira, too, but she took the fortissimo tongue-lashing in the traditional way of the Oriental woman, silently and with eyes downcast, unlike her own daughter, who generally answered back, then sulked when scolded. . . .

Although the hajjas on the top floor were Egyptian, with the exception of myself, the lower floors were tenanted by pilgrims of different nationalities, Arabian, Egyptian, African, Syrian, and others. Immediately below us were two rooms, the first occupied by my husband and other men, the second by African families. Different colours, different backgrounds, different languages, yet all were living in harmony.

Water, an expensive necessity in Mecca, was carried daily to the house by sinewy young Yemeni water carriers accustomed to tramping up countless steep flights every day loaded with their heavy cans. The cans were slung from a yoke across their shoulders. Up the stone stairs they toiled to empty their cans with a satisfying splash into stone cisterns with taps at the base set in the washroom walls. The washrooms were kept clean by a thorough sluicing daily.

Next to my husband's room and overlooking a dusty light well festooned with bird droppings was a small room of the category we later heard described as "box" on our second Hajj. Having no daylight other than the meagre amount filtering down the light well, the room was rather dark. But, dark or not, it was highly valued by whoever rented it because of its privacy. As such, it was suitable for a married couple or a small family, and a small family was in occupation at the moment. Into the room's narrow L-shaped space were crammed an elderly and diminutive Gambian hajja and her four young grandchildren, not forgetting a perfect paraphernalia of boxes and pots and pans. Despite being a grandmother, the hajja was sprightlier than many a girl. Yusry and I had met this intrepid lady earlier, when we had shared a taxi, so ours was a cheerful reunion at Hajj Thakafy's.

Yusry kept the Primus on the landing between the rooms, and in the mornings he used to make tea to enjoy with his roommates, with whom he had many interesting discussions. He always reserved a cup for the Gambian hajja, who surely appreciated kindness in the midst of her preoccupation with caring for the children. In retrospect, I am full of admiration for her. How on earth did she manage travelling alone and coping with her brood? I can only conclude divine Providence saw to it a kindly hajji was always at hand whenever the handling of passports, papers, transport, luggage, or accommodation was involved!

Once, when sleeping arrangements became temporarily disorganized, Yusry asked if I might spend the night in her room. The hajja was most welcoming, clearing a space in the midst of her mass of belongings, augmented that day, she informed me, by the addition of the huge tin trunk gaily painted with flowers. The grandchildren were packed along the wall, where they lay under their blanket solemnly rolling their great eyes at me, without a sound.

Below us, every room, nook, and cranny were crammed with the faithful and their luggage. The old house was alive with the tramp of feet on stairs, the sound of voices as hajjis came and went to and from prayers at the Haram or carrying out the first rites. . . .

FRIDAY IN MECCA On my first Friday in Mecca, I went down [to the mosque] with the *hareem.* Even Hajja Wadida had struggled to her feet to join us, eager to attend congregational prayer. The crowds grew denser as we approached the Haram. Near the mosque, our eldest hajja declared she was feeling tired so would prefer to stay where she was. Around us were others also preparing to sit outside on their prayer rugs and then say the prayers led by the broadcast voice of the imam. This is the wiser course for anyone infirm, because the crowding at this time is at its maximum, when almost every pilgrim in Mecca joins the congregation.

Now some of us made for a side door so as to avoid the crush at the main entrance, where hajjis pausing to remove their sandals mingled with others making their way out. But the Turkish Tyrant, crimson faced and gesticulating masterfully from the steps of the main door, compelled us to follow her meekly. Holding on to each other, we struggled through the milling throng. At the same time, hundreds of hajjis were trying to get out because the prayers were not due to begin for a while, adding to the mêlée. The crush was unlike any other I had ever seen or experienced. Thousands of hajjis were pouring into the Haram in search of a space in which to wait and then pray on the prayer rugs most of them were carrying over their shoulders. Led with stentorian shouts by the Tyrant, our little Indian file forced its way inside. But once this objective was achieved, it was clearly impossible to get farther; so, urged on by more shouts, we made our way directly to the left. Here, there was a space flanked by shallow steps. At the top stood a line of armed soldiers. The Tyrant led us to a place near the wall, but the soldiers for some reason objected to this and urged us away with fierce cries and gesticulations. At this point, the Tyrant showed us she had a sense of humor; winking broadly in our direction, she sank to the ground and pretended to burst into tears to convince the soldiers of her womanly weakness and weariness, compelling her to stay where she was. Probably one of them noticed the wink, for we were moved forward firmly to find new places at their feet.

We had become part of a small sea of women of various types and colours. Now and then, a few worshippers threaded their way through our ranks towards the stairs leading to the upper balconies. A handful of intrepid men who tried to find space among the hajjas was repelled with disapproving cries of *"Hareem! Hareem!"* Despite the feminine objections, however, certain bold men battled their way to find places in the midst of the feminine throng, and there they stayed. Indeed, during the prayers, a hajji be-hind me gave me a sharp push for stepping inadvertently on his prayer mat. When later I remarked on this ungentlemanly behaviour to Yusry, he pointed out to me that probably the pilgrim in question was brought up to believe, wrongly, that the prayer mat when spread must not be touched by anyone but its owner.

Still the faithful came pouring in to the Haram, where there is room for everyone, even when it seems not an extra inch of space remains unoccupied.

Considering the vast numbers, the crowding, the unfamiliar languages, and the differing races and temperaments gathered together in close prox-imity, it is a wonder tempers are not lost more often. For the most part, everyone shows self-control and patience, but naturally occasions arise when fiery temperaments get the better of these virtues. The soldiers above us formed an amused audience for a little scene played out between two hajjas, one ebony and Junoesque, the other ivory and slightly built. A battle of wills was taking place for a few inches of room. Voices were raised. The next moment, the ivory hajja lost her temper and gave Juno a stinging slap across the face. At once cries of *"Haram! Haram!"* resounded from all sides. ("For-bidden! Forbidden!") Quieted, the ivory hajja sat down, but her adversary was making strange grimaces in the direction of the soldiers, rolling her eyes towards the other hajja and gesturing a knife stroke across the throat. Her meaning was clear enough, but the absurdity of it had the soldiers grinning. Eventually the injured party calmed down, soothed by the sympathy of her neighbours.

I must record the fact that throughout all my pilgrimages, this was the only incident of its kind I saw. . . .

MECCA TO MINA The taxis and buses, cars, vans, and lorries now pouring out of Mecca were loaded with pilgrims and their camping equipment. The chanting of *"Labayk Allahumma, labayk!"* from passing lorry loads of hajjis sounded every now and then above the roar of traffic. Yusry and I shared a taxi with the Gambian hajja and her solemn brood of grandchildren. I won-der how she managed during the tough period of camping; we lost sight of her once we arrived in Mina. We had decided to take with us only the cook-ing equipment, sufficient food for four days, a blanket, sheet, and pillows, all bundled into the old green rug.

Mina is only about four miles from Mecca, so it is soon reached. It is a small, attractive town encircled by rocky mountains. In summer, the heat there is said to be murderous; the mountains reflect the heat and keep out most of the cooling breezes. Now the mountains, dotted over with white tents, appeared to be sprouting mushrooms among the rocks. The houses of Mina looked surprisingly tall to me. Many of them are plastered in blue or grey with carved, unstained woodwork.

Mina's main street, long and broad, is the setting for one of the final rites of the Hajj; the symbolic stoning of the devil.

The house provided by Hajj Thakafy for his pilgrim guests was three storeys high. It had a very narrow entrance with a blue door and thick stone walls to keep out the worst of the summer heat. When we arrived, all the rooms were already occupied, mostly by hajjas on the upper floors, the Egyptian *hareem* occupying the largest room on the top floor. Two of the hajjas called to me to join them. They made room for me between their pallets, but they had hardly enough space for themselves. It would have been uncomfortably cramped sleeping there. I preferred to stay out of doors with my husband and other hajjis, both men and women, in the large tent pitched in the yard at the back of the house. I was glad to see Hajja Wadida settled among friends, her pallet against the wall. Safe with the Egyptian *hareem,* she had no need of Yusry's care then, although he was able to assist her a few days later. The formidable Turkish Tyrant had not yet arrived with the rest of her family, I noticed.

In the yard, Yusry and I found several tented areas sheltering Pakistani, Indian, Sudanese, and Egyptian hajjis. Suppers were prepared on spirit stoves. We were tired, and soon after supper we said our prayers, spread the rug and blankets on the ground, and quickly fell asleep. . . .

ARAFAT Arafat is a vast plateau ringed by low hills. . . . We stepped out of the taxi to see the entire plain and lower hillsides covered with a multitude of tents of every description. Tent sites belonging to individual *mutawwifs* were identified by large signs. Roadways through the encampment were alive with the din and bustle of arriving motor transport and disembarking passengers. Luckily for us, Hajj Thakafy's tents were pitched near the edge of the sea of canvas, or we could easily have lost our way.

The gigantic encampment was very well organized; there were tented accommodations for half a million or so hajjis, plentiful pure drinking water supplied from nearby reservoirs, and any number of individual tented latrines. The World Health Organization later congratulated Saudi Arabia on the complete absence of any epidemic, no mean achievement, considering that the entire pilgrim companionship is collected in this place for one day, and at Mina for three, under inevitably crowded conditions.

Not so very many years ago, serious epidemics used to break out among the pilgrim fellowship staying in the Holy Cities and making the journey.

Smallpox and cholera in particular took a deadly toll of casualties in certain years. Nowadays, when the Saudi authorities take such good care to prevent epidemics and to hospitalize at once any serious cases of illness among the hajjis, it is sad to read Doughty's account of the cholera years, when "the deceased and dying were trussed with cords upon the lurching camels' backs . . . and all was fear, no man not musing he might be one of the next to die and never come home to his house."

As Yusry and I gazed around, Hajj Thakafy emerged from one of his tents.

"The *hareem* are collecting in that tent with the Hajja," he told us, referring of course to his mother-in-law.

"Your wife would do best to join them," Thakafy said to Yusry; "the hajja will explain the rites of Arafat to her."

Yusry objected quickly, "I can explain them best to her—after all, I've done so from the beginning."

"The hajja will explain them better," Hajj Thakafy insisted, growing visibly annoyed.

"In English?" asked my husband pointedly. Thakafy looked daggers. Clearly, he was rarely crossed, and no doubt he thought me dreadfully rebellious. But how could his mother-in-law explain the rites to me when she knew no English and my Arabic was so elementary? The logic was inescapable. Besides, Yusry, with his experience of two previous pilgrimages and his extensive reading on Islamic subjects, was as well qualified as anyone to instruct me. Also, quite simply, I felt more comfortable with my husband.

Seeing Yusry was adamant, Hajj Thakafy pointed out another tent in which he found a space for us among its Pakistani occupants, who, as it happened, were not many. The hajjis were sitting in quiet meditation, reciting prayers or reading from their Qurans aloud or silently. . . .

RETURNING TO MINA Once again back at Hajj Thakafy's house, ready for a long drink of water, we noticed the well water had developed an unpleasant taste. In fact, the well was situated too near the overworked drains for health. We stopped even boiling the water for drinking, preferring to buy it from a purer source.

Our tent was pitched beside the back entrance to the yard, which led directly to the street. The cooking for the camp was done in giant iron cauldrons heated over wood fires that snapped and crackled a mere couple of yards beyond the canvas wall of the tent. At times, the heat became uncomfortable as the flames burned fiercely under the bubbling cauldrons. Alongside the cooking fires was a large pond for the slops, which seemed hourly in danger of overflowing and inundating the tent floor with greasy water and scraps of food. However, when I rather nervously asked Hasan, Hajj Thakafy's burly, good-natured assistant, if this could happen, he assured me with a beaming smile it was an impossibility.

Camping next to us was a little family of very poor Indian pilgrims. The poorest hajjis, often slightly built and frail, could not help showing their poverty-stricken condition by their emaciated physiques and clothing of the humblest kind. To achieve the Hajj obviously represented the expenditure of a lifetime's savings, leaving precious little over for everyday expenses once they arrived.

There was a marked contrast between these poorest of the faithful's physical condition and that of their more prosperous brethren, whose rounded forms were clearly used to comfort and plenty.

Our tentmates consisted of the young husband and his timid, silent wife and mother. No doubt to the little wife, our more numerous possessions suggested a more affluent state, because one morning, after exchanging smiles, as I cooked our meal, I suddenly felt a hand take mine from behind and a finger tickle my palm. It seemed the little Indian hajja was asking for money. I smiled at her, pretending not to understand, and when Yusry came, I told him about the incident. Yusry told me it was rare to find a pilgrim begging. For one thing, the Hajj is obligatory only for those who are financially able to accomplish it. Also, cases of want among pilgrims are generally looked after by charitable organizations representing various Islamic countries. The number of hajjis who are reduced to begging for money is very small, but of course it can happen that every penny gets spent on the journey and nothing is left for the stay. Later, in Medina, we were approached by a couple of hajjis, heads of families, who told us this is what had happened to them. We did not give the Indian hajja money but, instead, invited her small family to share some of our food. They accepted gladly, afterwards offering us a dish of their own made from wheat grain brought from their home village, where it was specially treated to be suitable for a dish similar to porridge. . . .

BACK IN MECCA Upstairs, the hajjas were making themselves at home again, sorting out their belongings. The suitcases had to be stowed on the roof, or the room would have been impossibly congested. The only drawback to this arrangement was that the morning sweep meant a different order of stacking each time. The result was a certain amount of confusion as to the whereabouts of a clean petticoat or headkerchief when needed.

As the days passed while we awaited permission from the authorities to move on to Medina, the hajjas grew to know each other a little better. We became very friendly with one another, and even our masterful landlady seemed less fierce. The picture remains in my mind's eye—the circle of ladies sitting chatting or lying in the little room, the Tyrant reclining odalisque fashion, her head tightly bound by a cotton kerchief, her ample form wrapped in the comfortable expanse of a purple flowered housedress. Contentedly she puffs at her hubble-bubble, every now and then suspending the mouth-piece to take part in the conversation.

The chief diversion was shopping, and everyone would compare pur-chases and prices in the evening. Mecca, Medina, and Jidda were a joy to shop in, particularly for anyone from Egypt, which country was suffering the inevitable shortages following a war. Watches, electrical appliances, dress materials, and perfume were items in great demand. Of course, everyone looked for the best prayer rugs and beads for herself as well as for gifts. Prayer rugs, chiefly in reds, greens, and blues, depicting the two Harams [in Mecca and Medina] are sold everywhere. Rosaries of a wide description can be found. Perhaps the prettiest are the ones of mother-of-pearl in the little shops around the Prophet's Mosque in Medina.

Mecca has a fascinating *souk,* a long, covered way sheltering a profu-sion of small, open-fronted shops whose goods glow and glitter in a riot of colour: ruby-, emerald-, and sapphire-hued prayer rugs; diaphanous saris and scarves of rose pink, midnight blue and snow white, threaded with gold; rich brocades and materials shimmering with sequins, golden earrings and brace-lets and tiny Quranic medallions, rosaries gleaming in pearl, garnet, jade green and jet; rosaries of wood and coloured glass; silver trays and platters; coffee cups and jugs with slender, gracefully curved spouts; perfumes in bottles of every size and shape; precious carpets from Persia and Afghanistan. And these are only a few of the wares displayed to tempt the pilgrim to part with too much too soon!

The perfumes of Mecca and Medina are popular with men who like to follow the Prophet's example of perfuming themselves before prayers. Another custom of the Prophet's was the use of a small tooth stick of aro-matic wood. Bunches of tooth sticks are sold today by pavement venders. When cut, the wood divides into bristles at one end, useful not only for the teeth but to massage the gums. Because of their association with the Prophet and the Holy Cities, perfume in small coloured vials and bunches of tooth sticks are valued gifts for pious men.

Day and night during the Hajj, the souk is a bustle of activity. The covered way, the shops, and narrow winding lanes on each side swarm with shoppers. Every now and then, a heavily laden porter calls out for people to make way for him. Shop owners are in their element as they parry the pilgrim's hopeful attempts at bargaining, often reclining at ease among their goods. . . .

Little shops sold a variety of imported goods, ranging from sophisticated Japanese tape recorders to packets of English cigarettes. There are no theatres, no cinemas, few advertisements, but many café owners entertain their clients with television in the evenings.

The Turkish Tyrant's Amira owned a set, and sometimes we hajjas would watch with her family. Mostly we liked to sit chatting outside on the roof as the nights grew warmer; later we would spread out mattresses out there and go to sleep under the stars.

But now the time had come for us to leave. About a week after our return from Mina, official permission was granted for us all to travel on to Medina. Porters came to fetch the baggage. One by one, we of the Egyptian *hareem* went to kiss the lady of the house good-bye. I had by this time become less intimidated by her. Perhaps I had imbibed some of the spirit of submissiveness shown toward her by all the hajjas. Anyway, I bent to kiss her rosy cheek, and suddenly . . . the trailing end of my veil caught for a moment in the glowing embers of her charcoal burner. I took that as my cue to vanish like the jinn in a cloud of smoke. . . .

THE MEANINGS OF THE HAJJ Yusry and I walked to the Haram to make what is known as the *tawaf* of Farewell, the final circling, out of respect to God. Like all pilgrims, we felt very sad at leaving the Haram, our inspiration, our comfort, and our refuge for most of the time we had been in Mecca.

Ahmad Kamal* has this to say about Mecca: "And yet Mecca is not so much a geographic location, or pilgrimage, or ritual, as it is a frame of mind. Pilgrims will discover in Mecca only what they take to Mecca. We are not come here in search of inspiration, but because we are inspired. Pilgrimage is a declaration of belief not a search for it."

There is a great deal of truth in what he says, yet I personally would differ with his opinion to the extent that pilgrimage does mean different things to different pilgrims. My husband, for instance, says that he goes on the Hajj to get his spiritual batteries recharged and to increase the spiritual sensitivity of his heart. For myself, the Hajj meant a voyage of discovery ending in the opening of a door to a far deeper spiritual experience, even though my travelling to Mecca was indeed a declaration of faith.

*Ahmad Kamal: contemporary Turkish novelist who also wrote a popular pilgrim guide, *The Sacred Journey* (1961). [Ed.]

23

Michael Wolfe
United States
1990

꽃꽃꽃

Like all the previous introductions here, this one presents a few remarks on back-ground and itinerary, setting the pilgrim traveler in a context for the reader. In this case, however, I was the traveler.

When I performed the Hajj in 1990, I had been a Muslim for about three years. As a much younger man, I had traveled for three years in North and West Africa, a region full of predominantly Muslim countries. As my interest in religion grew, in my forties, I found myself attracted to Islam. It was, after all, first cousin to the spiritual traditions I really knew—Christianity and Judaism. Moreover, I had spent some years with Muslims and seen the religion work in daily settings: its spirit was egalitarian and socially harmonious. Last but not least, the inclusion into its practice of a journey to a heartland appealed to the traveler in me.

Reasonable Hajj package tours were available from my home: three-week jaunts by air from California that permitted American-based Muslims to per-form the rites in Mecca, then return them to job and family. I had a longer trip in mind. Rather than travel with a group, I set out in March 1990 for what proved to be a three-month stay in Morocco, the account of which is briefly ex-cerpted here. I chose Morocco as a starting place because I wanted to pass Ramadan in a traditional Muslim country, one I liked and knew. In June, I flew to Mecca for the Hajj.

According to Saudi statistics, fifty-two pilgrims attended the Hajj from the Americas in 1972. In 1990, I found more Americans than this in my hotel. I have on my desk a photograph from that time, of four pilgrims posed on a rock wall in Medina. They wear head scarves and white robes and appear to have strolled out of old Arabia. Two of these men, however, are from Brazil, a third from La Paz, Bolivia, and the fourth from Los Angeles. We and a few dozen others from our hemisphere formed an impromptu New World delegation, trav-eling for four weeks and performing the Hajj together. We zoomed around Mecca in Japanese taxis. We placed long-distance telephone calls to Atlanta, Rio de

Janeiro, San Francisco. We discussed politics and the graces and risks of Western civilization while sitting in lobbies cooled by equipment produced in New Jersey. We watched NBA basketball games beamed in via satellite and rode out to the Plain of Arafat in German buses, through traffic controlled by computers and closed-circuit TV. I knew very soon that any book I wrote about the Hajj would differ from many that had come before. An already international convocation had become both global and highly technological in thirty years. At the same time, the essential rites remained unchanged. We turned the tawaf *in precisely the same way Naser-e Khosraw had performed it in 1050. At such times, we resembled modern vessels into which timeless emotions were being poured.*

   The Hadj: An American's Pilgrimage to Mecca* falls into two parts: 150 pages set in Morocco, followed by 150 pages set in the Hijaz. In Morocco, I felt on familiar social ground, in a domestic and largely personal situation. Nothing in my travels prepared me for Mecca. Today the city's resident population is largely composed of the ancestors of pilgrims who stayed on after the pilgrimage was over. It is further enriched and complicated by the arrival of several million visitors at a set time every year whose presence has nothing to do with vacations or commerce. The midsummer heat proved daunting, and I had never experienced such crowds. In such circumstances, I came to appreciate the ihram *laws, of which the two white robes are just a symbol. They protected the pilgrims, inspiring peaceful behavior in just the sort of jam-packed situation where people in other settings lose their heads.*

   Some lost their heads anyway, and the stress on most pilgrims as the Hajj built up was inescapable. Anyone who has read half the selections in this book must know by now that the Hajj has never been easy, that for pilgrims in every age the adage applies: If it weren't hard, it wouldn't be the Hajj. One way and another, the challenge before the pilgrim has always been the same: to wrest a spiritual experience from a physical struggle, to cultivate patience, concentration, and good instincts—to know when to follow the flow of events and when to pitch one's tent, dodge trouble, avoid exhaustion. Today, however, the physical risks do not take the form of raiding parties or death en route across infernal wastes. Air travel and a modern nation-state have dissolved those problems. Now it is the weight of the Hajj crowds and the motorized traffic that threaten to undermine you, the noise, the fumes, and man-made discomforts, the frustration of experiencing polar opposites at the wrong moment: where one expects peace there

---

*I used a variant spelling for *Hajj*, adding a *d*, subtracting a *j*, to distinguish my book from a current potboiler with racist overtones by Leon Uris, unfortunately entitled *The Hajj*. My use of the *d* was not an innovation. Earlier pilgrim authors, including John Lewis Burckhardt, spelled the word *Hadj*, too.

reigns confusion, and the like. The obstacles of the modern Hajj require pilgrims in good physical condition, able and willing to adapt to the inevitable. Elders and children, as always, suffer most.

The following extracts begin in the Marrakesh market during the months-long buildup to the Hajj. In this part of the book, I tried to demonstrate that, humanly speaking, the preparations for pilgrimage are in some ways as mean-ingful as the pilgrimage itself. The excerpts continue, two months later, with my arrival at the Jidda airport and a night ride into the Hijaz. These are followed, one last time, by a series of scenes depicting the initial rites in Mecca as performed near the end of the twentieth century. I have also included some strolls through town, some late-night scenes in the Haram Mosque, and excerpts that track the Arafat procession. By now this will be familiar territory. A few post-Hajj reflec-tions round out the entries.

from *The Hadj:*
An American's Pilgrimage to Mecca
by Michael Wolfe

MARRAKESH, MOROCCO. MAY 1, 1990 The lunar year rolled backward as the warm weather came on. Now that Ramadan was finished, the Hajj, that other engine of the Muslim calendar, began turning over. The rite would not take place until July, but a pilgrimage required preparation. The three-thousand-mile journey from Morocco to Saudi Arabia involved visas, reservations, and other arrangements. For many, these plans were already afoot, and the Hajj was becoming a topic in the medina. Every week the local papers carried more full-page advertisements for flights to Mecca. I began to meet a few pilgrims in the souk. They all were merchants.

Abd al-Hadi ran an electronics shop a few blocks from the Ben Yusef Medersa. He was fifty-five, a chunky man with baby-smooth skin and a hairline mustache. His store faced a busy square lined with vendors and fruit carts. I passed the place often. His floor stock never changed. In a storefront window misted with red dust were on display his few more modern items— three transistor radios, a videotape machine, two cassette recorders, and a color television. These never sold. . . . The shop did well because Abd al-Hadi could fix whatever you brought him. I never saw him sell a retail item. The real money, you felt, was in repairs.

Indoors, behind a waist-high counter, stacks of used equipment rose to the roof beams, and forests of wiring dangled everywhere. Vintage amplifiers sat balanced on torn speakers at odd angles. Empty TV consoles, rainbows of circuitry poking out the backs, leaned against piled crates of picture tubes. Because the dirham abroad is all but worthless, Moroccans (who save the flints from disposable lighters) do not easily part with imported goods. No matter how outmoded, when a piece of equipment fails, they bring it into stores like Abd al-Hadi's. The entire shop was twenty-five feet square.

Although he went to Mecca often, Abd al-Hadi was only marginally well off. Unable to take much profit from his shop, he paid for the journeys by acting as a guide to first-time pilgrims. This year, for instance, he had three women, a trio of rich sisters, lined up as clients. He was still arranging their plane tickets when we met. The first week after Ramadan, I found him filling out visa applications, which he posted the next day to Rabat. The following week he proudly showed me a return-mail packet of beribboned papers. I naturally took an interest in all this, having as yet no visa of my own. . . .

I asked Abd al-Hadi about his Mecca clients.

"Very old," he said. "One is blind. None of them has even a living brother. They want to go to Mecca before they die, and I have been there. *Alors,* they bought me a ticket. As their escort."

Like most religious journeys, the Hajj has been bound up with trade since it began. I wondered if he would do a little business.

"*Bien sûr.* The oil economy makes equipment cheap there. I'll bring back a couple of cameras, a TV."

I tried to picture Abd al-Hadi leading his trio through the heat waves, shouldering a twenty-one-inch screen. He wrote on a card the name of his hotel in downtown Mecca. I said, *Insh' Allah,* I would look them up. . . .

Islamic law requires the Hajj of those who can afford it. Its rewards act as a goad to the middle classes. All over Morocco, men work hard, sometimes for years, acquiring the economic edge to leave their shops for a spell and go to Mecca. Prior to airplanes, when the journey was more daunting, requiring months and sometimes years of travel, the pilgrim returned with elevated status. Nowadays the rewards are more personal. One's neighbors still pay attention when the suitcases come out, but a fiftyfold increase in hajjis has made the trip less impressive. These days one goes to fulfill a major obligation, to round out one's life, to renew one's spirit, often dampened in the swamps of commerce. Some mourn the passing of older, slower ways. Many feel it is better. Moroccans are family-oriented people. The airplane reduces the trek to a three-week absence, and more pilgrims with less money can undertake it. They go to complete a set of rites and to see the place they have bowed toward for a lifetime. They come home with a title in front of their names: al-Hajj.

The Hajj is the fifth pillar of Islam. No one I encountered planned to miss it. Even sophisticated city dwellers viewed the rite as transformative: your life could be changed by it forever. Elias Canetti had got it right in his book *Crowds and Power:* in the minds of most contemporary Muslims, you hadn't really lived till you'd made the Hajj.

Among Moroccans too poor to afford the trip, there were stories of miraculous transportations, astral projections, and magic-carpet rides to the holy shrine. These tales grow more plentiful the farther one lives from Mecca. Edward Westermarck's three-volume *Ritual and Belief in Morocco* retails dozens:

> One of [Sidi Hamed Buqudja's] followers expressed a wish to go to Mecca. The saint told him to go to the sea and throw himself in the water. He went there but could not persuade himself to follow the saint's advice. . . . A man came riding on horseback and asked him what he was doing. On hearing that . . . he would reach Mecca if he threw himself into the sea, the horseman fearlessly rode into the water. The saint, who was hidden in the sea, at once took the horse with the rider on his shoulders and carried them to Mecca.

In other stories, the shrine is brought to you:

> Moulay M'sish once told some of his followers to go with him to the top of the mountain . . . because he wanted to show them from there the Great Mosque in Mecca, and so he did. . . .
>
> Sidi al-Hajj al-Arbi of Wazzan caused the Ka'ba to come to Wazzan and walk around him seven times, just as the pilgrims walk around the Ka'ba in Mecca.

Originally instructive devices rather like Zen koans, stories like these were first invented to internalize a spiritual message. Later they became a part of local folklore and were accepted at face value or as hagiography. . . .

JIDDA AIRPORT. JUNE 21 I had chosen Morocco as my starting point because it was familiar territory. Previous visits over the years had accustomed me to its widely varied landscapes, its delicate foods, and its ancient mores. I was able to bargain in the local language and count in dirhams in my sleep. I knew the alleys of the major cities. I had friends there.

In Saudi Arabia, I knew nobody. I had never even been inside the country. I was only going now to perform a demanding set of rites whose complexities already made me nervous. I did not intend to add to this the task of measuring deserts or assessing its people. I would not be traveling, in any case. I would be almost exclusively in Mecca, Muhammad's birthplace and the least representative of Saudi cities.

As the airplane took off, I steeled myself a little. . . . Scattered here and there across the aisles were the makings of a group of men with whom I was going to spend the next month in Mecca. But I did not know that yet. The sun rolled down behind us, tinting the Red Sea a violent orange. Nobody spoke.

We landed about 8:00 P.M. at the Hajj airport in Jidda, and I followed a planeload of pilgrims down the ramps. The women among us were scarved and wore white caftans. Every man had on the white *ihram* garments. . . . The lower wrap fell from my waist to my shins. The top half hung loosely off the shoulders. This sacramental dress, ancient and pastoral, is a common motif on Sumerian statuary dating to 2000 B.C.E. Against the airport's high-tech background, we looked like shepherds emerging from a steam bath. The muggy Red Sea heat is legendary. I broke into a sweat leaving the plane.

We entered a stadium-size concourse full of hajjis. I stopped in my towels to gawk at the wing-spread roofs. Tented on all sides, they gave the effect of a Bedouin encampment. In overall area, this is the world's biggest airport. . . . This year, in a period of six weeks, a million pilgrims were going to set down here, a jumbo jet every five minutes, four thousand hajjis every hour. It was also the world's only "annual" airport, its systems too specialized to handle normal traffic. At the end of the season, a few weeks hence, the whole complex would close until next year.

Our group divided and subdivided, moving down the mall. I passed through customs, then joined a knot of three dozen pilgrims in a hallway. A Lebanese man with a curved stick took the lead. I had seen him on the airplane, wearing loafers and a Western business suit. [Now he sported the white *ihram*.] His staff was a saw on a pole, for pruning trees. His name was Mohamad Mardini. Offhand, cherubic, in his thirties, he seemed to know more than the others where we were going. The saw, he said, was a gift for a friend in the city. Its blade was covered by a cardboard scabbard. Walking, I kept my eye on him in the crowds. If we fell behind, he raised the saw to direct us. . . .

DRIVING INTO THE HIJAZ The night was moonless. Freeway lighting curtained off the land. Where it died away, I saw high desert dotted with scrubby thorn bushes and steppe grass. The road curved up through switchbacks, flattened to a plain, then climbed again. Isolated peaks poked up like islands. Now and then in fields beside the road, we passed small herds of camels. Oddly formal looking in the headlights, they raised their heads from grazing as we passed.

As we rode along, the men began chanting the Talbiyya:

I am here to serve you, Allah. Here I am!
I am here because nothing compares to you.
Here I am!
Praise, blessings, and the kingdom are yours.
Nothing compares to you.

These lines are the Hajj's hallmark, as much as the *ihram*. I heard them repeated day and night for weeks. The fifth line, echoing the second, wrapped back on the first line like an English round. The Arabic is chanted. . . . *Talbiyya* means "to wait, in a ready state, for an order or direction." One of its functions is to clear the mind, to prepare you for anything. In the van, it began the moment we left the airport. Before long, I would hear it in my dreams.

The *ihram* had a powerful impact on me, too. For one thing, it put an end to my months of arrangements. In a way, it put an end to me as well. The uniform cloth defeats class distinctions and cultural fashion. Rich and poor are lumped together in it, looking like penitents in a Bosch painting. The *ihram* is as democratic as a death shroud. This, I learned later, is intentional.

Mecca lies fifty miles east of the Red Sea. It is a modern city of one million people, splashing up the rim of a granite bowl a thousand feet above sea level. Barren peaks surround it on every side, but there are passes: one leading north toward Syria; one south to Yemen; one west to the coast. A fourth, a ring road, runs east to Ta'if. By day, the hills form a volcanic monotony. At night, they blend into the sky and disappear.

529

The first thing I discovered about Mecca was that I'd been spelling the name wrong. West of town we passed a fluorescent sign with glowing arrows and six letters sparkling in the headlights: MAKKAH. The orthography threw me. With its two hard *c*'s, Mecca is the most loaded Arabic word in the English language. Without them, what is it? No one here said MEH-ka. They said ma-KAH. The accent took getting used to, but English-speaking Meccans insisted on it. "Do you pronounce Manhattan men-HET-en?" one of them asked me.

A title was linked to Mecca on every road sign: al-Mukarramah, the Ennobled. With its special laws of sanctuary, with its status as the birthplace of Islam, the city is sacred ground, however you spell it. It is also strictly off-limits to nonbelievers. Another sign, at a freeway exit, read

STOP FOR INSPECTION
ENTRY PROHIBITED TO NON-MUSLIMS.

The van rolled to a stop beneath the sign. Two soldiers stepped out of a booth and played their flashlights through the cab. Visas were checked. The hajjis continued chanting. A few looked nervous.

Some Westerners think of Mecca as forbidden to foreigners. In fact, it exists to receive them and is largely composed of them. Most of the populace descends through thirteen centuries of migrant pilgrims who settled here after their Hajj and did not go home. The result is a cosmopolitan city, where every nation and race has taken root. Naturally it is completely Muslim. Only a Muslim has any business being here.

The officers brought back our passports in a basket. We left the checkpoint and continued on. Hijazi landscapes are studies in barren grimness. It was hard to imagine a sanctuary among these mangled limbs of Mother Nature. Bare hills rose in the headlights—treeless ridges reminiscent of Death Valley. The skyline looked straight out of Stephen Crane:

> *On the horizon*
> *The peaks assembled;*
> *And as I looked,*
> *The march of the mountains began.*
> *And as they marched, they sang,*
> *"Ay, we come! we come!"*

At the top of a final ridge, the road swept east and joined a freeway. The asphalt here was lit up like an airfield. Luminescence bathed the rubbled hills; then, at blinding speed, the van shot under a giant concrete book. I swung around in disbelief, staring back through the windows. There it stood: a sculpture the size of an overpass, a Claes Oldenburg mirage of huge arched crossbeams supporting a forty-ton Quran. *Did you see that?* Then we came over the lip of a canyon. The lights of Mecca lay fanned out in a bowl. . . .

ARRIVING IN MECCA [That same night], we were climbing with the crowds up Umm al-Qura Road. At the top of the rise, where the street was closed to cars, a throng of five thousand people moved up the pavement. Reaching the crest, I came up on my toes. Everyone knew what was down there, glowing at the bottom of the valley: the largest open-air temple in the world.

I fell in behind Mardini as we climbed. Soon I was being introduced to a Saudi guide named Shaykh Ibrahim, a professor of *hadith* at the local university. I asked him what the Prophet had said about the mosque. . . .

Ibrahim was a gentle man, the most taciturn of the four guides attached to our party. A few blocks farther on I asked again.

He said, "Just remember: the Ka'ba is a sacred building. But not so sacred as the people who surround it," and pointing to the ground, he made a circle with his finger. "Whatever you do here, don't hurt anyone, not even accidentally. We are going to perform the Umra now. We will greet the mosque, circle the Shrine, walk seven times between the hills, like Hagar. Think of it as a pilgrim's dress rehearsal. Don't rush, don't push. Take it easy. Get out of the way if anyone acts wild. If you harm someone, your performance might not be acceptable. You might do it for nothing."

Shaykh Ibrahim's explanation of the Umra . . . was the longest single speech I would hear him make in the next four weeks. The view from the brow of the hill cut off further discussion. Behind a concrete overpass rose the biggest minaret I'd ever seen.

Down below, a mosque in the shape of a mammoth door key completely filled the hollow.* Lit from above, roofless at the center, it seemed to enclose the valley bowl it covered. The proportions of this eccentric structure were staggering. The head of the key alone comprised a corral of several acres. In addition, attached to the east wall, the shaft of a two-story concourse ran on another quarter mile. For so much stone, the effect at night, beneath banks of floods, was airy, glowing, tentlike. Seven minarets pegged down the sides.

*See Figure 3.

This was the recent surrounding mosque that encapsulates a much older Ottoman courtyard. Ibrahim called it Haram al-Sharif, the Noble Sanctuary. Its 160,000 [square] yards of floor provided room, on a crowded day, for 1.2 million pilgrims. Galleries lit up the second story. Parapets ran right around the roof. From the crest of the hill, the minarets looked canted. I could not begin to guess the building's height. Its outer walls were faced in polished slabs of blue-gray marble, and the marine shades differed stone to stone. The veins shooting through them looked like ruffled surf. The minarets were spotlighted. On every side, the valley glowed.

I had never seen such a beguiling temple complex. Saint Peter's Basilica in Rome is roofed, and open to tourists. Palenque [in Mexico] covers more ground, but no one uses it. My aversion to sightseeing vanished before this pool of light and stone. All the must-see points were in one building.

We followed the road downhill beneath a bridge. Chunks of the mosque heaved into view as we went down, here a gallery, there a tower, shifting behind façades and concrete rooftops. Then the street curved sharply, and the building disappeared.

A hot breeze swept down the hillside. Behind, the hum of traffic died away. The lots, where cars and buses parked at quieter times of the year, were occupied tonight by camping pilgrims. Fires burned low between the groups. Bedrolls lay open under bridgeheads. At the edge of the road, we came upon a circle of Ghanaians reciting the Quran around a lamp. Most of the encampment was asleep now.

We entered a canyon lined with bazaars and food stalls. Where it leveled out, the mosque returned to view. Its second floor had a Coliseum-like curve to the upper galleries. Across the road we stopped before a gate, forming a huddle. Ibrahim addressed us. . . . When everything was settled, we waded into the crowds around the mosque.

THE MOSQUE Most hajjis arriving at Mecca enter the Haram through Bab al-Salaam, the Gate of Peace. Ibn Battuta went in by this gate; so did Ibn Jubayr, his predecessor, . . . Tonight crowds on the stairs kept us from fulfilling this tradition.

Mardini shrugged. We continued around the mosque to another gate, Bab al-Malik. A shallow flight of steps led up to a foyer. We deposited our sandals at the door and stepped across the threshold, right foot first.

Inside we offered the formulaic greeting:

This is your sanctuary.
This is your city.

I am your servant.
Peace is yours.
You are salvation.
Grant us salvation,
And guide us
Through the gates of Paradise.

Crossing the foyer, we entered a series of pillared, curving halls. In surrounding naves lit by chandeliers, fields of pilgrim families sat on carpets, reclining, conversing, reading the Quran. Their numbers increased as we moved deeper into the building. Books on waist-high shelves divided quiet colonnades. Brass fixtures overhead were interspersed with fans lazily turning. We continued down an aisle through the crowds. The Ka'ba, Islam's devotional epicenter, stood in an open courtyard dead ahead, but we could not see it. There were three hundred thousand pilgrims in the complex. Our walk from the outer gate took fifteen minutes.

The colonnades enclose an oval floor of about four acres. The oldest columns in the mosque flank the perimeter, columns that Burckhardt, Burton, al-Fasi, and Qutb al-Din all felt compelled to count and could never agree on.* On the east wing, they stood in quadruple rows; elsewhere they ran three deep into the building, making a courtyard portico.

I had read about this building and glimpsed it on Moroccan television, but taking its measure now was out of the question. Its proportions could not compete with its population, or with the emotional state of those I saw. To begin with, the aisles and carpets held an astounding racial microcosm: Berbers, Indians, Sudanese, Yemenis, Malaysians, and Pakistanis overlapped Nigerians, Indonesians, Baluchis, Bangladeshis, Turks, Iraqis, and Kurds. It was a calm crowd with almost no pushing. Our numbers did not result in agitation. The rush to reach Mecca was finished. The hajjis had arrived. Now the laws of sanctuary took over. This was the peace we had petitioned in the foyer. Everyone felt it.

Across the way a vigorous-looking Afghan in his eighties, six feet tall with burnished skin, stood praying into his open hands while big tears dropped onto his palms. A deep exhilaration knocked at my rib cage. Counting up columns in this became absurd.

---

*Qutb al-Din counted 555 pillars; al-Fasi, 586; Burckhardt, 450 to 554. The pillars stand twenty feet high, with varying diameters to about two feet. Most are carved from the local granite; half a dozen others look clearly Attic. Tradition claims they were brought from Panopolis, Egypt.

THE TAWAF As we walked, the aisles were subtly descending, conforming to the valley floor. We passed out of the covered portico and stepped down into the marble courtyard. This was the head of the key, the building's hub.

[All the other mosques in the world are] arranged in figures of four sides. The core of the mosque at Mecca is on the round, an open, roofless forum overlooked by tiered arcades. The marble floor is 560 feet on the long sides, 350 feet wide, and polished to the whiteness of an ice rink. At the center of this hub stands the Ka'ba, a four-story cube of rough granite covered in a black embroidered veil.

This monolith is Islam's most sacred shrine. Thomas Carlyle, the Scottish historian, called it an authentic fragment of the oldest past. It was already ancient when Muhammad's grandfather restored it in 580 C.E. Its tall simplicity and black reflection lend the mass an upward rhythm. Tonight a light breeze ruffled its cover, and the slabs felt strangely cool beneath my feet. After acres of ceilings, it was soothing to look up and see some stars.

We were fifty or sixty yards from the Ka'ba, moving around the outskirts of the forum. Knots of hajjis, stopped in their tracks, stood everywhere around. The first sight of the Shrine was literally stunning. Men wept and muttered verses where they stood. Women leaned against columns, crying the rarest sort of tears—of safe arrival, answered prayers, gratified desire. I shared these emotions. I also felt an urge to escape my skin, to swoop through the crowd like lines in a Whitman poem, looking out of every pilgrim's eyeballs. I heard [a fellow pilgrim named] Fayez call out as he hurried past, "We made it! We made it!"

A doughnut ring of pilgrims ten rows deep circled the Shrine, forming a revolving band of several thousand people. We kept to the edge of them, skirting the cube, and faced its eastern corner. Here a black stone in a silver bezel had been set into an angle of the building. This was its oldest relic, the lodestone of popular Islam. We faced the stone and stated our intention:

Allah, I plan to circle your Sacred House.
Make it easy for me,
And accept
My seven circuits in your name.

Each hajji began at the Black Stone and circled the Ka'ba counterclockwise. . . . At a distance, the wheeling pilgrims obscured its base, so that for a moment the block itself appeared to be revolving on its axis. As we came nearer, the Shrine increased dramatically in size. On the edge of the ring, we adjusted our *ihram*s and raised our hands to salute the Stone. Then we joined the circle.

Keeping the Shrine on our left, we began to turn. Ibrahim and Mardini went ahead, calling words over their shoulders as we followed. There were special supplications for every angle of the building, but not many pilgrims had them memorized. Now and then we passed someone reading set prayers from a handbook, but most people were speaking from the heart. I caught up to Mardini and asked him what was proper. The invocations all but drowned us out. "One God, many tongues!" he shouted. "Say what you want, or repeat what you hear. Or just say, 'God is great.'" I dropped back into the wheel and did all three.

The first three circuits of *tawaf* are performed at a brisk pace called *ramal,* or "moving the shoulders as if walking in sand." Richard Burton likened the step to the *pas gymnastique.* I had not imagined the Hajj would be so athletic. Each time a circuit returned to the Stone, it was all I could do to remember to raise my palms and shout, *"Allahu akbar!"* It was not the pace or the distance but the crowd that was distracting. On the perimeter of the ring, I noticed wooden litters passing, on which pilgrims weakened by age or illness were being borne around. These pallets marked the circle's outer edges.

Coming around the northwest wall, we included in each circuit a half circle of floor marked by a rail. Inside the rail lay two slabs of green stone said to mark the graves of Hagar and Ishmael. Directly above, a delicate golden rainspout protruded from the roof of the Ka'ba. The prayer at this spot alluded to the rainspout:

> *On that day*
> *When the only shade is yours,*
> *Take me into your shadow, Lord,*
> *and let me drink*
> *From the Prophet's trough*
> *To quench my thirst forever.*

The liturgy and the place were of a piece here.

We performed the quicker circuits near the Ka'ba, on the inside rim of the doughnut. When they were done, Mardini began taking side steps, distancing himself from the Shrine as we moved along. I followed suit, working my way to the outer edge of the circle, where we performed our last four rounds at a leisurely walk.

As the pace fell off, space opened around us. I could see the black drape rustle on a breeze. It hung down the Ka'ba on all sides, covering the cube in heavy silk. Its name is *al-kiswa.* I later heard it called the Shrine's *ihram.*

THE ZAMZAM WELL One had to perform the *tawaf* to comprehend it. Its choreographic message, with God's House at the center, only came clear to me in the final rounds. Orbiting shoulder to shoulder with so many others induced in the end an open heart and a mobile point of view.

The final circuit brought us back to the eastern corner. We saluted the Black Stone as we swept past, then washed up on an outer bank of marble, behind a copper enclosure the size of a phone booth. This was called the Station of Abraham. Prayers offered here acquired special grace. We faced the Ka'ba and performed two *rakat*s together.

Our rite of *tawaf* was complete now, but the evening was not over. Next we descended a flight of steps to a cavernous room containing the Zamzam Well. Cool air flooded the stairwell, cutting the night's heat as we went down.

In Ibn Battuta's day, the Zamzam Well was housed above ground in a large pavilion. Today, the floor has been cleared of these installations. The water drawers and leather buckets have vanished, too, and the profiteers who placed exorbitant fees on the concession. Even the well has been relocated, to a wedge-shaped amphitheater underground.

The air was deliciously damp the first night I went down there. The slanting stone floors ran with surplus water. Hajjis not content merely to drink dumped buckets of the liquid on their bodies, and strangers toweled off each other's backs. The atmosphere was like a friendly bathhouse. Here and there, on a dry patch, lay a solitary sleeper. . . .

Mecca would not exist without this well. Its appearance in the bone-dry Hijaz is a fundamental wonder: the first condition of desert urban life. For thousands of years, it supplied the whole town for drinking and ablutions. Seeing it, I understood why Muhammad had linked water to prayer and installed a purifying rite at the heart of his practice. Even in pre-Islamic times, the well was sacramental. Today, pilgrims drink from it to fulfill tradition. Minerals render it heavy, but I found the taste of Zamzam water sweet, not brackish, and very, very cold (its having passed through a cooling system in the basement). . . .

THE SA'Y Our last labor of the night was a ritual job between the hills. The rite, called *sa'y*, takes place in the concourse on the long side of the key. To reach it, we crossed the Ka'ba floor, saluted the Stone, then walked out of the courtyard, heading south.

A series of arches led through cloisters to a gate. Here the head of the mosque and its shaft were joined, forming a marble lane called the Masa'a. Later I heard one hajji refer to it as the racecourse. I was unprepared for the length of this passage: a quarter-mile stretch of covered mall, split in two lanes for pilgrims coming and going.

The course began at the top of a hill called Safa, jutting from the base of Mount Qubays. It ended at the second hill, Marwa, in the north of the building. I had never seen hillocks housed inside a building; domes had been set in the ceilings to accommodate their crowns. A complete lap covered about eight hundred yards. Here, as around the Ka'ba, old age and illness were shown consideration. Down the center of the Masa'a, on a median strip dividing the two lanes, frail pilgrims were being wheeled in rented chairs.

Saluting the Shrine at the top of each relay, we completed seven lengths, or about two miles. My legs began to throb in the third round. The contrast between the mystical *tawaf* and this linear, headlong rush could not have been greater. Wandering loosely between fixed points, doubling back on itself around the hills, the rite expressed persistence and survival. The *sa'y* was not a circle dance. Its intent seemed to be to instill compassion for the victimized and the exiled. This was the mall of necessitous desire.

We finished our run and stepped down onto a ramp beside al-Marwa. By now, our *ihram* towels were streaked with dirt and sweat. We had come through the Umra. We were *muta 'ammirin*. As we stood shaking hands (Mohamed Fayez high-fived me), two self-appointed barbers stepped from the wings, offering their services. In order to put aside the *ihram* clothes, a pilgrim who plans to return to them for the Hajj is supposed to have a desacralizing haircut. Generally this means a token snip of three or four neck hairs. When it was done, we returned to Bab al-Malik for our sandals.

THE GUIDES In the dark on the hill going back to the hotel, I noticed two or three men from the group trying to give Ibrahim money. Each time he refused.

This starkly contradicted the slanderous talk I had heard about the guides here. [More than one experienced hajji] in Marrakesh had warned me off these people like the plague. Their extortionate rates were a set piece in the oldest commentaries. Time after time pilgrims strapped for money, tried by exhaustion, cholera, and thieves, arrived at the site of their aspirations only to be fleeced by their *mutawwif.* Eldon Rutter, who made the pilgrimage in 1925, accused them of never missing an unearned tip and of eternally evolving new ways to get them. Ahmad Kamal wrote in 1961:

> All pilgrim guides belong to closed Meccan guilds. Each guild
> is organized to cater only to pilgrims of a particular nation or area,

whose languages or dialects the guild members speak, and with whose peculiarities they are familiar. Such knowledge is a two-edge blade, bleeding the unwary as often as it protects them. . . . Dwelling in close proximity to the Holy Ka'ba has not turned them into angels.

. . . I caught up to Mardini and asked him about it. The pilgrim guides were much maligned, he said. In the past, they had deserved it. Today, their activities are regulated. Some remained rapacious in their greed, but the majority performed a service fairly. They worked hard. Their earning periods were brief. And Ibrahim and his fellow shaykhs were different. They had day jobs to begin with, and PhDs. They were professors on vacation picking up a second wage, not cicerones. They worked in the hire of the Islamic Affairs Department, guiding official guests and delegations. . . .

Mardini's view of the guides opened my eyes. I wondered where our group would be without them. We had stepped off a bus and been plunged into a labyrinth of rites. It was the same for every hajji. Regardless of status, you reached Mecca exhausted and in a state of exultation and were required to perform on the first night. A good guide was indispensable, it seemed. It was not, as in Rome or at the Taj Mahal, a matter of missing the artwork. The correctness of your Hajj was at stake. For a vast majority of pilgrims, this was a once-in-a-lifetime event. They would not have the money or the chance to try again next year. Everyone needed to get it right the first time. . . .

JUNE 22 Having by now performed the rites of Umra, I saw, coming down the hill again, that the d shape of the mosque was far from eccentric. This design had been purposely devised to enclose two ritual arenas: the boulevardlike Masa'a and the rink of the Ka'ba. Both areas had been laid down in prerecorded time along the lines they occupy today. These lines show purpose. The *sacra via* runs on an east-west axis; the four-cornered cube still marks the compass points. Clearly, the lay of the mosque has been aligned by cosmographic logic, like Stonehenge or the sun temple at Thebes.

I could also appreciate its enlarged proportions. In the Hajj month of 1939, one hundred thousand pilgrims had come to Mecca. This month about the same number arrived each day. The mosque complex had been expanded in every direction to accommodate them. A lot of rock had been moved to make more room. . . .

MIDNIGHT HAJJIS Sunstroke in June was so common during Hajj that the Saudis, in their role as pilgrim hosts, had set up 150 centers equipped to treat it. In addition, Green Crescent nurses manned several hundred clinics in the town. The TV preached prevention every evening, and leaflets were passed out in the streets. The essential piece of advice—to avoid direct sunlight—went mostly unheeded. Visiting hajjis continued to choke the roads. Their guides had to work to keep up with them.

Our biggest adversary was the heat. Eventually it determined all my movements. To beat the sun, I began breaking up my trips to the mosque with long siestas—a three-hour nap between dawn and noon, another rest after lunch between *zuhr* and *asr*. Canonical hours shaped everybody's day. Rather than fall out of step, I kept to the schedule. I slept between prayers while the sun was up and visited the Haram every evening. Most of my time between dusk and dawn I spent at the mosque.

I became what Mardini called a midnight hajji. In June, it was a usual regime. Every summer on the weather maps Mecca, Yanbu, and Jidda competed for the hottest spot on Earth. Having spent two years in West Africa in my twenties, I arrived convinced that heat could not affect me. A few days in Mecca proved me wrong. The thermometer on the sill edged nearer 120 Fahrenheit every day. The sun, bouncing off the streets, added ten degrees. At night the buildings were radiators. Hijazi heat gave a new twist to Shabestari's* famous couplet:

> *If the smallest atom were broken apart*
> *You would find the sun at its very heart.*

Stepping out of the air-conditioned lobby, one opened up the door on a roaring stove.

The mosque was surprisingly cool in the evening hours. A network of cold-water pipes run under the floors, and some cloisters are air-conditioned. I often went there equipped to stay on until dawn, with a portable one-man prayer rug and my Quran. I found the mosque completely accommodating. There were water tanks in every hall, carpets to nap on, and food stalls on the street for midnight snacks. To simplify matters, I brought along a plastic bag to carry my foot gear. The Haram has sixty-four entries, and once inside I liked to stroll around, so that exiting later by my original gate might mean a long hike across the building. Worse, the piles of shoes to be searched through became confusing. With my flip-flops bagged, I could come and go as I liked and be sure to leave wearing the pair I had come in on.

*Shabestari: Sa'd od-Din Mahmud Shabestari (ca. 1250–1320), a Persian mystic, author of *The Mystic Rose Garden*, a classic Sufi work. [Ed.]

Every night the crowd and mood were different. Despite Fayez's claim, there was no best seat. The mosque, built on the round, provided countless perfect sight lines. Your view depended on time and elevation. The final prayers of a Muslim day, *maghrib* (just after sunset) and *'isha* (dusk), occurred within ninety minutes of each other. I tried to be on the roof during these hours. The crowds were smaller than on the lower levels, and oftentimes a breeze came down the hills. . . .

Coming back uphill at dawn, when the streets were less choked, I had a chance to poke around the town. The roads still lay in shadow then, and things were at their coolest. Under the porticoes on Bab al-Umra Street, coffee vendors set up tables on the sidewalks, and small bazaars were opening for business. Offices above them sprouted signs. Their English intrigued me:

EXPERIMENTAL ESTABLISHMENT

FOR PILGRIMS FROM NON-MUSLIM COUNTRIES

NO. 7

ONLY RIYALS

SACRIFICIAL COUPONS HEAR

Only Riyals was a gift shop. The government coupon dispenser sold pilgrims sacrificial sheep.

The perfumeries sparkled like bright museums with tall cases of pastel-colored scents in cut glass vials. There were delicatessens, *thobe* and *ihram* vendors, pharmacies, trinket shops, and many bookstores. My favorite bookshop had dark wood shelves and seventeen-foot ceilings. It specialized in classic Muslim texts, printed in Beirut and Riyadh. It sold posters, too, writing materials, and postcards displayed on sidewalk racks.

I was browsing here one morning when a dozen Tajik pilgrims came into the store. . . . These men were among the first post-Soviet hajjis in seventy years. They wore brown wool hats and cream-white robes belted at the waist with tasseled cords. They entered warily, elected a spokesman, and walked him to the counter. They watched his lips, to be sure he got the speech right. They did not want perfume, they wanted books. If the ruble was worthless outside Russia, they were ready to pay in deutsche marks. And the man produced a wallet filled with both currencies.

The Quran had been forbidden by the Soviets so long that a copy in Tashkent currently cost a hundred dollars. Here they cost five. The Tajiks left the shop with a dozen copies. . . .

* * *

The *tawaf* revolved day and night in the heart of the city. At any hour the oval floor was packed. I continued to walk to the mosque around five every evening, stayed until nine or ten, then returned after midnight. Transport was almost effortless. The constant streams of pedestrians moving past the hotel worked like a current, conveying us into the hollow and back home.

I'd been in a lot of crowds by now, but never one so at ease or densely threaded. Most crowds acquire thrust by a destination. The hajjis moved as if they had arrived. In that sense, the Haram resembled a roundhouse. Our pace became more stately day by day. This seemed preternatural in a city swollen to three million people, with lights and roads and horns and calls to prayer. Modern Mecca whirled around us, but the tempo was like a retreat. The city felt vital yet monasterial. When Burckhardt wrote that "in all my journeys in the East, I never enjoyed such perfect ease as at Mecca," he was affirming the tranquillity of the Hajj.

The delegation adjusted to new rhythms. We slept, we ate, we performed *salat,* we floated in robes along the street, moving with minimal effort, putting on lives of customary action. Like the airplanes over Jidda, we circled in holding patterns. We had managed to reach Mecca. Now we were waiting.

Every day thousands of new arrivals drove in from the airport. Performing the Umra rites took longer now. . . .

The mosque complex has sixty-four gates, some in much more frequent use than others. I investigated one evening and turned up Bab al-Nabi. It lies on the east wall of the Masa'a. It meant a long walk to the back of the building, but once inside it was easy to skirt Mount Safa and slip into the courtyard. Being nearest his house, Muhammad had used this gate often. There were always a few cats lounging by the door.

Coming in at whatever gate, you reach the Ka'ba by crossing arcades that radiate deep into the building. Despite its enormous population, I could always find room at the back of the mosque to sit. There might even be a pillar there to lean on. Far from the oval center, the cloisters lost their curvature, and the architecture became conventional. It was quieter, but I could not see the Shrine.

Occasionally it was possible to sit nearer. Where the porticoes meet the Ka'ba floor, three steps form a ledge around the courtyard. These steps are broad and deep, like bleachers, and ringed around with steel water tanks. . . . The ledge formed a natural curb above the fray, and it soon became my favorite place to rest. I had the Ka'ba in plain view, a hundred yards across the floor, and I had its precise reflection on the marble. Entirely serene, at times like these the mosque took on the mood of a summer palace —one of those ancient, well-appointed spreads designed to approximate Paradise, where poets and thinkers whiled away their evenings.

Groups of hajjis often paused to drink here. One night I saw a family of Pakistanis, three or four men with wives walking behind, followed by sons and daughters, cousins and nephews, fragile grandparents. The men wore the *shalwar kamiz,* a pajamalike top and blousy trousers, but when they spoke, it was in British English—the children less rapidly, with Bradford accents. I had wrongly assumed they were from Lahore.

Another night in about the same place, I met two young newlyweds from Atlanta. She was of Turkish background. He was blond, a novice insurance adjuster in his twenties. Both had grown up in the South, attended school there, just been married. I watched him fill a Zamzam cup and offer her a drink.

Haram honeymooners were not unusual. I sometimes passed them escorting each other through the galleries. Inside the mosque, they practiced shy decorum. On the street, when the crowds were large, they might hold hands. Mardini said that in families who could afford it, the Hajj was considered the best way to cement a marriage, before having children.

These two from Georgia were distinguished by their speech. When I asked whether they spoke Arabic, the man looked sheepish. His wife replied, "Ah do speak Turkish. But ah make ma prayahs in English."

MECCA TO MINA VALLEY The sky was growing red as we climbed on the bus. We had been coming to this moment for a week now. We were leaving for the desert. As the bus swayed forward through thick traffic, the mosque fell behind. At times, the pedestrian crowds moved faster than we did. With stops, we averaged fifteen miles an hour.

It was hard to imagine a time when the Hajj had not been up on wheels. Four-lane bands of glinting chrome snaked up the hillsides. Crowds dashed between bumpers. Vehicles spilled off the modern roads, taking shortcuts over sand and scabblings. In a little more than fifty years, a medieval city had been utterly transformed by modern transportation. I wondered what would come when the car was gone. It would take a lot more than a face-lift to rearrange things. The town had been remade for the rubber tire, the wider axle. A massive infrastructure of tunnels, freeways, and overpasses swooping impressively through granite hills physically walled us off from the 1930s, when the Hajj was still an occasion of the camel. Harry St. John Philby wrote then of the Mina caravan, "There must have been fifty thousand of them at least, and all moving forward together at the silent, hurried pace character-istic of the chief carrier of Arabia."

Today's chief carrier ran on gasoline. Bumper to bumper the trade-off appeared pathetic, and yet we were not figures in a frieze. The Hajj had been motorized for fifty years, and we were products of that history, a part of the blaring horns and squealing rubber, not the sweep of padded feet.

A camel can carry four hundred pounds of cargo, cover sixty miles a day for twenty days without a drink in temperatures of 120 degrees Fahren-heit—and still go five more days before it dies. Only a fool is not respectful of the camel. On the other hand, almost no one on the bus knew how to ride one. Rafiq, [a] Libyan, who did, only joked about it: "Imagine your-selves on that wooden saddle, wearing cotton towels!"

MINA TO ARAFAT At 7:00 A.M., all of Mina was in motion. Winding downhill to the parking lots, I had my first clear view of the whole valley: a mile-wide dun-colored corridor forming one continuous plane between two ranges, from its western edge against the spine of Mecca due east to Arafat, five miles away. The sky was still faintly pink in that direction, and traces of morning ground fog smudged the view. Past Muzdalifa, the visible end of the valley tapered off. Most of the way the land ran with tents and glints of chrome.

I had been through Super Bowl gridlock in San Francisco. I knew the rush-hour tunnels of New York. I had witnessed Woodstock and marched on Washington. I had never experienced a throng approaching this one. It was as if the twentieth century's thickest tie-up had embarked on an epic traveling back into Roman times. A tricky desert sky hung over everything, compressing volumes, curving distance, befuddling the eye.

As we boarded vans, a block-long hulk of yellow helicopter appeared above the cliffs over the road. It hovered long enough to drop a basket on a cable, then pluck a prostrate pilgrim from the crowds. It reeled him up and vanished over the hillside. Mardini referred to the craft as a flying hospital. The Saudi army had seven of these contraptions, with landing pads all over the valley.

We inched our way down the drive to Abd al-Aziz Street. The encamp-ments in this quarter were mostly filled with Pakistani peasants. The numbers of mothers with infants startled me. The Hajj in July with a baby on each hip seemed inconceivable. [Mardini] guessed that the children were here because of economics. Their parents could not afford to leave them with nursemaids.*

---

*Taking a child on the Hajj does not fulfill its obligation. Grace always attaches to the jour-ney, but the rites are void without mature intent, or *niya.*

The pressing heat and constant need for water weighed down older people, too. The camps were peppered with them, men and women seventy and eighty, bent over walking sticks, toothless, squinting. They were here by choice, of course, to do their duty and to soak up the Hajj's grace before they died. The women looked bird boned. The men in white towels, creaking down embankments, appeared to have one foot in the other world.

At the bottom of the hill, the crowds thinned out, and the cars and trucks and buses and vans took over. For several minutes, I saw nothing but steel hoods and blazing trunk lids. Then the road ran up into a viaduct and gave us a bird's-eye view of Mina Valley.

Night had all but erased the surrounding mountains. Now they dominated everything. Their bouldered bases tumbled to the sand's edge, forming up the narrows of the valley. The contrast of gray-blue rock on sable was exact, as if cut with a scalpel. Terraces in the rock face higher up formed tier upon tier of shelflike lofty bleachers holding single ranks of canvas tents. The shelves zagged like roads in a pit mine. The tents were distant flecks. The treeless ranges appeared to have poked up yesterday, but they held legends. The Prophet's cave on Mount Hira lay to the west. To the north stood Mount Thabir, where Abraham went to sacrifice his son, and where Gabriel stopped him. . . .

The van rolled down off the escarpment, taking a crossroad to the middle of the plain. Here we joined one of the many numbered ribbons of new pavement linking Mina to Muzdalifa and Arafat. These long, sand-leveed roads ran high and dry across the desert, like taffy stretched out in the sun. They paralleled each other through the sand, splitting the valley in quarter-mile channels, so that, crawling along at a snail's pace, we could gauge our progress by vans across the way on our left and right. Sometimes we saw whole vehicles. More often we made out only roofs, viewed over sand humps topped with hanks of thorn brush. There was something submarine about the valley. Low dunes lapped the canyon floor, as if a sea had boiled off it in the night.

A pedestrian walkway shaded with green roofing ran down the center of the plain. Thousands of hajjis flowed along it, keeping pace with the traffic, stirring up dust clouds. It ran unbroken for about three miles, dumping out crowds at the eastern end of the spillway. Seen from the air, the walkway would be a prominent feature. From the van it was hard to distinguish across the sand. Had Mardini not pointed it out, I might have missed it. It was difficult to hold any view in focus, especially where dust became involved. Heat waves curled off the sand. The sky was scored with corrugated ripples.

Where the valley narrowed, we crossed a riverbed, the Wadi Muhassir. Over its dry banks, we joined a track reserved for special cars. The traffic gained speed here, in keeping with a tradition that the Prophet spurred his camel through this pass.

The road climbed slightly, hills fell off to either side, and we entered the mile-wide basin of Muzdalifa. Again the valley ground was packed with tents, the hills dotted white like Mina's. In the acid light, objects melted to shades of solar brown. Lost between slopes, a worn gray runner of masonry and stone wound through the clinkers. This was the eighth-century aqueduct built by Zubayda, wife of the caliph of Baghdad. Easing the Hajj for centuries to come, Zubayda had paid to sink a hundred wells from al-Kufa in southern Iraq all the way to Mina. She and her husband, Harun al-Rashid, had performed the Hajj nine times along this route, once across a field of carpets rolled out every morning on the sand. . . .

Files of pedestrians swept by on roadside paths. Some waved staves with make-shift banners. With the men in *ihram,* it was hard to tell families apart or confirm nationalities, but the banners helped to keep the groups together. I saw Moors from Spanish North Africa, Libyan Berbers, blacks from the Sudan, Syrians, Palestinians, Kurds and Iraqis, Mongols, Circassians, Persians, Baluchis, Afghans, Malays, and Sinhalese. I became so immersed in this pageant I did not mind our lack of forward progress. Even Hajj congestion had a planetary character. The chunk of road we looked out on was as racially dense as a UN parking lot on Flag Day. . . .

We were heading toward a boundary line that divided Muzdalifa from the plains. Arafat proper, the site of the Hajj, lay a mile away. As the van gained ground, the enclosing ranges tapered, then opened like an hourglass below the waist. We passed a pair of whitewashed pillars at the mouth of the valley, marking the edge of Sacred Territory. Another dry river, the Wadi al-Arak, extended for some distance to our left. It was filled with a shrub that the Meccans prize for toothpicks. Behind sparse green tops, we picked out the spires of Namira mosque farther down the valley. Its minarets stood out like ships' masts in a harbor. There were four.

The enormity of my assumption, that words could take the measure of the Hajj, caught up to me on the Plain of Arafat. I saw now why men as observant as Rutter and Burckhardt had given it two pages. At Arafat, the Hajj became too big to be a subject, too sprawling, too amoebic. There were no hooks by which to hoist the vista. Its edges outran the verbal frames we place around things. Its center was everywhere, confounding reason, opening the heart.

The four-mile bowl of sand we entered now was lined with tents enclosed by granite mountains, identical white canvas rows, forming quads that lapped out of sight, fusing into dots on the horizon. Sweeps of momentarily homeless millions were divided here and there by two-lane roads winding through the camp like canals through Venice, coming and going in the mist. As we rolled to a stop in one of these canvas rivers, I gave up and slipped my notebook into my bag. I relinquished my post at the fort of objective inquiry. Chants of *"Labayk"* welled up from the plain.

The van rocked and pitched as we watched at the windows.

> *You wanted a look*
> *At Death*
> > *before you faced it?*
> *Now you have seen it*
> *with your eyes.* *

If Arafat *was* a dress rehearsal for Judgment Day, one thing seemed certain: no one would be alone there. The crowds on the road gleamed like figures from two worlds. The Hajj was at its most ethereal right now, vibrating between the real and the symbolic. Out on the sand, a man in towels marched past the van with a green flag. Suddenly it was as if we had driven into a Wallace Stevens poem. The figures in the street became figures of heaven. Men grew small in the distances of space. The blown banners seemed to change to wings. Then the van jerked suddenly forward, the crowd swam into focus, and we floated along together down the plain. . . .

ARAFAT The roads were little veins of pandemonium in the larger, calmer body of the Hajj. Once we had found our parking lot and left the van behind, I marveled at the quiet in the campsites. Laid out in quads, they occupied the largest part of the valley; the roads were no more than perimeter stripes around them. Each quad was further broken into blocks, great sandy courtyards edged by canvas tents and gravel walkways. The tents sat backed against these paths. Stalls and vendors collected at each crossroads.

In contrast to the roads, the camps felt cool and crisp and organized. Here life's minor rhythms carried on. A young man crouched to wash at a

*Quran III:143.

plastic bucket. Three Iraqi women sat around a Primus stove, sipping coffee. A baby whimpered.

The first real breeze in a week blew down the valley. It whipped up scraps of paper as we walked. The air smelled strongly of ozone. Tissue-thin, high clouds dulled the sun. After ten days and nights in the hollow, the plain felt cool. It was 93 degrees Fahrenheit at ten-thirty, a low unheard of in summertime Mecca. . . .

It was impossible to place ourselves in relation to the landscape. The corridors of tents blocked any view. Cut off, with no point of reference, I wondered if it were possible to attend the Hajj and miss it. Passing a rank of buses by the road, I stopped to look. They were locked, painted white, with sky-blue trim. At the back of one, a ladder ran up to the baggage racks. I let the others pass and climbed the ladder. From the roof, I had a good view of Jabal al-Rahma.

It lay at the closed end of the valley, butted against the foot of Mount Namira. Broad stone steps zagged up the eastern side to a gentle summit two hundred feet above the plain. This modest pile of boulders was the focal point of the Hajj. Every structure on the plain, tents included, faced or flowed toward it. A tall, whitewashed obelisk marked the summit. It looked the size of a matchstick from the bus. . . .

JABAL AL-RAHMA I was now on one of a dozen lanes that ran like spokes toward Mount Mercy. Wider than the aisles through the camps, these lanes were filled with hajjis like myself from the back of the enclave. Although the whole plain was Arafat, the *jabal* represented the heart of the action. Muhammad had stood on its peak. People wanted to see it.

A ring road circled the hill's perimeter. It looked less like a road from where I stood than like a moat full of shepherds. Ahead the feeder lane was a lake of hands. A government water truck had backed onto the road, and hajjis stood around it with their arms raised. I worked my way past them, wading through cast-off plastic. On the other side, I stood facing the mountain.

Broad stone steps ran up the southern flank, making a left, then a right-hand turn, leading to the summit with its column. Halfway up lay a pad with a wall around it. This, it was said, marked a spot where the prophet Adam first performed *salat*.* Hajjis leaned at the wall, enjoying the view there.

---

*The name Arafat derives from a root of meaning "to find, recognize, or know." It denotes the spot where, after their expulsion from the Garden, Adam and Eve crossed paths and became reacquainted—a primal lost-and-found for souls.

Earlier that week I had visited this hill when no one was on it. Now small figures perched on every rock. Some stood still like sentries, faces growing smaller near the summit. Others chatted under parasols or read from prayer books. Every few minutes a patch of two hundred people would stand together, wave their shoulder towels, and chant, *"Labayk Allahumma, labayk!"* An answering chorus rose up off the plain.

Behind the hill, a higher shelf of cliffs overlooked the quads. It formed a gallery fringed with tents and cars, where hundreds of thousands of locals were assembled. Meccans considered these perches the best seats in the house, and they drove out from town in packs to claim them early. . . . Their view across the plains would be superb.

Very few tents stood on the *jabal* proper. Bodies packed the rocks on every side, but the slopes were too oddly pitched for real camping, and the boulders looked jagged. A few stunted mimosas poked through cracks.

On the outer rim of the road, the crowds grew thinner. There were unexpected pockets of open ground and no trucks or cars. People strolled easily. Some walked arm in arm. Here and there I heard a vendor calling. Just then the crowd was moving in a counterclockwise direction, but this was coincidental. Circling Jabal al-Rahma is not a required rite of the Hajj. A minute later the crowd's flow changed direction. Something offhand, even idle, about the procession distinguished it from the purposeful *tawaf.*

On the inner edge of the road, near the base of the hill, emotions ran higher. Walking there, I passed a dozen Filipino women. They were weeping. Farther on, a distracted Kazakh pilgrim in a brilliant hennaed beard stood lost in meditation by the road. On the hill itself, blocks of *ihram*s went up, and the chanting swelled in sections. Mount Mercy induced a notable self-effacing ardor. The nearer I came, the more my mind went blank and the place took over.

I continued around the drive and soon crossed paths with an old Yemeni woman selling apples. . . . I impulsively bought all the woman's fruit and walked along the road passing them out. The apples were small and red, perhaps from San'a. They gave my hands something to do while I strolled around. I saw nothing out of the ordinary, really—shoulders, elbows, bare heads, tear-streaked faces. The mood was self-possessed, not at all trancelike. Now and then I felt a swell move through us—the unifying agency of the Hajj.

Time passed quickly at the mountain. When my supply of fruit ran out, I started winding back to the pavilion. The sky grew hazy as I went. The sun declined toward the Meccan hills.

MAKKAH. JULY 15 As my stay wound down in Mecca, I spent more time [at the Haram], marking my notebooks, meditating, reading. I strolled, performed my circuits, sat and watched. At mealtimes, I ducked out of the mosque to eat from wooden stalls in the jewelry market.

I [now possessed] an overview of the Hajj different from the Hajj I had imagined, and I wanted to fix it while my thoughts were fresh. I began to fill a notebook with summations. From California, I had viewed the Hajj as a journey to a physical destination. In fact, the Hajj was protean, all process. It surprised me now to see how off I'd been. In the West, the notion of pilgrimage centered on going, on reaching, on arrival. Nailing this moribund image to the Hajj was a mistake, like claiming that going home to dinner began with getting off work and ended when you reached the porch—omitting any mention of the meal.

Reaching Mecca was only a beginning. The goal of the Hajj was to perform it well. The rites were hard, sometimes unfathomable—like living. Yet they provided a counterweight to the usual view of life as a dog-and-cat fight. Elsewhere, except at the best of times, every person looked out for himself. During the Hajj, people looked out for each other. The Hajj is a shared rite of passage. I saw it through the eyes of others as much as through my own. In that way, it was like an act of love. . . .

I especially admired the way the sweat and the symbols flowed together. By an act of imagination and exertion, a spiritual rite of some duration fulfilled a private quest. For all its public aspects, the experience was intensely personal. By giving the pilgrim a chance to choose his moment, it provided a service missing in the West since the days of the medieval palmers: it offered a climax to religious life.

Maps

❦

Variant Spellings

Numbers in brackets refer to the figure on which the variant spelling appears. The spelling following the colon is the one used in this book.

'Adan [6]: Aden
Aqabeh [12]: Aqaba
Bijaya [9]: Bejaïa
Buraida [16]: Burayda
Cyrenaica [9]: eastern Libya
Dhu l-Hulaifa [10]: Dhu al-Halifah
Dimashk [6]: Damascus
Esfahan [12]: Isfahan
Fatimah [1, 2], Fat'mah [4]: Fatima
Ghazza [4, 6]: Gaza
Hail [16]: Ha'il
Hejaz [4, 7]: Hijaz
Jauf [16]: al-Jawf
Jebel Abu Qubes [4]: Abu Qubays
Jedda [12, 13], Jeddah [4], Jiddah [1, 2]: Jidda

al-Kahira [6]: Cairo
Khorasan [7]: Khurasan
Ma'abdah [4]: Ma'abida
Makkah [1, 2], Mekka [4]: Mecca
Madrasah [4]: *madrasa*
el-Merwa [4]: Marwa
mu'addhin [4]: muezzin
Nimira [3]: Namira
Qadhi [4]: Qadi
Sawakin [6]: Suwakin
esh-Shebeka [4]: al-Shubayka
sheik [4]: shaykh
sherif [4]: sharif
Ta'ef [7], Taif [4]: Ta'if
Tripolitania [9]: western Libya
Yanbo' [12, 13]: Yanbu

551

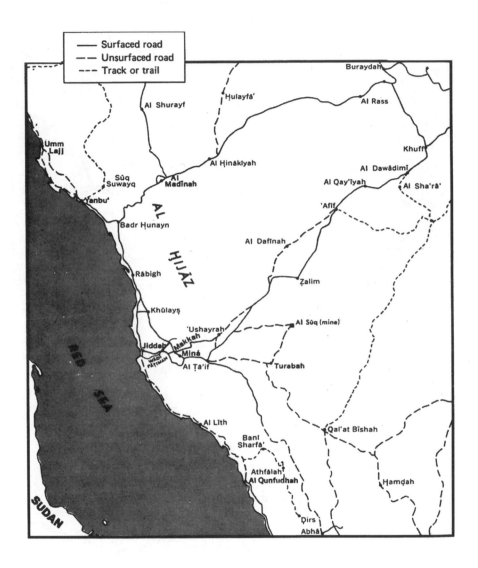

The Red Sea Region of the Arabian Hijaz

FIGURE I

Reprinted from *The Hajj Today: A Survey of the Contemporary Pilgrimage to Makkah* by David Edwin Long, Albany: 1979. By permission of the State University of New York Press.

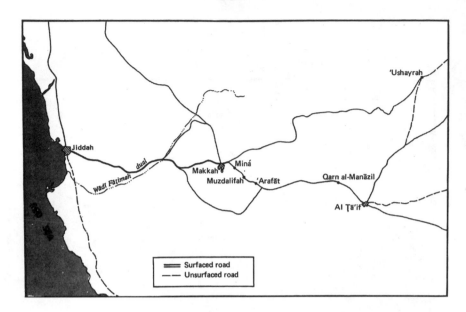

Mecca and Its Environs
FIGURE 2

Reprinted from *The Hajj Today: A Survey of the Contemporary Pilgrimage to Makkah* by David Edwin Long, Albany: 1979. By permission of the State University of New York Press.

The Pilgrim Route from Mecca to Mina, Arafat, and Muzdalifa
FIGURE 3

Reprinted from *The Hadj,* by Michael Wolfe, London: 1994. By permission of Reed Consumer Books.

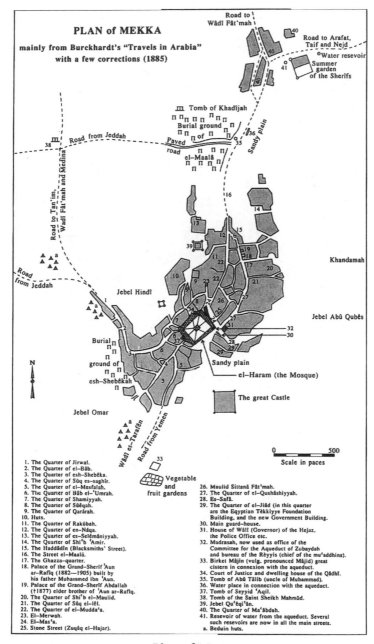

PLAN of MEKKA

mainly from Burckhardt's "Travels in Arabia"
with a few corrections (1885)

Road to
Wâdî Fât'mah

Road to Arafat,
Taif and Nejd

Water resevoir

Summer
garden
of the Sherifs

Tomb of Khadîjah

Burial ground
of

Paved
road

el-Maalâ

Road from Jeddah

Road to Tan'im,
Wadî Fât'mah and Medina

Sandy plain

Road
from
Jeddah

Jebel Hindî

Khandamah

Jebel Abû Qubês

Burial

ground of

esh-Shebêkah

Sandy plain

el-Haram (the Mosque)

N

The great Castle

Jebel Omar

Wâdî el-Tarafên

Road from Yemen

Vegetable
and
fruit gardens

0   500
Scale in paces

1. The Quarter of Jirwal.
2. The Quarter of el-Bâb.
3. The Quarter of esh-Shebêka.
4. The Quarter of Sûq es-saghîr.
5. The Quarter of el-Mesfalah.
6. The Quarter of Bâb el-'Umrah.
7. The Quarter of Shamiyyah.
8. The Quarter of Sûêqah.
9. The Quarter of Qarârah.
10. Huts.
11. The Quarter of Rakûbah.
12. The Quarter of en-Nâqa.
13. The Quarter of es-Selêmâniyyah.
14. The Quarter of Shi'b 'Amir.
15. The Haddâdîn (Blacksmiths' Street).
16. The Street el-Maalâ.
17. The Ghazza-quarter.
18. Palace of the Grand-Sherif 'Aun
    ar-Rafîq (1882—1905) built by
    his father Muhammed ibn 'Aun.
19. Palace of the Grand-Sherif Abdallah
    (†1877) elder brother of 'Aun ar-Rafîq.
20. The Quarter of Shi'b el-Maulid.
21. The Quarter of Sûq el-lêl.
22. The Quarter of el-Mudda'a.
23. El-Merwah.
24. El-Mas'a.
25. Stone Street (Zuqâq el-Hajar).

26. Maulid Sittanâ Fât'mah.
27. The Quarter of el-Qushâshiyyah.
28. Es-Safâ.
29. The Quarter of el-Jiâd (in this quarter
    are the Egyptian Têkkiyye Foundation
    Building, and the new Government Building.
30. Main guard-house.
31. House of Wâlî (Governor) of the Hejaz,
    the Police Office etc.
32. Madrasah, now used as office of the
    Committee for the Aqueduct of Zubaydah
    and bureau of the Rèyyis (chief of the mu'addhins).
33. Birket Mâjin (vulg. pronounced Mâjid) great
    cistern in connexion with the aqueduct.
34. Court of Justice and dwelling house of the Qâdhî.
35. Tomb of Abû Tâlib (uncle of Muhammad).
36. Water place in connection with the aqueduct.
37. Tomb of Seyyid 'Aqil.
38. Tomb of the Saint Sheikh Mahmûd.
39. Jebel Qu'êqi'ân.
40. The Quarter of Ma'âbdah.
41. Resevoir of water from the aqueduct. Several
    such resevoirs are now in all the main streets.
a. Beduin huts.

Plan of Mecca

FIGURE 4

Reprinted from *Mecca: A Literary History of the Muslim Holy Land,* New Jersey, 1994. By permission of Princeton University Press.

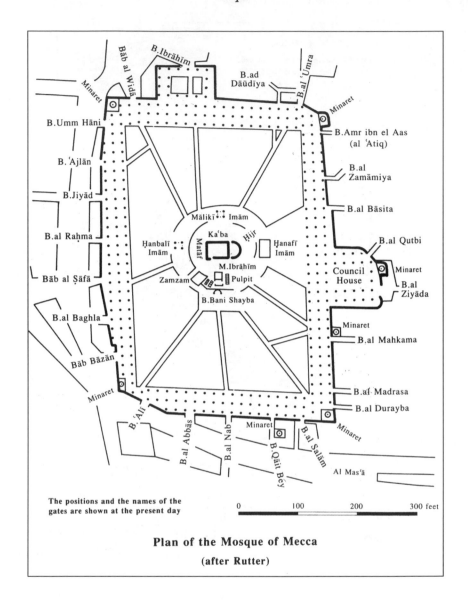

Plan of the Mosque of Mecca

(after Rutter)

Plan of the Mosque in Mecca

FIGURE 5

Reprinted from *Mecca: A Literary History of the Muslim Holy Land,* New Jersey, 1994. By permission of Princeton University Press.

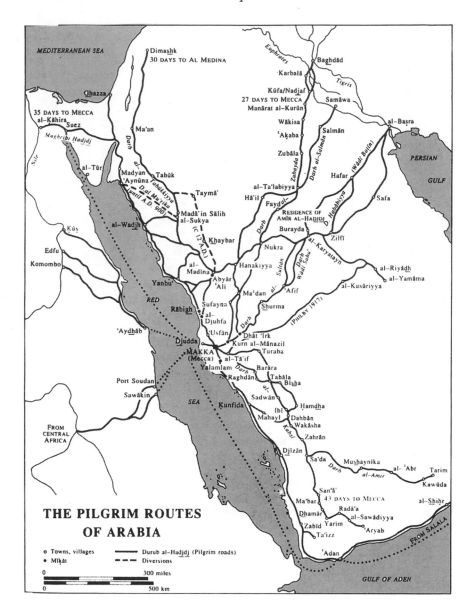

The Pilgrim Routes of Arabia

FIGURE 6

Reprinted from *Mecca: A Literary History of the Muslim Holy Land,* New Jersey, 1994. By permission of Princeton University Press.

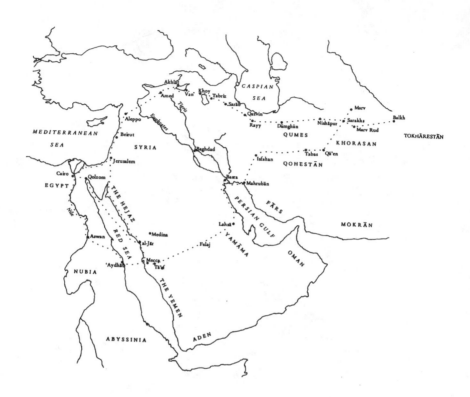

Naser-e Khosraw's Itinerary, 1046–52

FIGURE 7

Reprinted from *Naser-e Khosraw's Book of Travels,* translation, introduction, and notes by
W. M. Thackston, Jr., New York, 1986. By permission of Persian Heritage Foundation,
Bibliotheca Persica, Columbia University.

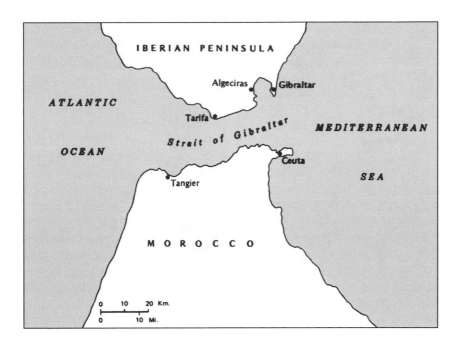

Region of the Strait of Gibraltar

FIGURE 8

Reprinted from *The Adventures of Ibn Battuta: A Muslim Traveler of the 14th Century*, by Ross E. Dunn, Berkeley and Los Angeles, 1989. By permission of the University of California.

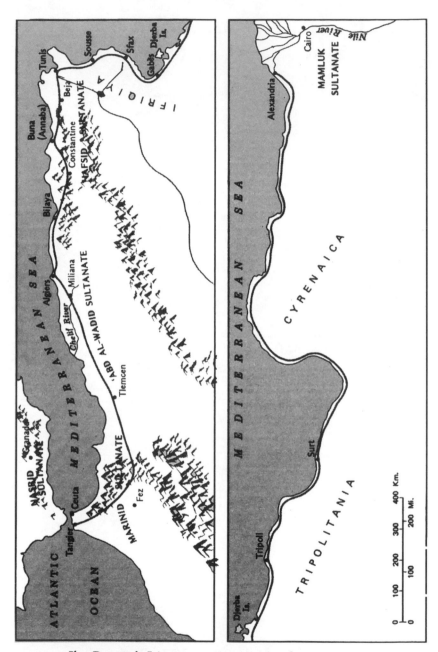

Ibn Battuta's Itinerary across North Africa, 1325–26.

FIGURE 9

Reprinted from *The Adventures of Ibn Battuta: A Muslim Traveler of the 14th Century,* by Ross E. Dunn, Berkeley and Los Angeles, 1989. By permission of the University of California.

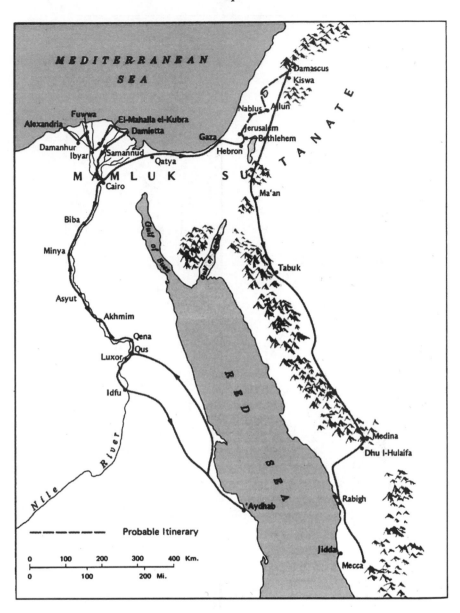

Ibn Battuta's Itinerary in Egypt, Syria, and Arabia, 1325–26.

FIGURE 10

Reprinted from *The Adventures of Ibn Battuta: A Muslim Traveler of the 14th Century,* by Ross
E. Dunn, Berkeley and Los Angeles, 1989. By permission of the University of California.

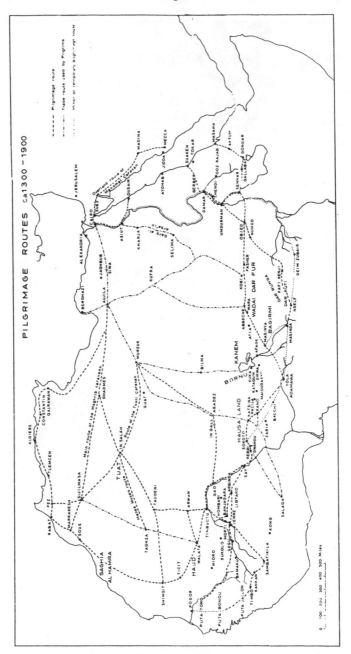

African Pilgrimage Routes to Mecca, ca. 1300–1900

FIGURE II

Reprinted from *The Pilgrimage Tradition in West Africa,* by Umar al-Naqar, Khartoum, Sudan, 1972. By permission of Khartoum University Press.

Maps

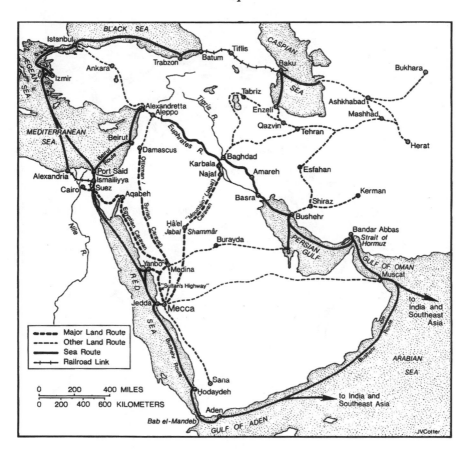

Major Pilgrimage Routes in the Nineteenth Century

FIGURE 12

Reprinted from *A Shi'ite Pilgrimage to Mecca, 1885–1886: The Safarnameh of Mirza Moham-mad Hosayn Farahani,* edited, translated, and annotated by Hafez Farmayan and Elton L. Daniel, Austin, 1990. By permission of University of Texas Press.

563

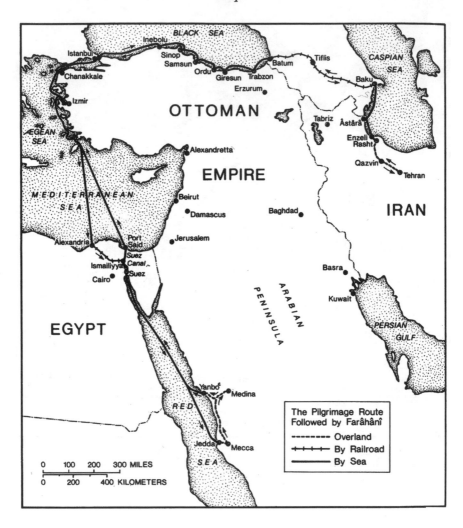

Farahani's Itinerary, 1885–86

FIGURE 13

Reprinted from *A Shiʿite Pilgrimage to Mecca, 1885–1886: The Safarnameh of Mirza Moham-mad Hosayn Farahani,* edited, translated, and annotated by Hafez Farmayan and Elton L. Daniel, Austin, 1990. By permission of University of Texas Press.

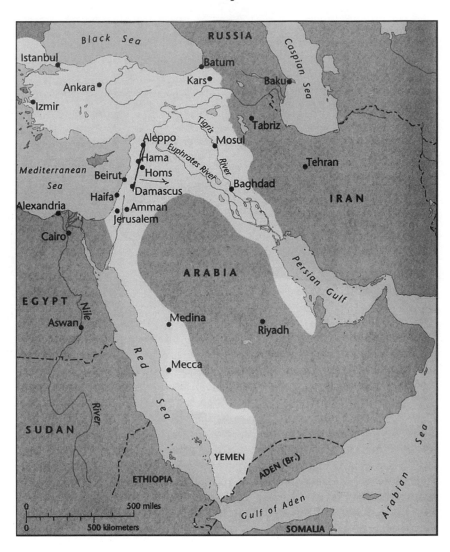

The Ottoman Empire in 1914

FIGURE 14

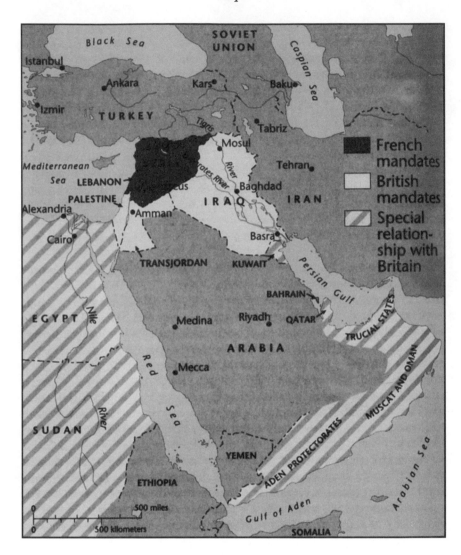

The Middle East in the Interwar Period

FIGURE 15

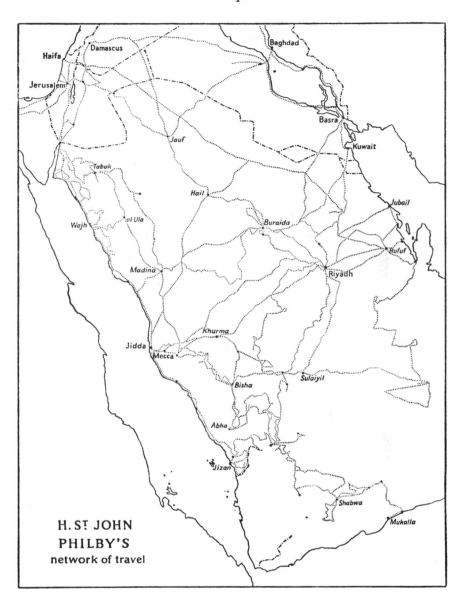

H. St. John Philby's Travels in Arabia, 1917–53

FIGURE 16

Reprinted from *Philby in Arabia,* by Elizabeth Monroe, New York, 1973. By permission of the Pitman Publishing Corporation.

Acknowledgments

Thanks go to my brother Daniel Wolfe for rescuing the initial notebook from which this collection grew. The project might have otherwise been abandoned. And to

- Abdullah Ankawi, Hajj scholar in Jidda, for documents and valuable discussion
- Professor Edmund Burke III, University of California at Santa Cruz, for instruction, direction, and advice
- Professor Julia Clancy-Smith, University of Arizona, for her responses to an early draft on Muslim Spain
- Vanessa Corrick, Assistant Librarian, Bodleian Library, Oxford University, for bibliographic assistance
- Professor Alan Abd al-Haqq Godlas, University of Georgia, for help with the Glossary
- Winmai Juniwan, in England, for bibliographic assistance
- Ibrahim Jastaniya, Office of the Vice-Minister of Hajj, Mecca, for documents on, and guidance in, Mecca
- Alex Kronemer, for valuable comments on the General Introduction
- Jamal Nasef, Acting Director, Department of Information, Royal Embassy of Saudi Arabia, Washington, D.C., for providing useful data in translation
- Professor Michael Pearson, University of South Wales, for valuable comments on the Indian Ocean Hajj
- Hatim Qadi, Vice Minister of Pilgrimage, for assistance in Mecca
- Alan Ritch, McHenry Library, University of California, Santa Cruz, for locating the hard-to-find volumes excerpted here
- Munir Sperling, for bringing Idries Shah's Hajj account to my attention
- Mahmud bin Muhammad Safar, Minister of Pilgrimages, Riyadh, Saudi Arabia, for detailed facts and statistics on the Hajj since 1945
- Abigail Winograd, for copy editing
- and to my friends Sam Amico, Kebir Helminski, Shaykh Khalil al-Khalil, Jo Menell, Jay Schumann, and Cathy Summa, all of whom were helpful in their ways

Permissions

Grateful acknowledgment is made to the following publishers for permission to reprint sections from the following works:

Lost in the Crowd, by Jalal Al-e Ahmad, translated by John Green, introduction by Michael Hillmann, 1984. By permission of Lynn Rienner, Publisher.

The Road to Mecca, by Muhammad Asad, 1952. By permission of Dar Al-Andalus Limited, Gibraltar.

The Sheltered Quarter: A Tale of a Boyhood in Mecca, by Hamza Bogary, 1991. By permission of the Center for Middle Eastern Studies at the University of Texas at Austin.

Pilgrimage to Mecca, by Evelyn Cobbold, 1934. By Permission of John Murray (Publishers) Ltd.

A Shiʿite Pilgrimage to Mecca, 1885–1886: The Safarnameh of Mirza Mohammad Hosayn Farahani. Edited, translated, and annotated by Hafez Farmayan and Elton L. Daniel, 1990. By permission of University of Texas Press.

The Fifth Pillar: The Story of a Pilgrimage to Mecca and Medina, by Saida Miller Khalifa, 1977. By permission of Exposition Press.

Naser-e Khosraw's Book of Travels, translation, introduction, and notes by W. M. Thackston, Jr., 1986. By permission of Persian Heritage Foundation, Bibliotheca Persica, Columbia University.

A Pilgrim in Arabia, by Harry St. John Bridger Philby, 1946. By permission of the Philby Estate.

Arabian Days, by Harry St. John Bridger Philby. By permission of the Philby Estate.

The Autobiography of Malcolm X, by Malcolm X with the assistance of Alex Haley, 1965. By permission of Ballantine Books.

Every effort has been made to locate the copyright holders of these works. Inquiries may be directed to the publisher.

Glossary:
Names and Terms

ABA   a man's overrobe, in Arabia.

ABBASID DYNASTY   second of the two great dynasties to rule the caliphate, the Abassids overthrew the **Umayyad Dynasty** in 750 and reigned until the destruction of Baghdad by the Mongols in 1258.

ABU BAKR   the first **caliph,** successor to Muhammad (reigned 632–34).

ADHAN   the Muslim call to prayer.

AGHA   a chief.

AISHA   daughter of **Abu Bakr** and Muhammad's favorite wife in his later years.

ALHAMDULILLAH   equivalent to "Gratitude is due to God"; a general expression.

ALI IBN ABU TALIB   (died 661). Cousin and son-in-law of the Prophet, considered by Shiʿites the rightful heir to the caliphate and the most inspired of the early companions of Muhammad. Ali's two sons by Muhammad's daughter Fatima were the Prophet's most direct male descendants. The Fatimid lineage descends from this union. Descendants of the elder son, **Hasan,** are often referred to as *sharif*s; those of the younger son, **Husayn,** are termed **sayyid**s.

ALID   a descendant of **Ali.**

AMIR   a general or other military commander; by extension, the governor of a territory.

AMIR AL-HAJJ   the official leader of a pilgrim caravan.

ARAFAT   the desert plain and mountain fifteen miles east of Mecca, where pilgrims perform the rite of standing (*wukuf*) during the high point of the **Hajj.**

ARAMCO   the Arabian American Oil Company, which explored and developed the Saudi Arabian oil concession beginning in the early 1930s. By 1964, American joint shareholders included Standard Oil Company of California, Texaco, Standard Oil Company of New Jersey (later Exxon), and Socony-Vacuum Company (later Mobil Oil Company). The Saudi government nationalized Aramco in 1973.

All cross-references appear in boldface type in an entry's definition.

ARNAUT   an Albanian; in particular, an Albanian Muslim soldier in the service of the Ottoman Empire, especially in eighteenth- and nineteenth-century Egypt.

ʿASHURA   a holiday on the tenth of the month of **Muharram** commemorating the martyrdom of Imam **Husayn** and his followers at Karbala in 680; of special importance to Shiʿite Muslims.

ASR   afternoon; in particular, the third prayer of the Muslim canonical day.

AYAT   a verse of the Quran; in general, any sign of God's work in nature.

AYYUBID DYNASTY   (1169–1250), founded at Cairo after the overthrow of the **Fatimid Dynasty** by Saladin; the rule of Egypt, northern Iraq, most of Syria, and Yemen passed to his descendants.

BAB   gate or doorway in a mosque, city wall, or house.

BAB AL-SALAAM   Gate of Peace; the traditional gate for entering the **Haram** in Mecca.

BADR   Site of an important battle during the Medina period (March 15, 624), between a small Muslim force led by Muhammad and a well-guarded **Quraysh** caravan returning from Gaza; a decisive victory for the Muslims.

BANU SHAYBA   the clan appointed by Muhammad in perpetuity as caretakers of the Meccan mosque.

BAQIYYAʿ   a Muslim cemetery in Medina where many of Muhammad's closest companions are buried; therefore, a major historic landmark.

BARAKA   spiritual power or blessedness; also, a miraculous force that emanates from certain people and places.

BAYRAM   feast; the Turkish equivalent to the Arabic *id*. The feast that marks the end of the **Ramadan** fast is Seker Bayrami (**Id al-Fitr**); the feast that marks the end of the **Hajj** is Kurban Bayrami (**Id al-Adha**).

BAYT ALLAH   *See Kaʿba*

BAYT AL-HARAM   the Sacred House; Arabic name of the Grand Mosque in Mecca.

BAZAN   public fountain, especially the one near the entry to **Arafat**.

BEDOUIN OR BEDAWI   traditional nomadic camel-breeding tribes of the Arabian desert.

BIDʿA   religious innovation; also, diverging from the established way to the point of heresy although not to the point of actual unbelief; the opposite of *sunna*.

BISMILLAH   in the name of God, the beginning of nearly every chapter of the Quran; also, a protective formula, frequently uttered before any action, from eating or drinking to entering a house.

BLACK STONE   an ancient relic mounted in the eastern corner of the **Kaʿba** about five feet above the ground and held in place by a silver band; in Arabic, al-Hajar al-Aswad. The Stone is kissed, touched, or saluted by passing pilgrims as a gesture of respect for the Prophet Muhammad, who did the same on his final pilgrimage to Mecca.

CALIPH   originally, any of the four successors of Muhammad, spiritual and temporal rulers of Islam; later, a figurehead of the Muslim world, whose significance waxed and waned over the centuries. *See also* **sultan.**

CUBIT   originally, the distance from the elbow to the tip of the middle finger; an ancient measurement equal to about 1.5 modern feet.

DAR AL-ISLAM   lands under Muslim rule; later, any lands where Muslim institutions are maintained.

DERVISH or DARWISH   a devotee or mendicant of a Muslim order or brotherhood. *See* **faqir.**

DEY   Ottoman governor or military commandant in North Africa.

DHU AL-HIJJA   the last lunar month of the Islamic calendar, during which the **Hajj** is undertaken.

DHU AL-QADA   the eleventh lunar month of the Islamic calendar.

DILUL   a fine breed of Arabian camel.

DIR'IYYA   original town of the Saudi **amirs,** near present-day Riyadh.

DISHDASHAH   See **thobe.**

ELL   an ancient unit of measure, between 1.5 and 2 feet.

FAJR   the first, predawn, prayer of the Muslim canonical day.

FAQIH   an expert in Islamic jurisprudence (*fiqh*). *See* **mufti.**

FAQIR (plural *FUQARA*)   member of a religious order; an adept. See **dervish.**

FARSAKH   a Persian measurement equivalent to between 2.3 and 4.2 miles. *See* **parasang.**

AL-FATIHA   the opening chapter (*sura*) of the Quran and the most frequently recited Muslim prayer.

FATIMA   daughter of the prophet Muhammad and wife of *Ali,* from whom the **Fatimid Dynasty** descends.

FATIMID DYNASTY   rulers of an empire in North Africa (909) and subsequently in the Middle East (960–1171); founders of Cairo (968).

FIRMAN   a decree or license issued by a ruler.

FRIDAY MOSQUE   a mosque where the Friday congregational prayer may be conducted.

HADITH (plural *AHADITH*)   often translated as "tradition"; a report of what the Prophet Muhammad, his companions, or one of the first four "rightly guided" *caliph*s said or did. Collectively, the *ahadith* form a large and active literature with the status of Scripture in the determination of precedent in Islamic law.

HAGAR   according to the Quran, one of Abraham's wives and the mother of Ishmael. Her search between **Safa** and **Marwa** for water for her son is commemorated during the **Hajj** by the rite called *sa'y.*

HAJJ   the annual Muslim pilgrimage to Mecca, required of every able Muslim at least once in a lifetime.

HAJJI (feminine HAJJA)   a prenominal title given to any Muslim who has made the **Hajj.**

HAMZA   an uncle of the Prophet Muhammad and a famous Muslim warrior and early martyr.

HANAFI   the **Sunni** system of jurisprudence ascribed to Abu Hanifah (699–767);

the predominant school of modern Turkey. Its adherents depend strongly on analogy in the interpretation of the Quran.

HANBALI   the **Sunni** system of jurisprudence ascribed to Ahmad ibn Hanbal (780–885); the majority sect in modern Saudi Arabia. This conservative movement "returns" interpretation to the Quran.

HARAM   a sacred precinct with special laws of asylum; also the area of any mosque.

HARAM   in Mecca, the walled court of the Great Mosque (**al-Haram al-Sharif**) or, the whole of Mecca, together with the surrounding territory within the **haram**, or sacred limits, as marked by pairs of stone pillars built beside the roads outside the city.

AL-HARAM AL-SHARIF   the Noble Sanctuary; popular name for the mosque complex at Mecca.

HARWALA   the quicker part of the *sa'y* rite.

HASAN   older son of **Ali** and **Fatima** (died 680).

HASHIMITE   the house of Hashim, originally Muhammad's clan; later, the name of the dynasty of **sharif**s who governed Mecca.

HATIM   the low semicircular wall built out from the northwest face of the **Ka'ba**, surrounding the *hijr* area.

HAWQALA   any of various Quranic verses said on difficult occasions to ward off evil.

HIJAB   Arabic term for the Muslim woman's veil; in Persian, *chador.*

HIJAZ   highland and Red Sea coastal region in the northwest of the Arabian Peninsula, containing Mecca, Medina, Rabigh Jidda, and the **Haram** Territory.

HIJR   semicircular area extending from the northwest face of the **Ka'ba**, traditionally identified as the burial place of Ishmael and **Hagar.**

HIJRA   the Prophet's departure from Mecca to Medina on July 16, 622; hence, the first day of the Muslim calendar and the system of dating marked A.H. (*anno hegirae*) in the West.

HUSAYN   younger son of **Ali** and **Fatima,** martyred at **Karbala** in 680 while attempting to gain control of the caliphate. Shi'ites consider Imam Husayn the pre-eminent figure of resistance against oppression and tyranny.

ID AL-FITR   feast that celebrates the end of the **Ramadan** fast; also called Id al-Seghir, the Little Feast; in Turkish, Seker Bayrami.

ID AL-ADHA   Feast of the Sacrifice marking the formal end of the *Hajj* on the tenth day of the last month of the Muslim calendar and continuing three more days; also called, Id al-Kebir, the Big Feast; in Persian, Ayd-e Azha, Ayd-e Qorban; in Turkish, Kurban Bayrami. It takes place at **Mina** for **Hajj** pilgrims.

IHRAM   the rites of purification that pilgrims complete before entering the Sacred Territory of Mecca to perform the **Hajj** or **Umra.** The term also applies to a manner of dress indicating this ritual status: for men, two lengths of unstitched cotton cloth worn during the Hajj or Umra rites at Mecca; for women, modest national dress; also called the attire of submission or the clothing of the next life.

IMAM   prayer leader in a mosque; also, by extension, the leader of a Muslim community.

INSH'ALLAH   God willing; a phrase that follows any statement or promise concerning the future.

IQAL   a circlet worn over the *kaffiya* to keep it in place.

'ISHA   the fifth, prayer of the Muslim day, occurring after dusk.

ISMA'ILIS   a sect of Islam, a branch of **Shi'ism.**

IZAR   the lower half of the *ihram* garment, covering the body from navel to knee.

JABAL NUR   Mountain of Light; the mountain in Mecca where Muhammad received the first Quranic revelation.

JABAL AL-RAHMA   Mount Mercy; Mountain of Pardon or of Forgiveness; a hill on the Plain of **Arafat** where the Prophet Muhammad delivered his farewell sermon and, thus, where a sermon is given each year during the high point of the **Hajj.**

JAMARAT   a group of three pillars—Jamarat al-Aqaba (the biggest), Jamarat al-Wusta (the middle sized), and Jamarat al-Ula (the smallest)—where pilgrims throw pebbles during the **Hajj;** also, the place they are located, the rite itself, or the pebbles thrown.

JEMAA or *JUMA*   the congregational Muslim Friday prayer.

JIHAD   effort; struggle. Islam distinguishes two jihads: the greater effort, applying to a person's struggle against base impulses, such as pride, envy, greed; and the lesser effort, a war in the defense of Islam and in accordance with **Sharia** law.

JINN   invisible beings, sometimes harmful, at other times helpful, to human beings.

JUMA   See *JEMAA.*

JUMADA I   the fifth lunar month of the Islamic calendar.

JUMADA II   the sixth lunar month of the Islamic calendar.

KA'BA   the shrine at the center of the mosque in Mecca, toward which Muslims face when they pray and around which they circle as pilgrims in the rite of *tawaf;* variously called the Shrine, the House of God (Bayt Allah), the House.

KAFFIYA   the checkered head scarf worn by Arab men in the Middle East.

KARBALA   the desert site sixty miles south-southwest of Baghdad where in 680, Imam **Husayn,** younger son of **Ali** and **Fatima** and grandson of the Prophet, leading an insurrection by Ali's family, was killed with seventy followers while trying to seize the Islamic caliphate from the second **Umayyad** ruler, Yazid ibn Mu'awiyya (reigned 680–683). The event is celebrated annually by pilgrimages to Karbala and marked as the year's great day of mourning by Shi'ite Muslims, for whom the passion play depicting this and other historical tragedies plays a central part.

KHADIJA   the Prophet Muhammad's first and only wife until she died, in 619.

KHAN   title for a ruler; also, a public hostel for travelers and pilgrims (caravansary).

KHAYBAR   site of a siege and subsequent battle fought between Muslims and Arabian Jews in May-June 628, located about a hundred miles north of Medina.

KISWA   the ceremonial black and gold cloth covering the **Ka'ba**, which is annually replaced during the **Hajj**.

LABAYK   I am here; I am ready; first word of the **Talbiyya**.

MADHAB   sometimes rendered "sect," "school," or "rite"; a system of jurisprudence, of which four have survived in **Sunni** Islam: **Hanafi, Hanbali, Maliki,** and **Shafi'i.**

MADRASA   a Muslim school in which traditional fields of Muslim scholarship are studied; in North Africa, *madersa.*

MAGHRIB   the West; Arab North Africa.

MAGHRIB   the fourth prayer hour of the Muslim day, just after sunset.

MAHMAL   a traditional camel-mounted palanquin accompanying the official **Hajj** caravan from Damascus and, later, Cairo as a symbol of sovereignty.

MALIKI   the **Sunni** system of jurisprudence ascribed to Malik ibn Anas (715–95); the predominant sect in present-day Morocco.

MAMLUK   originally, the slave-soldier corps of Saladin (reigned 1171–93), whose leaders replaced their Ayubbid masters in 1250 and continued to rule Egypt and its provinces until 1517; more generally, any member of their large army.

MAQAM IBRAHIM   Station of Abraham; a small shrine in the Meccan mosque marking a legendary boulder upon which Abraham reputedly stood to rebuild the **Ka'ba**; today, it is sheltered in a kiosk.

MAQSURA   an enclosed or screened-off portion of a mosque, originally reserved to protect a ruler while praying.

MARWA   one of two hills in Mecca about four hundred yards apart between which Ishmael's mother, **Hagar**, is said to have run in search of water; in Persian, Marveh.

MASA'A   the course, between the hills of **Safa** and **Marwa** in Mecca, along which the rite of *sa'y* is performed.

MASH'AR AL-HARAM   a pre-Islamic Sacred Grove; an area, marked by a mosque, in **Muzdalifa** where pilgrims spend the night after leaving **Arafat**, before they may return to **Mina**.

MASHRABIYA   protruding wood lattice window casement; also called *raushan.*

MIHRAB   the niche in a mosque wall indicating the *qibla*, or direction of the **Ka'ba** in Mecca, toward which Muslims pray.

MINA   a village and valley a few miles east of Mecca where the **Hajj** procession camps on its way to and from **Arafat**.

MINBAR   a portable staircase in a mosque from which the **imam** delivers a sermon; a form of pulpit.

MIQAT   the stations bordering the Sacred Territory where pilgrims purify themselves and put on the *ihram.*

MISHLAH   a loose cloak, often with golden threads on the fringes, worn loosely over other robes and clothing.

MOLVI or *MOULVI*   a religious teacher.

MUDAYYINA   Those Devoted to Religion; the proper and preferred name of the Wahhabis.

MUEZZIN   the mosque crier who calls Muslims to prayer from a minaret; from Turkish, and now the accepted English spelling of *mu'adhdhin.*

MUFTI   an expert in the **Sharia,** who gives public decisions. See *faqih.*

MUHARRAM   the first lunar month of the Islamic calendar.

MUHASSIR   a valley on the **Hajj** pilgrim route forming the boundary between **Mina** and **Muzdalifa.**

MUHRIM   a term applied to a pilgrim in the requisite state of ritual purity (*ihram*) for entering the Mecca shrine area.

MUJAWIR (pl. *MUJAWWIRIN*)   a sojourner; one who resides for an unusually long period near a holy place to receive the blessing associated with it.

MULLAH   a generic term for clergyman.

MURID   disciple of a **Sufi** *murshid,* or *pir.*

MURSHID or *PIR*   a **Sufi** master; one authorized to lead disciples on the **Sufi** path.

MUSSELMAN   older, variant European spelling of *Muslim;* probably from Persian, *musulman.*

MUTAWWIF   a guide who counsels and leads pilgrims on the proper performance of the **Hajj** rites.

MUZDALIFA   a small town about four miles from **Arafat,** the stopping place after Arafat on the route of the **Hajj** recessional.

MUZAWWIR   a pilgrim's guide in Medina.

NAFRA   the Pouring Forth or the Rush; a rapid movement undertaken en masse by all pilgrims on leaving **Arafat** for the night vigil at **Muzdalifa.**

NIYA   intention; the mental or verbalized statement of purpose preceding any ritual action in Islam.

OSMANLI   an Ottoman Turk.

OTTOMAN EMPIRE   an empire established by Turkish tribes in fourteenth-century Anatolia. The Ottomans ruled most of the Middle East from 1453 to 1922.

PARASANG   originally, the distance traveled by a caravan in one hour; equal to just under 3.5 modern miles (6 kilometers).

PASHA   a Turkish title, often equivalent to governor; in Arabic, *bashaw.*

PATROON   Algerian slave owner; in Spanish, *patrón.*

PORTE   the Sublime Porte in Istanbul; a widely accepted French term for the "high gate" (*babiali*) of the Grand Vizier's offices, for which the Ottoman government was named.

PROPHET'S MOSQUE   the site of Muhammad's home after leaving Mecca and of his grave; one of the three principal shrines of **Sunni** Muslims; the second destination of most **hajjis** while in the **Hijaz.**

QADI   a judge administering **Sharia** law.

QADIRIYYA   followers of Abd al-Qadir al-Jilani (died 1166); today, one of the largest **Sufi** orders.

QIBLA   the direction of the **Ka'ba** in Mecca, from wherever one is standing; the orientation point of prayer marked by a niche, or *mihrab,* in a mosque.

QIRBA   a waterskin.

QURAYSH   the tribe of Muhammad; traditional protectors of the **Haram** in Mecca and providers of security for **hajjis**.

RABI'I   the third lunar month of the Islamic calendar.

RABI' II   the fourth lunar month of the Islamic calendar.

RAJAB   the seventh lunar month of the Islamic calendar.

RAK'A (plural *RAKAT*)   a cycle of ritual daily prayer (**salat**) consisting of recitation, bowing, kneeling, and prostration. The five daily prayers are composed of two (predawn), four (noon or not long after), four (afternoon), three (near sunset), and four (dusk or not long after) *rakat*s.

RAMADAN   the ninth lunar month of the Islamic calendar, during which Muslims fast in the daylight hours.

RAMAL   the quickened pace of the first three circuits around the **Ka'ba** in *tawaf;* also, a meter in Arabic poetry.

RENEGADO   European volunteer in a Mamluk or other mercenary Muslim army, (ca. 1500–1900.)

RIDA   the upper half of the *ihram* garment.

SAFA   one of two hills in Mecca about four hundred yards apart between which **Hagar** is said to have run in search of water for her son, Ishmael.

SAFAR   the second lunar month of the Islamic calendar.

SALAAM ALAYKOUM   Peace be upon you; universal Arabic greeting.

SALAT   ritual daily prayer, as an act of piety and expression of humility; not an entreaty or supplication.

SA'Y   the hastening, the hurry, the running; a **Hajj** rite that commemorates **Hagar**'s search for water in the desert, comprising seven ritual laps between two hills, **Safa** and **Marwa**, at the **Haram** Mosque in Mecca.

SAYYID (feminine *SAYYIDA*)   originally, a descendant of the Prophet through **Husayn**, son of **Ali**, Muhammad's cousin and son-in-law, and Muhammad's daughter, **Fatima**; later, any noble; in Arabic, an honorific.

SELJUK DYNASTY   a ruling military family of Oguz Turkmen tribes who founded an empire in Persia and Mesopotamia (1038–1194) and in central and eastern Anatolia (1077–1307) that for a period also included Syria and Palestine.

SEPOY   soldier, especially in the Ottoman cavalry; also, *sipahi, spachi.*

SEQUIN   a gold piece; a ducat or dinar.

SHABAN   the eighth lunar month of the Islamic calendar; the month preceding **Ramadan**.

SHAFI'I   the **Sunni** system of jurisprudence ascribed to al-Shafi'i (767–820), deriving from the **Maliki** school and distinguished by a capacity to appeal to local authorities and traditions in resolving legal and religious questions.

SHARIA   the Path or Way; sometimes translated as Sacred Law or Canon Law; the whole body of moral law guiding the life of a Muslim, modeled on the Quran and **Sunna**.

SHARIF (feminine *SHARIFA*)   originally, a descendant of the Prophet through **Hasan,** son of Ali, Muhamamad's cousin and son-in-law, and Muhammad's daughter, **Fatima;** by extension, the ruling family of Mecca from ca. 1200 to 1924; more generally, any noble; an honorific.

SHAWAL   the tenth lunar month of the Islamic calendar.

SHAYKH (feminine *SHAYKA*)   elder; a person of knowledge or understanding; in **Sufi** circles, a guide or teacher; among the Arab **Bedouin,** a clan or tribal leader; in modern Middle Eastern society, a title of deference, eminence, or respect.

SHEVRIA or *SHUBREYA*   in the Hijaz, a square camel saddle made up like a small bed on which one rider sits.

SHI'ISM   a large and diverse group of Muslim sects that distinguish themselves from the **Sunni** rite by sharing a belief that Muhammad's cousin and son-in-law, Ali, was the legitimate **caliph** after the Prophet and that succession to the caliphate should be hereditary; also known as Shi'at Ali, Party of Ali.

SHUBREYA   See **shevria.**

SHUGDUF   two square panniers constructed around a framework of wood and rope-work and set on a camel, used to convey pilgrims in the Hijaz. Each pannier holds one person.

SIND   the Indus River territories; generally, modern-day Pakistan.

SOUK   an Arab market area, sometimes with covered lanes.

SUFI   a follower of Sufism, the mystical paths of Islam.

SULTAN   in early times, the actual ruler, often with military power, in contrast to the **caliph,** or spiritual head of the Muslim people; later, the usual term for a regional or imperial sovereign.

SUNNA   the practice and example of Muhammad, of which the *ahadith* are illustrations; the opposite of *bid'a;* by extension, acceptable behavior. As an adjective, it describes an action as either *sunna* or not.

SUNNI   the Way of the Customs of Muhammad; adherent of the majority sect of Islam; distinguished from **Shi'ism** by a belief that the post of **caliph** is elective, not hereditary; all Sunnis subscribe to one of the four schools, **Hanafi, Hanbali, Maliki,** or **Shafi'i.**

SURA   a chapterlike division of the Quran.

TA'IF   a mountain town almost overlooking Mecca.

TAKHTRUAN   a deluxe litter carried by two camels for conveying pilgrims in the **Hijaz.**

TALBIYYA   acquiescence; a prayer frequently chanted by pilgrims, the first word of which is *labayk,* "I am here"; an answer to a divine summons.

TAQIYYA   religious dissimulation or concealment, practiced by various minority Muslim sects at different times to escape persecution.

TARIQA   way; used especially to refer to the mystical paths of the Sufis; by extension, a **Sufi** group or order with a particular method of achieving complete spiritual and physical integration.

TAWAF turning or circumambulation; a pilgrim rite comprising seven circuits of the **Ka'ba.**

THOBE or *DISHDASHAH* the long-sleeved, ankle-length gown worn by Arab men; in Arabic, *thawb.*

TOMAN basic unit of Iranian currency.

TRAVEL LIAR a term coined by the American scholar Percy G. Adams, used here to describe a European travel author who wrote in a lifelike manner about journeys to places he had never been.

UHUD site of the first battle fought by Muslims.

ULAMA (singular, *'ALIM*) people learned in Islamic legal and religious studies; where institutionalized, a religious senate.

UMAYYAD DYNASTY first Muslim dynasty (661–750) to rule the caliphate, stretching at its peak (685–705) from Spain to India.

UMRA the Minor or Lesser Pilgrimage to Mecca, including the rites of *tawaf* and *sa'y* but excluding **Arafat.** Of a more individual nature than the **Hajj,** it may be carried out at any time.

VIZIER a ruler's administrator; anglicized form of the Arabic *wazir.*

WAHHABI Western term for a follower of Shaykh Muhammad ibn Abd al-Wahhab (1703–92) and his interpretation of the **Hanbali** teachings; more properly, **Mudayyina.** This religious movement provided the theological basis for the Sa'ud family's conquest and unification of the Arabian peninsula.

WAQF a pious endowment or mortmain dedicated, sometimes in perpetuity, to the upkeep of a mosque, hospital, or school. The mosques at Mecca and Medina were and are the recipients of many such endowments.

WONDER BOOK a fanciful atlas of unknown lands; a medieval European literary genre.

WUDU' the ritual ablution establishing a state of purity required before Muslim prayer.

WUKUF the **Hajj** rite of "standing together" at **Arafat.** This obligatory noon-to-sunset vigil is the high point of the pilgrimage.

YAWM AL-TARWIYYA the Day of Washing, on which the **Ka'ba** is given a ceremonial cleaning, following which a new *kiswa* is draped over the Shrine.

ZAKAT a ritual annual tax paid by Muslims and distributed to the poor.

ZAMZAM the sacred well inside the mosque at Mecca.

ZAMZAMI members of the Shrine guild who provide pilgrims with water from the **Zamzam** well.

ZAWIYA a Sufi center; in Persian, *khaniqah;* in Turkish, *tekke.*

ZUHR the second prayer hour of the Muslim day, usually falling in the hour beginning a few minutes after high noon.

Selected Bibliography

※※※

The following list of books includes the editions from which these selections were excerpted. A more extensive bibliography of secondary literature on the Hajj may be found in Sadar and Badawi, *Hajj Studies* (see below.)

General Introduction

Armstrong, Karen. *Muhammad: A Biography of the Prophet.* San Francisco: HarperCollins, 1992.

Crone, Patricia. *Meccan Trade and the Rise of Islam.* Princeton, N.J.: Princeton University Press, 1987.

Eickelman, Dale F., and James Piscatori, eds. *Muslim Travelers.* Berkeley: University of California Press, 1990.

Hourani, Albert. *A History of the Arab Peoples.* Cambridge, Mass.: Belknap Press of Harvard University, 1991.

Lings, Martin. *Muhammad: His Life Based on the Earliest Sources.* Rochester, Vt.: Inner Traditions, 1983.

Ministry of Information. *At the Service of Allah's Guests.* Riyadh: Kingdom of Saudi Arabia, Ministry of Information, 1992.

Peters, F. E. *Mecca: A Literary History of the Muslim Holy Land.* Princeton, N.J.: Princeton University Press, 1994.

———. *The Hajj: The Muslim Pilgrimage to Mecca and the Holy Places.* Princeton, N.J.: Princeton University Press, 1994.

Sardar, Ziauddin, and M. A. Zaki Badawi, eds. *Hajj Studies.* London: Croom Helm, for the Hajj Research Centre, King Abd al-Aziz University, Jidda, 1978.

Part One: The Medieval Period
INTRODUCTION

Campbell, Mary, B. *The Witness and the Other World: Exotic European Travel Writing, 400–1600.* Ithaca, N.Y.: Cornell University Press, 1988.

Dunn, Ross E. *The Adventures of Ibn Battuta: A Muslim Traveler of the Fourteenth Century.* Berkeley and Los Angeles: University of California Press, 1986.

Hodgson, Marshall G. S. *The Venture of Islam: Conscience and History in a World Civilization,* 3 vols. Chicago: University of Chicago Press, 1977.

Ohler, Norbert. *The Medieval Traveller.* Translated from German by Caroline Hillier. Suffolk, England: Boydell Press, 1989.

Wilson, Peter Lamborn. *Sacred Drift: Essays on the Margins of Islam.* San Francisco: City Lights Books, 1993.

NASER-E KHOSRAW

Corbin, Henry. "Nasir-i Khusrau and Iranian Isma'ilism." In *The Cambridge History of Iran,* vol. 4, pp. 520–42. London: Cambridge University Press, 1975.

Khosraw, Naser-e. *Book of Travels.* Translated from Persian with an introduction and notes by W. M. Thackston, Jr. New York: Persian Heritage Foundation, Bibliotheca Persica, Columbia University, 1986.

———. *Forty Poems from the Divan.* Translated from Persian with introductions and notes by Peter Lamborn Wilson and Gholam Reza Aavani. Tehran: Imperial Iranian Academy of Philosophy, 1977.

IBN JUBAYR

Dunn, Ross E. *The Adventures of Ibn Battuta.* Berkeley: University of California Press, 1986.

Fletcher, Richard. *Moorish Spain.* Berkeley and Los Angeles: University of California Press, 1992.

Hoffman, Eleanor. *Realm of the Evening Star: A History of Morocco and the Lands of the Moors.* New York: Chilton Books, 1965.

Ibn Jubayr, Muhammad ibn Ahmad. *Voyages.* Translated and annotated by Maurice Gaudefroy-Demombynes. 2 vols. Paris: Paul Guethner, 1949–51.

———. *The Travels of Ibn Jubayr: Being the Chronicle of a Mediaeval Spanish Moor concerning His Journey to the Egypt of Saladin, the Holy Cities of Arabia, Baghdad the City of the Caliphs, the Latin Kingdom of Jerusalem, and the Norman Kingdom of Sicily.* Translated by R.J.C. Broadhurst with an introduction and notes. London: Jonathan Cape, 1952.

Khadra, Salma, ed. *The Legacy of Muslim Spain.* Leiden, New York, and Cologne: E. J. Brill/Project of Translation from Arabic (PROTA), 1992.

Mahlouf, Amin. *The Crusades through Arab Eyes.* New York: Schocken Books, 1985.

Netton, Ian Richard. "Basic Structures and Signs of Alienation in the *Rihla* of Ibn Jubayr." In *Golden Roads: Migration, Pilgrimage, and Travel in Medieval and Modern Islam,* edited by I. R. Netton. Surrey, England: Curzon Press, 1993.

IBN BATTUTA

Dunn, Ross E. "International Migrations of Literate Muslims in the Later Middle Period: The Case of Ibn Battuta." In *Golden Roads: Migration, Pilgrimage, and Travel in Medieval and Modern Islam,* edited by I. R. Netton. Surrey, England: Curzon Press, 1993.

Ibn Battuta, Abu Abd Allah. *Voyages d'ibn Batoutah.* Annotated Arabic edition and French translation by C. Defremery and B. R. Sanguinetti. Paris: Société Asiatique, 1874–79.

————. *The Travels of Ibn Battuta: 1324–58,* vols. 1–2. Translated with revisions and notes by H.A.R. Gibb. Cambridge, England: Cambridge University Press, 1958.

Ohler, Norbert. *The Medieval Traveller.* Translated from German by Caroline Hillier. Suffolk, England: Boydell Press, 1989.

Part Two: Enter the Europeans
INTRODUCTION

Adams, Percy G. *Travelers and Travel Liars: 1660–1800.* Berkeley: University of California Press, 1962.

Campbell, Mary B. *The Witness and the Other World: Exotic European Travel Writing, 400–1600.* Ithaca, N.Y.: Cornell University Press, 1988.

Fabri, Felix. *The Wanderings of Felix Fabri.* Translated from Latin by Aubrey Stewart. Palestine Pilgrims' Texts Society, vol. 7, 1893. Reprint, New York: AMS Press, 1971, pp. 666–70.

Harff, Arnold von. *The Pilgrimage of Arnold von Harff.* Translated from German by Malcolm Letts. Hakluyt Society, 2d ser., vol. 94 (London, 1967), pp. 153–54.

Joseph, Roger. "Islam: Its Representation in the West." *The Maghreb Review* 10 (1985): 4–6.

Sabini, John. *Armies in the Sand: The Struggle for Mecca and Medina.* London: Thames and Hudson, 1981.

Southern, R. W. *Western Views of Islam in the Middle Ages.* Cambridge, Mass.: Harvard University Press, 1962.

LUDOVICO DI VARTHEMA

Varthema, Ludovico di. *The Travels of Ludovico di Varthema in Egypt, Syria, Arabia, Deserta, and Arabia Felix, in Persia, India, and Ethiopia,* A.D. *1503–08.* Translated from Italian, with a preface, by John Winter Jones and edited with notes and an introduction by George Percy Badger. Hakluyt Society, vol. 32, 1863. Reprint, New York: Burt Franklin, n.d.

PILGRIM WITH NO NAME

"A Description of the Yearely Voyage or Pilgrimage of the Mahumetans, Turks, and Moors unto Arabia." In *The Principal Navigations, Voyages, Traffiques, and Discoveries of the English Nation* by Richard Hakluyt, vol. 5, 1599. Reprint, Glasgow: MacLehose and Sons, 1904, pp. 329–65.

JOSEPH PITTS

Barnby, H. G. *The Prisoners of Algiers: An Account of the Forgotten American-Algerian War, 1785–97.* London: Oxford University Press, 1966.

Gaury, Gerald, de. *The Rulers of Mecca.* New York: Dorset Press, 1991.

Pitts, Joseph. *A Faithful Account of the Religion and Manners of the Mahometans,* 4th ed. London: T. Longman, 1738.

Pitts, Joseph. "An Account by Joseph Pitts of His Journey from Algiers to Mecca and Medina and Back." In *The Red Sea and Adjacent Countries at the End of the Seventeenth Century As Described by Joseph Pitts, William Daniel, and Charles Jacques Poncet.* Edited by Sir William Foster. Hakluyt Society, 1949. Reprint, Nendeln/Liechtenstein: Kraus Reprint, 1967.

ALI BEY AL-ABBASI

Al-Abbasi, Ali Bey [alias Domingo Badia y Leblich]. *Travels in Africa and Asia during the Years 1803–07.* Philadelphia: 1816.

Moorehead, Alan. *The Blue Nile.* New York: Vintage, Random House, 1983.

JOHN LEWIS BURCKHARDT

Bovill, E. W. *The Golden Trade of the Moors.* Oxford, England: Oxford University Press, 1978.

Burckhardt, John Lewis. *Travels in Arabia, Comprehending an Account of Those Territories in Hedjaz Which the Mohammedans Regard as Sacred.* London: Henry Colburn, 1829. Reprint, London: Frank Cass, 1968.

Moorehead, Alan. *The Blue Nile.* New York: Vintage, Random House, 1983.

al-Naqar, 'Umar. *The Pilgrimage Tradition in West Africa.* Khartoum, Sudan: Khartoum University Press, 1972.

Sims, Katherine. *Desert Traveller: The Life of John Lewis Burckhardt.* London: Victor Gollancz, 1969.

Part Three: Nineteenth-Century Changes

SIR RICHARD BURTON

Burton, Sir Richard. *A Personal Narrative of a Pilgrimage to al-Madinah and Meccah,* memorial ed. 2 vols. London: Tylston and Edwards, 1893.

Rice, Edward. *Captain Sir Richard Francis Burton: The Secret Agent Who Made the Pilgrimage to Mecca, Discovered* The Kama Sutra, *and Brought the Arabian Knights to the West.* New York: Charles Scribner's Sons, 1990.

Said, Edward W. *Orientalism.* New York: Vintage, Random House, 1979.

HER HIGHNESS SIKANDAR, THE BEGUM OF BHOPAL

The Nawab Sikandar, Begum of Bhopal. *A Pilgrimage to Mecca.* Translated from Urdu and edited by Mrs. Willoughby-Osborne. London: W. H. Allen, 1870.

Pearson, M. N. *Pious Passengers: The Hajj in Earlier Times.* London: C. Hurst, 1994.

JOHN F. KEANE

Keane, J. F. *Six Months in Meccah: An Account of the Mohammedan Pilgrimage to Meccah.* London: Tinsley Brothers, 1881.

MIRZA MOHAMMAD HOSAYN FARAHANI

Farahani, Mirza Mohammad Hosayn. *A Shiʿite Pilgrimage to Mecca, 1885–86.* Edited, translated from Persian, and annotated by Hafez Farmayan and Elton L. Daniel. Austin: University of Texas Press, 1990.

ARTHUR J. B. WAVELL

Dictionary of National Biography, 1912–21. London: Oxford University Press, 1927, pp. 559–60.

Wavell, Arthur J. B. *A Modern Pilgrim in Mecca and A Siege in Sanaa.* London: Constable, 1913.

Part Four: The Early Twentieth Century
INTRODUCTION

Cleveland, William L. *A History of the Modern Middle East.* Boulder, Colo.: Westview Press, 1994.

Fromkin, David. *A Peace to End All Peace: Creating the Modern Middle East, 1914–22.* New York: Henry Holt, 1989.

Hurgronje, Christian Snouck. *Mekka in the Latter Part of the Nineteenth Century.* London: Luzac, 1931.

———. *Makkah a Hundred Years Ago.* Edited by Angelo Pesce. London: Immel, 1986.

Long, David Edwin. *The Hajj Today.* Albany: State University of New York Press, 1979.

Nielsen, Jorgenson. *Muslims in Western Europe.* Edinburgh: Edinburgh University Press, 1995.

ELDON RUTTER

Rutter, Eldon. *The Holy Cities of Arabia.* 2 vols. London and New York: G. P. Putnam's Sons, 1927.

WINIFRED STEGAR

Stegar, Winifred. *Always Bells.* Sydney and London: Angus and Robertson, 1969.

MUHAMMAD ASAD

Asad, Muhammad. *The Road to Mecca.* London: Max Reinhardt, 1954.

Parker, Mushtaq. "Muhammad Asad." *The London Independent,* Sunday edition, March 1, 1992. [*As of this writing, most of Asad's books may be ordered from Threshold Books, Putney, Vermont.*]

HARRY ST. JOHN PHILBY
Monroe, Elizabeth. *Philby of Arabia.* London: Pitman, 1973.
Philby, Harry St. John Bridger. *A Pilgrim in Arabia.* London: Robert Hale, 1946.
————. *Arabian Days: An Autobiography.* London: Robert Hale, 1948.

LADY EVELYN COBBOLD
Cobbold, Lady Evelyn. *Pilgrimage to Mecca.* London: John Murray, 1934.

Part Five: The Jet Age Hajj
INTRODUCTION
Armstrong, Karen. *A History of God.* New York: Alfred A. Knopf, 1994.
Barboza, Steven. *American Jihad.* New York: Doubleday, 1994.
Braibanti, Ralph. *The Nature and Structure of the Islamic World,* position paper 1. Chicago: International Strategy and Policy Institute, 1995.
Esposito, John. *The Islamic Threat: Myth or Reality,* rev. ed. New York: Oxford University Press, 1995.
al-Farsi, Fuad. *Modernity and Tradition: The Saudi Equation.* Guernsey, England: Knight Communications, 1990.
Shah, the Sayyid Idries. *Destination Mecca.* London: Octagon Press, 1969.

HAMZA BOGARY
Bogary, Hamza. *The Sheltered Quarter: A Tale of a Boyhood in Mecca.* Translated from Arabic by Olive Kenny and Jeremy Reed, with an introduction by William Ochsenwald. Austin: Center for Middle Eastern Studies, University of Texas, 1991.
Holden, David, and Richard Johns. *The House of Saud.* New York: Holt, Rinehart and Winston, 1981.

JALAL AL-E AHMAD
Al-e Ahmad, Jalal. *Lost in the Crowd.* Translated from Persian by John Green, with an introduction by Michael Hillmann. Washington, D.C.: Three Continents Press, 1985.

MALCOLM X
Breitman, George. *The Evolution of a Revolutionary.* New York: Pathfinder Press, 1967.
DeCaro, Jr., Louis A. *On the Side of My People: A Religious Life of Malcolm X.* New York: New York University Press, 1996.
Dyson, Michael Eric. *Making Malcolm.* New York: Oxford University Press, 1995.
Malcolm X. *Speeches at Harvard.* London: Free Association Books, 1989.

Selected Bibliography

Essien-Udom, E. U. *Black Nationalism: The Search for an Identity in America.* Chicago: University of Illinois Press, 1963.

Malcolm X with the assistance of Alex Haley. *The Autobiography of Malcolm X.* New York: Grove Press, 1965.

West, Cornell. *Race Matters.* Boston: Beacon Press, 1993.

Wolfenstein, Eugene Victor. *The Victims of Democracy: Malcolm X and the Black Revolution.* London: Free Association Books, 1981.

SAIDA MILLER KHALIFA

Khalifa, Saida Miller. *The Fifth Pillar: The Story of a Pilgrimage to Mecca and Medina.* Hicksville, N.Y.: Exposition Press, 1977.

MICHAEL WOLFE

Wolfe, Michael. *The Hadj: An American's Pilgrimage to Mecca.* New York: Grove/ Atlantic, 1993.

index

Note: Page numbers in boldface refer to maps.